LIVES

OF THE

LORD CHANCELLORS OF ENGLAND.

LIVES

OF

THE LORD CHANCELLORS

AND

KEEPERS OF THE GREAT SEAL

OF

ENGLAND,

FROM THE EARLIEST TIMES TILL THE REIGN OF QUEEN VICTORIA.

BY

LORD CAMPBELL.

SEVENTH EDITION.

ILLUSTRATED.

VOL. VIII.

WILDSIDE PRESS

CONTENTS

OF

THE EIGHTH VOLUME.

CHAP.	PAGE
CLXXVI.—Life of Lord Chancellor Erskine from his birth till he was called to the bar,	1
CLXXVII.—Continuation of the Life of Lord Erskine till he entered the House of Commons,	13
CLXXVIII.—Continuation of the Life of Lord Erskine till the conclusion of the case of the Dean of St. Asaph,	45
CLXXIX.—Continuation of the Life of Lord Erskine till the commencement of the State trials in 1794,	66
CLXXX.—Continuation of the Life of Lord Erskine till the conclusion of the prosecutions for high treason against the advocates for a reform in Parliament,	96
CLXXXI.—Continuation of the Life of Lord Erskine till the trial of Hadfield for shooting at George III.,	121
CLXXXII.—Continuation of the Life of Lord Erskine till his visit to Paris during the peace of Amiens,	144
CLXXXIII.—Continuation of the Life of Lord Erskine till he became Lord Chancellor,	163
CLXXXIV.—Continuation of the Life of Lord Erskine while he was Lord Chancellor,	176
CLXXXV.—Continuation of the Life of Lord Erskine till he resigned the Great Seal,	202
CLXXXVI.—Continuation of the Life of Lord Erskine till the Prince of Wales, having become Regent, renounced the Whigs,	216
CLXXXVII.—Continuation of the Life of Lord Erskine till the General Peace in 1815,	233

CONTENTS.

CHAP.	PAGE
CLXXXVIII.—Continuation of the Life of Lord Erskine till the conclusion of the trial of Queen Caroline,	256
CLXXXIX.—Continuation of the Life of Lord Erskine till his last visit to Scotland,	272
CXC.—Conclusion of the Life of Lord Erskine,	288
CXCI.—Life of Lord Chancellor Eldon from his birth till his marriage,	324
CXCII.—Continuation of the Life of Lord Eldon till he was called to the bar,	356
CXCIII.—Continuation of the Life of Lord Eldon till he received a silk gown,	364
CXCIV.—Continuation of the Life of Lord Eldon till he was made Solicitor General,	386
CXCV.—Continuation of the Life of Lord Eldon till he became Attorney General,	403
CXCVI.—Continuation of the Life of Lord Eldon till he was made Chief Justice of the Common Pleas,	415
CXCVII.—Continuation of the Life of Lord Eldon till he was made Lord Chancellor,	438
CXCVIII.—Continuation of the Life of Lord Eldon till his first resignation of the Great Seal,	457
CXCIX.—Continuation of the Life of Lord Eldon till he was restored to the Woolsack,	494

LIVES

OF THE

LORD CHANCELLORS OF ENGLAND.

CHAPTER CLXXVI.

LIFE OF LORD CHANCELLOR ERSKINE FROM HIS BIRTH TILL HE WAS CALLED TO THE BAR.

I RESERVE Lord Loughborough's immediate successor for the conclusion of my work. After a short suspension of Lord Eldon's Chancellorship, it was prolonged above twenty years under George III., under the Regency, and under George IV. He lived down to the reign of Queen Victoria, and he took an active part in politics long after he quitted office—strenuously opposing the repeal of the Test Act, Catholic Emancipation, the Reform Bill, and the other measures which have placed our institutions, for good or for evil, in the condition in which we now behold them. The rival to whom he yielded for a brief space, nearly closed his public life—so brilliant, so useful to his country—when forced to resign the Great Seal in 1807, amidst cries that the *Church was in danger*, because it had been proposed that Roman Catholics might hold in the army the rank of field officer. It will, therefore, be more convenient that I should now proceed with the Life of this illustrious advocate and patriot.

I confess that I am impatient to behold him, and to attend him in his extraordinary career, as he ever engaged the affections as well as excited wonder and applause—from the time he learned "Shantrews" in the dancing school at St. Andrew's, till he presided on the Woolsack at the trial of Lord Melville. Since I accompanied to the tomb the venerable Camden, I have passed through many disagreeable scenes with the dull Bathurst, the overbearing Thurlow, and the faithless Loughborough. I have before me a long journey in the society of Eldon, with whom, notwithstanding his great abilities, profound learning, and delightful manners, I must often quarrel for his selfishness and insincerity, as well as for his bigotry. The subject of this memoir commands my love and my respect. He had imperfections, to which I am not blind, and which I shall not attempt to conceal; but he displayed genius united with public principle; he saved the liberties of his country; he was the brightest ornament of which the English Bar can boast; and from his vivacity, his courtesy, and his kindness of heart, he was the charm of every society which he entered.

On the 10th day of January, 1750, in a small and ill-furnished room in an upper "flat" of a very lofty house in the old town of Edinburgh, first saw the light the Honorable Thomas Erskine, the future defender of Stockdale, and Lord Chancellor of Great Britain.[1] He was the youngest son of Henry David, tenth Earl of Buchan, and counted in his ancient line many distinguished ancestors. The Erskines[2] are said originally to have been "of that ilk," deriving their name territorially from the domain of "Erskine" on the banks of the Clyde,—but they were so early ennobled, that Lord Hailes says "the title of Marr, which they bore, is one of those titles the origin of which is lost in their antiquity; it existed before our records, and before the æra of genuine history." MARTACUS, the first Earl of Marr of whom authentic mention is made, was contemporary with Malcolm Canmore and William the Conqueror. James Erskine, a younger son of James, the seventh Earl of Marr, and grandson of the Regent Marr, married the heiress of the Earldom of Buchan, which had existed in the time of William the Lion, and,

---

[1] The houses in Edinburgh, some of them sixteen stories high, were then let in stories, or "flats," as houses in Paris now are.

[2] The name was variously spelt "Ereskin," "Airskin," and "Areseskin." Voltaire, in his Letters on the English Nation, writes it "Hareskins." The common pronunciation in Scotland is "Askin," which gave rise to an often-told repartee of the famous Henry Erskine. A silly fellow at the Scotch Bar, not liking a question put to him by the witty Dean of Faculty, testily said, "Harry, I never meet you but I find you *Askin*"—to which he replied, "And I, Bob, never meet you but I find an *Anser*."

being descendible to females, had passed through the Stuarts, the Comyns, and other illustrious Scottish houses. Thereupon he had a new charter limiting it to his "heirs male and assigns whatever," and he is called the "sixth Earl of Buchan." He and his descendants wasted the ample patrimony once belonging to the title,—and in the middle of the 18th century, Henry David, the tenth Earl, with a numerous offspring, was reduced to an income of £200 a year.[1] However, his Countess, daughter of Sir James Stewart of Goodtrees in the county of Mid-Lothian, Baronet, was a woman of extraordinary intellect, which had been highly cultivated, and she was equally remarkable for eminent piety and for peculiar skill in housewifery. The family had been obliged to abandon an old castle standing on the last remnant of their estates, for the elevated but wretched habitation I have mentioned, in the metropolis of Scotland,—where their poverty could be better concealed and their children might be cheaply educated. The Countess herself taught them to read, and was at great pains to instil into their infant minds the doctrines of the true Presbyterian faith. The Erskines were reckoned a most "godly" race. The Earl's great grandfather had suffered in the Covenanting cause in the preceding century; and those pious men, Ralph and Ebenezer Erskine, who had recently seceded from the establishment, and whose sentiments have been adopted and acted upon by the Free Church of Scotland, were his "far-away cousins." Not only was the house frequented by the eloquent divines who then flourished in Edinburgh, but by the leaders of the "Parliament House," and by members of other families almost as noble and almost as reduced,—who came to partake of "a social dish of tea,"—so that young Tom, from his infancy, saw society well calculated to form his manners and to sharpen his intellect. He is said early to have discovered that buoyancy of spirit and playfulness of fancy which afterwards distinguished him. For some years he was kept at the High School of Edinburgh, still—according to the Scottish usage, which is attended with

---

[1] It is curious to observe, that notwithstanding the strict law of entail in Scotland, which is so injurious to the country, the nobles there have fallen into poverty much more than in England, where family estates are either unfettered, or are preserved by settlements made with the joint consent of father and son in each succeeding generation.

many advantages—eating his meals at home,—having oatmeal porridge for breakfast, and soup maigre, called "kail," for dinner. While he remained here he was generally "Dux" of his class, although he was pretty frequently subjected to the discipline of the "tawse."

With all Lady Buchan's economy and good management, the metropolis was found too expensive for the very slender finances of the family, and in the beginning of the year 1762 they removed to St. Andrew's, in the county of Fife, where house-rent was lower, and where they could entirely abstain from receiving company—the education being nothing inferior. Of Tom Erskine, at this period of his life, I can speak from undoubted authority; for he was in the same class with my own father, and with George Hill, afterwards Principal of St. Mary's College, my preceptor, both of whom I have frequently heard talk of him. They described him as of quick parts and retentive memory, rather idly inclined, but capable of great application—full of fun and frolic —and ever the favorite of his master and his playmates.

There is extant a very interesting letter, written by him while a school-boy here, to his eldest brother, Lord Cardross, who had been left behind with a relation at Edinburgh:—

'August 11, 1762.

"MY DEAR BROTHER,

"I received your letter, and it gave me great joy to hear that you were in health, which I hope will always continue. I am in my second month at the dancing-school. I have learned *shantrews*[1] and the single *hornpipe*, and am just now learning the *double hornpipe*. There is a pretty large Norway ship in the harbor: the captain took Harry and me into the cabin, and entertained us with French claret, Danish biscuit, and smoked salmon; and the captain was up in the town seeing Papa to-day. He is to sail on Friday, because the stream is great.

---

[1] The same *saltatory* course prevailed when I was at St. Andrew's. The name and dance of "shantrews" some ascribe to a Highland origin,—some to our ancient allies, the French. The memory of Lady Buchan was then green, and I was shown a cave on the sea-shore in which she used to drink tea, and make her toilette when she bathed—still called "Lady Buchan's Cove."

Yesterday I saw Captain Sutherland exercise his party of Highlanders, which I liked very well to see. In the time of the vacation Harry and me writes themes, reads Livy and French, with Mr. Douglas, between ten and eleven. Papa made me a present of a ring-dial, which I am very fond of, for it tells me what o'clock it is very exactly. You bid me, in your last letter, write to you when I had nothing better to do; but, I assure you, I think I can not employ myself better than to write to you, which I shall take care to do very often. Adieu, my dear brother, and believe me, with great affection,

"Yours,

"T. E."

At the grammar school of St. Andrew's, under Mr. Hacket, a zealous teacher, but not much of a scholar, he attained only a moderate proficiency in Latin, and learned little of Greek beyond the alphabet. But he was carefully taught to compose in English, as if it had been a foreign language; and, being fond of books, he read, in a desultory way, many English poems, plays, voyages, and travels. He never was matriculated in the University of St. Andrew's,[1] but in the session 1762-3[2] he attended the Mathematical and Natural Philosophy classes, taught by professors of considerable eminence, and from them he imbibed the small portion of science of which he could ever boast.

With a seriousness not to be expected from his years or his disposition, he began to consider how he was to make his way in the world, and he expressed a wish to be bred to some learned profession, in which he might distinguish himself. His father and mother truly told him, however, that they could not afford this expense as their means were entirely exhausted in sending his eldest brother, Cardross, to study at Leyden, and educating his second brother, Henry, for the Scotch Bar; and that they could do nothing better for him than send him to sea as a midshipman. Being earnestly bent on mental improvement, and having a particular aversion to the sea service,—if he must serve his Majesty, he prayed that a

---

[1] This I have ascertained by the assistance of Sir David Brewster, Principal of St. Leonard's and St. Salvator's—at present the great ornament of that seat of learning.

[2] The session begins in November and ends in May.

commission in the army might be procured for him. After a correspondence between his father and some old friends of the family, this point seemed to be conceded in his favor. Under that belief he wrote the following letter to his aunt, Lady Stewart, which I think is much to be admired for the ingenuous feelings and noble aspirations which it discloses:—

"Nov. 4, 1763.

" MY DEAR AUNT,

"I received your letter about a week ago with great pleasure, and thank you for the good advice contained in it, which I hope by God's assistance I shall be able to follow.

" I am extremely glad that you approve of my not going to sea. I shall tell my reasons for it.

" In the first place, Papa got a letter from Commodore Dennis, laying before him the disadvantages at present of the sea service on account of the many half-pay officers on the list, which all behoved to be promoted before me; he also acquainted Papa that he was sorry that if I did go he could be of no service to me, as he had at present no command, and had no prospect of getting any : he at the same time did not forget the advantages of it ; but when I weighed the two in scales, the disadvantages prevailed, and still more when added to my own objections, which are as follows :—In the first place, I could have no opportunity of improving my learning, whereas in the army the regiment is often quartered in places where I might have all advantages. I assure you I could by no means put up without improving myself in my studies, for I can be as happy as the day is long with them, and would ten times rather be at St. Andrew's, attending the classes there, and even those which I was at last year, viz. Natural Philosophy and Mathematics (both of which I am extremely fond of), than at the most beautiful place in the world, with all manner of diversions and amusements. My second objection is, that I would be obliged to keep company with a most abandoned set of people that would corrupt my morals; whereas in the army, though they be bad enough, yet I should have the advantage of choosing my company when I pleased, without being constrained to any particular set ;—and thirdly, I think my constitution would not agree with it, as I am

very subject to rheumatic pains.' [Then follow some little family matters and messages.]
" I shall now conclude with assuring you that I am, my dear aunt, your most affectionate nephew,
"THOMAS ERSKINE."[2]

However, a commission could not be obtained without purchase, and the original intention of sending him to sea was resumed. The case being properly stated to him, he submitted—fully resolved, under all circumstances, however adverse, to struggle for the acquisition of knowledge, and the development of his intellectual powers. In the spring of the following year it was arranged that he should be put under Sir David Lindsay, an experienced sea-captain, in command of the Tartar man-of-war. This officer, on the recommendation of his uncle, the Earl of Mansfield, who took an interest in the Buchan family, promised to be kind to the "young middy."

The lad being supplied with his blue jacket, cocked hat, and sword, was almost reconciled to his fate. Embarking at Leith, he took an affecting leave of his family, to whom he was very tenderly attached, and from whom he had not before been separated. His father he never again beheld alive, but his mother survived to encourage his entrance into a profession more suitable to his taste and his talents, and to witness the commencement of his brilliant career.

He left his native land with the disheartening prospect of dying a half-pay lieutenant;—but when he next revisited it he was an ex-Chancellor, a Peer, and a Knight of the Thistle—what was far more valuable, he had achieved for himself the reputation of the greatest forensic orator that Britain ever produced.

It is wonderful to think that the period of life, during which almost all those whose progress to greatness I have traced were stimulated to lay in stores of knowledge at public schools and universities, was passed by Erskine in the hold of a man-of-war, or in the barracks of a marching regiment. But his original passion for intellectual dis-

---

[1] These rheumatic pains were probably indicative of a constitutional tendency to the gout, of which his father and mother both afterwards died, and of which he himself had a smart attack three years after the date of this letter, at the age of eighteen—the first and last visit of this hereditary complaint.

[2] Communicated to me by his son, the Right Hon. Thomas Erskine.

tinction was only rendered more ardent by the difficulties which threatened to extinguish it.

He remained in the Tartar four years, cruising about in the West Indies and on the coast of America. The life of a midshipman has been much improved of late years by superior comforts, and by anxious attention to professional and general education while he is afloat; but in Erskine's time the interior of a man-of-war presented nearly the same spectacle which we find described in so lively a manner by *Roderick Random,*—and the young officers were taught little else than to smoke tobacco, to drink flip, and to eat salmagundy. Erskine, however,—never neglecting his professional duties,—contrived often to escape from the dark and noisy abode of the midshipmen to a quiet corner of the vessel, where he amused and improved himself in reading books which he had brought on board with him—picking up some new volume at every port he visited. He was soon reconciled to his situation—and his elastic spirits and gay temperament made him not only take a deep interest in the new scenes which presented themselves to him, but be pleased with all he saw. Joining in the gay dances of the negroes,—when he and they forgot their toil and their stripes,—he formed a favorable notion of slavery as a *status*, which influenced him after he became a member of the legislature; and he was so warm an admirer of the open, straightforward, light-hearted, brave, though thoughtless and indiscreet, character of English seamen, that he would not hear of any plan for rendering them more sober and orderly on shore, saying, "You may scour an old coin to make it legible; but if you go on scouring, it will be no coin at all." [1]

One letter which he wrote at this time from Jamaica to his eldest brother, is preserved, and, by its artless touches, shows the attachment he still retained to home, notwithstanding the *couleur de rose* medium through which he viewed foreign lands:—

"The longer I stay in the West Indies, I find the country more healthful and the climate more agreeable. I could not help smiling when Mamma mentioned in her letter, 'how much reason you had to be thankful that you gave up your commission, or you would have gone to the

[1] Armata.

most wretched climate on the earth.' I don't know, indeed, as to the rest of the West India Islands; but sure I am, if you had come here, you would have no reason to repent of it. To be sure, to stay here too long might weaken a constitution, though hardly that; but to stay here some time is extremely serviceable. . . . I begin now to draw indifferently. I am studying botany with Dr. Butt, so I will bring home drawings of all the curious plants, &c., and everything that I see. I have sent Mamma home a land turtle, to walk about Walcot garden: it is very pretty, particularly its back, which is all divided into square lozenges, and the shell is as hard as a coat of mail."

Sir David Lindsay, his captain, who behaved to him with great kindness, was replaced by Commodore Johnson. The "harsh demeanor" of this officer has been assigned as the reason for Erskine quitting the sea service —but this statement is incorrect, for, although his manners were rather rough, " Tom " was a favorite with him, and was appointed by him acting-lieutenant. In this capacity the future Chancellor made the voyage home to England,—reckoning with confidence on his promotion being confirmed, and hoping to rival Anson and Hawke. But, alas! on his arrival at Portsmouth, the ship was paid off, and he was told at the Admiralty that on account of the great number of midshipmen who had served longer than him, and whose friends were applying for their advancement, he could not yet have a lieutenant's commission, and there was no saying when his turn might come. He indignantly vowed that he would not again go to sea as a midshipman after having served as lieutenant.

While in perplexity as to his future destiny, he had the misfortune to lose his father. The old Earl died at Bath, where he had been for some years a resident, and had been a regular attendant at Lady Huntingdon's Chapel, established there under the ministry of the famous Whitfield. From this enthusiast we have a very striking account of his obsequies,—the future Chancellor appearing in the group of mourners: " All has been awful, and more than awful. On Saturday evening, before the corpse was taken from Buchan House, a word of exhortation was given, and a hymn sung, in the room where the corpse lay. The young Earl with his hand on the head of the coffin, the Countess-dowager on his right, Lady Anne and Lady Isabella on his left, and their brother, Thomas, next to their mother, with a few friends. On Sunday morning, all attending in mourning at early sacrament, they were seated by themselves at the foot of the corpse, and with their servants received first, and a particular address was made to them." Having mentioned the preparations for the second service at eleven the same day, when Whitefield himself was to preach the funeral sermon, he continues:—" The coffin being deposited on a space railed in for the purpose, the bereaved relations sat in order within, and their domestics outside the rail. Three hundred tickets of admission, signed by the present Earl, were given to the nobility and gentry. Ever since there hath been public service and preaching twice a day. This is to be continued till Friday morning;—then all is to be removed to Bristol, in order to be shipped for Scotland." The following was the pious inscription on the coffin :—

> " His life was honorable—his death blessed.
> He sought earnestly peace with God ;
> He found it
> Alone in the merits of our Saviour."

These solemnities made an impression on the mind of the young midshipman which was never effaced. But he was now obliged, with the advice of his surviving parent, to determine upon the course of life he was to pursue.

He had reached his eighteenth year, when, according to the common routine in England, he ought to have been going to commence his studies at Oxford or Cambridge. Most happy would he have been to do so, but the pittance which came to him under his father's will was quite insufficient to maintain him at an English university, and his talents had not yet sufficiently displayed themselves to justify the hope that he might triumph over the formidable obstacles he would have to encounter if he should study for the Bar. He resolved, therefore, to try his luck in the army; and, through the recommendation of John, Duke of Argyll, Colonel of the " Royals," or " First Regiment of Foot," he obtained an ensign's commission in that corps at the regulation price,—which absorbed the whole of his patrimony.

Of the first two years of his military life I find no account. During this time the regiment was quartered in different provincial towns at home, and we can only conjecture that the sprightly ensign, when he was not at drill, or carrying the colors on a field-day, employed himself in reading books which he borrowed from circulating libraries, and flirting with the pretty girls in the neighborhood. He fell in love with one of these, who was luckily of respectable family and connections, though without fortune—the daughter of Daniel Moore, Esq., M. P. for Marlow; and on the 21st of April, 1770, he led her to the altar.

This imprudent match turned out auspiciously. They lived together in uninterrupted harmony. Become a married man, he, without abating anything of his outward gaiety, thought more deeply, and was capable of more determined application to business, than would have been possible for him if he had only had himself to care for.

The Royals were soon after ordered to Minorca, then under the dominion of the British Crown; and thither his wife accompanied him. For two long years was he shut up in this island; but they were the most improving he ever spent; and it may be doubted whether his mind would have been better cultivated if he had devoted them to mathematics or the Greek measures, in hopes of a high degree on the banks of the Cam. Laboriously and systematically he went through a course of English literature. Milton was his chief delight, and "the noble speeches in PARADISE LOST may be deemed as good a substitute as could be discovered by the future orator for the immortal originals in the Greek models."[1] He was, likewise, so familiar with Shakespeare, that he could almost, like Porson, have held conversation on all subjects for days together in the phrases of this great dramatist. Dryden and Pope,—nearly laid aside, by the rising generation, for the mawkish sentimentality now alone allowed to be poetry,—he not only perused and reperused, but got almost entirely by heart. He likewise showed the versatility of his powers by acting as chaplain to the regiment, the real chaplain being at home on furlough by reason of ill health. At first he contented himself with

[1] Lord Brougham.

reading the service from the Liturgy; but he found that this was not altogether relished by the men, who were chiefly Presbyterians. Thereupon, his mind being imbued with the religious notions implanted in it by his mother and the godly divines whom she patronized, he would favor them with an extempore prayer; and he composed sermons, which he delivered to them with extreme solemnity and unction from the drum-head. He used always to remember and to talk of this portion of his life with peculiar satisfaction.[1]

While at Minorca he was much noticed by the Governor, General Mostyn; and he highly approved of the conduct of that officer in imprisoning and banishing Fabrigas, the Minorquin, accused of plotting against the English Government. It is well known that there was no sufficient ground for these severities, and that, an action having been brought to recover a compensation for them in the Court of Common Pleas at Westminster, the plaintiff secured a verdict with £3,000 damages. Erskine, in his old age, gave the following account of his indignation, at a time when TRIAL BY JURY would by no means have been selected by him as his motto:—

"I remember the news coming out to Malta of the verdict in the cause of Fabrigas and Mostyn. I was then in the garrison, and we all took the side of our worthy and popular Governor, whom we thought very ill used; and we drank that day at the mess a hearty damnation to the jury who brought in that verdict.

"Getting warm with indignation and wine, I lampooned the jury after dinner in some extempore verses, little thinking I should ever have anything to say to a jury myself.

"I forget exactly how they ran; but the idea was, that the ghost of great Alfred came from the abodes of the blest, to survey the result of the institutions he had founded when in life; and I supposed him present at the

---

[1] The following anecdote, related by a brother officer who served with him in the Royals, has recently been communicated to me:—" His first sermon appeared so wonderfully good, that he was suspected of having stolen it. He thereupon desired that he might have a text given him, and that he might be shut up in a room alone without any book, promising within a specified time to produce as good a sermon. The experiment was made, and within the specified time he produced a sermon on the subject assigned to him, allowed to be still more eloquent and edifying."—*3rd Edition.*

verdict of the jury against Governor Mostyn. The concluding verses were these:—

" The monarch's pale face was with blushes suffused,
To observe right and wrong by twelve villains confused,
And, kicking their ****s all round in a fury,
Cried, ' *Curs'd be the day I invented a jury !*' "[1]

The regiment returned from Minorca in 1772, Erskine being still an ensign; and he had leave of absence for near six months. The greatest part of this time he spent in London, where his high-born relations received him very kindly, and introduced him into general society. Making quite a sensation in town by his agreeable manners and graceful volubility, he was well received in the most distinguished literary circles. Often he enlivened the assemblies of Mrs. Montagu, frequented by Dr. Johnson, Sir Joshua Reynolds, the Bishop of St. Asaph, Dr. Burney, and other celebrated wits of that day.[2]

Boswell, in his inimitable " Life of Johnson," *ad ann.* 1772, says, " On Monday, April 6, I dined with him at Sir Alexander Macdonald's, where was a young officer in the regimentals of the Scots Royals, who talked with vivacity, fluency, and precision, so uncommon that he attracted particular attention. He proved to be the Honorable Thomas Erskine, youngest brother to the Earl of Buchan, who has since risen into such brilliant reputation at the Bar in Westminster Hall." It appears that, after the example of David and Goliah, the ensign ventured to combat the literary giant. A controversy arising about the respective merits of the authors of "Tom Jones," and " Clarissa;" and Johnson pronouncing Fielding to be " a blockhead " and " a barren rascal," and saying " there is more knowledge of the heart in one letter of Richardson's than in all Tom Jones,"—Erskine objected: " Surely, sir, Richardson is very tedious." He received only this answer, which, I think, is not very satisfactory: " Why, sir, if you were to read Richardson for the story, your impatience would be so much fretted, that you would hang yourself ! But you must read him for the sentiment, and consider the story as only giving occasion to the sentiment." The ensign then—showing an early instance of his egotistic propensity,—to the amusement and with the good will of the company, gave them a detailed account of his occu-

[1] See Fabrigas *v.* Mostyn, Cowper, 161. [2] Wraxall's Memoirs, i. 152.

pations in Minorca, and told them with particular glee how he read prayers and preached to the regiment.[1] He afterwards rather rashly objected to a passage in Scripture, where we are told that the Angel of the Lord, in one night, smote 185,000 Assyrians. "Sir," said Johnson, "you should recollect that there was a supernatural interposition; they were destroyed by pestilence. You are not to suppose that the Angel of the Lord went about and stabbed each of them with a dagger, or knocked them on the head man by man."[2]

Erskine now came forward as an author, and published a pamphlet, with the following title-page:—

"OBSERVATIONS
on the
PREVAILING ABUSES
in the
BRITISH ARMY,
arising from the
CORRUPTION OF CIVIL GOVERNMENT;
with a
PROPOSAL to the OFFICERS
Towards obtaining an Addition to their Pay.
By the Honorable . . . . ,
An Officer.
'Si omnes volumus, quod arguimur, non distinguemus voluntatem à facto: Omnes plectamur.'—*Tit. Liv.* lib. xiv."

The style of the Subaltern is much more stately and sententious than that afterwards assumed by the Chancellor; but in this production there breathes that ardor of sentiment which distinguished the author through life. A few specimens will be found amusing. Thus he starts off:—

"There is no task more difficult than to combat, with

---

[1] Mr. Croker, in his edition of Boswell, says,—"Lord Erskine was fond of this anecdote. He told it to the Editor the first time he had the honor of being in his company, and often repeated it, with an observation that he had been a sailor and a soldier, was a lawyer and a parson. The latter he affected to think the greatest of his efforts; and, to support that opinion, would quote the prayer for the clergy in the Liturgy, from the expression of which he would (in no commendable spirit of jocularity) infer, that the enlightening them was one of the greatest marvels that could be worked."—But any one might have remarked, without offense, that, upon a revision of the Liturgy, this introduction of the prayer for the clergy might be amended. The Right Hon. Thomas Erskine, in a letter to me, observes,—" His laugh at the prayer for the clergy showed no irreverence for religion, but was meant as a joke upon the Episcopacy, against which his mother, a strict Presbyterian, had always entertained the strongest prejudice."

[2] Boswell, ii. 177.

success, abuses of long standing; they borrow the appearance of right from immemorial custom, and it is almost impossible to rouse men to acute feelings of sufferings and oppressions, of which they themselves have not seen or felt the beginnings.

"But evils are still more insurmountable when their removal demands a steady and prompt unanimity in extensive communities. The various interests and opinions of men defeat the completion of this most powerful engine of human force; and great reformations are consequently either the fruits of long and often frustrated labor, or the birth of fortunate accidents.

"There may be, perhaps, two causes of the many feeble, ill concerted, and worse supported attempts towards an augmentation of the pay of the British troops, which seem now to be so submissively or indolently laid aside, and the grievance, with many others, so patiently supported, that to offer new proposals on the subject can not but carry with it the air of Quixotism.

"But as attempts that have been deemed unwarrantable from improbability of success, have often been found to be very easy on trial, and their apparent difficulties to be only the bugbears of irresolution; ardent, enterprising spirits are sometimes eminently useful as pioneers to regular and sober industry. Men who have virtue and talents for executing work which is put into their hands have not always fertile and progressive inventions, but treat everything as impossible and chimerical which presents any glaring difficulties; and the world would stand still, and every species of improvement be at an end, if nature did not provide another set of men, of irritable and restless dispositions, fretful under grievances, and ambitious of being the instruments of public advantage.

"It is this disposition, and perhaps this ambition, which led me to address myself to the officers of the British army, to demonstrate to them how shamefully, from the present miserable establishment of their pay, and other glaring abuses, they are cut off from their share in the prosperities of Great Britain; to show to them how far this insulting misfortune is owing to their absurd neglect of their own advantages, and to rouse them to a spirited yet constitutional demand of the rights of the most useful and laborious citizens.

"At first view, this may appear to be a dangerous subject, and highly incompatible with the arbitrary principles of military government. What is termed remonstrance in a citizen is supposed to be mutiny in a soldier; but mutiny I apprehend to be confined to the breach of discipline and subordination in an inferior towards a superior in military command; soldiers do not give up their general rights as members of a free community; they are amenable to civil and municipal laws, as well as to their own martial code, and are therefore entitled to all the privileges with which a free form of government invests every individual; nay, it is to their virtue that all the other parts of the community must ultimately trust for the enjoyment of their peaceable privileges; for, as Mr. Pitt (now Lord Chatham) in his strong figurative eloquence expressed himself in Parliament, 'To the virtue of the army we have hitherto trusted; to that virtue, small as the army is, we must still trust; and without that virtue, the Lords, the Commons, and the people of England may entrench themselves behind parchment up to the teeth, but the sword will find a passage to the vitals of the Constitution.'"—He afterwards goes on to show that, from the low pay of the army, none but the cadets of high families and persons of great wealth can enter it; and asks whether these men often deserve the honorable title of soldiers. "A commission," says he, "and a tour through Italy, are the finishing strokes to modern education; they are undertaken with the same serious intentions, and are prosecuted with equal improvement. So long as the battalions are encamped on native plains, or ensconced in peaceful barracks, so long these sons of riot and effeminacy maintain their posts. The brilliant orbit of Ranelagh glows with their scarlet, and the avenues of Vauxhall glitter with blades, drawn against unarmed apprentices in the honor of a strumpet,—which rust in their scabbards when their country calls. If for a review or a muster they are obliged to loll in their *vis-à-vis* to the quarters of their regiment, it is but to inflame the contempt and hatred of the people of England against the defenders of their peaceable privileges. They gallop again to town, after having filled the country with such horror at their debaucheries that hospitable doors are shut against officers of principle and reputation.—Such are the advantages which the military profession reaps from these apes in embroidery; such are the heroes that in the event of a war must lead the British troops to battle, for these men rise almost universally over the heads of officers grey with fatigues and rough with scars,—whose courage and abilities yet preserve the honor of the English name,—who, without money and without interest, languish in the subaltern ranks, unknown and unrespected,—who, after having braved all the terrors and calamities of war, and immortalized their country, sink into obscure graves, unwept and unremembered; without a tongue to speak their worth, or a stone to record their virtues. It is only upon the useful and valuable part of the army that all its grievances fall. To the stripling of the peaceable parade it is the limbo of vanity; to the veteran of the field it is a path sown with thorns."

In the same strain the pamphlet goes on at great length to point out abuses, and to call upon the injured officers to join together in obtaining a remedy, which he assures them they may safely do without danger of being punished for mutiny. From the excellent condition in which the army now is, under our illustrious Commander-in-chief, the Duke of Wellington,[1] we are not necessarily to suppose that these complaints are much exaggerated.

The American war breaking out soon after, the army was found to be in a very defective state, and the public derived considerable advantage from Erskine's suggestions for its improvement. This pamphlet had a wide circulation; the name of the author was well known, although it did not appear in the title-page; and he acquired much celebrity by the boldness and eloquence with which he had pleaded for his profession.

Having been some time the senior ensign in his regiment, on the 21st of April, 1773, he was raised to be a lieutenant. The pleasure of promotion speedily passed away, and he became more and more dissatisfied with his situation and his prospects. He was again moving about with his regiment from one country town to another. This mode of life had lost the charm of novelty which once made it endurable, and was now become doubly irksome from his having to keep a wife and family in a

[1] A.D. 1848.

barrack-room, or in lodgings, the expense of which he could ill afford. He had no money to purchase higher commissions, and he might wait many years before he gained another step by seniority. Notwithstanding some disputes with the American colonies, there was thought to be a probability of long and profound peace. He considered himself fit for better things than the wretched existence that seemed lengthening before him—to be spent in listlessness and penury.

It so happened that, in the midst of these lucubrations, the assizes were held in the town in which he was quartered. The lounging lieutenant entering the court in his regimentals, Lord Mansfield, the presiding judge, inquired who he was, and, finding that this was the youngest son of the late Earl of Buchan, who had sailed with his nephew, invited him to sit on the bench by his side, explained to him the nature of the proceedings that were going forward, and showed him the utmost civility. Erskine heard tried a cause of stirring interest, in which the counsel were supposed to display extraordinary eloquence. Never undervaluing his own powers, he thought within himself that he could have made a better speech than any of them, on which ever side he had been retained. Yet these gentlemen were the leaders of the circuit, each making a larger income than the pay of all the officers of the Royals put together,—with the chance of being raised by their own abilities to the Woolsack. The thought then suddenly struck him that it might not even now be too late for him to study the law and be called to the Bar. He saw the difficulties in his way, but there was no effort which he was not willing to make, no privation to which he would not cheerfully submit, that he might rescue himself from his present forlorn condition,—that he might have a chance of gaining intellectual distinction,—above all, that he might make a decent provision for his family. Lord Mansfield invited him to dinner, and being much struck with his conversation and pleased with his manners, detained him till late in the evening. When the rest of the company had withdrawn, the Lieutenant, who ever showed high moral courage, in consideration of the connection between the Murrays and Erskines, and the venerable Earl's great condescension and kindness, disclosed to him his plan of a change of profession, with a modest statement of his reasons. Lord Mansfield by no means discouraged him ; but advised him before he took a step so serious to consult his near relations.

He accordingly wrote to his mother, and she, justly appreciating the energy and perseverance as well as the enthusiasm belonging to his nature, strongly advised him to quit the army for the law. His brothers did not oppose—although Henry warned him of the thorny and uphill path on which he was entering. His resolution was now firmly taken, and he came up to London to carry it into effect. It was not till the spring of the following year that financial difficulties were so far removed as to render it possible for him to make the experiment. Craddock says,—" At the House of Admiral Walsingham I first met with Erskine and Sheridan, and it was there the scheme was laid that the former should exchange the army for the law;" but he had not been made acquainted with the previous consultations, or he would have said that "the plan was there *matured*, and the arrangements were made for his legal studies and his call to the Bar." The period of five years was then required by all the inns of court for a student to be on the books of the Society before he could be called—with this proviso, that it was reduced to three years for those who had the degree of M. A. from either of the universities of Oxford or Cambridge. It was resolved that Erskine should immediately be entered of an inn of court ; that he should likewise be matriculated at Cambridge and take a degree there; that he should keep his academical and law terms concurrently ; and that, as soon as it could be managed, he should become a pupil to some eminent special pleader, so as to be well grounded in the technicalities of his new craft.

Accordingly, on the 26th day of April, 1775, he was admitted a student of Lincoln's Inn ;[1] and on the 13th of January, 1776, he was matriculated at Cambridge, and entered on the books of Trinity College as a Fellow Com-

[1] "Lincoln's Inn.—The Honorable Thomas Erskine, third son of the Right Honorable Henry David, Earl of Buchan, is admitted into the Society of this Inn on the 26th day of April, in the fifteenth year of the reign of our Sovereign Lord, George the Third, by the grace of God of Great Britain, France, and Ireland King, Defender of the Faith, &c., and in the year of our Lord 1775 , and hath thereupon paid to the use of this Society the sum of three pounds, three shillings and four-pence.—Admitted by J. Cox."

moner,[1] with the privilege of wearing a *hat*. He had rooms in college, in which he resided the requisite periods to keep his terms, but, being entitled to a degree without examination, he paid no attention to the peculiar studies of the place. He despaired of becoming a great classical scholar, and he never either had or desired to have more than the slightest tincture of science which he had acquired at St. Andrew's. But he still assiduously applied to English *belles lettres*, and practiced English composition both in verse and prose. He gained some applause by a burlesque parody of Gray's "Bard." The author had been prevented from taking his place at dinner in the College Hall by the neglect of his barber, who failed to present himself in proper time to trim the *ailes de pigeon*, without which no one could then appear in public. In the moment of supposed disappointment, hunger, and irritation, the bard pours forth a violent malediction against the whole tribe of hair-dressers, and in a strain of prophetic denunciation foretells the overthrow of their dynasty in the future taste for cropped hair and unpowdered heads. He carried off the prize given by the College for English declamation. To this academical distinction he referred with complacency in his defense of Paine:—"I was formerly called upon, under the discipline of a college, to maintain these truths, and was rewarded for being thought to have successfully maintained that our present Constitution was by no means a remnant of Saxon liberty, nor any other institution of liberty, but the pure consequence of the oppression of the Norman tenures, which, spreading the spirit of freedom from one end of the kingdom to the other, enabled our brave fathers, not to reconquer, but for the first time to obtain, those privileges which are the inalienable inheritance of all mankind." In June, 1778, he took the honorary degree of A. M.

While still a student at Cambridge he contrived to keep his terms at Lincoln's Inn. He had not yet actually quitted the army, having obtained six months' leave of absence. It is said that during Easter and Trinity

[1] Jan. 13, 1776.—Admissus est Socio-comensalis Thomas Erskine, filius Henrici Davidis, Comitis Buchan, defuncti in academia Sancti Andreæ sub præsidio Magistri Dick, olim institutus ann. nat. 25. Mag. Collier et Atwood Tut."

Terms he excited a great sensation in the dining-hall by appearing with a student's black gown over the scarlet regimentals of the Royals, probably not having a decent suit of plain clothes to put on. He obtained a supply of cash by the sale of his lieutenancy on the 19th of September, 1775.[1]

As soon as it was practicable, he became a pupil in the chambers of Mr. Justice Buller, with whom he afterwards acted the famous scene in the trial of the Dean of St. Asaph; and when this great special pleader was made a judge, he entered himself with another not less celebrated, George Wood, afterwards made a Baron of the Exchequer, with whom he wisely continued nearly a year after he was called to the Bar, attending to the sage counsel of Littleton to his son, which ought to be impressed on the mind of every man who wishes to succeed in the profession of the law:—" Et sachez mon fitz que un des pluis honorables, et laudables, et profitables choses en nostre ley, est daver le sciens de un pleder en accions realx et personalx et pur c̄ ieo toy conseil especialmēt de mettr̄ tout ton corage et cure ce d'apprendr̄."[2]

Erskine never did become a profound jurist, but along with his lively imagination he had a logical understanding, and, by severe application at this period,[3] he made the respectable progress, which several who have been pushed high in our profession have never reached, of being able thoroughly to comprehend any question of law which he had occasion to consider,—to collect and arrange the authorities upon it, and to argue it lucidly and scientifically.

When Erskine was at Cambridge, no such debating society as the "Union" had been established; but when settled in London, he was in the habit of taking part in the debates of the Robin Hood, Coachmakers' Hall, and other spouting shops, which, according to the custom of

[1] I received this information almost with the celerity of the electric telegraph, from my right hon. friend, the present Secretary of War, accompanied by the following note:—
" My dear Campbell,—In your next volume pray *laud* the alacrity and regularity of the W. O., which can give you in two hours information regarding the sale of a commission seventy-one years since.—Yours truly,
" F. MAULE."
[2] Lit. s. 534.
[3] I have several of his commonplace books then compiled, showing great industry and perseverance.

the time, were attended by shoemakers, weavers, Quakers, law students, and Members of Parliament, each person paying sixpence, and being entitled to a glass of porter or a glass of punch, and in which there is said to have been often a display of high oratorical powers.

During the three years which followed his retirement from the army, notwithstanding the kind assistance of some of his friends, he was in great pecuniary straits He had an increasing family to maintain, besides defraying his own expenses as a Cambridge undergraduate and a student of law. Exercising the strictest economy and the most rigid self-denial, he often found it a sore matter to provide for the day which was passing over him. But, with a sanguine disposition, and a fixed determination of purpose, these difficulties only stimulated him to more vigorous exertion, that he might finally subdue them. "He had taken lodgings in Kentish Town, and would occasionally call for his wife at the house of a connection who kept a glass shop in Fleet Ditch, and used to talk of him as *our Tammy*."[1]

Jeremy Bentham, who had kept up an intercourse with him since the publication of his pamphlet on the Abuses of the Army, speaking of him at this time, says,—" I met him sometimes at Dr. Burton's. He was so shabbily dressed as to be quite remarkable. He was astonished when I told him I did not intend to practice. I remember his calling on me, and, not finding me at home, he wrote his name with chalk on my door."

Reynolds, the comic writer, in his "Life and Times," relates that at this time the villa of his father, an eminent solicitor, at Bromley, in Kent, was frequently visited by Erskine, of whom he gives the following lively description:—" The young student resided in small lodgings near Hampstead, and openly avowed that he lived on cow-beef because he could not afford any of a superior quality,[2] dressed shabbily, expressed the greatest gratitude to Mr. Harris for occasional free admissions to Covent Garden, and used boastingly to exclaim to my

[1] Townsend's Life of Erskine, on the authority of Mr. Pensam, the friend and Secretary of Bankrupts of Lord Eldon. The Right Hon. T. Erskine says, " The connection at whose house he is supposed (ex relatione Pensam) to have called was, I suspect, Mr. Moore, a jeweler on Ludgate Hill."

[2] I have often heard that he used to say that at this time he lived on " cow-heel and tripe."

father, 'Thank fortune, out of my own family I don't know a lord.' "[1]

But suddenly he was to be the idol of all ranks of the community, and to wallow in riches. Such a quick transition from misery to splendor is only equaled in the Arabian Nights, when the genii of the wonderful lamp appeared, to do the bidding of Aladdin. A sunrise within the tropics displays some fleeting crepuscular tints between utter darkness and the full solar blaze, and therefore can not be used to give a just notion of Erskine's first appearance to the dazzled eyes of the British public.

CHAPTER CLXXVII.

CONTINUATION OF THE LIFE OF ERSKINE TILL HE ENTERED THE HOUSE OF COMMONS.

ERSKINE was called to the Bar by the Honorable Society of Lincoln's Inn on the 3d day of July, 1778, in the end of Trinity Term;[2] but not having completed his special-pleading discipline, he continued working in the chambers of Baron Wood, and he might be considered as *in statu pupillari* till near the end of Michaelmas Term following. The 24th of November in that term was the critical day in his life, and exhibited the most remarkable scene ever witnessed in Westminster Hall.

Notwithstanding his agreeable manners, he seems to have made hardly any connections to be of use to him. No attorney or attorney's clerk was as yet aware of his

[1] This speech is very characteristic of the vanity which, under the guise of humility, he was accustomed to exhibit.

[2] "Lincoln's Inn.—At a Council there held the 3rd day of July, in the eighteenth year of the reign of our Sovereign Lord, King George the Third, and in the year of our Lord 1778,—Ordered, that the Honorable Thomas Erskine, one of the Fellows of this Society, having been regularly admitted to the Degree of Master of Arts in the University of Cambridge, and being thereby of full standing in this Society, according to the order of the 30th of June, 1762, and having kept twelve terms' commons, and conformed himself to the rules of this Society, be called to the Bar, on paying all his arrears and duties, and that he be published at the next Exercise in the Hall."

He was made Bencher in 1785; and Treasurer of the Society in 1795.

merit. But he had one retainer which came to him by an accident much like Thurlow's in the Douglas cause. Captain Baillie, a veteran seaman of genuine worth, having for his services been appointed Lieutenant Governor of Greenwich Hospital, discovered in that establishment gross abuses, by which those entitled to its advantages were defrauded. He presented successively petitions to the directors, to the governors, and to the Lords of Admiralty, praying for inquiry and redress. Meeting with no attention from any of them, he printed and circulated a statement of the case, detailing the real facts of it without any exaggeration, and reflecting with great but just severity upon Lord Sandwich, First Lord of the Admiralty, who, for electioneering purposes, had placed in the Hospital a large number of landsmen. Captain Baillie was immediately suspended by the Board of Admiralty. Lord Sandwich himself did not venture to appear openly as a prosecutor, but instigated by him, several of the inferior agents who had likewise been animadverted upon, although in much less severe terms, at the end of Trinity Term applied for and obtained from the Court of King's Bench a rule to show cause, in Michaelmas Term following, why a criminal information should not be filed against the author for a libel upon them. During the long vacation, Captain Baillie and Erskine, who had never seen each other before, met at a dinner party.[1] The Greenwich Hospital case, which had excited extraordinary interest, being mentioned, Erskine, not knowing that Captain Baillie was at table, entered upon it with glee, and, fired with indignation which he really felt, inveighed with much eloquence against the corrupt and tyrannical conduct of Lord Sandwich. Captain Baillie,

[1] The Right Hon. Thomas Erskine sends me the following account of his father casually becoming acquainted with his first client:—The circumstances that led to his meeting Captain Baillie was strikingly illustrative of the observation, that the slightest incidents are often providentially made the instruments of important results. My father had been engaged to spend the day with Mrs. Moore, the mother of his friend Charles Moore, and of Sir John Moore, and was proceeding with his friend C. M. across Spa Fields on foot, where a wide ditch tempted my father to prove his activity by leaping over it, which he accomplished; but, slipping on the other side, sprained his ankle, and was carried home. In the evening he was so much recovered that he determined to join a dinner party, to which he found an invitation on his return home. Captain Baillie was one of the party. If he had dined with Mrs. Moore, he might have waited for years before such an opportunity of showing what was in him might have presented itself."

finding out that he was a young lawyer just called to the Bar, who himself had been a sailor, swore that he would have him for one of his counsel. They parted without being introduced to each other; but the next day, while Erskine was sitting in his chambers in a fit of depression, and thinking that all his labor and sacrifices might be vain, as there seemed so little prospect of his ever having any opportunity to gain distinction,—a smart knock came to his door, and a slip of paper was brought to him with the words written upon it,—

" KING'S BENCH,
THE KING v. BAILLIE.
Retainer for the Defendant,
THE HONORABLE THOMAS ERSKINE,
ONE GUINEA."

and a yellow golden guinea was actually put into his hand.[1] He was vain enough to think that he was to be sole counsel to show cause against the rule, and he was much elated by his good fortune.

When Michaelmas Term came round, a brief was delivered to him in *Rex* v. *Baillie;* but what was his consternation to behold upon it—

" *With you, Mr. Bearcroft,*
Mr. Peckham,
Mr. Murphy, and
Mr. Hargrave."

He very reasonably despaired of being heard, or at all events of being listened to,—coming after so many seniors; and he gave himself no trouble to collect or to methodize the ideas upon the subject which had passed through his mind when he believed that the defense was to rest upon his own shoulders.

At a consultation, Bearcroft, Peckham, and Murphy were for consenting to a compromise which had been proposed by the prosecutors, that *the rule should be discharged, the defendant paying all costs.* " My advice, gentlemen," said the Junior, " may savor more of my late profession than my present, but I am against compromising." " I'll be d——d if I do !" said Captain Baillie, and he hugged Erskine in his arms, crying " You are the man for me !"

[1] This, his first fee, he used long to show as a curiosity; and I presume it is still preserved in the family.

About one o'clock in the afternoon of the 23rd of November, the Solicitor General, who had obtained the rule moved to make it absolute. Bearcroft began to show cause, and the affidavits being very long, and he and the three gentlemen who followed him being very prosy, and Mr. Hargrave, the last of them, having been several times while speaking obliged to leave the Court from indisposition, it was almost dark when he concluded his argument. Lord Mansfield, supposing that all the defendant's counsel had been heard, said, " We will go on with this case to-morrow morning." If the hearing had then proceeded, Erskine would not have done more than say a few words as a matter of form, and he might long have remained unknown.

When the Judges took their seats on the bench next day, the court was crowded in all parts, from the political aspect which the prosecution had assumed. The expectation was, that the Solicitor General would immediately proceed to support his rule, and would have no great difficulty in making it absolute;—but there rose from the back row a young gentleman whose name as well as whose face was unknown to almost all present, and who, in a collected, firm, but sweet, modest, and conciliating tone, thus began :—[1]

" My Lord, I am likewise of counsel for the author of this supposed libel; and if the matter for consideration had been merely a question of private wrong, I should have thought myself well justified, after the very able defense made by the learned gentlemen who have spoken before me, in sparing your Lordship, already fatigued with repetition, and in leaving my client to the judgment of the Court. But upon an occasion of this serious and dangerous complexion,— when a British subject is brought before a court of justice only for having ventured to attack abuses, which owe their continuance to the danger of attacking them,—when, without any motives but benevolence, justice, and public spirit, he has ventured to attack them, though supported by power, and in that department, too, where it was the duty of his office

---

[1] Under such appalling circumstances, it might rather have been expected, that, when he heard his own voice for the first time in a public assembly, the description would have been applicable to him—
" And back recoil'd, he knew not why,
E'en at the sound himself had made."

to detect and expose them,—I can not relinquish the high privilege of trying to do justice to such merit,—I will not give up even my small share of the honor of repelling and of exposing so odious a prosecution."— After some general observations on the common herd of libelers whom the Court had been accustomed to punish, he said, "I beseech your Lordships to compare these men and their works with my client and the publication before the Court. *Who is he? What was his duty? What has he written? To whom has he written? and what motive induced him to write?*" These few questions, which he answered *seriatim*, the advocate made the heads of his inimitable discourse—showing that his client had written nothing but the truth, and had acted strictly within the line of his duty. He was thus about to conclude:—"Such, my Lords, is the case. The defendant,—not a disappointed malicious informer, prying into official abuses, because without office himself—but himself a man in office;—not troublesomely inquisitive into other men's departments, but conscientiously correcting his own; —doing it pursuant to the rules of law, and, what heightens the character, doing it at the risk of his office, from which the effrontery of power has already suspended him, without proof of his guilt—a conduct not only unjust and illiberal, but highly disrespectful to this Court; whose judges sit in the double capacity of ministers of the law, and governors of this sacred and abused institution. Indeed, Lord Sandwich has in my mind acted such a part—" [*Here* (in the words of the report) Lord Mansfield, observing the counsel heated with his subject, and growing personal on the First Lord of the Admiralty, told him that Lord Sandwich was not before the Court.] *Erskine:* "I know that he is not formally before the Court, but for that very reason *I will bring him before the Court.* He has placed these men in the front of the battle in hopes to escape under their shelter, but I will not join in battle with them; *their* vices, though screwed up to the highest pitch of human depravity, are not of dignity enough to vindicate the combat with *me.* I will drag *him* to light who is the dark mover behind this scene of iniquity. I assert that the Earl of Sandwich has but one road to escape out of this business without pollution and disgrace,—and that is, by publicly disavowing the acts of the prosecutors, and restoring Captain Baillie to his command! If he does this, then his offense will be no more than the too common one of having suffered his own *personal* interest to prevail over his *public* duty in placing his voters in the Hospital. But if, on the contrary, he continues to protect the prosecutors, in spite of the evidence of their guilt, which has excited the abhorrence of the numerous audience who crowd this Court, IF HE KEEPS THIS INJURED MAN SUSPENDED, OR DARES TO TURN THAT SUSPENSION INTO A REMOVAL, I SHALL THEN NOT SCRUPLE TO DECLARE HIM AN ACCOMPLICE IN THEIR GUILT, A SHAMELESS OPPRESSOR, A DISGRACE TO HIS RANK, AND A TRAITOR TO HIS TRUST. But as I should be very sorry that the fortune of my brave and honorable friend should depend either upon the exercise of Lord Sandwich's virtues or the influence of his fears, I do most earnestly entreat the Court to mark the malignant object of this prosecution, and to defeat it.—I beseech you, my Lords, to consider that even by discharging the rule, and with costs, the defendant is neither protected nor restored. I trust, therefore, your Lordships will not rest satisfied with fulfilling your JUDICIAL duty, but, as the strongest evidence of foul abuses has by accident come collaterally before you, that you will protect a brave and public-spirited officer from the persecution this writing has brought upon him, and not suffer so dreadful an example to go abroad into the world, as the ruin of an upright man for having faithfully discharged his duty. My Lords, this matter is of the last importance. I speak not as an ADVOCATE alone—I speak to you AS A MAN—as a member of a state whose very existence depends upon her naval strength. If our fleets are to be crippled by the baneful influence of elections, WE ARE LOST INDEED. If the seaman, while he exposes his body to fatigues and dangers, looking forward to Greenwich as an asylum for infirmity and old age, sees the gates of it blocked up by corruption, and hears the riot and mirth of luxurious landsmen drowning the groans and complaints of the wounded, helpless companions of his glory,—he will tempt the seas no more. The Admiralty may press HIS BODY, indeed, at the expense of humanity and the Constitution, but they can not press *his mind,*—they can not press the heroic ardor of a British sailor; and instead of a fleet to carry terror all round the globe, the Admiralty may not be able much longer to amuse us with even the peaceable, unsubstantial pageant of a review.[1] FINE AND IMPRISONMENT! The man deserves a PALACE instead of a PRISON who prevents the palace built by the public bounty of his country from being converted into a dungeon, and who sacrifices his own security to the interests of humanity and virtue. And now, my Lords, I have done; but not without thanking your Lordships for the very indulgent attention I have received, though in so late a stage of this proceeding, and notwithstanding my great incapacity and inexperience. I resign my client into your hands, and I resign him with a well-founded confidence and hope; because that torrent of corruption which has unhappily overwhelmed every other part of the Constitution is, by the blessing of Providence, stopped HERE by the sacred independence of the Judges. I KNOW that your Lordships will determine ACCORDING TO LAW; and, therefore, if an information should be suffered to be filed, I shall bow to the sentence, and shall consider this meritorious publication to be, indeed, an offense against the laws of this country; but then I shall not scruple to say, that it is high time for every honest man to remove himself from a country in which he can no longer do his duty to the public with safety,—where cruelty and inhumanity are suffered to impeach virtue, — and where vice passes through a court of justice unpunished and unreproved."

The impression made upon the audience by this address is said to have been unprecedented; and I must own that, all the circumstances considered, it is the most wonderful forensic effort of which we have any account in our annals. It was the *debut* of a barrister just called and wholly unpracticed in public speaking — before a court crowded with men of the highest distinction, belonging to all parties in the state. He came after four eminent counsel, who might be supposed to have exhausted the subject. He was called to order by a venerable Judge, whose word had been law in that Hall above a quarter of a century. His exclamation, "I will bring him before the Court," and the crushing denunciation of Lord Sandwich,—in which he was enabled to persevere

[1] There had just before been a naval review at Portsmouth.

from the sympathy of the by-standers, and even of the Judges, who in strictness ought again to have checked his irregularity,—are as soul-stirring as anything in this species of eloquence presented to us by ancient or modern times. I hardly less admire his quiet peroration, which, with an appearance of modesty and submission, breathes confidence and defiance. A commonplace declaimer would have thought it necessary to conclude with some noisy, mouthing sentences. How much more effective must have been the lowered tone of the man who knew instinctively to touch the feelings—speaking in an assembly where every look was fixed upon him—where every syllable he uttered was eagerly caught up—where breathing was almost suspended—and as often as he paused a flake of snow would have been heard to fall!

Need I mention that the rule was discharged with costs? It would be easy to narrate the congratulations which the young counsel received in Court, and his ovation when, on retiring, he walked through the Hall. But who could adequately describe his own feelings, when all his anxieties were over, and he knew that he had conquered fame for himself, and secured all worldly comforts to those who were dear to him? This last consideration I believe was nearest his heart. Being asked how he had the courage to stand up so boldly against Lord Mansfield, he answered, that he thought his little children were plucking his robe, and that he heard them saying, " Now, father, is the time to get us bread." He himself is stated to have given, many years after, at the " King of Clubs," the following gay account of his start in the profession:—

" I had scarcely a shilling in my pocket when I got my first retainer. It was sent to me by a Captain Baillie, of the navy, who held an office at the Board of Greenwich Hospital; and I was to show cause, in the Michaelmas Term, against a rule that had been obtained in the preceding term, calling upon him to show cause why a criminal information for a libel, reflecting on Lord Sandwich's conduct as governor of that charity, should not be filed against him. I had met, during the long vacation, this Captain Baillie at a friend's table, and, after dinner, I expressed myself with some warmth, probably with some eloquence, on the corruption of Lord Sandwich as First

Lord of the Admiralty, and then adverted to the scandalous practices imputed to him with regard to Greenwich Hospital. Baillie nudged the person who sat next to him, and asked who I was? Being told that I had just been called to the Bar, and had been formerly in the navy, Baillie exclaimed, with an oath, 'Then I'll have him for my counsel!' I trudged down to Westminster Hall, when I got the brief, and, being the junior of five, who would be heard before me, never dreamed that the Court would hear me at all. Dunning, Bearcroft, Wallace, Bower,[1] Hargrave, were all heard at considerable length, and I was to follow. Hargrave was long-winded, and tired the Court. It was a bad omen: but, as my good fortune would have it, he was afflicted with the strangury, and was obliged to retire once or twice in the course of his argument. This protracted the cause so long that, when he had finished, Lord Mansfield said that the remaining counsel should be heard the next morning. This was exactly what I wished. I had the whole night to arrange, in my chambers, what I had to say the next morning, and I took the Court with their faculties awake and freshened, succeeded quite to my own satisfaction (sometimes the surest proof that you have satisfied others), and as I marched along the Hall, after the rising of the Judges, the attorneys flocked around me with their retainers. I have since flourished, but I have always blessed God for the providential strangury of poor Hargrave."[2]

Briefs and fees—large and small—now flowed in a continual stream into the chambers of the counselor who had so astonished the world. He was at once in full business; and it should be recorded, for the honor of the "long robe," that, although he passed over the heads of many who had fully established themselves, or were gradually beginning to establish themselves, in Westminster Hall, there was no caballing against him; he had not even to encounter envy or ill-will; he was hailed by his competitors as

---

[1] Erskine, or more likely his reporter, had forgot the names of the counsel. Dunning was on the other side; and Wallace and Bower were not engaged in the cause.

[2] Adair's Clubs of London. On other occasions he varied the circumstances a good deal, and he carried the number of retainers which he received before he left the Hall to the number of SIXTY-FIVE, inducing a suspicion that they had multiplied from narration.

conferring new honor upon them; and, bearing his faculties most meekly, he became, and ever continued a favorite with all ranks of the profession.

He practiced in the King's Bench. There he was very courteously treated by Lord Mansfield, who rejoiced to see the young officer of the Royals, whom he had invited to sit by him at the Assizes, transformed into the most eminent advocate at the English Bar. To this venerable peer, and to all other Judges, Erskine behaved with respect, but with uniform independence and freedom,— never basely surrendering a cause in which he knew that he was right, with a view to succeed, by favor, in others in which he might be wrong.

In the beginning of the following year, he gained additional *éclat* as counsel in the famous court-martial, held at Portsmouth, on Admiral Lord Keppel, to try the charges tardily brought against him by Sir Hugh Palliser, of incapacity and misconduct in the battle off Ushant, with the French Fleet, under the command of Count d'Orvilliers. This case, bearing a great resemblance to that of Admiral Byng, excited quite as much interest, and many thought would have the same fatal termination. The party accused, however, being not only innocent, but belonging to the Whigs, who, from the disasters of the war, had risen much in public opinion, was extremely popular. For his very triumphant acquittal, he was indebted to his advocate. He wished to be defended by Dunning and Lee: but they, giving him their general advice as to the line of defense he should take, recommended Erskine, who, in addition to his abilities, had the advantage of being well acquainted with naval language and naval maneuvers. The trial lasted thirteen days, during all which time Erskine exerted himself for his client with unabated zeal and consummate discretion. He was not allowed to examine the witnesses *viva voce*, nor to address the Court; but he suggested questions, which were put in writing,—and he composed the speech which Lord Keppel delivered on the merits of his case. Considering the plain understandings to which this was addressed, I think admirable tact is discovered by its simplicity:[1]

[1] In a memoir of Erskine in the "Gentlemen's Magazine," it is said that, "having drawn up Admiral Keppel's defense, he personally examined all

"After forty years spent in the service of my country," (said the hoary-headed Admiral in his peroration, which seemed to be the genuine effusion of his own mind,) "little did I think of being brought to a court-martial to answer to charges of misconduct, negligence in the performance of duty, and tarnishing the honor of the British navy. These charges, Sir, have been advanced by my accuser. Whether he has succeeded in proving them or not, the Court will determine. Before he brought me to a trial, it would have been candid in him to have given vent to his thoughts, and not, by a deceptive show of kindness, to lead me into the mistake of supposing a friend in the man who was my enemy in his heart, and was shortly to be my accuser. Yet, Sir, after all my misconduct,—after so much negligence in the performance of duty, and after tarnishing so deeply the honor of the British navy,—my accuser made no scruple to sail a second time with the man who had been the betrayer of his country. Nay, during the time we were on shore, he corresponded with me on terms of friendship; and even in his letters he approved of what had been done—of the part which he now condemns, and of the very negligent misconduct which has since been so offensive in his eyes. Such behavior, Sir, on the part of my accuser, gave me little reason to apprehend an accusation from him. Nor had I any reason to suppose that the State would criminate me. When I returned, his Majesty received me with the greatest applause. Even the First Lord of the Admiralty gave his flattering testimony to the rectitude of my conduct, and seemed, with vast sincerity, to applaud my zeal for the service. Yet, in the moment of approbation, it seems as if a scheme was concerting against my life; for, without any previous notice, five articles of charge were exhibited against me by Sir Hugh Palliser, who, most unfortunately for his cause, lay himself under an imputation for disobedience of orders, at the very time when he accused me of negligence. This, to be sure, was a very ingenious mode of getting the start of me. An accusation exhibited against a commander-in-chief might draw off the public attention for neglect of duty in

the Admirals and Captains of the fleet, and satisfied himself that he could substantiate the innocence of his client, before the speech which he had written for him was read."

an inferior officer. I could almost wish, in pity to my accuser, that appearances were not so strong against him. The trial has left my accuser without excuse, and he now cuts that sort of figure which I trust in God all accusers of innocence will ever exhibit! As to this Court, I entreat you, gentlemen, who compose it, to recollect that you sit here as a court of honor, as well as a court of justice; and I now stand before you, not merely to save my life, but for a purpose of infinitely greater moment—to clear my fame. My conscience is perfectly clear—I have no secret machination, no dark contrivance, to answer for. My heart does not reproach me. As to my enemies, I would not wish the greatest enemy I have in the world to be afflicted with so heavy a punishment as my accuser's conscience."

On the finishing of this speech, the Hall resounded with shouts of approbation. The Court, by an unanimous verdict, fully and honorably acquitted the Admiral, affirming that, far from having sullied the honor of the navy, he had acted as became a brave, judicious, and experienced officer. The cities of London and Westminster were illuminated two successive nights, and the mob breaking into the house of Sir Hugh Palliser destroyed his furniture and burned him in effigy.

Erskine did not on this occasion obtain much public applause, as the share he had had in the conduct of the defense was little known; but from his grateful client he received the munificent present of a thousand pounds. The correspondence between them is highly creditable to both:—

"Audley Square, Feb. 23, 1799."

"MY DEAR SIR,

"Do me the favor to accept the inclosed notes,[1] as an acknowledgment of the zealous and indefatigable industry you have shown in the long and tedious course of my court-martial. It is to your unremitting labors, together with the assistance of Mr. Dunning and Mr. Lee, that I chiefly owe its having been attended with so honorable a conclusion. I shall be very happy if I have been in any degree the means of furnishing you with opportunities of showing those talents which only wanted to be made known to carry you to the summit of your profession. I

[1] Two bank-notes of £500 each.

shall ever rejoice in this commencement of a friendship which I hope daily to improve,
"I am, &c.,
"A. KEPPEL."

Greatly delighted, Erskine called in Audley Square to return thanks in person; but, not finding the Admiral at home, wrote the following touching acknowledgment in the porter's hall:—

"Audley Square, Tuesday afternoon.

"You must no doubt, my dear Sir, have been very much surprised at receiving no answer to your most generous letter, but, I trust, you are well enough acquainted with my temper and feelings to find out the reason, and to pardon me. I was, indeed, altogether unable to answer it. I could not submit to do injustice to my gratitude and affection, and was therefore obliged to be silent, till I could wait upon you in person; and, having missed you, must be silent still. I shall, therefore, only say, that the generous present you have sent me is out of all kind of bounds and measure, even if the occasion had afforded me an opportunity of rendering them; how much more when your own ability and the absurdity of the occasion wholly disappointed my zeal! At all events, the honor of attending Admiral Keppel would have been in itself a most ample reward—an honor which, whatever my future fortunes may be, I shall ever consider as the brightest and happiest in my life, and which my children's children will hereafter claim as an inheritance.

"I do most sincerely pray God that every blessing may attend you, and that you may be spared for the protection of a country which has proved itself worthy of protection. My heart must ever be with you. Adieu, my dear Sir, and believe me to be, with the greatest respect and regard,
"Your most grateful and affectionate
"humble servant,
"T. ERSKINE."

He then, with a boyishness of disposition which distinguished him all his life, hurried to Bromley, and showing his wealth to the Reynoldses, exclaimed "*Voilà!* the nonsuit of *cow* beef, my good friends."

This spring he joined the Home Circuit, where his fame had preceded him, and he was immediately in full employment. Riding over a blasted heath between Lewes and Guildford with his friend William Adam, afterwards Lord Chief Commissioner of the Jury Court in Scotland,—(whether from some supernatural communication, or the workings of his own fancy, I know not) he exclaimed, after a long silence, "Willie, the time will come when I shall be invested with the robes of Lord Chancellor, and the Star of the Thistle shall blaze on my bosom!"

Soon after his return to London he was retained as counsel at the bar of the House of Commons, against a bill which caused much agitation, as it touched the liberty of the press. Under a grant from King James I., the Stationers' Company and the Universities of Oxford and Cambridge had enjoyed the exclusive right of printing almanacs, till its validity was denied by Mr. Carnan, a bookseller in St. Paul's Churchyard, who published other almanacs cheaper, more copious, and more correct. Legal proceedings being instituted against him, it was solemnly decided by the Court of Common Pleas and the Court of Exchequer that the grant was void. Lord North, Prime Minister and Chancellor of the University of Cambridge, thereupon introduced a bill into Parliament to vest the monopoly in the parties who had so long usurped it. Erskine's attack upon this unjust bill appears in the printed collection of his speeches which he himself revised, and it was not only highly esteemed by himself, but it has been loudly praised by others. I confess, however, that its merits seem to me to have been considerably overrated. Though sensible and judicious, it deals in commonplaces, and might have been made by a very inferior declaimer. Nevertheless, the tale is told,—so marvelous to those who have witnessed the utter neglect with which the best speeches of counsel at the bar of either chamber of Parliament are treated,—that "the House remained crowded till he had concluded, and that the rejection of the bill by a large majority, upon a division which immediately afterwards took place, was entirely to be ascribed to his eloquence." Lord Eliot, Member for Cornwall, who, at the desire of Lord North, his brother-in-law, had come from the extreme west to support the bill, certainly divided against it, declaring in the lobby that "after Mr. Erskine's speech he found it impossible to do otherwise.

But, although the advocate can not be denied the rare glory of having influenced one vote by argument, I suspect that the result is to be ascribed to the contemplated job which was finally perpetrated, whereby the monopolists were indemnified for their loss of the public revenue.[1]

His next appearance of which we have an account was as counsel for Lieutenant Bourne of the Royal Navy, brought up before the Court of King's Bench for having sent a challenge to Admiral Sir James Wallace, his commanding officer, who was said to have used him very tyrannically. The circumstances of the case are devoid of interest, but Erskine's speech must ever be curious, as showing how, even before English judges sitting on their tribunal, a practice could be spoken of which I hope will speedily be condemned as much by the fashionable world, as by law, reason, and religion. Thus he meekly began— being about to declare the conduct of the defendant to be so meritorious that he himself under the same circumstances would have pursued his old commander, Sir David Lindsay, the nephew of Lord Mansfield, through created space, that he might force him into the field:—

"I build my principal hope of a mild sentence upon much more that will be secretly felt by the Court than may be decently expressed from the bar; for though I am convinced that your Lordships have all those nice sensations which distinguish men of honor from the vulgar, and that your genuine feelings for the defendant must be rather compassion and approbation than resentment, yet I can not address myself to your Lordships sitting on that bench, and clothed in the robes of magistracy, in the same language by which I think I could insure your favor to my client in another place. It is indeed very unfortunate for the gentleman whose cause I am defending, that your Lordships are bound, as judges of the law, to consider that as a crime in him against the society in which he lived, which yet if he had not committed, that very society would have expelled him, like a wretch, from its communion; and that you must speak to him the words of reproach and reprobation for doing that, which if he had not done, your Lordships would scorn to speak to him at all as private men. Surely, My Lords,

[1] 20 Parl. Hist. 608–621. Ersk. Speeches, i. 38.

this is a harsh and a singular situation. . . . . I profess to think, with my worthy friend who spoke befor: me, that the practice of private dueling, and all that behavior which leads to it, is a high offense against the laws of God; and I agree with that great Prince (Frederick II. of Prussia), that it is highly destructive of good government among men,—a practice certainly unknown to the most refined and heroic people the revolutions of time and manners have produced in the world,—and by which the most amiable man in society may be lost by an inglorious death, depending upon mere chance. *But though I feel all this, as I think a Christian and a humane man ought to feel it, yet I am not ashamed to acknowledge that I would rather be pilloried by the Court in every square in London, than obey the law of England, which I thus profess so highly to respect, in a case where that custom, which I have reprobated, warned me that the public voice was in the other scale.* My Lords, every man who hears me feels that so would he; for, without the respect and good opinion of the world we live in, no matter upon what foundation it is built, life itself is a worse imprisonment than any which the laws can inflict; and the closest dungeon to which a court of justice can send an offender, is far better with the secret pity and even approbation of those that send him there, than the range of the universe with the contempt and scorn of its inhabitants." After referring to voluminous affidavits to his client's character, he continued:—"A man in possession of such a character as this, justly acquired, will not consent to sacrifice it to the pride of any man; it is a just and sacred pledge, and he to whom God in his providence has given it deserves every sort of reproach if he parts with it in a light cause. Unquestionably, the captain may desire every officer, whose duty it is to walk the quarter-deck, to go to the top of the mast of the ship; but he can not do that without an adequate cause, and without subjecting himself to the disgrace and punishment of a court-martial. I have had the honor to sail with a man who is an honor to that profession,—a gentleman, I believe, the most accomplished that this nation or world can produce, and who has the honor to be nearly allied to your Lordship. Under him I learned what idea ought to be entertained on this subject, and what respect ought to be paid to officers in all stations; and the result of what I saw there, joined with my own original feelings, is this—that, *although I was placed on board his ship, to reverence him as my father, by the command of my own, and although at this hour I do reverence him in that character, yet I feel that if he had treated me in that manner, I should not have made Jamaica or Bath the limit of my resentments, but would have sought him through all created space, till he had answer made and done me justice!* There are some injuries which even Christianity doth not call upon a man to forgive or to forget, because God, the author of Christianity, has not made our natures capable of forgiving or forgetting them. I must plead for the infirmities of human nature, and beseech your Lordships once more to consider what the honor of an officer is; consider that, and say what punishment this gentleman deserves. You have before you a young military man, jealous, as he ought to be, of his fame and honor, treated with the grossest indignity by his superior officer, smothering his honest resentment as long as the superior duties of military service required that painful sacrifice,—and afterwards pursuing the man who had dishonored him, with a perseverance, certainly in criminal opposition to the law, but in obedience to what I may, without offense even here, term the generous infirmity in his nature, nourished by the long-established, though erroneous, customs of the world. . . . . I rely with confidence upon the justice, the humanity, and the honor of the Court!"[1]

All that Erskine had yet done perhaps might have been accomplished by a skillful and fortunate rhetorician. He had now an opportunity of addressing to the feelings of a jury that fine union of argument and passion which constituted the character of his oratory, and of showing that by his intuitive knowledge of the principles of criminal law, by his steady patriotism and his undaunted courage, the liberties of his country, while he survived, were to be in no danger from the most violent assault that could be made upon them, through a perversion of judicial procedure.

Lord George Gordon, an ignorant and enthusiastic, but very well-meaning, young nobleman, having testified a violent horror of popery, had been elected "President of

[1] Townsend's Eminent Judges, i. 412.

the Protestant Association," and, at the head of upwards of forty thousand persons, had proceeded to the House of Commons to present a petition of the "Associated Protestants" for a repeal of certain slight modifications recently introduced into the atrocious penal code which then ground down our Roman Catholic fellow-citizens. This meeting, though rather tumultuary, had no aim against the Constitution of the country, and all who belonged to it were specially loyal to the King from sympathy of sentiment on religious subjects; but, unfortunately, it ushered in the fatal riots which for so many days desolated the metropolis, which shook, for a time, even the foundations of the Government, and the recital of which, under the misnomer of "Lord George Gordon's riots" still frightens us. Although guilty of imprudence in exciting the fanaticism of the multitude,—when he saw among them any inclination to violate the law, he exerted himself to restore order, and he accompanied the Sheriffs of London into the City to exercise his influence among his followers for that purpose. Yet, when tranquillity was restored, he was committed to the Tower, and he was indicted for high treason in levying war against the Crown. He certainly was in very serious jeopardy, for a universal panic had prevailed for some days among all those who were to be his jurymen: they had expected that their houses would be burnt down, and their wives and daughters would be violated; they actually had seen the prisons broken open, fires blazing, and blood flowing in various parts of the metropolis, while the magistrates were paralyzed with fear, and the soldiery could not act without orders—all these calamities being imputed to "the President of the Protestant Association." The Government likewise thought that it was necessary for the future tranquillity of the country, that a signal sacrifice should be offered up to the offended majesty of the laws, however much the victim might be deserving of pity; and, in consequence, the prosecution was conducted with all the power of the Crown, and with an earnest desire to obtain a conviction. But Erskine was counsel for the prisoner.

Regularly trained to the profession of the law—having practiced thirty years at the Bar—having been Attorney General above seven years—having been present at many

trials for high treason, and having conducted several
myself,—I again peruse with increased astonishment and
delight, the speech delivered on this occasion by him who
had recently thrown aside the scarlet uniform of a
subaltern in the army—which he had substituted for the
blue jacket of a midshipman, thrust upon him while he
was a school-boy. Here I find not only wonderful acuteness, powerful reasoning, enthusiastic zeal and burning
eloquence, but the most masterly view ever given of the
English law of high treason,—the foundation of all our
liberties.

The trial came on in the Court of King's Bench, before
Lord Mansfield and his brethren. There had been a
strange selection of a leading counsel against the Crown,
in Mr. Kenyon (afterwards Lord Kenyon), who, though
well acquainted with the technicalities of real property,
and the practice of Courts of Equity, had no talent for
public speaking, and was entirely devoid of constitutional
learning. Against the case made for the prosecution, he
delivered a very honest, but very inefficient, speech; and
when he sat down, the friends of Lord George were in an
agony of apprehension. According to the usual routine,
Erskine ought to have followed immediately; but, to
give the jurymen time to recover from the confusion into
which they had been thrown, he prayed that, according
to one precedent to be found in the "State Trials," his
speech might be postponed till after the evidence for the
prisoner had been closed. To this the Court assented,
and a great many witnesses were called, the weight of
whose evidence as to the personal demeanor of the
prisoner, was much weakened with the jury by what they
stated, on cross-examination, respecting the outrages
which were actually committed.

Erskine rose a little after midnight, and not only instantly dispelled all feeling of exhaustion and lassitude
from the minds of the jury, the Judges, and the
bystanders, but, while he spoke, they seemed all to be inspired with a new ethereal existence, and they listened as
if addressed by some pure Intelligence of Heaven, who
had appeared to instruct them!

His speech is too closely-reasoned and concatenated to
allow me to give any adequate notion of it by extracts.
After a most captivating proemium, he proceeded to lay

down the law in the able manner to which I have referred, asserting nothing that could be gainsaid—but artfully adapting the points he made most salient to the facts on which he was to comment. Thus he felicitously referred to the destruction of the house of the presiding Judge during these riots,—drawing from it an argument in favor of his client :—

" Can any man living believe that Lord George Gordon could possibly have excited the mob to destroy the house of that great and venerable magistrate, who has presided so long in this great and high tribunal, that the oldest of us do not remember him with any other impression than the awful form and figure of justice ; a magistrate, who had always been the friend of the Protestant Dissenters against the ill-timed jealousies of the Establishment ;— his countryman, too ; and, without adverting to the partiality not unjustly imputed to men of that country, a man of whom any country might be proud ?—No, gentlemen, it is not credible that a man of noble birth and liberal education (unless agitated by the most implacable personal resentment, which is not imputed to the prisoner), could possibly consent to this burning of the house of Lord Mansfield."

He then reviewed the whole of the evidence, varying his tone from mild explanation to furious invective,—always equally skillful and impressive, and ever carrying the sympathies of his hearers along with him in the most daring flights of his eloquence. Now was witnessed the single instance recorded in our judicial annals, of an advocate in a court of justice introducing an oath by the sacred name of the Divinity,—and it was introduced not only without any violation of taste, or offense to pious ears, but with the thrilling sensations of religious rapture, caught from the lips of the man who, as if by inspiration, uttered the awful sound. Arguing upon the construction of certain words attributed to Lord George Gordon, he exclaimed, " But this I will say, that he must be a *ruffian*, and not a lawyer, who would dare to tell an English jury that such ambiguous words, hemmed closely between others not only innocent, but meritorious, are to be adopted to constitute guilt by rejecting both introduction and sequel." Then, after noticing the offer made to the Goverment by the prisoner himself to quell the disturbance, he ventured upon the following bold and extraordinary sentence: " I say, BY GOD, that man is a ruffian, who shall, after this, presume to build upon such honest, artless conduct, as an evidence of guilt." The sensation produced by this daring appeal to the feelings of the jury, and by the magic of the voice, the eye, the face, the action with which it was uttered, is related by those present on this memorable occasion to have been electrical. Some have supposed that the oath was premeditated; but " intuitive and momentary impulse could alone have prompted a flight which it alone could sustain; and as its failure would, indeed, have been fatal, so its eminent success must be allowed to rank it among the most famous feats of oratory."[1]

When he had shown the futility of all the supposed proofs relied upon for the Crown, and dwelt upon the strong testimony adduced to establish the innocence of the prisoner, he thus proceeded:—

" What, then, has produced this trial for high treason? What! but the inversion of all justice, by judging from consequences, instead of from causes and designs? What! but the artful manner in which the Crown has endeavored to blend the petitioners in a body, and the zeal with which an animated disposition conducted it, with the melancholy crimes that followed—crimes which the shameful indolence of our magistrates, which the total extinction of all police and all government, suffered to be committed in broad day, in the delirium of drunkenness, by an unarmed banditti, without a head, without plan or object, and without a refuge from the instant gripe of justice; a banditti, with whom the Associated Protestants and their President had no manner of connection, and whose cause they overturned, dishonored, and ruined? How unchristian, then, is it to attempt, without evidence, to infect your imaginations, who are upon your oaths dispassionately and disinterestedly to try the offense of assembling a multitude to petition for the repeal of a law, —by blending it with the subsequent catastrophe, on which every man's mind may be supposed to retain some degree of irritation! O fie! O fie! it is taking advantage of all the infirmities of our nature. Do they wish you, while you are listening to the evidence, to connect it with

[1] Ed. Review, vol. xvi. p. 108.

consequences in spite of reason and truth, to hang the millstone of prejudice round his innocent neck to sink him? If there be such men, may God forgive them for the attempt, and inspire you with fortitude and wisdom to do your duty to your fellow-citizens with calm, steady, reflecting minds. I may now, therefore, relieve you from the pain of hearing me any longer, and be myself relieved from a subject which agitates and distresses me. Since Lord George Gordon stands clear of every hostile act or purpose against the legislature of his country or the rights of his fellow-subjects,—since the whole tenor of his conduct repels the belief of the traitorous intention charged by the indictment,—my task is finished. I shall make no address to your passions. I will not remind you of the long and rigorous imprisonment he has suffered; I will not speak to you of his great youth, of his illustrious birth, or of his uniformly animated and generous zeal in Parliament for the Constitution of his country. Such topics might be useful in the balance of a doubtful case. At present, the plain and rigid rules of justice and truth are sufficient to entitle me to your verdict: and may God Almighty, who is the sacred author of both, fill your minds with the deepest impression of them, and with virtue to follow those impressions! You will then restore my innocent client to liberty, and me to that peace of mind which, since the protection of his innocence in any part depended upon me, I have never known."

Perhaps there is nothing in the speech more admirable than the soft, quiet, complacent key in which it concludes. Without arrogance or presumption, he considers that the cause is won—no further exertion is necessary,—" *radit iter liquidum.*" By a quick interchange of thought the sentiment is imbibed by the jury, that their verdict is already unanimously settled, and that they have only to go through the form of pronouncing it. Accordingly they were proof against the reply of the Solicitor General; and, after a rather severe summing up from Lord Mansfield, at a quarter past five in the morning they said, NOT GUILTY. All reasonable men rejoiced. Even Dr. Johnson said " he was glad Lord George Gordon had escaped, rather than that a precedent should be established for hanging a man for *constructive treason;*" " which," adds

Boswell, "in consistency with his true, manly, constitutional Toryism, he considered would be a dangerous engine of arbitrary power."[1] If the precedent had been established in this instance, it certainly would have been followed in 1794, and our lost liberties could only have been restored by some dreadful convulsion. But a just notion of the offense of compassing the death of the King, and of levying war against him in his realm, was now impressed upon the English nation by the exertions of Erskine; and afterwards, in the "Reign of Terror," when the grand struggle came, he was enabled to march from victory to victory.[2]

CHAPTER CLXXVIII.

CONTINUATION OF THE LIFE OF LORD ERSKINE TILL THE CONCLUSION OF THE CASE OF THE DEAN OF ST. ASAPH.

WE are next to see our illustrious advocate on the political stage,—where his success was by no means so brilliant. He was of a Whig family, and he ever adhered steadily to the Whig party. Its three great leaders, when he appeared in public life, were all in the meridian of their reputation,—the "Coalition" not yet having dimmed the luster of Fox's name—Burke not yet having been disturbed from his liberal course by the French Revolution,—and the fatal web of pecuniary embarrassment not yet having been wound round the soul of Sheridan, leading him to discreditable actions and degrading habits. These men rapturously hailed the rising genius of one likely to prove so powerful an auxiliary ; but they advised that with his full occupation in his profession he should not enter Parliament either while Lord North was minister, or during the Governments of Lord Rockingham or Lord Shelburne. When the "Coalition" was formed, however, a long tenure of power was expected by his friends, his promotion to be a law officer of the Crown on the first vacancy was promised to him, and his assistance was wanted against a host of lawyers who,

[1] Vol. iv. p. 92. [2] State Trials, vol. xxi. p. 485–647.

joining the Opposition, were now obstructing business in the House of Commons, although the Ministry could command large majorities upon a division. There was some difficulty in finding a seat for the aspirant. But Sir William Gordon, who represented Portsmouth, was prevailed upon to take the Chiltern Hundreds, in consideration of a comfortable provision made for him; and Erskine succeeded him, making himself popular with the inhabitants by boasting of his maritime education, and his warm attachment to the naval service. The "Point" afforded scope for innumerable jests against him from Jekyll, and his other friends in Westminster Hall; but he bore them all with great good humor, and took off the effect of a bad pun by a worse.[1]

There was great eagerness to hear his maiden speech in St. Stephen's Chapel. Almost all mankind anticipated that he would still raise his reputation by being a match for the younger Pitt, who had recently, all at once, placed himself in the very highest class of parliamentary orators; but a few judicious men, who knew Erskine best, had misgivings as to his success in a new field, in which, if not higher, very different qualifications were required from those he had hitherto displayed. Thus wrote one of his professional friends to another, detailing the gossip of the robing-room:—

"Nov. 3, 1783.

"Wallace is gone down to Teignmouth, the place where Dunning died,—in all probability on the same errand. Everybody says that Erskine will be Solicitor General, and if he is, and indeed whether he is or not, he will have had the most rapid rise that has been known at the Bar. It is four years and a half since he was called, and in that time he has cleared £8,000 or £9,000 besides paying his debts,—got a silk gown, and business of at least £3,000 a year—a seat in Parliament—and, over and above, has made his brother Lord Advocate. For my part I have great doubts whether his coming into Parliament was a wise thing. He sacrificed his House of Commons business, which was very profitable. He has

---

[1] Jekyll said to him, "Having been long a wanderer, I hope you *will now stick to the Point*." He answered, "Yes, I have an eye to the *pole* since I know where the *Pointers* are." My readers have probably heard of the Point at Portsmouth, and its inhabitants.

several of Burke's defects, and is not unlikely to have his fate, and the expectation from him will be too great to be satisfied. We expect a match between him and Pitt, and another between Fox and Flood."

Deep was the disappointment of the Opposition—loud was the exultation of the Ministers—when the new champion in the political arena had essayed his prowess. It is a curious coincidence that Erskine and John Scott, afterwards Lord Eldon, of whom but slender expectations were then entertained, first addressed the House of Commons in the same debate,—upon the introduction of Mr. Fox's famous India Bill. Alas! neither of them raised the reputation of lawyers for parliamentary oratory. The Equity man took the precedence, but was dull and prosy. Our great common lawyer despised such an antagonist, and lay by for Pitt—but (*impar congressus!*) disgrace fell on both sides of Westminster Hall. The speech of the honorable member for Portsmouth could not have been so wretchedly bad as it is represented in the Parliamentary History,—from which I can not extract a sentence of any meaning, except the concluding one— that " he considered the present bill as holding out the helping, not the avenging, hand of Government."[1] But all agreed in considering the effort a failure. The most favorable account of it I find is by Sir Nathaniel Wraxall; " Mr. Erskine, who, like Mr. Scott, has since attained to the highest honors and dignities of the Bar, first spoke as a member of the House of Commons in support of this obnoxious measure. His enemies pronounced the performance tame, and destitute of the animation which so powerfully characterized his speeches in Westminster Hall. They maintained that, however resplendent he appeared as an advocate while addressing a jury, he fell to the level of an ordinary man, if not below it, when seated on the Ministerial bench, where another species of oratory was demanded to impress conviction or to extort admiration. To me, who, having never witnessed his jurisprudential talents, could not make any such comparison, he appeared to exhibit shining powers of declamation."[2]

[1] 23 Parl. Hist. 1215. In answer to the argument from the violation of the charters of the East India Company, he seems to have taunted Pitt with the little respect he showed for the ancient privileges of the rotten boroughs by his plan of Parliamentary Reform. This could not have been well received on either side of the House. [2] Memoirs, ii. 436.

According to one most graphic representation of the scene, Erskine's faculties upon this occasion were paralysed by the by-play of his opponent: "Pitt, evidently intending to reply, sat with pen and paper in his hand, prepared to catch the arguments of this formidable adversary. He wrote a word or two. Erskine proceeded; but, with every additional sentence, Pitt's attention to the paper relaxed, his look became more careless, and he obviously began to think the orator less and less worthy of his attention. At length, while every eye in the House was fixed upon him, with a contemptuous smile he dashed the pen through the paper and flung them both on the floor. Erskine never recovered from this expression of disdain;—his voice faltered, he struggled through the remainder of his speech, and sank into his seat dispirited and shorn of his fame."¹—A discussion is said to have arisen at the time, whether Pitt's pantomimic display of contempt was premeditated, or arose from the feeling of the moment; but the probability is, that expecting an antagonist from whose discomfiture he anticipated fresh renown, he really had been preparing in good earnest for the encounter, and that, more displeased than gratified at the tyros political feebleness, he threw away the pen and the paper as the readiest mode of marking his disappointment.

While Pitt remained at the Bar they had been apparently very good friends, although Mr. Espinasse conjectures (I think without reason) that the future Prime Minister had then conceived a grudge against the future Chancellor. "Pitt," says he, "had been once in a cause with him at Westminster, and attended a consultation. Erskine was the kindest of leaders, and the most gentle and encouraging to his juniors; but possibly some of his vagaries had offended the precise and serious young gentlemen, who perhaps felt somewhat of the alarm that I have known the clients of the great advocate feel on attending a consultation on their case. Certain it is that Pitt never justly appreciated that illustrious man, and always took a pleasure in mortifying him in the House." It must be matter of conjecture which would have had the advantage if they had been rivals in Westminster Hall—but it can not be denied that Erskine was much inferior

¹ Croly's Life of George IV.

in power and splendor as a parliamentary debater. "He was overpowered by the commanding tone, the sarcastic invective, and the cutting irony of Pitt."[1] "At a dinner given by Mr. Dundas at Wimbledon, Addington, Sheridan, and Erskine being present, the last was rallied on his not taking so prominent a position in the debates in Parliament as his high talents and reputation entitled him to assume,—when Sheridan said, "I'll tell you how it happens, Erskine; you are afraid of Pitt, and that is the flabby part of your character."[2]

Erskine spoke again on the second reading of the Bill, and with better effect. He now took an able view of our territorial acquisitions in the East, contending that they belonged to the Crown of Great Britain, and that the Parliament of Great Britain had a right to regulate the government of them as part of the British Empire,—ridiculing the notion that the East India Company was now to be dealt with as a private mercantile partnership. He further showed that charters such as those granted to the East India Company were necessarily subject to the control of Parliament, and that these very charters had been on several former occasions modified by Parliament for the benefit of our fellow-subjects in India, without any complaint of bad faith or unconstitutional legislation. Having then vindicated the details of the measure, he thus concluded: "I declare solemnly upon my honor, (which has never, I thank God, been called in question in public or in private), that I give my support most conscientiously to this urgently necessary reform. My original opinion in its favor is confirmed by the support it has received, in conduct and in argument, from the wise and eloquent statesman who presented it to the House,— whose talents seem to be formed by Providence to retrieve this still great country from its fallen and oppressed condition. Let my right honorable friend go on with firmness, and risk his office at every step he takes; and I will combat, as I now do, by his side, ready to sacrifice every prospect of ambition. Let him by guided by his own manly understanding, and the integrity of his own heart, and I will stand for ever by him, or sink with him in his fall."[3]

---

[1] Fraser's Magazine. [2] Pellew's Memoirs of Lord Sidmouth.
[3] 23 Parl. Hist. 1292. This peroration was maliciously compared to the

The Bill being defeated in the House of Lords, and the Coalition Ministry being dismissed, Erskine was true to his pledge. He started in Opposition before the new ministerial arrangements were completed, by moving a resolution, " That this House will consider as an enemy to the country any person who shall presume to advise his Majesty to dissolve Parliament in the present juncture of affairs." The gallery having been shut during this debate, which was of a very inflammatory nature, his speech is lost, but we know that he carried his motion by a majority of 73.[1] On a subsequent day he moved an address to the Crown, founded on this resolution, contending, in a speech of great length, but not much distinguished for constitutional learning, that the House of Commons might properly interfere with the exercise of any of the prerogatives of the Crown, and that a dissolution at that time would be highly injurious to the interests of the public. He smartly observed. " Should Parliament be now dissolved, and my constituents should ask me *why?* I must really be at a loss for an answer. They may say, ' Is it because the supplies have been withheld?' I must reply, ' That can not be the reason, for the Commons have liberally granted all the supplies that Government has called for.' ' Have the Commons, then, thrown any obstacle in the way of his Majesty's Executive Government?' 'So far is this from being the case, I must say that in all their deliberations they have gone hand in hand with his Majesty's Ministers, and never negatived a single proposition that has been made to them.' If I am then asked, ' Is it because they have no confidence in his Majesty's Ministers?' my answer must be, ' No, but because his Majesty's Ministers have no confidence in them; and therefore, as they are not Ministers to suit the Parliament, a Parliament is wanted to suit the Ministers.'" Getting upon his own ground he argued very keenly upon the insufficiency of Lord Temple's denial that he declared the King's hostility to the India Bill by merely saying " he had not used the words imputed to him." "Suppose that a doctor should have been suspected of having poisoned

---

saying of the sailor in Joe Miller, who, in a time when there was a cry that the Church was in danger, patted with his hand one of the pillars of St. Paul, crying out, " Don't be afraid; I will stand by you."
[1] 24 Parl. Hist. 224-25.

a patient with *tinctura thebaica*, and that a friend should wait upon him, and acquaint him that such a suspicion, so injurious to his character, was rumored abroad, and the doctor should say, " My dear friend, I assure you, upon my honor, I never administered to the patient, *tinctura thebaica*,'—would this answer satisfy any man that the doctor was innocent? Nay, I insist it would fix upon him the strongest suspicion that he had poisoned his patient with some other drug. This is what lawyers call a *negative pregnant*, or a denial bearing an admission of the truth of the charge." The motion was carried, and Erskine, going up with the address, was surprised to hear the King say, " I assure you I will not interrupt your meeting by any exercise of my prerogative, either of prorogation or dissolution." The Coalitionists were not yet sufficiently unpopular, and his Majesty " bided his time." [1]

On the day when Mr. Pitt, the new Prime Minister, resumed his seat in the House of Commons, after his re-election, Mr. Fox brought forward his motion for going into a committee on "the state of the nation." Erskine, on this occasion, came down with a prepared, but not very felicitous oration :—

" The question was," he said, " whether this country was to be governed by men whom the House of Commons could confide in, or whether the representatives of the people were to be the sport of any junto that might hope to rule over them by an unseen and inexplicable principle of government utterly unknown to the Constitution. The total removal of all the executive servants of the Crown, while they were in full possession of the confidence of that House, and, indeed without any other visible or avowed cause than their enjoyment of that confidence, and the appointment of others with no pretension except that they enjoyed it not, appeared to him a most alarming and portentous attack on public freedom. If the right honorable gentleman retains his opinions, which are in direct contradiction to those repeatedly avowed by this House, he enters upon office without the most distant prospect of serving the public. He brings on a struggle between executive and legislative authority, when they were harmoniously working together for the

[1] 24 Parl. Hist. 239-263.

common good. But whoever stands upon secret influence against the confidence of this House, will find that his abilities, however great they may be, or may be fancied, instead of being a support and protection to him, will only be like the convulsions of a strong man in the agonies of disease, which exhaust the vital spirit faster than the languishing of debility, and bring on death the sooner. Such, in a few hours, I trust, will be the fate of the right honorable gentleman at the head of the present Government. Indeed, I never compare in my own mind his first appearance in this House, when under the banners of my right honorable friend, he supported the genuine cause of liberty, with his present melancholy, ridiculous situation in it, but I am drawn into an involuntary parody of the scene of Hamlet and his mother in the closet :—

> ' Look here upon this picture, and on this :
> See what a grace was seated in his youth,
> His father's fire—the soul of Pitt himself,
> A tongue like his to soften or command ;
> A station like the genius of England
> New lighted on this top of Freedom's hill ;
> A combination and a form indeed,
> Where every God did seem to set his seal
> To give his country earnest of a patriot.
> —— Look you now what follows :
> Dark secret influence, like a mildew'd ear,
> Blasting his public virtue : has he eyes ?
> Could he this bright assembly leave to please,—
> To batten on that bench ?'

" The right honorable gentleman may profit the less by these observations, from believing that I seek them, and that I have pleasure in making them. If he thinks so, let me assure him, upon my honor, that he is mistaken— so very much mistaken, that the inconveniences which the world suffers at this moment from the want of a settled government, are greatly heightened to my feelings from the reflection that they are caused by his misguided ambition. Our fathers were friends, and I was taught from infancy to reverence the name of Pitt. This original predilection, instead of being diminished, was greatly strengthened by a personal acquaintance with the right honorable gentleman himself—which I was cultivating with pleasure, when he was taken from his profession into a different scene. Let him not think me the less his friend, or that I am the mean envier of his talents, if I suggest to him that they have been too much talked of, and that both he and his country are now reaping the bitter fruits of the intemperate praises bestowed upon them. 'It is good,' says Solomon, 'for a man to bear the yoke in his youth.' If the right honorable gentleman had attended to that maxim, he would have been contented, in a subordinate situation, to have assisted in carrying on the affairs of the nation, instead of declaring that none is fit for him but the highest, and thus for a time, at least, (the spirit of the House will take care that it is not long,) disturbing and distracting the whole range of public affairs. How very different has been the progress of my right honorable friend who sits near me! He was not hatched into a Prime Minister by the heat of his own ambition, but, *bearing the yoke in his youth*, as it was *good for him*, passed through subordinate offices, matured his talents in long Oppositions, and reached by the natural progress of his powerful mind, a superiority of political wisdom and comprehension which all sides in this House have long, with delight and satisfaction, acknowledged."[1]

In a subsequent part of the same debate (the House sitting from two o'clock in the afternoon till eight next morning), Erskine made an extempore attack on the Premier, in which, being cheered on by his friends, he succeeded much better. Pitt had declared that he took the Government on the plain and intelligible ground that he might save the country from the India Bill; and he was thus answered:—

"After the inconsistencies of the day, I am not surprised to hear the right honorable gentleman assert the India Bill to be the cause of his assuming the government; but I shall be surprised indeed if anybody believes him. No man of common sense—at least no man of common memory—sitting in this House will believe him, for all have heard him a hundred and a hundred times declaim upon his determined purpose to destroy the late Government before the India Bill was thought of. He could not act with the '*Coalition*,' forsooth,—not he! because of the obnoxious principles of the noble lord in the blue ribbon—and yet he flies at the same moment

[1] 24 Parl. Hist. 272.

into the arms of the pure and patriotic Lord Advocate; as if he had been attached to him by magnetism. I suppose it may be owing to a sort of political Methodism, which operates by faith, to the total exclusion of works, and by which the most obdurate sinner may be converted in a moment, without giving up any of the amusements of the flesh. It is, Sir, an affront to human reason to say that it was inconsistent for the right honorable gentleman to act in concert with the noble lord in the blue ribbon—while he is content to sit in the Cabinet with Lord Gower, the uniform supporter of that noble lord, and with Lord Thurlow, who, if not the instigator, was the zealous defender, of the worst errors of the Administration by which America was lost to us,—though, perhaps, the right honorable gentleman may say he has accommodated matters with these two noble lords, that, sinking other differences, he may have their sure co-operation in his grand plan of parliamentary reform, on which he still declares that he rests his own reputation, and which he still maintains to be necessary for the salvation of the state! [much laughter.] I should, indeed, admire the rigidity of that man's muscles who can withstand the childish, impertinent inconsistencies in these political partialities and aversions—although melancholy is the reflection, that to such pretenses the interests of this miserable, devoted country are to be sacrificed." [1]

When Mr. Pitt's India Bill was introduced, under which our Eastern possessions have been so long and auspiciously governed, Erskine described it as " such a monstrous production as never did, and he trusted never would disfigure the Statute Book of this realm ;"—as " a mere piece of patchwork, which could only disgrace the contriver ;" adding, " that it would deluge this country with profligacy and venality of every kind, that it would ruin the East India Company, and that it would lead to the oppression and misery of the inhabitants of Indostan, till they would rise and shake off our yoke." He then contrasted it with the rejected India Bill, the merits of which he once more detailed at great length to the House.[2]

On a subsequent day he justified the Resolution of the Commons which had been censured by the House of

[1] 24 Parl. Hist. 313.   [2] Ib. 402.

Lords directing the Lords of the Treasury not to make certain payments out of the public revenue. He contended that it was only declaratory of the law, and did not try to make a new law, as the Lords pretended. "What have been the pitiful tricks," he asked, "employed to support a set of Ministers who have defied the jurisdiction of this House? They have tried to delude the public mind, and to obtain addresses in their favor by stratagem and imposture. The prejudices against the measures of the late Government, and against my right honorable friend, originated in misrepresentation and falsehood."[1]

Erskine's last speech in the House of Commons, till seven years had rolled away, was on the motion for stopping the supplies, in consequence of the King's refusal to dismiss his Ministers in pursuance of the address of the House of Commons praying him to do so. In answer to the objection that ministers should have been tried before they were condemned, he justified the resolutions of the House against them, from the famous work of Lord Somers, written in answer to the declaration of King Charles II. to the people of England on the dissolution of Parliament in 1681;—reading several passages, which made the distinction between impeachments to *punish*, and addresses and resolutions to *remove*, Ministers,—the first requiring accusation and trial—the last resting on opinion, which may depend upon matters palpable and certain, though beyond the reach of legal proof, and which may be reasonably destructive of all confidence, though not a foundation for punishment.[2]

The motion was carried, and soon after Parliament was dissolved, the public being highly disgusted with the coalitionists, and indignant at the factious attempts which had been made to subvert Mr. Pitt's Government,—so that he could now with confidence appeal to the constituencies. Erskine, sharing the fate of many of his Whig friends, lost his seat for Portsmouth, and could not gain admission into the new Parliament. If he had been able justly to estimate his own powers, he must have felt little regret; for he had clearly proved to the world that the *forum*, not the *senate*, was the proper field for their display.

Notwithstanding these political checks and mortifica-

[1] 24 Parl. Hist. 563.   [2] Ib. 615.

tions, his professional career went on with increasing brilliancy. During the Coalition Ministry, while the Great Seal was in commission, he had obtained a patent of precedence, which entitled him to wear a silk gown and sit within the bar. Lord Loughborough, the First Lord Commissioner, was most active in conferring this dignity upon him, but the step was said to have been suggested by Lord Mansfield, in consideration of his great eminence in the Court of the King's Bench; and, although he had not yet been five years at the Bar, the whole profession concurred in the propriety of it. He had refused to hold junior briefs; and while he wore a stuff gown, taking rank only from his standing at the Bar, a number of venerable juniors, who at the age of fifty or sixty still wore the same garb, were thrown out of business, as they could not be retained with him in the same cause. His consequence depended less than that of any other man who has ever been in the profession on the place from which he spoke, or the robe which he wore,—but he was pleased with his promotion; for a silk gown, from its rarity, was then a great distinction, and even *he* was sensible that his weight on common occasions, both with judges and jurymen, was enhanced by belonging to the chosen few who enjoyed the highest rank at the Bar.[1]

Now began his special retainers, by which he was taken to the assizes in all parts of England and Wales, with a fee of at least 300 guineas.[2] The first of these was in the case of the Dean of St. Asaph.

[1] There was much difficulty in settling the precedence of those now promoted. It was wished to give the *pas* to Erskine, who was by far the most distinguished, but was the junior in standing at the bar. Pigot, afterwards Attorney General, yielded to his claim. It has been said, "He was probably despised by Erskine for this voluntary humiliation, and to a feeling of contempt may be ascribed that bitterness against the pusillanimous senior which excited general surprise."* The Right Hon. T. Erskine writes to me, —"I can not believe that this charge of bitterness against Pigot had any other foundation than some misconstrued ebullitions of professional zeal. I have often heard my father speak of Pigot in terms of admiration and regard; and it is to me inconceivable that a man so overflowing with generous kindness should have selected as the single object of personal rancor one whose only offense was the tender of the highest compliment that one competitor in a professional struggle can pay to his rival. The imputation is disproved by the whole current of his life, and obvious character of his disposition."

[2] According to the etiquette of our profession, no barrister may go to plead a cause on a different circuit from that which he usually attends, except on a

* Townsend's Lives of Eminent Judges, i. 423.

The famous Sir William Jones, the most accomplished man of his age, had written a very harmless little tract illustrating the general principles of government, and recommending parliamentary reform, entitled "A Dialogue between a Gentleman and a Farmer." His brother-in-law, Dr. Shipley, approving of it, recommended it to a society of reformers in Wales, and caused it to be reprinted. Thereupon the Honorable Mr. Fitzmaurice, brother to the first Marquis of Lansdowne, preferred an indictment against the Dean at the Great Sessions for Denbighshire, for a seditious libel; and in the autumn of 1783 it stood for trial at Wrexham, before Lord Kenyon, then Chief Justice of Chester, and his brother judge, Mr. Justice Barrington. Erskine attended, and thousands flocked to this dirty Wesh village in the hope of hearing him. There was a general feeling in favor of the defendant, so that his acquittal was anticipated, for not only had the pamphlet been generally read and approved of, but it was well known that the Attorney and Solicitor General, being applied to, had refused on the part of the Government to prosecute the author. At the sitting of the Court, however, a motion was made by the prosecutor's counsel to postpone the trial, on the ground that a paper had been printed and extensively circulated in the neighborhood, which, without mentioning or alluding to the pending prosecution, argued that in all cases of libel the jury are judges of the law as well as of the fact, and contained various extracts from legal writers to establish this position. There was no allegation that this was done by the defendant, and he made an affidavit, positively denying all knowledge of it. Notwithstanding an animated address from Erskine upon the unreasonableness of the motion and the extreme hardship which delay would cause to his client, the judges, without hearing the reply, ordered the trial to be postponed; and upon a suggestion by Erskine that a letter of the prosecutor could be proved, showing that he was acting vindictively, the following speech is said to have been made by the

special retainer; and, if he wears a silk gown, he can not take a fee less than 300 guineas. This is to prevent the unseemly scramble for business which might otherwise take place. Some say that special retainers began with Erskine; but I doubt the fact. From this time till he left the Bar he had, upon an average, twelve special retainers a year.

presiding judge, Lord Chief Justice Kenyon : "*Modus in rebus*--there must be an end of things."[1]

The case again stood for trial before the same tribunal in the spring of 1784, and Erskine again repaired to Wrexham ; but this time he had not the opportunity of even making a complaint, for, alighting from his post-chaise, he found that by a writ of *certiorari* served the same day, the indictment was removed from the Great Sessions in Wales into the Court of King's Bench.

The trial actually did come on at the following Summer Assizes for Salop, the next adjoining English county, before Mr. Justice Buller—when a scene was acted ever memorable in our juridical annals. Bearcroft, leading counsel for the prosecution, although he expressed his own opinion that the Dialogue was a libel, aware that no twelve Englishmen would find it to be so, boldly affirmed that this was no question for the jury, and that they were bound to convict the defendant if they believed that he caused it to be published, and that it was "of and concerning the King and his Government,"—leaving him to move the Court in arrest of judgment, or to bring a writ of error if he was advised that its sentiments and language were innocent.

"The only difficulty which I feel," said Erskine, " in resisting so false and malevolent an accusation is to be able to repress the feeling excited by its folly and injustice within those bounds which may leave my faculties in their natural and unclouded operation; for I solemnly declare to you, that if he had been indicted as a libeler of our holy religion, only for publishing that the world was made by its Almighty Author, my astonishment could not have been greater than it is at this moment, to see the little book which I hold in my hand presented by a Grand Jury of English subjects as a libel upon the Government of England. Every sentiment contained in it (if the interpretation of words is to be settled, not according to fancy, but by the common rules of language)

[1] 21 State Trials, 875. There were several Latin quotations which this distinguished lawyer had picked up, and which he generally misapplied,—insomuch that George III. gave him the friendly advice, "Stick to your *good law*, and leave off your *bad Latin*." He was very acute, very deeply learned in his profession, and a very honest man ; but it was rather humiliating that the successor of such an accomplished scholar as Lord Mansfield should hardly have had the rudiments of a classical education.

is to be found in the brightest pages of English literature, and in the most sacred volume of English laws: if any one sentence, from the beginning to the end of it, be seditious or libelous, the Bill of Rights was a seditious libel; the Revolution was a wicked rebellion; the existing Government is a traitorous conspiracy against the hereditary monarchy of England; and our gracious Sovereign, whose title I am persuaded we are all of us prepared to defend with our blood, is an usurper of the crown he wears. That all these absurd, preposterous, and treasonable conclusions follow necessarily and unavoidably from a conclusion that this Dialogue is a libel,— copying the example of my learned friend who has pledged *his* personal veracity in support of his sentiments,—I assert, upon *my* honor, to be my unaltered, I may say unalterable opinion, formed upon the most mature deliberation; and I choose to place that opinion in the very front of my address to you, that you may not, in the course of it, mistake the energies of truth for the zeal of professional duty. This declaration of my own sentiments, even if my friend had not set me the example by giving you his, I should have considered to be my duty on this occasion; for although, in ordinary cases, where the private right of the party accused is alone in discussion, and no general consequences can follow from the decision, the advocate and the private man ought in sound discretion to be kept asunder, yet there are occasions when such separation would be treachery and meanness. In a case where the dearest rights of society are involved in the resistance of a prosecution,—where the party accused is, as in this instance, a mere name,— where the whole community is wounded through his sides,—and where the conviction of the private individual is the subversion or surrender of public privileges,—the advocate has a more extensive charge—the duty of the patriot citizen then mixes itself with his obligation to his client—and he disgraces himself, dishonors his profession and betrays his country, if he does not step forth in his personal character, and vindicate the rights of all his fellow-citizens, which are attacked through the medium of the man he is defending. Gentlemen, I do not mean to shrink from that responsibility upon this occasion; I desire to be considered the fellow-criminal of the defendant — if by your verdict he should be found one—by publishing in advised speaking (which is substantially equal in guilt to the publication that he is accused of before you) my hearty approbation of every sentiment contained in this little book, promising here in the face of the world to publish them upon every suitable occasion, among that part of the community within reach of my precept, influence, and example. If there be any more prosecutors like the present abroad among us, they know how to take advantage of these declarations." Then, well knowing Buller's opinion respecting the rights of jurors to consider the question of *libel or no libel*, and the direction that would certainly be given by him in this case,—with admirable calmness and tact he thus proceeds: —"Gentlemen,—when I reflect upon the danger which has often attended the liberty of the press in former times, from the arbitrary proceedings of abject, unprincipled, and dependent Judges, raised to their situations without ability or worth, in proportion to their servility to power, I can not help congratulating the public that you are to try this indictment with the assistance of the learned Judge before you,—much too instructed in the laws of this land to mislead you by mistake, and too conscientious to misinstruct you by design. The days, indeed, I hope are now past when judges and jurymen upon state trials were constantly pulling in different directions,—the Court endeavoring to annihilate altogether the province of the jury, and the jury in return listening with disgust, jealousy, and alienation to the directions of the Court. Questions of libel may now be expected to be tried with that harmony which is the beauty of our legal constitution,—the jury preserving their independence in judging of the intention, which is the essence of every crime,—but listening to the opinion of the judge upon the evidence, and upon the law, with that respect and attention which dignity, learning, and honest intention in a magistrate must and ought always to carry along with them. Having received my earliest information in my profession from the learned Judge himself, and having daily occasion to observe his able administration of justice, you may believe that I anticipate nothing from the Bench unfavorable to innocence; and I have experienced his regard in too many instances not to be sure of every indulgence that is personal to myself. These considerations enable me with more freedom to make my address to you upon the merits of this prosecution, in the issue of which your own general rights, as members of a free state, are not less involved than the private rights of the individual I am defending.

So, without laying himself open to any interruption from the Judge, whom he appeared to treat with great courtesy and respect, he assumed that the jury were to determine upon the true character of the paper charged as libelous. Having then pointed out the extreme hardship his client had suffered in the trial being twice postponed, and at last brought on at such a distance from his home, he came to the "DIALOGUE;" and, taking it sentence by sentence, in a speech of several hours, which never flagged for an instant, he showed that most Englishmen would concur in its doctrines—which were the foundation for the Bill to reform the representation of the people several times brought forward by the present Prime Minister, and that, at all events, it stated nothing which in a free country might not be lawfully brought forward for consideration and debate. Finding that he had the jury " breast high" with him, he returned to the subject of their power to deal with the question of *libel or no libel*, which he asserted in still bolder language— and thus he took leave of them:—" Let me therefore conclude with reminding you, gentlemen, that if you find the defendant GUILTY, not believing the thing published to be a libel, or the intention of the publisher seditious, your verdict and your opinion will be at variance, and it will then be between God and your own consciences to reconcile the contradiction."

Mr. Justice Buller, however, began his summing up by telling the jury that, there being no doubt as to the *innuendoes*, the only question they had to decide was, "whether the defendant was or was not proved to have published the pamphlet?" He overruled all that had been contented for on this subject by the defendant's counsel, saying, " How this doctrine ever comes to be now seriously contended for is a matter of some astonishment to me, for I do not know any one question in the law which is more thoroughly established;"—and, after a great many similar observations, he thus concluded; " Therefore, I can only say, that if you are satisfied that the defendant did publish this pamphlet, and are satisfied as to the truth of the innuendoes, you ought in point of law to find him guilty."

The jury withdrew, and in about half an hour returned into court. When their names had been called over, the following scene was enacted.—*Clerk:* "Gentlemen of the jury, do you find the defendant guilty or not guilty?" *Foreman:* "Guilty of publishing only." *Erskine:* "You find him guilty of publishing only?" *A Juror:* "Guilty only of publishing." *Buller, J.:* "I believe that is a verdict not quite correct. You must explain that, one way or the other. The indictment has stated that *G.* means 'Gentleman,' *F.* 'Farmer,' *the King* 'the King of Great Britain,' and *the Parliament* 'the Parliament of Great Britain.'" *Juror:* "We have no doubt about that." *Buller, J.:* "If you find him guilty of publishing, you must not say the word 'only.'" *Erskine:* "By that they mean to find there was no sedition." *Juror:* "We only find him guilty of publishing. We do not find anything else." *Erskine:* "I beg your Lordship's pardon; with great submission, I am sure that I mean nothing that is irregular. I understand they say, 'We only find him guilty of publishing.'" *Juror:* "Certainly, that is all we do find." *Buller, J.:* "If you only attend to what is said, there is no question or doubt." *Erskine:* "Gentlemen, I desire to know whether you mean the word '*only*' to stand in your verdict?" *Jurymen:* "Certainly." *Buller, J.:* "Gentlemen, if you add the word '*only*,' it will be negativing the innuendoes." *Erskine:* "I desire your Lordship, sitting here as Judge, to record the verdict as given by the Jury." *Buller, J.:* "You say he is guilty of publishing the pamphlet, and that the meaning of the innuendoes is as stated in the indictment?" *Juror:* "Certainly." *Erskine:* "Is the word 'only' to stand part of the verdict?" *Juror:* "Certainly." *Erskine:* "Then I insist it shall be recorded." *Buller, J.:* "Then the verdict must be misunderstood; let me understand the jury." *Erskine:* "The Jury do understand their verdict." *Buller, J.:* "Sir, I will not be interrupted." *Erskine:* "I stand here as an advocate for a brother citizen, and I desire that the word '*only*' may be recorded." *Buller J.:* "SIT DOWN, SIR; RE-

MEMBER YOUR DUTY, OR I SHALL BE OBLIGED TO PRO-
CEED IN ANOTHER MANNER." *Erskine:* "YOUR LORD-
SHIP MAY PROCEED IN WHAT MANNER YOU THINK FIT; I
KNOW MY DUTY AS WELL AS YOUR LORDSHIP KNOWS
YOURS. I SHALL NOT ALTER MY CONDUCT."

The learned Judge took no notice of this reply, and, quailing under the rebuke of his pupil, did not repeat the menace of commitment. This noble stand for the independence of the Bar would of itself have entitled Erskine to the statue which the profession affectionately erected to his memory, in Lincoln's Inn Hall. We are to admire the decency and propriety of his demeanor during the struggle, no less than its spirit and and the felicitous precision with which he meted out the requisite and justifiable portion of defiance. The example has had a salutary effect in illustrating and establishing the relative duties of Judge and Advocate in England.

The jury, confounded by the altercation, expressed a wish to withdraw, and the verdict was finally entered,—" Guilty of publishing, but whether a libel or not, we do not find."

In the ensuing Michaelmas Term, a rule was obtained to show cause why the verdict should not be set aside, and a new trial granted, on the ground of misdirection by the Judge.[1] Erskine's addresses to the Court in moving, and afterwards in supporting, his rule, display beyond all comparison the most perfect union of argument and eloquence ever exhibited in Westminster Hall. He laid down five propositions most logically framed and connected—which, if true, completely established his case—

[1] In a copy of the trial, which had formerly belonged to Lord Erskine himself, I find in his own handwriting, after the verdict at Shrewsbury, the following memorandum :—" In Michaelmas T., which immediately followed, I moved the Court of King's Bench for a new trial, for a misdirection of the Judge, and misconduct after the verdict was returned into Court. I made the motion from no hope of success, but from a fixed resolution to expose to public contempt the doctrines fastened on the public as law by Lord Chie Justice Mansfield, and to excite, if possible, the attention of Parliament to so great an object of national freedom." Then there follows an observation which I do not understand : " The latter object miscarried from a circumstance which will hereafter be a curious piece of history, and show upon what small and strange pivots the greatest national events turn and depend." I presume that this had been written before Mr. Fox introduced his Libel Bill, which was not till 1791 ; and that a reference is made to some unknown circumstance which had delayed, and was thought to have defeated, that measure.

and he supported them with a depth of learning which would have done honor to Selden or Hale, while he was animated by an enthusiasm which was peculiarly his own. Though appealing to Judges who heard him with aversion or indifference, he was as spirited as if the decision had depended on a favorable jury, whose feelings were entirely under his control. So thoroughly had he mastered the subject, and so clear did he make it, that he captivated alike old black-letter lawyers and statesmen of taste and refinement. Charles Fox was not present in court, and could not have been carried away by the exciting manner of the advocate; yet, having read the second speech, delivered in moving to make the rule absolute, he often declared it to be the finest piece of reasoning in the English language. But it made no impression on the Judges. Erskine himself, in his defense of Paine, some years afterwards, gives rather a striking description of the manner in which they received it: " I ventured to maintain this very right of a jury over the question of libel, under the same ancient constitution, before a noble and reverend magistrate of the most exalted understanding and of the most uncorrupted integrity. He treated me—not with contempt, indeed, for of that his nature was incapable—but he put me aside with indulgence, as you do a child when it is lisping its prattle out of season." Of the closely-knit arguments and beautiful illustrations which constituted this speech, it would be impossible by extracts to convey an idea.

Lord Mansfield, in giving judgment, relied upon the practice that had long prevailed, and mainly upon the words of a ballad made on the acquittal of the " CRAFTSMAN," prosecuted by Sir Philip Yorke—which he misquoted, saying,—

"Sir Philip well knows,
That his innuendoes
Will serve him no longer
In verse or in prose;
For twelve honest men have decided the cause
Who are judges of fact, though not judges of laws."

Whereas the true rendering of the last line is—

"*Who are judges alike of the facts and the laws.*"

Erskine then moved in arrest of judgment, saying, that "all who knew him, in and out of the profession, could witness for him, that he had ever treated the idea of ultimately prevailing against the defendant upon such an indictment to be perfectly ridiculous, and that his only object, in all the trouble he had given to their Lordships and to himself, in discussing the right to a new trial, was to resist a precedent which he originally thought, and still continued to think, was illegal and unjustifiable: the warfare was safe for his client, because he knew he could put an end to the prosecution any hour he pleased, by the objection he would now, at last, submit to the Court." He was contending that the "Dialogue" was an entirely innocent production, when the counsel for the prosecution were required to point out any part of it, as charged in the indictment, which could be considered criminal, and they being unable to do so, JUDGMENT WAS ARRESTED.

So ended this famous prosecution. It seemed to establish for ever the fatal doctrine, that *libel or no libel* was a pure question of law, for the exclusive determination of Judges appointed by the Crown. But it led to the subversion of that doctrine, and the establishment of the liberty of the press, under the guardianship of English juries. The public mind was so alarmed by the consequences of this decision, that Mr. Fox's Libel Bill was called for, which *declared* the rights of jurors in cases of libel; and I rejoice always to think that it passed as a *declaratory* act, although all the Judges unanimously gave an opinion in the House of Lords, that it was inconsistent with the common law. I have said, and I still think, that this great constitutional triumph is mainly to be ascribed to Lord Camden, who had been fighting in the cause for half a century, and uttered his last words in the House of Lords in its support; but had he not received the invaluable assistance of Erskine, as counsel for the Dean of St. Asaph, the Star Chamber might have been re-established in this country."[1]

[1] 21 St. Tr. 847–1045. Erskine's Speeches, i. 137–393.

CHAPTER CLXXIX.

CONTINUATION OF THE LIFE OF LORD ERSKINE TILL THE COMMENCEMENT OF THE STATE TRIALS IN 1794.

WHILE out of Parliament, Erskine several times appeared as counsel at the bar of the House of Commons, using very considerable freedoms with this august assembly. Being retained upon the petition respecting the "Westminster Scrutiny," in cross-examining a witness who had imputed misconduct to Mr. Fox's agents he put the question, "Why do you infer that they were Mr. Fox's agents?" and the witness replying, "Because they appeared to be his friends," he exclaimed, "If all Mr. Fox's friends are to be taken to be his agents, every honest man may be so esteemed who is not a member of this House." The counsel was ordered to withdraw, and the Speaker was severely blamed for allowing such language to pass unnoticed. Cornwall apologized— admitting what had been said at the bar to be highly irregular, and a vote of censure on the counsel was then moved. Erskine, who was within hearing, was turning in his mind the spirited speech he should make in answer, when he was deeply mortified by hearing Pitt say, in a most supercilious tone, "I rather think, Sir, it is not worth our while to take any further notice of the language of the learned gentleman, as it probably formed part of his instructions!!!"

Appearing to support a petition against certain clauses of the new Bill for regulating the affairs of the East India Company, he denounced the whole measure as a vile imposture practiced on a credulous nation, eulogizing in the warmest terms the rejected bill of his right honorable friend. An admonition to regularity at last coming from the chair, he said, "If, Mr. Speaker, I have been guilty of any irregularity, it arises solely from a diminution of that respect which I was accustomed to feel for this assembly before it was shorn of its dignity—but which no longer animates me." He then, in an ironical and taunting tone, observed upon the humility of his present situation, standing at the bar of that House of which he had formerly been a member, and on the respect due to an assembly which was supposed to be so pure, so elevated, and so wise. At last he tried to restore good humor by a bad joke—saying, " I am well aware, Sir, that addresses from counsel are never much relished by the members of this House, and are rather submitted to by way of *physic*, as it were, for the benefit of the *constitution*. I promise, therefore, to make my dose as palatable as the nature of the patient's case will admit." This the House would not swallow, and the Speaker again interrupted him, desiring him to confine himself to the prayer of the petition. *Erskine:* "At this late hour, Sir, the House ought not to enter upon the consideration of so important a subject." *Speaker:* " Sir, it does not become counsel at the bar to intimate when this House ought to adjourn. The House will govern its own proceedings as it thinks proper; and, unless you wish to make some further observations for your client, you may withdraw." Erskine continued his speech, but with little effect, as the feeling on both sides was against him, and he required as a stimulus to his oratory the sympathy of his audience.

Although he could never very successfully adapt himself to the trim of the House of Commons, such rebuffs were soon forgotten amidst his triumphs in the adjoining Hall. Bearcroft, Pigot, and the other King's counsel opposed to him were completely overmatched by him; he had formidable influence with judges as well as jurymen; and the saying went, that "in the Court of King's Bench he was like a bull in a china shop."[1] He now gave up his circuit entirely, and confined himself to special retainers—being the first English barrister who ever took so bold a step.

While excluded from Parliament, he kept up a strict political connection with the Opposition leaders, and was particularly intimate with Fox and Sheridan. He had a transcendent admiration of Burke, whose writings he perused almost as much as those of Milton and Shakes-

---

[1] It might have been said of him, as it afterwards was of Scarlett, that " he had invented a machine by the secret use of which in court he could always make the head of a judge nod assent to his propositions; whereas his rivals, who tried to pirate it, always made the head of the judge move dissentingly from side to side."

peare. But the feeling was not reciprocal. Burke disliked all lawyers, and, considering the new ally of the party rather shallow and ill-informed, is said to have envied the fame and fortune he was acquiring. But Erskine was a very great favorite with the Prince of Wales, who was at this time a zealous Whig, and, forming his establishment as heir apparent, made him his Attorney General; intimating that if of longer standing at the Bar he should have been appointed Chancellor of the Duchy of Cornwall—but that this office should be kept vacant for him.

I mention the next case, in which he particularly attracted the attention of the public, chiefly for the purpose of showing the defective state of the administration of the criminal law which still prevailed. A gentleman of the name of Motherill, who certainly was of bad moral character as well as of deformed person, but who, like all the King's subjects, was entitled to a fair trial stood capitally charged for an assault upon Miss Wade, a young lady between sixteen and seventeen years of age, the daughter of an officer in the army, then Master of the Ceremonies at Brighton. Erskine was brought special to the Sussex Assizes, and, although there was a strong prejudice against the prisoner, and no speech from counsel could be heard for him, thus addressed the jury, without being checked by the Judge, and I presume, without being supposed to outstep the line of his duty,—the inflammatory language of the harangue being rendered more objectionable by its affected candor:—

"I beseech you, gentlemen, to discharge from your minds everything you have heard of the prisoner, and I might add, too, everything you have seen; for I am told *this wicked and unfortunate wretch* has been this morning led about the streets for the benefit of air, and may probably have excited your compassion. I have no objection that you should compassionate him; a man is more an object of compassion because he is an object of justice,—because his crimes are objects of horror." After exciting the sympathies of the jury for the afflicted father—praising his gallantry when in the service to which he had himself belonged,—he introduces the daughter with an affecting picture of her beauty and purity—preparing the jury for some inconsistencies in her evidence by insinuating that she was rather weak in her understanding. He then continues:—" When she is attentively observed by you, you will probably make this remark, that I confess I made myself upon seeing her, that if you could conceive a painter of the finest genius to be desirous of representing the character of artless simplicity and innocence, he would fix upon the countenance and figure of Miss Wade.—(What a venial offense is even murder compared with that of which the prisoner is accused!)—It seems at first view, and it has often struck me as a very great hardship, that the prisoner's counsel can not make those observations which in the commonest civil-law action every man's counsel is enabled to make for him; but the law is much wiser than me or any other individual. Custom comes to the protection of the prisoner, and imposes as a duty upon those who prosecute, that, which perhaps the law does not enforce, viz., that with whatever strength, with whatever clearness, with whatever conclusion the evidence on the part of the prosecution shall appear to-day, and whatever art and ingenuity may be employed to defeat the ends of justice, I shall, I can, make no reply If I should see the strength of my evidence as clear as the sun at noontide, and if I should see the weakness of any observations on the effect of any cross-examination of this young lady, so that I might drag him to justice by the power of your enlightened understanding, I shall be silent as the grave." After a highly colored sketch of the facts, he thus concludes:—" If there is any probability in favor of the prisoner at the bar, in God's name let him have it. But there is no probability in his favor, none that any reasonable mind can for a moment entertain; for, let me ask you this question, whether it be consistent with anything you ever saw, heard, or read of, that a young lady of hitherto chaste and virtuous life, artless, simple, and innocent in her manners, should all of a sudden go out on a tempestuous night—leave her father's house, not to throw herself into the arms of a lover who had addressed her and endeavored to seduce her, but into the arms of a stranger, with nothing to recommend him, with nothing upon earth to captivate or seduce the fancy? It is repugnant to reason to believe it—it is a thing incredible, that the most viciously-disposed woman could go into the arms of the squalid wretch before you! I do not mean to insult him by the expression; his wickedness renders him an object of compassion. But if he is not to be insulted, a virtuous, innocent, miserable, ruined lady is not to pass unredressed; nor the breach of God's laws and the country's to pass unrevenged. If he dies, he suffers less than her who lives. Oh, fie! it is a solemn and an unpleasant duty you have to perform. You are humane, I have no doubt, and I am glad you are so. Those who are not humane, can not be just. Justice is all I ask at your hands. If in your consciences you believe that the prisoner at the bar did commit this offense, so shocking to the individual and repugnant to all the principles of justice, you are bound in duty to God and to your country, to convict him. If you can go home to-night, and satisfy yourselves that this young lady either has not been violated in point of fact, or that, having been so, it has been with her own consent; if you can persuade yourselves of that absurd and improbable proposition, after you shall have heard the evidence, I shall not call your mercy in question; it is a matter which will rest with your own consciences."

Although circumstances appeared which induced the jury very reluctantly to pronounce a verdict of NOT GUILTY, it is impossible to say that they could be in a fit state of mind to discharge their duty, after listening to this appeal to their passions. Soon after, by a well-understood rule in the profession, a counsel for the Crown, on a charge of felony, was confined to a dry statement of the facts, with a view to enable the jury to understand the evidence; and now, thank God! the Prisoner's Counsel Bill has entirely removed the stain which so long deformed our criminal procedure.

Several years rolled on prosperously in the common routine of the profession, without producing any other celebrated cause or any political event to affect the for tunes of Erskine. In Trinity Term, 1788, the increasing infirmities of Lord Mansfield induced him to retire from his office, after having presided with distinguished luster as head of the Common Law for upwards of thirty-two years. On this occasion, Erskine, as the organ of the counsel practicing in his Court, wrote and presented to him the following address:—

" *To the Earl of Mansfield.*

" MY LORD,

" It was our wish to have waited personally upon your Lordship, in a body, to have taken our public leave of you, on your retiring from the office of Chief Justice of England; but judging of your Lordship's feelings upon such an occasion by our own, and considering, besides, that our numbers might be inconvenient, we desire, in this manner, affectionately to assure your Lordship, that we regret, with a just sensibility, the loss of a magistrate whose conspicuous and exalted talents conferred dignity upon the profession, whose enlightened and regular administration of justice made its duties less difficult and laborious, and whose manners rendered them pleasant and respectable.

" But, while we lament our loss, we remember with peculiar satisfaction, that your Lordship is not cut off from us by the sudden stroke of painful distemper, or the more distressing ebb of those extraordinary faculties which have so long distinguished you among men ; but that it has pleased God to allow to the evening of a useful and illustrious life, the purest enjoyments which Nature has ever allotted to it—the unclouded reflections of a superior and unfading mind over its varied events, and the happy consciousness that it has been faithfully and eminently devoted to the highest duties of human society, in the most distinguished nation upon earth.

" May the season of this high satisfaction bear its proportion to the lengthened days of your activity and strength !"

To this address, Lord Mansfield immediately returned the following answer :—

" *To the Honorable T. Erskine, Sergeant's Inn.*

" DEAR SIR,

" I can not but be extremely flattered by the letter which I this moment have the honor to receive.

" If I have given satisfaction, it is owing to the learning and candor of the Bar; the liberality and integrity of their practice freed the judicial investigation of truth and justice from difficulties. The memory of the assistance I have received from them, and the deep impression which the extraordinary mark they have now given me of their approbation and affection has made upon my mind will

be a source of perpetual consolation in my decline of life, under the pressure of bodily infirmities which made it my duty to retire. "I am, dear Sir,
   "With gratitude to you and the other gentlemen,
      "Your most affectionate
         "And obliged humble servant,
                                          "MANSFIELD.
"Caen Wood, June 18, 1788."

It was thought that this change might be prejudicial to the ascendency of Erskine; but he was, if possible, a greater favorite with the new Chief Justice, Lord Kenyon, than he had been with Lord Mansfield, and he always continued to have "the ear of the Court,"—a great felicity for an advocate, when it is not obtained by servility.

Not being in the House of Commons during the King's illness, which occurred in the following autumn, he was debarred from taking any part in the debates, and I do not find him much engaged in the intrigues about the Regency, although he strongly concurred in the doctrine, that during the incapacity of the reigning sovereign from mental alienation the heir apparent was entitled, *de jure*, to take upon himself the exercise of the prerogatives of the Crown. It was settled that he should be Attorney General to the new Ministry, but I do not believe that the Prince much consulted him about the course to be adopted—being entirely under the more experienced guidance of Lord Loughborough.

The Attorney General-elect felt a good deal cast down when the prospects of himself and his party were so completely blasted by the King's recovery in the beginning of 1789; but his spirits soon rallied, and before that year expired he acquired glory much more to be envied than the power or the pelf belonging to the highest offices in the state. As counsel for Stockdale he made the finest speech ever delivered at the English Bar, and he won a verdict which forever established the freedom of the press in England.

Pending the impeachment of Mr. Hastings, after the articles against him drawn up by Mr. Burke in very inflamed language had appeared in every newspaper, together with the vituperative speeches of the eloquent managers at the bar of the House of Lords, Mr. Logan, a

minister of the Church of Scotland, wrote a pamphlet in
his defense, which certainly contained some rather free
and offensive observations upon the prosecution. The
charges against Mr. Hastings were said to "originate
from misrepresentation and falsehood;" the House of
Commons, in making one of those charges, was compared
to "a tribunal of inquisition rather than a court of
Parliament:" others of them were stigmatized as " so insignificant in themselves, or founded on such gross misrepresentations, that they would not affect an obscure
individual, much less a public character:" and after a
good deal of invective and sarcasm, the impeachment was
said to be "carried on from motives of personal animosity, not from regard to public justice." But the
author entered into the merits of the case very deliberately, and very powerfully, and seemed animated by a
sincere desire to show the innocence of the accused.
This pamphlet was published by Mr. Stockdale, a respectable bookseller in Piccadilly, in the way of his trade. Mr.
Fox, instigated by Burke, complained of it in his place
as a libel upon the managers and upon the whole House
of Commons; and an address was carried, praying the
King to direct his Attorney General to prosecute the
publisher. Accordingly, a criminal information was filed
by Sir Archibald Macdonald, the then Attorney General,
against Mr. Stockdale, and it came on to be tried before
Lord Kenyon and a special jury in the Court of King's
Bench, at Westminster.

Justly to appreciate Erskine's inimitable speech upon
this occasion, the whole must be perused over and over
again—when an admirable chain of reasoning will be
found to run through it,—principles will be seen clearly
enunciated, illustrated, and established,—and the facts
of the case will demonstrably appear to be brought within
the scope of these principles, so as to entitle the defendant to an acquittal;—the reader all along admiring the
exquisite fancy with which the sentiments are embellished, and the harmonious and touching language in
which they are conveyed. " It is justly regarded by all
English lawyers as a consummate specimen of the art of
addressing a jury—as a standard, a sort of precedent for
treating cases of libel."[1] But a few extracts, which may be

[1] Edinburgh Review, xvi. 109.

introduced into a biographical memoir, will give a notion, although an inadequate one, of its transcendent merit. To excite a little compassion for Mr. Hastings, and to prepare the minds of the jury favorably to consider a publication written in his defense—in which some intemperance of language might be expected—he gives the following picturesque description of the trial in Westminster Hall:—

"There the most august and striking spectacle was daily exhibited which the world ever witnessed. A vast stage of justice was erected, awful from its high authority, splendid from its illustrious dignity, venerable from the learning and wisdom of its judges, captivating and affecting from the mighty concourse of all ranks and conditions which daily flocked into it as into a theater of pleasure. Here, when the whole public mind was at once awed and softened to the impression of every human affection, there appeared day after day, one after another, men of the most powerful and exalted talents, eclipsing by their accusing eloquence the most boasted harangues of antiquity; rousing the pride of national resentment by the boldest invectives against broken faith and violated treaties, and shaking the bosom with alternate pity and horror by the most glowing pictures of insulted nature and humanity;—ever animated and energetic, from the love of fame, which is the inherent passion of genius;—firm and indefatigable, from a strong prepossession of the justice of their cause. Gentlemen, when the author sat down to write the book now before you, all this terrible, unceasing, exhaustless artillery of warm zeal, matchless vigor of understanding, consuming and devouring eloquence, united with the highest dignity, was daily, and without prospect of conclusion, pouring forth upon one private, unprotected man, who was bound to hear it in the face of the whole people of England, with reverential submission and silence. I do not complain of this as I did of the publication of the charges, because it is what the law allowed and sanctioned in the course of a public trial: but when it is remembered that we are not angels, but weak, fallible men, and that even the noble Judges of that high tribunal are clothed beneath their ermines with the common infirmities of man's nature, it will bring us all to a proper temper for considering the book itself, which will in a few moments be laid before you. But, first, let me once more remind you, that it was under all these circumstances, and amid the blaze of passion and prejudice which the scene I have been endeavoring faintly to describe to you might be supposed likely to produce, that the author sat down to compose the book which is prosecuted to-day as a libel."

After some compliments to the character of that gentleman, the advocate thus strikingly and skillfully states the motive by which he had been actuated, and the question which the jury had to determine:—

" He felt for the situation of a fellow-citizen, exposed to a trial which, whether right or wrong, is undoubtedly a severe one;—a trial certainly not confined to a few criminal acts, like those we are accustomed to, but comprehending the transactions of a whole life, and the complicated policies of numerous and distant nations;—a trial which had neither visible limits to its duration, bounds to its expense, nor circumscribed compass for the grasp of memory or understanding;—a trial which had, therefore, broke loose from the common form of decision, and had become the universal topic of discussion in the world, superseding not only every grave pursuit, but every fashionable dissipation. Gentlemen, the question you have, therefore, to try upon all this matter, is extremely simple. It is neither more nor less than this. At a time when the charges against Mr. Hastings were, by the implied consent of the Commons, in every hand and on every table;—when by their harangues the lightning of eloquence was incessantly consuming him, and flashing in the eyes of the public:—when every man was, with perfect impunity, saying, and writing, and publishing just what he pleased of the supposed plunderer and devastator of nations; would it have been criminal *in Mr. Hastings himself* to have reminded the public that he was a native of this free land, entitled to the common protection of her justice, and that he had a defense in his turn to offer them, the outlines of which he implored them, in the meantime, to receive as an antidote to the unlimited and unpunished poison in circulation against him? THIS is, without color or exaggeration, the true question you are to decide. Gentlemen, I tremble with indignation to be driven to put such a question in England. Shall it be endured that a subject of this country—instead of being arraigned and tried for some single act in her ordinary courts, where the accusation, as soon at least as it is made public, is followed in a few hours by the decision—may be impeached by the Commons for the transactions of twenty years,—that the accusation shall spread as wide as the region of letters,—that the accused shall stand, day after day and year after year, as a spectacle before the public, which shall be kept in a perpetual state of inflammation against him ;—yet that he shall not, without the severest penalties, be permitted to submit anything to the judgment of mankind in his defense. If this be law (which it is for you to-day to decide), such a man has NO TRIAL; that great Hall, built by our fathers for English justice, is no longer a court, but an altar;—and an Englishman, instead of being judged in it by GOD AND HIS COUNTRY, is A VICTIM AND A SACRIFICE. If you think, gentlemen, that the common duty of self-preservation in the accused himself, which nature writes as a law upon the hearts of even savages and brutes, is nevertheless too high a privilege to be enjoyed by an impeached and suffering Englishman ;—or, if you think it beyond the offices of humanity and justice, when brought home to the hand of a brother or a friend, you will say so by your verdict of GUILTY. The decision will then be *yours*, and the consolation *mine*, that I labored to avert it. A very small part of the misery which will follow from it is likely to light upon *me ;* the rest will be divided among *yourselves and your children.*"

Having at great length, and with unflagging spirit, examined the contents of the pamphlet, and commented on the passages charged in the information to be libelous,—with the view of ingratiating Mr. Hastings's defender with the jury, he proceeds to take a favorable view of the conduct of Mr. Hastings himself; not venturing to defend all his acts, but palliating them so as to make them be forgiven, or even applauded, from the circumstances in which he was placed, and the instructions which he had received. Then follows the finest passage to be found in ancient or modern oratory—for imagery, for passion, for pathos, for variety and beauty of cadence, for the concealment of art, for effect in gaining the object of the orator :—

"If your dependencies have been secured, and their interests promoted, I am driven, in the defense of my client, to remark, that it is mad and preposterous to bring to the standard of justice and humanity the exercise of a dominion founded upon violence and terror. It may and must be true that Mr. Hastings has repeatedly offended against the rights and privileges of Asiatic government, if he was the faithful deputy of a power which could not maintain itself for an hour without trampling upon both; —he may and must have offended against the laws of God and nature, if he was the faithful viceroy of an empire wrested in blood from the people to whom God and nature had given it;—he may and must have preserved that unjust dominion over timorous and abject nations by a terrifying, overbearing, and insulting superiority, if he was the faithful administrator of your government, which, having no root in consent or affection, no foundation in similarity of interests, nor support from any one principle that cements men together in society, could only be upheld by alternate stratagem and force. The unhappy people of India, feeble and effeminate as they are from the softness of their climate, and subdued and broken as they have been by the knavery and strength of civilization, still occasionally start up in all the vigor and intelligence of insulted nature;—to be governed at all, they must be governed with a rod of iron; and our empire in the East would have been long since lost to Great Britain, if civil and military prowess had not united their efforts to support an authority which Heaven never gave,—by means which it never can sanction.

"Gentlemen, I think I can observe that you are touched with this way of considering the subject; and I can account for it. I have not been considering it through the cold medium of books, but have been speaking of man and his nature, and of human dominion, from what I have seen of them myself, among reluctant nations submitting to our authority. I know what they feel, and how such feelings can alone be repressed. I have heard them in my youth from a naked savage in the indignant character of a prince surrounded by his subjects, addressing the governor of a British colony, holding a bundle of sticks as the notes of his unlettered eloquence. 'Who is it,' said the jealous ruler over the desert encroached upon by the restless foot of English adventurers, 'who is it that causes this river to rise in the high mountains, and to empty itself into the ocean? Who is it that causes to blow the loud winds of winter, and that calms them again in the summer? Who is it that rears up the shade of those lofty forests, and blasts them with the quick lightning at his pleasure? The same Being who gave to you a country on the other side of the waters, and gave ours to us; and by this title we will defend it,' said the warrior, throwing down his tomahawk upon the ground, and raising the war-sound of his nation. These are the feelings of subjugated men all round the globe; and, depend upon it, nothing but fear will control where it is vain to look for affection.

"But under the pressure of such constant difficulties, so dangerous to national honor, it might be better, perhaps, to think of effectually securing it altogether, by recalling our troops and our merchants, and abandoning our Asiatic empire. Until this be done, neither religion nor philosophy can be pressed very far into the aid of reformation and punishment. If England, from a lust of ambition and dominion, will insist on maintaining despotic rule over distant and hostile nations, beyond all comparison more numerous and extended than herself, and gives commission to her viceroys to govern them, with no other instructions than to preserve them and to secure permanently their revenues,—with what color or consistency of reason can she place herself in the moral chair, and affect to be shocked at the execution of her own orders, adverting to the exact measure of wickedness and injustice necessary to their execution, and complaining only of the *excess* as the immorality;—considering her authority as a dispensation for breaking the command of God, and the breach of them as only punishable when contrary to the ordinances of man? Such a proceeding, gentlemen, begets serious reflections. It would be, perhaps, better for the masters and servants of all such governments to join in supplication that the great Author of violated humanity may not confound them together in one common judgment."

I will only add the conclusion of this reasoning against punishing every license of expression into which writers, warm with their subjects, may be betrayed:—

"From minds thus subdued by the terrors of punishment there could issue no works of genius to expand the empire of human reason, nor any masterly compositions on the general nature of government, by the help of which the great commonwealths of mankind have founded their establishments; much less any of those useful applications of them to critical conjectures, by which, from time to time, our own constitution, by the exertions of patriot citizens, has been brought back to its standard. Under such terrors all the great lights of science and civilization must be extinguished; for men can not communicate their free thoughts to one another with a lash held over their heads. It is the nature of everything that is great and useful, both in the animate and inanimate world, to be wild and irregular; and we must be contented to take them with the alloys which belong to them, or live without them. Genius breaks from the fetters of criticism, but its wanderings are sanctioned by its majesty and wisdom when it advances in its path; subject it to the critic, and you tame it into dullness. Mighty rivers break down their banks in the winter, sweeping to death the flocks which are fattened on the soil that they fertilize in the summer. Tempests occasionally shake our dwellings and dissipate our commerce; but they scourge before them the lazy elements which without them would stagnate into pestilence. In like manner, Liberty herself, the last and best gift of God to his creatures, must be taken just as she is. You might pare her down into bashful regularity, and shape her into a perfect model of severe scrupulous law; but she would then be Liberty no longer; and you must be content to die under the lash of this inexorable justice, which you had exchanged for the banners of freedom."

I have been told by my father-in-law, the late Lord Abinger, who was present in court when the speech was delivered, that the effect upon the audience was wholly unexampled;—they all actually believed that they saw before them the Indian chief with his bundle of sticks and his tomahawk;—their breasts thrilled with the notes of his unlettered eloquence,—and they thought they heard him raise the war-sound of his nation. When we now in our closet read the speech with enthusiasm, what must, indeed, have been the feelings of those on whom its impression was aided by the voice, the eye, the action of the speaker!—It is a curious fact, however, that the jury deliberated two hours before they found a verdict of NOT GUILTY. In mitigation of their doubts, and to add to the triumph of the advocate, it should be stated that this trial took place before Mr. Fox's Libel Act, at a time when juries were told by judges that their only province was to consider whether the writing alleged to be libelous had been published by the defendant.[1]

After his special retainers for the summer circuit were over, the fatigued barrister went to Paris for a few weeks to witness the progress of the Revolution, and when he came back he expressed high admiration of what he had seen;—but I rather suspect that, from his love of fun and frolic, he had mystified a little the solemn and severe Romilly, who, in a letter then written to Dumont, says, "Erskine is returned from Paris a violent democrat. He has had a coat made of the uniform of the Jacobins, with buttons bearing this inscription, '*Vivre libre ou mourir;*' and he says he intends to wear it in the House of Commons."[2]

On the dissolution of Parliament, which took place in the autumn of this year, Erskine was again returned for Portsmouth, and he continued to represent that borough till he was raised to the peerage. Upon various occasions he added considerable weight to the resistance offered by the Whig Opposition to unconstitutional measures; but, perhaps, it would have been as well if had contented himself with the fame of a great advocate, which his genius had shown to be at least equal to that of a great parliamentary debater.

On the first question which drew him forth I think he was decidedly wrong. Misled by pity for Hastings, or by dislike to Burke, he went against his party and against clear principles of constitutional law, in contending that the grand impeachment was at an end by the dissolution. In his speech on this subject he actually broke down— and, suddenly resuming his seat, he pleaded as an excuse the fatigue he had gone through in the early part of the day, and the extreme heat of the House. Next evening he resumed his argument—but with no success, although

[1] 22 St. Tr. 237-308. Erskine's Speeches, ii. 205-288.
[2] Romilly's Memoirs, i. 408.

he spoke from copious notes of all the authorities in point. Pitt, following, was very severe upon him ; and, in answer to his remark that the country should be governed by law, Burke observed that " he should be glad to see the country governed by law, *but not by lawyers.*" In replying to the complaint of the enormous length of the trial, Burke asked " whether the learned gentleman remembered, that if the trial had continued three years, the oppressions had continued twenty ?—whether, after all, there were hour-glasses for measuring the grievances of mankind ?—or whether they whose ideas never traveled beyond a nisi prius case were better qualified to judge what ought to be the length of an impeachment, than a rabbit who breeds six times a year was able to judge of the time proper for the gestation of an elephant ?" Burke likewise sneered at his note book—first calling it a " pamphlet," and then likening him to David armed with a stone and a sling—" but with the difference in his case that they could do no execution." Erskine declared that the " pamphlet " was nothing more than a collection of precedents copied by a friend of his for his greater convenience in referring to them.—He was properly beaten by 143 to 30.[1] He likewise ineffectually opposed the appointment of new managers to conduct the impeachment against the sense of a great majority of both parties.[2]

When the " Law of Libel " was brought under the consideration of the House, the learned member for Portsmouth might have been expected to be at last placed upon a pinnacle ; but, even then, he did not advance his parliamentary reputation. In rising to second Mr. Fox's motion—for leave to bring in " a Bill to declare the Rights of Jurors to decide generally on the merits of the case in Prosecutions for Libel," he offended the House by making his professional character too prominent, and by an unlucky touch of vanity. He observed that he had nothing new to bring forward on the subject; for, having been counsel in numerous trials (*which were in everybody's hand*) involving the existence of the liberty of the Press, he had urged all that could be said, and that to attempt again to speak upon the same subject appeared to him " like telling a tale that has been told." He did, nevertheless, speak at considerable length ; and bringing

[1] Parl. Hist. 1035, 1074, 1168, 1171.   [2] Ibid. 1238.

out his commonplaces, without freshness or life, they seem only to have vexed the dull ear of the drowsy listeners.¹

On Mr. Grey's motion for a reform in Parliament, however, he defended with animation the proceedings of the Society of the Friends of the People, of which he was a member; and he animadverted with good effect on the tergiversation of Mr. Pitt, who, having been the most zealous of reformers, was now an enemy to all reform.

From the progress of the French Revolution the world was rapidly assuming a new aspect. In England there was a division among the Whigs,—one section of the party viewing the movement as favorable to general liberty, and another dreading that it would introduce confusion into this country. To the former belonged Erskine; and to the latter his patron, the Prince of Wales. Whoever may question the prudence of his conduct at this juncture, all must admire his spirit and his disinterestedness. Regardless of present favor and of future promotion, as compared with the discharge of his duty, he resisted all solicitations to join the "Alarmists," although, if he had done so, he was sure of immediately sharing with them the patronage of the Crown. At the commencement of his political career he had attached himself to Mr. Fox; and to *his* principles, through good report and through evil report, he ever adhered.

In consequence, he severely censured the policy of seeking to oppose Jacobinism by new penal laws. On one occasion he observed with much force: "The question is, whether the Constitution is to be preserved by coercion, or in its own spirit and by its own principles— whether you choose to create disaffection and enmity in the people, or to conciliate them by the language of confidence and affection? Say to them frankly and sincerely, 'There is your Constitution, handed down to you from your fathers—created by their courage, and preserved and improved from age to age by their wisdom and virtue; it is now yours, with all its blessings, and it depends upon your love and attachment for its support.' Instead of loading them with abuse and calumny, we ought to meet their complaints, to redress their grievances, and, by

¹ 29 Parl. Hist. 577, 593, 598.

granting them a fair representation, remove the ground of their discontent."[1]

In a violent attack on the "Traitorous Correspondence Bill," he said: "It is urged that the circumstances of the time call for this extraordinary measure. I desire to know what are those circumstances which can justify lessening or endangering the freedom of the country. I know of nothing which has happened, except that a false alarm has been propagated for the purpose of strengthening the hands of Government, and weakening public liberty; and by this artifice Ministers are to have unbounded confidence, and their opponents are to be stigmatized by distrust, and libeled by suspicions of treason and rebellion."[2]

He made another elaborate speech in favor of parliamentary reform, bringing forward most of the arguments which proved triumphant forty years after,—but so low was the cause at that time that the motion was rejected by a majority of 282 to 41.[3]

We must again attend Erskine to the Forum. His firmness was now put to a severe trial—and he gave a memorable example of what may be expected from an English advocate. Wisely, the Government had taken no notice of the "First Part of Paine's Rights of Man," and it had attracted little notice: but the "Second Part," containing some offensive ribaldry about William III. and George I., with very indecorous aspersions upon the monarchical and aristocratical branches of our Government, its circulation was infinitely increased by the Attorney General filing an *ex-officio* information against the author. A retainer for the defendant was sent to Erskine, and the question was, "whether he should accept it?" He himself did not hesitate one moment; for although if he had read the publication he must have highly disapproved of it, the cause was to be tried in the Court in which he practiced as a barrister; and he was bound, when called upon, to defend the party accused, to the best of his ability, by all legal and honorable means.

However, several of his friends earnestly persuaded him to refuse the retainer, and among these was Lord Loughborough, who ought to have known better, but who thought that at last he had the Great Seal within his

[1] 30 Parl. Hist. 58. [2] Ibid. 590. [3] Ibid. 826, 925.

grasp. Erskine himself, many years after, gave the following amusing account of their interview:—" In walking home one dark November evening across Hampstead Heath, I met Loughborough coming in an opposite direction, apparently with the intention of meeting me. He was also on foot. 'Erskine,' he said, 'I was seeking you, for I have something important to communicate to you.' There was an unusual solemnity in his manner, and a deep hollowness in his voice. We were alone. The place was solitary. The dusk was gathering around us, and not a voice—not a footstep—was within hearing. I felt as Hubert felt when John half opened, half suppressed, the purpose of his soul, in that awful conference which Shakespeare has so finely imagined. After a portentous pause he began:—'Erskine, you must not take Paine's brief.'—'But I have been retained, and I will take it, by G—d,' was my reply." Messages to the same effect were brought to him from the Prince of Wales; but he was inexorable. By many well-meaning people, ignorant of professional etiquette, and of what is required by a due regard for the proper administration of criminal justice, his obstinacy was much condemned, and scurrilous attacks were made upon him in the Government newspapers.

At last the day of trial arrived, and he was at his post. Here he met with an unexpected difficulty, for the Attorney General produced a letter, lately written from Paris by Thomas Paine's own hand, in which he acknowledged himself to be the author, and applied a number of most opprobrious epithets both to the King and the Prince of Wales. Erskine, almost appalled, thus began :—

"Gentlemen, if the Attorney General felt the painful embarrassments he has described, you may imagine what MINE must be; he can only feel for the august character he represents in this place as a subject for his Sovereign—too far removed by custom from the intercourse which generates affection to produce any other sentiments than those that flow from a relation common to us all; but it will be remembered that I stand in the same relation towards another great person more deeply implicated by this supposed letter, who, not restrained from the cultivation of personal attachments by those qualifications which must always secure them, has exalted my duty to a Prince into a warm and honest affection between man and man." He next alludes to the attacks made upon himself, connected with this cause : " Every man within hearing at this moment, nay, the whole people of England, have been witnesses to the calumnious clamor that, by every art, has been raised and kept up against me. In every place where business or pleasure collects the people together, day after day, my name and character have been the topics of injurious reflection. And for what? only for not having shrunk from the discharge of a duty which no personal advantage recommended, and which a thousand difficulties repelled. But, gentlemen, I have no complaint to make against the printers of these libels, nor even against their authors : the greater part of them, hurried perhaps away by honest prejudices, may have believed they were serving their country by rendering me the object of its suspicion and contempt; and if there have been among them others who have mixed in it from personal malice and unkindness, I thank God I can forgive *them* also. Little indeed did they know me, who thought that such calumnies would influence my conduct ; I will forever—at all hazards—assert the dignity, independence, and integrity of the ENGLISH BAR, without which impartial justice, the most valuable part of the English Constitution, can have no existence. From the moment that any advocate can be permitted to say that he *will*, or will *not*, stand between the Crown and the subject arraigned in the Court where he daily sits to practice, from that moment the liberties of England are at an end. If the advocate refuses to defend from what *he may think* of the charge or of the defense, he assumes the character of the Judge ; nay, he assumes it before the hour of judgment; and, in proportion to his rank and reputation, puts the heavy influence of perhaps a mistaken opinion into the scale against the accused, in whose favor the benevolent principle of English law makes all presumptions, and which commands the very Judge to be his counsel." He then proceeds to the defense, and lays down, with admirable discrimination, the limits of free discussion on political subjects : " The proposition which I mean to maintain, as the basis of the liberty of the press, and without which it is an empty sound, is this;—that every man not intending to mislead, but seeking to enlighten others with what his own reason and conscience, however erroneously, have dictated to him as truth, may address himself to the universal reason of a whole nation, either upon the subject of governments in general, or upon that of our own particular country; that he may analyze the principles of its constitution, point out its errors and defects, examine and publish its corruptions, and warn his fellow-citizens against their ruinous consequences, and exert his whole faculties in pointing out the most advantageous changes in establishments which he considers to be radically defective, or sliding from their object by abuse. All this, every subject of this country has a right to do, if he contemplates only what he thinks would be for its advantage, and but seeks to change the public mind by the conviction that flows from reasonings dictated by conscience. If, indeed, he writes what he does not think; if, contemplating the misery of others, he wickedly condemns what his own understanding approves; or, even admitting his real disgust against the government or its corruptions, if he calumniates living magistrates, or holds out to individuals that they have a right to run before the public mind in their conduct; that they may oppose by contumacy or force what private reason only disapproves; that they may disobey the law, because their judgment only condemns it; or resist the public will, because they honestly wish to change it,—he is then a criminal upon every principle of rational policy, as well as upon the immemorial precedents of English justice; because such a person seeks to disunite individuals from their duty to the whole, and excites to overt acts of misconduct in a part of the community, instead of endeavoring to change, by the impulse of reason, that universal assent, which in this and every country constitutes the law for all."

But his difficulty was to bring Paine's book within the category of useful publications; and so little impression did he now make upon the jury, that as soon as he had concluded, without hearing the reply or the summing up, they found a verdict of GUILTY.

As a reward for the brave and honest defense which his duty compelled him to make for his client, he was, to the lasting disgrace of those from whom the measure proceeded, removed from his office of Attorney General to the Prince of Wales. He thus adverted to the fact in his defense of Horne Tooke:—" Gentlemen, Mr. Tooke had an additional and a generous motive for appearing to be the supporter of Mr. Paine;—the Constitution was wounded through his sides. I blush, as a Briton, to recollect that a conspiracy was formed among the highest orders to deprive this man of a British trial. This is the clue to Mr. Tooke's conduct, and to which, if there should be no other witnesses, I will step forward to be examined. I assert that there was a conspiracy to shut out Mr. Paine from the privilege of being defended: he was to be deprived of counsel, and I, who now speak to you, was threatened with the loss of office if I appeared as his advocate. I was told in plain terms that I must not defend Mr. Paine. I did defend him, and I did lose my office." Of this transaction, Lord Erskine, a few years before his death, gave a detailed account, in a letter addressed to Mr. Howell, editor of the State Trials:[1]—

"When Attorney General to the Prince of Wales, I was retained by Thomas Paine in person to defend him on his approaching trial for publishing the Second Part of his 'Rights of Man;' but it was soon intimated to me by high authority, that it was considered to be incompatible with my situation, and the Prince himself, in the most friendly manner, acquainted me that it was highly displeasing to the King, and that I ought to endeavor to explain my conduct, which I immediately did in a letter to his Majesty himself, in which, after expressing my sincere attachment to his person, and to the constitution of the kingdom, attacked in the work which was to be defended, I took the liberty to claim, as an invaluable part of that very constitution, the unquestionable right of the subject to make his defense by any counsel of his own free choice, if not previously retained or engaged by office from the Crown; and that there was no other way of deciding whether that was or was not my own situation as Attorney General to the Prince, than by referring, according to custom, that question to the Bar, which I was perfectly willing, and even desirous, to do. In a few days afterwards, I received, through my friend, the late Admiral Paine, a most gracious message from the Prince, expressing his deep regret in feeling himself obliged to receive

[1] St. Tr. vol. xxvi. p. 715.

my resignation, which was accordingly sent. But I owe it to his Royal Highness to express my opinion, that, circumstanced as he was, he had no other course to take in those disgraceful and disgusting times, and that my retainer for Paine was made a pretext by the King's Ministers for my removal, because my worthy and excellent friend, Sir A. Pigot, was removed from the office of the Prince's Solicitor General at the very same moment, although he had nothing whatever to do with Mr. Paine or his book. The fact is, that we were both, I believe, at that time members of a society for the reform of Parliament, called 'The Friends of the People.' It would, however, be most unjust, as well as ungrateful, to the Prince Regent, not to add, that in a few years afterwards, his Royal Highness, of his own mere motion, sent for me to Carlton House, while he was still in bed under a severe illness, and, taking me most graciously by the hand, said to me, that though he was not at all qualified to judge of retainers, nor to appreciate the correctness or incorrectness of my conduct in the instance that had separated us, yet that, being convinced I had acted from the purest motives, he wished most publicly to manifest that opinion, and therefore directed me to go immediately to Somerset House, and to bring with me, for his execution, the patent of Chancellor to his Royal Highness, which he said he had always designed for me; adding, that, owing to my being too young when his establishment was first fixed, he had declined having a Chancellor at that time; that during our separation he had been more than once asked to revive it, which he had refused to do, looking forward to this occasion; and I accordingly held the revived office of Chancellor to the Prince of Wales until I was appointed Chancellor to the King, when I resigned it, in conformity with the only precedent in the records of the Duchy of Cornwall, viz. that of Lord Bacon, who was Chancellor to Henry, Prince of Wales, and whose resignation is there recorded, because of his acceptance of the Great Seal in the reign of King James the First."

Whether the prosecution of "Paine's Rights of Man" was *discreet* or not, no one could justly complain of it as an infringement of public liberty, but Lord Loughborough was soon after Chancellor, and the " Reign of Terror" began. If not resisted by Erskine, to what might it not have led? I have already mentioned the case of John Frost, the first victim, prosecuted on the information of a man who had acted the part of a Government spy, for foolish words he had spoken after drinking freely in a coffee-house.[1] In the speech delivered by Erskine in defense, there were some passages of uncommon power and beauty:—

"Gentlemen, it is impossible for me to form any other judgment of the impression which such a proceeding altogether is likely to make upon your minds, than that which it makes upon my own. In the first place, is society to be protected by the breach of those confidences and by the destruction of that security and tranquillity which constitute its very essence everywhere, but which, till of late, most emphatically characterized the life of an Englishman? Is Government to derive dignity and safety by means which render it impossible for any man who has the least spark of honor to step forward to serve it? Is the time come when obedience to the law and correctness of conduct are not a sufficient protection to the subject,—but that he must measure his steps, select his expressions, and adjust his very looks, in the most common and private intercourses of life? Must an English gentleman in future fill his wine by a measure, lest in the openness of his soul, and while believing his neighbors are joining with him in that happy relaxation and freedom of thought which is the prime blessing of life, he should find his character blasted, and his person in a prison? Does any man put such constraint upon himself in the most private moments of his life, that he would be contented to have his loosest and lightest words recorded, and set in array against him in a court of justice? Thank God, the world lives very differently, or it would not be worth living in. There are moments when jarring opinions may be given without inconsistency, when Truth herself may be sported with without the breach of veracity, and when well-imagined nonsense is not only superior to, but is the very index to, wit and wisdom. I might safely assert,— taking, too, for the standard of my assertion the most honorably correct and enlightened societies in the kingdom,—that if malignant spies were properly posted,

[1] Ante, vol. vii. p. 452.

scarcely a dinner would end without a duel and an indictment.—When I came down this morning, and found, contrary to my expectation, that we were to be stuffed into this miserable hole in the wall [*the Court of Common Pleas*], to consume our constitutions, suppose I had muttered, passing along through the gloomy passages, 'What! **is** this cursed trial of Hastings going on again? **Are we** to have no respite? Are we to die of **asthma in this** damned corner? I wish to God the **roof** would come down, and abate the **impeachment**,—Lords, Commons, and all together.' *Such a wish proceeding from the mind* would be desperate wickedness, and the serious expression of it a high and criminal contempt of Parliament. Perhaps the bare utterance of such words without meaning would be irreverent and foolish; but still, if such expressions had been gravely imputed to me as the result of a malignant mind, seeking the destruction of the Lords and Commons of England, how would they have been treated in the House of Commons on a motion for my expulsion? How! the witness would have been laughed out of the House before he had half finished his evidence, and would have been voted to be too great a blockhead to deserve a worse character. Many things are, indeed, wrong and reprehensible, that neither do nor can become the object of criminal justice, because the happiness and security of social life, which are the very end and object of all law and justice, forbid the communication of them; because the spirit of a gentleman, which is the most refined morality, either shuts men's ears against what should not be heard, or closes their lips with the sacred seal of honor! This tacit but well-understood and delightful compact of social life is perfectly consistent with its safety. The security of free governments, and the unsuspecting confidence of every man who lives under them, are not only compatible but inseparable. It is easy to distinguish where the public duty calls for the violation of the private one. Criminal intention—but not indecent levities—not even grave opinions unconnected with conduct, are to be exposed to the magistrate; and when men, which happens but seldom, without the honor or the sense to make the due distinctions, force complaints upon Governments which they can neither approve of nor refuse to act upon, it becomes the office of juries—as it is yours to-day—to draw the true line in their judgments, measuring men's conduct by the safe standards of human life and experience."

Such was the infelicity of the times, however, that Frost was set in the pillory, expelled from his profession, and ruined for life.

The next prosecution of this sort had an issue which should have warned the Government that English juries were still awake to a sense of their duty, as guardians of the rights of Englishmen. The " Morning Chronicle," conducted with great ability and with a uniform respect for private character, as well as for the principles of our limited monarchy, had become exceedingly obnoxious by supporting parliamentary reform and the other measures for which the Foxite Whigs were contending; and the Attorney General filed *ex-officio* information against Mr. Perry and Mr. Gray, the proprietors of that journal, for having inserted in it an address of a society for political information, held at Derby, complaining of the state of the representation of the people, and other abuses, which they alleged required a remedy. When the case first stood for trial, only seven special jurors attending, the Attorney General would not pray a *tales*, but, the next term, moved to have another special jury struck. Erskine opposed this proceeding and established a most important doctrine, that " the special jury originally summoned must be resummoned, and try the cause;" so as to deprive the Crown officers of the power of postponing a trial till they have a jury to their mind.[1] When the case again came on before the same jury, Erskine began his address by saying,—

" If I had the slightest idea that the two gentlemen prosecuted as proprietors of the ' Morning Chronicle,' with whom I have an intimate acquaintance, were guilty of malicious and wicked designs against the state, as charged in the information, I should leave the task of defending them to others. Not that I conceive I have a right to refuse my professional assistance to any person who asks it; but I have for a day or two past been so seriously indisposed, that I feel myself scarcely equal to the common exertion of addressing the Court; and it is

[1] Lord Kenyon was at first very adverse, and said, "it would be very strange if the law were so."

only from the fullest confidence in the innocence of the defendants that I come forward for a very short space, to solicit the attention of the jury. You, gentlemen, indeed, are the sole arbitrators in this cause, and to you it belongs to decide on the whole merits of the question."—This being the first trial under the Libel Act, he said, "No one ought now to contend, as the Attorney General has done, that the criminality of the defendant in such a case is an inference of law from the fact, but (if, as one of the authors of the statute, I may be allowed to interpret its meaning) it connects and involves the law and the fact together, and obliges the jury to find in this crime, as in all others, by extrinsic as well as intrinsic means, the mind and intention with which the fact was committed. If you, gentlemen, can think that the defendants were actuated by the motive—not of wishing to reform and restore the beautiful fabric of our Constitution, somewhat impaired by time, but to subvert and destroy it, and to raise on its ruins a democracy or anarchy—an idea at which the mind of every honest man must shudder—you will find them guilty. Nay, if any one man knows or believes them to be capable of entertaining such a wish, or will say he ever heard, or had cause to know, that one sentence intimating anything of that nature ever fell from the lips of any one of them, I will give them up. But it seems the circumstances of the times render any opinion in favor of a reform of parliament peculiarly improper, and even dangerous; and the recommendation of it, in the present moment, must be ascribed to mischievous intentions. Were I to address you, gentlemen, to petition for a reform of parliament, I would address you NOW, as the season most fit for the purpose; I would address you NOW, because we have seen in other countries the effect of suffering evils to prevail so long in a government, and to increase to such a pitch, that it became impossible to correct them without bringing on greater evils than those which it was the first object of the people to remove; that it became impossible to remedy abuses without opening a door to revolution and anarchy. There are many diseases which might be removed by gentle medicines in their beginning, and even corrected by timely regimen, which, when neglected, are sure to bring their victims to the grave."—Having commented at considerable length upon the article alleged to be libelous, he said, " My learned friend can not produce a single instance in the course of seventeen years—the term of my acquaintance with the defendants—in which they have been charged in any court with public libel, or with private defamation; and I challenge the world to produce a single instance in which they have made their journal the vehicle of slander, or in which they have published a single paragraph to disturb the happiness of domestic life, to wound the sensibility of innocence, or to outrage the decencies of well-regulated society. They have displayed in the conduct of their paper a degree of learning, taste, and genius, superior to what has distinguished any similar undertaking. You may differ in opinion with them on public questions, but you would not for that reason consign them to a jail. I appeal to you, gentlemen, whether the abuses pointed out in this article do not exist in the Constitution, and whether their existence has not been admitted by all parties, both the enemies and the friends of reform? I will not say which party is right, but God forbid that honest opinion should ever become a crime."

Lord Kenyon: " There may be morality and virtue in this paper, and yet, *apparently*, LATET ANGUIS IN HERBA. There may be much that is good in it, and yet there may be much to censure."

The jury, after long deliberation, returned a verdict of " Publishing, but with no malicious intent;" and the Judge refusing to record this verdict, they found a general verdict of NOT GUILTY.[1]

The next Government prosecution assumed a very serious aspect, but was likewise so unfounded that the parties accused, being ably defended by Erskine, were acquitted, notwithstanding the prejudice excited against them as parliamentary reformers. Mr. Walker, a respectable master manufacturer at Manchester, and several others, were arrested for high treason, and were tried for a conspiracy to overturn the Constitution, and to assist the French in invading the realm. Some arms having been found in Mr. Walker's house, Dunn, a Government spy, swore that they had been purchased for the purpose of rebellion, and that he had been present at several consul-

[1] Erskine's Speeches, ii. 371–453.

tations among the prisoners, when an insurrection had been planned, in which the arms were to be used against the King's troops. Erskine demolished him in cross-examination, and made an admirable speech to the jury —opening the evidence he was to give, to prove that the arms (which were by no means of a formidable description) had been procured to enable Mr. Walker to defend his house against the attacks of a mob. Finding that the jury were completely with him, and that his clients were safe—in a manner very unusual with him, he concluded by indulging himself in a vein of pleasantry:

"This," said he, "is the genuine history of the business, and it must therefore not a little surprise you, that when the charge is wholly confined to the use of arms, Mr. Law should not even have hinted to you that Mr. Walker's house had been attacked, and that he was driven to stand upon his defense,—as if such a thing had never had an existence. Indeed, the armory which must have been exhibited in such a statement, would have but ill suited the indictment or the evidence, and I must therefore undertake a description of it myself. The arms having been locked up, as I told you, in the bed-chamber, I was shown, last week, into this house of conspiracy, treason, and death, and saw exposed to view this mighty armory, which was to level the beautiful fabric of our Constitution, and to destroy the lives and properties of ten millions of people. It consisted, first, of six little swivels, purchased two years ago, at the sale of Livesay, Hargrave & Co., by Mr. Jackson, a gentleman of Manchester, who is also one of the defendants, and who gave them to Master Walker, a boy of about ten years of age. Swivels, you know, are guns, so called because they turn upon a pivot; but these were taken off their props, were painted, and put upon blocks resembling the carriages of heavy cannon, and in that shape may fairly be called 'children's toys.' You frequently see them in the neighborhood of London, adorning the houses of sober citizens, who, preferring grandeur to taste, place them upon their ramparts at Mile End or at Islington. Having, like Mr. Dunn,—I hope I resemble him in nothing else,—having, like him, served his Majesty as a soldier (and I am ready to serve again if my country's safety should require it), I took a close review of all I saw, and observing that the muzzle of one of them was broken off, I was curious to know how far this famous conspiracy had proceeded, and whether they had come into action; when I found that the accident had happened on firing a *feu de joie* upon his Majesty's happy recovery, and that they had been afterwards fired upon the Prince of Wales's birthday. These are the only times that, in the hands of these conspirators, these cannon, big with destruction, had opened their little mouths;—once to commemorate the indulgent and benign favor of Providence in the recovery of the Sovereign, and once as a congratulation to the Heir Apparent of his crown on the anniversary of his birth. I went next, under the protection of the master-general of this ordnance (Mr. Walker's chambermaid), to visit the rest of this formidable array of death, and found a little musketoon, about so high *(describing it)*. I put my thumb upon it, when out started a little bayonet, like the jack-in-the-box which we buy for children at a fair. In short, not to weary you, gentlemen, there was just such a parcel of arms, of different sorts and sizes, as a man collecting them among his friends for his defense, against the sudden violence of a riotous multitude, might be expected to have collected. Here lay three or four rusty guns of different dimensions, and here and there a bayonet or broadsword, covered over with dust and rust, so as to be almost undistinguishable. We will prove by witness after witness, till you desire us to finish, that they were principally collected on the 11th of December, the day of the riot, and that from the 12th in the evening, or the 13th in the morning, they have lain untouched, as I have described them; that their use began and ended with the necessity, and that from that time to the present, there never has been in the warehouse any machine of war, or weapon of destruction, from a piece of artillery to a pop-gun."

The case became so clear, that Mr. Law abandoned the prosecution, and the Government spy was convicted of perjury at the same assizes.[1]

[1] 23 St. Tr. 1055–1166. Erskine's Speeches, iii. 1–52.

CHAPTER CLXXX.

CONTINUATION OF THE LIFE OF LORD ERSKINE TILL THE CONCLUSION OF THE PROSECUTIONS FOR HIGH TREASON AGAINST THE ADVOCATES FOR A REFORM IN PARLIAMENT.

NOTWITHSTANDING the unfortunate result of the late State prosecutions, Ministers (it is supposed with a division of opinion in the Cabinet) resolved upon a much more extensive and a much bolder attack on public liberty, which if it had succeeded, would have placed the lives of the great body of their opponents at their mercy. There were now several societies existing for the professed object of Parliamentary Reform —particularly the "Corresponding Society," and the "Society for Constitutional Information"—having branch societies in most of the large towns of Great Britain. At their meetings inflammatory and indiscreet speeches were occasionally made, and some of their resolutions and printed addresses were of a very objectionable character, although the principal leaders and the great bulk of the members were attached to the Constitution. Their evil designs and their influence were much over-estimated by the Government, and a still graver error was committed in the means adopted for putting them down. It would have been highly proper to prosecute for a *misdemeanor* the individuals who could have been proved to have uttered seditious language, or to have published seditious writings,—making each party accused answerable for his own acts. But it was thought better to resort to the law of "constructive treason," which had received such a blow on the trial of Lord George Gordon,—to assert that these societies intended to bring about a revolution,—and therefore to insist that all who belonged to them were to be considered guilty of "compassing the death of our Lord the King," and ought to die the death of traitors. I have not a doubt that most of those who advised this mode of proceeding, far from being animated by any bloodthirsty disposition, or love of arbitrary power, really believed it the only means of saving the country from anarchy; although I suspect that some of them were well pleased to increase the alarm in the public mind,—to throw obloquy upon their political rivals, and to strengthen the foundation of their own power. But, in my humble opinion, severe censure is due either to their judgment or their intentions. Indeed, in our times, when an arbitrary application of the criminal law has been abandoned by all parties in the state, we are at a loss to account for an attempt which seems to us not only very unconstitutional, but very foolish,—as it was not accompanied by the abolition of trial by jury.

First came secret committees of the two Houses of Parliament, and upon their reports a bill was passed suspending the Habeas Corpus Act, and containing this most reprehensible recital, to be referred to as *proof* in the prosecutions which were to follow—" that a treacherous and detestable conspiracy had been formed for subverting the existing laws and Constitution, and for introducing the system of anarchy and confusion which had lately prevailed in France."[1] This was more exceptionable in principle than anything done during the reign of Charles II.; for then the fabricators of the Popish Plot did not think of corroborating the testimony of Oates and Bedloe by a public statute; and there, if the facts alleged had been true, they would have amounted to a plain case of actual treason: whereas here, admitting the truth of all the facts alleged, there was no pretense for saying that any treason contemplated by the legislature had been committed. If this scheme had succeeded, not only would there have been a sacrifice of life contrary to law, but all political " agitation " must have been extinguished in England, as there would have been a precedent for holding that the effort to carry a measure by influencing public opinion through the means openly resorted to in our days, is a " compassing of the death of the sovereign." The only chance of escaping servitude would have been civil war. It is frightful to think of the perils to which the nation was exposed; for, on account of the horror justly caused in England by the murder of Louis XVI. and the other atrocities which had recently

---

[1] Stat. 34 Geo. 3, c. 54. This declaration, the work of a ministerial committee and a ministerial majority, was relied upon in the treason trials as proof of the conspiracy.

been perpetrated at Paris, an attempt which in former days would have excited universal disgust and indignation was now received with considerable favor, and might have been crowned with success. But Erskine and the crisis were framed for each other. He might have passed through life a well employed barrister, admired by his contemporaries for his skill in winning verdicts, and forgotten as soon as the grave had closed over him. But his contemporaries, who without him might have seen the extinction of freedom among us, saw it, by his peculiar powers, placed upon an imperishable basis.

The Grand Jury for the county of Middlesex found an indictment for high treason against twelve persons who had belonged to these societies, and had professed themselves warm friends to parliamentary reform,—the overt act laid being that they had engaged in a conspiracy to call a convention, the object of which was to bring about a revolution in the country—but it was not suggested that there was any plot against the King's life, or any preparation for force.

The prisoners, upon their arraignment, had Erskine assigned as their counsel, with Gibbs, hitherto only known as a good lawyer, but from the distinction he now acquired, afterwards Attorney General and Chief Justice of the Common Pleas. On their declining to be tried jointly, the Attorney General selected Thomas Hardy, a shoemaker, as the one against whom he could make the strongest case.

This memorable trial began on Tuesday, the 28th of October, 1794, at the Old Bailey, before Lord Chief Justice Eyre, and several other Judges, sitting under a special commission of oyer and terminer. Sir John Scott spoke nine hours in opening the case for the prosecution. In the annals of English criminal jurisprudence there had not yet been an instance of a trial for high treason that had not been finished in a single day. When the hour of midnight struck, scarcely any progress had been made in adducing the evidence for the Crown, which was to consist of innumerable speeches made, and resolutions passed, during many months, not only in London, but at Manchester, Sheffield, Norwich, Edinburgh, and many other places, when the prisoner had been at a distance of hundreds of miles,—of toasts at anniversary dinners,—and of voluminous publications issued by the obnoxious societies, or which the societies had approved of, or which had for their authors individual members of the societies supposed to be implicated in the conspiracy.

Erskine, who did not despise any arts by which he might conciliate the jury, expressed his readiness to consent that they should go to their several homes, saying, " I am willing that they shall be as free as air, with the single restriction that they will not suffer themselves to be approached in the way of influence ; and the gentlemen will not think it much that this should be required, *considering the very peculiar nature of this case.*"

An objection, however, was made to the jurymen separating ; and it was agreed that they should pass the night under the care of four bailiffs in a large room in an adjoining tavern, in which couches were strewed for them. But before they retired to talk over the subject together, and to ruminate upon it, Erskine, perceiving that a deep impression had been made upon them by the solemn and seemingly candid address of the Attorney General, was determined to give them some other topic of conversation, and some other food for reflection. As soon, therefore, as the four bailiffs had been sworn to do their duty, he thus spoke, while the jury listened :—

" My Lord, all this immense body of papers has been seized, and been a long time in the hands of the officers of the Crown. We applied to see them, but were refused—we applied to the Privy Counsel, and were refused—we were referred to your Lordship, because they knew that your Lordship could not grant such a request. Here we are, therefore, with all these papers tumbled upon our hands, without the least opportunity of examining them ; and yet from this load of papers, which the Attorney General took nine hours to read, the act of compassing the King's death is to be collected. I trust your Lordships will be disposed to indulge me—indeed I shall expect, in justice to the prisoner, that I may have an opportunity, before I address the jury upon this mass of evidence, to know what is in it. I declare, upon my honor, as far as relates to myself and my friend who is assigned as counsel for the prisoner, we have no design whatever to trespass upon the patience of the Court, and your

Lordships may have seen to-day how little of your time we have consumed. We have no desire upon earth but to do our best to save the man for whom your Lordships have assigned us to be counsel, and whom we believe to be innocent."

The Court sat day by day at eight o'clock in the morning, and continued sitting till past midnight. Erskine's attention was never for one moment relaxed, and he was ever on the watch for an opportunity of exciting the sympathy of the jury by interlocutory speeches,—particularly in arguing questions of evidence.

The proceedings of the Convention at Edinburgh being proffered, he objected that the Crown must first show that they were approved of by Mr. Hardy, saying:—

"I confess I am not very anxious to shut out any evidence—I very probably do not understand it; but I do not see how it bears upon the case. He is charged with 'compassing and imagining the death of our Sovereign Lord the King,' whose life is dear, my Lord, to all the kingdom. No act can be given in evidence before your Lordships; nor will I sit silent to hear any act given in evidence that does not tend to show the prisoner at the bar to have had that wicked intention. When I stand here defending the man who holds his life under the law (and I am not defending his life only, but my own life, and the life of every man in the country), I must take care that the rules of evidence are observed."

On a subsequent occasion, in objecting to similar evidence, he tried to awaken the jury to the consequences of this proceeding by observing,—

"How many thousands of his Majesty's subjects are to be brought to this place, I can not tell; for the conspiracy which is alleged comprehends all the members of every one of these societies. I say, in my judgment, upon the evidence that is before the Court, every man who has been a member of any of these societies, every man who has been connected with their proceedings, is liable to be put in the same situation as Mr. Hardy, and, according to the rule contended for, anything written by any one person belonging to any of these societies would be equally evidence against him."

His object was to keep in check, without insulting, Lord Chief Justice Eyre, who had, in addressing the

Grand Jury, referred to the recent Act of Parliament as proof of the conspiracy, and who, though he very conscientiously ruled the questions of law which arose, evidently had a leaning towards the prosecution.

While a Crown witness was under cross-examination, and equivocating so as to revolt the jury, the Chief Justice, interposing, took him out of the counsel's hands, and in a coaxing manner repeated the question to him. *Erskine:* " I am entitled to have the benefit of this gentleman's deportment, if your Lordship will just indulge me for one moment." *L. C. J. Eyre :* " Give him fair play." *Erskine :* " He has certainly had fair play. I wish *we* had as fair play,—but that is not addressed to the Court." *Attorney General:* " Whom do you mean ?" *Erskine :* " I say the prisoner has a right to fair play." *Garrow:* " But you declared that it was not said to the Court." *Erskine:* " I am not to be called to order by the Bar."

Being exceedingly afraid that an impression might be made upon the minds of the jury, which he might not be able to remove, by an infamous paper pretending to be a play-bill, to announce " an entertaining farce called LA GUILLOTINE, or GEORGE'S HEAD IN A BASKET,"—before it was read he said, most irregularly, but with an air that in him alone excused the irregularity, " The paper was fabricated by the spies who support the prosecution !" *Attorney General :* " You shall not say that till you prove it." *Erskine :* " I shall prove it."

He showed admirable skill in regulating his questions to the Crown witnesses by the disposition which they displayed. One ex-member of the Corresponding Society, whom he found very pliable, he thus interrogated. *Q.* " Had you any idea, when you became a member, or while you continued there, by parliamentary reform to touch the King's Majesty or the House of Lords ? " *A.* " No, never ; I never had that idea." *Q.* " Never in your life ? " *A.* " No." *Q.* " I ask you, in the presence of God, to whom you will answer, had you any idea of destroying the King or the House of Lords ? " *A.* " No, God forbid ! " *Q.* " Then I understand you to say, upon the oath you have taken, and subject to the consequences here and hereafter, that there was no such idea either in your own mind, or, from what you know from others, from what they said and what they did, in the minds of any other of the members?" *A.* "Never." *Q.* "Have you any reason to believe—I ask you to look upon your own soul when you answer the question—that, though they might not intend mischief originally, when associated they began to intend mischief?" *A.* "No, never."

Wishing to exhibit the consummate conductor of a cause before a jury, not a mere rhetorician, I add the following dialogue, which at least to those familiar with such scenes, strikingly exhibits his bearing to the Court and to his adversary. A witness, who pretended to relate from notes he said he had taken of the proceedings of a reform society, having been asked for a date, and having answered that he *thought* it was about such a time. Erskine exclaimed, "None of your *thinking*, when you have the paper in your hands!" *Witness:* "I have not a memorandum of the date." *Erskine:* "What date have you taken, good Mr. Spy?" *Witness:* "I do not think on such an occasion being a spy is any disgrace." *Eyre, C. J.:* "These observations are more proper when you come to address the jury." *Attorney General:* "Really, that is not a proper way to examine witnesses. Lord Holt held strong language to such sort of an address from a counsel to a witness who avowed himself a spy." *Erskine:* "I am sure I shall always pay that attention to the Court which is due from me; but I am not to be told by the Attorney General how I am to examine a witness!" *Attorney General:* "I thought you had not heard his Lordship." *Erskine:* "I am much obliged to his Lordship for the admonition he gave me. I heard his Lordship, and I heard you,—whom I should not have heard."

He would even try to ingratiate himself with the jury by being facetious, although there was such a weight upon his own mind. He asked a spy, who had assumed the name of *Douglas*, what was his true name? *Witness:* "As for taking the name of Douglas, I took it from a play-bill." *Erskine:* "Pray how long did *you play the part of Norval?*" The jury laughed, and disbelieved all the witness had said.

At last, when the Court was about to adjourn, at two o'clock on Saturday morning to the usual hour of eight the same day, the Attorney General intimated that he should not take above forty minutes longer to finish his case. Erskine then, pointing out very feelingly the embarrassment of his situation, as he had not had time to read any part of the evidence, prayed a few hours to enable him to arrange his papers and prepare for the defense. Eyre, most indecently, under pretense of consulting the convenience of the jury, refused the request, and proposed that the evidence for the prisoner should proceed while the counsel was preparing his speech, observing very coolly, that "it was a matter of indifference in what order they were presented." *Erskine :* " I should be sorry to put the jury to any inconvenience : I do not shrink from my duty, but I assure your Lordship that during the week, I have been nearly without natural rest, and that my physical strength is quite exhausted." *Eyre, C. J.:* " What is it you ask for ? " *Erskine :* " As I stated before, the Attorney General found it necessary to consume nine hours. I should not consume half that time, if I had an opportunity of doing that which I humbly request of the Court." *Eyre, C. J. :* " We have offered you an expedient : neither of you say whether you accept it." Gibbs spurned at it ; and then Erskine, pointing out how it might prejudice the prisoner, on trial for his life, proposed an adjournment till twelve next day. Eyre reluctantly agreed to eleven, but would make no further concession. *Erskine :* " I should be glad if your Lordships would allow another hour." *Eyre, C. J.:* " I feel so much for the situation of the jury, that, on their account, I can not think of it." *Erskine :* " My Lord, I never was placed in such a situation in the whole course of my practice before ;—however, I will try to do my duty." *Jury :* " My Lord, we are extremely willing to allow Mr. Erskine another hour, if your Lordship thinks proper." *Eyre, C. J. :* " As the jury ask it for you, I will not refuse you."

Cheered by this good omen, Erskine went home, and, after a short repose, arranged the materials of " a speech which will live forever." [1]

He began at two o'clock on Saturday afternoon, and spoke seven hours—a period that seemed very short to

[1] "I have been indulged by Mr. Rogers, the celebrated author of the 'Pleasures of Memory,' and other poems, with Mr. Horne Tooke's copy of Hardy's trial, where I find in Mr. Tooke's handwriting, at the end of this argument, the following remarkable note : 'THIS SPEECH WILL LIVE FOREVER.' "—*Editor of the State Trials,* vol. xxiv. p. 877.—I have myself been ately favored with a view of the book and of the note.

his hearers, and in reality was so, considering the subjects he had to deal with, and the constitutional learning, the powerful reasoning, the wit, and the eloquence which he condensed into it. This wonderful performance must be studied as a whole by all who are capable of understanding its merits ; for the enunciation of principles is so connected with the inferences to be drawn from the evidence, and there is such an artful, though seemingly natural succession of topics to call for the pity and the indignation of the jury—to captivate their affections, and to convince their understandings—that the full beauty of detached passages can not properly be appreciated. But some I must introduce, or this memoir might be considered very defective. Having judiciously commenced with eulogizing the Constitution of England, and reprobating the violence which had disgraced the revolution in France, he prayed that, if this prosecution had been commenced to avert from us the calamities incident to civil confusion, the prisoner should not be made a sacrifice :—

"Let not *him* suffer under vague expositions of tyrannical laws more tyrannically executed. Let not *him* be hurried away to predoomed execution, from an honest enthusiasm for the public safety. I ask for him a trial by this applauded Constitution of our country : I call upon you to administer the law to *him* according to our own wholesome institutions, by its strict and rigid letter. However you may eventually disapprove of any part of his conduct, or, viewing it through a false medium, may think it even wicked, I claim for him, as a subject of England, that the law shall decide upon its criminal denomination. I protest in his name against all speculations respecting *consequences* when the law commands us to look only to INTENTIONS. If the state be threatened with evils, let Parliament administer a *prospective* remedy ; but let the prisoner hold his life UNDER THE LAW. Gentlemen, I ask this solemnly of the Court, whose justice I am persuaded will afford it to me ; I ask it more emphatically of you, the *jury*, who are called upon by your oaths to make a true deliverance of your countryman from this charge ; but lastly and chiefly I implore it of HIM in whose hands are all the issues of life, whose merciful eye expands itself over all the transactions of mankind,—at whose command nations rise and fall, and are regenerated. I implore it of

GOD HIMSELF that HE will fill your minds with the spirit of truth, so that you may be able to find your way through the labyrinth of matter laid before you—a labyrinth in which no man's life was ever before involved in the whole history of human justice or injustice."

He then proceeds to analyze the indictment, and to lay down the law,—contending, with great subtlety:

" That the compassing of the King's death, or, in other words, the traitorous intention to destroy his *natural existence*, is the treason, and not the overt acts, which are only laid as manifestations of the traitorous intention, or, in other words, as EVIDENCE competent to be left to a jury to prove it; and that no conspiracy to levy war against the King, nor any conspiracy against his *regal character* or *capacity*, is a good overt act of compassing *his death*, unless some force be exerted or in contemplation against the KING'S PERSON; and that such force, so exerted and in contemplation, is not substantively the treason of compassing, but only competent in point of law to establish it, if the jury, by their verdict of *Guilty*, draw that conclusion of fact from the evidence of the overt act."

Discussing how far the charge was substantiated, he says: " The unfortunate man whose innocence I am defending is arraigned before you of high treason, upon evidence not only repugnant to the statute, but such as never yet was heard of in any capital trial—evidence which, even with all the attention you have given to it, I defy any one of you at this moment to say of what it consists— evidence (I tremble for my boldness, in standing up for the life of a man, when I am conscious I am incapable of understanding from it even what acts are imputed to him) —evidence which has consumed four days in the reading, made up from the unconnected writings of men unknown to one another, upon a hundred different subjects—evidence the very listening to which has filled my mind with unremitting distress and agitation, and which, from its discordant nature, has suffered me to reap no advantage from your indulgence, but which, on the contrary, has almost set my brain on fire with the vain endeavor to analyze it . . . But read these books over and over again, and let us stand here a year and a day in discoursing concerning them, still the question must return to what you, and you only, can resolve—Is he guilty of that base, detestable intention to destroy the King?—not whether you suspect, nor whether it be probable—not whether he *may* be guilty—no, but that '*provably*' he is guilty. If you can say this upon the evidence, it is your duty to say so, and you may with a tranquil conscience return to your families, though by your judgment the unhappy object of it must return no more to his. Alas! gentlemen, what do I say? He has no family to return to ; the affectionate partner of his life has already fallen a victim to the surprise and horror which attended the scene now transacting. But let that melancholy reflection pass —it should not, perhaps, have been introduced—it certainly ought to have no weight with you, who are to judge upon your oaths. I do not stand here to desire you to commit perjury from compassion ; but, at the same time, my earnestness may be forgiven, since it proceeds from a weakness common to us all. I claim no merit with the prisoner for my zeal ; it proceeds from a selfish principle inherent in the human heart. I am counsel, gentlemen, for myself. In every word I utter, I feel that I am pleading for the safety of my own life, for the lives of my ohildren after me, for the happiness of my country, and for the universal condition of civil society throughout the world."

He then showed that the Societies impeached had only adopted the doctrines of Lord Chatham and other great reformers whose loyalty had not been doubted, and that the Duke of Richmond had gone much further than Mr. Hardy :—

"Gentlemen, the Duke of Richmond's plan was universal suffrage and annual parliaments ; and urged, too, with a boldness which, when the comparison comes to be made, will leave in the background the strongest figures in the writings on the table. I do not say this sarcastically ; I mean to speak with the greatest respect of his Grace, both as to the wisdom and integrity of his conduct ; for, although I think, with Mr. Fox, that annual parliaments and universal suffrage would be nothing like an improvement in the Constitution, yet I confess that I find it easier to say so than to answer the arguments which the Duke of Richmond has adduced in support of his sweeping measure of reform."

Having pointed out that the present Prime Minister himself, who must be supposed to have directed these prosecutions against associates and disciples, had been a reformer like the prisoner at the bar, he says:—

"It would be the height of injustice and wickedness to torture expressions, and pervert conduct into treason and rebellion which had recently lifted up others to the love of the Nation, to the confidence of the Sovereign, and to all the honors of the State! Why is everything to be held up as *bonâ fide* when the example is set, and *malâ fide* when it is followed? Why have not I as good a claim to take credit for honest purpose in the poor man I am defending—against whom not a contumelious expression has been proved—as when we find the same expressions in the mouths of the Duke of Richmond and Mr. Pitt?"

In palliating the sympathy of the Societies with the French Republic, which was likely to make an unfavorable impression on the jury, he dwelt with much force upon the combination of the Continental Sovereigns to extinguish liberty in France, and thus, in his own person, avowed the sentiments which were urged as proof to support the charge of high treason:—

"Men may assert the right of every people to choose their government without seeking to destroy their own. This accounts for many expressions imputed to the unfortunate prisoners, which I have often uttered myself, and shall continue to utter every day of my life, and call upon the spies of Government to record them. I will say anywhere without fear—nay, I will say in this Court where I stand—that 'an attempt to interfere by despotic combination and violence with any government which a people choose to give to themselves, whether it be good or evil, is an oppression and subversion of the natural and inalienable rights of man;' and, though the Government of this country should countenance such a system, it would not only be still legal for me to express my detestation of it, as I here deliberately express it, but it would become my interest and my duty to do so. For, if combinations of despotism can accomplish such a purpose, who shall tell me what other nation may not be the prey of their ambition? Upon the very principle of denying to a people the right of governing themselves, how are we to resist the French, should they attempt by violence to fasten their government upon us? or what inducement would there be for resistance to preserve laws which are not, it seems, our own, but which are unalterably imposed upon us? The very argument strikes, as with a palsy, the arm and vigor of the nation. I hold dear the privileges I am contending for, not as privileges hostile to the Constitution, but as necessary for its preservation; and if the French were to intrude by force upon the government of our own free choice, I should leave these papers, and return to a profession *that perhaps I better understand.*"[1]

Having the jury now under his control, he returns with renewed force to the consideration of the tremendous consequence of the principle on which the prosecution was founded:—

"The delegates who attended the meetings could not be supposed to have met with a different intention from those who sent them; and if the answer to that is, that the constituents are involved in the guilt of their representatives, we get back to the monstrous position from which I observed you before to shrink with visible horror when I stated it—as it involves in the fate of this single trial every man who corresponded with these societies, or who, as a member of societies in any part of the kingdom, consented to the meeting which was assembled, or to the meeting which was in prospect. Upwards of forty thousand persons, upon the lowest calculation, must alike be liable to the pains and penalties of the law, and hold themselves as tenants at will under the ministers of the Crown. The campaign of Judge Jeffreys in the west was nothing to what may follow. In whatever aspect, therefore, this prosecution is regarded, new difficulties and new uncertainties and terrors surround it."

But I must give a specimen of the manner of his commenting upon the testimony of the witnesses—which, after all, is the most important function of an advocate before a jury. Thus he handled one of the Government spies who had been examined:—

[1] We may conceive to what a pitch he had worked up the feelings of the jury when he could venture upon this martial ebullition, which, in cooler moments, would have excited a titter. In reality, he had no taste for the art of war, and never had made greater progress in it than being able, in the absence of the captain, pretty tolerably to put his company of the Royals through the manual of platoon exercise.

"Mr. Grove professed to speak from notes, yet I observed him frequently looking up to the ceiling while he was speaking—when I said to him, 'Are you now speaking from a note? Have you got any note of what you are now saying?' He answered, 'Oh no; this is from recollection.' Good God Almighty! *Recollection* mixing itself up with *notes* in a case of HIGH TREASON. He did not even take down the words; nay, to do the man justice, he did not even affect to have taken the words, but only the *substance*, as he himself expressed it. Oh, excellent evidence! The substance of words taken down by a spy, and supplied where defective by his memory! But I must not call him a spy, for it seems he took them *bonâ fide* as a delegate, and yet *bonâ fide* as an informer. What a happy combination of fidelity! faithful to serve, and faithful to betray!—correct to record for the benefit of the society, and correct to dissolve and to punish it! In the last precedent which could be cited of the production of such testimony, the case of Lord Stafford, accused of being concerned in the Popish plot—all the proceedings were ordered to be taken off the file and burned, 'to the intent that the same might no longer be visible to after ages,'—an order dictated, no doubt, by a pious tenderness for national honor, and meant as a charitable covering for the crimes of our fathers. But it was a sin against posterity; it was a treason against society; for, instead of being burned, they should have been directed to be blazoned in large letters upon the walls of our courts of justice, that, like the characters deciphered by the prophet of God to the Eastern tyrant, they might enlarge and blacken in your sight to terrify you from acts of injustice."

I must refrain from copying more than a few sentences of the peroration:—

"My firmest wish is, that we may not conjure up a spirit to destroy ourselves, nor set the example here of what in another country we deplore. Let us cherish the old and venerable laws of our forefathers. Let our judicial administration be strict and pure; and let the jury of the land preserve the life of a fellow-subject, who only asks it from them on the same terms under which they hold their own lives, and all that is dear to them and their posterity forever. Let me repeat the wish with which I began my address to you, and which proceeds from the very bottom of my heart: May it please God, who is the author of all mercies to mankind, whose providence I am persuaded guides and superintends the transactions of the world, and whose guardian Spirit has ever hovered over this prosperous island, to direct and fortify your judgments! I am aware I have not acquitted myself to the unfortunate man who has put his trust in me in the manner I could have wished; yet I am unable to proceed any further — exhausted in spirit and in strength—but confident in the expectation of justice."

It is said that from his extraordinary exertions he had become quite hoarse, and that for ten minutes before he sat down, leaning for support on the table, he could only whisper to the jury; but, that, so intense was the stillness—such breathless eagerness was there to catch every syllable which fell from him, his faint accents were heard in the remotest corner of the court, and produced a deeper effect than was ever witnessed from tones the most powerful and mellifluous.

As soon as he had concluded, an irresistible acclamation pervaded the court, and was repeated to an immense distance around. The streets seemed to be filled with the whole population of London, and it was for some time impossible for the Judges to get to their carriages. Erskine, thereupon, making a noble and triumphant use of his popularity, went out and addressed the multitude, desiring them to confide in the justice of the country—reminding them that the only security of Englishmen was under the inestimable laws of England, and that any attempt to overawe or bias them would not only be an affront to public justice, but would endanger the lives of the accused. He then besought them to retire,—and in a few minutes there was no one to be seen within half a mile of the court except a casual passer-by, unconscious of what had happened, or a drowsy watchman on his round, announcing, according to ancient custom, the hour of the night and the state of the weather.

The result of this memorable trial is well known. After important evidence as to the objects of the Societies and the loyal and peaceable character of the prisoner,—an argumentative and able address from Sir Vicary Gibbs,—a very lengthy reply from Lord Redesdale, then Solicitor

General,—and an unexceptionable summing up from Chief Justice Eyre, the jury found a verdict of NOT GUILTY,— which gave rise to rapturous rejoicings among the reformers, and was received with satisfaction by the judicious of all parties.

I am wholly at a loss to account for the infatuated obstinacy which was now exhibited. The almost invariable practice has been, that after an acquittal of the first man tried of several jointly charged with high treason, the prosecution has been abandoned as to the others; and one would have thought that here the Government would eagerly have withdrawn from an attempt which had been so unfortunate, and which was so universally condemned. Yet, to the amazement of the public, it was announced that another prisoner was to be tried on the same charge and the same evidence, and that this prisoner was JOHN HORNE TOOKE, a man popular by his agreeable manners, admired for his literary acquirements, who had ever conducted himself with caution and discretion; known to be aristocratic in his inclinations, although he was a demagogue;--and for assailing and annoying antagonists in a forensic proceeding having proved himself to have unrivaled powers,[1] which were sure to be called in aid to follow up the destructive onslaught of Erskine, now flushed with victory.

Yes! John Horne Tooke, with a constitution broken by age and disease, but a mind as alert and youthful as when he wrote against Junius, and spoke against Thurlow, was next called upon to hold up his hand at the bar of the Old Bailey, and having heard the jargon of the indictment read, was asked how he would be tried? Although perfectly confident of an acquittal, he gave a foretaste of what might be expected during the trial, by putting on the aspect of a man weighed down by his oppressors, by looking round the Court some seconds with an air of significant meaning, which few assumed better, and by answering, while he emphatically shook his head, " I would be tried by God and my country! But——" Here

[1] *E. g.* He had been his own counsel in the action brought against him by Mr. Fox for the expenses of the Westminster election petition, and thus began his address to the jury: " Gentlemen, there are here three parties to be considered—YOU, *Mr. Fox*, and *myself*. As for the *Judge* and the *crier*, they are sent here to preserve order, and they are both well paid for their trouble."

he paused, having intimated with sufficient distinctness that he feared much he should not have this advantage.

An application having been made that, on account of his infirmities, he might be permitted to sit beside his counsel, he was told that "this *indulgence* should be shown him." Instead of humbly thanking the Judge in whose hands he was, and who was by and by to direct the jury on the question of his life or death, he observed, in a very quiet, familiar tone, "I can not help saying, my Lord, that if I were a Judge, that word '*indulgence*' should never issue from my lips. My Lord, you have no indulgence to show: you are bound to be just; and to be just, is to do that which is ordered."

Once seated at the table with the counsel, he was the most facetious and light-hearted of mortals, and seemed to have as much enjoyment in the proceeding as a young advocate who has unexpectedly got a brief with a good fee in a winning cause, which has excited great interest, and by which he expects to make his fortune. "Cool and prompt, ready at repartee, and fond of notoriety, he trod the boards of the Old Bailey like some amateur actor, pleased with his part, and resolved to make the most of of it, even though the catastrophe should terminate in his death. After the acquittal of Hardy, the reverend agitator would have deprecated his not being brought to trial as a personal misfortune. It is impossible to read this grave state prosecution without frequently indulging in an involuntary smile. From the constant merriment which rewarded his sallies, it might be guessed that a madder wag never stood at the bar; and yet he rarely laughed himself, but glanced around, from his keen and arch eyes, a satirical look of triumph."[1] To the credit of Erskine be it stated, that he was not at all annoyed by the sallies of his client, although they were sometimes unseasonable, nor jealous of the *éclat* which they brought him; but on the contrary, encouraged him to interpose, and rejoiced in the success of his hits. While the evidence for the prosecution was going on, he seemed content with the office of being second to one so perfect in the art of forensic dueling.

I may mention one or two of the quips of Horne Tooke, which Erskine applauded.

[1] Townsend's Twelve Eminent Judges, ii. 24.

Passages being read from pamphlets published by the Societies, abusing the King and the Lords, he offered to prove that much abuse of himself had been printed on *earthenware vessels*.—A witness having said that a treasonable song had been sung at a public meeting, he proposed that it should be sung in court, so that the jury might ascertain whether there was anything treasonable, resembling *Ca ira* or the Marseillaise Hymn in the tune. He not unfrequently succeeded in arguing questions of evidence; and if found out to be clearly wrong, he took a pinch of snuff, and quietly apologized by saying that "he was only a student of forty years' standing." On one occasion, when he objected to the admissibility of evidence of a particular fact, on the ground that he was not connected with it, Eyre reminded him, that if there were two or three links to make a chain, they must go to one first, and then to another, and see whether the chain was made." *Horne Tooke:* "I beg your pardon, my Lord, but is not a chain composed of links? and may I not disjoin each link? and do I not thereby destroy the chain?' *Eyre, C. J.:* "I rather think not, till the links are put together and form the chain." *Horne Tooke:* "Nay, my Lord, with great submission to your Lordship, I rather think that I may, because it is my business to prevent the forming of that chain."—To show him to be a Republican, evidence was given that a society, of which he was a member, had approved of certain proceedings in the National Assembly. "Egad," said he, "it is lucky we did not say there were some good things in the Koran, or we should have been charged to be Mohammedans."—Having put questions to show that at public meetings they had often disapproved of his sentiments and his conduct, he gave a knowing nod to the jury, and said, "My object, gentlemen, was to show that, after I had deposed our Lord the King I was likely to have very troublesome subjects, for I was constantly received with hisses."—By putting the following question, he excited a roar of laughter against the solemn and empty Beaufoy, who pretended hardly to know him, and denied all recollection of a date to which he was interrogated: "Now witness, upon your oath, was it not the very day that you complained so bitterly to me you could not sleep because, notwithstanding all your

. services to Mr. Pitt, and all the money you had spent in his cause, he had refused to return your bow?" Few were aware, at the time, that this was pure invention to expose a tuft-hunter. The Attorney General, in repelling some insinuations thrown out against him for the manner in which he had instituted these prosecutions, said "he could endure anything but an attack on his *good name:* it was the *little patrimony* he had to leave to his children, and, with God's help, he would leave it unimpaired." He then burst into tears, which, from his lachrymose habit, surprised no one; but, to the wonder of all, the Solicitor General, not known to be of the melting mood, became equally affected, and sobbed in concert with his friend. Tooke, afraid that this sympathy might extend to the jury, exclaimed in a stage whisper, " Do you know what Sir John Mitford is crying about? He is thinking of the destitute condition of Sir John Scott's children, and the *little patrimony* they are likely to divide among them."

When the time arrived for the prisoner's counsel addressing the jury, Erskine was again the observed of all observers, and almost surpassed his performance in defending Hardy. On that occasion, notwithstanding his assumed boldness, he evidently entertained great apprehensions as to the result. He could now even venture to be jocular. In commenting upon the authorities cited by the Attorney General, he said :—

" To give the case of Lord Lovat any bearing upon the present, you must first prove that our design was to arm, and I shall then admit the argument and the conclusion. But has such proof been given on the present trial? It has not been attempted; the abortive evidence of arms has been abandoned. Even the solitary pike that formerly glared rebellion from the corner of the court, no longer makes its appearance, and the knives have returned to their ancient office of carving. Happy was it indeed for me that they were ever produced; for so perfectly common were they throughout all England, and so notoriously in use for the most ordinary purposes, that public justice and benevolence, shocked at the perversion of truth in the evidence concerning them, kept pouring them in upon me from all quarters. The box before me is half full of them; and if all other trades fail me, I might now set up a cutler's shop."

Thus he pointed out the improbability of the charge against the aged philologist :—

"Yet this gentleman, greatly advanced in years, and broken in health, who was shut up then, and long before, within the compass of his house and garden at Wimbledon, where he used to wish an act of parliament might confine him for life, who was painfully devoting the greatest portion of his time to the advancement of learning, who was absorbed in researches which will hereafter astound the world—who was at that very moment engaged in a work such as the labor of man hardly ever undertook, nor perhaps his ingenuity ever accomplished —who never saw the Constitutional Society but in the courtesy of a few short moments after dining with some of the most respectable members, and who positively objected to the very measure which is the whole foundation of this prosecution,—is yet gravely considered to be the master-spirit which was continually directing all the movements of a conspiracy as extensive as the island—the planner of a revolution in the government, and the active head of an armed rebellion. Gentlemen, is this a proposition to be submitted to the judgment of honest and enlightened men, upon a trial of life and death? Why, there is nothing in the *Arabian Nights* or in the Tales of the Fairies which is not dull matter of fact compared with it. . . . Filled with indignation that an innocent man should be consigned to a prison for treading in the very steps which had conducted the Premier to his present situation, Mr. Horne Tooke did write 'that if ever that man should be brought to trial for his desertion of the cause of parliamentary reform, he hoped the country would not consent to send him to Botany Bay;' but whatever you may think of this sentiment, Mr. Tooke is not indicted for compassing and imagining the death of William Pitt."

In combating the unfair course of inferring that every opinion in a book is adopted by him who praises the author, he pointed out that a work of Mr. Burke contained a dangerous principle destructive of British liberty, and thus proceeded :—

"What then ? Ought I to seek its suppression ? Ought I to pronounce him to be a criminal who promotes its circulation? On the contrary, I shall take care to put it into the hands of those whose principles are left to my formation. I shall take care that they have the advantage of doing, in the regular progression of youthful study, what I have done even in the short intervals of laborious life;—that they shall transcribe with their own hands, from all the works of this most extraordinary person, the soundest truths of religion—the justest principles of morals, inculcated and rendered delightful by the most sublime eloquence—the highest reach of philosophy brought down to the level of common minds—the most enlightened observations on history, and the most copious collection of useful maxims from the experience of life. All this they shall do, and separate *for themselves* the good from the evil—taking the one as far more than a counterpoise for the other."[1]

The case against Horne Tooke rested chiefly upon the following letter, found in his possession, addressed to him by Joyce, one of the alleged conspirators:—

"Dear Citizen,—This morning at six o'clock Citizen Hardy was taken away by order from the Secretary of State's office; they seized everything they could lay hands on. *Query—Is it possible to get ready by Thursday?*"

The conclusive proof of rebellion was thus disposed of by Erskine:—

"This letter, being intercepted, was packed into the green box, and reserved to establish the plot. It is another lesson of caution against vague suspicions. Mr. Tooke having undertaken to collect from the Court Calendar a list of the titles, offices, and pensions bestowed by Mr. Pitt on his relations, friends, and dependents, and being too correct to come out with a work of that magnitude and extent upon a short notice, had fixed no time for it—which induced Mr. Joyce, who was anxious for its publication, to ask if he could be ready with it by Thursday; using the French designation of '*citizen*' for the purpose of turning it into ridicule!"

So confident had he become, that he even ventured to treat with some severity a juryman who appeared to disapprove of his argument;—

"To expose further the extreme absurdity of this ac-

---

[1] The Right Hon. T. Erskine, in reference to this passage, writes to me,—"This resolution he put in practice by giving us, as boys, passages from Burke's works to transcribe and learn by heart."

cusation, if it be possible to expose it, let me imagine that we are again at peace with France, while the other nations who are now our allies should continue to prosecute the war,—would it *then* be criminal to congratulate France upon her success against them? When that time arrives, might I not honestly wish the triumph of the French armies? And might I not lawfully express that wish? I know certainly that I might—and I know also that I would? *I observe that this sentiment seems a bold one;* but who is prepared to tell me that I shall not? I WILL assert the freedom of an Englishman; I WILL maintain the dignity of man. I WILL vindicate and glory in the principles which raised this country to her preeminence among the nations of the earth; and as she shone the bright star of the morning to shed the light of liberty upon nations which now enjoy it, so may she continue in her radiant sphere to revive the ancient privileges of the world, which have been lost, and still to bring them forward to tongues and people who have never yet known them, in the mysterious progression of things."

Instead of an impassioned peroration, he now merely said, as if he considered the battle won,—

"I can not conclude without observing that the conduct of this abused and unfortunate gentleman throughout the whole of this trial has certainly entitled him to admiration and respect. I had undoubtedly prepared myself to conduct his cause in a manner totally different from that which I have pursued. It was my purpose to have selected those parts of the evidence only by which he was affected, and to have separated him from the rest. By such a course I could have steered his vessel safely through all perils, and brought her without damage into a harbor of safety, while the other unfortunate prisoners were left to ride out this awful tempest. But he would not suffer his defense to be put upon the footing which discretion would have suggested. Though not implicated in the supposed conspiracy, he has charged me to waste and destroy my strength to prove that no such guilt can be brought home to others. I rejoice in having been made the humble instrument of so much good—my heart was never so much in any cause."

When the evidence came to be adduced, he strenuously assisted Mr. Tooke in examining the witnesses, and particularly in trying to refresh the memory of Mr. Pitt respecting a meeting of delegates, at which the young patriot had been present previous to one of his motions for parliamentary reform ; but could extract no answer from him, except that he *did not recollect*. The Minister evidently quailed under the discipline of his former associates, and of the man whom in the House of Commons he had treated with such contempt. Indeed, this was the most humiliating passage of his whole life, and the recollection of it must have been painful to him amid all his subsequent triumphs over political foes.[1]

Although Hardy's jury had deliberated several hours, Horne Tooke was acquitted as soon as the Judge had concluded the summing up—when he gracefully returned thanks to the Bench and the jury for the fair trial which had ended so auspiciously, and above all for the noble exertions of his counsel, who had done such effectual service to public liberty.

Still the Government was not satisfied, and a third prisoner, Thelwall, was put upon his trial. They would have had a better chance of a conviction if they had begun with him, as he had taken a much more active part in the societies than either of the other two. The effort now was, to shorten the case for the prosecution, and it ended early on the third day. Erskine expressed some embarrassment at being so unexpectedly called upon to enter on the defense, but he executed the task with his never-failing ability and energy.[2] I must content myself with giving one passage from it, in which he tried to take off the effect of most intemperate words against the Government imputed to the prisoner by a spy. After attacking the credibility of the witness, he thus proceeded :—

" Even if the very phrase had not been exaggerated, if the particular sentence had not been colored or discolored,

---

[1] It is curious that, after the examination of Sheridan, Pitt voluntarily declared that he *did* recollect a meeting at the Duke of Richmond's, at whic were present delegates from different county meetings, and from several cities and towns. At this moment he must have wished that he had been true to the cause of Parliamentary Reform, instead of grasping supreme power in the state.

[2] It is said that Thelwall was a very troublesome client, and frequently interfered indiscreetly in the defense. At one time he was so much dissatisfied, that he wrote on a piece of paper, which he threw to Erskine, " I'll be hanged if I don't plead my own cause ;" upon which his counsel returned for answer, " You'll be hanged if you do."

what allowance ought there not to be made for infirmity of temper, and the faults of the tongue, in a period of intense excitement! Let me ask, who would be safe, if every loose word, if every vague expression, uttered in the moment of inadvertence or irritation, were to be admitted as sufficient evidence of a criminal purpose of the most atrocious nature? In the judgment of God we should, indeed, be safe, because He knows the heart—He knows the infirmities with which He hath clothed us, and makes allowance for those errors which arise from the imperfect state of our nature. From that perfect acquaintance which He possesses with our frame, He is qualified to regard in their proper point of view the involuntary errors of the misguided mind, and the intemperate effusions of the honest heart. With respect to these, in the words of a beautiful moral writer, 'the accusing angel, who flies up to Heaven's chancery, blushes as he gives them in, and the recording angel, as he writes them down, drops a tear upon the words and blots them out forever.' Who is there that in the moment of levity or of passion has not adopted the language of profaneness, and even trifled with the name of the God whom he adores? Who has not, in an unguarded hour, from a strong sense of abuse, or a quick resentment of public misconduct, inveighed against the Government to which he is most firmly attached? Who has not, under the impulse of peevishness and misapprehension, made use of harsh and unkind expressions, even with respect to his best and dearest relations—expressions which, if they were supposed to proceed from the heart, would destroy all the affection and confidence of private life? If there is such a man present so uniformly correct in expression, so guarded from mistake, so superior to passion, let him stand forth, let him claim all the praise due to a character so superior to the common state of humanity. For myself, I will only say, *I am not the man.*"

The Jury found a verdict of NOT GUILTY.

At last the Attorney General said he should proceed no further, and all the other prisoners were acquitted without any evidence being offered against them.

Even Adolphus, the zealous advocate of all the measures of Mr. Pitt's Administration which can be praised or excused, is obliged to say,—" Considering calmly these prosecutions, they appear in every point of view to have been unfortunate, not to say unwise. .... It was desirable to frustrate the schemes of desperate innovators; but the British public, who had ever been accustomed to meet, to associate, to proclaim their political opinions and predilections, to devise means and to recommend measures for removal of their grievances, and improvement of their social condition, viewed with anxiety and alarm those measures which tended to plunge individuals into the dreadful gulf of high treason, when they had unintentionally, perhaps, exceeded the bounds which an exact knowledge of the laws and a timid prudence would have prescribed." [1]

There were strong manifestations of public gratitude for the services which Erskine had rendered in saving the country from the peril with which it had been threatened. On the last night of the trials his horses were taken from his chariot,—amidst bonfires and blazing flambeaux, he was drawn home by the huzzaing populace to his house in Sergeant's Inn,—and they obeyed his injunction, when, addressing them from a window, with Gibbs by his side, he said, " Injured innocence still obtains protection from a British jury, and I am sure, in the honest effusions of your hearts, you will retire in peace and bless God."[2] The freedom of many corporations was voted to him, and his portraits and busts were sold in thousands all over Great Britain. What was more gratifying, his speeches for the prisoners were read and applauded by all men of taste, his political consequence was much enhanced with his party, and he had full revenge for the sarcasms of Pitt. He now occupied a position as an advocate which no man before had reached, and which no man hereafter is ever likely to reach at the English Bar.

It is delightful to find the same individual a few weeks after thus writing to a friend:—"I am now very busy flying my boy's kite, shooting with the bow and arrow, and talking to an old Scotch gardener ten hours a-day, about the same things, which, taken altogether, are not of the value or importance of a Birmingham half-pen-

[1] Vol. vi. p. 71.
[2] When he used to boast of this ovation, some of his friends sought to mortify him by asserting (I know not with what truth) that the patriots who took his horses from his carriage, *forgot to return them.*

ny, and am scarcely up to the exertion of reading the daily papers. How much happier it would be for England and the world if the King's ministers were employed in a course so much more innocent than theirs, and *so perfectly suitable to their capacities!* "[1]

CHAPTER CLXXXI.

CONTINUATION OF THE LIFE OF LORD ERSKINE TILL THE TRIAL OF HADFIELD FOR SHOOTING AT GEORGE III.

WHEN the victorious advocate again spoke in the House of Commons, his reception there was much more flattering than any he had previously experienced. The occasion was a motion for a repeal of the " Habeas Corpus Suspension Act," when he went through the history of the late State Trials, contending that they proved "a conspiracy to alarm the country, and to deceive Parliament." Having stated the opinion of the Judge against the objection that the prisoners were not privy to the plans of the obnoxious societies, he proceeded:—

" The Judge said true: we forebore to urge it, because we knew that it was not tenable ground, though we were firmly convinced that the defense was invulnerable in point of law, not only by the statute, but even by all the authorities; yet we did not expect that the jury would prefer our statement as advocates to the judgment of the Court, whether well or ill founded ; but we looked to the great sheet-anchor of the cause—the gross falsehood and absurdity of the supposed conspiracy. On that we relied, and on that we prevailed." Thus he concluded:—" If the threat of invasion is carried into effect, who is to defend the country? Who, but this insulted people, whom you calumniate? The people only can do it, and they will do it only as they feel an interest worth the exertion. Let the Chancellor of the Exchequer attend to the maxim happily expressed by the poet, and no less happily

[1] Letter to Dr. Parr.

applied by his great father to the case of alienated America :

> 'Be to their virtues very kind,
> Be to their faults a little blind ;
> Let all their ways be unconfin'd,
> And clap a padlock on their mind.'"[1]

In a very violent speech which he made against the Seditious Meetings' Bill, he resorted to an oath as in Lord George Gordon's case, but not with the same success :—
"If the Government resolve to rob the people of their rights, the people will be justified in resisting such glaring oppression. I will say again and again, that it is the right of the people to resist a Government which exercises tyranny. It is certainly bold to say that the people have a right to resist, and that they ought to rise; but there are some occasions which render the boldest language warrantable. 'If the King's servants,' said Lord Chatham, ' will not permit a constitutional question to be decided according to the forms and on the principles of the Constitution, it must then be decided in some other manner; and rather than it should be given up— rather than that the nation should surrender their birthright to a despotic Minister, I hope, my Lords, old as I am, I shall see the question brought to issue, and fairly tried between the people and the Government!' Sanctioned by the sentiments of that venerable and illustrious man, I maintain that the people of England should defend their rights, if necessary, by the last extremity to which freemen can resort. For my own part, I shall never cease to struggle in support of liberty. In no situation will I desert the cause. I was born a freeman, and, BY GOD, I will never die a slave."[2]

One of the best speeches he ever delivered in Parliament was against the bill for making "a conspiracy to levy war" HIGH TREASON,—without any overt act which could be considered a levying of war. He here gives a most admirable exposition of the statute of Edward III., showing the wisdom of the distinction between "a conspiracy to levy war" and "a conspiracy against the life of the Sovereign:"—illustrating from English history the evils produced by departing from that statute and tyrannically creating the new treasons which had all been

[1] 31 Parl. Hist. 1087-1177. [2] 32 Parl. Hist. 310.

repealed in better times. I would earnestly implore statesmen to read and to ponder his arguments before proposing to repress crimes against the state by severer penal laws. But happily, in the present generation, such admonitions are little wanted, and I am delighted to think that I can freely stand up for constitutional maxims without incurring any suspicion of reflecting on political opponents : whatever questions may still divide existing parties, I believe that, from the improved spirit of the age, we are all equally united in the conviction that the governors should respect the Constitution if they wish it to be respected by the governed. Of the passionate declamation which Erskine mixed up with his reasoning, the reader may form an opinion from the following specimen :—

" I have no right to ask a Royal audience, but I declare that I feel a strong inclination to rush into the closet of my Sovereign, forgetful of the usual forms of decorum, and to implore him, upon my knees, to withhold his assent from a bill which goes to destroy his throne in the hearts of his subjects, and to invest him with the insignia of a tyrant. I can not believe that his Majesty, convinced as he must necessarily be of the loyalty and attachment of his people, will ever give his approbation to a law which, under the pretext of providing for his safety, contains a gross and unfounded libel on the character of his subjects. When it pleased God to remove from the Sovereign the hand of affliction, what demonstrations of loyalty and affection appeared in the metropolis, as his Majesty passed to St. Paul's to give thanks to Heaven for his deliverance ! The nation appeared one great family rejoicing at the recovery of their common father. And notwithstanding all this tumult of congratulatory joy, notwithstanding that banquet of affection on which it is the fortune of the present Monarch daily to regale, his Ministers would inspire him with jealousy and distrust. An alarm is sounded throughout the kingdom, and spies and informers echo back the cry. Whence the framers of the bill borrowed the enactment against ' expressing, publishing, uttering, or declaring any words or sentences to incite or stir up the people,' I can not conceive. After this, a sigh or a groan may be construed into treason. I have in vain searched for it in the history of former tyrannies, and I can only suppose it to have been suggested by the description of the poet:—

> 'In the vaulted roof
> The tyrant sat, and through a secret channel
> Collected every sound; heard each complaint
> Of martyr'd virtue; kept a register
> Of sighs and groans, by cruelty extorted;
> Noted the honest language of the heart;
> Then on the victims wreak'd his murd'rous rage,
> For yielding to the feelings of their nature.'

"The annals of Britain do not furnish an instance in which the statute of Edward III., the *statutum benedictum*, as it is emphatically called, has not accomplished all that law can accomplish to protect the King and his Government; but the present bill wantonly creates new and undefined treasons, disorganizes the system of our jurisprudence, and, by sanctioning grievous and vexatious measures, will excite disaffection and engender discord."[1]

While this bill was pending, a controversy arose in which, I am sorry to say, Erskine and the Whig Opposition appeared to little advantage;—nay, to speak the whole truth, most inconsistently, grossly, and flagrantly violated the principles of free discussion which they had been so loudly contending for. Mr. John Reeves, president of the "Society against Republicans and Levelers," —a gentleman of considerable literary distinction,—had published a somewhat silly, but a very harmless, book, entitled "Thoughts on the English Government," in which was to be found this passage: "The government of England is a monarchy; the monarchy is the ancient stock from which have sprung those goodly branches of the legislature,—the Lords and Commons, that at the same time give ornament to the tree, and afford shelter to those who seek protection under it. But these are still branches, and derive their origin and their nutriment from their common parent; they may be lopped off, and the tree is a tree still;—shorn, indeed, of its honors, but not, like them, cast into the fire. The kingly government may go on in all its functions, without Lords or Commons; it has heretofore done so for years together, and in our times it does so during every recess of Parliament; but without the King, his Parliament is no more." I blush while I relate that the defender of Stockdale, of Hardy,

[1] 32 Parl. Hist. 470.

and of Horne Tooke,—while still meditating his purpose of rushing into the King's presence, to implore, upon his bended knees, that the royal assent should be withheld from a bill to fetter free inquiry into political subjects,— zealously and effectually supported a resolution that this book was "a breach of the privileges of the House of Commons, and that the Attorney General should be directed to prosecute the author for a libel;" saying, "What a glorious representative of the people of England, would that House appear to be, if they passed by the pamphlet which had been read to them that night, in which they were represented as a mere council for the Crown, and that in this consisted their greatest utility,— that all the vigor they were supposed to have, as an emanation from the people, was a mere chimera! If they voted that this was no libel, the public would see that they did so because it was in favor of the Crown against the rights of the people; and he was quite sure, that if the Attorney General called for the verdict of a jury upon it, they would not require that time to deliberate upon it which members opposite seem to desire." Mr. Pitt and his colleagues, very sensibly and laudably, tried to keep the House out of the scrape into which they were rushing, and succeeded so far as to have the matter referred to a Committee of Privileges: but, after two reports from the Committee, the motion for a prosecution, being supported by Mr. Fox, Mr. Sheridan, and Mr. Grey, was carried, without a division. Accordingly, a criminal information was filed by the Attorney General, and brought to trial, before Lord Kenyon—when the jury, taking a much juster view of the subject than had been anticipated by the champion of the liberty of the press, after an hour's deliberation returned this verdict: "My Lord, we are of opinion that the pamphlet, which has been proved to have written been by John Reeves, Esq., is a very improper publication,—but we think his motives not such as are alleged in the information, and therefore we find him NOT GUILTY."[1] So end all such House of Commons' prosecutions!!! I hope that, as a punishment for this hallucination, Erskine was present when Plumer, who was counsel for the defense, spoke with much applause,

[1] 32 Parl. Hist. 610, 620, 634, 680.

and that he heard the shouts of rejoicing with which the verdict was received.¹

Whether ashamed to show himself in the House of Commons or not, the fact is, that the next time Erskine rose to take a part in debate,—notwithstanding all his experience and all his success,—he "broke down" soon after he began to address the House. The occasion was rather a formidable one. After the rupture of the negotiation for peace with the French Republic, Pitt, in one of the most splendid orations he ever delivered took a comprehensive and masterly view of our foreign affairs, and moved an address to the King, recommending a vigorous prosecution of the war. The defeated prosecutor for libel immediately followed, with the intention of answering him, and moving an amendment; but when he was observing that "France had formerly offered terms, the obtaining of which now would make the right honorable gentleman be worshiped as a God,"— he became confused, and after a pause sat down. Fox instantly rushed in to the rescue,—thus beginning: "Sorry indeed am I, on account of my honorable and learned friend, whose indisposition has suddenly compelled him to resume his seat; sorry for the sake of the House, whose information, from the train of argument he had adopted has been thus unpleasantly interrupted; and sorry for the cause which would have had such an advocate—sorry for the sake of England, which Ministers, by their imprudent councils and infatuated policy, seem determined to push to the last verge of ruin,—that I am thus so unexpectedly called upon to address the House. I feel it, however, incumbent on me to step forward, knowing that my opinion on the subject entirely coincides with that of my honorable and learned friend—but lamenting that the arguments on this momentous question must considerably suffer from the want of that ability with which he would have enforced them." He then went on so as to make Erskine's failure soon forgotten, and once more to divide the opinion of impartial judges whether the palm of oratory should be awarded to him or to his adversary.²

¹ Quevedo, the Spanish Poet, says that the punishment of fiddlers in hell will be to stand by and listen while the other fiddlers play.
² 32 Parl. Hist. 1464.

For several years afterwards, Erskine very rarely spoke, or even attended the House. The policy which he condemned was not only triumphant in Parliament, but was approved by the great bulk of the nation; and he said that he saved himself for more auspicious times. He joined Fox and the other principal Whig leaders in their ill-judged secession.

In this interval he published a pamphlet, entitled, "A View of the Causes and Consequences of the present War with France," which was so popular, that it was said to have run through thirty-seven editions. However, I can not say that it adds much to his permanent fame. It contains some forcible passages, but it deals in commonplaces, and the style is careless. Having received some gentle hints on this subject from his friend, Dr. Parr, he replied: "I can not say how much I thank you for remarking the negligence with which it can not but be filled. I wonder it is not nonsense from beginning to end, for I wrote it amidst constant interruption, great part of it in open court, during the trial of causes. Fifteen thousand copies have been sold in England, besides editions printed at Dublin and Edinburgh, where the sale has been unusual." The most amusing part of it is the history of the Prime Minister as connected with parliamentary reform, which thus begins: "Towards the close of the American War, Mr. Pitt (a boy almost) saw the corrupt condition of Parliament, from the defect of the representation of the people, with the eyes of a mature statesman: the eagle eyes of his father had seen it before him, and the thunder of his eloquence had made it tremble. Lord Chatham had detected and exposed the rank corruption of the House of Commons, as the sole cause of that fatal quarrel, and left it as a legacy to his son to avenge and to correct them. The youthful exertions of Mr. Pitt were worthy of the delegation. From my acquaintance with him, both before and after his first entrance into public life, I have no doubt of his perfect sincerity in the cause he then undertook; and the maturity of his judgment, even at that time, with which I was well acquainted, secures his conduct from the rashness of unthinking youth." He then traces him to his fall from virtue, and the degradation he reached when he became the accuser of his old friends. This made Pitt very indignant, and he several times alluded to the pamphlet with bitter scorn.

Erskine's next appearance in the House was in seconding Mr. Grey's annual motion for a Reform in Parliament. He now, in a very long speech, reiterated all his former arguments, and thus again showed his enmity to the Premier: "The right honorable gentleman, not contented with apostatizing from the principles which he once professed, has resisted them in a spirit and language of the loftiest pride and arrogance. In his humiliation and disgrace unfortunately this once mighty nation has also been humbled and disgraced. The cause of reform was to be, at all events, put down, and all who maintained it were to be stigmatized, persecuted, and oppressed. Here is the clue to every measure of Government, from the hour of the right honorable gentleman's apostasy to the present. But the insolence with which the hopeful changes of the rising world were denounced within these walls is an awful lesson to mankind. It has taught that there is an arm fighting against the oppressors of freedom, stronger than any arm of flesh, and that the great progressions of the world, in spite of the confederacies of power and the conspiracies of corruption, move on with a steady pace, and arrive in the end at a happy and glorious consummation." Pitt followed, but on this occasion his sarcasms were dulled by the sense of his own inconsistency, and he made but a feeble opposition to the motion,—objecting to the argument of imprescriptible right by which it had been supported, and relying upon the inflamed state of the public mind, which rendered any constitutional change too perilous.[1]

Reprobating the unfortunate rejection of the overtures of peace by Bonaparte when he became First Consul, Erskine made an excellent speech, and called forth a reply from Pitt, which, although in a bad cause, is one of the finest efforts of his genius.[2] There was no other great battle between them before the time when Pitt, having seen the ruinous effects of his policy, for a time withdrew from office, that others might negotiate with a victorious General, to whom he had prescribed, as a condition of forgiveness, the restoration of the Bourbons.

[1] 33 Parl. Hist. 653. [2] 34 Ibid. 1285.

In the meanwhile Erskine spoke several times on miscellaneous subjects—in favor of the Bill for making adultery an indictable offense,[1] and the Bill for checking the institution of monastic societies in this country;[2] and against the Bill for preventing ordained clergymen from sitting in the House of Commons,[3] On all these subjects he spoke sensibly, without saying anything very brilliant.

We must now look back to what was passing in the Courts of Law, where his ascendency remained unimpaired. The Government having very properly brought to trial, for high treason, William Stone, a merchant of London, against whom there was strong evidence that he had "adhered to the King's enemies," by inviting an invasion from France, Erskine was his counsel, and conducted the defense with infinite tact and dexterity. There was here no ground to complain of any perversion of the law of treason, or of any attack on public liberty. In a very moderate tone, therefore, he confined himself to an examination of the evidence, contending that it was all consistent with the prisoner's innocence, and observing, that "it was not enough for the Crown to raise so thick a cloud that the jury could not be sure which way to walk, but that a clear light must be shed upon the path leading to conviction, before they could venture to tread it." After long deliberation, there was a verdict of NOT GUILTY.

His speech in defense of the Bishop of Bangor, delivered at Shrewsbury, was corrected by him, and published under his sanction; but the occasion did not offer an opportunity for a display of his higher powers as an advocate. The Right Reverend Prelate, along with a body of his clergy, having somewhat irregularly and violently broken into the office of the Registrar for the diocese, and ejected from it a Mr. Grindley, who pretended to be the lawful Registrar, this gentleman indicted them all for a riot and assault. The prosecutor was a very intemperate and wrong-headed person, but the law hardly justified the proceeding of the defendants, and their counsel was evidently under very considerable alarm. I must content myself with introducing the piece of acting to which he

[1] 35 Parl. Hist. 309.   [2] Ibid. 361.   [3] Ibid. 1335, 1397,
[4] 25 St. Tr. 1153–1438.

thought he was justified in resorting at the conclusion of his address. Although he knew that he could not alter the facts by calling witnesses, and he had resolved that none should be called, he observed,—

"I am instructed, gentlemen, and, indeed, pressed, by the anxiety of the Bishop's friends, to call many witnesses to show that he was by no means disturbed with passion, as has been represented; and that, so far from it, he even repressed those whose zeal for order, and whose affection for his person, prompted them to interfere, saying to them, 'The law will interpose in due season.' I have witnesses, to a great number, whom I am pressed to call before you, who would contradict Mr. Grindley in the most material parts of his testimony; but then I feel the advantage he would derive from this unnecessary course; he would have an opportunity from it to deprive the Right Reverend Prelate of the testimony and protection of your approbation. He would say, no doubt, 'Oh! I made out the case which vindicated my prosecution, though it was afterwards overturned by the testimony of persons in the Bishop's suit, and implicitly devoted to his service; I laid facts before a jury from which a conviction must have followed, and I am not answerable for the false glosses by which *his witnesses have perverted them.*' This would be the language of the prosecutor; and I am, therefore, extremely anxious that your verdict should proceed *upon the facts as they now stand before the Court;* and that you should repel with indignation a charge which is defeated by the very evidence that has been given to support it. I can not, besides, endure the humiliation of fighting with a shadow, and the imprudence of giving importance to what I hold to be *nothing*, by putting *anything* in the scale against it,—a conduct which would amount to a confession that *something* had been proved which demanded an answer. How far those from whom my instructions come may think me warranted in pursuing this course, I do not know; but the decision of that question will not rest with either of us, *if your good sense and consciences should, as I am persuaded they will, give an immediate and seasonable sanction to this conclusion of the trial.*"

He was in hopes that on this invitation the jury would at once have risen, and, without turning round to deliberate, have said it was unnecessary to proceed further, and pronounced a verdict of NOT GUILTY;—but they all kept their seats, and maintained a deep silence. Thereupon, considerably disconcerted, he pretended to consult a few minutes with Mr. Plumer, Mr. Leycester, and Mr. Milles, who were counsel along with him for the defendants, and with the attorney who instructed them,—and then, with an assumed air of satisfaction, said, " he was happy to inform the Court that his advice was followed, and he should give no evidence."

Mr. Justice Heath summed up for a conviction,[1] and said to the jury, " Considering that all individuals are to be tried by the law of the land, notwithstanding their high station and the character they may heretofore have maintained, if you believe the prosecutor's witnesses, and think that a case has been made out against the defendants, it will be your duty to find them guilty; but if you have any *reasonable doubt* whether they are guilty or not, you will acquit them." The jury,—from a laudable reluctance to send an aged prelate, venerated for his piety and good works, and a number of respectable clergymen of the Church of England, who had been actuated by a desire of supporting their Diocesan, to stand on the floor of the King's Bench as malefactors, there to receive sentence of fine and imprisonment,—had sufficient doubts to induce them to pronounce a verdict of acquittal; and Erskine,—after having been some time in a state of painful suspense, — as usual, returned to London victorious.[2]

We are next to see him in a new capacity—conducting a prosecution for a blasphemous libel. Paine's " Age of Reason," a most scurrilous and insulting attack on the Christian religion, had lately appeared—which rendered the author and publisher liable to severe punishment; leaving only one question for consideration,—whether more mischief was likely to arise to the community from the wider circulation the infamous work might obtain by the notoriety of a public trial, or from allowing it to pass with entire impunity? The Government abstained from prosecuting but " The Society for the Suppression of

---

[1] This Judge was supposed generally rather to lean against Erskine; he used to say, " I am always on my guard against these 300-guinea gentry."

[2] Erskine's Speeches, v. 93-168; 26 St. Tr. 463-529.

Vice and Immorality" preferred an indictment against a bookseller of the name of Williams, at whose shop it was sold, and retained Erskine for their counsel as prosecutors. I shall give a few extracts from his beautiful address to the jury :—

"For my own part, gentlemen, I have been ever deeply devoted to the truths of Christianity; and my firm belief in the Holy Gospel is by no means owing to the prejudices of education (though I was religiously educated by the best of parents), but has arisen from the fullest and most continued reflections of my riper years and understanding. It forms at this moment the great consolation of a life which as a shadow passes away; and without it I should consider my long course of health and prosperity (too long, perhaps, and too uninterrupted to be good for any man) only as the dust which the wind scatters, and rather as a snare than as a blessing." Having read and commented on some of the most obnoxious parts of the book, he continued: "In running the mind over the long list of sincere and devout Christians, I can not help lamenting that Newton had not lived to this day to have had the darkness of his understanding illuminated by this new flood of light. But the subject is too awful for irony. I will speak plainly and directly. Newton was a Christian!—Newton, whose mind burst forth from the fetters fastened by nature upon our finite conceptions!—Newton, who carried the line and rule to the uttermost barriers of creation, and explained the principles by which all created matter exists and is held together!" In a similar strain, he appealed to the testimony of Boyle, Locke, and Hale, and then introduced a still greater name : "But it is said by the author that the Christian's fable is but the tale of the more ancient superstitions of the world, and may be easily detected by a proper understanding of the mythologies of the Heathens. Did Milton understand these mythologies? Was HE less versed than Mr. Paine in the superstitions of the world? No! they were the subjects of his immortal song, and he poured them forth from the stores of a memory rich with all that man ever knew, and laid them in their order as the illustration of real and exalted faith—the unquestionable source of that fervid genius which has cast a shade on the other works of man :—

> He pass'd the flaming bounds of place and time,
> The living throne, the sapphire blaze,
> Where angels tremble while they gaze.
> He saw—but, blasted with excess of light,
> Closed his eyes in endless night.'

But it was the light of the body only which was extinguished. The celestial light shone inward, and enabled him to '*justify the ways of God to man.*'" He does not conclude without a tribute to the benefits of free and enlightened discussion: "I do not dread the reasonings of Deists against the existence of Christianity itself, because, as was said by its Divine Author, '*if it be of God, it will stand.*' An intellectual book, however erroneous, addressed to the intellectual world, upon so profound and complicated a subject, can never work the mischief which this indictment is calculated to repress. Such works will only incite the minds of men, cultivated by study, to a closer investigation of a subject well worthy of their deepest and continued contemplation. The changes produced by such reciprocations of lights and intelligences are certain in their progression, and make their way imperceptibly by the final and irresistible power of truth. If Christianity be founded in falsehood, let us become Deists in this manner, and I am contented. But this book has no such object, and no such capacity: it presents no arguments to the wise and the educated ; on the contrary, it treats the faith and opinions held sacred by the British people, with scoffing and ribaldry, and tends to make the thoughtless multitude view with contempt the obligations of law and the precepts of morality."

A Mr. Stewart Kid, counsel for the defendant, having, without the authority of his client, delivered a most indecent address to the jury, defending the sentiments and the language of "The Age of Reason," Erskine, in reply, entered at considerable length into the evidences of the Christian religion. He asked :—

"Is there a person of the least knowledge who suffers himself to doubt, that, in the most comprehensive meaning of Scripture, the prophecy of its universal reception is fast fulfilling, and certainly must be fulfilled ? For my own part, gentlemen of the jury, I have no difficulty in saying to you, not as counsel in this cause, *but speaking, upon my honor, for myself* (and I claim to be considered as an equal authority, at least, to Mr. Paine, on the evidence which ought to establish any truth), that the universal dispersion of the Jews throughout the world, their unexampled sufferings, and their invariably distinguished characteristics, when compared with the histories of all other nations, and with the most ancient predictions of their own lawgivers and prophets concerning them, would be amply sufficient to support the truths of the Christian religion, if every other record and testimony on which they stand, had irrecoverably perished."[1]

The jury instantly found a verdict of GUILTY.

In the ensuing term, Erskine moved for judgment, and the defendant was committed to jail, while the Judges considered what sentence they should pronounce. In the meantime, the learned counsel saw reason to decline being longer concerned for the "Society," and returned their retainer. A statement of the circumstances which

---

[1] Erskine's declaration was soon after referred to from the pulpit by a right reverend prelate: "In our own times, more particularly, a man of distinguished talents and acknowledged eminence in his profession, and in the constant habit of weighing, sifting, and scrutinizing evidence with the minutest accuracy in courts of justice, has publicly declared that he considered this prophecy, if there were nothing else to support Christianity, as *absolutely irresistible.*"—*Lectures by Porteus, Bishop of London,* ii. 212. 10th edit.

In a letter from Erskine, now lying before me, in reference to this prosecution, he says, "My opening speech, correctly as it was uttered in court, is in Mr. Ridgway's collection of my speeches at the Bar. It was first printed by the Society, and circulated to a very wide extent,—which gave me the greatest satisfaction; as I would rather that all my other speeches were committed to the flames, or in any manner buried in oblivion, than that a single page of it should be lost."

Some of his liberal admirers were a little alarmed by the part he had taken in this prosecution. The following is his answer to the famous TIM BROWN, who had called upon him for an explanation :—

"My dear Sir,

"I had the pleasure of your letter last night on my return from Bridgewater. I shall find no difficulty in giving you the explanation you desire respecting the trial of the 'Age of Reason,' but I can do it more completely over a bottle of your white Hermitage at Camberwell than by writing, and that I will do as soon as you please. If you read my opening as copied from the Times, it is a very correct representation; in which you will find nothing that considers every writing to be a libel which questions the principles of the establishment of the *National Church, of which I have a very indifferen opinion, and in which I take no sort of interest.* The grounds on which I arraigned the 'Age of Reason' are the simplest and most obvious in the world; and I scarcely know any subject so important, but so totally misunderstood, as the true principles and the proper limits of the liberty of the press,—the abuse of which is as destructive of all society and of the blessings to be derived under it, as the use of it is the corner-stone of society.

"Most faithfully yours, "T. ERSKINE.

"August 28th, 1797."

induced him to adopt this unusual step, he communicated, many years afterwards, in an interesting letter to the Editor of the "State Trials:"—

"Having convicted Williams, as will appear by your report of his trial, and before he had notice to attend the Court to receive judgment, I happened to pass one day through the Old Turnstile, from Holborn, in my way to Lincoln's Inn Fields, when in the narrowest part of it I felt something pulling me by the coat: on turning round, I saw a woman at my feet bathed in tears, and emaciated with disease and sorrow, who continued almost to drag me into a miserable hovel in the passage, where I found she was attending upon two or three unhappy children in the confluent small-pox, and in the same apartment, not above ten or twelve feet square, the wretched man whom I had convicted was sewing up little religious tracts, which had been his principal employment in his trade; and I was fully convinced that his poverty, and not his will, had led to the publication of this infamous book, as, without any kind of stipulation for mercy on my part, he voluntarily and eagerly engaged to find out all the copies in circulation, and to bring them to me to be destroyed. I was most deeply affected with what I had seen; and feeling the strongest impression that he offered a happy opportunity to the prosecutors of vindicating, and rendering universally popular, the cause in which they had succeeded, I wrote my opinion to that effect, observing (if I well remember) that mercy being the grand characteristic of the Christian religion, which had been defamed and insulted, it might be here exercised not only safely, but more usefully to the objects of the prosecution, than by the most severe judgment, which must be attended with the ruin of this helpless family. My advice was most respectfully received by the Society, and I have no doubt honestly rejected, because that most excellent prelate Bishop Porteus, and many other honorable persons, concurred in rejecting it; but I had still a duty of my own to perform, considering myself not as counsel for the Society, but for the Crown. If I had been engaged for all or any of the individuals composing it, prosecuting by indictment for any personal injury punishable by indictment, and had convicted a defendant, I must have implicitly followed my instructions, however inconsistent with my own ideas of humanity or moderation; because every man who is injured has a clear right to demand the highest penalty which the law will inflict: but in the present instance I was only responsible to the Crown for my conduct. Such a voluntary Society, however respectable or useful, having received no injury, could not erect itself into a *custos morum,* and claim a right to dictate to counsel who had consented to be employed on the part of the King for the ends of justice only. Whether I was right or wrong, I will not undertake to say; but I am most decidedly of opinion that, if my advice had been followed, and the repentant publisher had been made the willing instrument of stigmatizing and suppressing what he had published, Paine's Age of Reason would never again have been printed in England."

The defendant was sentenced to a year's imprisonment, with hard labor, in the House of Correction for the county of Middlesex.[1]

It has often been remarked, that men most accustomed to appear before the public, when examined in a court of justice make the worst witnesses. Garrick being called to explain what is "a free benefit," nothing could be got out of him except that "a free benefit is a free benefit." Erskine now exemplified the same remark by talking too much. Arthur O'Connor being tried for high treason, on a charge which afterwards turned out to be perfectly well founded, although the Crown could not produce sufficient evidence against him, the whole body of the Opposition, from whom he had concealed his traitorous correspondence with France, came forward to give him a character for loyalty. Erskine's evidence will be amusing—at least to my professional readers, who remember the rules by which he ought to have been bound:—

Q. "You know Mr. O'Connor?"—*A.* "I do."—*Q.* "How long have you known him?"—*A.* "I have known him between two and three years, and I live a great deal with those with whom Mr. O'Connor lives much when he is in this country. Mr. O'Connor's friends in this country are principally those persons who are my friends. [The Attorney General interposing]—I do not stand here to

---

[1] 26 St. Tr. 653–720; Erskine's Speeches, ii 183.

argue the admissibility of evidence; and you may depend upon it I shall strictly adhere to giving answers to questions. Mr. O'Connor has principally lived with persons of high rank in the public world—Mr. Fox, Mr. Grey, Mr. Sheridan—all that class of gentlemen with whom I have acted in Parliament. I know Mr. O'Connor's character as well as I can be acquainted with the character of any gentlemen who lives' principally in another country, but whom I have seen frequently here."—*Q.* "Shall I beg the favor of you to state what that character is?"—*A.* "In my opinion, the best character that any man can possibly possess. I have a sincere regard and esteem for Mr. O'Connor, founded upon my opinion and belief that he is a man of the strictest honor and integrity—a man not only capable of making, but who has made, great sacrifices to what he thinks right. If there be any more prominent feature in his character than another, as far as I am acquainted with it,—and I am much acquainted with it,—it is a noble-mindedness and a high spirit of honor; and I therefore feel myself not only entitled, but bound upon my oath, to say, in the face of God and my country, as a British gentleman, which is the best thing any man can be, that he is incapable in my judgment of acting with treachery or duplicity to any man, but most of all to those for whom he professes friendship and regard; and I do know positively, of my own knowledge, that he has been in the constant course of professing, not only regard, but admiration and enthusiasm, for the persons whose names I mentioned."—*Q.* "Did you ever observe any difference, either upon public or private subjects, between himself and you?"—*A.* "Recollecting the station I hold in the law, I should be little desirous to urge upon the Court anything that could be at all questionable in point of evidence; otherwise I could, if the Court thought it right, state many instances of his persevering in the same opinions and in the same regards; this I may say generally, that upon my oath I never had any reason to think that Mr. O'Connor's principles and opinions differed from my own." The Attorney General having again objected, the witness continued:—" I am obliged to Mr. Attorney General, but I do assure the Court that I might have been in another situation, where those objections could not have been made; I might have been defending Mr. O'Connor as one of his counsel, but I felt my situation as a witness, so that I declined."[1]

There is said to have been much tittering in court excited by this egotistical garrulity.

Shortly afterwards, Erskine, again in his proper sphere as an advocate, was beheld with universal respect and admiration. Arthur O'Connor, having been acquitted by the jury at Maidstone, where he was tried,—conscious of the fresh charges which might be brought against him,—wished to leave the court as soon as the verdict was pronounced; but a new warrant had been issued to arrest him,—which the officer now attempted to execute. A scuffle took place, in court, between those who wished to seize him and those who favored his escape. The Government, rather vindictively, alleged, that in the latter class were Sackeville, Earl of Thanet, a great Whig nobleman, and Mr. Cutlar Fergusson, a young barrister of fine talents and high honor, afterwards Advocate General at Calcutta, and Judge Advocate to Queen Victoria,—with several others of inferior note,—and included them all in a prosecution for a conspiracy to rescue Mr. O'Connor from the custody of the sheriff of Kent. The case was tried at the King's Bench bar, before Lord Kenyon and his brethren.

Erskine, on this occasion, as counsel for the defendants, displayed consummate ability in commenting upon the evidence, and was most successful in showing that no sufficient case was was made for the Crown by Mr. Justice Heath and the respectable witnesses who were called, and that the Bow-street officers, who themselves had wantonly begun the riot, were not to be believed. His speech is the best specimen I know of this most difficult and important species of eloquence, upon which the fortune, the life, and the fame of our fellow-citizens frequently depend; but it can only be relished in a critical perusal of the whole trial. Drawing to the conclusion, he said:—

"The noble and learned Lord who presides here today, where the proofs have been much stronger, has been in the habit of saying to juries, 'This is not a case for conviction; the defendant *may* be guilty, but there is not a sufficient preponderance in the evidence to pro-

[1] 27 St. Tr. 38.

nounce a penal judgment.' These are the maxims, gentlemen, which have given to British courts of justice their value in the country and with mankind. These are the maxims which have placed a guard around them in the opinions and affections of the people. I admit that this consideration deeply enhances the guilt of him who would disturb the administration of such an admirable jurisprudence. But if the Courts of England are so popular and estimable—if they have been through ages after ages the source of public glory and private happiness—*why is this trial to furnish an exception?* For myself, I can only say, that I wish to do my duty, and nothing beyond it. Govern us who will, I desire only to see my country prosperous, the laws faithfully administered, and the people living under them happy and contented. Let England be secure, and no ambition of mine shall ever disturb her. I should rather say, if I were once disengaged from the duties which bind me to my profession,—

> ' Oh for a lodge in some vast wilderness,
> Some boundless contiguity of shade,
> Where rumor of oppression and deceit,
> Of unsuccessful and successful war,
> Might never reach me more!'"

There can be little doubt that there would have been an acquittal, if Mr. Sheridan had not, unfortunately, been called to give evidence for the defendants, and presented to the world another instance of the difference between a great orator and a good witness. On cross-examination by Mr. Law, he was asked this question, " Whether, from the conduct of the defendants, as it fell under his observation, he did not believe they meant to favor the escape of Mr. O'Connor?" Now, he was not asked, and could not lawfully have been asked, his belief as to their *secret wishes*—and he was only to give an opinion upon their conduct as it fell under his observation. But he chose to say, " My belief is, that they *wished* him to escape; but, from anything I saw of their conduct upon that occasion, I am not justified in saying so;" and though he swore positively, on re-examination, that "he did not believe they took any part in rescuing Mr. O Connor," the jury, never getting over his declaration as to their *wishes*, found them all guilty.

Mr. Fergusson, in addressing the Court when he was

brought up to receive sentence, declined to dwell upon the nature of the charge, the proofs by which it was supported, or his own peculiar situation—saying," I can not so soon have forgotten the manner in which these topics were urged, in your Lordship's presence, in the course of that defense which was made for me by the most zealous of friends, the most able and eloquent of men "—and he thus concluded a Preface to a report of the trial which he published :—" Of his defense, let those who heard it judge. It is sufficient to say—and more can not be said—that it equaled any of those former exertions by which he has forever shut out all higher praise. I have long enjoyed a portion, perhaps beyond my merits, of his countenance and friendship. It had ever been my study to seek the approbation of a man whom, for the mild and amiable features of his private character, I esteem and love—whom, for the noble and manly features which mark his public conduct, I admire and venerate—whom the force of genius and eloquence has raised to a height in his profession where he excites no envy, and whose whole life—a life not untried on the slippery stage of politics, nor unexposed to the allurements of corrupt ambition—has been a life of honor, integrity, and independence. During a period of twenty years, he has fought every arduous contest in which the rights of his countrymen and the cause of general liberty have been involved. So many and splendid have been the triumphs of his eloquence, that they have left him no further honors to attain :—

    ———' Nil jam, Theodore, relictum
    Quo virtus animo crescat, vel splendor honore,
    Culmen utrumque tenes.' "——[1]

From a doubtful case, I have to go to one that was clearly most discreditable, both to the Judge and jury who decided upon it, although they were solemnly warned of their duty by the great advocate whose splendid career

[1] 27 St. Tr. 821–986. Erskine's Speeches, iv. 139–411., The Court for some time doubted whether, as the riot was laid to have taken place " before the King's Judges," they were not bound to pronounce the specific judgment "that the right arm of each defendant should be cut off ;" but finally sentenced Lord Thanet to a year's imprisonment, and a fine of £1,000, and Mr. Fergusson to the same length of imprisonment, and a fine of £100. They both made affidavits of their innocence, and their conviction and punishment are sad proofs of the violence of the times.

we are following. The throne of Russia was now filled by that madman, Paul, who, among other freaks, had lately published, in the most wanton manner, an edict prohibiting the exportation of timber, deals, and other naval stores, whereby the commerce of this country was greatly crippled, and a severe injury was inflicted on his own subjects. The following paragraph, which had previously appeared in several other journals, was copied in the Commercial Intelligence of the "Courier," a newspaper then in strong opposition to the Government:—
"The Emperor of Russia is rendering himself obnoxious to his subjects by various acts of tyranny, and ridiculous in the eyes of Europe by his inconsistency; he has now passed an edict prohibiting the exportation of timber, deals, &c. In consequence of this ill-timed law, upwards of one hundred sail of vessels are likely to return to this kingdom without freights." For this, the Attorney General filed a criminal information against the proprietor, printer, and publisher of the "Courier." In vain did Erskine point out, that, as the facts stated in the paragraph were allowed to be true, the commentary upon them was justifiable, and that there was here no malicious defamation of a foreign government, but only a wish to point out the wrongs of British subjects. However, Lord Kenyon, sneering at the late Libel Act, said, "I am bound by my oath to declare my own opinion, and I should forget my duty if I were not to say to you that it is a *gross libel*."[1] The jury found the defendants guilty, and they were sentenced to fine and imprisonment.[2]

In the present Memoir, I have only one other case of libel to mention, and this likewise should make us gratefully to rejoice that we live in better times. Mr. Cuthell, one of the most respectable booksellers in London, dealt almost exclusively in classical works, and had published the philological writings of the Rev. Gilbert Wakefield. That eminent scholar, being the

---

[1] Mr. Fox's Act only requires the Judges to give their opinion on matter of law in libel cases as in other cases. But did any Judge ever say, "Gentlemen, I am of opinion that this is a willful, malicious, and atrocious murder?" For a considerable time after the Act passed against the unanimous opposition of the Judges, they almost all spitefully followed this course. I myself heard one Judge say, "As the legislature requires me to give my own opinion in the present case, I am of opinion that this a diabolically atrocious libel."

[2] St. Tr. 627–642.

author of a political pamphlet in answer to one by the Bishop of Llandaff, employed Mr. Johnson, of St. Paul's Church Yard, to publish it; but some copies were sent to Mr. Cuthell's shop, and his servant, without authority, sold a few of them. As soon as Mr. Cuthell was aware of the nature of the publication, he stopped the sale of it. Nevertheless, in addition to criminal informations against the author and the publisher, a criminal information was filed against Mr. Cuthell, which came on for trial at Guildhall, before Lord Kenyon. The pamphlet was such as would not now be noticed by the Attorney General, — consisting chiefly of strong charges of misconduct against the existing Administration, with an exaggerated picture of the deplorable condition to which the country was reduced. But Erskine, as counsel for the defendant, declined entering into the question of libel or no libel; contending, by the following unanswerable arguments, that the defendant was not criminally responsible, having been ignorant of the contents of the pamphlet, and the publication having been without his authority:—

" In case of the *civil* action—throughout the whole range of civil injuries—the master is always *civiliter* answerable for the acts of his servant or agent; and accident or neglect can therefore be no answer to a plaintiff complaining of consequential wrong. If the driver of a public carriage, by gross negligence, overturns the passengers on the road while the proprietor is asleep in his bed at a hundred miles distance, the proprietor must unquestionably pay the damages to the last farthing. The servant may be liable to indictment, and to suffer an infamous judgment; *could the master also become the object of such a prosecution?* CERTAINLY NOT! In the same manner, partners in trade are *civilly* answerable for bills drawn by one another, or by their agents under procuration, though fraudulently and in abuse of their trust; but if one partner commits a fraud by forgery, or fictitious indorsements, so as to subject *himself* to death or other punishment by indictment, *could the other partners be indicted?* To answer such a question here would be folly; because it not only answers itself in the *negative*, but exposes to scorn every argument which would confound indictments with civil actions. Why, then, is *printing and publishing* to be an exception to every other human act? Why is a man to be answerable *criminaliter* for the act of his servant in this case more than in all others? As far, indeed, as damages go, the principle is intelligible and universal ; but as it establishes a *crime*, and inflicts a punishment, it is shocking to humanity, and insulting to common sense. The Court of King's Bench, since I have been at the Bar, (very long, I admit, before the noble Lord presided in it, but under the administration of a truly great Judge), pronounced the infamous judgment of the pillory on a most respectable proprietor of a newspaper, for a libel on the Russian Ambassdor, copied, too, out of another paper, but which I myself showed to the Court, by the affidavit of his physician, appeared in the first as well as in the second paper while the defendant was on his sickbed in the country, delirious in a fever. I believe that affidavit is still on the files of the Court. I have thought of it often—I have dreamed of it, and started from my sleep—sunk back to sleep—and started from it again. The painful recollection of it I shall die with. How is this to be vindicated?—from the *supposed* necessity of the case. An indictment for a libel is, *therefore*, considered to be an anomaly in the law. *It* WAS *held so, undoubtedly;* but the exposition of that *error* lies before me;—the Libel Act lies before me, which expressely and in terms directs that the trial of a libel shall be conducted *like* every other trial for every other crime ; and that the jury shall decide, not upon the mere fact of *printing and publishing*, but *upon the whole matter put in issue*, i. e. the publication of the libel WITH THE INTENTION CHARGED BY THE INDICTMENT. This is the rule by the Libel Act, and you, the jury, as well as the Court, are bound by it."

Lord Kenyon, however, acting on former precedents, and saying that the passing of the Libel Bill was " a race for popularity between two seemingly contending parties, who then chose to run amicably together," the defendant was found *guilty*.—The case was so revolting, that after a short imprisonment he was discharged on paying a fine of thirty marks.[1]

[1] 27 St. Tr. 641–680. Erskine's Speeches, vol. v. 213–246. There had been one case the (the King against the Rev. Bate Dudley, proprietor of the *Morning Post*) in which Erskine, having William Pitt for his junior, had obtained an acquittal under similar circumstances against the summing up of Lord Mansfield. Unfortunately there is no report of this trial extant.—The

CHAPTER CLXXXII.

CONTINUATION OF THE LIFE OF LORD ERSKINE TILL HIS VISIT TO PARIS DURING THE PEACE OF AMIENS.

I COME to Erskine's last, and perhaps his greatest, display of genius in defending a party prosecuted by the Crown—his speech as counsel for James Hadfield, indicted for shooting at King George III. in Drury Lane Theater. It is now, and will ever be, studied by medical men for its philosophic views of mental disease,—by lawyers for its admirable distinctions as to the degree of alienation of mind which will exempt from penal responsibility, — by logicians for its severe and connected reasoning, — and by all lovers of genuine eloquence for its touching appeals to human feeling. A few detached extracts can only excite a desire to peruse the whole composition, the different parts of which will be found beautifully to illustrate and to give force to each other. It should be remembered that a strong impression had been made by the case for the prosecution, and that the Judges, the jury, and all present viewed with just horror the attempt proved to have been made by an assassin upon the life of a beloved Sovereign. Thus Erskine began, in a subdued and solemn tone, to win the sympathies of his hearers, and to prepare them for the discussion of the awful and mysterious question arising from the distinction between the insanity of passion, unaccompanied by delusion, and that total derangement of the intellectual faculties which ought to exempt from punishment acts the most atrocious :—

" The scene which we are engaged in, and the duty which I am not merely *privileged* but *appointed* by the authority of the Court to perform, exhibits to the whole civilized world a perpetual monument of our national justice. The transaction, indeed, in every part of it, as it

grievance is at last effectually redressed by " Lord Campbell's Libel Bill," which expressly admits the defense to an indictment or criminal information for a libel, that the publication was by a servant without any authority from the defendant.

stands recorded in the evidence already before us, places our country and its government and its inhabitants upon the highest pinnacle of human elevation. It appears that upon the 15th of May last, his Majesty, after a reign of forty years, not merely in sovereign power, but spontaneously in the very hearts of his people, was openly shot at (or to all appearance shot at) in a public theater in the center of his capital, and amidst the loyal plaudits of his subjects; YET NOT A HAIR OF THE HEAD OF THE SUPPOSED ASSASSIN WAS TOUCHED. In this unparalleled scene of calm forbearance, the King himself, though he stood first in personal interest and feeling, as well as in command, was a singular and fortunate example. The least appearance of emotion on the part of that august personage must unavoidably have produced a scene quite different and far less honorable than the Court is now witnessing: but his Majesty remained unmoved, and the person *apparently* offending was only secured, without injury or reproach, for the business of this day." After the advocate had gracefully insinuated himself into the favor of the jury by an appeal to their loyal sympathies, he comes to discuss the question on which their verdict was to depend:—" It is agreed by all jurists, and is established by the law of this and every other country, that it is the reason of man which makes him accountable for his actions, and that the deprivation of reason acquits him of crime. This principle is indisputable: yet so fearfully and wonderfully are we made,—so infinitely subtle is the spiritual part of our being,—so difficult is it to trace with accuracy the effect of diseased intellect upon human action, that I may appeal to all who hear me, whether there are any causes more difficult, or which, indeed, so often confound the learning of the Judges themselves, as when insanity, or the effects and consequences of insanity, become the subjects of legal consideration and judgment? Your province, to-day, will be to decide whether the prisoner, when he did the act, was under the uncontrollable dominion of insanity, and was impelled to it by a morbid delusion ; or whether it was the act of a man who, though occasionally mad, or even at the time not perfectly collected, was yet not actuated by the disease, but by the suggestion of a wicked and malignant disposition. It is true, indeed, that in some, perhaps in many, cases the human mind is stormed in its citadel, and laid prostrate under the stroke of frenzy: these unhappy sufferers, however, are not so much considered by physicians as maniacs, as in a state of delirium from fever. There, indeed, all the ideas are overwhelmed, for Reason is not merely disturbed, but driven from her seat. Such unhappy patients are unconscious, therefore, except at short intervals, even of external objects, or at least are wholly incapable of understanding their relations. Such persons, and such persons alone (except idiots), are wholly deprived of their understandings, in the Attorney General's sense of that expression. But these cases are not only extremely rare, but can never become the subjects of judicial difficulty. There can be but one judgment concerning them. In other cases Reason is not driven from her seat, but Distraction sits down upon it along with her, holds her trembling upon it, and frightens her from her propriety. Such patients are victims to delusion of the most alarming description, which so overpower the faculties, and usurp so firmly the power of realities, as not to be dislodged and shaken by the organs of perception and sense; in such cases the images frequently vary, but in the same subjects are generally of the same terrific character. *Delusion*, therefore, where there is no frenzy or raving madness, is the true character of insanity; and where it can not be predicated of a man standing for life or death for a crime, he ought not, in my opinion, to be acquitted; and if courts of law were to be governed by any other principle, every departure from sober, rational conduct would be an emancipation from criminal justice. I shall place my claim to your verdict upon no such dangerous foundation. I must convince you not only that the unhappy prisoner was a lunatic within my own definition of lunacy, but that the act in question was the IMMEDIATE UNQUALIFIED OFFSPRING OF THE DISEASE."[1]

Having at considerable length, and with never-failing spirit and distinctness, propounded and illustrated his doctrine, he proceeded to give a most interesting narra-

[1] When I quoted this last sentence on the trial of Oxford for shooting at Queen Victoria, Lord Denman said, "he thought the criterion here proposed was rather too unfavorable to the party accused, and that Erskine, on this occasion felt himself safe in extending criminal responsibility so far, knowing that he could prove a clear case of positive delusion as a defense for his client."

tive of the life of his unhappy client, who had served
abroad as a soldier,—who was brave and orderly, who
had received in battle a wound which laid his head open
to the brain,—who had ever after been subject to
fits of insanity, for which he had been in confinement,—who had recently taken up the notion that
his immediate death by violence if he did not commit suicide, would produce some great benefit to
mankind,—and who although he was loyally attached
to the King, and the whole royal family, had formed
the resolution to fire at his Majesty from the pit of
the theater, so that he might be sure to be apprehended
and executed for high treason. The evidence of the Duke
of York had made a very deep impression on the jury,
as he said, " I saw the prisoner in a room at Drury Lane
immediately after his apprehension; the moment I entered, he said, ' God bless you, I know your Royal Highness; you are the Duke of York—I served under you.'
I said, ' I think you have been one of my orderlies.' He
answered, ' Yes, I have.' •I then asked him particularly
' when?' he said, ' The day after the battle of Fraymar.'
I had a long conversation with him, during which he
seemed perfectly to understand the subjects on which we
conversed. He said once or twice that he knew perfectly
well that his life was forfeited. He said that he was tired
of life, and he regretted nothing but the fate of a woman
who was his wife. There was no irregularity in his conversation from which I could collect any existing derangement of his understanding; on the contrary, he appeared
to speak as connectedly as possibly could be." Erskine
completely took off the effect by introducing some anecdotes, which, while they amused the attention of the
jury, bore directly on the issue they had to try:—

" I conceive, gentlemen, that I am more in the habit of
examination than either that illustrious person, or the
witnesses who have spoken in similar terms; yet I well
remember (indeed I never can forget it) that since the
noble and learned Judge has presided in this Court, I examined for the greater part a day, in this very place an
unfortunate gentleman, who had indicted a most affectionate brother, together with the keeper of a mad-house
at Hoxton, for having imprisoned him as a lunatic, while,
according to his own evidence, he was in his perfect senses.

I was unfortunately not instructed in what his lunacy consisted, although my instructions left me no doubt of the fact; but not having the clue, he completely foiled me in every attempt to expose his infirmity. You may believe I left no means unemployed which long experience dictated, but without the smallest effect. The day was wasted; and the prosecutor, by the most affecting history of unmerited suffering, appeared to the Judge and jury, and to a humane English audience, as the victim of most wanton and barbarous oppression. At last Dr. Sims came into Court, who had been prevented by business from an earlier attendance. From him I learned that the person who, under my long examination, had appeared to be so rational, intelligent, and ill-used, believed himself to be the Lord and Saviour of mankind—not merely at the time of his confinement, which was alone necessary for my defense, but during the whole time he had been triumphing over every attempt to surprise him in the concealment of his disease. I then affected to lament the indecency of my ignorant examination,—when he expressed his forgiveness, and said, with the utmost gravity and emphasis, in the face of the whole Court, 'I AM THE CHRIST:'—and so the cause ended." He then related, in the words of Lord Mansfield, a still more extraordinary instance of monomania, accompanied with cunning to conceal it:—"A man of the name of Wood had indicted Dr. Munro, for keeping him as a prisoner when he was sane. He underwent a most severe cross-examination from the defendant's counsel without exposing his infirmity; but Dr. Battye having come upon the bench by me, and having desired me to ask him 'what was become of the princess with whom he had corresponded in cherry-juice,' he showed in a moment what he was. He answered, that 'there was nothing at all in that, because having been (as every body knew) imprisoned in a high tower, and being debarred the use of ink, he had no other means of correspondence but by writing his letters in cherry-juice, and throwing them into the river which surrounded the tower, where the princess received them in a boat.' There existed of course no tower, no imprisonment, no writing in cherry-juice, no river, no boat, no princess,—but the whole was the inveterate phantom of a morbid imagination. I immediately directed Dr. Munro

·to be acquitted. But this madman again indicted Dr. Munro, in the city of London, through a part of which he had been carried to his place of confinement. Knowing that he had lost his cause by speaking of the princess, at Westminster, (such is the wonderful subtlety of madmen,)—when he was cross-examined on the trial in London, as he had successfully been before, in order to expose his madness, all the ingenuity of the Bar and all the authority of the Court could not make him say a single syllable upon that topic which had put an end to the indictment before, although he still had the same indelible impression upon his mind, as he signified to those who were near him; but, conscious that the delusion had caused his former defeat, he obstinately persisted in holding it back. His evidence at Westminster was then proved against him by the short-hand writer;—and I again directed an acquittal."

Erskine opened in the following affecting words, which are said to have drawn tears from almost all present,—the evidence he was to give of a recent attempt by the prisoner upon the life of a child whom he tenderly loved:

"To proceed to the proofs of his insanity down to the very period of his supposed guilt: This unfortunate man before you is the father of an infant of eight months, and I have no doubt whatever that, if the boy had been brought into court (but this is a grave place for the admistration of justice, and not a theater for stage effect)— I say, I have no doubt whatever that, if this poor infant had been brought into court, you would have seen the father writhing with all the emotions of parental affection; —yet upon the Tuesday preceding the Thursday when he went to the play-house, you will find his disease still urging him forward, with the impression that the time was come when he must be destroyed for the benefit of mankind; and in the confusion, or rather delirium, of this wild conception, he came to the bed of the mother who had this infant in her arms, and, snatching it from her, was about to dash out its brains against the wall in her presence, when his arm was arrested from the dreadful attempt."

Having clearly distinguished this case from that of Lord Ferrers and others of the same class,—confidently anticipating an acquittal, he thus quietly concluded, as if he had been the judge summing up the case to the jury:

"Nothing can more tend to the security of his Majesty and his Government than the scene which this day exhibits, in the calm, humane, and impartial administration of justice. I declare to you solemnly, that my only aim has been to secure for the prisoner at the bar, whose life and death are in the balance, that he should be judged rigidly by the evidence and the law. I have made no appeal to your passions—you have no right to be swayed by them. This is not even a case in which, if the prisoner be found guilty, the royal mercy should be counseled to interfere: he is either an accountable being or not accountable: if he was *unconscious* of the mischief he was engaged in, he is *not guilty;* but if, when the evidence closes, you think he was conscious, and that he maliciously meditated the treason he is charged with, it is impossible to conceive a crime more detestable; and I should consider the King's life to be ill attended to indeed, if not protected by the full vigor of the laws, which are watchful over the security of the meanest of his subjects. It is a most important consideration, both as it regards the prisoner and the community of which he is a member. Gentlemen, I leave it with you." [1]

He had perceived some time, from the looks and nods of the jury, that they were impatient to acquit. After a few witnesses had been been examined, Lord Kenyon stopped the trial, on the ground that a case of insanity, at the very time when the pistol was fired, had been clearly made out. An Act of Parliament passed (40 Geo. 3, c. 94) for the detention, during the pleasure of the Crown, of persons acquitted of treason or felony on the ground of insanity. Under this Act, Hadfield was confined in Bedlam many years; and it is said that he not only survived George III., but all the judges, all the jurymen, and all the counsel, who had taken part in hi trial.[2]

[1] Lord Erskine, in a letter (now lying before me) to Mr. Howell, the very learned editor of the "State Trials," says,—"It is lucky you have got Hadfield. I hope you have printed my speech as published by Ridgway, as there were many blunders in Gurney's copy, who was then getting very old. None of my speeches have been so much read and approved."

[2] When he had become a very old man, I was introduced to him by Dr. Haslam, the author of several works upon madness,—to which calamity he

I should give a defective sketch of Erskine's career at the Bar if I did not mention his merits as an advocate in civil actions. Unfortunately very few specimens of his eloquence in this kind have been preserved; but we know, from undoubted contemporary authority, that he here shone unrivaled,—varying in the display of talent according to the opportunity of displaying it. For many years he was in almost every cause tried at *Nisi prius* at Westminster and at the Guildhall of the City of London, before Lord Mansfield and Lord Kenyon. He was generally retained by the plaintiff; and, whether his client sued on a bill of exchange, or on a policy of insurance, or for an assault, or for defamation, or to establish a doubtful pedigree, or to impeach the validity of a will, or for a breach of promise of marriage, or for the seduction of a daughter or a wife, he did all for his client that could be effected by zeal, ingenuity, boldness, discretion, insight into the human heart, and control over human feelings.

He was almost invariably successful when he went upon special retainers. Indeed, to preserve the *prestige* of his invincibility, he declined (as he was entitled to do, according to professional etiquette) being counsel in a desperate case to be tried in a Court in which he did not usually practice.—He met with one signal defeat, which he recollected with deep mortification to the close of his life. This was in *Day* v. *Day*, tried at the Huntingdon Assizes, before Mr. Justice Heath, in the year 1797. It turned out to be the Douglas cause over again in miniature,—the question being, whether the defendant, who had been brought up as heir to a considerable family and a large estate, was not a suppositious child purchased from a poor woman in a workhouse. Erskine was for the plaintiff, and he himself considered his speech on this occasion as among his very best forensic efforts. Secure of victory, he thus magnanimously spoke of the defendant:

" Notwithstanding the suspicions which from the beginning obscured and questioned his birth, he was, nevertheless, acknowledged by his family, and has arrived at man's estate
contended all men were subject, less or more. The supposed assassin was reading a newspaper, and talked very rationally upon the topics of the day; but he continued at times subject to strong delusion, and it would have been unsafe to have discharged him from custody.

See **27** St. Tr. 1281-1356. Erskine's Speeches, v. 1-48.

with the feelings of a gentleman. I learn, indeed, that his conduct and character are every way worthy of a genuine descent. I hear the very best report of him from all quarters, and it makes a strong and painful impression upon me. I am wholly a stranger in this place, utterly unknown, I believe, to all of you whom I am addressing; but I might safely appeal to those around the table who have long known me, whether they think me capable of enjoying any triumph or gratification in being even the instrument of the justice I seek at your hands, when the administration of it must give so much pain to a deserving individual wholly guiltless of the fraud which placed him in his present station. In such a case the best minds find it the most difficult to be just; because the understanding shrinks back from its office, and the heart pulls against the faithful discharge of such a distressing jurisdiction. But it is necessary, in equal justice, to contemplate the other side of the case, and to be made impartial by revolving in your minds the situation of the plaintiff if the defendant's birth be really suppositious."

The case as opened was sworn to by several witnesses; but their credit was a good deal shaken in cross-examination— and after a summing up from Mr. Justice Heath, which appears to me very fair, the jury found a verdict for the defendant.

Erskine, on his return to London, wrote a letter to the plaintiff's attorney, in which he says, "The charge of the Judge is a reproach to the administration of English justice, being, from the beginning to the end of it, a mass of consummate absurdity, and ignorance of the first rules of evidence. If he had done his duty, I think the verdict would have been otherwise. You, however, have the consolation to reflect, that you have not been wanting in any part of the duty cast upon you; and I have the greatest pleasure in assuring you that, in the whole course of my professional life, I never saw greater vigilance, nor a more enlightened course of proceeding, than has marked and distinguished you in this unfortunate business." A rule for setting aside the verdict, and for a trial at bar, having, after long argument, been discharged, Erskine, more indignant, thus addressed the attorney: "My opinion of Mr. Day's cause you can scarcely believe to be at all altered; my mind must be indeed shallow in the extreme if anything which passed in the King's Bench could make any other impression upon it than that of utter contempt for the prejudices of judges in the blind support of one another's errors. Kenyon's mind is of a size, and generally speaking, of a character, to disdain such a course; but he appears to me to have laid aside his reason in the speech he delivered." Many years after, he said, in a letter to the plaintiff, who was then about to publish the trial, " Take care not to abridge a syllable of Mr. Justice Heath's charge; when the whole appears together, nothing but the utmost contempt can follow." And when the publication came out, he thus again addressed him: "Nothing could be more perfectly honorable and just than your conduct throughout in the painful and unprosperous endeavor to establish your inheritance. The best possible vindication of your conduct is to have published, *as you have done*, a faithful account of the proceedings. I should be sorry, however, if I had been formerly a Common-Law Judge, that the public should have to read such evidence as you have printed, and *such a summing up* of mine."[1]

It was in actions for *criminal conversation* that he was thought chiefly to excel. He joined with all right-judging persons in condemning the English law that permits, and, indeed, with a view to a divorce, requires, an injured husband to seek a pecuniary compensation for his dishonor: but when called upon to dwell upon the happiness arising from the purity of domestic life, and the ruin produced by its contamination, while performing his forensic duties, he inculcated morality, perhaps, more forcibly than some orthodox divines from their pulpits. His two most celebrated speeches upon this subject—one when he was for the plaintiff, and the other when he was for the defendant—are preserved, having been published under his own superintendence. The first was *Markham* v.

[1] ...." Manet altâ mente repostum
Judicium Paridis."—
This letter bears date 2nd Feb. 1823, within a few months of Lord Erskine's death.
I have heard an anecdote (which was probably a pure invention) that he thus successfully took off the effect of another strong summing up against him in an important cause. Old Mr. Justice Gould, the presiding Judge, being hardly audible, and quite unintelligible to the jury, Erskine, sitting in their view, nodded assent to all that was said; and—making them believe that the law was laid down altogether in his favor—obtained the verdict.

Faucet, in which the action was brought by a clergyman, the son of the Archbishop of York, against a country gentleman who lived in his parish, and with whom he had been on terms of great intimacy. After describing the long-continued friendship of the parties, he thus continued :—

" Yet, dreadful to relate, and it is the bitterest evil of which the plaintiff has to complain, a criminal intercourse, for nearly five years before the discovery of the connection, had most probably taken place. I will leave you to consider what must have been the feelings of such a husband, upon the fatal discovery that his wife—and such a wife—had conducted herself in a manner that not merely deprived him of her comfort and society, but placed him in a situation too horrible to be described. . . . He does not know at what time this heavy calamity fell upon him. He is tortured by the most afflicting of all human sensations. When he looks at the children whom he is by law bound to protect and to provide for, and from whose existence he ought to receive the delightful return which the union of instinct and reason has provided for the continuation of the world, he knows not whether he is lavishing his fondness and affection upon his own children, or upon the seed of a villain, sown in the bed of his honor and his delight. He starts back with horror, when, instead of seeing his own image reflected from their infant features, he thinks he sees the destroyer of his happiness, —a midnight robber introduced into his house under professions of friendship and brotherhood,—a plunderer, not in the repositories of his treasure, which may be supplied, or lived without,—' *but there where he had garnered up his hopes—where either he must live, or bear no life.*' God himself, as he has constituted human nature, has no means of alleviating such an injury as this. While the sensibilities, affections, and feelings which he has given to man, remain, it is impossible to heal a wound which strikes so deep into the soul. . . . I have established a claim for damages that has no parallel in the annals of fashionable adultery. It is rather like the entrance of sin and death into this lower world. The pair were living like our first parents in Paradise, till this Demon saw and envied their happy condition. Like them, they were in a moment cast down from the pinnacle of human happiness into the very lowest abyss of sorrow and despair. In one point, indeed, the resemblance does not hold, which, while it aggravates the crime, redoubles the sense of suffering. 'It was not an enemy that hath done me this dishonor, for then I could have borne it. Neither was it mine adversary that did magnify himself against me; for then peradventure I would have hid myself from him: but it was even thou, my companion, my guide, mine own familiar friend.'"[1]

In *Howard* v. *Bingham*, which was an action of the same description, by the heir presumptive to the Duke of Norfolk, against the eldest son of the Earl of Luçan, Erskine was counsel for the defendant, but made his client appear the party aggrieved. There had been a mutual attachment between the lady, a daughter of Lord Fauconberg, and the defendant: they had been engaged to be married, before her acquaintance with the plaintiff, and her parents had broken off that match for what appeared the superior advantages of a new offer. This was the theme of Erskine's splendid apology, or rather retaliation, and countercharge:—

"I have the noble Judge's authority for saying, that the gist of this action is *the plaintiff's loss of the comfort and society of his wife by the seduction of the defendant*. The loss of her affection and of domestic happiness, are the only foundations of his complaint. Now, before anything can be lost, it must have *existed*,—before anything can be taken away from a man, he must have had it,—before the seduction of a woman's affections from her husband can take place, he must have possessed her affections. . . . In order, therefore to examine this matter (and I shall support every syllable that I utter, with the most precise and incontrovertible proofs), I will begin by drawing up the curtain of this blessed marriage-bed, whose joys are supposed to be nipped in the bud by the defendant's adulterous seduction. Nothing certainly is more delightful to the human fancy than the possession of a beautiful woman in the prime of health and youthful passion; it is, beyond all doubt, the highest enjoyment which God in his benevolence and for the wisest purposes has bestowed upon his own image; I reverence as I ought that mysterious union of mind and body which, while it

[1] Erskine's Speeches, v. 169–195.

continues our species, is the source of all our affections, —which builds up and dignifies the condition of human life,—which binds the husband to the wife by ties more indissoluble than laws can possibly create, and which, by the reciprocal endearments arising from a mutual passion, a mutual interest, and a mutual honor, lays the foundation of that parental affection which dies in the brutes with the necessities of nature, but which reflects back upon the human parents the unspeakable sympathies of their offspring, and all the sweet, delightful relations of social existence. While the curtains, therefore, are still closed on this bridal scene, your imaginations will naturally represent to you this charming woman, endeavoring to conceal sensations which modesty forbids the sex, however enamored, too openly to reveal,—wishing, beyond adequate expression, what she must not even attempt to express, and seemingly resisting what she burns to enjoy. Alas, gentlemen! you must prepare to see in the room of this, a scene of horror and of sorrow; you must prepare to see a noble lady, whose birth surely required no further illustration; who had been courted to marriage before she heard even her husband's name; and whose affections were irretrievably bestowed upon and pledged to my honorable and unfortunate client. You must behold her given up to the plaintiff by the infatuation of parents, and stretched upon the bridal bed as upon a rack,—torn from the arms of a beloved and impassioned youth, himself of noble birth,—only to secure the honors of a higher title,—a legal victim on the altar of heraldry. Gentleman, this is no high coloring for the purpose of a cause; no words of an advocate can go beyond the plain unadorned effect of the evidence: I will prove to you that when she prepared to retire to her chamber, she threw her desponding arms around the neck of her confidential attendant, and wept upon her as a criminal preparing for execution: I will prove to you that she met her bridegroom with sighs and tears—the sighs and tears of afflicted love for Mr. Bingham, and of rooted aversion to her husband. Gentlemen, this was not the sudden burst of youthful disappointment, but the fixed and settled habit of a mind deserving of a happier fate. I shall prove that she frequently spent her nights upon a couch, in her own apartments, dissolved in tears; that she frequently declared to her woman that she would rather go to Newgate than to Mr. Howard's bed; and it will appear by her own confession that for months subsequent to the marriage she distinctly refused him the privileges of a husband. . . . My learned friend deprecates the power of what he terms my pathetic eloquence. Alas, gentlemen, if I possessed it, the occasion forbids its exertion, because Mr. Bingham has only to defend himself, and can not demand damages from Mr. Howard for depriving him of what was *his* by a title superior to any law which man has a moral right to make. Mr. Howard was NEVER MARRIED: God and nature forbade the bans of such a marriage. If, indeed, Mr. Bingham this day could have by me addressed to you his wrongs in the character of a plaintiff demanding reparation, what damages might I not have asked for him!—and without the aid of this imputed eloquence, what damages might I not have expected! I would have brought before you a noble youth, who had fixed his affections upon one of the most beautiful of her sex, and who enjoyed hers in return,—I would have shown you their suitable condition,—I would have painted the expectation of an honorable union, and would have concluded by showing her to you in the arms of another, by the legal prostitution of parental choice in the teeth of affection,—with child by a rival, and only reclaimed at last, after so cruel and so afflicting a divorce, with her freshest charms despoiled and her very morals in a manner impeached, by asserting the purity and virtue of her original and spotless choice. Good God! imagine my client to be PLAINTIFF, and what damages are you not prepared to give him! And yet he is here as DEFENDANT, and damages are demanded against him. Oh, monstrous conclusion!"

He went on in the same strain above an hour longer, taking occasion to warn the aristocracy of the ruin which the mercenary spirit which was here displayed would bring upon their order. The jury, as they afterwards declared, were resolved to find a verdict for the defendant, with heavy damages to be paid to him,—till they were reminded by the Judge that no blame was imputable to the plaintiff, as he had not been made aware of the previous engagement; that when the lady, under whatever influence, had vowed to be his at the altar, and their hands had been joined by the priest, she became his wife according to the laws both of God and man; that their sacred union ought to have been respected by the defendant, however much he was to be pitied, as his wrongs were irremediable; that it was his duty to have fled from temptation, instead of cherishing a guilty flame; that he had inflicted an injury for which he was liable to make compensation, by rendering it impossible for the plaintiff ever to win the affections of his wife, or to behold her more; that the jury were bound by their oaths to find a verdict for the plaintiff, if they believed that the adultery had been committed, and that they would not be justified in affixing a brand upon him by awarding trifling damages. The jury at last did find for the plaintiff, damages £500.—£10,000 being the lowest sum which in such cases was then usually awarded.[1]

In the case of *Dunning* v. *Sir Thomas Turton*, of which we have a very imperfect report, Erskine appears to have produced, perhaps, a still greater effect by describing the state of a husband fondly attached to his wife, but suspecting her fidelity,—painting in the most lively colors the different emotions of his soul—the agonies of suspense —the feverish irritation of unrelieved doubt—the struggles of the wounded spirit as to a fact which, while the heart wanted to disbelieve, reason told him was but too true. The advocate excited the most thrilling emotions when he quoted from Othello—

"Oh! what damned minutes tells he o'er
Who dotes, yet doubts; suspects, yet strongly loves!"

"But," added he, with overwhelming force, "when suspicion is realized into certainty, and his dishonor is placed beyond the reach of doubt, Despair assumes her dominion over the afflicted man, and well might he exclaim from the same page—

....' Had it pleased Heaven
To try me with affliction; Had He rain'd
All kinds of sores and shames on my bare head;
Steep'd me in poverty to the very lips;
Given to captivity me and my hopes,
I should have found in some place in my soul
A drop of patience. But now———'"

He stopped, and tears filled every eye. His recitation

[1] Erskine's Speeches, v. 195–212.

was perfect; and his felicitous quotations, though carefully premeditated, seemed the spontaneous recollections of the moment.'

It is with unfeigned sorrow that I must take leave of Erskine as an advocate at the Bar, where his superiority to the rest of mankind was so striking,—and that I must now attend him through scenes in which he acted a subordinate part and in which justice requires that he should sometimes be severely censured.

During the concluding years of Mr. Pitt's first Administration, Erskine almost entirely absented himself from the House of Commons, despairing of his party and of the country, and defending the measures of secession to which the Opposition leaders then imprudently resorted. I do not much wonder that he should have refused to take part in the debates concerning the conduct of the war; for the prostrate Whigs were not able to get a hearing either in or out of Parliament, when they attempted to touch upon this subject,—tremendous majorities approving of the expedition to Holland,—of the expedition to Ferrol,—of the expedition to Quiberon,—and of wasting the strength of the nation in taking sugar islands in the West Indies, for the extension of the slave trade. But it is remarkable that he should have been silent upon the Union with Ireland, and other great constitutional questions which were from time to time brought before the House of Commons. He probably persuaded himself that it was better for the public that he should offer no resistance to the measures of the Government; and he had no pleasure in going from Westminster Hall, where he was applauded and triumphant, to St. Stephen's Chapel, where his powers of persuasion utterly failed, and where he was sometimes even slighted. He did speak in favor of several bills not connected with politics; but he considered it vain to combat the supremacy of Pitt, who having carried the Irish Union, and annihilated the Whig Opposition, seemed more firmly established in power than at any former period.

At the opening of the first session of the United Par-

---

[1] I was told by a barrister who had often been in causes with him that he used to produce his proposed quotations at consultation the night before, and take the opinion of his juniors upon them; but my learned informant was noted for " shooting with a long bow."

liament of Great Britain and Ireland, a rumor arose, that, from the failure of his attempt to grant Catholic emancipation, or from a desire that peace should be negotiated by another Minister, Pitt was about voluntarily to descend into the rank of a private citizen. This strange Ministerial crisis, prolonged by the mental alienation of the King, I have described in the Life of Lord Loughborough, and I must recur to it in the Life of Lord Eldon, as it terminated in transferring the Great Seal from the one to the other. But Erskine had no share in it; for the Whigs had only to look on as spectators—the struggle being between different sections of their opponents,—and no prospect appeared of their ever being restored to power. When Mr. Addington was, at last, installed in office, several of them, with a view to rescue him from the thraldom of Pitt, were inclined to support him; and there actually was a negotiation opened for Erskine becoming Attorney General.

"During the Administration of Addington," says Mr. Moore, "Erskine, led by the example of Lord Moira, Sheridan, Tierney and others of the friends with whom he usually acted, manifested a willingness to support the new Minister, and was even on the point of accepting the office of Attorney General. Overtures to that effect having been transmitted to him by Mr. Addington, he thought it his duty to lay them before the Prince of Wales, whose service, in case of an acceptance of the office, it would be necessary for him to relinquish. In his answer, conveyed through Mr. Sheridan, the Prince, while he expressed the most friendly feelings towards Erskine, declined, at the same time, giving any opinion as to either his acceptance or refusal of the office of Attorney General if offered to him under the present circumstances. His Royal Highness also added the expression of his sincere regret that a proposal of this nature should have been submitted to his consideration by one of whose attachment and fidelity to himself he was well convinced, but who ought to have felt, from the line of conduct adopted and persevered in by his Royal Highness, that he was the very last person who should have been applied to for either his opinion or concurrence respecting the political conduct or connections of any public character, especially of one so intimately connected with him and belonging to his family. Upon this expression of the Prince's sentiments, the offer was of course declined."[1]

By listening to this overture Erskine incurred no suspicion of vacillation; for he really believed, at the time, that Mr. Addington not only was desirous of making peace, but that he meant to depart from the arbitrary policy which had been adopted, since the year 1792, with respect to the internal government of the country.[2]

He showed his steady adherence to his old principles by the part which he soon after took in the projected coalition with the "Grenville-Windhamites," as they were called,—a section of Mr. Pitt's colleagues that had gone out with him, and were now desirous of having Mr. Fox for their leader, with a view of vigorously pushing on the prosecution of the war.—He was one of those who met at Norfolk House, for the purpose of frankly remonstrating with Mr. Fox against the offered alliance; and the remonstrance then agreed to, strongly marked by generous sentiments of private friendship and of enlightened patriotism, was said to have been drawn up by him.[3]

Without joining the Adminstration, he gave it his countenance. The peace of Amiens being concluded, he voted with the majority in approving of it; and he made a vigorous speech in defense of the Convention with Russia for defining some of our controverted belligerent rights against neutrals. On this occasion he said:

[1] Life of Sheridan, ii. 323.
[2] The following are extracts of letters which he wrote to a friend while this negotiation was going on:—" I know and feel my own high station in the profession (which, I may say in a private letter, no man ever held before for such a number of years), and I know and feel also the etiquette it imposes upon me with regard to my juniors, however accidentally placed above me by temporary political offices. But so far am I on that account from wishing to stand in the way of the advantages which such accidents may be thought, from custom, to have conferred, or may hereafter confer, upon those who hold them, that I should be the very last man in the world to take the least interest in finding any precedents if any were wanting, for supporting any disposition in any body to support my advancement out of the proper course of things."...." For myself, I can say positively, that if *all* the high offices in the law were to fall vacant to-morrow, and to be filled up without any thought of me, it would not in the slightest degree affect the conduct which I have prescribed to myself, from the best attention I have been able to give to that line of conduct which the public ought to expect from me, and which my conscience approves.".. "I am in a lucrative and honorable situation, and I will remain in it till the time comes (if it ever does) when I can vindicate to friends and foes the change in my situation."
[3] Moore's Life of Sheridan, ii. 324.

"I can not, Sir, refuse myself the pleasure of expressing the most unqualified approbation of the manner in which the Convention has been so happily concluded. Not long ago I saw three great nations of the North confederated against the vital interests of our country; yet in so short a time afterwards I now see the same powers pledged to concur with us in their support, by upholding our ancient system of international law. The effect of such a successful conspiracy must have been to establish universally, that free bottoms should make free goods, because they who denied the right of search, and enforced the refusal, annihilated every regulation against enemies' property as contraband of war, since it is only by search that the invasion of neutrality can be detected. The right of search is now recognized as the general law of civilized states. We have preserved the honor and interests of our own country by not forgetting that other countries have honor and interests also. Without this reasonable compromise we could not have had a peace so likely to continue, for it will be pursued as it was made—in the spirit of peace. I wish France and every other nation to see that our divisions are at an end. We have made many sacrifices in the course of the late contest, and we must make many more to redeem our country from the consequences of a war, the continuance of which might have been fatal to it and to the whole civilized world. I hope, Sir, that Ministers will now pursue towards their fellow-subjects the same liberal policy which upon this occasion they have shown towards adversaries. This is still wanting. I am now looking forwards, and confidently maintain that, if the people of Great Britain and Ireland were governed according to the spirit of our laws, mildly administered, they would, to use the language of Mr. Burke, 'forever cling and grapple to you, and nothing could tear them from their allegiance.' Nothing, indeed, can estrange them from our invaluable Constitution but shutting them out from its benefits."[1]

During the present session, Erskine again came forward in the debate caused by Mr. Nicholl's motion to "thank the Crown for the removal of Mr. Pitt;" and Sir H. Mildmay's amendment, "That Mr. Pitt, for his services while Minister, deserved the gratitude of the House."

[1] 36 Parl. Hist. 278.

He was particularly severe on Mr. Pitt's injudicious refusals to treat for peace with Bonaparte; and on his resignation,—which he represented as "a desertion of the vessel of the state when she was laboring in the tempest, and in danger of being dashed to pieces among the rocks which surrounded her." The vote of thanks, however, was carried by a majority of 224 to 52,[1] partly from the recollection of Pitt's former Administration, and still more from the anticipation that he must ere long be Minister again.

CHAPTER CLXXXIII.

CONTINUATION OF THE LIFE OF LORD ERSKINE TILL HE BECAME LORD CHANCELLOR.

IN the long vacation of this year, Erskine went to Paris, where he expected that he must be gazed at— on account of his fame as an advocate, and the leading part which he conceived he had taken for many years in the House of Commons; but his vanity was considerably mortified by his reception there. He knew hardly anything of the French language, so that he could not assist in spreading his own fame;—none of his forensic speeches had been translated into French, and his political consequence was utterly extinguished by the presence of Fox, who had gone over to collect materials for his " History of the Reign of James, II.," and was run after as a prodigy. We have the following account from an eye-witness of our hero's reception by the First Consul:—

" Bonaparte, at the levee, made a long florid address to Fox, to which the modest statesman made no reply. Erskine's presentation followed. I am tempted to think that he felt some disappointment at not being recognized by the First Consul; there was some dfficulty at first, as Erskine was understood to speak little French. Monsieur Talleyrand's impatient whisper to me, I fancy I yet hear: ' *Parle-t-il François ?* ' Mr. Merry, the English Consul, already fatigued with his presentations, and dreading a host to come, imperfectly designated Erskine—

[1] 36 Parl. Hist. 6:6, 653.

when the killing question followed, '*Etes-vous légiste?*' This was pronounced by Bonaparte with great indifference, or, at least, without any marked attention."[1]

Erskine was better treated at the Cour de Cassation, if we may credit Monsieur Berryer the Elder, who, in his "*Souvenirs*," is rather imaginative:—

"One morning," says he, in narrating his visit to London in 1822, "I repaired to the Court of King's Bench, accompanied by a solicitor, with no other intention than that of being present as a looker-on at one of its sittings. The Attorney General perceives my white head, the only one in the crowd; he sends a *huissier, bearing a wand of ivory*, to speak to me. The *huissier* presses through the crowd, reaches the place where I stand, and in a few words of English, translated by my solicitor, invites me to follow him to the bar of the amphitheater set apart for the advocates. The bar opens. Two young advocates, in wigs, *à la Louis Quatorze*, came forward to introduce me. All the advocates—the Broughams, the Scarletts, being of the number—rise to salute me. I was dressed in a plain black surtout. My two young attendants assigned me a seat between them. They keep me, during the sitting, *au courant* of what is going on. It was a bankruptcy matter, under an inquiry by a jury. The jury having retired to deliberate, I took a respectful leave of the advocates *en masse*.—All the London newspapers of the day following gave a report, highly flattering to both countries, on this solemn reception of a Parisian advocate. I have since ascertained that it was by way of return for

[1] Trotter's Memoirs of Fox, p. 268. However, the Right Hon. Thomas Erskine writes to me,—" Mr. Trotter has misunderstood the circumstance to which he alludes, obviously in no friendly spirit. My father was introduced to Bonaparte, not by name, but by his official title as Chancellor to the Prince of Wales. The First Consul, not knowing the nature of this office, or the name of the individual who filled it, put the question, '*Etes-vous légiste?*' When my father was afterwards, at an evening party given by Madame Josephine, introduced to the hero by his name, Napoleon alluded to his former interview by saying, 'You are better known to me by your name than your office.'"

Curran, who was then likewise at Paris, escaped the mortification of such a question being addressed to him, by luckily keeping away from Bonaparte's levee. Thus he wrote to a friend while still in some doubt upon the subject:—"I don't suppose I shall get myself presented to the Consul; not having been privately baptized at St. James's would be a difficulty;—to get over it a favor; and then the trouble of getting myself costumed for the show;—and then the small value of being driven like the beasts of the field before Adam when he named them. I think I shan't mind it."

my having, twenty years before, procured the famous Erskine a reception equally warm from all my brethren at one of the sittings of the Appeal Court at Paris."

But if Erskine had not more to boast of from the attention paid to him by his brethren at Paris than Berryer had in London, I can testify, from having been present at the scene so pompously described, that much was left to be supplied by self-complaisance and imagination. I well recollect regretting that more was not done to testify our sense of the honor conferred upon us by a visit from such a distinuished foreign jurist. We could not have summoned him by a *huissier* with *a wand of ivory*, having no officer with any such emblem of dignity; and it would have been contrary to our customs to have interrupted a jury-trial by the Bar all rising in a body to do homage to any stranger, however distinguished,—were he even a crowned head. But we ought to have taken care that M. Berryer was placed on the bench, by the side of the Judge, whereas he was squeezed in among the barristers; and although several of them spoke to him very courteously, he remained in an inconvenient seat during a tedious trial respecting an act of bankruptcy, which could not be made intelligible to him; and when the jury withdrew to consider their verdict he left the court, with his "solicitor," almost unnoticed.

During this visit to Paris, Erskine was placed in a situation of great embarrassment by meeting in society the man whose political principles he had vouched to be exactly the same as his own, and who had since, having confessed his treasons, been banished by Act of Parliament, and had engaged in the military service of France. "At a sumptuous dinner given by Madame Cabarras, *ci-devant* Tallien, to Fox, Erskine, and other distinguished foreigners, to the surprise and displeasure of some, Arthur O'Connor was a guest. Erskine was extremely uneasy, remembering how much he had been deceived in his testimony at Maidstone, and afraid lest evil report should misrepresent this matter in England; but Fox treated it as unavoidable, though unlucky. He spoke to O'Connor as usual."[1] I confess that this seems to me to have been carrying complaisance to a hurtful extreme, and that Erskine did better by avoiding all conversation with a

[1] Trotter's Memoirs of Fox.

man who had violated alike the duties of allegiance and of friendship.

Erskine was well pleased to return to England, and he never again revisited the Continent—not even after the battle of Waterloo, when he might have seen his kilted countrymen encamped in the Champs Elysées, and, clad in tartan, mounting guard with claymore in hand at the Louvre. He was hardly acquainted with any modern language except his own, and he felt a great loss of comfort and of consequence when he found himself in company where that was not spoken. It must likewise be confessed that, although his mind was highly cultivated and his taste exquisitely formed by an intense study of the English classics, he was not familiar with foreign literature, and he had but a small stock of general political science; so that, even with the assistance of an interpreter, he was not well qualified to shine in the Parisian salons, notwithstanding his elegant manners, which announced his birth and breeding wherever he appeared.

Soon after his return he gave a striking proof of the unenvious disposition, and the generosity to those who might be considered rivals, which distinguished him through life. We were now at peace with France, and Napoleon Bonaparte, made Consul for life, was acknowledged by us as the Chief Magistrate of that state. On the complaint of his minister,—Mr. Perceval, the Attorney General, had filed an *ex-officio* information against Peltier, the editor of the Ambigu, a French newspaper, published in London, for a libel,—and this *cause célèbre* attracted the attention of all Europe. Erskine would have been well pleased with the *éclat* of being counsel for the defendant, and with the opportunity of defending the liberty of the press in England from such an attack upon it by a foreign despot. Yet he heard without repining that this task was intrusted to Mackintosh; and when the day of the trial arrived, instead of sulkily absenting himself, he attended as one of the audience to listen to the author of the VINDICIÆ GALLICÆ, and to countenance and encourage him.[1] Before going to bed, the admired, though defeated, orator received the following hearty tribute of praise:—

[1] See 28 St. Tr. 530.

" DEAR MACKINTOSH,
" I can not shake off from my nerves the effect of your most powerful and wonderful speech, which so completely disqualifies you for Trinidad or India. I could not help saying to myself as you were speaking, ' O terram illam beatam, quæ hunc virum acceperit, hanc ingratam si ejecerit, miseram si amiserit.' I perfectly approve of the verdict, but the manner in which you opposed it I shall always'consider as one of the most splendid monuments of genius, learning, and eloquence.
" Yours ever,
" T. E.
" Monday evening."

And he felt as he wrote. He was not made wretched by the success of another man in a department in which he himself had succeeded; nor did he incite dependants to malignant criticisms in reviews, nor himself descend to annoymous slander in the newspapers, for the purpose of mitigating the anguish of his alarmed vanity. On the contrary, he not only received Mackintosh with a smiling countenance when they met, but, behind his back and in all societies, cordially strove to swell his reputation and to advance his fortune.[1]

Soon after followed the rupture of the peace of Amiens; and so general was the conviction that this was forced on by the First Consul, that the Whigs almost all joined in openly applauding the recommencement of hostilities, and in the pledge to carry on the war with vigor. According to the Parliamentary History, " Mr. Erskine warmly expressed his sense of the vindictive disposition and proceedings of France. To some parts of the conduct of Ministers in the negotiation and of the address he urged objections; but he assured them of his readiness to contribute at all times and by every method in his power toward the effectual resistance of all aggression either upon the dominion, the interests, or the honor of the country."[2] The same record informs us that when

[1] Life of Sir James Mackintosh, vol. i. p. 182. Adolphus, in giving an account of Peltier's trial, says,—" The speech pronounced for him was highly complimented by the most eminent of advocates, and in print it displays a masterly specimen of vigorous conception, glowing description, and powerful reasoning; but in Court it produced no effect, for without a moment's hesitation, the jury returned a verdict of *guilty*."—Vol. vii. p. 055.
[2] Vol. xxxvi. 1386.

the Property Tax was first proposed, "Mr. Erskine declared himself ready to support it—not that he approved of it in principle, but he was convinced of the necessity of making great exertions at so perilous a moment as the present. He felt it necessary that great sacrifices should be made ; and although he felt that his own professional income was not worth above two years' purchase, he would gladly give up any part that could be asked for the general service of the country."[1]

The population of this island now exhibited that military spirit which is so well described by Walter Scott in the "Antiquary," which I, myself, witnessed when a student in the Inns of Court, and which I trust would, under similar circumstances, again blaze forth with equal ardor. Bonaparte was collecting his mighty armament at Boulogne with the avowed intention of invading our shores, and he had foolishly exasperated the quarrel by detaining in custody all British subjects in his power at the renewal of the war,—whereby he in no degree weakened our means of resistance, while he considerably increased among us the rancor against himself, and the readiness to submit to every sacrifice in the hope of being revenged. Of the 300,000 volunteers enrolled and disciplined, the lawyers in the metropolis raised two regiments—the B. I. C. A., or Bloomsbury and Inns of Court Association, and the "Temple Corps," generally called "The Devil's Own." The command of the latter was conferred upon Erskine. Having myself served in the ranks of the former, I am not able from personal observation to criticize his military prowess,[2] but I well remember we heard many stories of the blunders which he committed, and we thought ourselves lucky to be under the orders of Lieutenant Colonel Cox, a warlike Master in Chancery.[3] While our rivals could boast of most of the dignitaries of the law, and were renowned for their

[1] Parl. Hist. xxxvi. 1663.
[2] I did once, and once only, see him putting his men through their maneuvers, on a summer's evening in the Temple Gardens ; and I well recollect that he gave the word of command from a paper which he held before him, and in which I conjectured that his " instructions " were written out as in a *Brief*.
[3] Of the other two most noted volunteer commandants in the metropolis, one had been a miller, and went by the name of Marshal *Sacks ;* and the other actually was a pastry-cook in the City, famous for selling good turtle-soup, and he was dubbed Marshal *Tureen.*

"*belly-gerent*" appearance,[1] we consisted chiefly of lean students and briefless barristers;[2] so that we were in great hopes that, if we did go into the field, before the end of the campaign fatigue alone would make great openings for us in Westminster Hall and on all the circuits. We had drills every morning, and many field days; but we never had any harder service than being reviewed by George III. in Hyde Park, along with all the volunteers of the metropolis, on a very rainy day. Both the Law corps were especially noticed by his Majesty, who caused much jealousy among us of the B. I. C. A. by his particularly gracious return to the salute of Lieutenant Colonel Erskine. Many severe colds were caught, but there was no casualty to cause any promotion in the profession, the servants of the seniors waiting for them with cloaks and umbrellas as soon as they were dismissed from the parade. Lord Eldon in his old age gave the following account of this spectacle:—" I think the finest sight I ever beheld was the great review in Hyde Park before George III. The King in passing addressed Tom Erskine, who was Colonel, asking him the name of his corps. He answered, 'The Devil's Own.' The Lincoln's Inn volunteers[3] always went by the name of 'The Devil's Invincibles.'"[4]

Soon afterwards, Bonaparte having broken up his encampment at Boulogne, and marched into Germany, the military ardor of the lawyers greatly subsided; and although Erskine nominally retained the command of his corps, he became remiss in the discharge of his regimental duties—being entirely above the affectation of pretending

[1] Law, the then Attorney General, afterwards Lord Chief Justice Ellenborough, was reported to be a fair specimen of them; for, even with the help of chalk, he never could be taught the difference between marching with his right or his left foot foremost; and all the time he was in the service he continued in the awkward squad.
[2] There were likewise a good many attorneys belonging to us, who brought down many jests upon us—among others, that upon the word being given "prepare to charge," they all pulled out pen, ink, and paper; and being ordered to "charge," they wrote down 6s. 8d. or 13s. 4d.—The soul of our corps was our adjutant, my poor friend Will Harrison, who with us could talk of nothing but battles, and seemed to think himself as great a military genius as Napoleon, although he talked much law at regimental messes, which he was fond of dining at,—so that it was said he was "a General among Lawyers, and a Lawyer among Generals."
[3] Meaning the B. I. C. A.
[4] Twiss's Life of Eldon, i. 283.

to a knowledge of strategy, and the folly of " playing at soldiers."[1]

He now came before the public in a manner much more to his taste. Other civilians, as well as the lawyers, were weary of military maneuvers when the danger of invasion had passed by, and longed to retire; but the Government wished to keep up the force on its present footing, and insisted that they were bound to serve during the war. The Attorney and Solicitor General having given an opinion to this effect, Erskine was consulted, and thus expressed himself respecting the nature and extent of the engagement of volunteers:—" If the term *volunteer* is supposed to be satisfied by the original spontaneousness of the enrollment, leaving him afterwards indefinitely bound, then every enlisted soldier must equally be considered to be a volunteer, and, with the difference of receiving money, and the local extent of service excepted, would be upon an equal footing, both as to merit and independence. Such a doctrine appears to me to be equally unjust and impolitic: unjust, because for the volunteer's engagement there is no consideration but the sense of honor and duty, the reward of which is sullied if the service does not continue to be voluntary;—impolitic, because it is overlooking a motive of action infinitely more powerful than the force of any human authority, to take no account of that invincible sensibility in the mind of man for the opinion of his fellow-creatures." He further examined the statutes upon the subject, and came to the clear conclusion that any member of a volunteer corps might resign at pleasure, although while he continued to serve he was subject to military law. The conflicting opinions were published in all the newspapers, and caused general confusion, till the question was regularly brought before the Court of King's Bench, of which Lord Ellenborough was now the distinguished head. The case having been elaborately argued by Perceval the Attorney General on the one side, and Erskine on the other, the Judges unanimously determined in favor of the power of resignation;[2] and the champion

---

[1] I know not what he did with his sword when he was made Lord Chancellor. I still preserve my musket, which I mean to hand down as an heirloom in my family.

[2] Rex *v.* Dowley, 4 East, 512.

of it was extolled as a great lawyer as well as advocate, if not as a great military commander.

The regulation of the volunteer force occasioned much discussion in the House of Commons, and was finally made the subject on which Mr. Addington was turned out of office. In truth, while his intentions were allowed to be excellent, and his private character was above exception, he had not the confidence of any party, and there was a general wish in the nation that the government should be in abler hands, although the King continued highly pleased with his Minister, and would have much preferred him to Pitt as well as to Fox.

A clause having (contrary to the decision of the Court of King's Bench) been introduced into the " Volunteer Consolidation Bill" to prevent the resignation of volunteers till the conclusion of a general peace, Erskine strenuously opposed it, saying, "The foundation of the decision of the Court of King's Bench was the nature of the service. If a man comes out under arms upon the occasion of an invasion, what is the duration of his engagement? The duration of his engagement is as long as the enemy continues in the country; but that continuance is not necessarily and at all events the same as the duration of the war. From the obstinacy of our enemies, or from a legitimate desire to retaliate upon them, and to reduce their power within safe bounds, we may be obliged to carry on war with them long after all danger of invasion—all apprehension of invasion—has ceased. Till then you may safely trust to that patriotism which has animated the whole population of the country with the desire of fighting for her independence. If there are volunteer corps who wish to extend their services, and to carry arms till the conclusion of a general peace, let them be authorized hereafter to do so; but do not touch the right of resignation now enjoyed under the solemn judgment of the highest Court in Westminster Hall." The clause was withdrawn.[1]

Although Erskine continued a member of the House of Commons nearly two years longer, this was his last speech in that assembly.

In a few weeks afterwards Mr. Addington's Administration came to an end, and Mr. Pitt resumed the reins of

[1] Parl. Debates, vol. i. p. 934.

government, which he held with undivided and uncontrolled power till his death. A Coalition Government had been expected, including Mr. Fox with the "old Opposition" and Lord Grenville with the "new Opposition;" but Lord Grenville would not accept office without Mr. Fox, and the King's prejudice against that statesman could not yet be surmounted. It is very doubtful whether Mr. Pitt used much urgency to gain this end, although, ir the very critical state of public affairs, it was generally desired by the nation. I am afraid he was well pleased to find that he had in the Cabinet no one whom he did not consider his creature and dependent. He paid a dreadful penalty for the supremacy he grasped. While planning his new coalition against Napoleon, he was, no doubt, buoyed up by the hope of a successful issue to the contest, which would have placed his name even above that of his illustrious sire; but after the man whom he hoped to conquer had taken Ulm, and gained the battle of Austerlitz, he saw nothing before himself but disgrace and despair; and he not only found that it would be impossible for him much longer to retain his position as Minister, but, notwithstanding our naval triumphs, the safety of the state was endangered by the policy he had pursued. His brave heart was broken, and death relieved him from the mortification of being exposed, in the House of Commons, to the reproaches and sneers of those whose advice and predictions he had despised. Erskine, although he had invariably been opposed in politics to the departed statesman, and had often been the object of his sarcasms, on the present melancholy occasion generously joined with those who only recollected his splendid talents and his elevated patriotism, and concurred in voting a public funeral to him and in granting a sum of money for the payment of his debts.

The mind of our illustrious advocate was now softened by deep domestic grief. A few weeks before, he had lost his wife, to whom he was tenderly attached, who had been his faithful companion in his early struggles against penury, and who had enjoyed more than himself the fame and high position which he afterwards achieved. On a tablet erected to her memory in Hampstead Church, he thus recorded her virtues:—

> "Near this place
> lies buried
> THE HONORABLE FRANCES ERSKINE,
> the most faithful
> and
> most affectionate of Women.
> Her husband,
> THOMAS, LORD ERSKINE,
> an Inhabitant of this Parish,
> raised this monument
> to
> her lamented memory,
> A. D. 1807."[1]

After a feeble attempt to reconstruct the Cabinet under Lord Hawkesbury, who remained Chief only long enough to appoint himself Mr. Pitt's successor as Lord Warden of the Cinque Ports, Lord Grenville was sent for by the King to form a new Administration; and his Majesty, being told that Mr. Fox must be included it, had the magnanimity to say, "I thought so, and I meant it so; he is a gentleman."[2]

The chief difficulty experienced was in disposing of the Great Seal. Lord Eldon, if he had been willing to retain it, could not possibly be allowed to sit in the new Cabinet, the overthrow of which, whether in or out of office, all foresaw that he would unscrupulously plot. The offer of it was made to Lord Ellenborough, who declined it, as he could not run the risk of the proposed exchange on account of his large family; and to Sir James Mansfield, Chief Justice of the Court of Common Pleas, who pleaded his advanced age. Lord Grenville and Mr. Fox then asked the King's permission to offer it to Mr. Erskine—when his Majesty exclaimed, "What! what! Well! well!—but, remember, he is your Chancellor, not

[1] On a marble tablet in the same church is the following inscription in honor of the ninth Earl of Buchan:
> "Near this place lies buried
> THE RIGHT HONORABLE DAVID ERSKINE,
> EARL OF BUCHAN,
> LORD CARDROSS,
> LORD AUCHTERHOUSE, &c., &c.
> Died October 14th, O. S., A. D. 1745.
> Aged 73.
> This stone was erected to his memory
> by his Grandson,
> THOMAS, LORD ERSKINE,
> an Inhabitant of this Parish."

[2] On the authority of Lord Grenville, who related the anecdote to the late Earl of Essex.

mine." I am afraid that the royal objection arose from the recollection that he not only had always professed and acted upon Whig principles, but that by his eloquence he had defeated many prosecutions which his Majesty had deemed necessary for the public tranquillity. Had the King been aware (which could hardly be expected) of the professional qualifications necessary for a Chancellor, and this had been the source of his reluctance, he ought to be honored for his discernment.

I must confess that the appointment was not justifiable—being prompted by political convenience, and not by a due regard to the administration of justice in the Court of Chancery. The mere circumstance of a barrister having practiced chiefly in the courts of common law, I hold to be no disqualification for the office, and, on the contrary, I think he is likely to fill it more for the public benefit than a man reared in an equity draughtsman's office, who has never attended a circuit or quarter-sessions, and has exclusively employed his days and nights in drawing bills and answers, and conning over equity practice. If Erskine had been well versed in the civil law,—if he had scientifically studied general jurisprudence,—if he had been in the habit of pleading at the bar of the House of Lords,—and if he had been initiated in equity proceedings, by having been occasionally retained in great cases in the Court of Chancery,—he might have been expected to turn out as great an Equity Judge as Lord Eldon himself, who always ascribed his own proficiency to the circumstance that he began with the common law. But, unfortunately, Erskine was only a clever *nisi prius* pleader; and although he had sufficient acuteness to be made to understand any legal question, however abstruse, he was only familiar with the rules of evidence and the points likely to occur in the conduct of a cause before a jury, or in the common routine of a King's Bench leader in banco. I doubt whether he had ever opened the Institutes of Justinian, or glanced at the codes of any of the continental nations; and he could hardly go so far as Lord Holt, who said, "I have been counsel in *one* equity suit, which I lost;" for in his time, the equity leaders having been well drilled in common law, the custom had not begun, which has become very usual since, of calling

in upon important occasions the assistance of the common-
law leaders. Erskine, declining to accept briefs in the
House of Lords, or before the Privy Council, had seldom
to travel beyond the Term Reports and Buller's Nisi
Prius. He could hardly have expected to be an adequate
successor of Lord Nottingham, Lord Somers, and Lord
Hardwicke; and if he had consulted his own comfort and
his own glory he would have declined the offer, however
tempting it might appear to vulgar men. Better would it
have been for him to accept the office of Attorney General; in the expectation that a common-law chiefship
might become vacant, the duties of which he might have
adequately performed; or to have been contented with
being by far the first advocate who had ever practiced at
the English Bar—a position more enviable than that of
an indifferent Chancellor, notwithstanding the precedence
and the power which the Great Seal confers. In an evil
hour he yielded to the temptation of "the pestiferous
lump of metal"[1] which has proved fatal to so many;
and, ere long, from being the "beheld of all beholders,"
he sunk into comparative insignificance. He can not be
accused of having deserted his party, or ever done a dis-
honorable or mean act to obtain it. When Fox was
Prime Minister, nothing could be more natural than that
Erskine should be Chancellor. Politically, the arrangement was laudable; but, judicially, it was not to be defended. Romilly, in his Diary, speaking of the new Administration, says, "There are some few appointments
which have been received by the public with much dis-
satisfaction, and none with more than that of Erskine to
be Lord Chancellor. The truth undoubtedly is, that he
is totally unfit for his situation. His practice has never
led him into Courts of Equity, and the doctrines which
prevail in them are to him almost like the law of a foreign
country. It is true that he has a great deal of quickness,
and is capable of much application; but, at his time of
life, with the continual occupations which the duties of
his office will give him, and the immense arrear of business left him by his tardy and doubting predecessor, it is
quite impossible that he should find the means of making
himself master of that extensive and complicated system
of law which he will have to administer. He acts, indeed,

[1] Roger North.

very ingenuously on the subject; he feels his unfitness for the office, and seems almost overcome with the idea of the difficulties which he foresees that he will have to encounter. He called on me a few days ago, and told me that he should stand in great need of my assistance, that I must tell him what to read, and how best to fit himself for his situation. 'You must,' these are the very words he used to me, 'You must make me a Chancellor now, that I *may afterwards make you one.*" [1]

CHAPTER CLXXXIV.

CONTINUATION OF THE LIFE OF LORD ERSKINE WHILE HE WAS LORD CHANCELLOR.

THE transfer of the Great Seal took place at the Queen's Palace on the 7th of February, 1806, when, being delivered up by Lord Eldon, his Majesty *multa gemens* put it into the hand of Erskine, declaring him Lord Chancellor of Great Britain, and directed him to be sworn of the Privy Council. The same day the new head of the law was created a Peer of the United Kingdom, by the title of Baron Erskine of Restormel Castle, in the county of Cornwall, this locality being designated as a mark of favor by the Heir Apparent, because it was the ancient residence of the Princes of Wales.

The following day an honor was conferred upon him by which, I make no doubt, he was far more gratified. A meeting of the bar was held in Westminster Hall, and although a vast majority of those present were high Tories, the following resolution was carried unanimously:

"That we can not deny ourselves the satisfaction of presenting our sincere congratulations to the R[t]. Hon[ble]. Thomas, Lord Erskine, on his appointment to the office of Lord High Chancellor of Great Britain, and of expressing the deep impression made upon us by the uniform kindness and attention which we have at all times experienced from him during his long and extensive practice among us; and we further beg leave to assure his Lord-

[1] Memoirs, ii. 128.

ship that, in retiring from us, he is accompanied by our best wishes for his health and happiness."

This being presented to him in the name of the Bar, by the two senior barristers, the following was his reply:—

"GENTLEMEN,

"I can not express what I felt upon receiving your address, and what I must ever feel upon the recollection of it. I came originally into the profession under great disadvantages. Bred in military life, a total stranger to the whole Bar, and not entitled to expect any favorable reception from similar habits or private friendships, my sudden advancement into great business before I could rank in study or in learning with others who were my seniors also, was calculated to produce *in common minds* nothing but prejudice and disgust. How, then, can I look back without gratitude upon the unparalleled liberality and kindness which for seven-and-twenty years I uniformly experienced among you, and which alone, I feel a pride as well as a duty in acknowledging, enabled me to surmount many painful difficulties, and converted what would otherwise have been a condition of oppressive labor into an uninterrupted enjoyment of ease and satisfaction? I am happy that your partiality has given me the occasion of putting upon record this just tribute to the character and honor of the English Bar. My only merit has been, that I was not insensible to so much goodness. The perpetual and irresistible impulses of mind, deeply affected by innumerable obligations, could not but produce that behavior which you have so kindly and so publicly rewarded. I shall forever remain,

"Gentlemen,

"Your affectionate and faithful humble servant,

"ERSKINE.

"Lincoln's Inn Fields, Feb. 9, 1806."[1]

Considering how political enmities and private jealousies oppose such an expression of good-will to a barrister on his elevation to the woolsack, we need not wonder that this is a solitary instance of it in the annals of our profession; and we may form some conception of the fascinating manners and real kindness of heart, as well as of the brilliant genius which called it forth.

I must, however, relate that he caused a good deal of

[1] Annual Register, 1806, p. 363.

merriment in Westminster Hall, by the heraldic honors which, on his own suggestion, were accorded to him. Retaining his family shield and crest, he took for supporters "a Griffin, wings elevated, gules, charged with a mullet, and a Heron, wings mounted, holding in the beak an eel proper," (on which many jokes were made);[1] and he took for his motto, "TRIAL BY JURY." That of his father being "JUDGE NOUGHT," all allowed that it would not have been very appropriate; but it was said that "BY BILL IN EQUITY" would have been a better substitution on his going into the Court of Chancery, and that "Trial by Jury" was a vain imitation of Lord Camden's motto from Magna Charta, "Judicium Parium aut Lex Terræ."[2]

He took his seat on the woolsack on the 10th of February,[3] and on the last day of Hilary Term Lord Chancellor Erskine, seated in a state carriage, adorned with this blazonry, rode in grand procession from his house in Lincoln's Inn Fields to Westminster Hall, accompanied by his Royal Highness the Duke of Clarence, afterwards William IV., many peers and privy councillors, and all the Judges and King's counsel. The oaths were administered to him with due solemnity, and he commenced his judicial career.[4]

[1] The Buchan supporters were two ostriches.
[2] Soon after, a barrister whom I knew well, setting up his carriage—in still worse taste put upon the panels, "Causes produce Effects,"—equal to the tobacconist's "Quid rides," or the water-doctor's ducks crying *Quack! quack!*
[3] The following is a copy from the Lords' Journals on his taking his seat as a peer:—
"10th Feb. 1806.—His Royal Highness, the Duke of Clarence, acquainted the House 'That his Majesty had been pleased to create the Right Honorable Thomas Erskine, Lord Chancellor of that part of the United Kingdom of Great Britain and Ireland called Great Britain, a Peer of these realms.'
"Whereupon his Lordship, taking in hand the purse with the Great Seal, retired to the lower end of the House, and having there put on his robes, was introduced between the Lord Holland and the Lord Rawdon (also in their robes), the Yeoman Usher of the Black Rod, Garter King at Arms, and the Earl Marshal preceding.
"His Lordship laid down his patent upon the chair of state, kneeling; and from thence took and delivered it to the clerk, who read the same at the table.
"Then his Lordship at the table took the oaths, and made and subscribed the declaration; and also took and subscribed the oath of abjuration, pursuant to the statutes.
"Which done, his Lordship took his seat at the lower end of the Baron's Bench; from whence he went to the upper end of the Earl's bench, and sat there as Lord Chancellor, and then returned to the woolsack."
[4] "12th February, 1806.—John, Lord Eldon, Lord High Chancellor of that part of the United Kingdom of Great Britain and Ireland called Great

The Equity Counsel behaved to him with much liberality. He had been in the constant habit of jeering, although in a good-natured way, at their complicated and interminable proceedings, which he contrasted with the simplicity and dispatch of the Common Law. They had been often taunted in society with his pathetic appeal to Lord Kenyon, who recommended that his client should apply to Chancery for relief.—"Would your Lordship send a dog you loved there?"[1] and the answer was handed about which he had lately given to a question connected with equity: "My opinion is, that the present case should be sent to some gentleman conversant with this branch of practice." Yet they not only behaved to him with much respect and courtesy, but abstained from seeking to derive any unfair advantage from his inexperience, and showed a general disposition to keep him out of "*scrapes.*" His demeanor in his new office, to all who approached him, was so noble and so benevolent, that it conquered all prejudices, repressed the natural ebullitions of envy and of selfishness, and created an emulation of reciprocal good feeling. He continued all the officers of his predecessor in their situations; he did not dismiss one commissioner of bankrupts;[2] and as, by a

Britain, having delivered the Great Seal to the King, at the Queen's Palace, on Friday, the 7th day of February, 1806, his Majesty the same day delivered it to the Honorable Thomas Erskine, with the title of Lord High Chancellor of Great Britain, who was then sworn into the said office before his Majesty in Council; and on Wednesday, the 12th day of February, 1806, being the last day of Hilary Term, he went in state from his House in Lincoln's Inn Fields to Westminster Hall, accompanied by the Judges, King's Sergeants, King's Counsel, and several other persons. The Lord Chancellor proceeded into the Court of Chancery, where, before he entered upon business, in the presence of his Royal Highness the Duke of Clarence, and several other peers, he took the oaths of allegiance and supremacy, and the oath of Chancellor, the same being administered by the Deputy Clerk of the Crown, his Honor, the Master of the Rolls, holding the book, and three other Masters being present; which being done, the Attorney General moved that it might be recorded. Then his Royal Highness and the other Lords departed, leaving the Lord Chancellor in Court."—*Min. Book*, No. 2. fol. 80.

[1] The proper pendant to this sarcasm is the advice given to send a dog that could not be confined at home, and went astray doing mischief, into the Court of Chancery, "for no living thing once there can ever get out again."

[2] This was in the time of the "Septuagint," or Seventy Commissioners, who were all removable at pleasure. I was then a student of law, and having had a promise of a commissionership from the new Chancellor, in respect of his friendship for my father, felt disappointed, like other expectants, that there was not a "*scratch*"—or turning out of those who were wealthy and inefficient.

combination of independence and deference, he had been a model of what is due to the Court from an advocate, he now, by his uniform patience, impartiality, firmness, and politeness, showed what is due from a Judge to the Bar. As to higher qualifications, he was not only above all suspicion of corruption, but most devotedly anxious that full justice should be done to all the suitors who came before him; and while he sat in court, notwithstanding his love of desultory amusement, he rigidly confined his attention to the business in hand, however irksome it might be, and however dull and boring the counsel who treated it. There lie before me many quarto volumes of notes which he took during his short tenure of office, proving that he had assiduously listened to, and labored to understand, all who addressed him,—there being as large a space allotted to the plodding draughtsmen as to Romilly and Perceval. I expected to extract some amusement from the mass; but, to my disappointment and his credit, I can not discover a single humorous sally in the whole series of his note-taking labors. When a sixth counsel was creeping over the oft-trodden ground, still he had not relieved the tedium he must have felt by penning an epigram, or drawing a caricature, in the margin of his note-book.

Further, he was not only very quick, but very cautious; and he had the discretion, on most occasions, to say little, notwithstanding his general love of talking—recollecting, that although his judgment might be right, there was serious danger of his reasons being wrong.

But here my commendation of him as a Judge must cease. Well aware of his own deficiency in the professional knowledge requisite for the satisfactory discharge of his duty, he took no pains to supply it; and the examples of Lord Nottingham and Lord Hardwicke, who, though far better prepared, had entered on a laborious course of study when they received the Great Seal, were unknown to him, or neglected by him. Being entirely unacquainted with the law of real property, which is so peculiarly essential in a Court of Equity, he did purchase a copy of the most popular Digest upon this subject; and being caught with a volume of it under his arm, he said "he was taking a little from his *Cruise* daily, without any prospect of coming to the end of it." But I can not find that he made any systematic or vigorous effort to initiate himself in the doctrines of equity; and, on the contrary, I have been told that, finding he got on more smoothly in the Court of Chancery than he expected, he undervalued the difficulties of his situation, and was not much dissatisfied with his own qualifications and his own performances. Gratifying Hargrave with a silk gown, he got this deep though dull lawyer to work out the authorities for him; and, with such assistance, he thought himself equal to most of his predecessors.

He had to boast that "there was only one of his decrees appealed against, and this was affirmed." From the peculiar nature of the jurisdiction of the Court of Chancery, however, the test of appeals and reversals very inadequately tries the merits of a Chancellor. A court of appeal is very reluctant to take a different view of facts from the judge below; and in the course of an equity suit, there is often a difficulty in raising a question of law so distinctly as that it may be submitted to a superior tribunal. However erroneous the vulgar notion that an Equity judge may do what he likes according to his own notions of natural justice, there is often much left to his discretion, and his decree is not to be altered unless it be erroneous. Had Lord Erskine presided only the same length of time in the Court of King's Bench as in the Court of Chancery, although he certainly would have done his work infinitely better, there probably would have been many writs of error from his judgments, and some of them would have been reversed.

The decisions "Tempore Erskine" are to be found in the 12th and 13th volumes of the Reports of Vesey, Junior. I believe that but little bad doctrine is to be found in them; yet although they are not to be "*tabooed*," or denominated the "APOCRYPHA," as some coxcombical Equity practitioners have proposed, it must be admitted that, generally speaking, there is a striking tenuity about them; that if they do not do injustice to the parties, they lay down few useful rules; and that, if they do not disturb, they do little to advance, our equitable code. In the whole series of them I do not think that there is once any allusion to the civil law or foreign jurists; and the illustrations are drawn from NISI PRIUS more frequently than from the general principles established by the successive occupiers of the "MARBLE CHAIR." Luckily for the public, the office of Master of the Rolls was at this time held by Sir William Grant, who comes up to the highest notion that can be formed of judicial excellence.

I will try to select a few of Lord Erskine's decisions which are most likely to interest the general reader.

In *Matthewson* v. *Stockdale*,[1] the question arose, whether there was a copyright in a compilation entitled "East India Calendar or Directory," objection being made that it afforded no scope for a display of literary merit, and that the same materials were open to all mankind :—

Lord Chancellor: "In the case of Dr. Trusler's Chronology, all the remarkable events, the accounts of eminent persons, every matter of curiosity and interest, were subjects of information past and gone by,—which could not be altered. All human events are equally open to all who wish to write an original work. No man can monopolize such a subject. Therefore Dr. Trusler would have had no right to complain of another who employed his mind in a new compilation, endeavoring to make additions and improvements. But it was stated by the Court, that if the defendant's work was a copy from the other, with alterations merely colorable, Dr. Trusler was entitled to a verdict; and finally he obtained a decision in his favor. Then came the case of a map of St. Domingo, attached to the work of the late Mr. Bryan Edwards. The defendant said, ' How can there be copyright in a map of the Island of St. Domingo? Must not the mountains have the same position—the rivers the same course? Must not the points of land—the coast connecting them—the names of places—everything constituting a map, be the same in every map which is accurate?' The answer was, that the subject of the plaintiff's claim was a map made at a great expense, from actual surveys—distinguished from former maps by improvements which were manifest; while the defendant' map was a servile imitation of it, requiring no ingenuity or expense beyond engraving on a plate of copper a copy of the original.—When I was at the Bar, I unsuccessfully resisted an action for pirating a chart of the English Channel—urging that the latitude and longitude of the several

[1] 12 Ves. 270.

points on the adjoining shore, and the soundings, must be in all charts as they are fixed by nature. So Cary, the author of the 'Road Book,' succeeded against Patterson's imitation of it, which was shown to have extended to its blunders,—the beautiful place in the Isle of Wight called *the Priory* being stated by the defendant, as well as by the plaintiff, to belong to Mr. Justice GRO, instead of Mr. Justice GROSE. There is no copyright in the title of 'East India Calendar;' but if a man, by considerable expense and labor, has procured all the names and appointments on the Indian Establishment, he has a copyright in that individual work. I have compared these books, and find that, in a long list of casualties, removals, and appointments, there is not the least variation even as to situation in the page. Upon such evidence, in a court of law, there would hardly be anything to try; and though I do not approve extending copyright too far, I am bound, under these circumstances, to continue the injunction to the hearing."

In *Sanders* v. *Pope*, he granted relief against the forfeiture of a lease for breach of a covenant to lay out a specific sum in repairs in a given time, where compensation can be made to the landlord :—

" There is no branch of the jurisdiction of this Court more delicate," said he, " than that which goes to restrain the exercise of a legal right. That jurisdiction rests only upon this principle,—that one party is taking advantage of a forfeiture; and as a rigid exercise of the legal right would produce a hardship, while the other party may have the full benefit of the contract as originally framed, the Court will interfere. In the common case of a covenant in a lease to pay rent—with a clause of forfeiture for non-payment, equity is in the constant course of relieving the tenant, the rent and all expenses being paid, although the failure to pay at the day did not arise from accident or disease. I think the case rests on the same principle, for the landlord may be placed in the same situation as if the covenant had been strictly performed."[1]

In *White* v. *Wilson*, he laid down the law very distinctly upon the delicate and difficult subject of incapacity to make a will by reason of insanity. An issue having been

[1] 12 Ves. 289. This judgment, however, has been much questioned. See 10 Ves. 70; 12 Ibid. 334.

directed to try the validity of the will of Lord Chedworth, it appeared that for many years he had acted as Chairman of Quarter Sessions, and had attended and voted in the House of Lords—although there were some suspicions as to his sanity, from the eccentricity of his manner and singularity of his dress. The jury found for the will; but a motion was made for a new trial upon an affidavit of Dr. Parr, expressing his opinion that the testator had never been of perfectly sound mind. On the other side, several letters from Dr. Parr to the testator were produced, consulting his Lordship on subjects of literature, expressing in strong terms an opinion of his taste and talents, and, in one instance, recommending a clergyman for a living in his Lordship's gift:—

The Lord Chancellor: "The rule upon this subject I take to be, that where the party has been subject to a commission, or to any restraint permitted by law, even a domestic restraint, clearly and plainly imposed upon him in consequence of undisputed insanity, the proof is thrown upon the side which maintains his sanity. On the other hand, where insanity has not been imputed by relations or friends, or even by common fame, the proof of insanity is thrown upon the other side—and it is not to be made out by rambling through the whole life of the party, but must be applied to the particular date of the transaction. A deviation from that rule will produce great uncertainty. In such a case as this, therefore, it must be shown that a man exercising all these great public duties, which it was proved this testator did exercise, had nevertheless a morbid image in his mind upon a particular subject, wide from sound understanding and clear reason. In my experience I know only one instance of a verdict of lunacy under such circumstances—that of Mr. Greenwood, who was bred to the bar, and, like Lord Chedworth, acted as chairman at the Quarter Sessions, but becoming diseased, and receiving in a fever a draught from the hand of his brother, the delirium connected itself with that idea, and he considered his brother as having given him a potion with a view to destroy him. He recovered in all other respects; but that morbid image never departed, and that idea appeared connected with the will by which he disinherited his brother, Nevertheless, it was considered so necessary to have some precise rule, that though a verdict had been obtained in the Court of Common Pleas against the will, the Judge strongly advised the jury to find the other way, and they did accordingly find in favor of the will. Further proceedings took place afterwards, and concluded in a compromise. But is this case of that sort? Is there any evidence of a morbid image in the mind of this testator, connected with his will, or at any other period? Dr. Parr, when he speaks of specific facts, is obliged to go back to the time when they were boys together at Harrow, and appears afterwards to have had a high opinion of his discrimination and good sense." *A new trial was refused.*[1]

In the case of *Ex parte Cranmer*, he made several other striking observations on the law of lunacy, which he had much considered. Under a commission to inquire whether Henry Cranmer, Esq., was a lunatic? the jury found "that he is so far debilitated in his mind as to be incapable of the general management of his affairs," the fact being that his faculties were in a state of great decay from old age:—

Lord Chancellor: "There ought to be an Act of Parliament to authorize the Chancellor to deal with a case of this kind in a different fashion. Unless the party be expressly declared to be a lunatic, or of unsound mind, I have no jurisdiction; but I feel, as Lord Eldon seems to have felt, that persons who are above all others entitled to protection ought not to go unprotected. A man may have passed a useful and illustrious life, and, by the course of nature, his faculties may decay, so that he may not be fit either to govern himself or his affairs; it is unseemly that he should be put upon the footing of a lunatic, and that, in the ordinary course, a commission should issue against him, which in after times may affect the fortunes of his posterity. He ought to have the guardianship of the Court in his second infancy as he had in his first. If it falls to the King, by his prerogative, to take care of those who can not take care of themselves, and I have jurisdiction,—at all events there must be a congruity between the commission and the finding. The verdict must either be in the words of the commission, or in equipollent words. The jury can not find a special verdict referring the question to the

[1] 18 Ves. 98.

Court, and saying, 'Whether he be a lunatic or not we can not tell, but we refer it upon the evidence to the Court.' I have no authority to act upon his liberty or his property except under a legal verdict. I make no doubt that I have jurisdiction in a case like this, if the proceedings are regular. Lord Coke considers the word 'lunaticus' as by no means material, only classing it with '*amens*,' '*demens*,' &c., and there is no doubt that the moon has no influence over lunatics."[1] *The commission was quashed, with directions that another commission should issue.*[2]

Soon after, a case came before him which excited great public interest, and of which we have the following account from Sir Samuel Romilly; strongly characteristic both of the judge and the reporter:—

"A bill was filed some time ago by a lady of the name of Purcell against John M'Namara, to set aside several deeds conveying to him a moiety which she was entitled to of a very valuable estate in the island of Tortola, as having been obtained from her by advantage taken of her ignorance, and an abuse of the confidence she had reposed in him. The cause was heard by Lord Eldon when Chancellor, and he decreed that all the deeds should be delivered up by M'Namara to be canceled, and that he should pay the costs of the suit. As soon as the present Chancellor succeeded to the Great Seal, M'Namara petitioned to have the cause reheard. It seems that he had in early life been an acquaintance of the Chancellor's; and he had the folly to boast that he should certainly obtain a reversal of the decree, and to invite his friends to come and witness his triumph. The Chancellor, not choosing to trust himself with the sole decision of the cause, or thinking that there might be considerable difficulty in the case, desired the Master of the Rolls to assist him. During the first two or three days of the cause being reheard, the Chancellor, with great rashness, expressed a very strong opinion that the decree could not be supported. The Master of the Rolls, after his usual

---

[1] Vesey, Jr., represents this as *a point of law* decided by Lord Erskine; and puts in the margin of his report, "In cases of lunacy, the notion that the moon has an influence is erroneous." To complete the *ridicule* at which, were it not for his simplicity, one would suppose that he had maliciously aimed, he put in his index, "LUNATIC, see LORD CHANCELLOR."

[2] 12 Vesey, Jr., 445–457.

manner, remained perfectly silent. In truth, the Lord Chancellor did not, at the time he discovered his opinion, at all understand the cause, nor had he then heard of some of the most important facts in it ; for M'Namara's counsel began, and, as might be supposed, did not open a very strong case against their own client. When he had heard the counsel for Miss Purcell, and talked with the Master of the Rolls upon the case, he became sensible that it was impossible to reverse or even to alter the decree. In truth it was a very gross case, in which M'Namara, under pretense of rendering service to the plaintiff, her brother and her sister, had obtained from them a conveyance of everything they were possessed of, and had reduced them to subsist upon small annuities received from himself, and for which he compelled the plaintiff to sign receipts, acknowledging that she had no right to her annuity, but owed it to his generosity and charity. The decree was affirmed."[1]

Lord Chancellor Erskine's judgment is not given by Vesey, but there is a copy of it extant, which shows that he at last was complete master of the case, and that he was very anxious to decide it justly. Thus he began :

" I had not, I believe, sat here quite a week, when a petition was presented to me to rehear this most important cause. And when I recollected that it had been heard at great length—that it had been pleaded by counsel of eminence who are not now at the Bar, having been since raised by his Majesty's favor to seats on the benches of justice—that the decree under review was pronounced by a noble and learned lord, who had spent the greatest part of his professional life in the practice of this Court, and presided in it for several years with so much reputation,—and when I considered the example of those who have adorned the place which I now fill, I thought it highly incumbent on me to pursue that course, of asking the assistance of his Honor the Master of the Rolls, to

[1] Life of Sir S. Romilly, ii. 166. During the argument at the Bar, Mr. M'Namara sent a challenge to Sir Samuel, who very properly declined it, for he had strictly confined himself within the discharge of his professional duty. " M'Namara," says Romilly, " who had been concerned in the course of his life in several duels, had vainly attempted during the hearing of the cause to intimidate Miss Purcell's counsel from doing their duty. Some years afterwards, having recovered from a very dangerous illness, he wrote a letter to a friend of mine, in which, after telling him how near dying he had been, he added, ' but I was prepared to meet the event *like a man of honor.*' "

which I am entitled by the jurisdiction and constitution of this Court on difficult and complicated points, in the same manner as, when any question of law mixes in the consideration of any subject before the Court, I am entitled to the assistance of the learned Judges. In the present case, I have another reason for pursuing this course. I have had occasion more than once to remark that, consistently with the habits of English life and manners, a Judge who is to administer justice can not be always a stranger to the contesting parties; and, whenever the decisions of the Courts of Common Law respect facts, this consideration renders the trial by jury of such inestimable value. Of the plaintiff in this cause I know nothing. From the evidence, she appears to be a woman friendless and unprotected. She was a total stranger to me till this cause presented itself in court. With the defendant, it is quite otherwise; I have known him all my life; I have a particular acquaintance with him, and certainly I have always had great good-will towards him; and therefore, though I have that confidence in myself which it may be indecent to express, and though my judgment was not likely to be surprised, yet, as it might have turned out that it might be my duty to reverse that decree,—not from anything personal to myself, but that the character of English justice might stand pure and unsuspected, I wished to be assisted, as I have been, and I return my thanks to the Master of the Rolls for the learned opinion which he has delivered. But, greatly as I am bound to respect his Honor, if I had not agreed with him, I should have paused, and taken time to consider; for the judgment must be mine, and I am responsible for the justice or injustice of it."

He then entered very elaborately into the evidence, and came to the clear conclusion that the deeds were fraudulent, and must be set aside. The following day there appeared in the newspapers a report of the case, furnished by M'Namara, misrepresenting the facts, the arguments of counsel, and the judgment of the Court—representing the suit to have originated in a shameful conspiracy between the plaintiff, her attorney, and a discarded steward of the defendant, to destroy his character.

"So scandalous an attempt on the part of M'Namara," wrote Sir Samuel Romilly in his Diary, "to impose on the public, to convert the proceedings of a court of justice into a vehicle of calumny, and to draw down the infamy which belonged to himself upon the heads of his victims, called for the severest animadversion ; and, as counsel for Miss Purcell, I moved the Court that M'Namara, and the person whom he had employed and paid to draw up the account, should be committed for a contempt of the Court. I represented to the Chancellor, in the strongest way that I could, the hard situation in which the suitors, witnesses, and solicitors in his court must be placed, if he could not protect them against such libels. I pressed him to consider how much the preservation of the liberty of the press depended upon not suffering such an abuse to pass unpunished. I represented to him how much the offense was aggravated by the condition of the parties, who did not now even pretend that the account published was meant to be accurate ; who attempted no apology, expressed no contrition, offered no atonement ; but, already anticipating, as it were, their triumph over the Court, contended that they had done no more than they had a right to do ; and pretty clearly intimated that they were ready to misrepresent the future proceedings of the Court, just as they had misrepresented the past. I called upon him to assert the honor of his situation ; and I ventured to tell him that, although he would probably be disposed to disregard an indignity offered to himself, he should consider how much others, how much all his Majesty's subjects, were interested in his maintaining the respect due to the high Court in which he presided. I added, that as there could be no doubt that his office had become more honorable and dignified in passing through the hands of the Somerses, the Talbots, the Hardwickes, the Camdens, and his other illustrious predecessors, so it would be transmitted by him undiminished in splendor and dignity to his successor. When I concluded, the Chancellor immediately delivered his opinion. The Court was extremely crowded, for a good deal of interest and curiosity had been excited to see how he would conduct himself. He said that there could not be any doubt of the authority of the Court to commit in such a case ; that the fact of M'Namara being the publisher was clearly established, and the article was a gross misstatement of the proceedings of the Court, and was manifestly printed for the purpose of exculpating the defendant in the public opinion, and of rendering odious his opponents. After dilating on these topics at considerable length, and raising an universal expectation of the only decision which it was supposed possible could follow such a speech, he added, that, 'though this was certainly a case in which the Court might commit the offenders as for a contempt, it still remained to be considered whether, in the exercise of the discretion which the Court must necessarily have in such a case, it ought to do so, and that, exercising that discretion, he would certainly *not* commit them.'"

Romilly goes on to state that a proposal being made that the papers should be laid before the Attorney General, with a view to a prosecution for a libel, Lord Erskine sent for Miss Purcell's solicitor, to discourage any such proceeding, and adds, "This conduct of the Chancellor to a person not well acquainted with his character, must seem incomprehensible; for myself I have no doubt that it has not proceeded from regard to M'Namara, but merely from the fear of losing or endangering that vulgar popularity which he values a great deal too highly." But he brings forward a serious charge of inconsistency against Lord Erskine:—" The Chancellor was so sensible of the loss of reputation which he has sustained by this, that about ten days after, upon a complaint against a man and his wife for a publication relative to the proceedings of the Court in a lunacy, he immediately committed them and their printer to the Fleet, although the case was much less flagrant than that of M'Namara."[1] This was *Exparte Jones*,[2] where, pending a petition to remove the committee of a lunatic, an application was made against the committee and his wife, and other persons, as the authors, printers, and publishers of a pamphlet on lunacy, with a dedication to the Lord Chancellor, reflecting on the conduct of the petitioners:—

Lord Chancellor: " As to remedy at law, the subject of this application is not the libel against the petitioners. Whatever may be said as to a constructive contempt through the medium of a libel against persons engaged in controversy in the Court, it never has been or can be denied that a publication, not only with an obvious tendency, but with the design to obstruct the ordinary course of

[1] Life of Romilly, ii. 172. [2] 13 Ves. 237.

justice, is a very high contempt. Lord Hardwicke considered persons concerned in the business of the Court as being under the protection of the Court. But, without considering whether this is or is not a libel upon the petitioners, what excuse can be alleged for the whole tenor of this book? Stripped of dedication, it could be published with no other intention than to obstruct the course of justice, and to bring into contempt the orders which the Court has made. But in the dedication the object is avowed to influence the decision of the Court in the particular case, to obtain a decision contrary to the established rules of the Court, and, by flattering the Judge, to taint the source of justice. Let the committee and his wife and the printer be committed to the Fleet prison."[1]

Notwithstanding the harsh observation of Romilly, I am not at all clear that the two decisions may not be reconciled, as the publication in the former case might be considered only a libel on individuals, and in the latter case it was a direct obstruction to the administration of justice.

There is at present a disposition to attempt to do away all distinction between the transfer of real and personal property, in forgetfulness of the essential difference between the two which ought ever to be had in remembrance. This is well expressed by Lord Chancellor Erskine in the case of *Hiern* v. *Mill*,[2] on the effect of notice of a prior incumbrance to a purchaser:—

"The law distinguishes between a real estate and a personal chattel. The latter is held by possession,—a real estate by title. Possession of a real estate is not even *primâ facie* evidence of title; it may be by lease or at will, or by sufferance; and real property can not answer the purposes of society, unless various interests may be carved out of it, which can only be evidenced by writing."[3]

The great boast of Lord Erskine's Chancellorship was his decision in *Thelluson* v. *Woodford*. The famous will of Peter Isaac Thelluson contained this clause:—" In

[1] 13 Ves. 240. [2] Ibid. 119.
[3] Possession never can be evidence of title to real estate; but I hope that, before long, no deeds affecting real estate will have any validity unless they be registered.

case I shall in my lifetime enter into any contracts for the purchase of any lands, and I shall happen to die before the necessary conveyances thereof are executed, I order and direct that all such contracts so entered into by me shall be completed and carried into execution by my said trustees after my death, and that the purchase-moneys shall be paid by them by, with, and out of my personal estate, and that the conveyances thereto shall be made to them, their heirs and assigns, and that they shall be seized and possessed of the premises so to be conveyed on the same trusts as are by this my will created concerning the estates directed to be purchased in manner aforesaid." The testator, after making his will, and within a month before his death, had contracted for the purchase of real estates to the amount of £30,000. These estates, as the law then stood, could not pass by the will, and vested in the heir at law; but the trustees contended that, according to the doctrine of "*election*," he must renounce all benefit under the will, or let the devise take effect:—

Lord Chancellor: "I give the judgment which I find myself bound to pronounce, with some reluctance,—considering this will as dictated by feelings not altogether consistent with convenience. But this appears to me to be a case of *election*. The jurisdiction exercised by this Court compelling election, may be thus described:—' A person shall not claim an interest under an instrument, without giving full effect to that instrument as far as he can.' If, therefore, a testator, intending to dispose of his property, and making all his arrangements, under the impression that he has the power to dispose of everything made the subject of his will, mixes in his disposition property that belongs to another person, or property as to which another person has a right to defeat his disposition, giving to that person an interest by his will,—that person shall not be permitted to defeat the disposition, and yet take under the will. The reason is, the implied condition that he shall not take both, and the consequence is, that there must be an *election;* for though the mistake of the testator can not affect the property of another, yet devisee shall not take the testator's property unless in the manner intended by the testator. But it is said that the testator here labored under a mistake, and *non constat* what he would have done had he been aware of the true state of the circumstances. The best answer to such reasoning was given by Lord Alvanley in the case of *Whistler* v. *Webster*,—that no man shall claim a benefit under a will unless he confirms as far as he is able, and gives effect to everything contained it, without reference to the consideration whether the testator had any knowledge of the extent of his power or not. Nothing can be more dangerous than to speculate on what he would have done if he had known one thing or another. It is enough to say that he has manifested the intention that the property over which he professes to exercise a testamentary power, should go in such a manner. Whether he thought he had the right, or, knowing the extent of his authority, intended to exceed it, is immaterial." After reviewing the prior decisions he said :—" It can not be argued that the rule does not reach an heir at law. Lord Hardwicke would not put the case of an heir at law by way of illustration, if the heir could not under any circumstances be put to election. Mr. Thelluson's heir takes these estates as if his father had not made a will; but my opinion is, that he can not also take what is given to him by the will. He must therefore *elect*." There was an appeal against this decree, but it was affirmed by the House of Lords.[1]

With questions of evidence our Chancellor was very familiar, and it was a great comfort to him when they came before him. In a pedigree cause a new trial was applied for on the ground, 1st, That hearsay evidence of a husband as to the legitimacy of his wife had been rejected because he was not her relation by blood; and 2ndly, That a forged register had been produced by the party who had gained the verdict :—

Lord Chancellor: " First. Consider whether the knowledge of the husband, as to the legitimacy of his wife, is not likely to be more intimate than that of any relation, however near in blood. He has every motive to inquire into the fact, with the means of ascertaining it. If she is entitled to any freehold estate of inheritance, he is tenant by the courtesy. So, as to personal estate, he is entitled to all that comes to her. The honor of the husband and the family are connected with her pedigree, and the subject must often be discussed between them. How much or how little weight the evidence ought to

[1] 1 Dow. 249.

have, will be the subject of consideration for the jury. Here we are to consider, whether it ought to be admitted or not; and upon that point I think there must be a new trial. Secondly. I likewise think, that there ought to have been a new trial on the ground of the forged register, although, giving faith to the rest of the evidence of the party who obtained the verdict, his case might be established without it. I do not say that the forgery was necessarily fatal—but sufficient weight was not given to it. Two conflicting decisions have occurred upon this subject in the House of Lords. In the *Douglas cause*, every branch of the written evidence that went to prove the descent of Lady Jane Douglas was known to be manufactured by Sir John Stewart, who, having neglected to secure evidence of birth, had recourse to those 'feigned letters,' as they were called, in support of his son's legitimacy, and that was considered, both by Lord Mansfield and Lord Camden, as not throwing any obstacle in the way. But, in the more recent case of *Lord Valentia*, although his father and mother, before and at the time of his birth, had lived together as man and wife, and his father had often declared that he was married to the mother, and that the claimant was the legitimate son of that marriage, a forged certificate of marriage having been given in evidence, Lord Mansfield said, 'Truth does not require the aid of forgery; if the marriage was real, they might have relied upon the evidence belonging to it;' and judgment was given against Lord Valentia.[1] These two cases stand in opposition to each other. A rule is not to be laid down either way, but every case must depend upon its own circumstances."[2]

I will mention only one other decision of Lord Erskine in the Court of Chancery, which he pronounced the day he gave up the Great Seal. The House of Lords, according to many precedents, having made an order, "That the Lord Chancellor should give orders for the printing and publishing the trial of Lord Melville, and the several questions put to the Judges, with their answers thereto, and that no other person should presume to print or publish the same," the Lord Chancellor appointed Mr. Gurney, the famous short-hand writer, who, with his

---

[1] However, he was held legitimate by the House of Lords in Ireland.
[2] See Vowles *v.* Young, 13 Ves. 140–148.

assistants, had taken down the whole in short-hand, and was preparing to publish it—when the defendant advertised another report of the same trial and proceedings; a bill was filed, and a motion made for an injunction:—

Lord Chancellor: " Notwithstanding the high authority of the House of Lords, the copyright existing by my order under the direction of the House, I should not have been justified in granting the injunction without hearing the defendant, and I feel so forcibly the arguments that have been pressed for him, that if the case of *Bathurst* v. *Kearsley* had not been produced, which can not be distinguished from this, I should not have been disposed to grant the injunction in the first instance, as it is not sufficient that privileges, however high, have been exercised, unless they have been judicially recognized. I shall therefore follow the example of Lord Eldon in the case of *Bruce* v. *Bruce,* upon a dispute between the King's printers in this country and in Scotland, great consideration being necessary to arrive at a right judgment between their contending patents. When I then pressed him with the argument, that injunctions proceeding upon legal rights ought to have their foundation in legal title, receiving consummation by legal judgment, he answered, that the same question had been decided by Sir Joseph Jekyll, and his decree affirmed by the Lord Chancellor, and that the Court granting the injunction till the hearing did not decide ultimately upon the rights of the parties. I feel so much the detriment to the defendant from an injunction upon a publication of this temporary nature, calculated merely for the gratification of present curiosity, that unless I had a strong impression that at the hearing I should continue of the same opinion, and decree a perpetual injunction, I should not grant the injunction now. The facts are all admitted, and the question rests on the mere right of the plaintiff to a monopoly of this subject. This case turns on the authority of the Lords to exercise the privilege of appointing a person with exclusive power to print and publish their proceedings. The privilege has been uniformly asserted by the Lords, and it is confirmed by Lord Hardwicke and Lord Northington. The case of *Bathurst* v. *Kearsley* had a favorable circumstance for the defendant, which the present wants. There, the

House of Lords had permitted the Duchess of Kingston to employ a person to take notes on her behalf; she delivered the notes to the counsel to be corrected, and afterwards sent them so corrected to the defendant, with directions to publish them for her protection. The present defendant does not claim under Lord Melville; but stands upon the liberty of every individual to publish an account of this trial. The trial of Dr. Sacheverell was published by the same authority which the plaintiff has obtained; and there are many other instances of which I have selected a few, not only on articles of impeachment by the House of Commons, but also in trials for felony and treason." He then went through Lord Winton's trial, Lord Oxford's, Lord Lovat's, Lord Ferrers's, the Duchess of Kingston's, and Mr. Hastings's. He added, " I do not proceed on anything like literary property, but upon this only, that the plaintiff is in the same situation as to this particular subject. At the hearing it is possible that a different view may be taken of the case. In *Miller* v. *Taylor* it appeared that the Crown had been in the constant course of granting the right of printing Almanacs; and at last King James II. granted that right to the Stationers' Company and the two Universities; for a century they kept up that monopoly by prosecutions; at length Carnan, an obstinate man, insisted on printing an almanac of his own. An injunction was applied for to the Court of Exchequer, and granted till the hearing; but at the hearing, that Court, sitting in equity, directed the question to be put to the Court of Common Pleas, whether the King had power to grant the exclusive right of printing and publishing Almanacs? After the case had been twice argued, the Court of Common Pleas returned for answer that the grant was void. The injunction was accordingly dissolved, and the House of Commons threw out a bill introduced for the purpose of continuing the monopoly."[1]

It is impossible, with any justice, to praise Erskine as a magistrate, while we view him presiding in the Court of Chancery; but, luckily for his judicial fame,—while he held the Great Seal, the impeachment of Lord Melville, which had been voted in the lifetime of Mr. Pitt, came to be tried before the House of Peers. Mr. Hastings's trial

[1] Gurney *v.* Longman, 13 Ves. 493–509.

had brought this mode of proceeding against state
offenders into much disrepute, and to Erskine belongs
the merit of proving that it may still be so conducted as
to prove an efficient safeguard of the Constitution. Instead of the House sitting to hear the case a few days in
a year, and when sitting being converted from a Court of
Justice into a theater for rhetorical display, he insisted
that it should sit, like every other criminal tribunal, *de
die in diem*, till the verdict was delivered; and he enforced, both upon the managers of the House of Commons, and on the counsel for the defendant, the wholesome rules of procedure established for the detection of
crime and the protection of innocence. During the fourteen days the trial lasted, his demeanor on the woolsack
excited universal admiration for dignity, for courtesy, for
impartiality, for firmness, and for discrimination. His
nisi prius experience was now of infinite service to him,
and he was able in few minutes satisfactorily to decide
questions of evidence which might have consumed whole
days in arguments and in references to the Judges, and in
processions from Westminster Hall to the Chamber of
Parliament, and from the Chamber of Parliament to
Westminster Hall. Entire deference was properly shown
to his opinion respecting the mode of examining the witnesses and the admissibility of written documents, and
without any intrusive interference, not unfrequently by a
question which he put, or a suggestion which he offered,
he materially assisted both the prosecution and the defense. As the evidence turned very much on matters of
account, it is difficult to convey any idea of the points
which were ruled; but as a specimen I will mention the
decision upon the question, whether the contents of a
book kept in an iron chest in the Pay Office could be read
against Lord Melville.—Mr. Whitbread, Sir S. Romilly,
and Sergeant Best contending for the Commons, that he
must be presumed to be cognizant of them, and his counsel, Mr. Plumer and Mr. Adam, insisting that, as the book
was not kept by him or under his authority, he could not
be affected by it:—

Lord Chancellor: "Unless any noble lord shall think
that this matter ought to be further considered in the
Chamber of Parliament, I will now state what I think of
it. I am of opinion that the entry proposed to be read

from this book ought not to be received. I am persuaded that the honorable managers offered it to the Court from a sense of duty and justice; and I am persuaded that every one of your Lordships feels, as I do, the greatest possible respect for their dignity and learning; but it is the office and duty of the House, as a Court of Justice, to pronounce upon the legality of the evidence which is offered to it; and I am anxious, in the few words I mean to deliver, to make it manifest that the House has administered, as it will always administer, consistent justice. The certificate of Mr. Andrew Douglas, as to the receipt of money at the Exchequer was received yesterday, because he was proved to have acted under a power of attorney from Lord Melville, and that certificate was shown to have been given in the universal and public course by which the receipt of such money was to be manifested. But this is a book which can not be received on any principle of justice. If it had been an official document to which Lord Melville had access, and which it was his duty to examine, he might have been presumed to be aware of its contents; but no such character has been imputed to it; or if he could have been proved to have referred to it, or to have adopted it, it would have been evidence against his Lordship, whether it be public or private; but the honorable managers did not profess to be possessed of any such proof—saying only that the noble lord had admitted a balance similar to that which the House would have found recorded in the book if it had been received."

The House unanimously concurred in this opinion, and without further discussion the book was rejected.

When Mr. Tierney, one of the managers for the Commons, was called as a witness, he claimed as a privilege to be examined from his place in the gallery set apart for the Commons' use. *Lord Chancellor:* " I think there ought to be no distinction between one witness and another, as to the place in which he is to be examined. It is the privilege of the Lords to say where a witness is to be placed upon his examination."—Mr. Tierney, counting, perhaps, on former intimacy and partisanship with the Chancellor, was beginning to remonstrate, when the Chancellor stopped him by saying very gravely, " I apprehend we can hear no further argument on this subject from a member of the House of Commons; ano if the gentleman is to be examined, he must stand in the proper place for witnesses."—Mr. Tierney was obliged to descend to the witness-box, and being asked by Mr. Whitbread whether he had been at any time Treasurer of the Navy? thus vented his spleen: "My Lords, before I answer that question, I presume I may be permitted to clear myself from what may otherwise apppear to be a want of respect to your Lordships. There was nothing more remote from my intention than to show anything inconsistent with the most complete deference to the order and proceeding of this Court; neither have I any personal motive for presuming to protest as to the place in which I am examined. I felt that the courtesy of every Court in the kingdom would have allowed me to be examined in any place in which I might be sitting when called as a witness; and being in the gallery, as one of the Commons, not an indifferent spectator, but as member of a committee of the whole House, to make good the charge against Lord Melville, I did feel that I should be wanting in the respect which is due to them, did I not endeavor to maintain my right and privilege, of being examined in my place, in which, as one of the representatives of the people, I attended. Having protested against the place in which I now stand, I will proceed to answer the questions of the honorable manager."[1]

In strong contrast to the rudeness and unfairness I have witnessed in Judges refusing, at a late hour of the night, the reasonable request of counsel for an adjournment before entering on the defense of their clients, Lord Chancellor Erskine, while the day was not yet far spent, when he saw that Mr. Plumer appeared fatigued from the effort of having spoken some hours for Lord Melville, thus spontaneously addressed the weary advocate:—"If you seek for a resting-place, in a cause so complicated and extensive as this, you may freely choose it for yourself. This Court, which ought to be an example to all other Courts, will ever hold in the highest reverence the indulgent character of British justice. I am persuaded, without calling for the formal consent of their Lordships, that if you find it more consistent with the duty which you owe to your client, or more comfortable to yourself, you may rest

[1] Hatsell's Precedents, iv. 288.

here, and proceed to-morrow morning in your defense." The indulgence was gratefully accepted.

On the other hand, the Chancellor husbanded the time of the Court by stopping, with some severity of observation, all frivolous inquiries and discussions. Thus the managers, after showing that a document, which they wished to give in evidence, had been admitted to be genuine by Lord Melville, having tried to give it validity by proving that it had been treated as genuine by the Lords of the Treasury, he exclaimed—"Lord Melville having recognized the document, it is already admissible in evidence; but the opinion of the Lords of the Treasury upon it is of no more consequence than the color of their clothes."[1]

When the verdict was to be given, the Chancellor merely said, " My Lords, your Lordships having fully heard and considered the evidence and the arguments in this case, have agreed upon several questions which are severally to be put to your Lordships, and the first question is this: Is Henry, Viscount Melville, guilty of the high crimes and misdemeanors charged upon him in the first article of the impeachment, or not guilty? John, Lord Crewe, what says your Lordship on this first article?"— He afterwards put the like question to all the peers present, on each of the ten articles. He himself voted last,—saying, " NOT GUILTY," to the 1st, 4th, 5th, 8th, 9th, and 10th; and "GUILTY," to the 2nd, 3rd, 6th, and 7th articles. But on summing up the votes, there was a majority in favor of the defendant on all; and the Chancellor thus spoke:—" My Lords, a majority of the Lords have acquitted Henry, Viscount Melville, of the high crimes and misdemeanors charged upon him by the impeachment of the Commons, and of all things contained therein. Henry, Viscount Melville, I am to acquaint your Lordship, that you are acquitted of the articles of impeachment exhibited against you by the Commons for

[1] The last day Lord Tenterden ever sat in Court (which was on the trial of the magistrates of Bristol), wishing to rebuke a counsel who was wasting time by irrelevant questions respecting a journey performed by the mayor in a post-chaise and four,—he observed with much solemnity, " Sir, you have forgot to ask him the color of the jackets of the postilions." He was taken dangerously ill the same night; and having in his delirium still dreamed of the trial, he expired with these words on his lips: "Gentlemen of the jury you will now consider of your verdict."

high crimes and misdemeanors, and of all things contained
therein."—Lord Melville, in recognition of the fairness of
his trial, made a low bow to the Chancellor, and withdrew.[1]

To finish what I have to say of Lord Erskine as a
Judge, I have only to advert to the appeal business in the
House of Lords while he presided there. Having the assistance of Lord Eldon and Lord Redesdale, to whom he
generally deferred, he disposed of it satisfactorily,—with
one exception, which I mention with pain, because it
threw some suspicion upon the impartial administration
of justice in the court of last resort. A daughter of Lord
Hugh Seymour, being left an orphan by the death of both
her parents soon after her birth, remained under the care
of Mrs. Fitzherbert till she was between five and six
years old, when her family required her to return to
them, and filed a bill in the Court of Chancery to have
guardians appointed to her. The Master to whom the
matter was referred approved of Lord Euston and Lord
Henry Seymour as guardians, and from his decision Mrs.
Fitzherbert, who was much attached to the child, appealed to Lord Chancellor Eldon, who, after a long hearing and with less than his usual hesitation, confirmed the
Master's report. "While the cause was depending, the
Prince of Wales, who lived in Mrs. Fitzherbert's house as
his own, was extremely anxious about the event of it.
He loved the child with paternal affection, and the idea
of having her torn from him seemed to be as painful to
him as it was to Mrs. Fitzherbert." An appeal being
brought to the House of Lords against Lord Eldon's
order, His Royal Highness made his wishes on the subject generally known, and actively canvassed Peers to attend and vote for a reversal. The hearing of the appeal
excited more interest than any judicial proceeding in the
House since the Douglas cause. All notion of Mrs. Fitzherbert being appointed guardian was abandoned, but the
effort was to have the Marquis and Marchioness of Hertford appointed, there being an understanding with them
that they would not remove the child from Mrs. Fitzherbert. Lord Eldon having stated the reasons for his decree, to which he adhered, left the House. Lord Chancellor Erskine moved a reversal of the decree, and that

[1] 29 St. Tr. 549-1482

the Marquis and Marchioness of Hertford should be appointed guardians, on the ground that the Marquis was nearest in blood to the infant. Sir Samuel Romilly, who was counsel for the appellant, says, "Several Peers voted against this, but there was no division. I counted between eighty and ninety Peers who were present: the Prince, who was as anxious that Mrs. Fitzherbert should continue to have the care of the child as he could have been if the child had been his own, and who knew that Lord and Lady Hertford would not remove her, had earnestly entreated all his friends to attend. I had, on the Prince's account, done everything that depended on me to prevent this; and which was only to represent to Colonel M'Mahon what I thought of such a proceeding. The question was certainly one which involved no legal consideration whatever, and which every Peer was as competent to decide as a lawyer could be, but yet to canvass votes for a judicial decision, is that which can not be too strongly reprobated." [1]

CHAPTER CLXXXV.

CONTINUATION OF THE LIFE OF LORD ERSKINE TILL HE RESIGNED THE GREAT SEAL.

WE must now regard Erskine in his political capacity while he was a member of the Fox and Grenville Government. He does not seem to have had any great weight either in Parliament or in the Cabinet. He rather shocked the Peers by the egotism of his maiden speech among them, which was upon the bill to indemnify witnesses who were to be examined on the trial of Lord Melville:—

" I feel it my duty, my Lords," said he, " to communicate my sentiments on a subject of so much consequence to proceedings in Courts of Law. I have been seven-and-twenty years engaged in the duties of a laborious profession, and while I have been so employed I have had the opportunity of a more extensive experience in the Courts than any other individual of this generation. In

[1] Life of Romilly, ii. 146

the profession there have been and there now are men of much more learning and ability than I pretend to, but it is very singular that in these twenty-seven years I have not for a single day been prevented from attending in the Courts by any indisposition or corporal infirmity.' Within much the greater part of this period I was honored with a patent of precedency, and have been engaged in every important cause in the Court of King's Bench. Your Lordships would have no concern with the history of my political life were it not connected with the present inquiry; but when I declare that I have never known an objection taken to an interrogatory, 'that the answer might subject the witness to a civil suit,' it is material for your Lordships to know that my experience is not only equal to that of any individual Judge, but of all the Judges collectively. A decision of Lord Kenyon to the contrary has been cited; but the report must be wrong, for I was counsel in the cause, and I have no recollection of such a point having been mooted, and the opinion imputed to Lord Kenyon is different from what I have often heard him express. I must, therefore, oppose this bill, and recommend that our legislation on the occasion be confined to an act *declaring* the existing law; and that, I think, will be sufficient to obviate the danger of witnesses refusing to be examined because their answers may affect their civil rights, and if no other Lord more competent will undertake the task, I will myself bring forward a measure which will place the question forever in repose."

He accordingly introduced a declaratory act to that effect, which passed both Houses, and received the royal assent.

The first hostile discussion which took place in the House of Lords after the formation of the new Government was upon the appointment of Lord Ellenborough, Chief Justice of the King's Bench, to a seat in the Cabinet. Lord Eldon and other Peers having strongly condemned it on the ground that the Cabinet Minister might have, as a Judge, to try the prosecution, for treason or sedition, which he had recommended, and on the event of which the stability of the Government might depend, the Chancellor left the Woolsack to plead for it, but was not very successful. After a labored panegyric upon the learning and talents of Lord Ellenborough, he contended that the King was entitled to the assistance in council of all his subjects, and that no office, civil or military, lay or ecclesiastical, was a disqualification to a subject performing the duties of a Privy Councillor. He denied that the summoning of the Chief Justice of the King's Bench to the Committee of the Privy Council, commonly called the CABINET, was either illegal or unconstitutional:—

"*The Cabinet*," said he, "is a word never mentioned in any Act of Parliament, or in any parliamentary proceeding, and is wholly unknown to the law and the constitution. The King has his Great Council, consisting of the two Houses of the Legislature, and his Privy Council, consisting of such individuals as he chooses to swear to give him faithful advice on affairs of state. He seldom summons all these in a body into his presence, referring particular subjects to particular members of the Privy Council, who are responsible respectively for the advice which they give to him. No one denies that a Judge may properly be sworn of the Privy Council, and since the Revolution the chiefs of the Courts in Westminster Hall have generally had this honor conferred upon them. But it would be an unqualified interference with the King's prerogative to tell him that he shall not ask advice of a Privy Councillor. It has not been usual for the Chief Justice of the King's Bench to be summoned to the Committee of the Privy Council, called the Cabinet; but that venerable magistrate Lord Mansfield was constantly so summoned, during several administrations, without any complaint or suspicion that thereby the law or the constitution had been violated. There have been repeatedly Lords Justices named to exercise the functions of the Executive Government in the absence of the Sovereign, and the Lord Chief Justice of the King's Bench for the time being has generally been one of them, without any suspicion being cast upon his judicial purity. As to prosecutions for treason, Judges, members of the Privy Council, have often attended when persons arrested on charges of treason have been examined, and I believe that prosecutions for libel are left to the Attorney General and the Home Secretary. Notwithstanding the elevated situation which I occupy in this House, by the pleasure of my Sovereign, I will never

forget my duty to the people, whose partiality I have so
long enjoyed. I will ever bear in mind the active and
successful part which I have taken to support TRIAL BY
JURY; and if I saw any danger to public liberty in the appointment of Lord Ellenborough to a seat in the Cabinet,
I should have been the first to oppose it; but taking a
totally different view of the subject, I shall be glad, sitting by the side of my noble and learned friend, to consult, in conjunction with him, for the public welfare."

The resolution of censure was negatived without a
division,[1] but the appointment was condemned by the
public voice, and justly brought a great slur upon "ALL
THE TALENTS." To urge that the "Cabinet is not known
to the law" is a mere quibble.[2] By our constitution in
practice, it is a defined and acknowledged body for carrying on the executive government of the country, and the
question can not be evaded, whether a judge employed in
administering the criminal law may constitutionally belong to it? I without hesitation answer in the negative.
The duties of Criminal Judge and Member of the Cabinet
are incompatible. I can say from my own experience
under Lord Grey's administration, which may now be referred to as matter of history, that the policy of instituting prosecutions both for treason and seditious libels
does and must come under the consideration of the Cabinet. Suppose that the Chief Justice of the King's Bench,
being a member of the Cabinet, absents himself from
such discussions, how are the public to know that he was
absent when he comes to preside at the trials ordered by
his colleagues?—and if he were to proclaim the fact, how
can he, without suspicion, give an opinion upon the seditious tendency of a publication which contains much
abuse of the public measures to which he is a party? The
evil does not cease with the Government to which he belonged, for when that is dissolved and his political rivals
are in power,—being stamped with the character of a

[1] Parl. Deb., vols. vi. vii.
[2] It might be very convenient for a Prime Minister, upon a requisition by
some aspiring subordinate to be introduced into the Cabinet, to be able to
say to him,—" My dear friend, the Constitution knows nothing of the CABINET: you are already a 'Privy Councillor,' and, in point of law, all Privy
Councillors are equal. I am glad that I have not to refuse a request of
yours: do not let me hear another word about the Cabinet; you and I have
an equal right to be consulted by the Sovereign, when the advice of either of
us is wanted."

partisan, he is in danger of being suspected of a wish to thwart their prosecutions, and thereby to hasten their fall.¹—I do not think there is now much danger of the precedent being followed.²

On the next question which arose in the House of Lords I must likewise use the freedom of dissenting from Lord Chancellor Erskine. He moved a resolution that, pending Lord Melville's trial on the impeachment by the Commons, no part of the proceedings should be published; and even after the hearing of the case was over, he supported a further resolution, that the prohibition should be continued "until after the House shall have delivered its final judgment upon the said impeachment,"—with much *palaver* about the dignity of the House and the danger to the administration of justice from partial reports.³ But the House of Lords during an impeachment is a court of justice sitting *foribus apertis*,—that is, the public being admitted as far as there is accommodation for them,—and an accurate report of the proceedings is merely an enlargement of the Court, admitting all to be virtually present who choose to read a newspaper. Where there is a trial lasting many days, it is utterly impossible that by any other means than a daily publication, the bulk of the community can ever be made acquainted with the merits of the case. It is absurd to suppose that judges or jurymen can be biased by an accurate report of what they have heard, and improper comments upon the merits are likely to be more mischievous if not corrected

¹ When Mr. Perry, the proprietor of the "Morning Chronicle," was tried in the year 1810, for a libel on George III., and was acquitted under the direction of Lord Ellenborough, I happened to be sitting, along with several other juniors, immediately behind Sir Vicary Gibbs, the Attorney General, who turned round to us and said in a loud whisper, "We shall never again get a verdict for the Crown while the Chief Justice is in opposition." Yet the acquittal was allowed by all impartial persons to be highly proper,—the alleged libel merely alluding, not disrespectfully, to the prejudices of the reigning Sovereign against his Roman Catholic subjects. Gibbs had a spite against Ellenborough, who said of him that " his nose would take ink stains out linen."—*Sir Vicary* went generally by the soubriquet of SIR VINEGAR ; and one fine summer's day, looking more than usually *acetous*, the phenomenon was thus accounted for:

" The Sun's bless'd beam turns VINEGAR more sour."

² This was written in 1847, when I was myself a member of the Cabinet, holding the office of Chancellor of the Duchy of Lancaster. Being made Chief Justice of England in 1850, I of course attended the Cabinet no more. —*Note to 4th Edition, 1857.*

³ 6 Parl. Deb. 928 ; vii. 250.

by a full statement of what has actually passed. The House was obeyed in this instance, but such an injunction was not issued on the trial of Queen Caroline, and would not now be endured.

On the motion for the removal, by an address to the throne, of the Irish Judge Fox, accused of misconduct in his office, the Chancellor made a very characteristic speech:—

"My noble and learned friend who spoke last, alluded to the motto which I have selected, which ornaments the panel of the carriage at your Lordships' door, and which is to be borne, with the insignia of the Erskine family, through all future generations. For 'TRIAL BY JURY' I have fought in the hottest times, and shall ever fight; but I do not imply anything in favor of the Jury separate from the Judge who presides at the trial; it is the trial of Judge and Jury which attracts my respect and admiration, and I do not stand up for the Jury more than for the Judge. Let us proceed against Mr. Justice Fox constitutionally. I have been no flatterer of Judges. Did ever any man go further to remind Judges of their duties to the country? For my boldness I have received public rebukes, which I have returned I trust with honest indignation. It is my pride that I was honored with a gown of precedence, which permitted me to be counsel against the Crown, and the recollection of what I did on these occasions for my country constitutes no inconsiderable portion of the happiness of my life. Feeling as I do, I join with peculiar fervor in the wish of my noble and learned friend, that Judges may not be placed above the law, and permitted to trample on the rights of the subject. The true question is, what is the proper mode of investigation to be adopted in this case? Witnesses have been examined at your bar, but in the absence of the accused; and though your Lordships are exalted, enlightened, and learned, you are still men, and subject to all the infirmities of human nature. The witnesses have said, that this learned Judge condescended to bully the jury—but what a spectacle has this House exhibited! While we are arraigning the Judge, what are we doing ourselves? Have you not, behind his back, been haranguing one another? —inflaming one another? Must not all justice perish if such proceedings are sanctioned? Suppose when you

ask the Commons to concur in your address they were to
to say 'We choose to proceed by impeachment,' in what
a situation would you be, having already prejudged the
man whom you would be called upon to try? Your
Lordships would do better by referring the case to the
ordinary tribunals, and letting the guilt or innocence of
the learned Judge be decided by a jury upon a *scire facias*
to repeal the patent by which he holds his office. At all
events, let not your Lordships prejudge a cause which
you may probably be called upon judicially to determine."[1]

The bill for the immediate abolition of the Slave Trade
—the great glory of the Fox and Grenville administration, was supported by their Chancellor, who took occasion to announce his change of opinion upon this subject.
"I was in the West Indies," said he, "some years ago in
the service of my country, and the condition of the slaves
there seemed to me to be comfortable; they were generally treated in the kind manner used by great families in
England to their ancient domestics. Believing them to
be happy and contented, I could not be hostile to a system which produced such results. I have since had
reason to think that I was deceived by outward appearances, and that, without evil, man can never be the property of man. The horrors of a Guinea ship have been
lately disclosed to me in the course of my profession.
During the trial of a policy of insurance on a cargo of
slaves it appeared, that having risen on the crew in hopes
of liberty, and being fired upon,—some of them were
mortally wounded, some voluntarily jumped overboard a
prey to the sharks,—while others, who remained on
board, died, from refusing to take food,—and a British
jury was called upon to say, for which of these classes the
underwriters were to make compensation to the slave
dealers? This country is the morning star which has enlightened Europe, and let us now set an example of humanity and justice which may be followed by all the
nations of the earth."[2] He had the satisfaction, as First
Lord Commissioner, to announce the royal assent to this
bill.

When the session closed he delivered the royal speech,
and was observed, in accordance with the opinions he had

[1] 7 Parl. Deb. 76   [2] Ibid. 807.

so often expressed since the commencement of the war, to read with peculiar emphasis the sentence announcing that " His Majesty being always anxious for the restoration of peace on just and honorable terms, was engaged in discussion with a view to the accomplishment of this most desirable end."[1] But these hopes proved delusive; through the ambition and obstinacy of Napoleon, hostilities continued to rage in Europe for many years,—till the hour appointed for his overthrow at last arrived.

During the recess, all the friends of civil and religious liberty were deeply afflicted by the death of Mr. Fox, at a time when his countrymen, having renounced the prejudices they had long fostered against him, were eager to avail themselves of his services in negotiating a peace or in conducting the war,—which all agreed had been hitherto sadly mismanaged. Erskine felt the blow with peculiar severity, for he had not only, since his first entrance into public life, looked up to this great patriot and most amiable man as his political chief, but he had cherished for him an uninterrupted and ardent private friendship. On the melancholy day when the mortal remains of Charles James Fox were deposited in Westminster Abbey, near those of his illustrious rival William Pitt,—their deaths being divided only by a few short months,— Erskine was one of the pall-bearers, and could ill conceal his agitation as the coffin was lowered into the grave, and the awful words were pronounced. " Earth to earth—ashes to ashes—dust to dust."[2]

He continued to hold the Great Seal, but he was not much consulted about the measures of the Government. From the meeting of the new Parliament in December till the Ministerial crisis in March following, he did not

[1] 7 Parl. Deb. 1262.
[2] " Most of the persons present seemed as if they had lost a most intimate and a most affectionate friend."—*Romilly's Diary.* Even a bitter political opponent soon after sang—
" For talents mourn untimely lost,
When best employ'd and wanted most ;
Mourn genius high and lore profound,
And wit that lov'd to play, not wound ;
And all the reasoning powers divine
To penetrate, resolve, combine ;
And feelings keen, and fancy's glow,—
They sleep with him who sleeps below."
Introduction to the First Canto of "*Marmion.*"

speak in the House of Lords, except on occasions of form and ceremony. Lord Grenville himself proposed and carried through the bill for introducing into Scotland jury trial in civil cases; and bills brought up from the other House by Romilly to subject real estates to simple contract debts, and for other law reforms, remained unnoticed.

From the beginning of March nothing was talked of or thought of but the bill moved by Lord Howick; now the leader of the House of Commons, for allowing Roman Catholic officers in England to hold commissions in the army in the same manner as since the year 1793 they had been permitted to do in Ireland. This bill was not mentioned to Lord Erskine till it was about to be brought in; and then, strange to say! he disapproved of it, although he did not think it of sufficient consequence to require his resignation. He concurred in the propriety of withdrawing it when it was found so obnoxious to the King; but he strenuously supported Lords Grenville and Howick in their resisting the unconstitutional requisition by the King, that they should give him a written promise, signed with their names, never again to propose any measure for further relaxing the penal laws against the Roman Catholics.

His Majesty not yielding to the representations made to him on the impropriety of his demand, Lord Erskine, as the Keeper of his Conscience,—in a long interview with him,—attempted to bring him to reason. Of this we have the following amusing narrative in the Diary of Sir Samuel Romilly:—

"*March* 19th.—The Chancellor gave Pigot and me a long account of a very serious conversation he had yesterday with the King; I should rather say, of a long speech he made to the King. When he went in to his Majesty, and had told him that the Recorder's report was to be made, he says that, though it is contrary to all court *etiquette* to speak on any subject which the King has not first mentioned, he proceeded somewhat to this effect. He said he was about to do what he believed was very much out of order; but he hoped that his Majesty would excuse it in consideration of the very extraordinary conjuncture in which the country was placed; that he was sensible, when he first entered into his Majesty's service, his Majesty had entertained a prejudice against him ; that he was quite satisfied that this prejudice was now entirely removed ; and that his Majesty did him the justice to believe that he had served him faithfully; that upon the measure which had been the original occasion of the present state of things (meaning the Catholic Bill, as it has been not very properly called) he thought, both religiously and morally, exactly as his Majesty himself did ; that, however, after what had passed, it appeared to him that the Ministers who had signed the minute of council could not possibly, with any consistency of character, retract it ; and that to give a pledge not to offer advice to his Majesty on measures which the state of public affairs might render necessary, would be, if not an impeachable offense, yet, at least, that which, constitutionally, could not be justified. He then said that he thought it his indispensable duty to represent to the King the situation in which he stood; that he was on the brink of a precipice ; that nothing could be more fatal than to persevere in the resolution which his Majesty had formed of dismissing his Ministers ; that the day on which that resolution was announced in Ireland would be a day of jubilee to the Catholics; that they would desire nothing more than to have a ministry who were supported by *all the talents* and weight of property in the country go out upon such a measure; that he ventured to tell his Majesty that, if he proceeded with his resolution, he would never know another hour of comfort or tranquillity. The King, he says, listened to all this without once interrupting him ; that he could observe, however, by his countenance, that he was greatly agitated ; and when the Chancellor had concluded, the King said to him, ' You are a very honest man, my Lord, and I am very much obliged to you ;'—and this was all. The Chancellor thinks that he has made a great impression, and half flatters himself that the King will retract his resolution." [1]

Several days elapsed quietly; and Erskine, ignorant of the intrigues of Lord Eldon and the Duke of Cumberland, who were then negotiating for the formation of a new Government, really believed that the danger had passed by, and that he might remain in office, under George III., till his patron and friend, the Heir Apparent, should

[1] Life of Romilly, ii. 187.

mount the throne,—when he expected that the chief power would be vested in his own hands. He was in this frame of mind when, late at night on the 24th of March, he received a summons to attend the King on the morrow before twelve o'clock, to deliver up the Great Seal.

Notice had been put up in Lincoln's Inn Hall that judgment would be pronounced the next day in another branch of the cause of *Purcell* v. *M'Namara*, which had been argued before him, assisted by the Master of the Rolls. Soon after ten he entered the Court, which was densely crowded,—his Honor following him; and when they were seated, he addressed the bar in these words:—

"I had fixed this morning as the earliest and most convenient time for finishing, with the assistance of his Honor the Master of the Rolls, at least the judicial part of this long and important case; but late last night,—much too late to make it possible for me to apprise you of it,—I had notice to attend his Majesty, with his other Ministers, before twelve o'clock this day. I shall, therefore, ask his Honor to deliver his opinion, in which I heartily concur,—his Honor and myself having had long deliberations upon the subject. With regard to the other matters which stand for my own judgment, I shall not have time to deliver them in open Court. Adopting the same course as my Lord Eldon when he retired from the office of Lord Chancellor, I shall send them to the register.

"If I should be called out of this world as suddenly as I have been out of this place, it will be a happy thing for me if I can render as clear an account of my conduct through life as of my administration of justice during the period I have presided here. I believe it would not have taken an hour by the clock to have delivered all the judgments that remain for me to pronounce,—I have altered nothing here.—I have removed no man.—But I can not, with justice to myself, or with propriety as it regards you, retire from this Court, without returning you my most sincere thanks for the kind, honorable, and liberal manner in which you have uniformly conducted yourselves towards me.—I approach the threshold of my high office with conscious pride and satisfaction,—particularly when I consider the complicated nature of the

duties I have had to fulfill, and their newness to me. I
am happy to acknowledge that it is to the learning of the
Bar, and the assistance I have derived from you, that I
am indebted for having been enabled to administer these
duties with justice and equity.—In retiring to private
life, it will be my delight to cultivate that acquaintance
which I have had with you in my public station."

Mr. Attorney General (Sir A. Pigot):—" I am sure, my
Lord, I should not do justice to the sentiments of the
Bar, if I were to suffer your Lordship to leave this Court
without expressing their grateful sense of the kindness
shown to them while your Lordship has presided here."

The whole Bar rose and bowed to his Lordship, who
instantly after retired.[1]

He then proceeded to the Palace. There he found all
his colleagues assembled, and they were introduced one
by one into the royal closet, for the purpose of resigning
their wands, seals, keys, and other insignia of office. To
the general surprise, Erskine returned still bearing in his
hand the purse containing the Great Seal; and some supposed that, by reason of his concurrence of sentiment
with his Majesty as to the propriety of refusing any further
concession to the Catholics, he had been invited, and
had consented, to serve under the " No-Popery Ministry."
But the explanation of this phenomenon was, that " the
King, understanding that there were some causes which
had been argued, but in which the Chancellor had not
yet pronounced his decrees, desired him to remain a week
longer in office, that he might finish the business in his
Court." [2]

The following day came the Ministerial explanations in
the House of Lords; and Lord Erskine said,—

" He considered the subject of the Catholic question as
completely irrelevant as any other whatever to the
change in his Majesty's councils, although it happened to
be the subject which led to such a conjuncture. Although
a member of the late Government, he was decidedly adverse to the measure, and should not have advised it, because he did not see the political necessity for it which
had induced the great majority of his colleagues to recommend it to his Majesty. Yet he thought they were highly
commendable in giving his Majesty such advice as they

[1] Annual Register, 1807, p. 415.   [2] Life of Romilly, ii. 189.

in their conscience thought just—as well as in declining to be bound by any pledge to refrain from giving to their Sovereign, upon this or any subject, such advice as they conceived was for the public good. The firmness with which his Majesty had maintained his own conscientious opinions, by resisting the bill in the extent to which it went, had also his respectful approbation; but he must say his colleagues did right in declining to be bound never again to advise the measure under any possible pressure of circumstances. At the moment when his Majesty's late Ministers relinquished the bill in concession to his Majesty's scruples, they stood in the same situation as on their first accession to office. The right of his Majesty to change his Ministers no man would deny; but for them to have remained in power upon any such condition as the pledge alluded to, would have been, in his opinion, contrary to every principle of Ministerial duty, and directly in violation of the Constitution. Their dismissal for no other reason than their declining the pledge, he was afraid was a declaration to the Catholics, that the penalties and disabilities under which they labored were to be considered an essential part of our system of rule; what the result might be of such a conviction taking possession of their minds, he was afraid even to conjecture."

Impartiality requires me to mention a circumstance which, I recollect, was generally censured at the time,—that although Lord Erskine had been allowed to retain the Great Seal for a week only to give judgment in causes which had been argued before him, he employed the interval to concoct a job for the benefit of a member of his family. It is thus related by Romilly :—

"Two days before Lord Erskine parted with the Seal, he appointed his son-in-law, Edward Morris, a Master in Chancery. Sir William Pepys was prevailed upon to make a vacancy by resigning. This is surely a most improper act of Lord Erskine's. He ought to have considered himself as out of office last Wednesday. Morris, though a very clever and very deserving man, has no knowledge in his profession of that particular kind which is necessary to qualify a man to discharge the duties of a Master. This is a matter which will draw reproach on the whole Administration, though in every other department they have most scrupulously, as I understand, abstained from making any promotions."[1]

He had, no doubt, supposed, that while he held the Great Seal, all its powers, privileges, and patronage belonged to him; and I believe that if the vacancy had occurred in this interval by death, he would have been justified, according to established usage, in filling it up.

Having cleared off his arrear of judgments, and on the 1st of April granted the injunction which I have mentioned in the case of *Gurney* v. *Longman.*[2]—without any fresh leave-taking, he made his bow to the Bar, and proceeded to the Queen's Palace. There he finally parted with the Great Seal, and it was delivered to Lord Eldon, who kept it in his firm grasp for a continuous period of above twenty years.

From Lord Erskine's farewell address to the Bar, it appears that he was himself well satisfied with the manner in which he had performed the duties of Chancellor; and, though he did not do much to advance the science of equity, the suitors who came before him seem to have had little cause to complain of his decisions; but I am afraid that Romilly, ruminating upon the probable disposal of the Great Seal upon a contemplated change of Ministry a few months after, expresses the general opinion of his own profession and of the public:—

"The present Ministry can hardly, considering what the crisis is to which public affairs are hasting, be very long in power; and if those whom they have supplanted should recover their authority, the Great Seal can scarcely be again intrusted to the hands of Lord Erskine; with all his talents, (and very great they undoubtedly are), his incapacity for the office was too forcibly and too generally felt for him to be again placed in it."[3]

His faults as a judge were afterwards greatly exaggerated, and a report was spread abroad that most of his decrees were reversed. This having reached the United States of America, gave rise to a wager, which the parties, with Transatlantic coolness, referred to himself for decision. His reply to the American senator who had taken the *reversal* side of the question is extant, and is a striking instance of his buoyancy of spirit and frank good opinion of himself.

[1] Life of Romilly, ii. 192. [2] Ante, p. 196. [3] Life of Romilly, ii. 394.

"Upper Berkeley Street, Nov. 13, 1819.
"SIR.
"I certainly was appointed Chancellor under the Administration in which Mr. Fox was Secretary of State, in 1806, and could have been Chancellor under no Administration in which he had not had a part; nor would have accepted, without him, any office whatsoever. I believe the Administration was said, by all the *Blockheads*, to be made up of all the *Talents* in the country.

"But you have certainly lost your bet on the subject of my decrees. None of them were appealed against, except one, upon a branch of Mr. Thelluson's will—but *it was affirmed* without a dissentient voice, on the motion of Lord Eldon, then and now Lord Chancellor. If you think I was no lawyer, you may continue to think so. It is plain you are no lawyer yourself; but I wish every man to retain his opinions, though at the cost of three dozen of port.

"Your humble servant,
"ERSKINE.

"To save you from spending your money upon bets you are sure to lose, remember, that no man can be a great advocate who is no lawyer. The thing is impossible."

CHAPTER CLXXXVI.

CONTINUATION OF THE LIFE OF LORD ERSKINE TILL THE PRINCE OF WALES, BECOME REGENT, RENOUNCED THE WHIGS.

SOME have regretted that Erskine did not close his mortal career on the day when he resigned his office; but although he can not by any means be held up as a model for ex-Chancellors, he continued for many years, occasionally, to render important services to the public. He began with good resolutions—thus writing to a friend: "I am now retired—most probably for life—and am living what for me may be considered an idle, but I hope not a useless, life—as I keep up my reading, in case the chances of this changeable world should give me the opportunity of turning it to public account. Should I, however, remain long out of a public station, I shall find healthful and interesting occupation in the cultivation of the grateful Earth, who, if well cultivated, is less capricious in the distribution of her favors than Courts or Princes."

The late change of Government had been so highly unconstitutional, that "all the Talents" for some time thought they must speedily be restored to power. They had a decided majority in the House of Commons returned after an appeal by them to the people, and all the measures which they proposed had passed the other House of Parliament. The bill on which they had differed with the King was allowed by unprejudiced men to be salutary, and no one had ventured to say a word in defense of the pledge he had demanded from them. Accordingly, the Marquis of Stafford moved a resolution, "That it is the first duty of the responsible Ministers of the Crown not to restrain themselves by any pledge from giving any advice to his Majesty which, to the best of their judgment, the course of circumstances may render necessary for the honor of his Majesty's crown, and the security of his dominions." On this occasion Erskine spoke early in the debate, and thus began:—

"The particular situation in which I was placed in his Majesty's late councils, as it regards the subject now under consideration, and the many public references which have been made in various places to my office, and to my opinions respecting it, make it not unfit, I hope, that I should seek the earliest opportunity, consistently with the forms of the House, of explaining to your Lordships why I think the resolution deserves your support. My Lords, it has been the fashion to represent the introduction of the bill which led to the dissolution of the late Administration as an extravagant act of political suicide —as a rash, useless, and wanton propositon, dictated by no expediency, and opposed by insurmountable obstacles, within the knowledge of those who introduced it. Nay, my Lords, charges much more serious have been made. It has been more than insinuated that, to overcome these obstacles, recourse was had to the most unworthy arts of deception. Nothing is more easy, my Lords, for those who have an interest in such misrepresentations than to invent and propagate them; but it is not so easy to obtain belief (except in the surprise of the moment) that persons of acknowledged skill and ability as statesmen should suddenly conduct themselves so absurdly, or that distinguished and characteristic integrity should suddenly give place to dishonor and falsehood." Having at great length explained the existing state of the law with respect to Roman Catholics bearing military commissions in Ireland and in England,—with the proposed alteration of it, and the course which the affair had taken between the King and his Ministers, he thus proceeds:—"I never, therefore, at the time the Ministry was on the eve of dissolving, could discover any just or rational ground for its dissolution; and I could never, therefore, persuade myself that their removal was the spontaneous act of the King, because, having the highest opinion of his Majesty's honor and fairness, I could not reconcile their removal with either. A pledge was tendered, which is not only not argued to be legal, but the illegality of which is considered as a childish truism, utterly unfit for debate in Parliament: and yet this refusal, without further parley or explanation, and in the midst of the most respectful and affectionate submission, was made the only ground of a total, indiscriminate dismission. I believe that independently of the avowed cause, the fate of the late Ministry had been settled by some secret advisers. We all know, my Lords, that in political life there are wheels within wheels, as many almost, as in a silk-mill,—that the smallest, and apparently the most insignificant, are sometimes, from their situations, the most operative; and that some of them besides are sunk so deep in the dirt that it it is very difficult to find their places, though one can very easily find their tracks and their effects. It is admitted that, consistent with the coronation oath, Roman Catholics may be ensigns, lieutenants, captains, majors, and lieutenant-colonels in the army; but it is argued that they can not rise to the rank of general officers without a violation of the King's solemn obligation to support the Protestant establishment of the Church of England. What, in the name of wonder, can the Church have to do with this distinction? Whether it was expedient, as a question of state, to open the army to Catholics at all, the thing is done. We are therefore confined only to the mysterious enigma of the *perjury* in carrying on their promotion to be officers of the staff. My Lords, as I was no party at all to the bill, I can not but feel a most natural anxiety to deliver myself from the possible imputation of such gross stupidity and folly as to have ever objected to it on that principle. It should be remembered, My Lords, that, by the coronation oath, his Majesty swore to govern his people according to the laws and customs of this realm; and that, to require a pledge of his Ministers not to give him counsel on any subject, was manifestly contrary to the constitution and the laws and customs of the realm. To say, therefore, that the King, without an adviser, was the author of this, was to say that he had undoubtedly broken his coronation oath."[1] He concluded with the following characteristic disclaimer of being at all tainted by any leaning to Popery:—" My Lords, I have now only to assure you that no man can be more deeply impressed than I am with reverence to God and religion, and for all the ministers and professors of the Christian faith : I am sure that I need not except even the right reverend prelates in whose presence I make this solemn declaration. My Lords, I glory in the opportunity of making it. Would to God that my life could be as pure as my faith! I consider the Reformation, and its irresistible progress in the age which has succeeded it, as the grand era in which the Divine Providence began most visibly to fulfill the sacred and encouraging promises of the Gospel. I look forward, my Lords, with an anxiety which I cannot express, but with a hope which is inextinguishable, to the time when all the nations of the earth shall be collected under its shadow, and united in the enjoyment of its blessings. It is by that feeling, my Lords, mixed perhaps with what may be considered as the prejudices of education, but which I can not myself consider to be prejudices, that I have been kept back from going the full length of Catholic expectation. I consider the Roman Catholic faith as a gross superstition—not chargeable upon the present generation, which contains thousands and tens of thousands of sincere and enlightened persons—but the result of the darkness of former ages, and which is fast giving way under the hourly increasing lights of religion and philo-

---

[1] Romilly says with astonishment, "No notice was taken of this by any of the Peers who spoke after."—*Life*, ii. 197.

sophical truth,—not that vain and contemptible jargon which has usurped the name of philosophy—but the philosophy of nature, which lifts up the mind to the contemplation of the Almighty, by approaching to him nearer, and discovering his attributes in the majesty and harmony of his works."[1]

The motion was negatived by 171 to 81, and all hope of disturbing the new Government was cut off by a more mortifying defeat in the Lower House, where a similar motion was made by Mr. Brand, and where the Whigs had calculated on a large majority.[2]

Erskine was, for a time, a good deal dejected and disturbed by the prostrate condition of his party,—which, in private, he imputed to their own imprudence. The author of the "Rejected Addresses," alluding to his demeanor about this time, says, "I never saw him apparently vexed, except at a *fete champetre* given by Richard Wilson, at Fulham. I there walked with him round the grounds, when he spoke very peevishly about Lord Grenville and the recently shattered Whig Administration, exclaiming, several times—'A rope of sand!'"

The only other occasion on which he addressed the House of Lords, before the end of the session, was in support of the "Scotch Judicature Bill," when he rendered himself ridiculous by one of those displays of egotism and vanity which so much detracted from his dignity and usefulness, and made hearers believe it impossible that he should be the same man who had so nobly and successfully defended public liberty. Trial by jury being about to be introduced into Scotland, he took occasion to remind the House of his devoted attachment to this institution. The Duke of Cumberland, now King of Hanover, excusably joined in a titter occasioned by the repetition of what their Lordships had so often heard—when the indignant orator thus burst forth:

"I observe an illustrious personage on the benches op-

[1] 9 Parl. Deb. 353.
[2] " 7th April. I dined at Lord Howick's with a large party of the late Ministers and their friends. They are very sanguine as to carrying, by a considerable majority, Mr. Brand's motion.

"8th. The debate was a very extraordinary one. Perceval declared that the King had no advisers in the measure. While we were locked up in the lobby, we supposed ourselves the majority by about 20, but there was a majority of 32 against us."—*Life of Romilly*, ii. 195.

posite smile, and I must be bold to tell him that such a smile is inconsistent with the decorum with which this House is in the habit of hearing every noble lord express his sentiments. But it is particularly indecorous and indecent in that illustrious personage to smile at a panegyric upon the the 'trial by jury.' 'Trial by jury' placed the present royal family on the throne of England, and 'trial by jury' has preserved our most gracious Sovereign, that illustrious person's father, throughout a long and glorious reign. 'Trial by jury' is the best security for the rights of your Lordships, and of every order in the state; and I can never cease to feel that 'trial by jury' has enabled me to address your Lordships upon equal terms with the highest man among you."[1]

Soon after, the Parliament elected under Whig rule was dissolved, although the House of Commons had come to no resolution hostile to the present Government, except against the grant to Mr. Perceval of the Duchy of Lancaster for life; but it was thought right to take full advantage of the "No Popery" cry which now resounded through the length and breadth of the land. In vain did the Whig candidates boast of the good measures of the late Ministry, and complain of the unconstitutional manner in which it had been dismissed. The maxim that "the King can do no wrong," framed to establish the responsibility of his advisers, the nation translated into a declaration "that the King is infallible, and his will is not to be questioned." Accordingly, a Parliament was chosen in which the Whigs were not much more numerous than when they were vainly struggling against the ascendency of Pitt.

On the first day of the session, however, an amendment to the Address was moved in both Houses,—when Erskine made a last effort to persuade the Peers that the personal inclinations of the Sovereign ought not to be regarded as law under a Constitutional Monarchy, and strongly inveighed against the late dissolution, saying that "Ministers should yield to Parliaments, and not Parliaments to Ministers."—But he found himself in a minority of 67 to 160,[2] and there being a majority of near 200[3] in favor of Ministers in the House of Commons, he abandoned systematic opposition in despair.

[1] 9 Parl. Deb. 487.   [2] Ibid. 591.   [3] Ibid. 658.

For many years he only came forward on rare occasions, to record his dissent to measures which he considered particularly objectionable. He violently condemned the expedition to Copenhagen,[1] and supported a motion for restoring the Danish fleet.[2] He took an active part in censuring the famous "Orders in Council," respecting neutral navigation,—truly foretelling, that they would lead to a war with America, and that, being found injurious to our own commerce, they must be abandoned.[3]

In opposing the infamous and ludicrous attempt to conquer France by prohibiting the exportation of Jesuits' bark to the continent of Europe, he for a time revived his ancient fame. I can speak with confidence of the great talent as well as zeal he displayed on this occasion, for I then appeared for the first time at the bar of the House of Lords, soon after the commencement of my professional career.—Firmin de Tastet, a wealthy Spanish merchant, had imported several large cargoes of Jesuits' bark from South America into England with the view of forwarding them to different continental ports in the usual course of his trade; and he petitioned against the bill, on the ground of the heavy loss it would inflict upon him.—I was his counsel, and I well recollect my consternation when the great doors of the House were suddenly thrown open, and I was marched up to the bar by the Black Rod, who thrice stopped me to make my *congées*. The House was very crowded, and in a state of great excitement.—Erskine, seeing my trepidation, most kindly came to the bar, shook hands with me, and did everything in his power to encourage me. I stated my case with some boldness, and got through pretty well with the examination of my witnesses,—he putting questions to them to bring out the facts more prominently than I could do from my inexperience. I then moved, that on account of the complication of the evidence and the numerous arithmetical calculations into which the witnesses had entered, I should be allowed till the following day to sum up; and he warmly supported my application—pointing out from his own practice the difficulty of counsel doing justice without preparation in such a case, and urging that the fate of one of the first merchants in the world might depend upon their Lordships understanding it.

[1] 10 Parl. Deb. 354.   [2] Ibid. 653.   [3] Ibid. 929, 975. 1149. 1245, 1321.

The Government resisting the application, he divided the House; but there was a considerable majority against us. —I replied with some energy ; and, throwing figures and calculations overboard, I not only dwelt upon the grievous private injury which the bill would inflict on my client, but—contrary to the caution I had received from the Lord Chancellor—I ventured to glance at its general inexpediency, and the discredit which it would bring upon the British name.—A very animated debate then took place on the question, whether the bill should be read a third time ? No notion can be formed of Erskine's admirable speech from the miserable report of it to be found in print. Even now I have a lively recollection of his impassioned tones, of his piercing eye, of his noble action, as witnessed on this occasion ; but I can not attempt to follow the course of his reasoning, or to describe the manner in which he conjured the right reverend prelates, as ministers of Him who went about healing the sick, to save us from the curse that must follow such unchristian conduct. The bill being carried by a majority of 110 to 44 he embodied his objections to it in the following protest :—

" 1. Because the Jesuits' bark, the exportation of which is prohibited by this bill, has been found by long experience to be a specific for many dangerous diseases which war has a tendency to spread and exasperate, and because to employ, as an engine of war, privation of the only remedy for some of the greatest sufferings which war is capable of inflicting, is manifestly repugnant to the principles of the Christian religion, contrary to humanity, and not justified by the usage of civilized nations. 2. Because the means to which recourse has been hitherto had in war, have no analogy to the barbarous enactment of this bill, inasmuch as it is not even contended that the privation to be created by it has any tendency whatever to self-defense, or to compel the enemy to the restoration of peace—the only legitimate objects by which the infliction of the calamities of war can in any case be justified. 3. Because the only possible answer to these objections is, that the bill will not produce the privation which is held forth as its ostensible object, inasmuch as the Jesuits' bark may be exported under licenses from the Crown ; but such an answer would only prove the bill to be wholly useless to its purposes, while it would still leave in full operation the odious precedent of having resorted in cold blood, for the mere speculative sale of our manufactures, even to the possible infliction of miseries not to be vindicated but by the view of self-preservation, or in the extremities of war, directed to that justifiable object. 4. Because, as no scarcity of the Jesuits' bark appears to exist in France, and as, in the contrary case, no possible exertion on the part of this country could effectually prevent its importation into the numerous ports under the dominion and control of the French government, the bill is grossly vicious in principle, while it is absolutely nugatory in practice, and is therefore, in every point of view, disgraceful and absurd. 5. Because, if it were even just, expedient, or practicable to force the importation of our manufactures upon our enemies by withholding the Jesuits' bark, but upon condition of their permitting such importation, that principle should have been distinctly expressed in the bill, and the conditions specifically declared in it, instead of vesting in the Crown an arbitrary discretion to dispense with the prohibition by licenses—a power destructive of the equality of British commerce, and dangerous to the freedom of the British Constitution.

"ERSKINE."[1]

He next opposed unsuccessfully a bill very wantonly and offensively brought forward by Sir Vicary Gibbs, to enable the Attorney General to arrest and hold to bail any persons against whom he has filed an *ex-officio* information for a libel. It was aimed against proprietors and printers of newspapers who attacked the Government; but there never had been an instance of defendants so prosecuted not duly pleading and taking their trial; and if they actually were to fly the country, nothing could more effectually answer the purpose of prosecuting them. Erskine in vain showed that the bill was wholly unnecessary, and was a dangerous innovation, as it proceeded from a systematic desire to put down the discussion of public grievances. I doubt whether Sir Vicary ever did more than hang it *in terrorem* over the heads of the old ladies against whom he filed his informations, because they happened to have annuities payable out of newspapers in consequence of family settlements; and although

[1] Parl. Deb. 1320-1326.

it still disgraces the Statute Book, certainly no Attorney General since his time has ever thought of putting it in force.

When Erskine gave his opinion on military matters, although he had been a soldier in his youth, he by no means did himself so much credit. He considered it impossible that we should be able to defend Portugal, much less drive the French out of Spain. When thanks were moved to the army after the battle of Corunna, while he praised the gallantry of Sir John Moore and the other British officers who had gloriously fallen there, he said, "but for their immortal renown, it would have been better for them—certainly much better for their country —to have shot them on the parade of St. James's Park."[1] He afterwards asserted, "the men who were sent to Spain were sent there to be massacred, without any prospect of their ever being able to do any good."[2] Nay, he held the same language after the battle of Talavera had been won, saying "he would put an hypothetical case: suppose that the result of fighting a battle should be, although a victory was claimed, the failure of the main purposes of the campaign,—would it not be essential to have information with respect to the reasons for adopting that measure before they voted thanks for a victory which had produced only disastrous consequences?"[3] And afterwards, when the plan of establishing our ascendency in the Peninsula was discussed, he said "it might as well, in fact, be expected to accomplish this by sending over the woolsack, with my noble and learned friend upon it."[4]

But, leaving such vagaries, he almost entirely confined himself for some years to a subject which he made peculiarly his own, and with which his name will ever continue to be associated. Thus he began his speech in moving the second reading of his bill "For the Prevention of Cruelty to Animals:"—

"I am now to propose to the humane consideration of the House a subject which has long occupied my attention, and which I own to your Lordships is very near my heart. It would be a painful and disgusting detail if I were to endeavor to bring before you the almost innumerable instances of cruelty to animals which are daily

[1] 12 Parl. Deb. 136. [2] 14 Ibid. 169. [3] 15 Ibid. 107.
[4] 15 Ibid. 534.

occurring in this country, and which, unfortunately, only gather strength by any efforts of humanity in individuals to repress them without the aid of the law. These unmanly and disgusting outrages are most frequently perpetrated by the basest and most worthless—incapable, for the most part, of any reproof which can reach the mind, and who know no more of the law than that it suffers them to indulge their savage disposition with impunity. Nothing is more notorious than that it is not only useless, but dangerous to poor suffering animals, for a humane man to reprove their oppressors, or to threaten them with punishment. The general answer, with the addition of bitter oaths and increased cruelty, is, '*What is that to you?*'—If the offender be a servant, he curses you, and asks '*if you are his master?*'—and if he be a master, he tells you that '*the animal is his own.*' The validity of this most infamous and stupid defense arises from that defect in the law which I seek to remedy. Animals are considered as *property* only. To destroy or to abuse them, from malice to the proprietor, or with an intention injurious to his interest in them, is criminal,—but the animals themselves are without protection—the law regards them not—they have no RIGHTS. I am to ask your Lordships, in the name of that God who gave to man his dominion over the lower world, to acknowledge and recognize that dominion to be a MORAL TRUST."—After enlarging on this topic with great beauty, and fully explaining the preamble and enactments of the bill, he observed: "As to the tendency of barbarous sports, of any description whatsoever, to nourish the national characteristic of manliness and courage,—the only shadow of argument I ever heard on such occasions,—all I can say is this—that from the mercenary battles of the lowest of beasts—human boxers—up to those of the highest and noblest that are tormented by Man for his degrading pastime, I enter this public protest against such reasoning. I never knew a man remarkable for heroic bearing whose very aspect was not lighted up by gentleness and humanity, nor a *kill-and-eat-him* countenance that did not cover the heart of a bully or a poltroon."[1]

When the bill was in committee, he said,—
"During the thirty years of my parliamentary life, I

[1] 14 Parl. Deb. 553.

have never till now proposed any alteration in the law. I possess no ostentatious wish to couple a statute with my name, and, on the present occasion, your Lordships will, I trust, give me credit for being actuated by a better motive. I venture to say firmly to your Lordships, that 'the bill I now propose to you, if it shall receive the sanction of Parliament, will not only be an honor to the country, but an era in the history of the world.'"

The bill passed the Lords after a slight opposition from Lord Ellenborough, but was thrown out in the Commons by a speech of Windham's, who thus sneered at its author:—

"We ought to be cautious how we begin 'new eras of legislation,' and ought to have a reasonable distrust of the founders of 'eras,' lest they should be a little led away by an object of such splendid ambition, and be thinking more of themselves than of the credit of the laws or the interest of the community. To be the first who has stood up as the champion of the 'rights of brutes' is, indeed, a marked distinction. But I wish to know why, to tarnish his glory, he has excluded from protection animals not tamed or reclaimed; for one would have supposed that their '*rights*' were more unqualified and more unquestionable. It is said they are *feræ naturæ*—a learned distinction, but never before so whimsically applied. Again, we are told, if never treated with cruelty, they would become too numerous and *overrun the earth*; but how does this apply to a class of animals with which we are accustomed to make very free—*the fishes?* If it is to be a misdemeanor to beat a donkey, surely to crimp a cod, or to skin an eel, ought to be felony without benefit of clergy. What a pretty figure shall we make in the world, if, in one column of a newspaper, we read a string of commitments under the 'Cruelty to Animals' Act,' and, in another, the account of a grand *Battue*—attended by princes of the blood, and ministers of state—or of 'a glorious run, five horses only being in at the death, of fifty who started,—several having died in the field!' If the horses be within the purview of the statute, the hounds are not, and, at all events, the 'rights of the fox' are violated with impunity!"[1]

Erskine again introduced his bill, with some amend-

[1] 17 Parl. Hist. 1207.

ments, in the next session, and it underwent much discussion, but finding that he was not likely to carry it through the House of Commons, he withdrew it after it had passed the committee.[1] When Windham was gone, and the passion for bull-baiting and boxing had subsided, it was introduced there by Martin of Galway, and finally, in Erskine's lifetime, received the sanction of the Legislature.[2] Independently of "the rights of brutes," which it may be difficult to protect by human laws, although the subject of religious and moral obligation, I think there can be no doubt that any malicious and wanton cruelty to animals in public outrages the feelings,—has a tendency to injure the moral character of those who witness it,—and may therefore be treated as a crime.

When the dispute arose upon the commitment of Sir Francis Burdett to the Tower, Erskine yielding to the sin which most easily beset him,—the love of popularity,—took a violent part against the House of Commons, and maintained that all questions of privilege ought to be decided by the courts of common law. He dwelt upon the danger of either House of Parliament exceeding its jurisdiction,—forgetting the danger, which has since been exemplified, of judges, with the best intentions in the world, attempting to deprive the two Houses of Parliament of powers "essential to the due and effectual exercise and discharge of their functions and duties, and to the promotion of wise legislation."[3] In a very unnecessary ebullition of bravery, after referring to the fact of Chief Justice Pemberton being sent to Newgate by the House of Commons, he exclaimed, "If a similar attack were made upon my noble and learned friend who sits next me [Lord Ellenborough], for the exercise of his legal jurisdiction, I would resist the usurpation with my strength, and bones, and blood."[4] Nay, he went so far as to lay down for law, contrary to repeated decisions of all the Courts in Westminster Hall, that a warrant of commitment by either House of Parliament must upon the face of it specify the particular facts alleged to constitute a breach of privilege, for the consideration of the Common-law Judges upon a writ of habeas corpus.[5] It certainly would be desirable,

[1] 16 Parl. Deb. 726, 845, 881, 883, 1017.
[2] See stat. 3 Geo. 4, c. 71; stat. 5 & 6 Wm. 4, c. 59.
[3] See 3 Vict. c. 9.   [4] 16 Parl. Deb. 851.   [5] Ibid. 588, 598.

for public information, that such warrants were so drawn ; but the pretension of judges to review the cause of commitment renders this course impossible, without subjecting all parliamentary privilege to their summary caprice, —and the established sufficiency of a warrant of commitment, generally alleging a breach of privilege, is the only practical security retained by the two Houses for the undisturbed enjoyment of the powers which they have hitherto exercised, and which the public good requires that they should continue to exercise. Although Erskine had nobly repelled attacks on public liberty, I can not hold him up as an accomplished jurist or a great authority on constitutional law.

I am happy to say that he gradually took a more liberal view of the claims of the Roman Catholics: he was not yet prepared to put them, as to civil rights, on an equal footing with Protestants, but he supported Lord Donoughmore's motion for referring their petitions to a committee, saying, " The question now to be decided is— not whether the Roman Catholic religion be good or evil as a religion, but whether, so long as it exists among so large a proportion of the population of Ireland, we are not called upon so to deal with its professors as to make them safe and sound members of the British empire." [1]

I could have wished much, for his fame, that he had been more active in leading or assisting the efforts which now began strenuously to be made to soften the atrocious severity of our penal code: but I can only find that he once offered a few observations, and voted in a small minority, in favor of the bill for taking away capital punishment from the offense of stealing in a shop to the value of *five shillings*.[2]

The Whigs were again tantalized by the seemingly certain prospect of a speedy accession to power. In the end of the year 1810, the mental illness of King George III. was so aggravated that it could not be concealed from the public, and the functions of the Executive Government could not be carried on without the intervention of Parliament. The belief became general, which was verified by the event, that his Majesty was now permanently disabled from personally performing the duties of his high office. Notwithstanding the democratic doctrine adopted

[1] 17 Parl. Deb. 395.   [2] Ibid. 198.

in 1788, that on such an emergency the two Houses of Parliament were entitled to elect any individual at their pleasure as Regent, and to confer on, or withhold from him, any of the prerogatives of the Crown, it was easily foreseen that the Heir Apparent would soon be to all practical purposes upon the throne. After a little vacillation, in consequence of a supposed revolutionary movement in the country at the commencement of the war, he had remained true to the political party to which he attached himself in his youth; and at this very time he was living on terms of the most familiar intimacy with the leaders of it—talking to them of the distribution of the great offices of state among them as soon as they were his to bestow. Erskine, in particular, was in high favor with him; and when they met, his Royal Highness, without loss of dignity, laying aside court etiquette, addressed him by the endearing appellative of TOM. If the ex-Chancellor again desired the Great Seal, it seemed within his reach.

Upon the question as to the mode of proceeding to supply the deficiency in the exercise of the royal functions, he laid down what I consider the true doctrine—that the two Houses, as the states of the realm, should find and declare the fact of the incapacity of the Sovereign, and that then the Heir Apparent, by right of birth, should carry on the government while that incapacity continues. He said, "Not having been in Parliament in the year 1788, I had not then an opportunity publicly to declare my sentiments upon the subject, but I considered it most anxiously and deliberately, and I came to the conclusion that the power of election, arrogated to themselves by the two Houses of Parliament, is wholly inconsistent with the principles of hereditary monarchy, and may lead to all the horrors of civil war. There is no analogy between this case and the Revolution of 1688; for then the throne was vacant, and the two Houses were driven by necessity to fill it by calling in a new dynasty. But the throne is not now vacant, and the two Houses have no jurisdiction to assume or to change the royal authority."[1] This short statement seems absolutely conclusive against the proceeding by bill; for that proceeding can not take place without the direct assumption of the royal author-

[1] 18 Parl. Deb. 72.

ity, however strongly this usurpation may be disavowed. The Great Seal is not the organ of the two Houses, but of the King only. The Great Seal is used in judicial proceedings by virtue of the King's general authority; but for such solemn acts of state as opening Parliament or giving the royal assent to bills, it is the symbol of the King's mind and intention, signified by the indispensable sign-manual. To employ the Great Seal for such purposes by the two Houses of Parliament is, therefore, a manifest violation of the Constitution. The proposed plan assumes the power of the two Houses to exercise the royal authority during the King's incapacity—by which evil men may introduce confusion, not likely to terminate with one generation. This is no visionary fancy; the Constitution has fallen a sacrifice to the principle of separating the political power from the natural person of the Sovereign, and may again lead to the levy of armies in his name to fight against him.

When the restrictions to be put upon the Regent came to be discussed, Erskine strenuously opposed them, contending that they were wholly unnecessary for the purpose of insuring his Majesty's resumption of his royal authority on his recovery; and he denounced the prohibitions against promotions in the peerage as particularly disrespectful to that House, because they conveyed an insinuation " that their Lordships were ready to barter their allegiance against additional balls or strawberry-leaves for their coronets."

On the clause respecting the patronage of the household, the Government was beaten by a small majority in the committee, where proxies could not be used; and proxies being called on the " Report " to reverse this decision, the question arose whether, under the circumstances, the right of voting by proxy at all existed. Erskine contended that their Lordships were not sitting as a House of Parliament under the sanction of the King, so that the custom of voting by proxy did not apply; and, at any rate, that the custom, being always under the control of the House, ought not to be permitted on this occasion; "for what could be more calculated to bring it into utter contempt, and to cover it with the derision of the public, than to see a most momentous question decided by a majority of the Lords present at the end of long arguments, and in ten minutes afterwards to see that decision reversed by the very same assembly without an additional living man coming into the House, by the proxies of absent Lords, who, had they been present and heard the arguments, would very probably have confirmed the decision which they were supposed to condemn?" The Earl of Liverpool was so much ashamed, or so much afraid, of an adverse division, that he withdrew his call for proxies; and the clause, as amended in the committee, stood part of the bill.[1]

Another violent altercation took place on Lord King's motion, that Lord Eldon should be excluded from being a member of the Queen's Council, to assist her in taking care of the King's person,—on the ground that he had frequently obtained the King's signature for commissions when his Majesty, on account of mental disease, was under the care of physicians, who declared that he was incompetent to act. Erskine did not speak on this very delicate topic, but he voted for the motion, and joined in a strong protest against its rejection,[2] setting forth the instances in which this practice had been followed, and concluding with the allegation, that "John, Lord Eldon, having so conducted himself, is not a person to whom the sacred trust of acting as one of her Majesty's Council in the care of his Majesty's person, and in the discharge of the other most important duties committed to the said Council, can with propriety or safety be committed."

The Regency Act having received the royal assent by means of the "phantom," or sham commission ordered by the two Houses of Parliament, in t e King's name, the Whigs expected to be in office next morning; but, instead of a summons to attend the Regent at Carlton House, they received certain intelligence that his Royal Highness had written a letter to Mr. Perceval, intimating that "he felt it incumbent upon him, in the present juncture, not to remove from their stations those whom he found there as his Majesty's official servants." An attempt was made to soften this disappointment, by holding out a hope, which proved to be illusory, that, as soon as the period of restrictions had expired, and the Regent could freely follow his own inclination, he would get rid

[1] 18 Parl. Hist. 786, 805, 976.   [2] 18 Parl. Deb. 1086.

of the Ministers with whom he had been constantly at
enmity, and by whom he considered himself personally
ill used, for the purpose of forming a close and permanent
connection with his early friends. Erskine was not deluded by any such prospects, and soon perceived that his
old patron had now contracted a mortal aversion to the
Whigs and their principles, and was as firmly resolved as
ever his father had been to prevent them from obtaining
power.

CHAPTER CLXXXVII.

CONTINUATION OF THE LIFE OF LORD ERSKINE TILL THE GENERAL PEACE IN 1815.

FROM this time our ex-Chancellor seems to have renounced all thoughts of official employment, and to
have become rather indifferent about the estimation
in which he was held as a public man. He had paid very
little attention to the judicial business of the House of
Lords since his resignation, and now he was seldom
present at its political discussions. Giving up all professional reading, and without any serious occupation, he
led the idle life of a man of wit and pleasure about town,
spreading hilarity and mirth wherever he appeared,—
seemingly cheerful and happy himself, but spending
many listless and melancholy hours in private,—sometimes mixing in scenes which his friends heard of with
pain, and which brought upon him distress as well as discredit.

He as yet retained his beautiful villa at Hampstead,
near Caen Wood, called " Evergreen Hall." Here he
gave gay parties, of which he was the life by his goodhumor and whimsicalities. We have a lively description
of one of these from Sir Samuel Romilly, to whose
gravity they were not quite suitable :—

" I dined to-day at Lord Erskine's. It was what might
be called a great Opposition dinner: the party consisted
of the Duke of Norfolk, Lord Grenville, Lord Grey, Lord
Holland, Lord Ellenborough, Lord Lauderdale, Lord
Henry Petty, Thomas Grenville, Pigott, Adam, Edward

Morris (Erskine's son-in-law), and myself. This was the whole company, with the addition of one person; but that one, the man most unfit to be invited to such a party that could have been found, if such a man had been anxiously looked for. It was no other than Mr. Pinkney, the American Minister—this at a time when the Opposition are accused of favoring America to the injury of their own country, and when Erskine himself is charged with being particularly devoted to the Americans. These are topics which are every day insisted on with the utmost malevolence in all the Ministerial newspapers, and particularly in Cobbett. If, however, the most malignant enemies of Erskine had been present, they would have admitted that nothing could be more innocent than the conversation which passed. Politics were hardly mentioned, and Mr. Pinkney's presence evidently imposed a restraint upon everybody. Among the light and trifling topics of conversation after dinner, it may be worth while to mention one, as it strongly characterizes Lord Erskine. He has always expressed and felt a great sympathy for animals. He has talked for years of a bill he was to bring into Parliament to prevent cruelty towards them. He has always had several favorite animals to whom he has been much attached, and of whom all his acquaintance have a number of anecdotes to relate:—a favorite dog which he used to bring, when he was at the Bar, to all his consultations,—another favorite dog, which, at the time when he was Lord Chancellor, he himself rescued in the street from some boys who were about to kill it under pretense of its being mad,—a favorite goose, which followed him wherever he walked about his grounds,—a favorite macaw,—and other dumb favorites without number. He told us now that he had got two favorite leeches. He had been blooded by them last autumn when he had been taken dangerously ill at Portsmouth; they had saved his life, and he had brought them with him to town,—had ever since kept them in a glass,—had himself every day given them fresh water, and had formed a friendship with them. He said he was sure they both knew him, and were grateful to him. He had given them different names, HOME and CLINE (the names of two celebrated surgeons), their dispositions being quite different. After a good deal of conversation about them, he went himself, brought them out of his library, and placed them in their glass upon the table. It is impossible, however, without the vivacity, the tones, the details, and the gestures of Lord Erskine, to give an adequate idea of this singular scene."[1]

The ex-Chancellor used (but I believe only when he expected his friends to detect him in the act) to take a spade in his hand and pretend to work in his kitchen garden. On such occasions he would say, "Here I am, enjoying my 'otium cum *diggin a taity.*'"—The garden was under the care of a Scotch gardener, who once coming to complain to him, as of grievance to be remedied, that the drought had burnt up all the vegetables and was killing the shrubs, he said to him, "Well, John, all that I can do for you is, to order the hay to be cut down to-morrow morning; and if that does not bring rain, nothing will."—He encouraged the jokes of others when even a little at his expense. Boasting of his fine flock of Southdowns, he joined in the laugh when Colman exclaimed, "I perceive your Lordship has still an eye to the *Woolsack.*"

He afterwards parted with his property at Hampstead, and bought an estate in Sussex, which turned out an unfortunate speculation, for it produced nothing but stunted birch-trees, and was found irreclaimable. To lessen his loss, he set up a manufactory of brooms. One of the men he employed to sell them about the country being taken before a magistrate for doing so without a license, contrary to the "Hawkers' and Pedlars Act," he went in person to defend him, and contended there was a clause to meet this very case. Being asked which it was, he answered, "The *sweeping* clause, your worship—which is further fortified by a proviso, that 'nothing herein contained shall prevent or be construed to prevent any proprietor of land from vending the produce thereof in any manner that to him shall seem fit.'"

With a view to improve this property, he began to study farming, and put himself under the celebrated agriculturist Coke of Norfolk, afterwards Earl of Leicester, observing that "having been instructed by *Coke* at Westminster, he was now to be instructed by *Coke,* as great a man in his way, at Holkham." But the master boasted

[1] Life of Romilly, ii. 253.

little of the pupil, relating this anecdote of his progress:
—"Coming to a finely cultivated field of wheat, the first
specimen he had seen of drill husbandry, Erskine exclaimed in a delighted tone, 'What a beautiful piece of
lavender ! ! !'"[1] I have been favored by a valued friend
with the following reminiscence of one of the Holkham
"sheep-shearing" at which he was present:—

"On the morning following my arrival at Holkham,
happening to be rather late, I found that Mr. Coke, with
a large party, had been examining a ram that had been
brought out of Sussex by Lord Erskine, as a specimen of
his excellent breed of sheep. Our worthy host, however,
and the Norfolk farmers did not seem to estimate his
merits very highly, for they left him without expressing
much commendation. I found Lord Erskine still lingering about his favorite animal. He was engaged in a dissertation, or rather lecture, upon a subject which at that
time engaged, and still does engage, the attention of the
agricultural world, viz., the advantage of thick or thin
sowing. His arguments were rather of a theological than
of a practical character. 'The great God of nature,' he
said, 'did not create the wire-worm or the caterpillar or
the turnip-fly in vain; they have a right to their sustenance as well as man. I therefore highly commend the
practice of my excellent friend Mr. Coke, who sows
turnip-seed in sufficient quantity to feed the fly during
the summer, as well as his own cattle in the winter.' In
pursuing this argument, he had placed himself upon his
sheep's back, where I found him surrounded by twenty
or thirty farmers. The animal at first bore his Lordship's
weight, a light one, with great patience, but at length,
growing weary, it made a sudden move, the result of
which was to throw the ex-Chancellor sprawling in the
dust. He got up, and, deliberately wiping the dirt from
his clothes, exclaimed, 'I vow to God I thought I was on
the woolsack! and give me leave to observe that this is
not the first time that I have been unceremoniously
kicked off it.' We then walked out together, and he eloquently expatiated upon all that he beheld; but that

---

[1] I once puzzled a legal friend of mine, who certainly said he should know *oats* from *wheat* if he saw them growing together, by asking him if he should know *barley* from *malt* if he saw them growing together? He said he thought he should, but he was not quite so sure.

which more particularly excited his surprise and admiration was a monstrous heap of oyster-shells. At first he could only account for this by the large and well-known hospitality exercised at Holkham. Upon further inquiry he found that oyster-shells, when pounded and burnt, had lately been introduced as a valuable manure. 'Now,' said Lord Erskine, 'is the time to do justice to the members of the maligned and much injured profession to which I have so many years belonged. You have doubtless all heard the story of the advocate who swallows the oyster himself, and hands over an empty shell to each of his clients. In doing so it is perfectly clear that he was acting a most disinterested part, for while he contented himself with the poor cold fish for his own share, he gave to those for whom he was engaged the means of improving their lands, and of acquiring unlimited wealth.'— With jokes like these he proceeded to amuse the company, and succeeded in converting a grave didactic meeting into a scene of universal merriment and fun."

By way of lounge, he would not unfrequently come to Westminster Hall, to chat with his old friends—ever expressing regret that he had left the Bar. Once he jumped on the table in the robing-room, and said, in a pitiful tone, "Here is the first day of term, and I have not a single brief in my bag."—I remember, on another occasion, when a group of us gathered round him to hear his stories, we flattered him much by asking him to introduce into his "Cruelty to Animals' Bill," a clause "for the protection of JUNIORS"—telling him truly that we had suffered much bad treatment since he had left us.—Remaining a Bencher of Lincoln's Inn, he often dined in the Hall, and was much more light-hearted than when he sat there with the Great Seal before him.—Yet, when pinched by returning poverty, he would occasionally think with regret of the very short period he had enjoyed his lucrative office. Captain Parry, the famous navigator, being asked at a dinner party, what he and his crew had lived upon when they were frozen up in the Polar Sea, said, "they lived upon *Seals*." "And very good living, too, exclaimed Erskine, "*if you keep them long enough.*"

Soon after his resignation, he was invited to a fete at Oatlands, where the Duchess of York had upon the lawn a number of rare animals, and among others, a remarkable monkey with a long, white, hairy mantle gracefully over his head and shoulders. Erskine was late in appearing: but, at last, while the Prince of Wales, the Duke of York, and other royal personages, were standing in a group near the entrance to the court-yard, he arrived in a very mean-looking one-horse chaise. He immediately alighted; but, instead of paying his duty to the "Royalties" before him, he suddenly stepped up to the monkey; and, taking off his hat in a very dignified manner, and making three *congées*, he addressed the animal in these words, amidst the hearty laugh of all present: "Sir, I sincerely wish you joy—*You wear your wig for life.*"[1]

He used to dine occasionally at the "Stakes"—saying, that he had once consulted a Bishop, whether it was lawful for him, an ex-Chancellor to do so, and received this oracular answer, "*Cut* them," which he thought himself bound to take *in mitiori sensu.*

He frequently presided at the ceremony of laying the foundation stone of buildings for literary institutions, and at the anniversary dinners of societies of all sorts—when he used to make very amusing speeches, which the audience were not sorry to find often embellished with anecdotes of himself. I remember being present at an address from him to the members of the Law Life Insurance Society, at Freemasons' Tavern, when he gave us this account of one of his earliest opinions:—" A case was laid before me by my veteran friend, the Duke of Queensberry—better known as 'old Q.'—as to whether he could sue a tradesman for a breach of contract about the painting of his house? and all the evidence he had to adduce was detailed—which was wholly insufficient; whereupon I wrote, 'I am of opinion, that this action will *not lie*, unless the witnesses *do.*'"

He was at all fashionable breakfasts and balls of peculiar *éclat;* and whereas formerly he had risen at five in the morning to sit down to his briefs, before the ladies of his family had returned from such parties, it was now sometimes later before he went to bed,—and at any hour next day he might have adopted the excuse of Thomson, the

[1] On the authority of a gentleman who was present.—The Oatlands Monkey was a specimen of the Simia Rosalia,—"small red feet—hair very fine, soft, long, of bright yellow color, resembling yellow silk—round the face hair much longer than in other parts, so as to form a large mane like that of a lion—native of Guiana—the *Marikina* of Buffon."

poet, "Why should I get up when I have nothing to do?"

"Idleness of mind," says Burton, in his ANATOMY OF MELANCHOLY, "is the nurse of naughtiness, the stepmother of discipline, the cushion upon which the devil reposes, and a great cause of melancholy." Erskine's present mode of life, I am afraid, was no exception to the general rule—but his frailties were never obtruded on the world, and I am not bound to pry into them. When they were alluded to,—as he still displayed so many fine qualities, mankind were disposed to repeat the words of Lord Kenyon, applied to him in former times "Spots on the sun!—spots on the sun!" although, as it has been observed in no unfriendly tone, "as the luster of the luminary became more dim, the spots did not contract in their dimensions."[1]

Erskine now sought to relieve his *ennui*, and to recover his consequence, by becoming an author, and he published an octavo volume under the title of "ARMATA." This is a close imitation of "Utopia" and "Gulliver's Travels," but is very inferior to those immortal productions, though by no means without cleverness. "Morvin," the narrator, is supposed to have been shipwrecked, and, getting somehow into another planet, to have reached a very distant region called "ARMATA" (England), with a neighboring island under the same government, called "PATRICIA" (Ireland) having for its great rival in power another state, called "CAPETIA" (France). There are two Parts—one historical and political, the other describing manners and customs. I will copy a few extracts from it, to convey a notion of its contents, as the book is now very scarce. In an attempt to show that if the French Revolution had been treated differently by foreign nations, its excesses would not have been provoked, and war might have been avoided, he thus introduces the great patriot of "ARMATA"—who is no other than Charles James Fox:

"My confidence in this opinion," says the personage who is giving us an insight into Armatan politics, "is the more unshaken from the recollection that I held it, at any time, in common with a man whom to have known as I did would have repaid all the toils and perils you have

[1] Lord Brougham's Statesmen, i. 244.

undergone. I look upon you, indeed, as a benighted traveler, to have been cast upon our shores after this great light was set. Never was a being gifted with an understanding so perfect. He was never known to omit anything which, in the slightest degree, could affect the matter to be considered, nor to confound things at all distinguishable, however apparently the same; and his conclusions were always so luminous and convincing, that you might as firmly depend upon them as when substances in nature lie before you in the palpable forms assigned to them from the foundation of the world. Such were his qualifications for the office of a statesman; and his profound knowledge, always under the guidance of the sublime simplicity of his heart, softening without unnerving the giant strength of his intellect, gave a character to his eloquence which I shall not attempt to describe, knowing nothing by which it may be compared. Had the counsels of this great man been accepted,—much more if he himself had lived to carry them into execution with his eminent companions,—I must ever think that the peace of our world might have been preserved."

Thus the traveler, giving an account of the Armatans, shadows forth Burke, and the state prosecutions launched most oppressively by the two Houses of Parliament in the year 1794, when he himself acquired such glory:—

"Alas! the very voice which had breathed so happily the gentle accents of peace, was now heard louder than the trumpet of war to collect our world to battle,—spreading throughout the land an universal panic, until the public councils complained of sedition. Instead of leaving it to the Sovereign, in the ordinary course of law, to bring the suspected to trial, they exalted it into treason of the highest order, and the evidence was published by their command. It was, no doubt, within their jurisdiction, and it was their highest duty to protect the state,—to proclaim a conspiracy if they believed it existed, and to direct prosecutions against the offenders; but it was repugnant to the very elements of the Armatan constitution to involve individuals in the accusations, and to circulate among the people the accusing testimonies, stamped with their supreme authority, when inferior tribunals were afterwards to judge them. In any other country the consequences to the accused must have been *fatal;* but there is a talisman in Armata, which, while it is preserved inviolate, will make her immortal!—HER COURTS OF JUSTICE SPOKE ALOUD TO HER PARLIAMENT: THUS FAR SHALT THOU GO, AND NO FURTHER."

I ought to mention that, from modesty, not a word is introduced respecting the great ADVOCATE in whose hands the " talisman " was so powerful.

He made ample amends in a subsequent edition for the slight the author had cast upon Wellington's early career. Morvin, in alluding to a fight which we easily discover to be WATERLOO, says:—

" The hardy sons of Patricia were in all our ranks, and her soil produced the immortal hero who conducted the battle. No victory in human annals ever produced results so sudden and extraordinary. The adversary, who had built a thousand vessels to convey his armies to our shores, and who was then erecting a column, *even within our view*, to be crowned with his colossal statue, pointing at us with his finger for his own, now fled when no one was pursuing and gave himself up as a prisoner to the commander of a single ship."

I am sorry to say that Morvin's political economy is exceedingly bad, although supposed to be very sound by the author, and meant to guide us in England. He strongly reprobates the importation of foreign wool or foreign corn, as well as of any foreign manufactured goods; he is not contented with *protection*, but would have *bounties;* and he scouts the doctrine that population can ever be excessive, thus concluding: " Be assured that the very being of your country, *above all at this moment*, depends upon your making your own soil support your most extended population ; and that to consider population as an evil is to be wiser than God, who commanded man to *increase and multiply*." Erskine, however, knew as much about these matters as Sheridan, Grey, or Fox himself. Of that generation of statesmen, Pitt alone had studied Adam Smith.

I am surprised to find the following recommendation of wearing official costume in general society from Erskine, who, above all his contemporaries, appeared to despise formality and humbug :—

" We have," said Morvin, " robes of magistracy even

in the lowest of our Courts; and not only our Judges, but all their inferior officers and attendants, have grave and suitable habits of distinction, but which are cast off the moment the business of our councils and courts is over; when the highest of them are to be seen shouldered and jostled in the crowd, with the pickpockets whose imprisonments have just expired, and with the culprits they have amerced. This is by no means an ancient custom among us, but one of late years, most ignorantly and thoughtlessly introduced. Supreme Judges, and, indeed, magistrates of every description,—above all, when coming immediately and publicly from their tribunals,—should have some suitable distinctions, to point out their stations, and to continue, by habits of association, the reverence inspired by their dignified appearance when administering the government or the laws." "Then," adds the traveler in his own person, "I could not help smiling to myself at the ludicrous idea of all Palace Yard in an uproar at the astonishing sight of our Judges coming out of Westminster Hall in such shabby frocks and brown scratches as would infallibly subject them to be rejected as bail in their own Courts, even for £10, though they were to swear themselves black in the face."

Thus he boldly censures the abolition of ancient sinecure offices:—

"To say they are useless because they have no useful duties, may be a false conclusion. A critic of this description might reason in the same manner with Nature, and accuse her of the most senseless profusion, for dressing out a cock pheasant and a peacock quite differently from a jackdaw or a crow. How unmercifully those poor birds would be plucked! Not a feather would be left in their *sinecure* tails!"

He pathetically laments the loss of his "Cruelty to Animals' Bill:"—

"It went down almost by acclamation to the other council for its assent, where its success would have been equally certain if the resolutions of public assemblies were invariably the result of general convictions; but as the bravest armies have been put to flight by the panic of a single soldier, so the wisest councils, by the influence of individual error, may be turned out of the course of wisdom." He then goes on to have his revenge of Windham, on whom he charges "*monomania, or insanity quoad hoc.*"

He concludes the book in a strain of philosophical piety, by which I believe he was systematically animated, notwithstanding the occasional levity of his conversation or his conduct. After calculating that, at the swiftest rate of traveling then known, it would take ninety-one millions of years to reach the nearest of the fixed stars, he thus proceeds:—

"When I reflect that God has given to inferior animals no instincts nor faculties that are not immediately subservient to the ends and purposes of their beings, I can not but conclude that the reason and faculties of man were bestowed upon the same principle, and are connected with his superior nature. When I find him, therefore, endowed with powers to carry as it were the line and rule to the most distant worlds, I consider it as conclusive evidence of a future and more exalted destination, because I can not believe that the creator of the universe would depart from all the analogies of the lower creation in the formation of his highest creature, by gifting him with a capacity not only utterly useless, but destructive of his contentment and happiness, if his existence were to terminate in the grave."

"Armata" came out first anonymously, but the author avowed himself to his friends, and was well satisfied with his performance. He accompanied a presentation copy with the following note to Colman:—

"DEAR SIR,

"As men of real genius are always the most indulgent critics, I send you my little romance without fear. The two parts are very different. The first was intended to be a kind of bolus to swallow my old politics in, which were too long past to be a political pamphlet; and having gone out of this our world without going to that from whose bourne no traveler returns, I was obliged to come back again to town, describing it, however, as if in the world I had just left. I should like to know whether you think my remarks upon the stage are correct.

"Yours most faithfully,
"ERSKINE."

Dr. Parr pronounced the romance to be most valuable, and Erskine's name carried it through several editions:

but, as the story is devoid of novelty or interest, and the great bulk of the observations are without much wit or point, it soon fell into neglect.

The year 1812 seemed propitious to the prospects of the Whigs, and Erskine was often congratulated on his certain and speedy return to office. At the expiration of the restrictions imposed upon the exercise of the royal authority by the Regency Act, the Regent, through the Duke of York, professed a desire that "some of those persons with whom the early habits of his public life were formed would strengthen his hands and constitute a part of his Government;" but it was found that this was only to be under the ascendency of his new friends, Lord Eldon and Mr. Perceval,—and Lords Grey and Grenville declared the impossibility of their uniting with the present Government, as their differences of opinion were too important to admit of such a union; and, in particular, the first advice they should tender to his Royal Highness would be to repeal those civil disabilities under which so large a portion of his Majesty's subjects still labored on account of their religious opinions. In a debate in the House of Lords on this correspondence, Erskine said:—

"Happy should I have been, and ever shall be to manifest my attachment to the Prince. I stand in a peculiar relation to his Royal Highness; I have been in his service for thirty years, and have received many marks of kindness and confidence from him; and as I consider steadiness in friendship to be the source of all honor and usefulness, public and private, I am anxious to explain why it is not in my power, consistently with the attachment I must ever retain for the Prince, or the duty I owe to my country, to give the smallest support to the present Administration." After taking a very able view of their policy, domestic and foreign, he observed that "if a cabinet were to be formed by the proposed union, like *plus* and *minus* in equations they would destroy one another; —one-half determined upon a perpetual exclusion of the Catholics—the other half convinced that to refuse the claims of the Catholics was to dissolve the Empire;— one-half resolved to keep up the Orders in Council,—the other half thinking that the Orders in Council were unjust to neutral nations, and ruinous to our own commerce and manufactures. I deeply lament the present inauspicious state of affairs; but as there is no unmixed good in this world, there is seldom evil unmixed with good, and some advantage may arise out of the present conjuncture; it will furnish an unanswerable, and I hope, a final, refutation of one of the falsest and most dangerous opinions which can be propagated among the lower orders of the people,—that their superiors are all alike— all equally corrupt—all looking only to office by the sacrifice of all principle. The public may now be convinced, that what has been too frequently and invidiously stigmatized as *party*, may be better described as an honorable and useful union of men, of great talents and influence, esteeming one another in private life, and pledged to their country and to each other by similar political principles. I am persuaded, that a firm phalanx of such men, who have acquired general confidence, which they can only hope to preserve by sacrificing their own advancement to the interests of the people, is one of the most important safeguards of the British constitution." In a subsequent part of the debate, he said by way of explanation, " I should have approved of all that was proposed by the Cabinet of which I was a member, and much more than from circumstances they could venture to propose, had I not thought that, from the King's prejudices, this course would dissolve the Administration. [' Hear! hear!' from the other side of the House.] I am glad of that cheer—I laid a trap for it,—as it most strikingly marks the general disposition to impute to public men the love of office as the ruling principle of their conduct. Surely this error is now refuted."

Upon a division, however, the Government had a majority of 165 to 93.[1]

Three months afterwards arose another Ministerial crisis, on the assassination of Mr. Perceval, when Erskine again behaved with spirit and disinterestedness. The Whig leaders were offered the power of forming an entirely new Cabinet, on a condition to which it was known they could not accede—that the officers of the household should not be changed. Although this novel and unconstitutional arrangement was defended by the Earl of Moira, and even by Sheridan, Erskine stoutly asserted that " Lords Grey and Grenville were bound to see that

[1] 22 Parl. Deb. 62, 69, 89.

they had all the facilities and securities which were usual upon changes of Administration, to enable them to carry on the functions of Government with effect."[1]

During the five following years, Erskine never opened his lips in Parliament. Lord Liverpool, much ridiculed when a youth for his proposed "March to Paris," and certainly one of the dullest of men, was now Prime Minister, and under him our military operations on the Continent of Europe were more brilliant than under any of his predecessors since the time of Godolphin. Opposition almost entirely ceased, and all orders and parties joined in the effort to maintain our independence against the ambition of Napoleon.

During this long interval, Erskine devoted himself almost entirely to the enjoyments of private society; but of the space which he still occupied in the eyes of mankind we may judge from the following entries respecting him in the Diary of Lord Byron:—"On Tuesday dined with Rogers, Madame De Stael, Mackintosh, Sheridan, Erskine, Payne, Knight, and others. Sheridan told a very good story of himself and Madame Recamier's handkerchief. Erskine a few stories of himself only." . . . "Lord Erskine called and gave me his favorite pamphlet, with a marginal note and corrections in his handwriting.—Sent it to be bound superbly, and shall treasure it." . . . "Lord Erskine called to-day. He means to carry out his productions on the war, or rather wars, to the present day. I trust that he will. Must send to Mr. Murray to get the binding of my copy of his pamphlet finished, as Lord Erskine has promised me to correct it and add marginal notes to it. Any thing in his handwriting will be a treasure, which will gather compound interest from years. Lord Erskine thinks the Ministers must be in peril of going out. So much the better for him."[2]

[1] 23 Parl. Deb. 346, 596.
[2] This copy, now belonging to my friend Mr. Murray, of Albemarle Street, lies before me. It contains the following memorandum, in the handwriting of Lord Erskine:—

"I have no other copy of the pamphlet but this spurious edition—full of gross errors. After Debrett had become a bankrupt, having published forty-eight editions, the present edition appears to have been published with a print which I am sanguine enough to hope was intended as a caricature.* E."

* The print, although a likeness, is certainly by no means flattering.

The ex-Chancellor's abstinence from mixing in political debates at such a season might be proper; but his neglect of law reform can not be palliated. Romilly, in his Diary, says, under date 20th June, 1814, " Lord Erskine told me on Saturday that he should certainly bring on my bill, which he has taken charge of, on this day. He had not, however, given any notice of his intention, or required that the Lords should be summoned: and though he had formerly presided in the House as Chancellor for above a year, he was ignorant, till he learned from me with surprise and evident mortification, that a previous notice was, according to constant usage, necessary before he could move the second reading of any bill." And again, under date 5th March, 1815: "I called this morning on Lord Grenville to endeavor to prevail upon him to take the charge, in the House of Lords, of my bill for subjecting freehold estates to the payment of simple contract debts; for if it continues this year, as it was the last, in the hands of Lord Erskine, who does not understand the subject, and is incapable of answering any objections that are made to it, there is no chance of its being carried." [1]

I can not, however, join in the censure of the ex-Chancellor's political conduct at this period. He had, excusably, although not magnanimously, accepted an unsolicited and unexpected offer, made to him out of personal regard by the Regent, of a " green ribbon;" and I am afraid he was rather too much gratified in wearing it, and showing in public the star of the order of the Thistle on his breast.[2] But, while the affair was creditable to the one party, I do not think that it ought to derogate from our respect for the other. At a recent public dinner, Erskine, in commenting on the arbitrary policy of the existing

There are added the two following memoranda in the handwriting of Lord Byron:—
" The corrections and erasures in this volume are made by Lord Erskine's own hand, previous to his honoring me with the present of this volume.
"Oct. 12th 1814. B."
" This copy was given to me by Lord Erskine in November (I think), 1813.
" Oct. 15th, 1814. B."
The corrections are few and immaterial.
[1] Life, iii. 141, 156.
[2] It should likewise be recollected that this was the fulfillment of the prophecy he had uttered when crossing the blasted heath, forty years ago, as related by Lord Commissioner Adam. Ante, p. 36.

Government, had entered into a warm defense of "those principles which had placed the House of Brunswick on the throne of Great Britain;" and his Royal Highness, on reading a report of this speech in the newspapers, had observed, "They are principles which would unseat any family from any throne."—However, as, upon Napoleon's escape from Elba, the new Knight concurred, with almost the whole of his party, in supporting the preparations for renewing the war, he is thus disparagingly noticed by Romilly: "Erskine, who has lately accepted a green ribbon from the Regent, voted with the Ministers, but did not speak. One might have expected, however, that he would have explained how it happened that his opinions now were so different from those which he entertained during the last war, and which he published in a pamphlet that had great celebrity. This pamphlet I remember his carrying with him to Paris after the Peace of Amiens, and giving to a number of persons there, telling every one of them that there had been still later editions than that which he gave them, which was the twenty-sixth, or some other great number, for I do not recollect exactly which it was." But, whatever doubts might be entertained of the necessity for carrying on the war with the French Republic, almost all were convinced that peace with the emperor was now impossible.

Having published a pamphlet in vindication of the Whigs, he was answered in "A Letter from an Elector of Westminster," who thus assailed him:—

"It was on the 9th of November, 1794, that I harnessed myself to the carriage of the Hon. Thomas Erskine, when that distinguished barrister was drawn through the streets of the metropolis amidst the blessings and the tears of a people whom he had saved from the gripe of oppression. . . . No time, no, nor your Lordship's subsequent conduct, shall obliterate your share in the glorious struggle that gave a breathing-time to the last defenders of their country. The congratulations belong to the rescued prisoner, but the praise was all your own; you were the saviour of the innocent, the restorer of liberty, the champion of law, of justice, and of truth. Dazzled by your eloquence—animated by your courage—sympathizing with your success—your fellow-countrymen sunk under their admiration, their gratitude, and their joy, and bowed down before the idol of their hearts. My Lord, you should have died when you descended from the triumph of that memorable day. The timely end, which is the sole protection against the reverses of fortune, would have preserved you from that more lamentable change which could have been occasioned only by yourself. Had your life closed with the procession, you would have gone down to posterity pure and entire. As it is, your admirers have nothing left for it but to separate your early career from your present state, and to look at the record of your former exploits as belonging more to history than to you."

He then enumerates specifically the imputed misdeeds down to the acceptance of the " green ribbon." Erskine published an answer,—from which I copy his characteristic defense upon the last accusation :—

" To this vulgar jest I reply, that if the author holds in republican contempt the most ancient distinctions of a monarchical state, he is undoubtedly well justified in considering the green ribbon as a laughable thing; but he fails altogether when his wit is not pointed at that *knighthood* but *personally against me*. It is well known that the order of the Thistle is a distinction for the nobility of Scotland ; and that, ever since the Union, it has been the custom to invest with it two English Peers. Now, as the author repeatedly taunts me with my STUART ancestors, he, perhaps, has inadvertently let down the force of the sarcasm he aimed at ; because I am of the family of the King who instituted the order, and had been for many years in the service of the present Sovereign, it seems difficult to find fault, either with the Prince Regent for bestowing it on me, or to make out my disqualification to receive it ; but if the insinuation was pointed to convey that the accepting it was a departure from my principles or friendships, I hold the slander in the utmost contempt, because my whole life is its unanswerable refutation. I stood towards the Prince Regent in a relation quite different from that of my friends in Parliament, having been in his Royal Highness's service from the first formation of his establishment. The appointment of those Ministers who still continue in office might for a season produce a corresponding coolness among public men, but which could not, with any propriety, involve *me*, from my particular situation, and from many personal obligations. I was bound to fulfill *all my duties*. I remained, and still remain, faithful to the Prince of Wales, but faithful alike to my principles and friends;—defying any man, as I now do, to charge me with the slightest deviation from the most perfect integrity and consistency as a member of Parliament for nearly forty years. I value the distinction alluded to, because it was a fit one of my rank and birth; and I value it the more, because it was given to me by the Prince as a mark of his personal regard, and without any wish or expectation that it could at all affect my public conduct. So much for the 'Green Ribbon,'—which I have only at all adverted to because I will not suffer even a squib to come across the unsullied path of my public life without publicly treading it out."

A collection being published about this time of the speeches of his great leader, to whom he had ever been faithful, and to whose memory he was most affectionately attached, he thus addressed Mr. Wright, the editor :—

"The expression of my regret that the utmost care and attention could give but a very faint representation of their merit is, however, no preface to my wishing they should be suppressed. Far from it. It would be an absurd objection to a bust of Demosthenes or Cicero, that the vigor of the eye was lost in the marble, and the lips cold and silent, which were the sources of his fame. It would be as strange a criticism in a cabinet of natural history, that rare animals, however ingeniously preserved, were but feeble representations of them when living,— that, though we observed the form of a lion, we could not hear him roar, nor see him stalking over the desert in the tremendous majesty of his dominion,—or that, though we could not but admire the form and plumage of an eagle, we should account it nothing, because his vast wings were not in motion, nor his prey flying dismayed under their shadow. Eloquence, which consists more in the dexterous structure of periods, and in the powers of harmony of delivery, than in the extraordinary vigor of the understanding, may be compared to a human body, not so much surpassing the dimensions of ordinary nature, as remarkable for the symmetry and beauty of its parts. If the short-hand writer, like the statuary or painter, has made no memorial of such an orator, little is left to distinguish him;—but in the most imperfect relics of Fox's speeches the bones of a giant are to be discovered. I can not but look back as to the highest and most honorable circumstance of my life, that I thought and acted with Mr. Fox through so considerable a part of his time, and that now, in my retirement from the world (for so I have considered it, since my professional course has been closed forever), I have had the opportunity of thus publicly expressing my veneration for his memory. When I followed him to the grave, I was unable, from sorrow, to support with decent firmness the high place which my situation at that period assigned me in the funeral procession; and even now, when thus engaged in the review of his splendid and useful career, I can not but feel the most affectionate and painful regret,—seeking a kind of consolation, with his numerous friends, from his being in a manner still living in the representatives of his family."[1]

Although Erskine at this period of his life never mingled in the political discussions of the House of Lords, a peerage case came on in which he took a deep interest, and on which he bestowed immense labor—the claim of Lieutenant Colonel Knollys to the earldom of Banbury.[2] He has been highly extolled by those who have hitherto written any account of his life, for his efforts on this occasion; but, although the zeal and the eloquence which he displayed are much to be admired, I think he took an entirely erroneous view of the subject, trying, without any sufficient reason, to set at variance legal presumption and physical fact.—William Knollys, the first Earl of Banbury, when an old man, married the Lady Elizabeth Howard, a girl of nineteen, and she had for her lover the young Lord Vaux. While often in the company of her husband she twice became pregnant, but concealed her pregnancy from him, and she bore two

[1] This is a well-merited compliment to the genius and amiable qualities of his friend, Lord Holland,—alas! no more,—from whom I myself received more personal kindness than from any political leader with whom I have ever been associated.

[2] I am in possession of his MSS. connected with this case, which shows in a very striking manner, the industry he could still, when necessary, call into action. These contain full notes of all the arguments at the Bar—an abstract of all the facts of the case—a collection of all the authorities upon legitimacy —his long speech in support of the claim—and his elaborate protest against the decision.

sons during his lifetime, but concealed their birth and
their existence from him. Very soon after his death she
married Lord Vaux, and the boys taking the name Vaux
were long treated as Lord Vaux's children. Shortly before the old peer died, King Charles I. prevailed upon the
House of Lords to allow him precedence for his life over
Earls created before him, "considering how old a man
this lord is, *and childless.*" His will made no mention
of any son; and an inquisition taken after his death, respecting the lands of which he was seized, found that he
died without heirs male of his body. But Edward, the
elder son, afterwards claiming to be Earl of Banbury, it
was found under a commission from the Court of Wards
that he was the son and heir of the late Earl, and having
assumed the title, he was killed abroad during his minority. Nicholas, the younger son, then called himself, and
was generally called by others, Earl of Banbury. He was
allowed to sit under that title in the Convention Parliament, which assembled in 1660, but he was not summoned to the next Parliament. A committee of privileges reported that in the eye of the law he was the son
of the late Earl—but still a writ was refused to him on
the opinion of the Attorney General, and he died without being allowed to take his seat. His son Charles was
likewise excluded. He assumed the title, however, and,
being indicted for murder, petitioned the Lords that he
might be tried as a Peer, but they decided against him.
He then pleaded his peerage in abatement, and the decision of the House of Lords being replied, Holt, C. J.,
to the great wrath of the Peers, with perfect propriety
allowed the plea, as the decision of the Peers was not
founded on any reference by the Crown. His descendants continued to call themselves Earls of Banbury, but
were not summoned to the House of Lords, and did not
again take any proceeding to establish their right till the
petition presented by the present claimant. Erskine, being his private friend and thoroughly convinced that his
claim was well-founded in law, delivered a very animated
speech in the Committee of Privileges, to which it was
referred:—

"I admit," said he, "that the claimant labors under
great disadvantages. The facts, in his case, are extraordinary, and the grave has long since been closed over all

the individuals whose evidence could afford him any assistance. His claim is almost as old as the patent of his ancestor, and successive generations have passed away without any recognition of it by this House. Yet time would be the instrument of injustice, if it operated to raise any legal bar to the claimant's right. Questions of peerage are not fettered by the rules of law that prescribe the limitation of actions, and it is one of the brightest privileges of our order that we transmit to our descendants a title to the honors we have inherited or earned, which is incapable either of alienation or surrender. .... The rule relating to the bastardy of children born in wedlock may be reduced to a single point—' the presumption in favor of the legitimacy of the child must stand, until the contrary be proved by the *impossibility* of the husband being the father, and this impossibility must arise either from his physical inability or from non-access.' It has been urged, that strong improbability is sufficient; but this I confidently deny. We do not sit here to balance improbabilities on such a topic as this. If access can be proved, the inference from it is irresistible,—whatever moral probability there may exist of the adulterer being the father, whatever suspicions may arise from the conduct of the wife, or the situation of the family,—the issue must be legitimate. Such is the law of the land. Women are not shut up here as in the Eastern world, and the presumption of their virtue is inseparable from their liberty. If the presumption were once overthrown, the field would be laid open to unlimited inquiries into the privacy of domestic life; no man's legitimacy would be secure, and the law would be accessory to the perpetration of every species of imposture and iniquity. A fixed rule may give rise to occasional deviations from justice; but these amount to nothing more than the price which every member of the community may be called upon to pay for the advantage of an enlightened code. No laws can be framed sufficiently comprehensive to embrace the infinite varieties of human action, and the labors of the lawgiver must be confined to the development of those principles which constitute the support and security of society. He views man with reference to the general good, and that alone. He legislates for men in general,—

not for particular cases. No one can doubt that the interests of society are best consulted by making a question of such frequent occurrence as *legitimacy* to rest on a limited number of distinct facts—easy to be proved, but not to be counterfeited—instead of leaving it to be the result of inference from a series of indefinite circumstances, separately trifling, and only of importance collectively, from the object to which they are applied. Marriage and cohabitation afford us a more sure solution of the question of legitimacy than we could arrive at by any reasoning on the conduct of the husband and wife: As to the advanced age of the husband in this case, there is no statute of limitations on the powers and faculties of man. Instances of robust longevity might be cited still more extraordinary. Sir Stephen Fox married at the age of seventy-seven, and had four children; the first child was born when the father was seventy-eight; the second and third were twins in the following year, and the fourth was born when the father was eighty-one. The Earl of Ilchester and Lord Holland can vouch for the accuracy of this statement, and I believe their genealogy has stood hitherto unquestioned. Parr became a father when his first-born son was of a more advanced age than the old Earl of Banbury. Moreover, his Lordship seems to have kept all his faculties both of body and mind in full exercise. Though eighty-four or eighty-five years of age, not only does it appear, from the evidence of one of the witnesses, that he went out hawking up to his death, but the Journals of this House furnish us with the best evidence of his attention to more important matters. Then, my Lords, why is the bounty of Lord Vaux to his step-son to be ascribed to another motive than what belonged to such a relationship? Why is Nicholas to be supposed to have repudiated the title of Banbury, because in his childhood he had been called by the name of Vaux? These are weak arms to encounter a presumption so strong as that which exists in favor of legitimacy. The same rights have descended to the present petitioner, and I trust they will be recognized by your Lordships."

But it is quite clear, both from reason and authority, that although the husband and wife may have had an opportunity of being in the society of each other about the time to which the origin of the child is to be ascribed, —without proof of the *impossibility* of the husband being the father, there may be circumstances to lead to the conclusion that they did not live together as husband and wife, and that the paramour of the wife may be considered the father of the child. In the present case the concealment of the birth of the two boys from the Earl of Banbury, and the treatment of them as adulterous bastards, both by their mother and by Lord Vaux, afforded abundant ground for these inferences.—Lord Eldon, Lord Redesdale, and Lord Ellenborough accordingly gave a strong opinion against the claim. But such an impression was made by the plausible arguments in support of it, that upon a division in the committee it was only negatived by a majority of 21 to 13.[1] Erskine in a great rage, drew up a strong protest, which was signed by three royal Dukes and seven other peers,—and, writing about it to a friend, said:—" The Protest gives our opponents every fact and all arguments, but they are without a single voice in Westminster Hall from one end to the other." The decision, however, is in conformity to the Code Napoleon, which, on the birth of a child born in wedlock being concealed from the husband, admits proof that it is the child of an adulterer, and having been followed in several cases since, which have been carried by appeal to the House of Lords, it is now universally acquiesced in and considered to be law.[2]

[1] It was said that among the twenty-one were four spiritual Peers who had never attended, and ten lay Peers who attended only occasionally ; while the whole of the thirteen had attended constantly,—being, I presume, stanch partisans.
[2] See Morris *v.* Davis, Clark and Finelly's Reports, vol. v. 163, where all the authorities are collected.—The Judges all say, that if it be believed that intercourse did take place between the husband and wife, whereby the child by possibility may be the child of the husband, it is *presumptio juris et de jure*, —or an invariable rule of law,—that the child is legitimate ; but put the supposable, though not probable case, that the husband and wife are *whites,* that the paramour is a *negro,* and that the child is a *mulatto. Quid juris ?*

CHAPTER CLXXXVIII.

CONTINUATION OF THE LIFE OF LORD ERSKINE TILL THE
CONCLUSION OF THE TRIAL OF QUEEN CAROLINE.

THE battle of Waterloo being gained, and Napoleon relegated to St. Helena,—a measure necessary for the repose of the world,—party warfare likewise ceased for a time; but Erskine was at his post when hostilities against the Constitution were renewed, and he opposed with all his ancient vigor the "Seditious Meetings' Bill" and the suspension of the "Habeas Corpus Act," denouncing these measures as sure to excite instead of allay discontent, and as more injurious to the Constitution than any passed in the "Reign of Terror," under Mr. Pitt, when a foreign war and apparent danger from the spread of French principles, afforded some pretext for such arbitrary legislation.[1] In opposing a new "Seditious Meetings' Bill," he said,—

"If the authors of this bill had the government of the seasons, they would no doubt set about a reformation upon their own system; and the elements of fire, water, and air would no longer have their immemorial liberties, but would be put under such politic restraints as we are now about to lay upon the civil world. To *Fire*, they would say, 'You are an excellent servant, most beneficial when under due discipline and control, but most dangerous when left unrestrained. You may, therefore continue to blaze in our kitchen and in our chambers, but you shall no longer descend from heaven with electric flashes, destroying our persons and property, and striking even the spires of our churches with sacrilegious violence.' To *Water* they would say, 'We are delighted with your smooth face upon our calm, transparent lakes, and with your ripplings in our summer streams; but you must no longer come down from the hills in winter torrents, sweeping away our flocks and their masters.' To the *Air* they would say, 'Be free as air; it is even a proverb, and we will support it; continue, therefore, to be free as air, at least in our improved sense of freedom. But not more

[1] 35 Parl. Deb. 1213, 1224, 1226; 36 Ibid. 981.

than fifty clouds shall in future come together, without an order from seven farmers or graziers ; and if you shall presume to blight our fruit-trees or destroy our harvests, you shall be driven back to your caverns by a single justice of the peace.'"[1]

He likewise brought in a bill to prevent arrest for libel before indictment found against the libeler. This measure he supported in a most elaborate speech, but it was rejected on the second reading by a large majority.[2]

In the following stormy session, in which the "Six Acts" were passed—(I hope the last trial of the coercive system for England)—Erskine was active and energetic. He began by supporting Lord Grey's amendment to the Address; when he condemned in severe terms "the massacre at Manchester," on the dispersion of Mr. Hunt's meeting there,—and the Secretary of State's letter, approving of the violent conduct of the magistrates and the military without any previous inquiry.[3]

On Lord Landsdowne's motion for a committee to inquire into the state of the country, Erskine said, with much feeling,—

"My Lords, I am now an old man, and have been

[1] 57 Geo. 3, c. 3. [2] 38 Parl. Deb.
[3] 41 Parl. Deb. 26, 40. An anecdote which he then told, in the vain hope of inducing Lord Eldon to retract an opinion he had uttered, deserves to be recorded in his own language :—" There shoots across my mind at this moment a striking instance of candor which I have long treasured up in my memory, having a strong interest to remember it, because it was useful to me in the beginning of my professional life. Having been engaged in a cause in which that great Chief Justice [Lord Mansfield] had expressed a strong opinion in favor of my client, the jury found a corresponding verdict ; but a rule having been obtained to set it aside for the Judge's misdirection, I had to support his opinion in the Court of King's Bench. When I had finished my argument he said—I fear with more indulgence than truth—' This case has been remarkably well argued ; so well, indeed, that while the learned counsel was defending my direction, I began to think I had been in the right, whereas I never was more mistaken in my life. I totally misunderstood the case, and misdirected the jury; so there must be a new trial, and without of time. Did this lower Lord Mansfield ? So far from it, that having persuaded himself his first opinion was the best, I could not help saying at the time that if I had not been convinced of his integrity, I should have thought he was practicing a fraud to advance his reputation. It was indeed a justice to truth, which weak men are afraid of rendering, and therefore it is so seldom rendered."—I have myself often been surprised at the pusillanimous anxiety of Judges in *Banc* to support their rulings at *Nisi Prius*. Very different was the conduct of a Judge in recent times, who after all his brethren on the bench had pronounced judgment in his favor, said, " For the reasons given by my Lord and the rest of the Court, I think that I was entirely wrong, and that there ought to be a new trial."

nearly forty years in Parliament; yet I declare solemnly that I never felt more unqualified regret for any proceeding in it than the rejection of the amendment proposed by my noble friend, and so eloquently pressed upon our attention on the first day of the session. If your Lordships had fortunately adopted it, you could have had nothing further to consider on this painful subject, and would have escaped the second error of rejecting the proposition of the noble marquis to-night, which I can not but painfully foresee. You would then have had an unanimous Parliament reprobating all seditious combinations, calling upon both magistrates and people, by the combined authorities of the state to support the Constitution, and to maintain public order and tranquillity. The amendment asked nothing more than that the people should not be condemned unheard. I have had many more opportunities of knowing the sentiments and feelings of those who are classed as seditious subjects than most of your Lordships can have had, and it is my unalterable belief that a system of alarm, supported by mysterious green bags and the array of special commissions, followed as they have been, and will be, by convictions sufficiently numerous to inspire terror—not sufficiently numerous to enforce subjugation—only exasperate evils the unfortunate existence of which we all deplore. The present discontent may be silenced by severity, but it will be a dangerous silence." "As to the *Spenceans,*" he said, "they can not be gravely considered objects of criminal justice. Instead of the warrants of magistrates, the certificates of apothecaries may secure their persons if they become dangerous. What other prison, indeed, but a madhouse can be opened to receive persons so completely insane as to entertain an expectation that in such a country as England they can bring its whole surface and property into general division and distribution. By an ordinary display of spirit and resolution, insurrection may be repressed without violating the law or the Constitution. In the riots of 1780, when the mob were preparing to attack the house of Lord Mansfield, I offered to defend it with a small military force; but this offer was unluckily rejected; and afterwards, being in the Temple when the rioters were preparing to force the gate and had fired several times, I went forward to the gate, opened it, and showed them a field-piece which I was prepared to discharge in case the attack was persisted in; they were daunted, fell back, and dispersed."

After this somewhat vain-glorious narrative of his martial prowess (for which I find no other authority, he entered at great length into the law respecting public meetings; and, having commented upon the late conduct of the Government on this subject, he observed,—

"The threatened severe measures can not restore confidence, nor willing obedience to government. *Confide yourselves in the people*, and all murmurs and discontents will be at an end. For my own part, while I have life and strength to raise my voice, I will continue to protest against them *here and everywhere*. I will not repeat with the same oath what I swore in the House of Commons when similar restrictions were in agitation,[1] but I will say firmly, that I was born a freeman, and I will not die a slave."[2]

Dissatisfied with himself, he thus apologized for what he considered his want of energy in Parliament as compared with his forensic efforts:—

"I despair altogether of making any impression by anything I can say—a feeling which disqualifies me from speaking as I ought. I have been accustomed during the greatest part of my life to be animated by the hope and expectation that I might not be speaking in vain,—without which there can be no spirit in discourse. I have often heard it said, and I believe it to be true, that even the most eloquent man living (how then must I be disabled!) and however deeply impressed with his subject, could scarcely find utterance, if he were to be standing up alone, and speaking only against a dead wall."

As the several bills came forward, he strenuously, though ineffectually, opposed them in every stage;[3] but I do not dwell upon their odious enactments, as in better times they have all been repealed or allowed to expire, and there seems no danger of their ever again being pro-

[1] Perhaps he recollected the lines in the "Pursuits of Literature" in which the author of that satire, among things impossible ("Sooner," &c.) says,
"Or Erskine cease from impotent grimace,
And his appeals to God,—his prime disgrace."
[2] 41 Parl. Deb. 441.
[3] Ibid. 682, 695, 706, 966, 981, 1304, 1307, 1310, 1374.

posed, as, with a much greater disposition to insurrection among the lower orders than then existed, both the great parties in the state have wisely and successfully trusted to a vigorous and judicious use of the ordinary powers of the law.[1]

While these discussions were pending, George III. expired. Although the government had still been carried on in his name, he had long since ceased to control or to be conscious of public events; and for many years, as if already sleeping in the grave—

> ...."Nor steel nor poison,
> Malice domestic, foreign levy, nothing
> Could touch him further."

The Prince of Wales, under the title of REGENT, had exercised without restriction all the prerogatives of the Crown, and this event merely changed his title to that of George IV., without at all affecting his political position.

But the lady to whom he had given his hand, instead of being an outcast, wandering in foreign countries, sometimes under a feigned name, with hardly pecuniary supplies to defray the expenses of her slender suite, was suddenly Queen of England, entitled by law to share the throne, and to enjoy many powers and privileges suitable to her exalted rank. The new Sovereign was now to pay a dreadful penalty for the manner in which he had insulted and abandoned her. Owing to the levity of her conduct, after the "Letter of License" he had given her—whether she had actually broken her marriage vow or not—he could not receive her back as his wife without dishonor, and he could take no proceedings to obtain a divorce from her without exciting the sympathies of all mankind in her favor, and exposing his conduct towards her in a manner which must not only be fatal to his own reputation, but even dangerous to the monarchy. With prudence, an arrangement could perhaps have been made by which she might have remained quietly abroad, her title and an adequate establishment being conceded to her; but he still continued under the rule of his vindictive

---

[1] I allude to the Whig Government in 1839-40, and to the Conservative in 1841-42. I must again express my joy at being at liberty to reprobate the whole system of coercion, without being liable even to the suspicion of trying to throw odium on political opponents.

passions, and, to his lasting misfortune, and to the unspeakable prejudice of the nation, his Ministers had not the firmness to resist the mad measures which he suggested against her. Instead of entering into negotiation with her, the first rash proceeding of the new reign was illegally to exclude her name from the Liturgy, as if already convicted of some great crime, although the meanest subject in the realm was entitled to the presumption of innocence till proved to be guilty. In spite of the threats held out to her, she boldly came to this country to claim her rights,—and in an evil hour Lord Liverpool and Lord Eldon yielded to the desire of her husband, that she should be brought to a public trial for adultery. This did not, as in the time of Henry VIII., take the shape of an indictment for high treason, as not only were her alleged offenses committed beyond the seas, but it was not supposed that, under the circumstances, even if she had been convicted, the public would have endured to see her share the fate of Anne Boleyn or Katherine Howard. All that was asked was, that, being declared guilty of adultery, her marriage with his Majesty should be dissolved, and she should be degraded from her state and dignity as Queen. Little did the authors of this measure calculate upon her spirit, or upon the love of justice which ever actuates the inhabitants of Britain.

In the proceedings which followed, Erskine took a very prominent part, and, as it may be considered the close of his public life, I particularly rejoice to think that it was altogether worthy of him. Closely connected as he had been for so many years with the royal prosecutor, who regarded with indignation and abhorrence all opposition to his will on this subject, he exercised an impartial and independent judgment on the merits of the case, and gave his opinion and his vote on every question which arose in it, as if he had been sitting in an ordinary criminal court to decide upon his oath between humble individuals of whose names he had never before heard.

Differing with most of the members of his party, he supported the preliminary motion for submitting to a secret committee the contents of the "green bag" alleged to be sufficient to establish the Queen's guilt, as he thought the King was entitled to a hearing, and his step was analogous to the finding of an indictment by a grand jury.[1] But when, after the report of the committee, the "Bill of Pains and Penalties" had been presented, and a day was fixed for the second reading, which was to be the commencement of the open trial, he moved that before that day arrived the Queen should be furnished with a list of the witnesses to be produced against her:—

"This proceeding," said he "is so rare, or rather so anomalous, that no precedent can be found exactly to apply to it: but, in trying to hold the scales of justice equal between the accuser and accused, we may be guided by the spirit of the excellent statute of William III. for the protection of persons charged with high treason—whereby, before the Court is opened, the prisoner is to be furnished with a list of the witnesses, as well as a copy of the indictment. What is the principle of this admirable enactment, conferring a privilege which, in ordinary cases, is denied?—Because the prisoner has not to contend with an equal accuser—and therefore he is covered all over with the armor of the law. Is not the present case of the same description? I do not mean to speak invidiously, but only to point out the situation of the illustrious accused. She has to contend against the Crown and its Ministers, and against all the powers and influences which they possess. In most cases of high treason, the Crown and its Ministers have no personal wrongs to stimulate resentment, nor any other interest in conviction than a general interest in the safety of the state: but here the King himself is the individual charged to be personally wronged, and he may be said to be personally the accuser; the illustrious accused is charged directly in the bill with 'a violation of the duty she owed to his Majesty,'—not as his subject, but in violation of her duty as his wife. This gives an increased force to the great fountain of influence against which she has to contend. Ministers have staked their credit—perhaps their existence—on the success of the course they have recommended or assented to. Let it not, however, be thought that I am charging the Sovereign with making unworthy exertions in the prosecution even of a personal wrong, or his ministers with a design corruptly to concur in them; but the general presumption of law is entirely founded upon the probable abuse of power in trials for offense against the

[1] Hansard, new series, i. 922, 1116, 1211.

state, and it is impossible to resist or evade that presumption by arguing against any probable injustice in any particular case, without overthrowing the principle upon which the very law you yourselves have enacted, and have so long abided by, can alone rest for its support. I am well aware that no rules can bind us; but how shall we escape from reproach if we refuse to abide by those rules which we have made binding upon others, the reason for their obligation applying equally, or more forcibly, to ourselves? The generality of the charge also in the preamble of this bill adds most imperiously to the demand of the statute of King William. It is in effect a criminal charge, or it is nothing; yet it in no way resembles any other criminal charge ever exhibited, here or elsewhere, before any court of justice. Above all, it has none of the precision which is the very characteristic of English law. Her Majesty is not charged with any specific act of adultery, but with 'an adulterous intercourse'—and this not at any specified time or times, but during her whole absence from England, for six years together—which exposes her to criminating evidence, not only as to acts, but general deportment on every one day or hour of the day throughout all that time;—and this also not confined to any place or places, though it was known she had been traveling in countries remotely distant from each other. I do not mention this as an arraignment of the framers of the bill; it is enough for my view of the subject, that this unparalleled generality of accusation creates an unparalleled difficulty of defense, and renders a list of the witnesses indispensably necessary for the ends of justice. As the adulterous intercourse is alleged to have taken place with one whose station required his constant attendance on her person, through the many countries she visited, it is obviously impossible to anticipate, within whole years, or within thousands of miles, the assaults to be made upon her acts, or even upon her general deportment, which the bill calls upon her to defend. Another analogy between this Bill of Pains and Penalties and a trial for high treason arises from the punishment to be inflicted on conviction. What, my Lords, is death, which in a moment ends us, to the lingering and degrading suffering which the accused may, under our judgment, be sentenced to endure? Born a Princess, of the same illustrious house as the King, her consort, and now raised to wear the imperial crown of the greatest nation that ever flourished on the earth,—she may be suddenly cast down to shame and sorrow,—and not only excluded from the society of her exalted kindred, but forever deprived of the esteem and affection of the whole female world. For my own part, my Lords, this appears to me the heaviest and most intolerable punishment which any human tribunal can inflict. These are my sentiments, and no person surely can reasonably accuse or suspect me of any leaning beyond that of justice to the cause of the illustrious accused: my leanings, if I could suffer their intrusion, would rather draw me to the opposite side. All your Lordships must know that I have spent a great part of my life in the service of the present King. I remember, indeed, so well, and feel so strongly, the warm interest taken by his Majesty in my prosperity and happiness, in some of the most important periods of my progress, that I could not be unjust to him. The habits of my professional life are, I hope, a useful shield against every bias whatsoever. I was bred, in my early youth, in two professions, the characteristic of which is honor. But, after the experience of very many years, I can say with truth, that they can not stand higher for honor than the profession of the law. Amidst unexampled temptations, which, through human frailty, have produced their victims, the great bulk of the members of it are sound; and the cause is obvious—there is something so beautiful and exalted in the faithful administration of justice, and departure from it is so odious and disgusting, that a perpetual monitor is raised up in the mind against the accesses of corruption. The same protection ought also to apply to us, the highest of the Judges. When this House shall have deliberately and solemnly decided that the restraints imposed by common law and by statute, to shut out all the approaches to mistake, influence, or corruption, may be set at naught, will not the reserve and caution of all inferior judicatures be impaired?—will not the consequence be the disregard, perhaps even the repeal, of those admirable and now ancient rules by which, though we have enacted them to govern others, we ourselves have refused to be governed? Believe me, my Lords, I feel upon this part of the subject, so inseparably connected with the illustration of our country, much more than by any words I can express. It may be superstition, perhaps, but I can not alter the nature and character of my undertanding, which, as long as I can look back, has dictated to me, as a comforting truth, that the DIVINE PROVIDENCE singles out particular nations, and perhaps even individual men, to carry on the slow and mysterious system of the world. This island, although placed on the very margin of civilization, has been its example and its protector,—spreading the blessings of a pure religion and of equal laws to the remotest ends of the earth. My impression, my Lords, has always been, that such an unparalleled dominion is but a more exalted trust, and that, if we fall off from the character which bestowed it, and which fitted us for its fulfillment, we shall be deservedly treated like sentinels who desert, or who sleep upon, their posts. Let us stand by the principles of the Revolution, which so happily made us what we are, and by adhering to which we shall remain what we ought to be. My Lords, I have not made these observations from any desire to disappoint or obstruct the course we are engaged in. When the Court assembles, I will do my duty as if all the angels of heaven were taking notes of whatever passes through my mind on the subject."

But upon a division there were for the motion only 28, —against it 78.[1] A few days after, Erskine presented a petition from the Queen, lamenting that the House of Lords had deemed it proper to refuse her a list of the witnesses, and praying for "a specification of the place or places in which the criminal acts charged upon her are alleged to have been committed—without which she could only adequately prepare for her defense by bringing from every place she had visited during the last six years every person who had had the means of observing any part of her conduct." Although he enforced a motion to this effect by another able speech, on this occasion only eleven Peers voted along with him,[2]—so inauspiciously did the defense of Queen Caroline begin. But these flagrant outrages shocked public feeling, and greatly contributed to rouse that general sympathy in her favor which finally proved irresistible.[3]

[1] Hansard, ii. 314, 428, 470, 472.   [2] Ib. 574, 586.
[3] In Scotland a list of the witnesses is given in every criminal case; and

When the trial actually began, the eyes of mankind were chiefly turned on Mr. Brougham and Mr. Denman, whose heroic exertions in favor of their oppressed, if not innocent, client shed fresh luster on English forensic eloquence. Erskine was still distinguished in striving for impartial justice between the parties, by watching the procedure and enforcing the rules of evidence. A discussion arising respecting the mode of swearing the witnesses, he related the following anecdote, to great amusement of the House:—

"My Lords, when I was counsel in a cause tried in the Court of King's Bench, an important witness called against me, without describing himself to be of any particular sect, so as to be entitled to indulgence, stated, that from certain ideas in his own mind he could not swear according to the usual form of the oath; that he would *hold up his hand* and would swear, but that he would not kiss the book. I have no difficulty in saying that I wished very much to get rid of that witness; and I asked what was his reason for refusing to be sworn in the usual form? He gave a reason, which seemed to me a very absurd one, '*Because it is written in the " Revelations," that the angel standing on the sea* HELD UP HIS HAND.' I said, '*This does not apply to your case; for, in the first place you are no angel, secondly, you can not tell how the angel would have sworn if he had stood on dry ground, as you do.*' Lord Kenyon sent into the Common Pleas, to consult Lord Chief Justice Eyre, who expressed himself of opinion, that although the witness was not of any particular sect, yet if he stated (whether his reason was a good or a bad one) that there was a particular mode of swearing most consistent with his feelings of the obligation of an oath, this mode ought to be adopted. So the witness was sworn in his own fashion. Whether he spoke the truth or not, unfortunately for my client, the witness was believed by the jury, and I felt that the Judge was right, so that there was no ground for moving to set aside the verdict."[1]

A motion being made by the Attorney General to adjourn the trial, that additional witnesses for the prosecution might have time to arrive, Erskine strenuously resisted it, saying that "no such instance has ever been in England, in an action for *crim. con.*, a specification as to times and places is ordered as a matter of course. [1] 2 Hansard, 911.

heard of in any court of justice: to grant such an application would be subversive of all those principles upon which the security and the life of every individual in the kingdom depend. I can believe that your Lordships will agree to it; but if you do, I shall feel it my duty to record my solemn protest against such a decision. I have attended, with great inconvenience to myself at my advanced age, humbly to assist your Lordships on points of law or evidence, with the result of my long experience; but if such an application as the present be granted, experience, reasoning, and precedent are no longer of any avail in this House; and it is time for me to retire." The Attorney General would still have had a large majority in his favor, if he had chosen to persist in his application; but, in consideration of the feeling which was rising out of doors, he prudently withdrew it.[1]

The case for the Crown being closed, and an adjournment of three weeks granted to enable her Majesty to prepare for her defense, Erskine made a very anomalous motion, which could only be excused by the peculiarity of the case, "That Mr. Brougham should then be allowed to comment on the King's witnesses, without being required to open the evidence he meant himself to adduce till the House met again." He urged with some effect the disadvantage under which the Queen had labored for want of a list of the witnesses, and a specification, with time and place, of the charges against her; and he pointed out the unfairness of allowing the evidence for the King, with the opening and summing up of his counsel, to remain so long in the minds of their Lordships and of the public without any answer. But precedent and convenience were on the other side, and, without any obloquy being on this occasion incurred by the House, the motion was properly negatived by a majority of 170 to 40.[2]

When all the evidence on both sides had been given, and the speeches at the bar were at last concluded, the important debate on the second reading of the bill was opened by the Lord Chancellor; and Erskine, rising to answer him, said:

"I am now drawing near to the close of a long life, and I must end it as I began it. If you strike out of it, my Lords, some efforts to secure the sacred privilege of im-

[1] 2 Hansard, 1326.   [2] 3 Id. 40.

partial trial to the people of this country, and by example to spread it throughout the world, what would be left to me? What else seated me here? What else would there be to distinguish me from the most useless and insignificant among mankind? Nothing—just nothing!—And shall I then consent to this suicide—this worse than suicide of the body, this destruction of what alone can remain to me after death—the good-will of my countrymen? I DARE NOT DO THAT.—Proceedings of this kind, my Lords, have never been countenanced but in the worst times—and have afterwards not only been reversed, but stigmatized. You were justly reminded at the bar, that they were ordered by succeeding Parliaments to be taken off the file and burned,—' to the end that the same might no longer be visible in after ages!' But upon that I desire to repeat a sentiment which I remember to have expressed in struggling against arbitrary prosecutions in former times—that, instead of directing these records to be burned, they ought rather to have been blazoned in our Parliaments, and in all our tribunals, that, like the characters which appearing on the wall were deciphered by the prophet of God to the Eastern tyrant, they might enlarge and blacken in our sight to terrify us from acts of injustice."

He was then proceeding to analyze the evidence, when, according to the Parliamentary History, " his voice suddenly ceased. The pause was not particularly noticed at first, as it appeared as if his Lordship were looking over the minutes placed on the table before him; but after some time had elapsed without his resuming his speech, some of the peers became alarmed, and rose from their seats to gather round him. The anxiety of the House was now roused as he fell forward senseless on the table. There were cries of '*Open the windows!*' and '*Some water!*' The Lord Chancellor and the Earl of Liverpool evinced the greatest concern, and proceeded immediately to Lord Erskine's assistance—along with Earls Grey and Carnarvon, Lord Holland and Mr. Baron Garrow;—but his speech and color were gone. They were obliged to carry him into an adjoining room, where medical aid was procured—and the house adjourned."[1] It was generally thought that his end was to resemble that of the great

[1] Hansard, 1469.

Earl of Chatham, and it certainly would have been well for his reputation if he had now expired in the discharge of his public duty; but it was found that he was suffering a violent temporary cramp in the stomach,—which was completely relieved soon after he had been conveyed home. When intelligence of his safety had been received, the House of Lords reassembled, and Lord Lauderdale continued the debate, contending, to the grief of his old political associates, that the proceeding against the Queen was laudable, and that her guilt was established by the witnesses she herself had called.

The following morning Erskine was so far recovered as to be able to attend in his place; but he did not then attempt to continue his argument, the day being exhausted by two very able speeches, on opposite sides, from Lord Grey and Lord Liverpool. But again appearing at the next sitting of the House, he resumed his discourse, and said:—

"It is no longer my intention to minutely examine the evidence which I was proceeding to do when attacked by sudden indisposition. I experienced kindness from your Lordships, for which I can never be sufficiently grateful. The admirable speech of my noble friend (Earl Grey), which, at every risk to my health, I yesterday attended to hear, renders such a course unnecessary. The attempt would only unsettle your minds from a conviction which must be impressed upon them by the perspicuity with which he laid the facts before you, and the cogency with which he drew the just inferences from them. I now offer myself to your Lordships rather as a kind of authority from long professional habits, than as a debater—omitting, however, none of the facts supposed to be established by the prosecutor—submitting to you, at the same time, the principles of law by which their truth or falsehood ought to be examined, and the just consequences which follow from such of them as are true. If I were a judge trying an action for adultery under similar circumstances, I think I should thus begin my summing up: 'Gentlemen of the Jury, I am under no small embarrassment in stating my opinion on the case before you, after having seen your box opened, and the plaintiff in the cause admitted to assist you in the verdict you are to pronounce: but on this I wish to be silent, as it is a matter to which we must now submit, and which is expected to be a valuable improvement of the Constitution. All things arrive but by degrees at perfection, and the prejudices of our ancestors regarding the trial by jury, and the securities provided by them for its independence, are likely to be superseded by this grand discovery of the present age. The defendant certainly has laid before you the most positive evidence of the foulest practices to corrupt the sources of justice.'—My Lords, I find I can not go on with a supposititious case, nor continue to address you as a jury; amidst such disgusting instances of fraud and perjury I can not preserve the coolness which becomes a Judge in a court of law, and I must speak with the freedom which may, in such a case, be not improperly exercised by a member of this House. A dark cloud hangs over the very beginning of the prosecution; and when we find the accusation to have been hatched in secret, and to have been supported by all the power and influence of foreign governments,—when we see that some of the witnesses have been thrust forward by force, and others by the same force have been kept back—and that the foulest subornation has been detected, —what security could we have had for the truth of any part of the evidence, even if it had not been impeached by the palpable perjuries which have been exposed? If her Majesty be really guilty, and the prosecution is therefore a just one, no false testimony could exist; false testimony is never found where a prosecution could be supported by truth, and one detected falsehood takes away from the credulity of testimony brought forward by the same party, although it stands without direct contradiction." Having commented at considerable length on all the principal witnesses, he said: "If I were in the Queen's situation, and I were convicted of adultery by your Lordships on such evidence as this, I would cast your decision in your face, and appeal to the other House of Parliament—to the representatives of the people. The House of Commons can not pass the bill against their own conviction, and against the national *nolle prosequi* which resounds from every quarter of the island.—Of the legal proof of adultery I can not be ignorant, having conducted every important case of that kind for thirty years, not only in Westminster Hall, but likewise on the circuits; and I am sure, my Lords, it is impossible to infer that the opinion I have formed on this unfortunate subject has arisen from prejudice or from partial inclination. To the King, who can not be an indifferent spectator of this proceeding, I have many, many obligations, from the warm interest formerly taken by his Majesty in my advancement and credit, and from my belief that I am still held by him in the same personal regard—though political changes have removed me to a greater distance from his person. If his Majesty should ever be exposed to any injurious treatment, I should be ready to protect him at the peril of my life. I would contribute to his happiness by every sacrifice but that of my duty. My principles I never have deserted, and never will desert."

He is said to have sat down amid loud cheers. The second reading was carried,—but only by a majority of 28.[1] The bill was further greatly damaged in the committee from an attack of Erskine, and still more from the diversity of opinion among the bishops, with respect to the canonical doctrine of divorce.

During the short debate on the third reading every one perceived that the measure was "*doomed*;" and Erskine declared that "he should content himself with saying, notwithstanding his great respect for the learning of his noble friend on the woolsack, he continued of the opinion he had formerly given on the effect of the evidence,"—asserting that, "if it were the last word he had to utter in this world, he should pronounce the evidence to be wholly insufficient to support the charge; and he was certain that it would not be held sufficient in any Court in which justice was duly administered." The third reading was carried, but only by a majority of 9.[2]

Lord Liverpool: "I can not be ignorant of the state of the public feeling, and this House has determined that the bill shall be read a third time by a majority of not more than nine votes. Had the third reading been carried by as considerable a number of Peers as the second, I and my colleagues would have felt it our duty to persevere, and to send the bill down to the other branch of the Legislature. In the present state of the country, however, and with the difference of sentiment among your Lordships so nearly balanced, we have come to the resolution not to proceed further with it. I move, there-

[1] 3 Hansard, 95 to 123. 1698.   [2] Ib. 99 to 108. 1744.

fore, that the further consideration of the bill be adjourned to this day six months."

Lord Erskine: "I see the fate of this odious measure consummated, and I heartily rejoice at the event. My Lords, I am an old man, and my life, whether it has been for good or for evil, has been passed under the sacred rule of the law. In this moment I feel my strength renovated by that rule being restored. The accursed charge wherewithal we had been menaced has passed over our heads. There is an end of that horrid and portentous excrescence of a new law—retrospective, oppressive, and iniquitous. Our Constitution is once more safe. My heart is too full of the escape we have just experienced to let me do more than try to express my sense of the blessings which we have regained:—but I can not praise them adequately myself, and I therefore prefer the langnage of one of the most eloquent writers of any age—Hooker—in his great work on Ecclesiastical Polity: 'Of Law, there can be no less acknowledged, than that her seat is the bosom of God; her voice, the harmony of the world: all things in heaven and in earth do her homage,—the very least as feeling her care, and the greatest as not exempted from her power:—both angels and men, and creatures of what condition soever,—though each in different sort and manner yet all with uniform concert,—admiring her as the mother of their peace and joy.'"[1]

This proved to be Erskine's last speech in the House of Lords; and it certainly was a glorious termination of his parliamentary career.

CHAPTER CLXXXIX.

CONTINUATION OF THE LIFE OF LORD ERSKINE TILL HIS LAST VISIT TO SCOTLAND.

AFTER the Queen's trial Erskine survived nearly three years, but he very rarely appeared in his place in Parliament, and he never again addressed the Peers except once or twice, in a tone of conversation, upon a point of order. However, his chivalrous defense of

[1] 3 Hansard, 1747.

Caroline of Brunswick, in the midst of strong temptations to side with her prosecutors, revived his ancient popularity; and, without any fresh exertion, he continued till his death the idol of the multitude, almost as much as he had been when exposing the danger to liberty from "constructive treason" in the defense of Hardy and Horne Tooke. He was loudly cheered as often as he appeared in public; addresses, and gold boxes containing grants of the freedom of corporations, poured in upon him from all parts of the country, and prints and busts of him ornamented every workshop and almost every cottage.

The Scotch, who, notwithstanding their alleged nationality, have always been cautiously slow in doing honor to their eminent men while alive,—although they were proud of the greatest advocate that had ever practiced at the English Bar, had never, hitherto, shown him any public mark of distinction—piqued, perhaps, by his seeming neglect of them, for he had not once visited his native land since he first left it in the uniform of a midshipman, more than half a century ago. At last, however, a general desire existed in all ranks beyond the Tweed to see among them, and publicly to honor, the man who had done so much to raise the national fame and to remove the prejudice that they were time-serving politicians—ever ready, for the sake of a job, to support and to praise the minister of the day. Accordingly, he was invited to a public dinner at Edinburgh, and he at once accepted the invitation,—not only from gratified vanity, but from a desire to revisit the scenes of his childhood, and, above all, from a curiosity to cross by a bridge the *loch* or lake which had been the northern boundary of AULD REEKIE, and to admire beyond it the splendid New Town of Edinburgh, where he had been accustomed to shoot wild ducks and snipes.

On his arrival in the Scottish metropolis he eagerly flew to his old haunts, particularly the "flat" in the lofty house inhabited by his father and mother,—the High School where he had smarted under the *tawse*,— and the close in which he believed he had conversed with the ghost of the old family butler. It is said that he was affected by deep melancholy when he found that a second generation of men had nearly passed away since he had run about there a thoughtless, bare-legged, curly-pated stripling, and when he reflected that he must himself soon be spoken of as among those who *had been*. Confessing himself to be *laudator temporis acti*, he would not allow that many of the changes which he saw were improvements; and, recollecting the luster shed upon their country by Hume, Robertson, and Adam Smith, he questioned whether Scotland prospered in literature as much as in material wealth. But after he had passed a few days in the society of FRANCIS JEFFREY, all these moody contemplations were banished from his mind, and he admitted that for valuable knowledge, for intellectual prowess, for refined taste, and for gentle manners, she could still show a man equal to the sons of whom she had been most proud in former days.

Unfortunately, party spirit was dreadfully embittered by the recent trial of the Queen, and now raged in Edinburgh with unexampled fury. For this reason the Tories considered themselves bound to keep aloof from him who had so crossed the wishes of the King, and who had rendered himself so obnoxious at Court. Walter Scott, whose benevolent disposition is to be admired not less than his genius, refused to meet him, and did everything in his power to disparage him.

Nevertheless, the dinner went off with *éclat*—Jeffrey, Cockburn, Cranstoun, Moncrieff, John Murray, Cunninghame, and the other leading Scotch Whigs, assisting to do honor to their illustrious guest. They drank the health of "Plain Thomas Erskine," thinking that such a designation would be more grateful to his feelings than a pompous enumeration of all the titles bestowed upon him and all the offices he had ever filled. His forensic triumphs were duly celebrated, and he was seen to shed tears at allusions to the glories of former days.

His own speech was distinguished by good feeling and taste. After a few introductory observations, he thus burst forth:

> "Breathes there a man with soul so dead
> Who never to himself has said,
>   'This is my own, my native land:'
> Whose heart has ne'er within him burn'd
> When home his footsteps he has turn'd
>   From wandering on a foreign strand?

The accomplished author well knew that there was no such Scotsman: no, I verily believe there is no such man—the great author of our nature having implanted in us all an instinctive love of our country. It is this which makes the heart throb and vibrate when the eye recalls even the inanimate scenes of our earliest youth. A waste covered with heath or broom—varied, perhaps, by no higher vegetation than a few stunted trees half dead with age, which are yet remembered—will more affect the imagination of every human being, and will fill him with a far higher delight, than the most splendid scenery which nature assisted by art ever produced. It is on this account that when I shall visit St. Andrew's, the sequestered place to which my excellent parents retired for so many years, to perform the most sacred duty to their children, I shall feel more than I can express. The lifeless, unadorned street, in which a traveler would read his book as he drove through it, will electrify me at every step. I shall gaze upon the old plastered church-wall (if it be yet standing) where I used to toil at fives when I was a boy, with more pleasure than St. Peter's at Rome could bestow.[1] Gentlemen, these sentiments are quite universal, and they illustrate the Divine Providence in the economy of the world. Some regions are covered with never-fading fruits and flowers, while in others vegetation sickens and human life almost goes out; but the instinctive love of country gives, in the estimation of the native, equal luster and enjoyment to them all. Without this attachment, indeed, there would be no such thing as a people, and we should be still, as in the earliest times, scattered tribes, roaming about in search of spots where acorns are most abundant, or wild animals may be most easily snared. Scotland has ever been proverbially and fondly pre-eminent for this useful, this virtuous attachment; and, however we may be driven to seek our fortunes in the most distant countries, we are still eager to return to our own." After dwelling at considerable length on the glory, martial and literary, which the Scotch had ac-

[1] As a St. Andrew's man, I feel rather hurt at the slighting manner in which he speaks of this seat of learning. The Presbyterian Church, against which he played at fives, is not much to be commended for exterior beauty; but the chapel of St. Salvator's College is a fine specimen of Gothic architecture, and the cathedral in ruins gives striking though melancholy evidence of the ancient splendor of the metropolitan see of Scotland.

quired by their love of country, he described his astonishment when he first saw the NEW TOWN, "not one stone of which stood upon another when, more than half a century ago, he left Old Edinburgh, which gave him birth." He then, rather in a discursive manner, touched on parliamentary reform and other topics, and concluded by saying, "I shall look back with delight on this day during the remainder of my life—a period which can not now be much prolonged—and I hope that all who shall ever be descended from me will hold it in perpetual remembrance."[1]

Of this dinner we have the following prejudiced account from Mrs. Grant of Laggan, who though she had now become an Edinburgh Tory, I must admit when she wrote her "Letters from the Mountains," displayed as much talent in describing Highland scenery and Highland manners as Madame de Sévigné in painting the characters and narrating the intrigues of the Court of Louis XIV.:—

"The party have been paying great homage to Lord Erskine, and talking of his return to Scotland after fifty-one years' absence as if a comet had re-appeared. I was asked to meet him last Saturday night, and saw him surrounded by all his satellites. He is a shattered wreck of a man, decked with a diamond star. This decoration he wore, I was told, as a Knight of the Thistle. I always thought of him with the deep straw bonnet which he wore on his Gretna Green expedition.[2] On Monday the great dinner was given to the ex-Chancellor. Several great persons were expected, but none of them came.[3] I observe that these despisers of rank are wonderfully vain of getting a title to grace their meetings."

The illustrious stranger next visited the Court of Justiciary, and appeared there with the star of the order of the Thistle blazing on his breast. The question to be considered was one which had occupied his thoughts

---

[1] An Edinburgh correspondent of mine, who was present at this dinner, says: "His Lordship's speech rather caused a feeling of disappointment,—it not having the brilliancy we looked for. I must grant, however, that this may have arisen from our want of good taste as to what a dinner speech should be. It was a light, rambling, and jocular speech—whereas our stock speakers at that time delivered on such occasions regular and formal spoken Essays."   [2] I know nothing of the story here alluded to.

[3] I suppose she means some Tory peers. All the truly great men in Edinburgh, except Walter Scott, were present at the dinner.

much when he was Lord Chancellor—how far judges should interpose to punish in a summary manner printed comments on their own proceedings? A schoolmaster at Glasgow had published in a newspaper a letter disapproving rather freely of a judgment of their Lordships, and the Lord Advocate complained of this as a contempt of Court, for which the culprit ought to be immediately committed to the *Tolbooth*. Mr. Cockburn, the defendant's counsel, argued that he had not exceeded the bounds of legitimate discussion, and that, at any rate, the case ought to be submitted to the determination of a jury, in the ordinary course of law. The Court, however, asserted its jurisdiction, and passed sentence of imprisonment. Lord Erskine decorously concealed all expression of opinion while he remained on the bench, but in private lamented that in Scotland "trial by jury" should be thus superseded.[1]

He afterwards went to the theater, to see the representation of "The Heart of Midlothian." It is a curious fact, that Walter Scott, who had studiously kept aloof from his society, was present on this occasion. The "Edinburgh Evening Courant," coupling them together, says, they were loudly cheered on their entrance and departure." It would have been highly becoming if they had been seen arm in arm, and it had been impossible to distinguish which of them had the greater share of applause: but I have learned from a private source, that, entering and departing at separate times, they sat on opposite sides of the house; and that the ex-Chancellor being the "great lion," much more attention was paid to him. This seems to have sunk very deep into the breast of Walter, who, years after, offered an ingenious solution of it to soothe his own feelings. In his diary,—after alluding to the old woman at Carlisle, in the year 1745, who, when the Highlanders had taken that city by assault, being afraid of violence to her person, and surprised that none was offered, called out, "When is the ravishing to begin?"—he considers how he should act if any public mark of respect should be shown to him at Paris, and thus proceeds:—"I am sure I shall neither hide myself to avoid applause which probably no one will

[1] His own conduct on such occasions had not been quite uniform and consistent. See ante, p. 189.

think of conferring, nor have the meanness to do anything which can indicate a desire of ravishment. I have seen, when the late Lord Erskine entered the Edinburgh theater, papers distributed in the boxes to mendicate a round of applause,—the natural reward of a poor player."[1]

Dining with Lord President Hope, he asked "Whose portrait is that?" looking at a very fine one of the famous lawyer, Sir Thomas Hope, the founder of this branch of that distinguished family. The venerable judge answering the question, and adding, "You are as nearly and directly descended from him as I am," Erskine exclaimed, with great interest and eagerness, "Ah! I never before knew whence I inherited my law."

Erskine wished much to cross over into Fife, that he might revisit St. Andrew's,—above all he said, "Lady Buchan's Cove," the " Scores," the "Witch Lake," across which he had often swam—and the room in which he had learned to dance "*shantrews*;" but these scenes he never again beheld, as he was summoned to preside at a great public dinner to be given in England, to celebrate the Queen's acquittal.

Having parted with his numerous friends and advisers in Auld Reekie, he took his passage for London in the smack Favorite, Mark Sanderson, master. It so happened that no vessel could get out of Leith harbor for several days, from want of water on the bar, a circumstance of rare occurrence; and his Lordship, with other disappointed passengers, were seen at tide hours, day by day, on Leith pier, waiting anxiously to be set afloat.

When the Favorite at last cleared the harbor, the ex-Chancellor's feelings were expressed in the following stanza:—

"Of depth profound, o'erflowing far,
I bless'd the Edinburgh bar;
Whilst muttering oaths between my teeth,
I curs'd the shallow bar of Leith."

Among the passengers was Mr. Ruthven, the inventor of the celebrated portable printing-press; and a motion was made, and carried unanimously, that this impromptu should forthwith be printed by him. With great glee he proceeded to gratify the company, and speedily executed

[1] Life, by Lockhart, vi. 369.

the task allotted to him, with the addition of these lines
by a Leith beauty on board the Favorite:

" *To Lord Erskine.*
" Spare, spare, my Lord, your angry feelings,
Nor leave us thus as if at.war;
'Twas only to retain you with us,
We at our harbor placed a bar."

The following tribute, by Lord Erskine, to the nautical
skill of Captain Sanderson, was also printed, at the desire
of the passengers, by Mr. Ruthven when the vessel had
reached the Nore :—

" *On Captain Mark Sanderson, of the Favorite.*
" All who in safety seek to be,
Should watch the safest *marks* at sea;
But, noting *sea-marks* one by one,
Commend me to MARK *Sanderson*."

The dinner to which he had been summoned passed off
with great *éclat*, and for some time Erskine's popularity
was unbounded; but when the rejoicings on account of
the Queen's acquittal had passed away he fell back into
the ordinary routine of private life, which I am deeply
concerned to say was no longer very happy for him, nor
very creditable. From his unlucky purchase of land in
Sussex, from a bad investment of a large sum in the
American funds, and from other acts of imprudence, he became straitened in his circumstances. A gentleman in Derbyshire, from admiration of his public character, had left
him by will a considerable landed estate; but the will
was defeated by the ignorance of a country attorney,
who recommended that the testator should "suffer a
recovery" to confirm it, whereby it was rendered invalid.[1]
Having parted with his splendid mansion in Lincoln's
Inn Fields, as well as his villa at Hampstead, he now
lived at a lodging in Arabella Row, Pimlico, moving
occasionally to a cottage in Sussex, which he called
Buchan Hill: and he had contracted a second marriage—
when, how, or with whom, I have not learned upon any
authority.

[1] He used to give an amusing account of the attorney who came to him
after the testator's death to announce the intelligence of his being now owner
of a great estate, concluding thus: " And your Lordship need have no doubt
as to the validity of the will ; for, after it was made, *we suffered a recovery* to
confirm it." This legal absurdity is corrected by a bill I had the honor to
introduce into Parliament.

I can not venture, *ex cathedrâ*, to say lightly, as Sheridan did,—

"When men like Erskine go astray,
Their stars are more in fault than they."

Considering his years, his station, the feelings of those who looked up to him, and his own lively perception of what was right, his errors are attended with considerable aggravation. "The usual course, on such occasions, is to say: *Taceamus de his*—but History neither asserts her greatest privilege, nor discharges her higher duties, when, dazzled by brilliant genius or astonished by splendid triumphs, or even softened by amiable qualities, she abstains from marking those defects which so often degrade the most sterling worth, and which the talents and the affections that they accompany may sometimes seduce men to imitate."[1] However, if I conceal none of his errors which have come to my knowledge, I hope I shall not be generally blamed for not curiously inquiring into them.

It is said, that, to relieve himself from the depression of spirits under which he sometimes labored, he got into the pernicious habit of eating opium; but I think this statement must be incorrect, for in his correspondence he ever continued to display his wonted playfulness, and when he appeared in society I can testify that he was gay, lively, and debonair.[2] Being asked by George Sinclair his opinion respecting a paper currency, he wrote back merrily, "his complaints now related more to the *quantity* than the *quality* of Bank-notes." We have an agreeable representation of the somewhat eccentric, but ever gentleman-like, manner which still marked him, in the Journal of an American minister:—

[1] Lord Brougham.
[2] So early as the year 1796, the "Pursuer of Literature" had impudently written,
"In state affairs all barristers are dull,
And Erskine nods,—*the opium in his skull;*"
adding, in a note, " Mr. Barrister Erskine is *famous* for taking opium." But no faith is to be given to this libeler, either when he attacks classes or individuals.
The Right Hon. T. Erskine has since written to me, "This story about the habit of taking opium I believe to be wholly without foundation. His constitutional hilarity and elasticity of spirit *never* required it. He always had the faculty of throwing off his mind upon entering into society all subjects of care and annoyance with the ease with which a man puts off his great coat upon entering into a house. He required neither stimulus nor anodyne."

"At an evening party at the Duke of Cumberland's a nobleman came up and addressed Mr. Rush abruptly: 'I'm going to bring a bill into Parliament, making it indictable in any stranger, whether ambassador from a republic, kingdom, or popedom, ever to leave his card without his address upon it. How do you do, Mr. Rush, how do you do? I've been trying to find you everywhere. I'm Lord Erskine:

> Cætera norunt
> Susquehanna, Hudson, Connecticut, Mississippi.'

The monologue continued as follows;—'I had a letter for you from my brother, the Earl of Buchan; but you have made me carry it so long in my pocket that I lost it. It had no secrets,—it was only to congratulate you on your arrival: he was long a correspondent and friend of your father, and wants to transfer his feelings to you,— that's all; so you can write to him as if you had received it.' His Lordship added, that 'he had always loved the United States, and hoped to visit them yet, as he was an old sailor and cared nothing for storms.'" In a subsequent entry in the same journal we have the following amusing notice :—" Lord Erskine called upon me according to promise. I pass by all, to come to what he said of Burke. My boys being in the room, he asked if I had found a good school for them? I said they were at present with Mr. Foothead in my neighborhood. 'You are lucky,' he said, 'if Burke's recommendation goes for anything, for he thought well of him as a teacher of the classics. What a prodigy Burke was!' he exclaimed. 'He came to see me not long before he died. I then lived on Hampstead Hill. "Come, Erskine," said he, holding out his hand, "let us forget all! I shall soon quit this stage, and wish to die in peace with everybody, especially you!" I reciprocated the sentiment, and we took a turn round the grounds. Suddenly he stopped. An extensive prospect broke upon him. He stood wrapt in thought, gazing on the sky as the sun was setting. "Ah, Erskine," he said, pointing towards it, "you can not spoil that because you can not reach it,—it would otherwise go,—yes, the firmament itself,—you and your reformers would tear it all down."[1] I was much pleased

---

[1] The Right Hon. T. Erskine says: Mr. Rush has spoiled Burke's sarcasm. Upon being conducted by my father to his garden, through a tunnel under

with his friendly familiarity, and we went into the house, where kind feelings between us were further improved. A short time afterwards he wrote that attack upon the Duke of Devonshire [Bedford?], Fox, and myself which flew all over England, and perhaps the United States.' All this his Lordship told in the best manner. In my form of repeating it I can not do him justice. Desiring to hear something of Burke's delivery from so high a source, I asked him about it. 'It was execrable,' said he. 'I was in the House of Commons when he made his great speech on American conciliation, the greatest he ever made. He drove everybody away. I wanted to go out with the rest; but was near him, and afraid to get up,—so I squeezed myself down and crawled under the benches like a dog, until I got to the door without his seeing me,— rejoicing in my escape. Next day I went to the Isle of Wight. When the speech followed me there, I read it over and over again. I could hardly think of anything else. I carried it about me, and thumbled it until it got like wadding for my gun.' Here he broke out with a quotation from the passage beginning, 'But what, says the financier, is peace without money?' which he gave with a fervor showing how he felt it. He said that he was in the House when he threw a dagger on the floor in his speech on the French Revolution, and 'it had like to have hit my foot, it was a sad failure; but Burke could bear it.' He sat upwards for an hour, leaving me to regret his departure."

Our ex-Chancellor had not for some years visited Westminster Hall,—all his old associates having disappeared, and a new race having sprung up who knew him only by reputation; but at the Alfred Club, to which he belonged, he would still occasionally mount upon a table and give a specimen of his rhetorical powers, again fighting over fields that he had won. Nay, though steadily professing a belief in the Queen's innocence, he criticised the manner in which the prosecution had been conducted, and showed the line of examination and of argument by which an adverse decision might have been obtained.

the road that divided the house from the shrubbery, all the beauty of Kenwood (Lord Mansfield's) and the distant prospects burst upon them. 'Oh,' said Burke, 'this is just the place for a Reformer—all the beauties are beyond your reach.'"

He likewise still kept up a correspondence with his absent friends, and sent them metrical scraps, with which he tried to fill up his leisure. The following is his last letter to one of the warmest of his admirers:—

"Buchan Hill, Feb. 17, 1822.

"MY VERY DEAR PARR,

"If you wonder why I have not sooner thanked you for your most kind and delightful letter, which I shall keep as an heir-loom, it can only be from not having duly considered how difficult it is to find words to acknowledge it. I have read it over and over again, and my children shall read it hereafter. There was an inaccuracy in my little sonnet upon the infant Hampden—which should run thus:—

> ' Thy infant years, dear child, had passed unknown.
> As wine had flown upon thy natal day;
> But that the name of Hampden fires each soul,
> To sit with rapture 'round thy birthday bowl—
> Honest remembrance of his high renown
> In the great cause of law and liberty.
>
> ' Should heaven extend thy days to man's estate,
> Follow his bright example ; scorn to yield
> To servile judgments ; boldly plead the claim
> Of British rights ; and should the sacred flame
> Of eloquence die in corrupt debate,
> Like Hampden, urge their justice in the field.'

"These last lines may one day get this young gentleman hanged, unless he can take one just turn in hanging very many who so richly deserve it.

"Yours, very affectionately,

"ERSKINE."

Dr. Parr, in his will, thus testified his feelings for his patriotic correspondent:—" I give to the Right Honorable Lord Erskine a mourning ring, as a mark of my unfeigned respect for his noble exertions in defending the constitutional rights of juries and the freedom of the press, and for his vigorous and effectual resistance to the odious principles of constructive and accumulative treasons,— and I thankfully add, for his disinterested acts of kindness to my sister and myself."[1]

[1] The lawyer and the divine had long been accustomed to praise each other very lavishly. Erskine writes, soon after the State Trials in 1794,—" The approbation of such an excellent judge of every accomplishment is a great prize. It was not for nothing that I left the full-moneyed term of last November at Westminster. No, I am no better than my neighbors,—I was only

To support the cause of the Greeks, in the autumn of the year 1822 Erskine published a pamphlet, in the shape of a "Letter to Lord Liverpool;" which, if it be marked by a growing false taste in composition, proves a true and unabated love of freedom. He presented a copy of it to a lady of literary celebrity, with the following note:—

"DEAR LADY MORGAN,

"A long time ago, in one of your works (all of which I have read with great satisfaction), I remember you expressed your approbation of my style of writing, with a wish that I would lose no occasion of rendering it useful. I wish I could agree with your Ladyship in your kind and partial opinion; but as there never was an occasion in which it can be more useful to excite popular feeling than in the cause of the Greeks, I send your Ladyship a copy of the second edition, published a few days ago.

"With regard and esteem, &c., &c. "E.

"No. 13, Arabella Row, Pimlico, London,
October 11, 1822."

Lady Morgan, when first introduced to him a good many years before, wrote this account of him to a friend: "I was a little disappointed to find that Erskine spoke like other persons,—was a thin, middle-aged gentleman, and wore a brown wig; but he was always delightful, always amusing, frequently incoherent; and, I thought, sometimes affectedly wild, at least paradoxical." Now she wrote, with great candor and kindness of heart: "The pamphlet for the Greeks is worth citing as a testimony to prove that years do not make age, and that freshness of feeling and youthful ardor in a great cause may survive the corporal decay which time never spares, even to protracted sensibility."

I give one or two specimens to justify this criticism:

prudently preaching in these days of innovation for coin not subject to be debased in the esteem and approbation of such men as yourself; and I have so far succeeded, by the dint of sheer honesty (for I have little else to boast of), as to be compared to Demosthenes and Cicero, by one of the very few who are capable of estimating either of them, and who ought to take the lead in England, whether ancient learning and eloquence are to be judged of in the abstract, or compared with the shadows which their descended radiance still gives birth to in our latter days." When the two met, their flattery seems to have been still more intense. On one occasion, Parr, at last, as the highest recompense that could be bestowed, said, "When you die, I will write your epitaph." Erskine replied, "This is almost a temptation, my dear doctor, instantly to commit suicide!"

"I feel, while I am writing, that the ink must first have become blood, to enable me fitly to express my detestation and abhorence of their Turkish oppressors. To judge of what the Greeks under good government are capable of being, we have only to look back to what they have been. Their pedigrees, in which we can trace so many great men who never should have died, ought to protect them from the Saracens, who can not show in all their escutcheons a single man who should have lived." Proposing to *eject* the Turks from Europe, he declares that "he would confide the matter to some long-practiced diplomatist, with the assistance of a lawyer to draw up the *notice to quit*." He does not go on to explain how the writ of *habere facias possessionem* was to be executed. But it should be recollected that at this time such sentiments were shared by the most distinguished men. Byron was actually carrying arms in the great enterprise ; and Lord Dudley, though a non-combatant, wrote to the Bishop of Llandaff, "I have always considered it the greatest disgrace of Christendom to suffer these hated barbarians, the Turks, to remain encamped upon the finest and most renowned part of Europe for upwards of four centuries— during at least two of which it has been in our power to drive them out whenever we pleased ; let us at least have one civilized and Christian quarter of the globe, although it be the smallest."

In thus addressing Lord Liverpool as an advocate for the liberty of the Greeks, Erskine showed that he had become a zealous convert to the abolition of the African slave trade,—forgetting even that he had once been deluded by the apparent happiness which he had seen the negroes enjoying in their midnight dances in the West Indies. After giving an affecting description of the horrors of the middle passage, particularly the slaves jumping overboard to be devoured by the sharks, which he says he had frequently beheld, he adds—" When, after all this, it fell at last to my lot, and through ways as unaccountable as unexampled, to preside in the Lord's House of Parliament, on their deliverance—to hold up in my hands the great charter of their freedom, and with my voice to pronounce that it should be law, your Lordship, I am sure, whom I respect and regard as a man of honor and feeling, will rather approve than condemn my retaining the whole subject of slavery in the most affecting remembrance."[1]

Erskine was thus employed during the visit of George IV. to the Scottish metropolis. He privately expressed a wish that he might have been of the party,—to point out the beauties of his "own romantic town" to the first Brunswick Sovereign who had "kept court in Holyrood;" but there was a complete alienation between "Tom" and his old patron, who now hated all liberal men as well as liberal principles, and could with great difficulty be persuaded by his Tory Ministers to agree to the emancipation of the Catholics.

Though no longer attending in Parliament, nor even making speeches at anniversary dinners, our ex-Chancellor was still desirous of keeping his name before the public,— or I ought, perhaps, rather to say, of rendering service to the country,—and, in the beginning of the year 1823, he published a pamphlet, which proved to be his last; for though his figure was still juvenile and his eye piercing, his career was near its close. The all absorbing subject of the day was "Agricultural Distress," which, notwithstanding the protecting sliding scale of 1815, intended to prevent the price of wheat falling under eighty shillings the quarter, was now said to be dreadful; and certainly Erskine's attempts to raise wheat on land intended by nature only for the production of birch-brooms had turned out very disastrous. In his "Letter to the Proprietors and Occupiers of Land, on the Causes and Remedies for the Decline of Agricultural Prosperity,"[2] he still harps upon "insufficient protection," and the "burdens on land;" but he makes some good observations on the abuses of the old Poor Law, which many are so eager to

[1] I am sorry to say that the lawyers were the last in the community to support the rights of their black brethren. Wilberforce, in his Diary, says,— "That the general bias of the Bar was in favor of an established trade in slaves with Africa, was confirmed by the defense which burst from the boisterous Thurlow, and for a moment trembled upon the lips of Erskine."
. . . . . "The Bar were all against us upon the question of the African Slave Trade. Fox could scarcely prevent Erskine from making a set speech in favor of the trade."

[2] "It was well observed by Mr. Holme Sumner, that a successful clamor for cheap bread, by the encouragement of foreign importers, would soon leave the people no bread at all. No schemes for the sustentation of the poor, however judicious, will be attended with any material relief to the country, until we shut our ports by a higher scale than we have adopted."— *Lord Erskine's Pamphlet.*

restore. He thus illustrates his objection to the "allowance system" (*i. e.* apportioning parish relief according to the number of the family and the price of corn) then prevailing over the south of England:—

"A friend of mine in Sussex had a useful servant, who managed his small farm, and, being satisfied with his services, gave him higher wages than the common rate, a comfortable house to live in, besides firewood, with some little advantages which occasionally occurred. Nevertheless, this innocent-minded man, in a state of breathless agitation, addressed his master as follows: 'Master, be I bound to maintain five children?' To which the master said, 'Whose children are they?' 'Why, I believe them to be my own,' was the answer, to which the gentleman replied, 'Who else should maintain them?' 'Why, *the parish*,' replied the countryman, still more agitated. 'What can you mean by that?' said the master; 'have you not sufficient wages to maintain your wife and children comfortably?' 'Why, to be sure, I have,' said the countryman, 'thanks to your honor's kindness; my wife is a sober, good woman, so that we lays by a few shillings a week; but why be I to have no money from the parish, when every one else is paid who has children?' The end of this dialogue was, that the man was directed never to think of the *parish* any more; and he now lives contented in his place."

The public was disposed to applaud what was good, without criticising severely what might be questionable in the writings or actions of an old favorite. He was now regarded with general fondness. Annually, at a dinner (which he was not asked to attend, that his praise might be sounded more freely) given to celebrate the acquittal of Hardy, in 1794, his health was drunk with increasing enthusiasm—the company, on account of the tergiversation of his colleague, drinking in solemn silence "The memory of Sir Vicary Gibbs." Ridgway, under his revision, had a few years before published a collection of his speeches at the Bar. To my utter astonishment, it never reached a second edition; but it was in the hands of all who had any taste for genuine oratory, and it proved that his great fame as an advocate was scarcely equal to his merits. The "Indian Chief" was declaimed by schoolboys,—lawyers conned night and day his arguments against constructive treason,—and his analysis of mental alienation in his defense of Hadfield was studied and admired by philosophers. He had lived sufficiently both to nature and to glory: and if he had survived much longer, his reputation might have been permanently dimmed by the faults and follies into which he might have fallen. But, while it seemed that the strength of his constitution could only be undermined by a long decay, an acute disorder saved him from these perils.

CHAPTER CXC.

CONCLUSION OF THE LIFE OF LORD ERSKINE.

DURING his short visit to Scotland, in the year 1820, Erskine had been in a perpetual hurry and bustle, and had been constantly subjected to the public gaze. He longed to contemplate in repose the scenes of his infancy, and to enjoy an affectionate intercourse with his surviving relatives. His eldest brother, the Earl of Buchan, was now residing at Dryburgh Abbey, in Berwickshire, and, having by long economy repaired the shattered fortunes of his family, was in comparative wealth. Henry, his second brother, had paid the debt of nature, but had left a widow—a lady of superior understanding and most agreeable manners, to whom, as well from her own merits as from a regard to the memory of the deceased, he was warmly attached. He likewise desired to form an acquaintance with the junior branches of his noble house, and for its honor to give them the advantage of his experience in directing their pursuits in life. He therefore resolved, in the autumn of 1823, to revisit his native land and to pass the ensuing winter there. When he intimated his wish to go by sea, he was reminded that the equinoctial gales were to be expected; but, expressing a great dislike of being boxed up in the mail-coach, or posting over 400 miles of dusty road, he added,— "What is a puff of wind on the German Ocean to an old sailor who has often combated a tornado in the West Indies?" Accordingly he embarked at Wapping in a Leith smack, accompanied by one of his sons.

At first the weather was propitious, but when they were abreast of Harwich a violent gale arose from the north-northeast, accompanied by rain and sleet. The "old sailor" would remain on deck to show his hardihood,—till he found himself seriously indisposed. In a few hours it turned out that he was attacked with inflammation in the chest—a complaint from which he had suffered before, and against which he ought cautiously to have guarded himself. When the ship reached Scarborough he was so seriously ill that it was necessary to put him ashore. He rallied to a certain degree, and was able by easy stages to reach Almondell, the residence of his sister-in-law. There he had skillful medical advice, and the tenderest attentions which affection and respect could prompt; but he experienced a relapse of his malady, and after suffering severe bodily pain with much fortitude, on the 17th of November, 1823, he expired, in the 73rd year of his age. I have not been able to obtain any further authentic particulars of his last hours; but we need not doubt that he then found consolation in the deep religious feelings by which, when he had leisure for reflection, he was ever influenced; and we may humbly express a hope, in his own beautiful language, that, "instead of a stern accuser exposing before the Author of his nature the frail passages in a life generally well directed, their guilt was mitigated by a merciful intercession, and true repentance blotted them out forever."[1]

Had he died in London, he certainly would have been

[1] Mr. Thomson, a very respectable gentleman, the son of Dr. Thomson, the physician who attended Lord Erskine in his last illness, thus writes to me:—" Either on the day before or on the day that Lord Erskine died, when he had fallen into the state of delirium by which death is so often preceded, and in which the last thoughts that fleet through the mind previous to its separation from its terrestrial associate are apt to be expressed in mutterings, my father heard him pronounce these words with some declamatory emphasis:—' They have neither talents nor virtue to govern a nation." Whether this sentiment had reference to the Government then actually existing, or to some other which his imagination had recalled, I must leave it to your Lordship's sagacity to determine. I have heard my father, in mentioning this anecdote, say that these words of Lord Erskine's forcibly brought to his recollection what Dr. Baillie had told him relative to Mr. Pitt's last hours: Dr. Baillie, having happened to arrive before the other medical attendants, entered his bedroom alone, when he heard him mutter in an irritable tone, and with a repetition of the expressions, " What, sir! haven't you got enough?' —an expostulatory interrogation which Dr. Baillie said he feared must have been directed, in the wandering imagination of the Premier, against the insatiable demands of some place-seeking countryman of his own."

honored with a public funeral, and his mortal remains would have been deposited in Westminster Abbey, near those of his distinguished contemporaries, Pitt, Fox, and Wilberforce. But they molder in the family burying-place at Uphall, a remote parish in the county or Linlithgow, —the hearse that conveyed them thither being attended only by a few relations and private friends. On this occasion, no solemn knell announced the approach of the illustrious deceased to his last resting-place, no priest in holy vestment, with book in hand, paced the churchyard, chanting "I am the resurrection and the life,"—no swelling anthem resounded through the fretted aisles of a Gothic minster. In a narrow vault covered by weeds, near a small church, erected since the Reformation, and scarcely to be distinguished from a barn, the unadorned coffin of the immortal Thomas Erskine was placed by the side of his brother Henry; and the company having reverentially remained silent and uncovered while the ceremony was performed, departed, after casting a sorrowful look at the spot where he was to repose till the last trumpet should summon him to judgment.—But, though the interment was conducted in the Presbyterian fashion the horror of Popish rites was so far relaxed in the country, that the Reverend Mr. Fergusson, the parish clergyman, prayed, and delivered an impressive address, before the simple procession moved from Almondell, and—without cassock or surplice—he followed it to the grave. Although it may be regretted that the beautiful funeral service in the English Liturgy is rejected, as superstitious, by our Scottish brethren, the extempore prayers and exhortations substituted in its place, for the edification and consolation of surviving relations and friends assembled in the house where the body lies, often produce an effect as touching and as salutary. Dr. Johnson himself has said,—

"Legitimas faciunt pectora pura preces."

There is no marble monument erected to Erskine's memory—nor any mural inscription to celebrate his genius and public services; but the Collection of his Speeches will preserve his name as long as the English language endures, and a simple narrative of his life will best show his claim to the gratitude of posterity.

On searching his papers the only will found was one dated so far back as the 15th of November, 1782. This had been made in contemplation of an affair of honor which proceeded to a hostile meeting in the field, but ended without bloodshed.[1] He prefaces the disposition of his property by a declaration that, "from a sense of honor, and not from any motive of personal resentment or revenge, he was about to expose his life to great peril." Nine thousand pounds in 3 per cent. consols, and one thousand pounds in bills, stated to be all acquired by his practice at the Bar, he left to his then wife, with the highest expressions of confidence and affection, for the maintenance of herself and her children,—they to inherit it, after her decease, in equal shares, as they attained twenty-one. But he provided that as, on account of her youth, she might probably marry again, and as such an event, though by no means deprecated by him, might be incompatible with the interests of his children, upon such second marriage the fund should be transferred to his sister, Lady Anne Erskine, in trust for the purposes above mentioned. By a codicil, dated October 2, 1786, when his property had greatly accumulated, he confirmed his will, and directed equal portions to after-born children. I am afraid that, at last there was little forthcoming for these bequests to operate upon; but his family prized more his splendid reputation than any riches which he could have transmitted to them, and, without a murmur, thought of him with unmixed veneration and thankfulness.

To be descended from such a parent was indeed a great inheritance. Many generations may pass away before his equal is presented to the admiration of mankind. Of course, I do not refer to his qualifications as a Judge; and can only say of him as a politician, that he was ever consistently attached to the principles of freedom, though by no means above the prejudices of education and country. As a parliamentary debater he was much inferior to several of his contemporaries: and even in our own degenerate age we could outmatch him.[2] But as an

[1] He was never fond of any allusion to this affair, as his antagonist was an apothecary. It arose out of an altercation in a ball-room at Lewes.
[2] Some have supposed that his senatorial efforts appear to us generally so indifferent from bad reporting; but the following letter from him to Mr.

Advocate in the forum, I hold him to be without an equal in ancient or in modern times. Notwithstanding the flippant observations of some who can write and speak very fine sentences, without any notion of the real business of life, and who pretend to despise that for which they themselves would have been found utterly unfit, I boldly affirm that there is no department of human intellect in which the *mens divinior* may be more refulgently displayed. I despise, as much as they can do, the man wearing a gown, be it of bombazine or of silk, who is merely "præco actionum cautor formularum, auceps syllabarum," or who sordidly thinks only of amassing money and regulates his attendance

Wright, the editor of the Parliamentary Debates" (the original of which is in my possession, a present from my friend Mr. Surtees), shows that he was quite contented with the reports of his speeches in that collection as being full and faithful:—

"Dear Sir:

"If I did not know from long experience your singular correctness regarding your papers, I should be almost quite sure that you had all the speeches you ever sent me in time for the publication, except two, which, coming too late, you were so kind as to say (and which I hope you will not forget) you would reprint in the manner you mentioned. I am naturally very anxious that after, through your kind attention, so many of my speeches in Parliament appear so nearly as they were spoken, that the one in question should have the same advantage. I shall be in town on Sunday, when I will call on you; and although you may not be able to cut out a copy as you did with the others, you might find the book from which the others were taken, from which I would correct it without a moment's delay.

"Yours very sincerely,
"Erskine.

"Buchan Hill, near Crawley, Nov. 26th, 1818."

However, he sometimes complained bitterly of the short-hand writers. In one of his letters to Mr. Howell, the editor of the "State Trials," now in my possession, he says: "I am used to the systematic bad grammar of the short-hand writers. None of them (Gurney excepted) ever use any tense but the *present*. If the speaker is speaking of a transaction as ancient as the flood, it is still the *present* tense, 'Noah enters into the ark.' I believe no man who ever spoke extempore ever was so correct in tenses as myself. I have accustomed myself so much to that correctness in common conversation, that I could not depart from it if I were to try; and yet there is hardly any line in the whole copy you sent me in which there is not put into my mouth the present tense, for all that forms the variety of our English verbs. It is truly disgusting with other similar blunders; but to * a person so conversant with their ignorance and stupidity as I am, it can be corrected in half an hour."

Referring to his speech for the "Courier," he says: "I put everything else aside, and turned the whole from the third person to the first. It is an admirably correct report."

---

* *Sic*, instead of "by,"—and rather careless in this boast of superior accuracy!

and his exertions according to the fee marked on his brief. But let us imagine to ourselves an advocate inspired by a generous love of fame, and desirous of honorably assisting in the administration of justice, by obtaining redress for the injured and defending the innocent,—who has liberally studied the science of jurisprudence, and has stored his mind and refined his taste by a general acquaintance with elegant literature,—who has an intuitive insight into human character and the workings of human passion,—who possesses discretion as well as courage, and caution along with enthusiasm,—who is not only able by his powers of persuasion to give the best chance of success to every client whom he represents in every variety of private causes, but who is able to defeat conspiracies against public liberty, founded upon a perversion of the criminal law,—and who, by the victories which he gains, and the principles which he establishes, places the free Constitution of his country on an imperishable basis! Such an advocate was Erskine; and although he did creditably maintain his family by professional *honoraries* voluntarily presented to him, he was careless as to their amount, and he was ready on every proper occasion to exert his best energies without any reward beyond the consciousness of doing his duty.[1] Such an advocate, in my opinion, stands quite as high in the scale of true greatness as the Parliamentary leader who ably opens a budget, who lucidly explains a new system of commercial policy, or who dexterously attacks the measures of the Government. Certainly, different qualities of mind as well as different acquirements are demanded for these two kinds of eloquence; and it may be admitted that in senatorial deliberations there is a wider scope for an enlarged view of human affairs, and that they alone afford an opportunity for discussing the relative rights, duties, and interests of nations. But the forensic proceeding, though between private parties, or between the state and individual citizens, and though confined to a comparatively narrow field of investigation and of argument, has great advantages, from the intense and continued interest which it excites,—for, like a grand drama, it has often a

[1] *E. g.* When counsel for Hardy, Horne Tooke, and Thelwall, he pleaded *for love*. Indeed, it is contrary to professional etiquette to take a fee in high treason.

well-involved plot, and a catastrophe which can not be anticipated, rousing all the most powerful sympathies of our nature; and sometimes, as on the impeachment of Lord Strafford, or the Treason Trials of 1794, the fate of the empire may depend upon the verdict. Look to the recorded efforts of genius in both departments. I will not here enter into a comparison of the respective merits of the different sorts of oratory handed down to us from antiquity, but I may be allowed to observe that, among ourselves, in the hundred and fifty volumes of Hansard there are no specimens of Parliamentary harangues which, as literary compositions, are comparable to the speeches of Erskine at the Bar, with the exception of Burke's,— and these were delivered to empty benches. Do not, therefore, let it be assumed that Erskine is to be degraded into an inferior class of artists because he was not a skillful debater. He would no doubt have been a yet more wonderful creature if he had been as transient in the Senate as in the Forum; but we should recollect that, in the department of eloquence in which he did shine, he he is allowed to have excelled, not only all his contemporaries, but all who have attempted it in this island, either in prior or in subsequent times,—while mankind are greatly divided as to the individual to whom the palm of Parliamentary eloquence should be awarded;— and there will again probably be a debater equal to Pitt the father, Pitt the son, Fox, Sheridan, Burke, or Grey, before there arises an advocate equal to Erskine.[1]

Some have denied the possibility of his exalted preeminence, on account of his limited stock of general knowledge; but, although much culture is indispensable

[1] "I find him thus compared with his rivals in the Court of King's Bench: —" He could not display the peculiar energy of Law, invigorated as it was by a Latinized phraseology, and a pronunciation slightly tinctured with a Northern burr. He had not the coarse humor of Mingay, the tormenting pertinacity of Gibbs, or the interrogative astuteness of Garrow; but he possessed an opulence of imagination, a fertility of fancy, a power of commanding at an instant all the resources of his mind, and a dexterity in applying them, which the whole united Bar of England could not equal."

I have heard much speculation respecting the probable success of the younger Pitt, had he remained at the Bar. I think it must have been splendid; but, unless he had exhibited greater variety of manner, and a more familiar acquaintance with the common feelings of mankind, it never could have approached that of Erskine. Fox, in arguing questions of law on Hasting's trial, excited the astonishment and admiration of the Judges; and in every branch of forensic practice he would have been supreme.

to the development of the intellectual powers, and to the refinement of taste, this culture may be applied without the knowledge of a great variety of languages, and without any deep insight into science. No Greek knew any language but that which he learned from his nurse, and Shakespeare could not have gone through an examination as difficult as that of many modern parish schools. Far be it from me to discourage the acquisition of classical and scientific lore: this is delightful in itself, and it gives the best chance of success in every liberal pursuit; but where true genius exists, it may be brought into full operation and efficiency by suitable discipline within very narrow limits; and a man may be superior to all others in his art, and be ignorant of many things which it is disgraceful to the common herd of mortals not to know. Let it not be said, therefore, that Erskine could not, better than any other man, lead the understandings and control the passions of his audience when arguing a point of constitutional law, or appealing to the affections of domestic life, because he talked nonsense if he indiscreetly offered an opinion upon a question of prosody or of political economy. His moderate acquaintance with the Latin poets, and his intense and unremitting study of the best English writers, both in prose and verse, had taught him to think, and had supplied him with a correct, chaste, forcible, and musical diction, in which to express his thoughts. Although, judged by his common conversation he was sometimes very lightly esteemed,—listen to his discourses when he is rescuing from destruction the intended victim of an arbitrary Government, or painting the anguish of an injured husband, and he appears to breathe celestial fire.

In considering the characteristics of his eloquence, it is observable that he not only was free from measured sententiousness and tiresome attempts at antithesis, but that he was not indebted for his success to riches of ornament, to felicity of illustration, to wit, to humor, or to sarcasm. His first great excellence was his devotion to his client; and, in the whole compass of his orations, there is not a single instance of the business in hand—the great work of persuading—being sacrificed to raise a laugh or to excite admiration of his own powers. He utterly forgot himself in the character he represented. Through life he was often ridiculed for vanity and egotism,—but not from anything he ever said or did in conducting a cause in a court of justice. There, from the moment the jury were sworn, he thought of nothing but the verdict, till it was recorded in his favor. Earnestness and energy were ever present throughout his speeches—impressing his argument on the mind of his hearer with a force which seemed to compel conviction. He never spoke at a tiresome length; throughout all his speeches no weakness, no dullness, no flagging is discoverable; and we have ever a lively statement of facts,—or reasoning pointed, logical and triumphant.

I think I ought particularly to mention the familiar knowledge he displays of the most secret workings of the human mind. How finely he paints the peril arising from the perversion of what is good! "Some of the darkest and most dangerous prejudices of men arise from the most honorable principles. When prejudices are caught up from bad passions, the worst of men feel intervals of remorse to soften and disperse them; but when they arise from a generous though mistaken source, they are hugged closer to the bosom, and the kindest and most compassionate natures feel a pleasure in fostering a blind and unjust resentment." He spoke as his clients respectively would have spoken had they been endowed with his genius. "The dervise in the fairy tale, who possessed the faculty of passing his own soul into the body of any whom he might select, could scarcely surpass Erskine in the power of impersonating for a time the feelings, wishes, and thoughts of others."[1]

I must likewise mention the delight I feel from the exquisite sweetness of his diction, which is pure, simple, and mellifluous,—the cadences not being borrowed from any model, nor following any rule, but marked by constant harmony and variety. The rhythm of the Indian Chief is, I think, more varied, richer and more perfect than that of any passage from any other composition in our language.

When the great Lord Chatham was to appear in public, he took much pains about his dress, and latterly he arranged his flannels in graceful folds. It need not then detract from our respect for Erskine, that on all occa-

[1] Townsend's Eminent Judges, i. 434.

sions he desired to look smart, and that when he went
down into the country on special retainers he anxiously
had recourse to all manner of innocent little artifices to
aid his purposes. He examined the court the night before the trial, in order to select the most advantageous
place for addressing the jury. On the cause being called,
the crowded audience were perhaps kept waiting a few
minutes before the celebrated stranger made his appearance; and when at length he gratified their impatient
curiosity, a particularly nice wig and a pair of new yellow
gloves distinguished and embellished his person beyond
the ordinary costume of the barristers of the circuit.[1]

It may be more useful to hold up for imitation his admirable demeanor while engaged in business at the Bar,
—to which, perhaps, his success was not less due than to
his talents. Respectful to the Judges, although ever
ready to assert his independence,—courteous to the jury,
while he boldly reminded them of their duties, free from
asperity towards his opponents,—constantly kind and considerate to his juniors,—treating the witnesses as persons,
generally speaking, reluctantly attending to assist in the
investigation of truth,—looking benevolently even on the
bystanders, and glad when he could accommodate them
with a seat,—of a gay and happy temperament, enjoying uninterruptedly a boyish flow of animal spirits, and
enlivening the dullest cause with his hilarity and good-
humor,—he was a universal favorite—there was a general desire, as far as law and justice would permit, that he
should succeed, and the *prestige* of his reputation was considered the sure forerunner of victory. I have myself
witnessed, from the students' box, towards the conclusion
of his career at the Bar, his daily skirmishes and triumphs; but it is vain to try by words to convey an idea
of the qualities which he displayed, or the effect which he
produced.

Perhaps I may here appropriately introduce the estimate of other writers, entitled to more weight than mine,
of his eloquence and professional qualifications. Butler,
who had frequently heard him, observes:—" He often rose
to the highest oratory, but it was always simple; and
even in his sublimest flights there was much that was
very familiar, but this rather set off than diminished their

[1] Roscoe, 390.

general effect."[1] "In examining those particular qualities of Lord Erskine's speeches," says Roscoe, "which contributed more obviously to their success, the most remarkable will appear to be the exact and sedulous adherence to some one great principle which they uniformly exhibit. In every case he proposed a great leading principle to which all his efforts were referable and subsidiary —which ran through the whole of his address, arranging, governing, and elucidating every portion. As the principle thus proposed was founded in truth and justice, whatever might be its application to the particular case, it necessarily gave to the whole of his speech an air of honesty and sincerity which a jury could with difficulty resist." "Juries have declared," says Lord Brougham, "that they felt it impossible to remove their looks from him when he had riveted, and, as it were, fascinated them, by his first glance. Then hear his voice, of surpassing sweetness, clear, flexible, strong, exquisitely fitted to strains of serious earnestness, deficient in compass, indeed, and much less fitted to express indignation, or even scorn, than pathos, but wholly free from harshness or monotony. No man made fewer mistakes, none left so few advantages unimproved; before none was it so dangerous for an adversary to slumber and be off his guard, for he was ever broad awake himself, and was as adventurous as he was skillful, and as apt to take advantage of any the least opening, as he was cautious to have none in his own battle." "His action," says Espinasse, "was always appropriate, chaste, easy, natural, in accordance with his slender and finely-proportioned figure and just stature. His features, regular, prepossessing, as well as harmonious, bespoke him of no vulgar extraction. The tones of his voice, though sharp, were full, destitute of any tinge of Scottish accent, and adequate to every emergency, almost scientifically modulated to the occasion. He enlivened those who surrounded him with whimsical conceits, and jokes of what was passing. I had a full share of his *jeux d'esprit*, as my place in court was directly at his back." "Adequately to estimate what Erskine was at this period," says another brother barrister, "we must forget all that the English Bar has produced after him. They will afford no criterion by which he can be appreciated. They are

[1] Butler's Rem. 72.

all of inferior clay,—the mere sweepings of the Hall, in comparison. Nor is it easy to form any tolerable idea of him but by having seen him from day to day, from year to year, in the prime and manhood of his intellect, running with graceful facility through the chaos of briefs before him; it is only by that personal experience that it is possible to form any notion of the admirable versatility with which he glided from one cause to another—the irony, the humor, the good-nature with which he laughed down the adverse cause, and the vehemence and spirit with which he sustained his own."

In describing his professional merits, I ought by no means to omit his skill in examining witnesses, upon which the event of a cause often depends much more than upon fine speaking. When he had to examine in chief,—not, as in common fashion, following the order of the proofs as set down in the brief,—seemingly without art or effort, he made the witness lucidly relate, so as to interest and captivate the jury, all the facts that were favorable to his client. In cross-examination he could be most searching and severe; but he never resorted to browbeating, nor was gratuitously rude. Often he carried his point by coaxing; and when the evidence could not be contradicted, he would try by pleasantry to lessen the effect of it. Having to cross-examine a coxcombical fellow, belonging to the self-important class of persons sent by the wholesale houses in London to scour the country for orders,—formerly called "Riders," now styling themselves "Travelers,"—he began, "You are a *Rider*, I understand?" "A Traveler, sir," was the answer. "I might have discovered," replied Erskine, "that you considered yourself *licensed* to use all the privileges of a *Traveler*."—Another of the fraternity having long baffled him, he suddenly remarked, "You were born and bred in Manchester, I perceive?" The witness said he could not deny it. "I knew it," said Erskine, carelessly, "from the absurd tie of your neck-cloth." The traveling dandy's weak point was touched; for he had been dressing after Beau Brummel; and his presence of mind being gone, he was made to unsay the greatest part of his evidence in chief. —On the trial of an action to recover the value of a quantity of whalebone, the defense turning on the quality of the article, a witness was called, of impenetrable stupidity, who could not be made to distinguish between the two well-known descriptions of this commodity—the "long" and the "thick." Still confounding *thick* whalebone with *long*, Erskine exclaimed, in seeming despair, "Why man, you do not seem to know the difference between what is *thick* and what is *long!* Now I tell you the difference. You are *thick*-headed, and you are not *long*-headed."—I myself remember, when a student, being present when he was counsel for the plaintiff in an action on a tailor's bill,—the defense being, that the clothes were very ill-made, and, particularly, that the two sleeves of a dress-coat were of unequal length. The defendant's witness accordingly swore, that " one of them was longer than the other;"—upon which Erskine thus began: " Now, sir, will you swear that one of them was not *shorter* than the other?" The witness negativing this proposition, after an amusing reply the plaintiff had the verdict. The more difficult and delicate task of re-examination he was in the habit of performing with equal dexterity,—not attempting clumsily to go over the same ground which he had before trod, but, by a few questions which strictly arose out of the cross-examination, restoring the credit of his witness, and tying together the broken threads of his case.

As a mere author, I doubt whether he would ever have emerged from obscurity. From his peculiar temperament he seems to have required the excitement of listeners, and of controversy, and of instant applause, to brighten his imagination and to sharpen his faculties. Most of his prose compositions passed through several editions, as people had a curiosity to see an ex-Chancellor become a romance writer, or a pamphleteer; but if they had been published anonymously, or as written by John Smith or Thomas Tomkins, they would not even have reached the dignity of being censured by gods or men, or the columns of a newspaper.

We have seen that he likewise dabbled in poetry; but he prudently did not attempt more than *vers de société*,—and some of his metrical effusions are well calculated to promote the amusement of a drawing-room. I will here add a few to those which I have already introduced.

He had a kindness for his countryman, Park, afterwards

a judge of the Court of Common Pleas, but occasionally quizzed him; and he wrote upon him the following lines, which, with a little alteration, might have been applied to himself:—

"James Allan Park
Came naked stark
    From Scotland;
But now wears clo'es
And lives with beaux
    In England."

On the long, lanky visage of Mr. Justice Ashurst, before whom he daily practiced, he penned the following couplet:—

"Judge Ashurst, with his *lantern jaws*,
Throws *light* upon the English laws."

The Clerk of the Rules, a most important officer in the King's Bench, then was Mr. Short, who, notwithstanding severe illness, had reached a great age. On his eightieth birthday Erskine threw him the following lines, written on a scrap of paper torn from a brief:

"Tho' SHORT thy name, yet long thy life,
Triumphant o'er disease's strife;
For man's short days are long and full
To those who live, like you, by RULE."

The paper was immediately tossed back to him, with this answer subjoined, which he handed up to the bench, for the private amusement of my Lords the Judges:

"Your *Rule's* discharged. 'Tis plain your life
Has been and is maintained by—strife:
May still thy bag with RULES be full;
But *live*, as heretofore, *sans* RULE."[2]

When Sir Walter Scott, with a view to profit rather than fame, published "Paul's Letters to his Kinsfolk," with some very indifferent verses to celebrate the battle of Waterloo, Erskine, sitting at table, came out with the following *impromptu:*

[1] It has been said that he was the author of the epigram on Judge Grose—
    "Qualis sit Grotius judex, uno accipe versu,
        Exclamat, dubitat, stridet, balbutit et errat;"
but Latin versifying was unknown at St. Andrew's in his time, and he would hardly (if he could) have given utterance to such a savage effusion.
[2] The original now lies before me, having been transmitted to me from the Antipodes, by Sir H. E. Young, Governor of South Australia, who is married to a granddaughter of Mr. Short.—*3rd Edition.*

> "On Waterloo's ensanguined plain
> Lie tens of thousands of the slain;
> But none, by saber or by shot,
> Fell half so flat as WALTER SCOTT."

However, Erskine was generally more inclined to be good humored and complimentary. Being much indisposed during dinner at Sir Ralph Payne's, in Grafton Street, he retired to another apartment, and reclined for some time on a sofa. In the course of the evening, being somewhat recovered, he rejoined the festive circle; and Lady Payne inquiring how he found himself, he presented to her the following couplet:

> "'Tis true I am ill, but I need not complain,
> For he never knew *pleasure* who never knew PAYNE."

The house of an eminent counsel in Red Lion Square being taken by an ironmonger, Erskine thus celebrated the event:

> "This house, where once a lawyer dwelt,
> Is now a smith's, alas!
> How rapidly the *iron* age
> Succeeds the age of *brass* !"

He composed the following lines to the memory of a beloved pony, "Jack," who had carried him on the Home Circuit when he was first called to the Bar and could not afford any more sumptuous mode of traveling:

> "Poor Jack! thy master's friend when he was poor,
> Whose heart was faithful, and whose step was sure,
> Should prosperous life debauch my erring heart,
> And whisp'ring pride repel the patriot's part;
> Should my foot falter at Ambition's shrine,
> And for mean lucre quit the path divine;
> Then may I think of thee when I was poor,
> Whose heart was faithful, and whose step was sure."

Having thus spoken, in one of his pamphlets, of Frederica, Duchess of York, "a lady whose talents, manners, and distinguished accomplishments I should have been more desirous to record in unfading numbers; but no man can add a cubit to his stature, and I must therefore content myself, in this note, to express my affection, admiration, and respect,"—and being afterwards at Oatlands, the company insisted on his inditing some verses, for which they maintained he had a genius. He extemporized this sextain:—

LORD ERSKINE.

"Tom Erskine was once sailor, soldier, and lawyer,
A cross, beyond doubt, 'tween the devil and Sawyer;
He tried all the tricks of the old common law,
Till to Chancery sent, which can cure every flaw;
So merrily, merrily let him live now,
A planter of trees, and a holder of plow."

On another visit at Oatlands, where he met Lewis, the dramatist, Lady Anne Cullen Smith, and other wits, male and female, the company amused themselves in writing, after dinner, what they called "Threadpaper Rhymes." Erskine, having borrowed Lewis's pencil, returned it with the following impromptu :—

"Your pencil I send, with thanks for the loan;
Yet, writing for fame now and then,
My wants I must still be content to bemoan,
Unless I could borrow—your pen."

Having, in another stanza, glanced with some severity at female failings, Lewis thus answered :—

"Lord Erskine, at women presuming to rail,
Says wives are tin canisters tied to our tail;
While fair Lady Anne, as the subject he carries on,
Feels hurt at his Lordship's degrading comparison.
Yet wherefore degrading? Consider'd aright,
A canister's useful, and polish'd, and bright;
And should dirt its original purity hide,
That's the fault of the puppy to whom it is tied."

Erskine immediately put in his rejoinder:—

"When smitten with love from the eyes of the fair,
If marriage should not be your lot,
A ball from a pistol will end your despair—
It's safer than canister-shot."

Impromptu written by LORD ERSKINE *at Oatlands, on receiving from the* DUCHESS OF YORK *a Lock of Hair of the late lamented* CHARLES JAMES FOX.

"Could relics, as at Rome they show,
Work miracles on earth below,
This little hallow'd lock of hair
Might soothe the patriot's anxious care;
Might, to St. Stephen's Chapel brought,
Inspire each virtuous, noble thought,
As when those ancient benches rung,
Whilst thunder roll'd o'er Fox's tongue;
Then might Old England hold more high
Her proud and matchless liberty.
Alas! alas! the vision's vain,
From the dark grave none come again."

He afterwards printed for private circulation a poem of considerable length, which he thus prefaced :—"The following lines were occasioned by my having, at the instance of my bailiff in Sussex, complained to a neighbor of his rookery,—the only one in that part of the country; but having been afterwards convinced of the utility of rooks, I countermanded my complaint, and wrote 'THE FARMER'S VISION.' The lines are very incorrect and unfinished, being sketched only as a domestic amusement to inspire humane and moral feelings in a new generation of my family, and with that view were inscribed to my eldest granddaughter, Frances Erskine, as the fair poetess of St. Leonard's Forest, who, not then sixteen years of age, could have handled the subject much better herself. It is indeed so capable of being made interesting, that I would have prolonged the vision, and worked it up into a poem, but for an insuperable objection, viz. that I am not a poet, It is not fit for publication; a few copies are only printed for friends, who asked for them, as it was too long to make them in writing.—*Buchan Hill, Sussex, Dec.* 25, 1818."—I copy a short specimen:—

> " Old Æsop taught vain man to look
> In Nature's much neglected book,
> To birds and beasts by giving speech,
> For lessons out of common reach.
> They whisper truths in reason's ear,
> If human pride would stoop to hear,—
> Nay, often in loud clamors crave
> The rights which bounteous Nature gave.
> A flock of rooks, my story goes,
> Of all our birds the most verbose———."

We are then told how the bailiff fired into a congregation of rooks and killed several of them,—when the wounded leader hoarsely thus *appealed to the superior court:*—

> " ' Before the Lord of this domain
> Sure justice should not plead in vain ;
> And shall he now, with such blind fury,
> In flat contempt of judge and jury,
> Foul murder sanction in broad day,
> Not on the King's, but God's, highway?'
>
> " Touch'd with the sharp but just appeal,
> Well turn'd at least to make *me feel,*
> Instant this solemn oath I took—
> NO HAND SHALL RISE AGAINST A ROOK.'

Then comes the " Vision:"—

> " A form angelic seem'd to fly
> On meteor wing across the sky :"—

and he discourses at much greater length, but not more poetically, than the rook, on the duty of humanity to the whole brute creation.

In the scarcity of 1801, the lawyers, under the presidency of the Master of the Rolls, having met and agreed to restrict their consumption of bread at all meals Erskine sent the following protest to his Honor:—

> "My early meal thy prudent care controls,
> Lord of the breakfast! Master of the Rolls!
> But as to dinner? What is that to thee?
> There COKE alone shall give the law to me!"

One day, in 1807, when engaged to dine on turtle with the Lord Mayor, he was obliged to sit late on the woolsack, Plumer pleading at the bar with extraordinary turbulence and tediousness, and justifying the saying that "his eloquence was like a tailor's goose, *hot and heavy*,"— the Chancellor was secretly very impatient and angry, but was observed to be writing diligently. Bishop Majendie then came up to Lord Grenville and said, "Lord Erskine seems very intent on this cause." Lord Grenville answered, "My Lord Chancellor always takes a note." Lord Holland, who was very familiar with him, and suspected from his manner that there was something unusual in his occupation, had overheard the conversation and asked for a sight of his note-book. Being produced, it was found to contain the following lines addressed to Plumer—the ink not yet dry:—

> "Oh that thy cursed balderdash
> Were swiftly changed to callipash!
> Thy bands so stiff, and snug toupee,
> Corrected were to callipee;
> That, since I can nor dine nor sup,
> I might arise and eat thee up!"

Being once in a festive party, where every one present was required to make a new riddle, he most indecorously proposed the following:—

> "DE QUODAM REGE.
> "I may not do right, though I ne'er can do wrong:
> I never can die, though I may not live long:
> My jowl it is purple, my head it is fat—
> Come, riddle my riddle. What is it? *What? What?*"[1]

He was, nevertheless, a devoted friend to monarchy, and

---

[1] George III., distinguished by his "purple jowl" and interjection of *What! What!*

in his graver mood he was ready to do justice to the firmness of purpose and domestic virtues belonging to the Monarch, with whose appearance and phraseology he now used such unjustifiable freedom.

Without any refined wit, and with only a moderate portion of humor, he had much success in society from his constant hilarity and well-bred respect for the feelings of others. Fond as he was of talking, he never attempted to engross the whole conversation to himself, and, in choosing his topics and the manner in which he enlarged upon them, he considered the company he was addressing —not declaiming interminably, as if the listeners, whether ladies, military officers, members of parliament, or judges, were pupils to be instructed in a lecture-room,—nor entering into a disquisition on some recondite question with another reckless controversialist, each of them caring as little for the rest of the company as if two were disputing together on Salisbury Plain. He paid to sex and station the deference due to them, and he was eager to bring forward into notice the most unobtrusive of all who were present.

It must be confessed that he much too often introduced stories of which he was himself the hero. His egotism is thus ingeniously and elegantly accounted for and palliated: "With an appetency of applause equal to that of which the celebrated Garrick was accused, he saw the evidences of his triumph daily, and was intoxicated with the incense. The loud laughter or tears of the audience, the occasional faintings in the boxes, could not more delight the soul of the modern Roscius, open to all the titillations of vanity, than did the visible emotions of jurymen—their relaxed muscles at the jest—the dark look of indignation at the invective—the plaudits, scarcely suppressed in deference to the Court—the favorable verdict—gladden the heart of the sensitive orator. Both were alike players, strutting their hour upon the stage, and would alike enact their parts over again, too frequently *encore* their best things at private rehearsals, making their homes a theater, and their friends an audience."[1]

This propensity of Erskine drew down upon him much satire—without being at all repressed. A newspaper

[1] Townsend's Eminent Judges, i. 458.

apologized for breaking off a speech of his at a public dinner, in the middle, because their stock of I's were quite exhausted. Caricatures of him were published, under the name of "Counselor Ego;"—and when he was to be raised to the peerage, it was proposed that he should take the title of " Baron Ego, of Eye, in the county of Suffolk." "The Pursuits of Literature" introduced this Dialogue between Octavius and the Author, who had been talking rather vaingloriously of his own exploits:—

" OCTAVIUS.
This of yourself?
AUTHOR.
'Tis so.
OCTAVIUS.
You're turn'd plain fool,
A vain, pert prater, bred in *Erskine's* school."

Canning, in the "Anti-Jacobin," in the following pretended report of his speech at a dinner of the " Whig Club," attempted to ridicule his admiration of himself and of the French Directory, then lately established in power:—

"He had not the advantage of being personally acquainted with any gentleman of the Directory:—he understood, however, that one of them (Mr. Merlin), previous to the last change, had stood in a situation similar to his own; he was, in fact, nothing less than a leading advocate and barrister, in the midst of a free, powerful, and enlightened people. The conduct of the Directory, with regard to the exiled deputies, had been objected to by some persons on the score of a pretended rigor. For his part, he should only say that, having been, as he had been, both a soldier and a sailor, if it had been his fortune to have stood in either of these two relations to the Directory— as a man and as a major-general he should not have scrupled to direct his artillery against the national representation:—as a naval officer he would undoubtedly have undertaken for the removal of the exiled deputies: admitting the exigency, under all its relations, as it appeared to him to exist, and the then circumstances of the times, with all their bearings and dependencies, branching out into an infinity of collateral considerations and involving in each a variety of objects, political, physical, and moral; and these, again, under their distinct and separate heads, ramifying into endless subdivisions, which it was foreign to his purpose to consider. Mr. Erskine concluded by recapitulating, in a strain of agonizing and impressive eloquence, the several more prominent heads of his speech: he had been a soldier and a sailor, and had a son at Winchester School,—he had been called by special retainers, during the summer, into many different and distant parts of the country,—travelling chiefly in post-chaises. He felt himself called upon to declare, that his poor faculties were at the service of his country—of the free and enlightened part of it at least. He stood here as a man—he stood in the eye, indeed, in the hand, of God—to whom (in the presence of the company and waiters) he solemnly appealed. He was of noble, perhaps royal, blood—he had a house at Hampstead—was convinced of the necessity of a thorough and radical reform. His pamphlets had gone through thirty editions—skipping alternately the odd and even numbers. He loved the Constitution, to which he would cling and grapple—and he was clothed with the infirmities of man's nature. He would apply to the present French rulers (particularly Barras and Rewell) the words of the poet—

> 'Be to their faults a little blind,
> Be to their virtues very kind;
> Let all their ways be unconfin'd,
> And clap the padlock on their mind.'

And for these reasons, thanking the gentleman who had done him the honor to drink his health, he should propose '*Merlin, the late Minster of Justice, and Trial by Jury.*'"

Cobbett about the same time published the following notice of one of his parliamentary harangues:—

"Mr. Erskine delivered a most animated speech in the House of Commons on the causes and consequences of the late war, which lasted thirteen hours, eighteen minutes and a second, by Mr. John Nicholl's stop watch. Mr. Erskine closed his speech with a dignified climax—'I was born free, and, by G—d, I'll remain so!' [A loud cry of *Hear, hear!* in the gallery, in which were citizens Tallien and Barrère.] On Monday three weeks, we shall have the extreme satisfaction of laying before the public a brief analysis of the above speech, our letter-founder having entered into an engagement to furnish a fresh font of I's."

This distributor of *honors* afterwards offered him the title of "Lord *Clack*mannon."

A stronger proof of his incorrigible habit, we have in the following entry in the Journal of his friend and general admirer, Lord Byron:—
"A goodly company of lords, ladies, and wits. There was Erskine, good, but intolerable: he jested, he talked, he did everything admirably; but then he would be applauded for the same thing twice over. He would read his own verses, his own paragraphs, and tell his own stories again and again—and then the TRIAL BY JURY!!! I almost wished it abolished, for I sat next him at dinner. As I had read his published speeches, there was no occasion to repeat them to me."

In the Life of Dr. Burney by his daughter, we have a very lively picture on the same subject: she is giving an account of a party at Mrs. Crewe's, at which Lord Loughborough and Mr. Burke were present:—

"Mr. Erskine had been enumerating fastidiously to Mrs. Crewe his avocations, their varieties, and their excess; till at length he mentioned very calmly, having a cause to plead soon against Mr. Crewe, upon a manor business in Cheshire. Mrs. Crewe hastily interrupted him, with an air of some disturbance, to inquire what he meant, and what might ensue to Mr. Crewe. 'Oh, nothing but losing the lordship of that spot,' he coolly answered, 'though I don't know that it will be given against him; I only know for certain that I shall have £300 for it.' Mrs. Crewe looked thoughtful; and Mr. Erskine then, finding he engaged not her whole attention, raised his voice as well as his manner, and began to speak of the new Association for Reform by the Friends of the People, —descanting in powerful, though rather ambiguous, terms upon the use they had thought fit in that Association to make of his name, though he had never yet been to the society; and I began to understand that he meant to disavow it; but presently he added, 'I don't know, I am uncertain whether I shall ever attend. I have so much to do—so little time—such interminable occupation! However, I don't yet know. I am not decided, for the people must be supported!'"—"This renowned orator," Madame D'Arblay satirically adds, "at a convivial meeting at his own house, fastened upon my father with all the volubility of his eloquence, and all the exuberance of his happy good-humor, in singing his own exploits and praises, without insisting that his hearer should join in the chorus; or rather, perhaps, without discovering, from his own self-absorption, that this ceremony was omitted."

His infirmity is likewise censured by Hannah More, who, I suppose, had been silenced when she wished to enlarge upon her own writings and her own good deeds:—

"Among the chief talkers at the Bishop of St. Asaph's," says she, "was Mr. Erskine. To me he is rather brilliant than pleasant. His animation is vehemence; and he contrives to make the conversation fall too much on himself —a sure way not to be agreeable in mixed company."

One celebrated "blue-stocking," however, seems to have been almost in love with him when she was well stricken in years, and she bestows enthusiastic commendation on his social powers:—

"The enchanting Mr. Erskine," writes Miss Seward, "honored me with frequent attentions in the ball-room at Buxton, and with frequents visits at my lodgings, where he often met Mr. Wilberforce. . . . Did Mr. Erskine tell you of our accidental *rencontre* on the the Chatsworth road? I said to my mind, 'What an elegant figure is that gentleman approaching us, who loitering with a book, now reads, and now holds the volume, in a drop hand, to contemplate the fine views on the right! There seems mind in every gesture, every step; and how like Mr. Erskine!' A few seconds converted resemblance into reality. After mutual exclamations, the graceful Being stopped the chaise, opened the door, and, putting one foot on the step, poured all his eloquence upon a retrospect of the hours we had passed together at Buxton, illuminating, as he flatteringly said, one of those seldom intervals of his busy life, in which his mind was left to enjoy undisturbed the luxury of intellectual intercourse."

All impartial persons allowed, that, however excessive Erskine's egotism might be, it was accompanied with much *bonhomie*, and was entirely free from arrogance or presumption. Though vain, he never felt envy or jealousy of others; and, instead of trying to stifle the reputation of rivals by open or secret means, he sincerely and cordially praised, and heard praise bestowed upon, what was meritorious in the departments which most excited his own emulation.'

[1] Since I wrote these observations, I have received a letter from the Right

When I entered Westminster Hall, it rang with Erskine's jokes, consisting chiefly of puns,—some of them very good, and some of them requiring his established reputation to make them circulate.—A junior barrister, joining the circuit, had the misfortune to have his trunk cut off from the back of his post-chaise, on which the jocund leader comforted him by saying, "Young gentleman henceforth imitate the elephant, the wisest of animals, *who always carries his* TRUNK *before him.*"

He afterwards embraced a favorable opportunity of repeating the same joke. *Polito*, the keeper of the wild beasts in Exeter 'Change, having brought an action against the proprietors of a stage-coach for negligence, whereby his portmanteau was stolen from the boot of the vehicle, he himself having been riding on the box,—" Why did he not," said the defendant's witty counsel, " take a lesson from his own sagacious elephant, and travel with his TRUNK *before him ?*"[1]

Crossing Hampstead Heath, he saw a ruffianly driver most unmercifully pummeling a miserable, bare-boned pack-horse,—and remonstrating with him, received this answer, " Why, it's my own! mayn't I use it as I please ?" As the fellow spoke, he discharged a fresh shower of blows on the raw back of his beast. Erskine, much irritated by this brutality, laid two or three sharp strokes of his walking-stick over the shoulders of the cowardly offender, who, crouching and grumbling, asked him what business he had

---

Hon. Thomas Erskine, in which, referring to Miss Burney's strictures on his illustrious father, he says,—" The merits of 'Evelina' were probably but little known to my father, who seldom read books of that sort. The clever authoress, with great *naïveté*, mentions the fact, that ' Mr. Erskine confined his attention exclusively to Mrs. Crewe ;' and thus unconsciously records another instance of the all-pervading infirmity of egotism. My poor father's fault was in not appreciating the sensitiveness of others, and in not perceiving the necessity for controlling this universal passion. He was too artless to disguise his love of praise ; but he is entitled to this distinction,—his thirst for approbation never led him to depreciate the merits of others; and his whole life pronounces him innocent of that bitterness of spirit which too often marks the impatience of genius and talent when the appetite of a rival for the common food is too little disguised."

[1] The Right Hon. Thomas Erskine, from whom I have this anecdote, adds,—" Polito's portmanteau was put into the boot behind by his own directions ; and the jury adopted my father's suggestion, that the loss was owing to his own indiscretion, and gave a verdict for the defendant, to the great indignation of Lord Kenyon, who had told them it was an undefended cause. The joke, perhaps, helped the conclusion."

to beat him with a stick? "Why," replied Erskine, "my stick is my own; mayn't I use it as I please?"

Being counsel for a person who while traveling in a stage-coach which started from the "Swan with two Necks," in Lad Lane, had been upset and had his arm broken, he thus with much gravity began :—"Gentlemen of the jury, the plaintiff in this case is Mr. Beverly, a respectable merchant of Liverpool, and the defendant is Mr. Nelson, proprietor of the Swan with two Necks, in Lad Lane,—a sign emblematical, I suppose, of the number of necks people ought to possess who ride in his vehicles."

In an action against a stable-keeper, for not taking proper care of a horse,—"The horse," said Mingay, who led for the plaintiff, ' was turned into a stable, with nothing to eat but musty hay. To such feelings the horse *demurred*." "He should have *gone to the country*," retorted Erskine. This, though *caviare to the multitude*, to a true special pleader is of exquisite relish,—" demurring," and "going to the country," being the technical terms for requiring a cause to be decided on a question of *law* by the judges, or on a question of *fact* by the jury.

I must have credit with non-professional readers for my assertion that the following is equally delectable. Billy Baldwin, a low practitioner in the King's Bench, was much employed in bail-business, and moving attachments against the sheriff "for not bringing in the body," *i. e.* for not arresting and imprisoning debtors. Being told that Billy had sold his house in Lincoln's Inn Fields, now Surgeons' Hall, to the Corporation of Surgeons, "I suppose," said Erskine, "it was recommended to them from Baldwin being so well acquainted *with the practice of bringing in the body*."

When he was Chancellor, being asked by the Secretary to the Treasury whether he would attend the grand Ministerial fish-dinner to be given at Greenwich at the end of the session, he answered, "To be sure I will; what would your fish-dinner be without the GREAT SEAL?"

I venture on one more, which, though it has a legal aspect, all will understand. His friend, Mr. Maylem, of Ramsgate, having observed that his physician had ordered him not to bathe, "Oh, then," said Erskine, "you are

malum prohibitum." "My wife, however," resumed the other, "does bathe." "Worse still," rejoined Erskine, "for she is *malum in* SE."
When about to be created a Knight of the *Thistle*, he was jeered by one of his friends, who observed, "I suppose you next mean to have the *Garter*." He answered, "You seem to suppose that, having been in the Navy, the Army, and the Law, I am now going to *take Orders*."

In the exuberance of his fun he was likewise fond of what may be called practical jokes. The late worthy Sir John Sinclair having proposed that a testimonial should be presented to himself by the British nation, for his eminent public services,—in answer to one of his circulars, Erskine wrote on the first page of a letter in a flowing hand these words, which filled it to the bottom:—
"MY DEAR SIR JOHN,
"I am certain there are few in this kingdom who set a higher value on your public services than myself—and I have the honor to subscribe"—
Then, on turning over the leaf, was to be found—
"Myself,
"Your most obedient faithful servant,
"T. ERSKINE."

He would produce his leeches at consultation under the name of "bottle conjurors," and argue the result of the cause according to the manner in which they swam or crawled;—and a still more favorite amusement with him was to make his large Newfoundland dog, Toss, personate the Judge. He had taught this animal to sit with much gravity upon a chair, with his paws placed on the table, and occasionally he would put a full-bottom wig on his head and a band round his neck—placing a black-letter folio before him. The clients, as we may suppose, were much startled by such exhibitions; but then was the time when he took his amusement, and, rising next morning at cock-crow, he read all his briefs before the Court met, and won all the verdicts.

His general urbanity of manner to all classes and degrees of men deserves to be specially recorded. Notwithstanding his occasional effusions about his "noble, if not royal descent," he was, in truth, free from the slightest taint of arrogance or *hauteur*. Once he asserted, in a marked manner, his precedence as an Earl's son. During the State Trials, in 1794, he thought that Eyre, from the bench, had treated him with indignity; and, both dining at the Old Bailey the same day, he ostentatiously took the *pas* of the Chief Justice. But on ordinary occasions he did not at all presume upon his birth, and he was willing to place himself on a footing of perfect equality with all who approached him.'

I ought further to mention that humanity to animals was not a mere subject of talk or of legislation with him, but was a constantly actuating principle of his life. Of this I find a striking instance recorded in the Annual Register:— ' Feb. 3rd, 1807. As the Lord Chancellor was passing through Holborn on foot, he observed a number of men and boys hunting and beating on the bead a little dog with sticks, under the idea of his being mad. The Ld. Chan., with great humanity, observing not the least symptom of madness, rushed into the crowd, seized the poor animal from the hands of its destroyers, and carried it some distance, till he met a boy, whom he hired to carry it home with him, to his Lordship's house in Lincoln's Inn Fields: when he gave it into the care of a servant to be taken to his stables."— Not only was he kind to such attached favorites as "faithful Jack," the goose who followed him about his grounds, and Toss, so like a judge; but he ever took delight in protecting from ill-usage any living creatures, in watching their sports, and adding to their enjoyments.

Although he sometimes talked with levity on sacred subjects, he had deep and sincere religious feelings, and he might be considered as inclining to superstition rather than to scepticism. He not only believed in the general moral government of God, but in particular interpositions of his power for the benefit of highly favored individuals. "At the famous State Trials, in 1794, he lost his voice on the evening before he was to address the jury. It returned to him just in time; and this, like other felicities of his career, he always ascribed to a special providence, with the habitually religious disposi-

---

[1] I have no doubt that his rank, being joined with poverty and energy, materially assisted his progress. It gave him confidence, and made him more favorably listened to, both by judges and jurymen.

tion of mind which was hereditary in the godly families that he sprung from."[1]

He either was, or pretended to be, a believer in *Second Sight* and *Ghosts*. Perhaps he worked himself up to the persuasion that he was sincere, in order that he might, with a good conscience, appear a very extraordinary man, and make people stare; but I suspect that he would occasionally, with deliberation, mystify his hearers. There being a round of Ghost-stories in a large company at the old Duchess of Gordon's, when it came to the turn of Erskine, then an ex-Chancellor, he spoke as follows: "I also believe in *Second Sight*, because I have been its subject. When I was a very young man, I had been for some time absent from home. On the morning of my arrival in Edinburgh, as I was descending the steps of a *close*, on coming out from a bookseller's shop, I met our old family butler. He looked greatly changed,—pale, wan, and shadowy as a ghost. 'Eh, old boy,' I said, 'what brings you here?' He replied, 'To meet your Honor, and solicit your interference with my Lord, to receive a sum due to me, which the steward, at our last settlement, did not pay.' Struck by his look and manner, I bade him follow me to the bookseller's, and into whose shop I stepped back. But when I turned round to him, he had vanished. I remembered that his wife carried on some little trade in the Old Town; I remembered even the house and *flat* she occupied, which I had often visited in my boyhood. Having made it out, I found the old woman in widow's mourning. Her husband had been dead for some months, and had told her, on his death-bed, that my father's steward had wronged him of some money, but 'that when Master Tom returned, he would see her righted.' This I promised to do, and I shortly after fulfilled my promise. The impression was indelible; and I am extremely cautious how I deny the possibility of such 'supernatural visitings' as those which your Grace has just instanced in your own family."

Erskine's personal advantages have been already alluded to. His constitution was remarkably strong; and it was mentioned by himself, in the House of Lords,[2] as a singular fact, that during the twenty-eight years of his

[1] Lord Brougham.　　　　　　[2] Parl. Deb. vi. 247.

practice at the Bar, he had never for a single day been prevented from attending to his professional duties.

Before coming to his descendants, I must briefly notice his two brothers, with whom he always kept up an affectionate intercourse during their respective lives. The Earl of Buchan who spent half a century in increasing his income by saving—from £200 to £2,000 a year, might by his talents have made a considerable figure in the world had it not been for his morbid vanity, which is said to have been more excessive than ever was seen in a human being. Having no children by his wife, he used often to observe, "According to Bacon, '*great men have no continuance*,' and in the present generation there are three examples of it, Frederick of Prussia, George Washington, and myself." At the University of Leyden, while bearing the title of Lord Cardross, he had been a fellow student with Lord Chatham, who afterwards kindly offered him the appointment of secretary of embassy at Lisbon; but he refused it because Sir James Gray, the ambassador, was only a baronet. To be sure Dr. Johnson ignorantly and foolishly said, "Sir, had he gone secretary while his inferior was ambassador, he would have been a traitor to his rank and family." There can be no doubt that he acted most absurdly. He comforted himself for the rest of his days in talking of his ancestors, and corresponding with great people. Observing to the Duchess of Gordon, "We inherit all our cleverness from our mother;" she answered, "I fear that, as is usually the case with the mother's fortune, it has all been settled on the younger children."

He still continued to write letters to Lord Chatham, and in one of these he curiously introduces the future Chancellor:—" A brother of mine is just arrived from our colonies of East and West Florida, and gives me but a very unfavorable account of the capabilities of those countries. He brought me likewise a curious account of a negro conqueror, who has subdued a great part of Africa, lying nearer our settlements, and has occasioned the building of our new fort on that coast. He carries eight Arabic secretaries, who record his feats in that language. My brother has also conversed with Commodore Byron's officers, and confirms the account of the Patagonian giants.'"

[1] The " Middy" seems to have considered himself " *licensed as a traveler*."

Occupying, like his father, a "flat" in the old town of Edinburgh, he thought to place himself at the head of the literati there, but was baffled in a attempt to found a "Society of Antiquaries," —when he thus complained to a distant friend :—" I have been ungenerously requited by my countrymen for endeavoring to make them happier and more respectable. This is the common lot of men who have a spirit above that of the age and country in which they act, and I appeal to posterity for my vindication. I could have passed my time much more agreeably among Englishmen, whose character I preferred to that of my own countrymen, in a charming country too, where my alliance with the noblest and best families in it, and my political sentiments, would have added much to my domestic as well as civil enjoyments; but I chose rather to forego my own happiness for the improvement of my native country, and expect hereafter that the children of those who have not known me, or received me as they ought to have done, will express their concern, and blush on account of the conduct of their parents. 'Præclarâ conscientiâ igitur sustentor, cùm cogito me de republicâ aut meruisse quum potuerim, aut certe nunquam nisi divinè cogitasse.'"

Soon after, he entirely abandoned the ungrateful city of Edinburgh, and concealed himself amid the shades of Dryburgh, where he had purchased an estate. On this occasion he published a general epistle in Latin, addressed to all the literati of the world. He afterwards thus apologized for not doing more to enlighten mankind :—" My insatiable thirst of knowledge, and a genius prone to splendid sciences and the fine arts, has distraced my attention so much that the candid must make ample allowances for me in any one department; but, considering myself as a nobleman and not a peer of Parliament,—a piece of ornamental china as it were,—I have been obliged to avail myself of my situation to do as much good as I possibly could without acting in a professional line, which my rank and my fate excluded me from. A discarded courtier, with a little estate, does not find it easy to make his voice be heard in any country, and least of all

and to have told as great wonders as of "the Anthropophagi, and men whose heads do grow beneath their shoulders."

in Scotland."—However, he contrived to persuade him whom he styled sometimes the "American Buchan," that he was really a great man, and sending him a snuff-box made from the oak which sheltered Wallace after the battle of Falkirk, received Washington's portrait in return, with the following acknowledgment: " I accept with sensibility and satisfaction the significant present of the box, which accompanied your Lordship's letter."

Lord Coke says, a man has in him all his posterity; and Lord Buchan thought that he had in himself all his ancestors, or that the whole line formed a corporation sole never visited by death. He always spoke, therefore, of their actions as his own; and a stranger, not aware of this habit, was amazed once, although his Lordship did look very old, to hear him say at a dinner table, " I remonstrated strongly, before it took place, against the execution of Charles I."

An uncle of mine, a clergyman, who lived in the neighborhood, once gave me a ludicrous account of the Earl's installation of a colossal statue to Sir William Wallace on the anniversary of the victory of Stirling Bridge, obtained in 1297. The following was the inscription on the base: "In the name of my brave and worthy country, I dedicate this monument, as sacred to the memory of Wallace,—

" 'The peerless Knight of Ellerslie,
Who woo'd on Ayr's romantic shore
The beaming torch of liberty;
And roaming round from sea to sea,
From glade obscure, or gloomy rock,
His bold compatriots called to free
The realm from Edward's iron yoke.' "

A great curtain was drawn before the statue, which dropped at the discharge of a cannon; and then the Knight of Ellerslie was discovered with a huge German tobacco-pipe in his mouth, which some wicked wag had placed there,—to the unspeakable consternation of the peer, and amusement of the company.

Nevertheless he did some good by his patronage of letters. He encouraged the early efforts of Burns, Scott, and other men of genius; and he founded an annual prize in the University of Aberdeen, as an incentive to the study of the classics. It must be confessed, however, that the prize was of very minute intrinsic value, and operated only like the crowns of laurel and parsley distributed at the Olympic games.

Of all his poetical writings there are now extant only four lines, which he wrote with his own hand on the wall of St. Bernard's Well, in the neighborhood of Edinburgh :—

> "O drink of me only ; O drink of this well,
> And fly from vile whiskey, that lighter of hell.
> If you drink of me only—or drink of good ale.—
> Long life will attend you—good spirits prevail."
> [*Quoth the Earl of Buchan.*]

He considered himself quite superior in genius to his younger brothers, and he was rather shocked that they had got on in the world by following a trade. Yet at times he would boast of their elevation,—taking all the credit of it to himself. He said to an English nobleman who visited him at Dryburgh, "My brothers Harry and Tom are certainly extraordinary men; but they owe everything to me." This observation occasioning an involuntary look of surprise in his guest, he continued, "Yes, it is true; they owe everything to me. On my father's death, they pressed me for a small annual allowance. I knew that this would have been their ruin, by relaxing their industry. So, making a sacrifice of my inclination to gratify them, I refused to give them a farthing ; and they have both thriven ever since,—*owing everything to me.*"

While the head of the family made himself so ridiculous, Henry Erskine, the second brother, was universally beloved and respected. After studying at the Universities of St. Andrew's and Edinburgh, he was called to the Scotch Bar, and became its brightest ornament. Like Lord Loughborough, he first distinguished himself as a Ruling Elder in the debates of the General Assembly, then the best theater for deliberative eloquence to be found in Scotland. He soon got into extensive practice, and he established a new æra in the history of the Parliament House. The old pleaders, reared at the Dutch Universities, were very learned, but confined themselves to heavy quotations from Craig, Vinius, and Voet. He, by no means deficient in professional learning, indulged in the boldest sallies of imagination ; and his *seria commixta iocis*, while they delighted the Judges and the crowd who came to listen to him, in all sperate cases secured the judgment of the Court in favor of his clients. He had the fervid genius of the youngest brother without any of his eccentricities, and only required the same field for a display of his powers to have excelled him. Yet while, by the unanimous suffrages of the public, he found himself placed without a rival at the head of a commanding profession, his general deportment was characterized by the most unaffected modesty and easy affability; and his talents were not less at the service of indigent but deserving clients, than of those whose wealth or influence enabled them most liberally to reward his exertions. Henry Erskine was in an eminent sense the "advocate of the people" throughout the long course of his professional career. It is said that a poor man, in a remote district of Scotland, thus answered an acquaintance who wished to dissuade him from engaging in a lawsuit with a wealthy neighbor, by representing the hopelessness of his being able to meet the expense of litigation: "Ye dinna ken what ye're saying, maister; there's no a puir man in a' Scotland need to want a friend, or fear an enemy, sae lang as Hairry Askin lives."

True to the Whig principles in which he was reared, he was in Opposition during nearly the whole of his life; but such was the habitual sweetness of his temper, and such the fascination of his manners, that, in times when political animosities were carried to a lamentable height, no one was known to speak or to think of him with anything approaching to personal hostility. By the choice of his brother advocates, he many years enjoyed the dignity of Dean of Faculty, and twice he tasted office under the Crown as Lord Advocate—first during the "Coalition Ministry" in 1783, and again under the "Talents," when Thomas was Chancellor. I remember then hearing him plead a cause at the bar of the House of Lords—all the Courts in Westminster Hall being deserted from a curiosity to compare the two brothers,—and full justice was done to the elder. He at that time represented Dumfries, but he never opened his mouth in the House of Commons; so that the often-debated question, how he was qualified to succeed there, remained unsolved. Though baffled in some of his pursuits, and disappointed of the honors to which his claim was universally admitted, he never allowed the slightest shade of discontent to rest upon his mind, nor the least drop of bitterness to mingle with his blood. On the approach of the infirmities of age, he retired to his beautiful villa of Almondell, in West Lothian. "Passing thus," says one who knew him well, "at once from all the bustle and excitement of public life to a scene of comparative inactivity, he never felt a moment of *ennui* or dejection; but retained unimpaired, till within a day or two of his death, not only all his intellectual activity and social affections, but when not under the immediate infliction of a painful and, incurable disease, all the gayety of spirit and all that playful and kindly sympathy with innocent enjoyment which made him the idol of the young and the object of cordial attachment and unenvying admiration to his friends of all ages."

Such was his fame for wit, that, besides the genuine offspring of his own brain, most of the good things of the day, and many of days long gone by, were imputed to him.[1] A few have been sent to me, which may be relied upon as *genuine*. Having been speaking in the Outer House, at the bar of Lord Swinton, a very good but a very slow and deaf Judge, he was called away to the bar of Lord Braxfield (the well-known Justice Clerk Macqueen), who was Lord Ordinary for the week. On his coming up, Lord Braxfield said to him, "Well, Dean, what is this you've been talking so loudly about to my Lord Swinton?" "About a cask of whiskey, my Lord" (replied Harry); "but I found it no easy matter to make it *run in his Lordship's head*."

Andrew Balfour, one of the commissaries of Edinburgh, was a man of much pomposity of manner, appearance, and expression. Harry met him one morning coming into the Court, and observing that he was lame, said to him, "What has happened, Commissary? I am sorry to see you limping." "I was visiting my brother in Fife," answered the commissary, "and I fell over his stile, and had nearly broken my leg." "'Twas lucky, Commissary" (replied Harry), "it was not your *own stile*, for you would then have broken your neck."

---

[1] For example, I well remember hearing, when a boy, that Harry Erskine, being told by a friend that "his coat was much too short," answered, "It will be *long enough* before I get another."—To be found in Swift's " Polite Conversation."

His brother, the Earl of Buchan, who aimed at being a jester as well as a philosopher and a poet, one day putting his head below the lock of the parlor-door, exclaimed, "See, Harry, here's 'Locke on the Human Understanding;'"—"Rather a poor edition, my Lord," replied Harry.

Succeeding Dundas as Lord Advocate, that good-humored politician offered to lend him his embroidered official gown, as he would not want it long. "No," said he in the same spirit, "I will not assume the *abandoned habits* of my predecessors."

These smart sayings were sometimes lost upon some of his countrymen—who at least required time to consider them. It is related that Lord Balmuto, sitting on the bench, would retain the most inflexible gravity, notwithstanding a mirth-moving jest from the Dean; and some hours after, when another cause was called, would suddenly grin and exclaim, "Oh! Mr. Erskine, I hae ye noo: very gude, very gude!"

Henry likewise displayed the family faculty for versifying—of which we have a specimen in the lines he improvised on reading Moore's translation of Anacreon:—

> "Oh! mourn not for Anacreon dead;
> Oh! weep not for Anacreon fled;
> The lyre still breathes he touch'd before,
> For we have one ANACREON MOORE."

Sir Walter Scott, in his Diary, thus speaks of the three brothers:—"April 20, 1829. Lord Buchan is dead, a person whose immense vanity, bordering upon insanity, obscured or rather eclipsed very considerable talents. His imagination was so fertile that he seemed really to believe the extraordinary things which he delighted in telling. His economy, most laudable in the early part of his life, when it enabled him from a small income to pay his father's debts, became a miserable habit, and led him to do mean things. He had a desire to be a great man, and a Mecænas *à bon marché*. The two great lawyers, his brothers, were not more gifted by nature than I think he was; but the restraints of a profession kept the eccentricity of the family in order. Henry Erskine was the best-natured man I ever knew—thoroughly a gentleman—and with but one fault; he could not say '*No*,' and thus sometimes misled those who trusted him. Tom Erskine was positively mad. I have heard him tell a cock-and-a-bull story of having seen the ghost of his father's servant, John Barnett, with as much gravity as if he believed every word he was saying. Both Henry and Thomas were saving men, yet both died very poor; the latter at one time possessed £200,000; the other had a considerable fortune. The Earl alone has died wealthy. It is saving, not getting, that is the mother of riches. They all had wit. The Earl's was crack-brained, and sometimes caustic. Henry's was of the very kindest, best-humored, and gayest sort that ever cheered society; that of Lord Erskine moody and muddish. But I never saw him in his best days." Sir Walter himself was at this time in declining health, his spirits affected by the pecuniary difficulties in which he was involved, and his judgment still biased by political animosity, which grew stronger as he approached the end of his career,—otherwise his kindly nature, and exquisite relish for the beautiful and the good, wherever to be discerned, would have induced him to speak more warmly of the merits, and more mercifully of the failings, of LORD CHANCELLOR ERSKINE.[1]

This extraordinary man,—who will be a greater boast to his descendants than any Earl of Buchan or of Mar, or any royal progenitor,—by his first marriage had eight children; Frances, married to the Reverend Dr. Holland, Prebendary of Chichester; Mary, married to Edward Morris, Esq., the Master in Chancery; David Montague, the present Lord, who has served his country as minister to the United States of America and at the Court of Wirtemburg; Thomas, a judge of the Court of Common Pleas, one of the most upright and amiable of men; and Esmé Stewart, an officer in the army, who fought gallantly at Waterloo, and died from the consequences of a severe wound he received from a cannon-shot near the end of the day, by the side of the Duke of Wellington.

[1] Walter could even utter a bitter joke at the funeral of the old Earl.— 'April 25th. Time to set out for Lord Buchan's funeral at Dryburgh. Hi Lordship's burial took place in a chapel among the ruins. His body wa in the grave with its feet pointing westwards. My cousin Maxpopple wa for taking notice of it; but I assured him 'that a man who had been wron; in the head all his life would scarce become right-headed after death.'" H concludes, however, with a touch of tenderness: "I felt something at parting with this old man, though but a trumpery body. He gave me the first approbation I ever obtained from a stranger."

I must now reluctantly take leave of a task which I feel that I have inadequately performed—having attempted to describe the mental powers and intellectual achievements of Erskine. With his external lineaments posterity will be rendered familiar from the admirable representations of him which remain, by eminent painters and sculptors. The best portrait of him is by Hoppner, in the royal gallery at Windsor; and there is an admirable bust of him in Holland House, by Nollekens, with the inscription:—

"Nostræ eloquentiæ forensis facile princeps."

But the likeness of him which I regard with most delight is a statue, by Westmacott, in Lincoln's Inn Hall. This is the produce of a subscription eagerly made soon after his death by the members of that profession which he had so much adorned. The attitude is dignified and commanding; and although it was beyond the art of sculpture to convey any notion of that speaking eye which so much heightened the effect of the varying sentiments which proceeded from his lips, all the other features of his countenance are admirably portrayed, and still seem animated by the fervid genius which burned in the bosom of the original. I hope this statue may long exercise a salutary influence, not only on the young student who enters the Hall in the course of discipline prescribed to him to qualify him for the Bar, but on all successful practitioners who come here to plead before the Lord Chancellor. Let it constantly remind them of the noble objects of our profession, and impress upon them the important truth,—that its highest rewards may be obtained without the sacrifice of honor or consistency.

CHAPTER CXCI.

LIFE OF LORD CHANCELLOR ELDON FROM HIS BIRTH TILL HIS MARRIAGE.

HAPPILY for myself and my readers, I approach the termination of my biographical labors—

——" nos immensum spatiis confecimus æquor
Et jam tempus equum fumantia solvere colla."

Only one deceased Chancellor remains to be recorded

by me. I began with Augmendus, who, in the seventh century, was Chancellor to Ethelbert, the first Christian Anglo-Saxon king, and I have to finish with John Scott, Lord Eldon, who was Chancellor to George III. and George IV., and having struggled to return to power under William IV., died in the reign of Queen Victoria.

I am now appalled by the difficulty of knowing too well the subject of my memoir, and by the consideration that it is to be read by surviving partisans and attached relatives of this great man. I often practiced before him, and I was honored with some notice from him in private;—but, unluckily, I took an interest in political strife for a large portion of the period during which he occupied the woolsack, almost uniformly differing from the principles which he professed;—and I afterwards actually held office under an Administration to whose measures he was violently opposed. Thus, with the advantage of personal observation, I have to encounter the suspicion of political enmity.

I have sufficient confidence, however, in my own impartiality to proceed with boldness; and while I trust that I shall not deal out praise to his merits with a niggardly hand, dread of the imputation of party bias shall not deter me from pointing out his defects, or censuring his misconduct.

We biographers generally make it equally redound to the credit of our hero, whether he be of illustrious or of humble parentage, saying, with the same complacency, " he was the worthy descendant of a long line of noble ancestors," or " he raised himself by his talents, being the first of his race ever known to fame." Although the latter glory undoubtedly belongs to Lord Eldon, an absurd attempt has been made to trace his pedigree to SIR MICHAEL SCOTT of Balwearie, in the county of Fife, who, in the fourteenth century, was one of the ambassadors sent to bring the " Maid of Norway " to Scotland, upon the death of ALEXANDER III., and who is celebrated for his magical incantations in the " INFERNO,"[1] and in the

---

[1] "Quell' altro che ne' fianchi è così poco
Michele Scotto fu, che veramente
Delle magiche frode seppe il giuoco."
Inferno, canto xx.

"LAY OF THE LAST MINSTREL."[1] He might with more probability have been connected with DUNS SCOTUS, the enemy of the *Thomists*, who undoubtedly was of a Northumbrian family; but the truth is, that both he and his brother, Lord Stowell, had much too great a share of good sense and good taste to set up an unfounded claim to gentility of blood. When they were rising in the world, and found it necessary to have arms,—the seal used by their father having had nothing engraved upon it except W. S., his initials,—after looking at the armorial bearings of the different families of the name of Scott, they accidentally chose the "three lions' heads erased, gules," formerly borne by the Scotts of Balwearie, and now the just boast of their representative, Sir William Scott of Ancrum. From the interesting " Sketch of the Lives of Lords Stowell and Eldon," by their relative, Mr. Surtees, it appears quite clear that they could not go further back in their genealogy than their grandfather, William Scott of Sandgate, who is said to have been clerk to a " fitter," and who, in the latter part of his life, himself became the owner of several " keels,"—a " fitter " being the person who buys and sells coals between the owner of the mine and the shipper, and who conveys them in " keels," or barges, from the higher parts of the Tyne to Newcastle or Shields, where they are loaded for exportation. Sandgate, an old street by the water side, beyond the walls of Newcastle, bearing a great resemblance to Wapping, had long been connected with this trade,—as we learn from an ancient ballad, set to a tune well known through the North as the " Keel-row,"—of which the following is the first stanza:—

" As I came thro' Sandgate, thro' Sandgate, thro' Sandgate,
As I came thro' Sandgate, I heard a lassie sing,
Weel may the keel row, the keel row, the keel row ;
Weel may the keel row that my laddie's in."[2]

---

[1] " In these far climes it was my lot
To meet the wondrous Michael Scott,
A wizard of such dreadful fame,
That when to Salamanca's cave
Him listed his magic wand to wave,
The bells would ring in Notre Dame."
Lay of Last Ministrel, canto ii.

I never heard the Chancellor accused of dealing in the *black art ;* and I do not discover any resemblance between him and his supposed ancestor.

[2] This is taken from a Fife song, which I was taught when a child :—

This William Scott had a son William, who, on the 1st of September, 1716, was bound apprentice for seven years to a coal-fitter in Newcastle, with a fee of £5,—and whose indenture of apprenticeship in the first written muniment of a family destined to such distinction. The boy is here described as " son of William Scott of Sandgate, yeoman." This is not at all inconsistent with the representation that he had become a keel-owner, for "yeoman" did not necessarily mean, as we now understand it, "the cultivator of his own little farm," but simply meant "a householder of too poor estate to allow of his designation either as a gentleman or merchant, yet raised above the ranks of servile drudgery." [1] The Scotts of Sandgate well exemplify the quaint definition which the venerable Fuller gives of this class : " The good yeoman is a gentleman in ore, whom the next age may see refined; and is the wax capable of a gentle impression when the Prince shall stamp it."

William, the younger, showed great prudence, steadiness, and shrewdness; and when out of his apprenticeship, becoming himself a " fitter," and commencing with the "keels" he inherited from his father, amassed considerable substance. To swell his profits, he is said at one time to have kept a sort of public-house, near the Quay at Newcastle, for the purpose of supplying his own keelmen with their liquor, on the principle of the truck system. He afterwards became a large ship-owner, and

" O weel may the boatie row,
  That fills a heavy creel,
And cleads us a', frae head to feet,
  And buys our parritch meal.
The boatie rows, the boatie rows,
  The boatie rows indeed ;
And happy be the lot of a'
  That wish the boatie speed."

One stanza is particularly touching :—

" When Jamie vow'd he would be mine,
  And wan frae me my heart,
O ! muckle lighter grew my creel !
  He swore we'd never part.
The boatie rows, the boatie rows,
  The boatie rows fu' weel,
And muckle lighter is the lade
  When love bears up the creel."*

---

[1] Surtees, p. 3.

* " *Creel* is the basket in which the Scottish *poissardes* carry fish on their backs to market."

engaged in the maritime insurance then in vogue, called "bottomry." By "servitude" he was entitled to the freedom of the town of Newcastle, which he took up on the 25th of August, 1724; and on the 7th of September, in the same year, he was admitted into the "Hoastmen's Company," which his sons used to observe was the most reputable in the whole corporation. He seems by his industry and frugality to have risen to high consideration among the trading community of his native town, although he mixed little in society, and read no books except his Bible and his ledger. He married the daughter of Mr. Atkinson of Newcastle, a woman who was the model of all the domestic virtues, and of such superior understanding that to her is traced the extraordinary talent which distinguished her two sons, William and John,— Lord Stowell and Lord Eldon.

Their destiny was materially influenced by the chivalrous effort, in the year 1745, to restore the House of Stuart to the throne. If Prince Charles and his gallant band had not crossed the Border, William would never have been a fellow of University College, Oxford, and in all probability John never would have been Lord Chancellor of Great Britain. Although William's birth certainly took place in the county of Durham instead of Northumberland from the advance of the rebel army to the Tyne, there are two representations of the circumstances attending his mother's flight previous to this event. According to the more romantic story, Mrs. Scott, dreading the violence of the Highlanders about whom the most frightful rumors were spread,—when they approached Newcastle, resolved to hide herself in the country; but she found all the gates shut and fortified, and egress strictly interdicted to all persons of every degree: whereupon, although very near her confinement, she caused herself to be hoisted over the wall in a large basket, and descended safely to the water-side; there a boat, lying in readiness to receive her, conveyed her to Heworth, a village distant only about four miles from Newcastle, but on the right bank of the Tyne. Here she was delivered the same night of twins, William and Barbara.—But the following is the account of the affair by Mrs. Foster, a granddaughter of Mrs. Scott, from whom she says she had heard it hundreds of times;—" My grandmother Scott being with child in the year of the rebellion, 1745, it was deemed more prudent for her to be confined at my grandfather's country-house at Heworth than in the town of Newcastle. She was therefore attended at Heworth by a midwife, who delivered her of a male infant (afterwards Lord Stowell): but some difficulty arising in the birth of the second child, a man on horseback was dispatched to Whickham for Dr. Askew, a medical practitioner of considerable eminence at that time. Dr. Askew not being at home, the man proceeded to Newcastle for Mr. Hallowel. When Mr. Hallowel reached the town gate, it was, on account of the Rebellion, closed for the night; and further delay becoming serious,—instead of waiting until permission was procured from the mayor for his egress, he was let down from the top of the town-wall, on the south side, and proceeded immediately to Heworth, where he delivered my grandmother."[1]

After the retreat of the Chevalier from Derby, by the western side of the island, she returned to her husband's house in Love Lane, Newcastle, and there, in 1751, on the 4th of June, the birthday of George III., she produced her son John, the future Chancellor, who was likewise accompanied by a twin sister, and was baptized along with her at All Saints' Church on the 4th day of July following. Love Lane is a narrow passage between two streets—in Scotland called a "wynd,"—and in Newcastle a "chare,"—the lower extremity being there called the "chare-foot;" and Lord Eldon, who had always genuine delight in referring to native localities, used to amuse the Chancery Bar by declaring that "he ought not to complain of a small and inconvenient Court, as he was born in a *chare-foot*."[2]

I find nothing remarkable related of our Chancellor's infancy—nor any omen of his future greatness—except that he showed he was born with the faculty of always *lighting on his legs*. His elder sister, Barbara, used to re-

[1] Letter to the present Earl of Eldon, 14th June, 1840.—*Twiss*, i. 23.
[2] Mr. Twiss tells a story, that "at the Newcastle Assizes, in a case where a witness swore that at a certain time he saw three men come out of the *foot of a chare*, the Judge who tried the indictment recommended it to the jury to take no notice of this evidence, as being obviously that of an insane person. The foreman of the jury, however, restored the credit of the witness by explaining that the *chare* from whose *foot* the three men had been seen to issue was not an article of furniture, but a 'narrow street.'" Vol. i. p. 26.

late that "during one of their mother's confinements, Master Jackey being in her room in a go-cart, the nurse quitted her for something that was wanted, leaving the door open: away went Master Jackey after her, tumbling down a whole flight of steps, go-cart and all; but though his mamma, who was unable to get out of the bed to stop him, got a dreadful fright, he took no harm and was found standing *bolt upright* in the passage below."

He was taught to read by a master whom I suspect to have been a Scotsman, from his being called *Dominie* Warden, and his mode of "*muffing* the consonants," in which I was myself initiated.[1] But the success in life of both brothers is mainly to be ascribed to the admirable instruction they received from the Rev. Mr. Moises, master of the Free Grammar School at Newcastle,—under whom they laid in a large stock of classical learning, and acquired a habit of steady application, enabling them to overcome every difficulty which they had afterwards to encounter. The only thing that could be said against this zealous teacher was, that he was too much accustomed to mix his conversation with grave appeals to his conscience and his God—setting an example which at least one of his pupils very sedulously followed.

We have a striking illustration of "the boy being the father of the man," in an authentic account of the difference between the two brothers in their Sunday evening performances: "When asked to give an account of the sermon, their father's weekly custom, William would repeat a sort of digest of the general argument—a condensed summary of what he had heard; John, on the other hand, would recapitulate the *minutiæ* of the discourse, and reiterate the very phrase of the preacher. He showed a memory the most complete and exact, but failed in giving the whole scope and clear general view of the sermon, embodied in half the number of words by the elder brother."[2] Lawyers immediately conceive themselves first delighted with a judgment of Lord Stowell, in Robinson's Reports, and then toiling through one of Lord Eldon, in Vesey, Junior.

Although we know that John Scott, under Mr. Moises,

[1] According to this mode of teaching the alphabet, a vowel is placed before, instead of after, the consonant.
[2] Townsend's Life of Lord Stowell.

was extremely diligent and well-behaved, and a prodigious favorite with his master,—when an ex-Chancellor, he used to relate anecdotes of his boyish days which would rather represent him as having been a *pickle*. "I remember," he said, "my father coming to my bed-side to accuse Henry[1] and me of robbing an orchard, of which some one had come to complain. Now my coat was lying by my bed with its pockets full of apples, and I had hid some more under the bed-clothes when I heard my father on the stairs, and I was at that moment suffering intolerable torture from those I had eaten. Yet I had the audacity to deny the fact. We were twice flogged for it, once by my father, and once by the schoolmaster. I do not know how it was, but we always considered robbing an orchard—'boxing the fox,' as we call it—as an honorable exploit. I remember once being carried before a magistrate for robbing an orchard. There were three of us, and the magistrate acted upon what I think was rather a curious law, for he fined our fathers each thirty shillings for our offense. *We* did not care for that, but then *they did:* so my father flogged me, and then sent a message to Moises, and Moises flogged me again."

He used to relate, likewise, how he was flogged for going without leave to Chester-le-Street, a place eight miles off, to buy "short-cake," for which the place was famous, and staying away a whole night—and again for the offense of playing truant three days from the writing-school, aggravated by a declaration to his father that he had been there punctually every day;[2] —how he possessed the art of blowing out the candles in the shops, and escaping detection;—and how, having lost his hat in a scuffle, his father made him go three months bareheaded, except on Sundays. He gave a very entertaining account of the manner in which his father applied the *taws*, or ferula, in the family, till this instrument of punishment was stolen by the children;[3] and of the distinguished manner in which he danced hornpipes at the

---

[1] Henry was another brother, who succeeded to his father's business.
[2] Yet he wrote a most beautiful hand, which he retained to extreme old age.
[3] The taws were preserved by Henry; and, after the father's death, were produced annually when the brothers met at Newcastle, and talked over, with glee and triumph, the exploit of stealing them.

annual Christmas ball given by his father to the keelmen. But, above all, he dwelt with complacency on his early gallantry; "I believe," he would say, "no shoemaker ever helped to put on more ladies' shoes than I have done. At the dancing-school the young ladies always brought their dancing shoes with them, and we deemed it a proper piece of etiquette to assist the pretty girls in putting them on. In those days, girls of the best families wore white stockings only on the Sundays, and one week-day, which was a sort of public day: on the other days they wore blue Doncaster woolen hose, with white tags. We used, early on the Sunday mornings, to steal flowers from the gardens in the neighborhood, and then we presented them to our sweethearts. Oh! those were happy days—we were always in love." It might be presumed that he had peculiar pleasure in helping the sweet Elizabeth Surtees to put on her dancing-shoes, and that he presented to her the most beautiful flowers: but this was not the fact; for he had not yet seen his destined bride.

In the midst of these wild pranks, which he took pleasure in exaggerating in his old age, he made great progress in his studies, and, while yet in his fifteenth year, he was not only a good classical scholar, but he was pretty well exercised in English composition—often so sadly neglected. He would afterwards occasionally regret that he had not had the advantage of being at Eton or Westminster. Talking of his illustrious class-fellow, Lord Collingwood, he once said, "We were placed at that school because neither his father nor mine could afford to place us elsewhere;" but he related that George III. expressing his surprise how a naval officer could write so excellent a dispatch as that which contained Collingwood's account of the battle of Trafalgar, his Majesty suddenly added, "I forgot that he was educated under Moises." And it is pleasing to think that Lord Eldon always retained a grateful and affectionate recollection of the High School of Newcastle. At the commencement of his "Anecdote Book," written by him for the amusement of his grandson, he says: "The head master was that eminent scholar and most excellent man, the Rev. Mr. Moises. I shall hold his memory in the utmost veneration while I continue to exist."—In one of the last judgments which he delivered in the Court of Chancery, respecting a grammar school, he observed, " I remember that when I had the benefit of an education at one of those grammar schools, the boys were headed by their venerable master to church constantly upon Sundays, and *that* part of the duty of a master of a grammar school was, in those days, as much attended to as teaching the scholars what else they ought there to acquire."—Jack Scott did not hold the Great Seal more than two days before he gladdened the heart of his old preceptor by appointing him one of his chaplains, and he afterwards pressed upon him high preferment in the Church, which was modestly declined.—Finally, several years after the death of Mr. Moises, Lord Eldon wrote the following very amiable letter to the Rev. J. Brewster, of Egglescliff, in Durham, who had been a class-fellow, and had sent him the copy of a Memoir, which he had privately printed, of their beloved preceptor :—

' DEAR SIR,

Pardon me if my engagements have made me too dilatory in acknowledging your kindness in sending me your Memoir of the late Master of the Grammar School in which we were both educated. It has highly gratified me to find that the public are in possession of such a record of that excellent person's merits and worth. I feel the obligation I owe you for the mention of my name in that work. Throughout a long life, in which it has pleased God to confer upon me many blessings, I have always deemed it one of the most valuable that I had in the earliest period of my life the benefit of being educated under Mr. Moises.

" I am your obliged servant.

" ELDON.

" Lincoln's Inn Hall, Wednesday, Aug. 20, 1825."[1]

In the spring of the year 1766 the worthy hoastman began to deliberate seriously respecting the way of life by which his son John was to earn his bread, and after due deliberation resolved to bind him apprentice to his own trade of a coal-fitter. He did not think it necessary to care

[1] By the kindness of my friend Mr. W. E. Surtees, I am in possession of a copy of this interesting memoir. Not only Lord Eldon and Lord Stowell, but Lord Collingwood, and several other very distinguished Northumbrians, were flogged into greatness by Moises. When the master of a public school is at once a fine scholar and an enthusiast in teaching, he is one of the most useful, and ought to be one of the most respected, members of society.

much about the boy's own inclination; but, before preparing the indentures, he wrote to his eldest son, William, then at Oxford, to inform him of his intention. Several years ago, this wonderful youth, when only sixteen, taking advantage of the accidental place of his birth, had gained a Durham scholarship at Corpus Christi College, and afterwards a Durham fellowship at University; and he enjoyed so high a reputation, that before he had completed his twentieth year he was appointed College tutor. Thinking his youngest brother was capable of higher things than buying and selling coals, and having much affection for him, he wrote back to his father, "Send Jack up to me; I can do better for him here." Accordingly, in the beginning of May, 1766, Jack was packed off for London in the Newcastle stage-coach, which, by reason of what was then considered its rapid traveling, was called the "Fly"—seeing that it was only three nights and four days on the journey; its panels bearing the modest inscription, "Sat cito, si sat bene."

Our young traveler amused himself by the way in making jests on an old Quaker, who was his fellow-passenger. When the coach stopped at the Inn at Tuxford, *Aminadab* desired the chambermaid to come to the door of the leathern conveyance, and gave her a six-pence, telling her that he forgot to give it to her when he slept there two years before. *Scott.* "Friend, hast thou seen the motto on this coach?"—*Quaker.* "No."—*Scott.* "Then look at it, for I think that giving her only six-pence now, for all she did for you two years ago, is neither *sat cito* nor *sat bene.*"—He afterwards moralized this motto, and used to say: "In all that I have had to do in life, professional and judicial, I always remembered the admonition on the panels of the vehicle which carried me from school, *Sat cito, si sat bene.* It was the impression of this which made me that deliberate judge—as some have said, *too* deliberate—and reflection upon all that is past will not authorize me to deny that while I have been thinking *sat cito, si sat bene*, I may not have sufficiently recollected whether *sat bene, si sat cito*, has had its due influence."

His brother William was waiting to receive him at the White Horse, in Fetter Lane, Holborn, and treated him to the play at Drury Lane, where he saw "The Devil to Pay," Love acting Jobson, and Miss Pope, Nell. On the 15th of

May, 1766, he was matriculated as a member of the University of Oxford, by Dr. Durell, the Vice Chancellor, and the same day signed the following form of admission to University College:—" Ego Johannes Scott, filius natu minimus Gulielmi Scott, Generosi, de Novo Castro super Tinam, in Com. Northum. lubens subscribo, sub tutamine Domini Scott, annos natus circiter quindecim." Though with a mind well cultivated, his manners were rather rustic; he spoke with a strong Northumbrian accent; and his stature was short, even for his tender years. Lord Stowell used afterwards to say, " I was quite ashamed of his appearance,—he looked such a mere boy."

After he had been a few weeks at Oxford, the Summer vacation arrived, and, returning to Newcastle, his father very judiciously, though much against the lad's inclination, replaced him, till the following term, under Mr. Moises, at the Grammar School,—where he was obliged to construe with his old school-fellows, but was exempt from the discipline of the rod; so that he had no occasion to complain, with Milton,—

" Nec duri libet usque minas perferre magistri,
Cæteraque ingenio non subeunda meo."

He at this time went, among his townsmen, by the name of the "Oxonian" rather, it would seem, derisively, from his puerile appearance, than out of respect to his new dignity.

In October he returned to Oxford, and contiuued to reside there, as an under-graduate, above three years. It has been stated, as a proof of his wonderful proficiency, that when he had just completed his sixteenth year, he was elected a fellow of his college; but he himself, with his usual candor, ascribed this promotion entirely to his brother, good-humoredly saying, " His birth in the vicinity of Durham qualified him to be a candidate for the fellowship in Oxford which he afterwards obtained, and his influence in that station procured for me the fellowship in Oxford which I afterwards obtained. These fellowships were of great use to both of us in our future success in life; and although we have ever been steadily attached to the THRONE, it may truly be said that 'we owe every thing to REBELLION.' "

Under the admirable tuition of his brother, he attended rather more to learning than was then usual at Oxford, and he was very regular in his habits; but he showed no enthusiasm in study, and he looked no higher than to qualify himself for what he considered his destination—to be the incumbent of a college living. Now he contracted the orthodox relish for port wine, to which he ever after adhered; and, from his strong head and robust constitution, he could with almost entire impunity imbibe a portion of this generous liquor which weaker men found to disturb their reasoning powers, and render them martyrs to the gout.

The most stirring emulation among the gownsmen at Oxford seems to have been to make bad puns. Some of these he used to repeat with glee, as if they had been his own composition. "The drinking-cups, or glasses, from their shape, were called *ox-eyes*. Some friends of a young student, after inducing him to fill his *ox-eye* much fuller and oftener than consistent with his equilibrium, took pity at last upon his helpless condition, and led or carried him to his rooms. He had just Latin enough at command to thank them at the stair-head with ' Pol, me *ox-eye*-distis, amici.' "—" Windham, then an under-graduate, hated a pun, good or bad. Reading Demosthenes one day with great admiration, and coming to $T\acute{\epsilon}\theta\nu\eta\varkappa\epsilon\ \Phi\iota\lambda\iota\pi\pi o\varsigma$; (Is Philip dead?) $O\dot{\upsilon},\ \mu\dot{\alpha}\ \varDelta\ell$ (No! by Jupiter!) he was put into a great passion by a fellow-student saying, ' No, Windham, you see he is *not dead;* the Greek words only say he *may die.*' "—" The Vice Chancellor, Dr. Leigh, of Balliol, a determined punster, having given offense to the young men by some act of discipline, when he next appeared amoug them he was saluted with much sibilation; whereupon, turning round, he said, ' Academici, laudamur ab *his ?*' which produced a change in his favor, and they loudly applauded him."—Smoking was common in those days, and a fellow secretly indulged even in the habit of chewing tobacco. Having once inadvertently squirted near the master's niece, who was passing by, he was thus admonished, " *Ne quid nigh Miss.*"—" A clergyman who had two small Corpus livings adjoining each other, NEWBURY and BIBURY, and who always performed the morning service in the former and the evening in the latter, being asked in the Hall why he did not divide the duties equally between them, made answer, ' I go to *nubere* in the morning because that is the time *to marry;* and I go

to *bibere* in the evening, because that is the time *to drink*.'"
—"When I was an under-graduate, I was skating on Christ Church meadow, and the ice breaking, I was let into a ditch up to my neck in water. I scrambled out, but was dripping from the collar, and oozing from the stockings. A brandy-vender, seeing my pitiable plight, shuffled towards me, and recommended a glass of something warm; upon which Ned Norton, of our college, a son of Lord Grantly, sweeping past, cried out to the retailer, 'None of your brandy for that *wet* young man; he never drinks but when he is *dry*.'"[1]

The approach of the time when John Scott was to be examined for his bachelor's degree caused him no trepidation. A form of examination was gone through,—but the term "double-first" had not yet been heard of on the banks of the Isis, and *plucking* was unknown. The following is the account, in his own words, of the trial he went through to test his proficiency:—" I was examined in Hebrew and history. 'What is the Hebrew for the *place of a skull?*' I replied 'Golgotha.' Who founded University College?' I stated (though by the way the point is sometimes doubted) 'that King Alfred founded it.' 'Very well, Sir,' said the Examiner, 'you are competent for your degree."' Accordingly, on the 20th of February, 1770, it was duly conferred upon him.

He did not then, according to modern custom, leave the University, but continued in its classic bowers to prosecute the studies which should qualify him for being a Master. Under his brother's advice he wrote for the prize lately established by the Earl of Lichfield, Chancellor of the University, for the best composition in English prose—the subject being "The Advantages and Disadvantages of Foreign Travel." The essay with the motto "Non alibi sis, sed alius," was decreed to the best, and this was found to have for its author JOHN SCOTT. His

[1] The proper pendant to this joke is that of the old Scotch woman, who, upon an *un*popular preacher coming into her house after being exposed to a heavy shower of rain, and asking leave to dry himself at her fire, advised him "to go into the *poopit*, where he would be sure to be *dry enough*."

Lord Eldon was soon cured of the punning propensity; but it adhered inveterately to his class-fellow and brother-in-law, the Rev. Dr. Ridley, afterwards prebendary of Gloucester,—a most good-humored, worthy man, from whom I had many excellent dinners when I attended the Gloucester Sessions and Assizes; paying, however, sometimes rather dear for them, by being obliged to laugh at his bad puns.

success gave much delight to his brother, but still more to his old preceptor, who, having heard the joyous news, rushed into the school with a copy of the prize essay in his hand, saying to the senior lads,—"See what John Scott has done!"[1] It has been published in "Talboy's Collection of Oxford English Prize Essays," and is certainly very creditable to a Northumbrian of twenty, who had never traveled except in the country between the Tyne and the Thames, but is much inferior to the "Athenian Letters" written at the sister university by younger men. He seems to have formed his style on the model of Dr. Johnson, who was then worshiped by Oxonians, although in former times they had refused him a degree. We might suppose that we were beginning an indifferent Rambler:—

"There are few principles of action which have been more immediately beneficial to society, and which therefore merit more assiduous cultivation, than the love of our country. But, while we have been studious to regard our parent with the tenderness of filial affection, we have imbibed the weak prejudices of children, and, like the undiscerning lover, have fondly gazed without discrimination upon her beauties and her deformities. He who overrates his own merits, will probably undervalue the deserts of others. From this arrogant conceit of our worth as a people, has sprung that uncharitable opinion which confines excellence to the boundaries of a small island, and, with the true spirit of ancient Greece and Italy, has adjudged every other people to be comparatively barbarous. This illiberal idea, it is confessed, has been attended with salutary consequences; it has aroused the soul of the warrior, and by teaching the brave defenders of our country to despise, it has taught them to conquer, their enemies."

Thus he contemplates a visit to the "Eternal City:"—

"Amidst a variety of objects which will challenge the attention of the traveler, few will prove more copious sources of delight, or supply him with ampler matter for useful reflection than those awful monuments of ancient

---

[1] "Mr. Moises afterwards, when any of his boys did well, would give them this qualified praise : 'Well done, very well done ! but I have had lads that would have done better;—the Scotts would have done better than that.' "—*Twiss*, i. 45.

industry and power, which seem to have been hitherto preserved as memorials of a destructive luxury, the havoc of which was felt when the shocks of time were yet imperceptible. How must the British statesman feel for his country when he surveys the venerable ruins of a senate which stood secure till gold was accepted as an equivalent for freedom, and the Roman legislature, softened by pleasure, embraced the shackles of slavery! While the eye is ravished, the mind can not be unemployed, but recurs to the virtues which established, and the vices which overthrew, the grandeur it surveys."

The superiority of modern Italy in painting and sculpture he thus patriotically scorns:—

"He who has not a single right to protect, may endeavor to render his servitude supportable by studying the arts of politeness; but let not the Briton be taught to leave his distinguishing privilege—his liberty—without defense, while he affects these elegant improvements!"

Afterwards, in pointing out the danger of exchanging prejudice *for*, to prejudices *against*, our country, he introduces some "protectionist" sentiments, which, together with his dislike of the Roman Catholics, and his support of the severe criminal code, make his memory precious to his indiscriminate admirers:—

"To this only can we attribute a prevailing passion for foreign productions, which, as it deprives our own artists of the rewards of their industry, claims and withholds from our manufacturer every encouragement which can animate his labors."

He gracefully concludes with a compliment to his ALMA MATER:—

"Where, then, shall we seek a remedy? Must it not be in that education which watches over the morals with the strictest vigilance, and, by fortifying the mind with the soundest principles of religion, enables it to pursue with safety those inferior accomplishments whose only merit is to heighten the beauty of virtue, and which become truly dangerous when they soften the deformities of vice?"

I concur in the candid and discriminating criticism on this Essay by Mr. Surtees: "Its matter and arrangement indicate the possession of strong sense by its writer, together with a disposition to heap conflicting doubts into each scale, and then to watch with delight the trembling of the uncertain balance; but there is not to be found in it an originality of thought or imagination which can entitle it to the highest praise; namely, that it is a work of genius." For the honor of the order of lawyers, for which I am always solicitous, I am afraid that, although Lord Eldon was the greatest Chancellor that had appeared since Lord Hardwicke, and enjoyed such a splendid reputation in Westminster Hall, he could hardly have made his bread by literature, and he would have been of small account in Paternoster Row.

In his hour of victory he was not only modest, but shamefaced. Sixty years later he was reminded by the Bishop of Clonfert of his embarrassment in the vestibule of the Shelden theater: "I," said the venerable prelate, "recited my prize poem first; and when I came out, you hesitated so much about going in, that I actually had to take you by the shoulders and push you in." But to this triumph Lord Eldon, in his old age, would often revert with honest pride and pleasure; dilating on the increased confidence he acquired by it, and the encouragement it afforded him in his future exertions.

We have a more favorable specimen of his English style in a letter (his earliest extant) written by him from Newcastle to his class-fellow, Henry Reay, from whom he seems to have received a tedious account of a tour in Cheshire. After some introductory matter he proceeds thus in merry vein:—

"With what modest diffidence, then, shall I enter upon the laborious task of describing this place of my residence! —a task I should not undertake (so unequal are my shoulders to the weight) unless to oblige you, my friend, by giving you such a description of Newcastle as may enable you to form a clear and distinct idea of this town, though you never saw it. Say, Muse, where shall I begin? At the bridge? This is an elegant structure of thirteen arches. The battlements are beautified with towers, houses, &c.; and, what is a very extraordinary circumstance, it is built over a river. From hence you proceed to the *Sandhill*. Here you have presented to your view the *Exchange*, and *Nelly's, Katy's* and *Harrison's* coffee-houses; from the windows of which you observe the operations of shaving, turnip and carrot selling, and the fish-market—if you turn your eyes that way. The quay is reckoned one of the best in England. The water makes the prospect very agreeable; and there is no deficiency of wood, in the shape of planks, tar-barrels, and trees of that kind. At the east end of this, passing through a magnificent arch, you come to a street called *Sandgate*, which, whether you consider the elegance of the buildings, or the number of the inhabitants, or that strict regard they pay to decency, is equaled by none in the kingdom."

So he goes on describing the dirt and misery of his native place—well known to his correspondent.

Notwithstanding such sallies,—now in his *baccalaureate* state he considered himself irrevocably destined to the Church—and, if in an ambitious mood, he would dream of being a dean or a prebendary, but in his ordinary frame of mind he looked no higher than a snug rectory or vicarage —anticipating with pleasure and contentment the *jucunda oblivia vitæ*. And there can be little doubt that he would have ended his days as a country parson, recorded only by some annalist, like " P. P., clerk of this parish," had it not been for an imprudent step, which at first was thought to be his utter ruin, but which, changing the whole color of his life, in its consequences made him a millionaire, an Earl, Lord Chancellor for a quarter of a century, a prominent character in history, and the founder of one of the most distinguished families in the peerage of England.

On a foggy morning in the month of November in the following year, Mr. Moises, with a very different countenance from that which he wore when announcing the prize essay, rushed into the school, beating his breast and exclaiming, "Jack Scott has run off with Bessy Surtees! The poor lad is undone! the poor lad is undone!"

I have now a love story to relate. But I must not say:—
> " How can I name love's very name,
> Nor wake my heart to notes of flame?"

I must remember that—not a minstrel pouring forth the unpremeditated lay—I am " a sad apprentice of the law" —chronicling the Life of a Lord Chancellor.

It has already been seen that my present hero had a very inflammable fancy. Romeo had been attached to

Rosaline before he beheld Juliet, and "Miss Allgood, daughter of Sir Launcelot Allgood," said Lord Eldon, was *my first love;* but she was scornful." While smarting from her disdain, it happened that as he was traveling he accidentally entered during divine service the fine old Gothic Church at Sedgefield, a pretty village in the county of Durham,—and there for the first time he beheld his future wife, then a blooming girl of sixteen, in company with an old maiden aunt. He instantly fell in love with her, and learned to his great surprise, that she was the daughter of his townsman, Aubone Surtees, the banker. The Surteeses holding their heads rather high in Newcastle, she had not been allowed to go to the dancing school,—or Jack Scott must often have helped her to put on her shoes, and have presented her with a nosegay. But they, quoting Camden, who says, "Rivers have imposed names to some men as they have to towns situated on them, as the Old Baron *Sur Tays,* that is *on the river Tays,*"—claimed to be a younger branch of the family of Surtees of Dinsdale, in Durham, on the banks of the Tees, who held the barony of Gosforth in the reign of Henry I.; and they did not stoop to a visiting acquaintance with the Scotts,—BANKERS and COAL-FITTERS being considered the opposite extremes of the trading world. John Scott contrived to be introduced to the aunt, who lived close by, and so made acquaintance with the niece. Being then a tall, handsome young man, with black eyes, regular features, and most pleasing manners, he made an auspicious impression upon her; and the fame of his prize essay, with which Newcastle had rung, no doubt helped the prepossession in favor of an admirer of whom she had heard so much, and who was supposed to be such a credit to the place of his nativity. He stayed a few days at a small inn at Sedgefield, and before he left the village they had plighted to each other their mutual troth.

When she returned to Newcastle, he was not permitted to see her at her father's house, but they had flirtations on the Shields road, where she used to ride, attended only by a man-servant, who was bribed to silence by an occasional half-crown. "The riding scheme," says Mr. John Surtees, her brother, "began in this way: Sir William Blackett, popularly called the King of Newcastle, then I suppose seventy years of age, used to lend Lady Eldon a handsome pony, and to accompany her on horseback. He was called to London to attend Parliament, and died soon after. She, riding one of my father's horses, continued her rides as before, and Lord Eldon used, I believe, to meet her." He then goes on to state, that although Sir William Blackett might have intended to court her, "she never considered him in any other light than that of a benign old man who was kind to her."

Miss Surtees came out at a Newcastle ball, given on the 1st of September, 1771, on the occassion of a visit paid to that town by Henry, Duke of Cumberland, brother to George III. John Scott was there, but he did not venture to ask her to dance,—and, to conceal his new passion, he wrote to his friends as if he had still been under the sway of Miss Allgood. In a letter sent by him next morning to Mr. Bray he says, "The ladies are, as we supposed, half mad about the Duke of Cumberland. Miss Surtees and my dear Bell, it seems, were frightened out of their wits when he danced with them." However, at the next weekly assembly he contrived to dance with his new Dulcinea, and the ice being broken, he openly paid her marked attention. Recollecting these scenes, he said in his old age to his grand-niece, Miss Foster, "At the Assembly Rooms at Newcastle there were two rooms and a stair-head between them, so we always danced down the large room across the stair-head, and into the other room. Then you know, Ellen, that was very convenient, for the small room was a snug one to flirt in."

These flirtations gave rise to much gossip in the town of Newcastle, and the families of both parties became well acquainted with the devoted attachment of the enamored pair. The Scotts very much regretted Jack's entanglement; but as the young lady herself was so charming, and her family was so respectable, they would not forbid the match, although they strongly counseled delay. Thus wrote Mr. William Scott to his father:—"In a letter from Jack I find that you are now fully acquainted with the affair between Miss Surtees and himself, and that you are kind enough to forgive any indiscretion which a rigid prudence might perhaps condemn. I must own I am clearly of opinion, that, in consenting to his wishes, you act with a true paternal regard to his happiness, which, as far as I can judge from my own experience, would not be much promoted by a long continuance in college. The business in wchih I am engaged is so extremely disagreeable in itself, and is so destructive to health (if carried on with such success as can render it at all considerable in point of profit), that I do not wonder at his unwillingness to succeed me in it. The kindness of his friends, therefore, would be very judiciously employed in providing for him in some manner more agreeable to his own inclinations, and more consistent with his health. The purchase of a next presentation to a living is the most obvious way of giving him an early settlement. If you determine upon this method, the sooner we make the necessary inquires the better. If you will give me leave, I will endeavor to procure what information I can."

The Surtees family, on the other hand, were most hostile to the proposed union. Their pride was hurt by stories about the public-house kept by old Scott for his keelmen, and they expected their daughter, who was such a beauty, to make some splendid alliance. Not only had she engaged the affections of old Sir William Blackett, the member for the town, but Mr. Spearman, a young gentleman of considerable landed property in the county of Durham, and of great talents, although a little eccentric and flighty, and Mr. Erington, with a large estate in Northumberland, and of respectable character, had already proposed to her, and had been rejected, for the sake of Mr. John Scott.

Mrs. Surtees had been a Miss Stephenson, and she had a brother, Mr. Henry Stephenson, who was very rich, with a splendid mansion in Park Lane, a country-house at Taplow in Berkshire, and a daughter, an only child. It was therefore resolved, that, to cut off all intercourse between Elizabeth and the coal-fitter's son, she should be sent to spend some months with her relations in the south—a hope being entertained that she might be noticed by the Duchess of Northumberland, and that, being so advantageously introduced into society, she might produce a sensation in the metropolis—a strict injunction being given that no intercourse, by word or letter or signal, should be allowed to her with Mr. John Scott. The old hoastman, hurt by this proceeding, likewise ordered Jack to think no more of Miss Surtees.

"Set vetuere patres, quod non potuere vetare,
Ex æquo captis ardebant mentibus ambo."

The eager lover followed his mistress to London, and there, meeting his cousin Reay, who was his confidant, contrived measures for seeing her. She was noticed, as had been expected, by the Duchess of Northumberland, who would sometimes take her by the arm at Northumberland House, and present her to the guests as "my Newcastle beauty." "The fellow of University" had then no means of introduction to the gay societies which she frequented; but he went to a masquerade, to Ranelagh, and to the Opera-house, in the vain hope of descrying her.[1] At last, by watching in Park Lane, he traced her to Hyde Park, and on several occasions, as she was walking there with a female companion, he contrived to have interviews with her—when they renewed their vows.

Being obliged to return to Oxford, he wrote the following letter to Reay, who remained in London :

"MON CHER AMI,

"After being almost choked with dust, and suffering other inconveniences too numerous to be related, we at length arrived once more upon this classic ground. Sad exchange, of Ranelagh for the High Street,—of dominos for gowns and caps,—of a stroll in Hyde Park *comitante Surtesiâ*, for a trot up the hill with the *bussar!* For your satisfaction, however, give me leave to inform you, that we both enjoy health of body, though strangers to peace of mind, and wear clean shirts, though we have not a guinea! As Fisher and I were reduced to a melancholy duet by the departure of Haverfield, we found no small pleasure in having an accession to our party by the arrival of Ridley and Young. As the latter has not opened his mouth nor his eyes since he came, though to my certain knowledge the bell rung thrice a day, we yet consider ourselves as but a trio. Harry, whom Nature formed in a very philosophic mold, and endued with such a seeming indifference to *place*, that one should conclude she intended him for a citizen of the world, expresses but little regret upon the occasion, and accommodates himself with great facility to the collegiate plan. How happy would it be for those who are doomed

---

[1] While at the latter place, it is said that when the hope of discovering his *inamorata* was gone, taking no pleasure in the music, he fell asleep,—and he used to say that he found it " *opera* atque labores."

to drag on a few more years here, if they could acquire this blessed versatility, and thus calmly acquiesce in what they can not avoid!

"I was about to begin my lamentations upon the invisibility of a certain fair one, but I am determined to check my inclination. If I do not take the advice contained in that salutary aphorism, 'Obsta principiis,' the subject is so favorite a one, the theme so much my darling, that I generally forget that there is something impertinent in *boring* others upon topics indifferent to them, however interesting to yourself. If you have experienced this from me, I know you will make charitable allowances. I confess my weakness, and will guard against it.

"The Count of the Flaxen Empire[1] intends visiting this seat of literature: I shall have the honor, I suppose, of escorting his mightiness around this place. His Burgundy must suffer for this in the long vacation. As to the dear little tigress of Taplow, I will not flatter myself with the hopes of seeing her, where a disappointment is so probable.

"I had some thoughts of delivering your compliments to the Countess of the Hill[2] *en passant*, but I was deterred by considerations of propriety, nor was I certain how far the awkwardness of a fellow of a college might have been detrimental to the interests of his friend with the lady.

"Come in!—'tis the little barber; which puts me in mind that I left the gentleman of Tanfield Court without paying him. It was his own fault; however, pray inform him that after our next charity sermon, he shall have his share of the collection: *i. e.* when I come to town again I will pay him; or, if he is in any great hurry for the cash, if you will ask him what sum his honor will be satisfied with, I will send it him by the first opportunity.

"Pray remember me to Bunney, Lane, &c.; and, if invisibility become visible, then remember me, who am, with great sincerity,   "Your affectionate friend,
"J. SCOTT.

"Univ. Coll., Wednesday."

It is said that "*Invisibility* did become *visible*," and that, traveling from Oxford in the night, at sunrise he

[1] Mr. Aubone Surtees.
[2] The Lady Mary O'Bryen, Countess of Orkney in her own right, who resided at Taplow Court.

had the happiness of some rencontres with the dear little tigress in the shady lanes near Taplow; but this rests on no sufficient authority.—The London season then ended in May; and after it was over she continued for some months in this charming retreat, along with her fair cousin, under a pretty strict *surveillance*. We have pleasing portraits of the young ladies as they appeared at this time, by Mr. W. E. Surtees. "Of the two cousins, Miss Surtees was the elder by some three years. Her figure was slight, and of a short middle size; her hair, of the deepest brown, streamed in rich ringlets over her neck. From her mother (the beauty of a preceding generation) she had inherited features of exquisite regularity, as well as a strongly marked character, and a warm temper, Miss Stephenson, though yielding nothing in beauty to her cousin, had features somewhat less symmetrical. The mouth, of an infantine simplicity, but as sweet as that of a smiling infant, indicated more of pliability and less of individual character."[1]

Miss Surtees returned to Newcastle in the autumn. We are informed of few particulars till the catastrophe which I am now about to narrate; but we know that a renewed offer of a very advantageous match was made to her,—that her parents strongly pressed her to accept it, thinking that her childish predilection had been effaced by absence;—that they expressed high displeasure when she talked of fidelity to her engagement,—and that they peremptorily told her she must comply with their wishes. John Scott being then at Newcastle, she contrived a meeting with him; and, when she had stated the force that was put upon her inclinations, he proposed, as the only resource remaining to them, that she should run away with him. She blushed and consented.

"The house in which Mr. Surtees lived was a very large old-fashioned building, in a row of houses called

[1] He afterwards says,—"She, too, had an early attachment; but this, in accordance with the more ambitious views of her parents, she was induced to forego, and she became the bride of the Earl of Mexborough. In her heyday, Almack's brightened at her smile; and there, also, in age was she seen with cheeks where art had vainly tried to retrieve the faded bloom of nature, and restore the rosy light of youth. She was a ruin, from the otherwise serene beauty of whose aspect much was detracted by the injudicious introduction of parterres filled with Spring's gayest flowers; but still, as it was said of her by one who could even then find sufficient traces of pristine brightness to command homage, she was '*the finest ruin in England*.'" (p. 10.)

Sand-hill, which fronts towards the town hall, the *Exchange*, and the river. The ground floor was occupied by the shop and warehouse of a Mr. Snow Clayton, an extensive clothier; but between the shop and the rest of the house there was no communication, each having a separate entrance.—Mr. John Scott had an early friend of the name of Wilkinson, and to him he confided a plan for an elopement. Wilkinson, who was a young man of some small independence, which he contemplated investing in trade, had apprenticed himself to Clayton, the clothier; and as Clayton's shop was under Mr. Surtees' residence, his apprentice must have possessed peculiar means of facilitating the escape.—The night of Wednesday, the 18th of November, 1772, was that selected for the elopement. At that time the garrison within the house at *Sand-hill* was weakened by the absence of Mr. Surtees' eldest son, William, who was on a visit of a few days' duration to some friends. He had been the school-fellow of Mr. John Scott, and, being nearly of the same age, would, if at home, have been very capable of either intercepting a flight or leading a pursuit.— Wilkinson was faithful to Scott in aiding and abetting the enterprise, and is supposed to have materially assisted him by concealing a ladder in the premises of Mr. Clayton below. A ladder, probably produced by Wilkinson, was placed against the most westerly window of the first floor; and down it Bessy Surtees, '*with an unthrift love*,' descended into the arms of John Scott."[1]

The young lady behaved most heroically; and, after great peril of being discovered and stopped, they reached a post-chaise which was in waiting for them. Instead of driving to Gretna Green and soliciting the aid of the blacksmith, they took the road by Morpeth up Coldstream, and "over the border and away;" they next morning reached the village of Blackshiels, close to Fala, only two stages from Edinburgh. Here they halted, and were married by

[1] W. E. Surtees, pp. 11–13, from "original sources of information." The faithful friend, so useful in this emergency, dying in 1801, Lord Eldon, in a letter to Reay, thus feelingly commemorates him: "Before I say a word about other matters, let me heave one sigh over James Wilkinson! It was but yesterday that we three were engaged in the follies of childhood and the sports of youth. The period which has since passed seems short,—how short, in all probability, must that appear, then, which is yet to pass before we shall be gathered together again !"

the Reverend Mr. Buchanan, who was not, as has been said, " the established Presbyterian minister," but the clergyman of an Episcopal congregation at Haddington.[1]

The following is the certificate of this marriage, which Lord Eldon had carefully preserved, and which was found among his papers after his death :—

" John Scott, of the parish of All Saints, Newcastle-upon-Tyne, gentleman, and Elizabeth Surtees, of St. Nicholas parish, in the same town, spinster, were married at Blackshiels, North Britain, according to the form of matrimony prescribed and used by the Church of England, on this 19th day of November, 1772, by

" J. BUCHANAN, Minister.

" In pres-) JAMES FAIRBAIRN.
 ence of) THOMAS FAIRBAIRN."

As soon as the ceremony was performed and duly recorded, the bride and bridegroom set off on their return for their own country, meaning to pass the wedding-night at Morpeth. When they arrived there, late in the evening, they found that a fair was holding in the town, a circumstance they had not noticed as had they hurried through in their journey to the north—and that all the inns were full. However, their peculiar situation becoming known, Mr. and Mrs. Nelson, of the Queen's Head, good-naturedly gave up their own room to the new-married couple.

Great had been the consternation at Newcastle, caused by their flight. Jane Scott, John's twin sister, had been his confidante ; and when she went to bed on Wednesday she burst out a-crying, saying to her sister, Barbara, " Oh, Babby, Jack has run away with Bessy Surtees to Scotland to be married—what will my father say?" They wept all night—but, bathing their eyes in cold water, they composed themselves as they best could, and went down to breakfast in the morning. A letter from Jack to the old gentleman he read and put into his pocket, without saying a word or altering his countenance—and all that day the

---

[1] The canons of the Church of Scotland are extremely strict about marriage, requiring a proclamation of banns and the intervention of a minister, although, for civil purposes, marriage is constituted by consent of the parties in the presence of any witness.

The circumstance of Mr. Buchanan usually residing at Haddington has induced others to represent this town as the scene of the marriage. How he came to be at Blackshiels, and how the runaway couple were introduced to him, I have not been able to ascertain.

family remained in a state of suspense with respect to the line of conduct which he would pursue. The following morning he was melted by a contrite epistle from Morpeth; and Henry, the third brother, was dispatched thither with a pardon and an invitation to the young couple to take up their residence in Love Lane. The bride used to describe the third day of their marriage as very sad:—" Our funds were exhausted; we had not a home to go to, and we knew not whether our friends would ever speak to us again. In this mournful dilemma I suddenly espied from the window a fine large wolf-dog, belonging to the family, called *Loup*, walking along the street,—a joyful sight, for I knew a friend was near, and in a few minutes John's brother, Mr. Henry Scott, entered the room with tidings of peace." The invitation to Love Lane was of course gladly accepted.

But the Surteeses were for some time implacable. Mrs. Surtees had been so affected by her daughter's flight that she had kept her bed for several days, and her mind fluctuated between sorrow and anger. She was still more irritated by receiving a letter from Mrs. Henry Stephenson, who, piqued that the good advice she had given her niece the preceding season had all been thrown away, said,—" Mr. and Mrs. John Scott can not be received in Park Lane, as our own family consists only of a daughter with a very pretty face and a very good fortune, before whom it would be imprudent to present a sanction to elopements." The old banker was so much displeased that he would not even speak to the old coal-fitter, with whom he used before to converse on friendly terms. But at last "MONTAGUE" broke through the reserve, and going up to "CAPULET" on the Exchange, said to him characteristically,—"Why should this marriage make you so cool with me? I was as little wishful for it as yourself; but, since what is done can not be undone,—for every hundred pounds you put down for your daughter, I will cover it with another for my son." The answer was,—" You are too forgiving; you are too forgiving; that would be rewarding disobedience."

When the news transpired at Oxford, Mr. William Scott said to a friend there, " I suppose you have heard of this very foolish act of my very foolish brother." The softening observation being made—" I hope it may turn out better than you anticipate," he replied, "Never, Sir, never! he is completely ruined, nor can anything now save him from beggary. You do not know how unhappy this makes me, for I had good hopes of him till this last confounded step has destroyed all."—The despair of Moises I have already commemorated.

A story is told that, in the present abject state of his fortunes, the future Chancellor was in imminent danger of being punished for his imprudence by being condemned to spend the remainder of his days in selling figs and raisins. It is said that an old and very wealthy grocer, being childless, went to Scott the father, and, saying "he took compassion on the destitute condition of John," offered at once to give him an equal share of his lucrative business without any premium,—that the father was well pleased with the proposal, but said, "he could not accept it without consulting his oldest son, who was at Oxford," —that he wrote to William accordingly, and that it was only upon William requesting that John might be sent back to his college, wife and all, and promising to do what he could for them, that the offer was rejected. But there is no written, and very slender parole, evidence for this statement, and it was probably invented to multiply the marvels of Lord Eldon's career. I do not believe that after his academical distinction he would ever have submitted to the degradation of standing behind a counter. At the very time when this negotiation is supposed to have been going on, conscious of his own upright intentions, and relying with some confidence on his own powers, he wrote the following spirited letter to his cousin Reay, then at Oxford:—

"MY DEAR REAY,

"It gives me some satisfaction to find that, amidst the censures of those frowns I despise, and the applause of others whose good opinion I am not very anxious to secure, a change of life on my part has not been attended with a change of sentiment on yours. Those who knew me not were at liberty to deal out their plaudits, or express their disapprobation, in as strong terms as they pleased; and while I expected, from impertinent ignorance or morose old age, reflections upon my honor and my prudence, I was contented that the latter should be suspected by those friends whose knowledge of me would lead them without hesitation (I flatter myself) to believe that I had acted with an unremitting attention to the former. *Virtute med me involvo:* and I can with the greatest confidence retire, from the harsh criticisms of a world which must ever remain ignorant of the justifying circumstances, to a heart which will never reproach me. I hope I shall not be suspected of vanity, if I assert that no man, who knew me thoroughly, would condemn me as consulting only the gratification of a boyish passion.

. . . . .

"You have long known me, Hal; you will not suspect me of dissimulation, if, where there is so little occasion for any other arguments to disarm you of any suspicions with respect to the rectitude of my conduct, I further assert in general terms, *that I have only acted the unavoidable part*; I can not honorably descend to such particulars as may prove the truth of the assertion. I should not have said so much, if I had not been writing to a person whose behavior has endeared him to me so greatly, that I should be uneasy under his disapprobation.

"Such are the motives upon which the scheme was undertaken: it was executed with some wonderful escapes, and exhibits in my conduct some very remarkable generalship: I eluded the vigilance of three watchmen stationed in the neighborhood, without the assistance of a bribe; and contrived to be sixty miles from Newcastle before it was discovered that I had left the place. My wife is a perfect heroine, and behaved with a courage which astonished me. In truth, *fortes Fortuna juvat;* how else can I account for the first intimations about a scheme which I should not have dreamed would ever have been thought of,—the success of a plan seemingly impracticable,—and the ready forgiveness of those whom I expected to have found unrelenting?—I have now, Reay, bid adieu to all ambitious projects, because my highest ambition is gratified: though a husband, I am yet so much of a lover, as to think the world well lost, while I retain the affections of one woman, the esteem of a few friends, and the good wishes of Reay. Some of the good folks here, as you surmised, have starved me, out of pure pity; but, though I shall not expire by a surfeit, I think I shall scarce die of hunger.

. . . . . .

"With respect to your being a candidate for my fellowship, the college will suffer no loss by my imprudence if I have such a successor. I expect to hear from you again soon; in the meantime, believe me to be, dear Reay,
"Your sincere friend, and
" (Upon your mother's authority)
"Your affectionate cousin,
"J. SCOTT.
"Wednesday."

"A love-match may be a very silly and selfish action or a very wise and disinterested one—the suggestion of a passing fancy, or the result of reflection and self-knowledge."[1] The elopement of Mr. Scott and Miss Surtees was of a very venial character, and is chiefly to be regretted as giving countenance to a practice which can seldom admit of such palliations. Her parents, though they might reasonably refuse their consent to her union with a young man unable to support her, had no right to insist on her marrying another, when her affections were pre-engaged. His family having once countenanced the courtship, were not justified in suddenly trying to put a stop to it; and it should always be remembered that he was ready to submit to all the exertions, privations, and sacrifices demanded by the relation he thus clandestinely contracted. Both made ample atonement to society for their offense, if it was one. There never was a more faithful or affectionate pair; and they afforded a beautiful example of the *consortium vitæ*, which constitutes the essence of the married state. She conformed to his tastes, and thought only of his advancement. One example is worth more than any amount of general praise. When her husband was qualifying himself for the Bar, she would sit up with him during his midnight studies, watching him with silent affection, and moving about on tiptoe that she might not disturb the connection of his thoughts. The faults of penuriousness and seclusion, which she afterwards displayed, grew out of the habits she acquired when exercising self-denial for his sake. He showed his deep sense of the obligations under which he had come—not only by his unwearied exertions to be able creditably to maintain her, but when youth and beauty were gone, and peculiarities of temper and manners ap-

[1] Words of Lord Eldon in his old age.

peared in her which were to be regretted, though excusable, he still treated her with fondness. Being told, after the clandestine match of his eldest daughter, Lady Elizabeth, that he should force Lady Eldon into society, in order to chaperon the younger daughter, Lady Frances, —he replied, " When she was young and beautiful, she gave up everything for me. What she is, I have made her; and I can not now bring myself to compel her inclinations. Our marriage prevented her mixing in society when it might have afforded her pleasure; it appears to give pain now, and why should I interpose?" When she was snatched away from him by death, he still tenderly cherished her memory. Within two or three years of his own decease, when a north-country friend came over to see him at Rushyford, the old peer observed to him, " I know my fellow-townsmen at Newcastle complain of my never coming to see them, but how can I pass that bridge?"—meaning the bridge across the Tyne, looking upon the *Sand-hill*. Then musing on the dead—with tears in his eyes,—after a pause he exclaimed, " Poor Bessie! if ever there was an angel on earth, she was one. The only reparation which one man can make to another for running away with his daughter, is to be exemplary in his conduct towards her."

But we have now to attend Mr. and Mrs. John Scott in Love Lane. She was, and therefore so was he, still most wretched, on account of the obduracy of her father, who vowed that he never would see her more, nor forgive her even on his death-bed. But at length the old gentleman, hearing of her anguish, and feeling the want of her pious attentions, in which he had so much delighted, gradually relented, and sent her his forgiveness and his blessing. Her brother John, who was the bearer of this message, said, " She threw her arms about me in a transport of joy, and kissed me for a considerable time without intermission."

They now removed to Mr. Surtees' house on *Sand-hill*, where they met with a kind reception.

Soon after, "Articles" were executed, whereby Mr. Scott settled upon them £2,000, and Mr. Surtees £1,000 (which he afterwards doubled), to bear interest at £5 per cent.

I need not formally refute the false statement which

has been so often repeated,—that Lord Eldon, never having been reconciled to Mr. Surtees, showed his thirst for revenge by sealing with his own hand, when Chancellor, a commission of bankruptcy against him. Mr. Surtees lived and died in affluent circumstances, although the bank to which he belonged long afterwards failed; and he lived with his son-in-law on terms of the greatest confidence and affection.[1]

To bring this matrimonial narrative to a conclusion, I have only to state, that although no doubt was entertained about the marriage celebrated at Blackshiels being sufficient, both in law and religion,—with a view to easy evidence of marriage in future times, it was thought right to follow the practice of the Chancellor with respect to his wards, and to have the parties remarried in England, in conformity to the provisions of Lord Hardwicke's Act. Accordingly, the ceremony was again performed in the parish church of St. Nicholas, Newcastle, in the presence of the father of the bride and the brother of the bridegroom, and the following entry was made of it in the register:—

"John Scott and Elizabeth Surtees, a minor, with the consent of her father, Aubone Surtees, Esq., and both of this parish, were married in this church, by license, the 19th day of January, 1773, by me,
"CUTH. WILSON, Curate.

"This marriage was solemnized between us,—
John Scott and   } In the presence of us,
Elizabeth Surtees   } Aubone Surtees, Henry Scott."

The bride and bridegroom, on this occasion, without trepidation, entered a post-chaise which waited for them at the church door,—and, rapidly crossing the Tyne, bade adieu to Newcastle.

"The world was all before them, where to choose
Their place of rest, and Providence their guide."

---

[1] Of this I have a very striking proof in a letter from the son-in-law, showing that he was afterwards employed by his father-in-law in the delicate matter of advising with him about the framing of his will.

CHAPTER CXCII.

CONTINUATION OF THE LIFE OF LORD ELDON TILL HE WAS CALLED TO THE BAR.

IT was now necessary that Mr. John Scott should form a new scheme of life. He could no longer look to the Church as a profession. After the year of grace his fellowship was lost by his marriage, and he had no other chance of ecclesiastical preferment. He resolved, if a college living should fall vacant within the year, to claim it, but immediately to begin the study of the law—having for a little time two strings to his bow. Although he by no means felt any enthusiasm for his new profession, he knew that from a sense of duty he should be able to submit to its labors. Accordingly, on his arrival in London, he was admitted of the Middle Temple. The following is a copy of his admission:

"Die 28 Januarii, 1773, Mar. Johannes Scott, filius tertius Gulielmi Scott de Novo Castello super Tinum, Armigeri, admissus est in Societatem Medii Templi Londini specialiter. Et dat pro fine £4."

Mr. and Mrs. John Scott proceeded to Oxford, which was to be the place of their residence while he was preparing for the Bar. A lady, who met them at a friend's house where they paid a visit on their way, observed, in a letter written many years after, " Her appearance was considered his sufficient apology, for she was extremely beautiful; and so very young as to give the impression of childhood, especially as her dress corresponded with that idea, the white frock and sash being in those days the distinguishing mark of a child, as well as the flowing ringlets which hung around her shoulders."

Sir Robert Chambers, Principal of New Inn Hall, and Vinerian Professor of Law, had just been appointed a Judge in the East Indies, and the job had been arranged that he should retain these appointments during his absence, performing their duties by deputy. Accordingly John Scott was named Vice-Principal of New Inn Hall, having rooms for his family in the Lodge, and Vice Law Professor with a salary of £60 a year, being employed merely to read the lectures written by his superior. He himself gave the following amusing account of his *début* in this line :—" The law professor sent me the first lecture which I had to read *immediately* to the students, and which I began without knowing a single word that was in it. It was upon the statute (4 & 5 P. & M. c. 8) ' Of young men running away with maidens.' Fancy me reading with about 140 boys and young men all giggling at the professor ! Such a tittering audience no one ever had.

He likewise eked out his income by private pupils sent to him from University College ; and with the aid of a quarterly present from his brother William, and of strict good management, he and his wife could make the two ends meet. Tea-parties were the only entertainments they could venture to give to their friends. At these *symposia* they sometimes had a no less distinguished guest than Dr. Samuel Johnson, and Mrs. John Scott used to relate that she herself helped him one evening to fifteen cups of his favorite beverage.

Lord Eldon does not seem, like his brother, Sir William Scott, to have cultivated literary society on removing to London ; but he watched the great Lexicographer with much attention, and was eager to get into his company during his visits to Alma Mater. " The Doctor was so absent," he would say, "that I have seen him standing for a long time without moving—with a foot on each side of the kennel, which was then in the middle of the High Street, Oxford,—with his eyes fixed on the running water." He related, that, " in the common room of University College, a controversialist having frequently interrupted Johnson during a narrative of what had fallen under his own observation, saying, ' I deny that,' he at last vociferated, ' Sir, Sir, you must have forgotten that an author has said, *Plus negabit unus asinus in unâ horâ, quam centum philosophi probaverint in centum annis.*' "—But the following is his best Johnsonian anecdote. " I had a walk in New Inn Hall Garden with Dr. Johnson, Sir Robert Chambers, and some other gentlemen. Sir Robert was gathering snails and throwing them over the wall into his neighbor's garden. The Doctor reproached him very roughly, asserting that this was unmannerly and unneighborly. ' Sir,' said Sir Robert ' my neighbor is a dissenter.' ' Oh,' said the Doctor, ' if so, Chambers, toss away, toss away, as hard as you can.'" The real good-humor here displayed makes us forget the apparent bigotry.

At this time Lord Eldon gave the first specimen of his judicial powers—which must be allowed to have been very promising, although as yet he had but a slender portion of jurisprudential lore. Being senior resident fellow of University College, two under-graduates came to complain to him, that "the cook had sent them up an apple-pie *that could not be eaten.*" The defendant being summoned, said, "I have a remarkably fine fillet of veal in the kitchen." The Judge immediately overruled this plea as tendering an immaterial issue, and ordered a *profert in curiam* of the apple-pie. The messenger sent to execute this order brought intelligence that the other under-graduates, taking advantage of the absence of the two plaintiffs, had eaten up the whole of the apple-pie. Thereupon judgment was thus pronounced: "The charge here is, that the cook has sent up an apple-pie that can not be eaten. Now that can not be said to be uneatable which has been eaten; and as this apple-pie has been eaten, it was eatable. Let the cook be absolved." He used to say, in telling the story, "I often wished, in after-life, that all the causes I had to decide had been *apple-pie causes*, and then no one could have complained of my *doubts* or *delays.*"

But, by gigantic efforts, he was now laying the foundation of the unrivaled fame as a great magistrate which he acquired when presiding on the woolsack. Having taken his Master's degree on the 13th of February, 1773, he began the study of the law with the most devoted resolution to conquer all its difficulties. There was but little chance of a college living falling in during his year of grace, and on the 19th of November following,—the anniversary of his Blackshiels marriage, he actually gave up his fellowship. His efforts were redoubled when his new profession afforded the only chance of his being able to maintain himself and his family. He rose in the morning at four—took little exercise—made short and abstemious meals, and sat up studying late at night, with a wet towel round his head to drive away drowsiness. I am grieved to hear that the reading of "Coke upon Littleton" is going out of fashion among law students. When I was commencing my legal curriculum, I was told this anecdote :— A young student asked Sir Vicary Gibbs how he should learn his profession. *Sir Vicary:* "Read Coke upon Littleton." *Student:* "I have read Coke upon Littleton." *Sir Vicary:* "Read Coke upon Littleton over again." *Student:* "I have read it twice over." *Sir Vicary:* "Thrice?" *Student:* "Yes, three times over very carefully." *Sir Vicary:* "You may now sit down and make an abstract of it." If my opinion is of any value, I would heartily join in the same advice. The book contains much that is obsolete, and much that is altered by statutable enactment; but no man can thoroughly understand the law as it is without knowing the changes it has undergone, and no man can be acquainted with its history without being familiar with the writings of Lord Coke. Nor is he by any means so dry and forbidding as is generally supposed. He is certainly immethodical, but he is singularly perspicuous, he fixes the attention, his quaintness is often most amusing, and he excites our admiration by the inexhaustible stores of erudition which, without any effort, he seems spontaneously to pour forth. Thus were our genuine lawyers trained. Lord Eldon read Coke upon Littleton once, twice, and thrice, and made an abstract of the whole work as a useful exercise—obeying the wise injunction, "Legere *multum*—non *multa*." On the 8th of March, 1774, he had a fresh incentive to industry in the birth of a son.

Soon after, his health suffering, he consulted a physician, who seriously advised him to be more moderate in his application; but he answered, "It is no matter—I must either do as I am now doing, or starve." He had a little relaxation in going for a few days, four times a year, to keep his terms in the Middle Temple; and during the general election in 1774 he paid a visit to his native place, when he took up his freedom as the son of a "hoastman," and voted for Sir William Blackett and Sir Matthew White Ridley. It is said that in this journey, coming late at night to the Hen and Chickens, at Birmingham, the house he used to frequent in traveling between Newcastle and Oxford, the landlady seeing him look so dreadfully ill, insisted on dressing something hot for his supper, saying "she was sure she should never see him again."

While residing in New Inn Hall, his brother Henry married, and he wrote a number of letters to his new sister-in-law and to his other relations in Newcastle, which are preserved; but they are dreadfully stiff and dull, and indicate an utter loss of his ante-nuptial sprightliness.¹

It was full time that he should be transferred to a livelier scene, and the approach of his call to the Bar rendered his residence in London indispensable. Accordingly, in the long vacation of 1775, he bade Oxford a final adieu, and he moved, with his family, to a small house in Cursitor Street, near Chancery Lane. This house he would point out to his friends late in life, saying, "There was my first perch: many a time have I run down from Cursitor Street to Fleet Market to buy six-penn'orth of sprats for our supper."

He now diligently attended the Courts in Westminster Hall, with his note-book in his hand. Lord Bathurst presiding in the Court of Chancery, from whom little was to learned, he took his place in the student's box in the Court of King's Bench, where Lord Mansfield shone in the zenith of his fame; but he never would acknowledge the extraordinary merits of this great judge, and was always disposed to sneer at him. One source of prejudice was the marked predilection of the Christ Church man for his college, and the slighting manner in which he would talk of "University" along with other colleges and halls at Oxford. This we shall find was the ostensible ground for Mr. Scott afterwards quitting the Common Law for Equity.

He seems to have been less struck by the learning of the judges than by that of Sergeant Hill—supposed to be the greatest black-letter lawyer since Maynard's time, and as much celebrated for his eccentricity as his learning—insomuch that on his wedding night, going to his chambers in the Temple, and continuing there reading cases till next morning, he

"Thought of the 'Year Books' and forgot his bride.".

Lord Eldon related that, at their first interview in Westminster Hall, being entire strangers, the following dialogue took place between them:—*Hill, stopping Scott:* "Pray, young gentleman, do you think herbage and pannage ratable to the poor's rate?" *Scott:* "Sir, I can not presume to give any opinion, inexperienced and unlearned as I am, to a person of your great knowledge and high character in the profession." *Hill:* "Upon my word you

¹ Twiss, ch. iv.

are a pretty sensible young gentlemen ; I don't often meet with such. If I had asked Mr. Burgess, a young man upon our circuit, the question, he would have told me that I was an old fool. You are an extraordinary sensible young gentleman."[1]

The custom having been introduced for law students to become pupils of a special pleader, or of an equity draughtsman, Mr. Scott would have been very glad to have conformed to it, if the state of his finances would have enabled him to pay the usual fee of a hundred guineas ; but this he could not do without borrowing,—a habit he ever held in abhorrence; and he would have been without any preliminary discipline of this sort, if Mr. Duane, an eminent Catholic conveyancer,[2] had not agreed to let him have "the run of his chambers," for six months, without a fee. He was particularly anxious to be initiated in this branch of the profession ; for, ever since he took to the law he cherished the plan of settling as a provincial counsel at Newcastle, where skill in conveyancing would have been essentially necessary to his success.[3]

Soon after making this arrangement, he wrote the following letter to his brother Henry :—

"DEAR BROTHER,

"I am at length settled in the circle of lawyers, and begin to breathe a little after the laborious task of removing a family, which is a work as difficult as that of removing a mountain. You know, probably, that this is only a step preparatory to a settlement among you, which I begin to

---

[1] The first day I dined in Lincoln's Inn Hall, a brother student, whose name I had not before heard of—but who has since deservedly reached high professional distinction—after a long silence in our mess, thus addressed me: " Pray, Sir, what is your opinion of the *scintilla juris ?*" I entered into a discussion with him about the *feeding of uses*—but I am afraid I never could induce him to think me " an extraordinary sensible young gentleman." I may now state that this was Lord St. Leonards, ex-Chancellor of Ireland and of Great Britain.

[2] At this time conveyancing was chiefly in the hands of Roman Catholics. Being long prevented by their religion from being called to the Bar, they practised successfully in chambers ; and being employed at first by their co-religionists, their industry and learning forced them into general business. Charles Butler, whom I well knew, may be considered the last of this race.

[3] So early as 28th May, 1774, he says, in a letter to his brother Henry : " I hope once more to see you, about this time two years. when I intend, if I can manage it, to come your circuit ; and in case of encouragement, I shall, some three years after that, perhaps, settle in Newcastle." There is no foundation for the common opinion that his plan of settling at Newcastle originated from his bad success in London.

think is a prospect that brightens upon me every day. I have been exceedingly fortunate in forming my previous connections, as the object which I had most at heart I have obtained. The great conveyancing of your country is done by Mr. Duane; it seemed to be, therefore, a most desirable thing to be connected with him, as his recommendation and instructions might probably operate much in my behalf hereafter. The great fear arose from his never having taken any person in the character of a pupil before, and the apprehension, that if he should now break through a general rule, it must be on terms with which I could not afford to comply; but he has offered me every assistance in his power, and is so extremely ready to forward my schemes, as to declare himself contented with the satisfaction he will enjoy in contributing to the success of a person whom he is so uncommonly kind as even to honor. This conduct of his has taken a great load of uneasiness off my mind, as in fact our profession is so exceedingly expensive that I almost sink under it. I have got a house barely sufficient to hold my small family, which (so great is the demand for them here) will in rent and taxes cost me annually sixty pounds. I thank God, it will be only for two years at most. I have been buying books, too, for the last ten years, and I have got the mortification to find, that before I can settle, that article of trade— for as such I consider it—will cost me near two hundred pounds:—not to mention the price of a voluminous wig." [1]

During the six months agreed upon, he worked at Mr. Duane's almost night and day, making a gigantic collection of precedents, and examining all the draughts and cases which went through the office. To this period of study he ascribed much of his success in the profession. When he referred, as he was fond of doing, to Mr. Duane's liberality in taking him without a fee, he would add, "That was a great kindness to me. He was a most worthy and excellent man. The knowledge I acquired of conveyancing in his office was of infinite service to me during a long life in the Court of Chancery."

I will here finish what I have to relate of his legal studies. To supply the deficiency arising from his not

[1] In a letter from William Scott to his brother Henry, dated Oxford, Nov. 7. 1775, he says: "Brother Jack is gone to town to settle there under a conveyancer. God grant him success in his profession; he deserves the best wishes of his friends."

having been with a special pleader or equity draughtsman, he copied all the MS. forms he could lay his hands upon. He was very proud of the volumes he thus compiled, and regretted their loss, suggesting that "he had lent them to friends *with a bad memory*." Unconscious of the joke which I have often heard circulated against himself,—that, when Chancellor, he greatly augmented his own library by borrowing books quoted at the Bar, and forgetting to return them,—he would say of such borrowers, "Though backward in *accounting*, they are well practiced in *bookkeeping*."

He engaged in a course of reading,—the expediency of which I should doubt. It is well for the student to peruse consecutively the Reports of Lord Coke and of Plowden; but Mr. Scott went through a systematic course of Reports, and, coming down to a reporter of such low credit as *Vernon*, he could tell the names of most of the cases reported, with the volume and page where they were to be found.

I wish I could add, that at the same time he attended to more elegant pursuits; but for such a combination I fear that human strength is insufficient. He seemed to have renounced all taste for classical learning with his academical cap and gown, and never to have taken the smallest interest in the literature of the day. He read a weekly newspaper, but no other periodical publication; and although when a boy he had studied the Rambler and Johnson's earlier works, he is not supposed to have spared time from copying precedents to read the "Journey to the Hebrides," or the "Lives of the Poets." Hence we have to desiderate in him the vein of classical allusion, and the beautiful diction, which gave such a charm to the conversation and compositions of Lord Stowell. But we ought to honor his unwearied industry, and to admire his stupendous acquirements in one department of human knowledge. Before he had ever pleaded a cause, he was fit to preside on the bench; and there he would have given more satisfaction than most other members of the profession, who could boast of their "lucubrationes viginti annorum." It must be remembered always, that he had by nature an admirable head for law, and that he seemed almost by an intuitive glance to penetrate into its most obscure mysteries.—He was ere long to reap the reward of his industry.

CHAPTER CXCIII.

CONTINUATION OF THE LIFE OF LORD CHANCELLOR ELDON TILL HE RECEIVED A SILK GOWN.

MR. JOHN SCOTT was called to the bar by the Honorable Society of the Middle Temple, on the 9th of February, 1776; but he did not begin to appear as a candidate for practice till Easter term following. He used in his latter years to talk much of his bad success at starting; but I am bound to say that this he greatly exaggerated. It seems to me, that, with a view to enhance the marvel of his ultimate rise, he was unconsciously disposed to dwell rather too much upon the difficulties he had overcome, and to forget the encouragements he had met with,—till at last, by oft repetition, he himself gave faith to a representation of his first years at the Bar considerably at variance with the genuine truth.

According to the following statement by himself, he was cheated of his maiden fee:—" I had been called to the Bar but a day or two, when on coming out of court one morning, I was accosted by a dapper-looking attorney's clerk, who handed me a motion paper, in some matter of course, which merely required to be authenticated by counsel's signature. I signed the paper, and the attorney's clerk, taking it back from me, said, 'a fine hand your's, Mr. Scott—an exceedingly fine hand! It would be well if gentlemen at the Bar would always take a little of your pains to insure legibility. A beautiful hand, sir.' While he spoke thus, the eloquent clerk was fumbling first in one pocket, then in the other, till, with a hurried air, he said, 'A—a—a——I really beg your pardon, Sir, but I have unfortunately left my purse on the table in the coffee-room opposite; pray do me the favor to remain here, and I will be back in one moment.' So speaking, the clerk vanished with the rapidity of lightning, and I never set eyes on him again."

He dilated often on the difficulty he had in procuring an equipage to go his first circuit. "At last," he continued, "I hired a horse for myself, and borrowed another for an inexperienced youth who was to ride behind me with my saddle-bags. But I thought my chance was gone; for having been engaged in a discussion with a traveling companion, on approaching the assize town I looked behind, but there was no appearance of my clerk, and I was obliged to ride back several miles, till I found him crying by the roadside, his horse at some distance from him, and the saddle-bags still further off; and it was not without great difficulty that I could accomplish the reunion between them, which he had in vain attempted. Had I failed, too, in this undertaking, I never should have been Lord Chancellor."

He represented his gains for twelve months after he put on his gown to amount to 9s. sterling, and no more. "When I was called to the Bar," he would say, "Bessy and I thought all our troubles were over; business was to pour in, and we were to be rich almost immediately. So I made a bargain with her, that during the following year all the money I should receive in the first eleven months should be mine, and whatever I should get in the twelfth month should be hers. That was our agreement, and how do you think it turned out? In the twelfth month I received half a guinea; eighteen pence went for charity, and Bessy got nine shillings.[1] In the other eleven months I got not one shilling." It may be true, although it is highly improbable, (considering his north-country connections, the friendship of Mr. Duane, and his own agreeable manners,) that he had no other business in London during his first year; but in the summer of this year he went the Northern Circuit, where we know, from undoubted authority, that he prospered. There is extant a letter from Sir William to their brother Henry, written on the 2nd of October, 1776, containing this passage:—
"My brother Jack seems highly pleased with his circuit success. I hope it is only the beginning of future triumphs. All appearances speak strongly in his favor. If he does not succeed, I will never venture a conjecture upon any one thing again. He is very industrious, and has made great progress in the knowledge of his profession."

Lord Eldon has fallen into the belief that his famous

---

[1] This must have been a half-guinea motion, the last day of term—when there was a deduction (it used to be only 1s. in the King's Bench) for the benefit of poor prisoners confined for debt.

argument in *Akroyd* v. *Smithson*, before Lord Thurlow, in the year 1780, was the first opportunity he ever enjoyed of gaining distinction. But it now appears, that early in the year 1777 he repeatedly harangued the freemen of Newcastle at a contested election for that borough, and that in the ensuing session of Parliament he was counsel before a committee of the House of Commons, upon a petition which arose out of it. Stoney Bowes had lately married the Countess of Strathmore, after fighting a sham duel, in defense of her honor, with the Reverend Bate Dudley, editor of the Morning Post,—and was now, in her right, become entitled to large estates in the county of Durham. During the honey-moon he announced himself as a candidate to represent Newcastle on the death of Sir William Blackett; and his absence being excused on account of the duties he had to discharge elsewhere, John Scott, retained as one of his counsel, not only argued the validity of votes on his behalf before the returning officer, but used to speak for him in public. "As a mob orator, his townsmen considered him to have failed; he proceeded with hesitation, stopped frequently, and with a nervous action raised his hand to his mouth, as though to pull out the reluctant words."[1] The printed poll-book shows that John Scott, along with his brothers William and Henry, as freemen of the Hoastmen's Company, voted for Bowes; but Trevelyan, the opposite candidate, had a majority of votes, and was returned.[2] The poll lasted fourteen days, and our young barrister received an *honorarium* of 200 guineas, which he must have carried back to Bessy with high glee, although somehow it afterwards slipped entirely from his recollection. But his forgotten good fortune did not end here. There being a petition against the return, he was retained for the petitioner, against Dunning, Sergeant Glynn, and Jack Lee —and, with mutual charges of bribery, the case was fiercely fought many days. While it was pending, he wrote a letter to his brother Henry, who had been one of Bowes's agents during the election; in which, after stating that he had summed up the evidence for the petition that

---

[1] W. E. Surtees, 51. In a humorous piece acted on the Italian stage, where there is a similar difficulty experienced, Punchinello runs his head into the stomach of the stammering orator—to make the words jump out.

[2] 1163 to 1063.

morning in a long speech,—that a greater impression had been made upon the committee than was expected, but that their witnesses had been rigorously cross-examined with a view to recrimination, he adds:—" I hope you have not been so zealous as to overleap the bounds of law and prudence, for I take it for granted that they will spare nobody—our case has irritated and surprised them so much. I think, upon the whole, it will not be a void election, but will contribute to establish Bowes's importance very much."

The committee at last reported that the sitting member was duly elected, when John Scott, in another letter to his brother Henry, says, "The committee cleared the room to take the sense of the majority; but, after debating two hours, they were so much divided, that they could not come to a determination. They met according to adjournment again yesterday, but again broke up without a decision. This morning they met a third time, and I am just informed the majority is against us. Thus this 'vexatious and frivolous petition' has proved respectable, though not successful." A few days afterwards Sir William wrote—" I am very happy to find that my brother John acquitted himself so much to the satisfaction of his friends in the matter of the petition. That affair is well ended for us all,—all circumstances considered."[1]

The same year Mr. John Scott, through the influence of his father-in-law, had a general retainer from the corporation of Newcastle, and received a brief, with several eminent leaders, to support a claim of the Duke of Northumberland to an ancient office against Lord Gwydir. Of this last employment he would often talk, saying, "It was only

[1] These election proceedings not having been communicated to Mr. Twiss, he does not refer to them in his first or second edition. In a note on the third he says.—" Among the papers left by Lord Eldon there has been found no trace of, or allusion to, Mr. Bowes's retainers, nor is any memory of them extant in the Eldon family." But the old Earl could hardly have forgotten " briefs, consultations, and refreshers," which must have been so important to him ; and I suspect he became ashamed of his connection with a client who turned out such a reprobate. Many years after, Sir John Scott was examined as a witness in the Court of Common Pleas to prove that, at the time of this contested election, Mr. Bowes and Lady Strathmore lived together on cordial terms. In a letter dated 1st May, 1778, he says: " I see your friend Bowes very often, but I dare not dine with him above once in three months, as there is no getting away before midnight ; and, indeed, one is sure to be in a condition in which no man would wish to be in the streets at any other season."

a handsome way of giving me twenty guineas a day for walking down to the House of Lords."[1]

This summer he again went the Northern Circuit, and had evidently taken root there, having various briefs in the Crown Court at Newcastle, where the attorneys showed a disposition to employ him, and were well pleased with his performances. Above all, Mr. Cuthbert, the topping attorney of the town, was his avowed patron.[2]

In the end of the preceding year he had lost his father, who, by his will, left him a legacy of £1,000. He placed a tablet with an unostentatious inscription, in St. Nicholas's church, to the memory of the worthy coal-fitter, and always behaved with kindness to his surviving parent, who lived to see him a peer.

At this time, rather attracted by the harvest which he thought was ripe for him in his native place, than despairing of ultimate success in the metropolis, he resolved at once to settle as a provincial counsel; and he actually hired a house in Pilgrim Street, on the bank of the Tyne;—the summit of his ambition being, as yet, the Recordership of Newcastle.

But before he had removed his family from London he altered his plans, and made over the lease of his house in Pilgrim Street to his brother Henry. What was the cause of this sudden change has not been cleared up to us. Mr. Heron, another leading Newcastle attorney well affected to him, strongly urged that London was the proper field for such powers and acquirements as his, and added, "Only go, and I'll give you a guinea now, on condition that you give me a thousand when you're Chancellor." So saying, he handed him a guinea, which Mr. John Scott, who did not like to refuse money, was proceeding to put it into his pocket. On this Sir William, who was present at the deliberation, exclaimed in a tone of remonstrance, " Jack,

---

[1] When the Duke was commander-in-chief of the northern forces during the American war, his headquarters being fixed at Newcastle, he was occasionally the guest of Mr. Surtees, when Mrs. John Scott and her infant son were there. His Grace would often take the boy on his knees, calling him his Captain, and saying good-humoredly, " You shall soon be an officer in my regiment."

[2] The importance attached by the family to this patronage appears by a letter written at this time by Sir William, complaining much of Cuthbert's conduct in some negotiation, in which he says,—" However, Jack's interest is concerned in not saying anything affronting to him; otherwise I should not spare him."

you're robbing Heron of his guinea," and it was returned. I suspect that London was at this time preferred on account of a promise given by Lord Thurlow, on the application of Lord Darlington,—though never fulfilled,—to confer upon Mr. John Scott a Commissionership of Bankrupts. Accustomed to doubt long on questions of law, he never showed great decision in acting where his own interests were concerned. " I much question," says Mr. W. E. Surtees, " whether, in his whole life, he was ever prevented by his doubts from undertaking any enterprise which promised advantage. His were the doubts of the courageous but cautious general, who, even while making his advance, prepares for the hard necessity of retreat."

In this transaction we have a striking instance of his characteristic caution and the liberties with fact which he deemed justifiable. Although he was to part with all interest in the house, and he had abandoned for the present all notion of settling in Newcastle, he writes from London to his brother Henry: " You will be so kind as to second my wishes to keep Newcastle open for me, in case I am defeated here, and, for that purpose, to assert that I have not relinquished, but only delayed for a short time, my plan of settling there." And in a subsequent letter he says to Henry, who seems himself actually to have been taken in by these statements : " I thought we had understood each other too well to make it possible for you to receive any disturbance upon the subject of the house. I wished only to have it held out to the world, and, among the rest, to Cuthbert himself, that I might have the house again at a short warning—by way of impressing them and him with so strong an idea of an intention in me hereafter to settle at N. C. as effectually to prevent any other person from taking that step in the meantime.[1] . . . Previous to my receiving Cuthbert's letter to-day, I had wrote to

[1] This explanation reminds one of the scene in Foote's farce of " THE LYAR," where even Papillon had been taken in by Young Wilding's circumstantial account of his marriage at Abingdon, in the county of Berks, to the imaginary Miss Lydia Sybthorp :—
Pap. " I am amazed, Sir, that you have so carefully concealed this transaction from me."
Y. Wild. " Heyday ! what, do *you* believe it too ?"
Pap. " Believe it ! Why, is not the story of the marriage true ?"
Y. Wild. " Not a syllable."
Pap. " And the cat, and the pistol, and the poker ?"
Y. Wild. " All invention ! And were *you* really taken in ?"
VIII.—24

him, proposing a different method of transferring my interest, and telling him that I had determined to part with the whole of it, contrary to his advice, and to run the risk of getting another when I wanted it. If he interprets this into an intention of giving N. C. up absolutely, you may give him the most positive assurances to the contrary,—*telling* him and other people (*for it is but a white lie*), that, as I have taken this step to suit your convenience, we shall easily settle any difficulty that may arise."—Henry accepted an assignment of the house, in spite of the remonstrance of Sir William, who thought it would involve him in too great expense, and had thus concluded a letter, inculcating upon him frugality and attention to business: "We inherit from our deceased father not only a provision, but, what is more, an example."

Mr. John Scott, moving from his "first perch" in Cursitor Street, now took a small house in Carey Street, which, from its vicinity to Lincoln's Inn, obviated the necessity of his holding chambers at the same time. Still continuing regularly to go the circuit, and so far considering himself a common lawyer, he had transferred himself to the Court of Chancery, as his usual place of practicing in London. Of this transfer he used to give the following account:—" The Court of Chancery was not my object when first called to the bar. I first took my seat in the King's Bench; but I soon perceived, or thought I perceived, a preference in Lord Mansfield for young lawyers who had been bred at Westminster School and Christ Church, and, as I had belonged neither to Westminster nor Christ Church, I thought I should not have a fair chance with my fellows, and therefore I crossed over to the other side of the Hall.''[1]

The experiment was at first by no means successful. The old Chancery practitioners were a little hurt at seeing among them a new candidate for business, who had not been regularly bred to their craft; but they felt no alarm, and they sneered at the notion of a man aspiring to be an equity lawyer who had never penned a bill or

[1] The number of counsel at that time practicing in Chancery is said not to have exceeded twelve or fifteen. Till many years after, the proceedings of that Court were never noticed in the newspapers; and an equity counsel, as such, was rather an obscure character.

answer in an equity draughtman's office. For a year or two their predictions were verified. In January, 1779, Sir William writes to his brother Henry,—'Business is very dull with poor Jack—very dull indeed ; and of consequence he is not very lively. I heartily wish that business may brisken a little, or he will be heartily sick of his profession. I do all I can to keep up his spirits, but he is very gloomy. But *mum!* not a word of this to the wife of your bosom."—He filled up his time by diligently reading everything to be found in print, connected with the practice and doctrine of courts of equity, till continued hard study, or continued low spirits from want of business in London, began to undermine his health. He consulted Dr. Heberden, who dispatched him to Bath, with an intimation that if in three or four weeks the waters should bring out the gout, all was well ; but if this result was not effected, he must prepare for the worst. In narrating this interview, he said, "I then put my hand into my pocket, meaning to give the doctor his fee ; but he stopped me, asking, 'Are you the young gentleman who gained the prize for the essay at Oxford?' I said I was. 'I will take no fee from you. Go to Bath, and let me see you when you return.' He was a very kind man ; he would never take a fee from me."—The Bath waters did produce a fit of the gout, and the patient's health was improved.

His professional prospects were still discouraging ; but he was afterwards in the habit of considerably overstating his supposed failure. He would say, "One year I did not go the circuit, because I could not afford it. I had borrowed of my brother for several circuits, without getting adequate remuneration." Whereas it is proved by the circuit records that he regularly attended the assizes in the four northern counties from the time when he first joined it, and that he could only have been absent one spring circuit from York and Lancaster, where, as yet, he was little known. In reference to his obscurity there, the Reverend Sydney Smith, in an assize sermon delivered in York Cathedral, in 1824, from the text, "And, behold, a certain lawyer stood up and tempted him,"[1]—for the encouragement of the desponding young barristers, said "Fifty years ago, the person at the head of his pro-

---

[1] Luke x. 25.

fession, the greatest lawyer now in England, perhaps in the world, stood in this church on such an occasion as the present, as obscure, as unknown, and as much doubting of his future prospects, as the humblest individual of the profession here present." But in the four northern counties he had almost from his first start a good share of business. It is curious to think that this chiefly consisted in defending prisoners in the Crown Court—or what is jocularly called in the profession, the " rope-walk." But he had not the common reputation of lawyers who are eminent in this line,—that they greatly assist in the execution of the criminal law by hanging their clients;—instead of getting out the truth by indiscreet cross-examinations, he was wont to say that he had been a most effective advocate for prisoners, as he had seldom put a question to the prosecutor. He told this story to illustrate his practice : " I was counsel for a highwaymen at Durham, who was certainly guilty, but against whom no sufficient case was made out by legal evidence; I would not aid the prosecution by cross-examination, and remaining quiet, my client was acquitted and discharged. Sitting in my lodgings in the evening, a very ill-looking fellow, whose face I had seen before, but could not at first recollect where—for he had changed his dress—burst in, my clerk being absent— and said, ' Lawyer Scott, you owe me two guineas. You were my counselor to-day, and you did nothing for me. I am, therefore, come to have my fee back again; and my fee I will have.' I seized the poker, and said, ' Sirrah, although you escaped to-day, when you deserved to be hanged, you shall be hanged to-morrow for attempting to rob me, unless you instantly depart.' At that moment my clerk luckily came in, and the highwayman slunk off, or I am not sure that he would not have carried away with him, not only his own fee, but all the fees I had received on the circuit."

He had for some time succeeded so much better in the country than in London, that he again seriously meditated becoming a provincial." I believe that, if there had not been a speedy turn in his metropolitan practice, he would have carried it into effect; and, considering the important part he played during the King's illnesses, and on the dissolution of several administrations, who can tell how the history of the country might have been changed if he had been only Recorder of Newcastle, instead of being Lord High Chancellor of Great Britain ? But his extraordinary merit as a lawyer was now about to be disclosed to all the world; and from this time his rise was rapid and steady. He had only one brief before Lord Chancellor Bathurst, who was then entirely under the dominion of Thurlow, the Attorney General. After Thurlow and Wedderburn had argued the case at considerable length for opposing parties, between whom it was supposed to lie, and Lord Bathurst had intimated a strong opinion in favor of Thurlow's client,—Scott, a very young man, and wholly unknown, appeared as counsel for a third party. The Chancellor was disposed (though with much courtesy) to conclude that the young counsel could not cast much light upon the controversy. Still he *suffered* him to speak,—but without indicating any symptom of being convinced—when Thurlow rose, and, in a very decided tone, exclaimed, " My Lord, Mr. Scott is right ;" and dictated a decree accordingly.[1]

The first reported case in which he seems to have been employed in the Court of Chancery was *Green* v. *Howard*,[2] in which he was junior to Mr. Ambler and Mr. Maddocks, and in vain tried to persuade Lord Thurlow, who had lately succeeded to the Great Seal, that a bequest to the testator's "relations" would extend beyond that class of relations who, had he died intestate, would have taken under the "Statute of Distributions." His argument on this occasion, though badly reported, seems to have been very creditable to him.

But his fortune was made by *Akroyd* v. *Smithson*.[3] Not more than three weeks before his death, he gave the following very interesting account of that case to Mr. Farrer, who was dining with him, and put a question to him respecting it :—

" Come, help yourself to a glass of Newcastle port, and give me a little. You must know that the testator in that cause had directed his real estate to be sold, and after paying his debts, and funeral and testamentary expenses, the res-

---
[1] This anecdote rests on Lord Eldon's own authority.—Sir Vicary Gibbs told me, that on the Western Circuit, when counsel for the plaintiff, Baron Graham was for deciding in his favor ; but he insisted on being nonsuited, conscious that the law was against him, and that his client would have been put to the expense of correcting the Judge's error.
[2] 6th Feb. 1779. Br. Chancery Cases, p. 31.   [3] Ib. vol. i. p. 503.

idue of the money to be divided into fifteen parts—which he gave to fifteen persons whom he named in his will. One of those persons died in the testator's lifetime. A bill was filed by the next of kin, claiming, among other things, the lapsed share. A brief was given me to consent for the heir at law, upon the hearing of the cause. I had nothing then to do but to pore over this brief. I went through all the cases in the books, and satisfied myself that the lapsed share was to be considered as real estate, and belonged to my client (the heir-at-law). The cause came on at the Rolls, before Sir Thomas Sewell. I told the solicitor, who sent me the brief, that I should consent for the heir at law, so far as regarded the due execution of the will, but that I must support the title of the heir to the one-fifteenth which had lapsed. Accordingly, I did argue it, and went through all the authorities. When Sir Thomas Sewell went out of Court, he asked the Register who that young man was. The Register told him it was Mr. Scott. 'He has argued very well,' said Sir Thomas Sewell, 'but I can not agree with him. This the Register told me. He decreed against my client. The cause having been carried by appeal, to the Lord Chancellor Thurlow, a guinea brief was again brought to me to consent. I told my client, if he meant by 'consent' to give up the claim of the heir to the lapsed share, he must take his brief elsewhere, for I would not hold it without arguing that point. He said something about young men being obstinate, but that I must do as I thought right. You see the lucky thing was, there being *two* other parties, and, the disappointed one not being content, there was an appeal to Lord Thurlow. In the meanwhile they had written to Mr. Johnston, Recorder of York, guardian to the young heir at law, and a clever man, but his answer was, 'Do not send good money after bad ; let Mr. Scott have a guinea, to give consent; and if he will argue, why let him do so, but give him no more.' So I went into Court, and when Lord Thurlow asked who was to appear for the heir at law, I rose, and said modestly, 'that I was; and as I could not but think (with much deference to the Master of the Rolls, for I might be wrong) that my client had the right to the property, if his Lordship would give me leave I would argue it.'—It was rather arduous for me to rise against all the eminent counsel. I do not say that their *opinions* were against me, but they were *employed* against me. However, I argued that the testator had ordered this fifteenth share of the property to be converted into personal property, for the benefit of one particular individual, and that therefore he never contemplated its coming into possession of either the next of kin, or the residuary legatee ; but, being land, at the death of the individual it came to the heir at law.—Well, Thurlow took three days to consider, and then delivered his judgment in accordance with my speech, and that speech is in print, and has decided all similar questions ever since. As I left the Hall, a respectable solicitor of the name of Fo-ster came up, and touched me on the shoulder, and said, ' Young man, your bread and butter is cut for life,' or ' You have cut your bread and butter.' But the story of *Akroyd* v. *Smithson* does not stop there. In the Chancellor's Court of Lancaster, where Dunning (Lord Ashburton) was Chancellor, a brief was given me in a cause in which the interest of my client would oblige me to support, by argument, the reverse of that which had been decided by the decree in *Akroyd* v *Smithson*. When I had stated to the Court the point I was going to argue, Dunning said, ' Sit down, young man.'—As I did not immediately comply, he repeated, ' Sit down, Sir, I won't hear you.'— I then sat down. Dunning said, ' I believe your name is Scott, Sir.'—I said it was. Upon which Dunning went on:—' Mr. Scott, did not you argue that case of *Akroyd* v. *Smithson?*'—I said that I did argue it.—Dunning then said, ' Mr. Scott, I have read your argument in that case of *Akroyd* v. *Smithson*, and I defy you, or any man in England, to answer it. I won't hear you.'"[1]

Mr. Scott's argument in *Akroyd* v. *Smithson* made a great sensation in Westminster Hall, and, in the words of Lord Byron, " next day he awoke and found himself famous,"—although from the nature of the subject the *éclat* could not be compared with that acquired nearly about the same time by Erskine as counsel for Captain Baillie. But erroneous accounts have been given of its immediate consequences. Several writers have said that Lord Thurlow immediately offered him a Mastership in Chancery. Such an offer would have been gladly accepted, but was never made. The fulfillment of the promise

[1] Twiss, vol. i. ch. vi.

of a Commissionership of Bankrupts was still in vain expected, and the Chancellor being some years afterwards interrogated on this subject, said that "from his high opinion of Scott he had not given him the appointment, as it might have been his ruin."[1] Again, it is said that not long afterwards an offer was made to him of the Recordership of Newcastle, and that, having accepted it, he caused a house to he engaged for him there; but Mr. W. S. Surtees has satisfactorily proved that he never was Recorder of Newcastle, and that no offer of that office could ever have been made to him. The story of the residence must have originated from the circumstance of his having actually, in 1777, engaged the house which he assigned over to his brother Henry.[2]

The year 1780 continued a very lucky one for him. On the dissolution of Parliament, Mr. Bowes being returned, with Sir Matthew White Ridley, for Newcastle, there was a petition against them by Mr. Delaval, the unsuccessful candidate; and Mr. Scott being their counsel, with Jack Lee—after the committee had sat many days, and many fees were received, the petition was voted "frivolous and vexatious."

He was about this time in serious peril from Lord George Gordon's mobs, and, what was worse, Mrs. Scott was exposed to insult—when he was taking her for safety to the Temple, which was fortified. I observe that the lawyers all pretended to great prowess in this emergency. We have seen Erskine's boasting narrative of his putting the insurgents to rout with a piece of artillery. Lord Eldon, after stating how his wife's hat was lost, and every article of her dress was torn, proceeded with much quiet humor: "We youngsters at the Temple determined that we would not remain inactive during such times; so we introduced ourselves into a troop to assist the military. We armed ourselves as well as we could, and the next morning we drew up in the court, ready to follow out a troop of soldiers who were there on guard. When, how-

---

[1] Lord Eldon said,—"I have now a letter in which Lord Thurlow promised me a Commissionership of Bankruptcy when it would have been most valuable to me in point of income; he never gave it me, and he always said it was a favor to me to withhold it. What he meant was, that he had learned (a clear truth) that I was by nature very indolent, and it was only want that could make me industrious." This could only have been meant as a bantering apology for a broken promise. [2] Surtees, ch. ii.

ever, the soldiers had passed through the gate, it was suddenly shut in our faces, and the officer in command shouted from the other side, 'Gentlemen, I am much obliged to you for your intended assistance, but I do not choose to allow my soldiers to be shot; so I have ordered you to be locked in,'—and away he galloped."

The following year saw Mr. Scott fully established in business, and an uninterrupted tide of prosperity flowed in upon him for the rest of his life. Fond of making people stare when he referred, in his old age. to his early history, he would sometimes ascribe all his success to the accident of being employed as counsel before the Clitheroe election committee—which he thus narrated:—
" Mr. (afterwards Lord) Curzon, and four or five gentlemen, came to my door and woke me, and when I inquired what they wanted, they stated that the Clitheroe election case was to come on that morning at ten o'clock, before a committee of the House of Commons; that Mr. Cooper had written to say he was detained at Oxford by illness, and could not arrive to lead the cause; and that Mr. Hardinge, the next counsel, refused to do so, because he was not prepared. 'Well, gentlemen,' said I, 'what do you expect me to do, that you are here?' They answered, 'they did not know what to expect or to do, for the cause must come on at ten o'clock, and they were totally unprepared, and had been recommended to me as a young and promising counsel.' I answered, 'I will tell you what I *can* do; I *can* undertake to make a dry statement of facts, if that will content you, gentlemen, but more 1 *can not* do, for I have no time to make myself acquainted with the law.' They said that must do; so I begged they would go down stairs and let me get up as fast as I could. Well, I did state the facts, and the cause went on for fifteen days. It found me poor enough, but I began to be rich before it was done: they left me fifty guineas at the beginning: then there were ten guineas every day, and five guineas every evening for a consultation—more money than I could count. But, better, still, the length of the cause gave me time to make myself thoroughly acquainted with the law.—On the morning on which the counsel for the petitioner was to reply, Hardinge came into the committee-room, meaning to reply. I saw the members of the committee put their heads together, and then one of them

said, 'Mr. Hardinge, Mr. Scott opened this case, and has attended it throughout, and the committee think, that, if he likes to reply, he ought to do so: Mr. Scott, would you like to reply?'—I answered 'that I would do my best.' I began my speech with a very bad joke. You must know that the leading counsel on the other side, Douglas, afterwards Lord Glenbervie, had made one of the longest speeches ever known before a committee, and had argued that the borough of Clitheroe was not a borough by prescription, for it had its origin within the memory of man. I began by saying, 'I will prove to the committee by the best evidence, that the borough of Clitheroe is a borough by prescription; that it had its origin before the memory of man. My learned friend will admit the commencement of this borough was before the commencement of his speech: but the commencement of his speech is beyond the memory of man: therefore the borough of Clitheroe must have commenced before the memory of man.' We were beaten in the committee by one vote. After this speech, Mansfield, afterwards Sir James Mansfield, came up to me in Westminster Hall, and said he heard that I was going to leave London, but strongly advised me to remain in London. I told him that I could not, that I had taken a house in Newcastle, that I had an increasing family, in short, that I was compelled to quit London. Afterwards Wilson came to me and pressed me in the same manner to remain in London, adding what was very kind, 'that he would insure me £400 the next year.' I gave him the same answer as I had given Mansfield. However, I did remain in London, and lived to make Mansfield Chief Justice of the Common Pleas, and Wilson a Puisne Judge.'[1]

This narrative is chargeable with several inaccuracies which show that Lord Eldon's senile reminiscences of his youth are to be taken with grains of allowance. How the counsel should have allowed the committee to encroach on the privileges of the Bar, and dictate who should reply, is rather incredible; and I can not help suspecting that the argument to prove the antiquity of the borough of Clitheroe had been premeditated, instead of being improvised. But if he asserted to Sir James Mansfield and Mr. Wilson that a house was then taken for him at New-

[1] Twiss, i. 87.

castle, this was "a white lie." His supposed determination then to retire from London, on account of professional disappointments and pecuniary embarrassment, must have been pure invention, as his fortune had been made, more than a year before, by *Akroyd* v. *Smithson*,—and (best of all!) Wilson—having been created a Judge of the Court of Common Pleas by Lord Thurlow,—died in the year 1793, eight years before Lord Eldon was Chancellor!

It is likewise said, that he first got into the lead of civil causes on the circuit by lucky hits. I am glad that the account very generally circulated of his earliest triumph in the North is not in the "ANECDOTE BOOK," as it must be fabulous. "He was retained as junior counsel in an action of assault by a Mr. Fermor against a Miss Saustern, an elderly maiden lady. His leader was absent; and, having addressed the jury, he proved by witnesses, that, the parties playing at whist, high words arose between them,—whereupon the defendant threw her cards at the plaintiff, which knocked him down. The defendant's counsel argued, 'that there was a fatal variance between the *allegata* and *probata*,—the declaration stating that the defendant assaulted the plaintiff with her *hand*,—whereas the assault was committed by *pieces of pasteboard* converted into missiles.' The plaintiff was about to be nonsuited, when Mr. Scott insisted 'that the proofs substantially supported the averment in the declaration of an assault committed *with the hand;* for that, in the common parlance of the card-table, which alone ought to be regarded in such a case, the 'hand' means the 'hand of cards,'—and therefore that Miss Saustern, having thrown her cards in Mr. Fermor's face, had clearly assaulted the plaintiff with *her hand.*' The Judge then overruled the objection, and the jury found a verdict for the plaintiff, with large damages."[1]

At times he would himself ascribe his success on the circuit to his having gained a verdict in a great mining cause against the summing up of Buller. "When I went to the ball, that evening," he would boast, "I was received with open arms by every one. Oh! my fame was established; I really think I might have married half the

[1] Last edition of Joe Miller's "Jest Book."

pretty girls in the room that night. Never was a man so courted!".

Then he would relate how, after going seven years to Carlisle without any business, he had a guinea brief delivered to him by accident, for the defendant in an assault case, where, the plaintiff's attorney's name being Hobson, he made a very obvious and bad joke about "Hobson's choice," and induced the jury to give one penny damages. Thus he concluded his narrative: "When I record that, at the same assizes, I received seventy guineas for this joke—for briefs came in rapidly—I record a fact, which proves that a lawyer may beginn to acquire wealth by a little pleasantry, who might long wait before professional knowledge introduced him into notice."

But he would assert, that he was "first brought into notice on the circuit by *breaking the Ten Commandments*,"—thus explaining the enigma;—" I was counsel in a cause, the fate of which depended on our being able to make out who was the founder of an ancient chapel. I went to view it. There was nothing to be observed that gave any indication of its date or history. However, I observed that the Ten Commandments were written on some old plaster, which, from its position, I conjectured might cover an arch. Acting on this, I bribed the clerk with five shillings, to allow me to chip away a part of the plaster; and, after two or three attempts, I found the key-stone of an arch, of which were engraved the arms of an ancestor of one of the parties. This evidence decided the cause; and I ever afterwards had reason to remember with much satisfaction my having, on that occasion, *broken the Ten Commandments*."

I may now safely dismiss the notion of his having made his fortune by any one great speech. Erskine certainly was miraculously, as it were, raised at once to the very top of his profession by his defense of Captain Baillie; but I can testify that there has been no such case for the last forty years,—I believe there have been very few such instances in any age,—and it is quite certain that Scott got on by the gradual discovery of his learning, ability, and usefulness.

While he attended most diligently to the interests of his clients, he entered with much spirit into all the gamesome proceedings of his brethren at the Bar. In the

Grand Courts held for the trial of mock offenses "against the peace of our Lord the Junior," he acted a distinguished part,—insomuch that, in 1780, he was appointed Solicitor General, and in 1781 Attorney General of the circuit,—being a terror to evil doers while he held these high offices,— and giving a foretaste of the activity with which he prosecuted traitors and libelers when he became a law officer of the Crown.[1]

Northern Circuit stories, according to the custom of Northern Circuit men, constituted the staple of Lord Eldon's jocular talk as long as he lived. I will mention a few of those which he most frequently repeated. "While Sir Thomas Davenport, a very dull orator, was making a long speech at the York Assizes, a chimney-sweeper's boy, who had climbed up to a dangerous place in front of a high gallery, having been put to sleep by him, fell down, and was killed. Whereupon I, being then Attorney General of the circuit, indicted Sir Thomas in our Grand Court[2] for the murder of the boy; and the indictment (according to the rule of law which requires that the weapon shall be described, and that there shall be an averment of its value, or that it is of *no value*[3]) alleged that the murder was committed with 'a certain blunt instrument of *no value* called a LONG SPEECH.'"

"When I first went the Northern Circuit, I employed my time, having no business of my own, in attending to the manner in which the leading counsel did their business. I left Lancaster at the end of a circuit, with my friend Jack Lee, at that period a leader upon the circuit. We supped and slept at Kirkby Lonsdale, or Kirkby Stephen. After supper I said to him, 'I have observed that throughout circuit, in all causes in which you are concerned, good, bad, indifferent, whatever their nature was,

---

[1] There was a corresponding field of ambition open on my circuit—the Oxford; but according to the obscurity of my career, I only reached the dignity of Crier,—holding a fire-shovel in my hand as the emblem of my office. An epitaph was made for me, in the natural expectation that I should die in this office,—thus charitably concluding :
  "He of the Circuit long was Crier,
  But now we hope he's somewhat higher."

[2] The Grand Court is holden with a view to the discipline of the Bar, but chiefly in the High Jinks fashion, to bring mock charges against the members.

[3] This was with a view to the deodand, and continued to be law, till, by a bill which I had the honor to introduce and carry through Parliament in the year 1846, all deodands were abolished.

you equally exerted yourself to the uttermost to gain verdicts, stating evidence and quoting cases, as such statement and quotation should give you a chance of success, the evidence and the cases not being stated clearly, or quoted with a strict attention to accuracy, and to fair and just representation. Can that,' said I, 'Lee, be right? Can it be justified?'—'Oh, yes,' he said, 'undoubtedly. Dr. Johnson has said that counsel were at liberty to state, as the parties themselves would state, what it was most for their interest to state.' After some interval, and when he had had his evening bowl of milk punch and two or three pipes of tobacco, he suddenly said, 'Come, Master Scott, let us go to bed. I have been thinking upon the question that you asked me, and I am not quite so sure that the conduct you represented will bring a man peace at last.'"

"Jack Lee, though a Yorkshireman, had attended the York Assizes several years without a brief. One day, after dinner, he said, 'I find a prophet has no honor in his own country, and as I have never yet received a single guinea at this place, I will shake the dust off my feet—leave it this very night, and never be seen in this room again.' Davenport and Wedderburn thereupon drew up a brief which they entitled REX v. INHABITANTS OF HUM-TOWN, and which in due form gave instructions in a prosecution for not repairing a road within the parish leading from Goose-green to Crackskull-common. This they sent to Lee's lodgings, with a guinea as the fee. In the evening the barristers assembled as usual in the circuit-room to sup and play at cards, and the discontented Yorkshireman appearing among them, Wedderburn said, 'Bless me, Lee, I thought you were gone!' 'Well,' said Jack, 'it is very extraordinary; I was just going, I was shaking the dust of this place off my feet as an abominable place that I would never see again, when, lo and behold, a brief is brought to me, and I must stay.' 'Well,' said Davenport, 'in what cause may it be.' Lee answered, 'In the King v. Hum-town.' 'Oh dear,' cried Davenport, 'they brought me a brief in that case with a bad guinea, and I would not take it. I dare say they have given you the bad guinea.' 'I have it in my pocket,' said Lee, 'here it is.' Davenport, looking at it, said, 'Yes, the very same guinea,' and put it in his pocket. They then told him the joke they had practiced upon him, that they might not lose the pleasure of his company. Although a good-natured man, he never forgave this joke, although it kept him at York, where, in a few years after, he led every cause."

As a pendant to this, Lord Eldon used to relate a story which he had actually thus recorded in his "Anecdote Book," but for which I think there could only have been a slight foundation of fact. " At an assizes at *Lancaster* we found Dr. Johnson's friend, Jemmy Boswell, lying upon the pavement—*inebriated*. We subscribed at supper a guinea for him, and half a crown for his clerk, and sent him, when he waked next morning, a brief with instructions to move for what we denominated the writ of ' Quare adhæsit pavimento,' with observations duly calculated to induce him to think that it required great learning to explain the necessity of granting it to the Judge before whom he was to move. Boswell sent all round the town to attorneys for books that might enable him to distinguish himself—but in vain. He moved, however, for the writ, making the best use he could of the observations in the brief. The Judge was perfectly astonished, and the audience amazed.—The Judge said, ' I never heard of such a writ—what can it be that adheres *pavimento ?*—Are any of you gentlemen at the Bar able to explain this ?' The Bar laughed. At last one of them said, ' My Lord, Mr. Boswell last night *adhæsit pavimento*. There was no moving him for some time. At last he was carried to bed, and he has been dreaming about himself and the pavement.' "[1]—But Jemmy Boswell, who has written one of the most entertaining and instructive books in the English language, and had often pleaded causes of great importance in the Court of Session, and at the bar of the House of Lords, could not by possibility have been taken in by such a palpable hoax. The scene here described could not have been acted before the King's Judges, but must be a reminiscence of something which had taken place in the Grand Court when the barristers were sitting in HIGH JINKS *foribus clausis*.

Lord Eldon is said to have given this amusing anecdote of a trial at York arising out of a horse-race : " One of the conditions was that ' each horse should be ridden by a *gentleman*.' In an action for the stakes, the question arose, ' whether the plaintiff was a *gentleman* or not ?' After

[1] Twiss, vol. i. ch. vi.

much evidence and oratory on both sides, the Judge thus summed up: 'Gentlemen of the Jury, when I see you in that box I call you *gentlemen*, for I know you are such there; but out of that box I do not know what may be the requisites that constitute a *gentleman;* therefore I can give you no direction, except that you will consider of your verdict.' The jury found for the defendant. Next morning the plaintiff challenged both Law and me, who were conducting the cause against him, for having said that he was *no gentleman*. We sent him this answer, 'that we could not think of fighting one who had been found *no gentleman* by the solemn verdict of twelve of his countrymen.'"[1]

He once had a narrow escape from a watery grave. From Ulverstone to Lancaster there is a short but very dangerous cut across the sands, and, being in a hurry, he was going to take it at the time of greatest peril,—when the tide was beginning to flow. But as he was setting off he asked the landlord whether any persons were ever lost in going to Lancaster by the sea-shore. "No, no," was the answer, "I think nobody has ever been *lost*—they have all been *found at low water*."[2]

To illustrate the unreasonable complaints against public functionaries, he would relate that on the circuit, stopping to bait at a place where many years before Mr. Moises had been curate, he had the curiosity to ask the landlord of the inn whether he remembered him? "Yes," answered he with an oath, "I well remember him. I have had

[1] Twiss, (vol. i. ch. vi.) on the authority of Mrs. Foster. An article in the "Law Review" (No. II. p. 279), attributed to Lord Brougham, says,—"This is a great mistake. The person in question blustered and talked big, and threatened to call out Mr. Law, who led the cause, and could alone have said the offensive words. That gallant individual put off his journey to Durham for half a day, and walked about, booted and spurred, before the coffee-house, the most public place in York, ready to repel force, if offered, by force—because personal chastisement had also been threatened. No message was sent, and no attempt was made to provoke a breach of the peace. It is very possible Lord Eldon may have said, and Lord Ellenborough too, that they were not bound to treat one in such a predicament as a gentleman, and hence the story has arisen in the lady's mind. The fact was well known on the Northern Circuit as was the answer of a witness to a question, whether the party had a right by his circumstances to keep a pack of fox-hounds: 'No more right than I to keep a pack of archbishops.'"
[2] There is an ancient office of "Guide across Ulverstone Sands," which is in the gift of the Chancellor of the Duchy of Lancaster, and to which, upon a vacancy, I have lately appointed; so that I hope to hear no more of 'bodies being *found at low water*."

reason enough to remember him. It was the worst day this parish ever saw that brought him here." The lawyer, afraid of hearing something hard on the character of his old master, said, with some solemnity, " Mr. Moises, I am certain, was a most respectable man." " That may be," cried Boniface, " but he married me to the worst wife that ever man was plagued with." " Oh! is that all? that was your own fault; she was your own choice, not Mr. Moises'." " Yes," concluded he, unconvinced—" but I could not have been married if there had not been a parson to marry us."

Lord Eldon had not quite as high a respect for " trial by jury" as Lord Erskine. He said, " I remember Mr. Justice Gould trying a cause at York, and when he had proceeded for about two hours, he observed, ' Here are only eleven jurymen; where is the twelfth?' ' Please you, my Lord,' said one of the eleven, ' he is gone away about some business, but he has left his verdict with me.' "[1] —Once, when leaving Newcastle, after a very successful assize, a farmer rode up to him, and said, " Well, lawyer Scott, I was glad that you carried the day so often; and if I had had my way, you should never once have been beaten. I was foreman of the jury, and you were sure of my vote, for you are my countryman, and we are proud of you."

Mr. Scott was now very prosperous. His " OPINIONS " contained so many " ifs," and " buts," and " thoughs," that the solicitors seldom laid cases before him,—while Kenyon, giving direct answers which could be acted upon, was making, by case-answering alone, £3,000 a year. He was, however, a zealous and not too scrupulous advocate, and from his circuit and town practice he began to count a yearly saving, which at length accumulated into a princely fortune. Still he was fond of grumbling. Giving an account of a sinecure of £400 a year, which his brother William had got in Doctors' Commons, the future Chancellor despondingly adds, " As to your humble servant, I have the younger brother's portion, a life of drudgery; our part of the profession has no places for young men, and it will wear me out before I cease to be such."

[1] This, after all, is pretty much like voting by proxy in a certain deliberative assembly; although there the fiction is, that the peer holding the proxy votes according to his own conscience; and holding two proxies, if he votes on opposite sides (as he may), he is supposed suddenly to have changed his opinion.

To relieve his melancholy at this period of his career, although he despised the sweetest warblings of Italian song, he would go on a Saturday night to witness the triumph of the histrionic art at Drury Lane Theater. "You will see," says he, in a letter to a friend, "the papers are full of accounts of a Mrs. Sidons,[1] a new actress. She is beyond all idea capital. I never saw an actress before. In my notion of just affecting action and elocution, she beats our deceased Roscius all to nothing."[2]—But excitement more congenial to him was at hand.

Though he wore a stuff gown, he was rapidly getting into the lead, and was throwing worthy plodders, who were his seniors, out of business. Therefore a silk gown was offered to him without solicitation. The moving cause to the promotion which now took place was the wish to advance Erskine, who had lately so much astonished the world by his eloquence, and was a special favorite with the reigning Administration. An attempt was made to place him at the head of the batch; but Mr. Scott, who was his senior, resolutely resisted this arrangement, and obtained a patent of precedence, which preserved his relative rank among those who took their places within the bar along with him.[3]

CHAPTER CXCIV.

CONTINUATION OF THE LIFE OF LORD ELDON TILL HE WAS MADE SOLICITOR GENERAL.

HITHERTO the successful lawyer had cautiously avoided mixing at all in party politics. He was known to be a good Oxford Tory, of genuine Church-and-King principles, which he did not seek to disguise; but in the struggles between Lord North and the Whigs, or between the different sections of the Whigs, after the death of Lord Rockingham, he had outwardly shown no interest—prudently devoting himself to his profession, without giving offense to any one. Corresponding with his brothers during the American war, he showed that he had a poor opinion of the Ministry, but thought

[1] *Sic.* [2] Surtees, p. 76. [3] Vide antè, Ch. CLXXVIII.

much worse of Opposition. When the intelligence arrived of the surrender of General Burgoyne and his army, he wrote to Henry: "You could not be more deeply concerned for the fate of the gallant Burgoyne, than were your two brothers and your sister. We mingled our tears for two days together, being English folks of the old stamp, and retaining, in spite of modern patriotism, some affection and reverence for the name of Old England. All people whose hearts lie in the same direction are extremely concerned. It is totally unknown, even to themselves, what the Ministry will do. I think they want common sense and common spirit, as much as the minority wants common honesty." He highly approved the sentiments, and he implicitly followed the advice, soon after communicated to him in a letter from Sir William: " For my own part, I am sick of politics—there is so much folly on the part of Ministers, and so much villainy on the other side, under the cloak of patriotism, that an honest man has nothing to do but to lament the fate of his country, and butter his own bread as well as he can. And I hope you take care to do so." Thus, in great perplexity, he expresses himself on the formation of Lord Shelburne's Administration: "We seem here to think that Charles Fox can't get in again, and that Lord Shelburne can not keep in, and that Lord North may rule the roast again whenever he pleases. I like the language of Lord North, better than that of any other man or set of men in the House, upon the subject of peace: all parties but his seem to be struggling who can give up most of the old rights of Old England."

However, when the "inglorious peace" had been censured by a vote of the House of Commons, and the "Coalition" had stormed the royal closet, Lord Thurlow, leading the Opposition, with the zealous aid of the King, urged Mr. Scott to enlist as a recruit under his banner,—arguing that, on public grounds, the Crown ought to be supported,—and pointing out the ambitious prospects which must open to him if he became a "King's friend," as soon as his Majesty should be rescued from the bondage to which his Majesty had been reduced, but which his Majesty was determined not to bear. A regard for prin ciple and for personal advantage recommended the proposal to one so much attached to the King and to himself,

—and he yielded. The ex-Chancellor undertook to procure him a seat in the House of Commons, and speedily succeeded through Lord Weymouth, owner of the borough of Weobly,—now, alas! disfranchised.¹ A stipulation being easily made, that "his conduct in parliament should be entirely independent of Lord Weymouth's political opinions,"—which corresponded exactly with his own,—he posted down to Weobly with the *congé d' élire* in his pocket, and, according to ancient custom, he proceeded to the house that contained the prettiest girl in the place, and began his canvass by giving her a kiss. At the hustings, the ceremony of election was to have been quietly gone through as usual, but he was addressed by a very old man, who said, with a true Herefordshire accent, " We hear how as you be a la'er, and if so be, you ought to tip us a speech—a thing not heard in Weobly this thirty year; and the more especially as Lord Surey has been telling the folks at Hereford as you be a Newcastle-upon-Tyne gentleman, sent down by a peer, and not having no connection with this here place." Lord Eldon gave the following good-humored account of the fresh effort he was driven to make as a mob orator—when he seems to have succeeded much better than in his native town.

" I got upon a heap of stones, and made them as good a speech upon politics in general as I could, and it had either the merit or demerit of being a long one. My audience liked it, on account, among other things, of its length. I concluded by drawing their attention to Lord Surrey's speech. I admitted that I was unknown to them. I said that I had explained my public principles, and how I meant to act in Parliament; that I should do all I had promised; and that, though then unknown to them, I hoped I should entitle myself to more of their confidence and regard than I could have claimed, if, being the son of the first Duke in England, I had held myself out as a reformer while riding, as the Earl of Surrey rode,

¹ I have already pointed out,* and I will not again dwell upon, the palpable misrepresentation of Lord Eldon respecting Fox's wish to have had Thurlow for Chancellor to the Coalition Ministry.† I must say, that on various occasions in Lord Eldon's old age his memory had failed him, or he conceived himself justified in using considerable liberties with truth.

* Life of Lord Thurlow, Vol. VII. Ch. CLVIII.   † Twiss, i. 100.

into the first town of the county, drunk, upon a cider cask, and talking, in that state, of 'reform.' My audience liked the speech, and I ended, as I had begun, by kissing the prettiest girl in the place;—very pleasant, indeed. Lord Surrey had often been my client, even at that early period of my life. He had heard of, or read my speech; and, when I met him afterwards in town, he good-humoredly said, 'I have had enough of meddling with you; I shall trouble you no more.'"

Of course he was returned without opposition. He took his seat before the prorogation of Parliament, but reserved his maiden speech till the ensuing session.

Then came the most deadly struggle recorded in our party annals. As I have already had occasion to state, Scott and Erskine, the hopes of the opposite parties, spoke for the first time in the debate on Fox's India Bill,—and both egregiously failed.[1] The Honorable Member for Weobly very characteristically required "more time to make up his mind upon the measure," but "was nevertheless clear to say that it seemed to him rather of a dangerous tendency; but he would not declare against it; he would rather wait till he got more light thrown upon the subject; and as he was attached to no particular party, he would then vote as justice seemed to direct. He meant hereafter to give an opinion upon the Bill; he could assure the House he would form it elaborately, and when he gave it, it should be an honest one."[2] Mr. Fox good-naturedly paid a compliment to the new member's professional reputation, but "could not refrain from remarking on his inconsistency; for, after stating the necessity for time to deliberate on the Bill, he had immediately, without any opportunity for deliberation, ventured to pronounce a decision against it, and with a good deal of positiveness."

To repair his misfortune, Scott formed the most insane scheme that ever entered the mind of a sensible man. He resolved, in the debate on the third reading of the Bill, to be revenged on Fox, by imitating the manner of Sheridan, and becoming witty and sarcastic. Accordingly, from a volume of Elegant Extracts, a new edition of Joe Miller, and the Bible, he crammed himself with quotations, jokes, and texts, as laboriously as if he had been preparing

[1] See Life of Erskine, Vol. VII. Ch. CLXVIII.   [2] 23 Parl. Hist. 1239.

to argue a case upon a contingent remainder before the twelve Judges. He began, however, *more suo*, by alluding to certain insinuations, "that agreeably to the common conduct of lawyers, he would not scruple to espouse any cause which he should be paid to defend. In the warmest terms he reprobated such unworthy imputations: he asserted the reluctance of his nature to such practices, and he declared that on this occasion he considered it his duty to deliver his sentiments—the solemn sentiments of his heart and conscience." Then, without having at all prepared his audience for the transition, he came to his *facetiæ*, and alluding to the popular caricature upon Mr. Fox as "CARLO KHAN," he affected to speak very courteously of the Whig chief, and observed, "As Brutus said of Cæsar—

> . . . . 'he would be crown'd !
> How that might change his nature,—there's the question.'"

In a moment the orator plunged into Scripture, saying, "It was an aggravation of the affliction that the cause of it should originate with one to whom the nation had so long looked up; a wound from him was doubly painful. Like Joab, he gave the shake of friendship, but the other hand held a dagger with which he dispatched the Constitution." He next pulled a New Testament from his pocket; and, after a proper apology for again alluding to anything recorded in sacred writ, read some verses in different chapters of the book of Revelation, which seemed to express the intended innovations in the affairs of the East India Company: "And I stood upon the sand of the sea, and saw a beast rise out of the sea, having seven heads and ten horns, and upon his horns ten crowns. And they worshiped the dragon which gave power to the beast ; and they worshiped the beast, saying, Who is like unto the beast? Who is able to make war with him? And there was given to him a mouth speaking great things; and power was given unto him to continue forty and two months." ["Here," said Mr. Scott, "I believe there is a mistake of six months."¹] "And he causeth all, both small and great, rich and poor, to receive a mark in their right hand, or in their forehead." [Here places, pensions, and peerages are clearly marked out.] "And he cried

---

¹ The Bill was to be in force only for three years,—*thirty-six* instead of *forty-two* months.

mightily with a strong voice, saying Babylon the Great" [plainly the East India Company] "is fallen, and is become the habitation of devils, the hold of every foul spirit, and the cage of every unclean bird." Having at great length continued to read these prophecies, and to show their fulfillment, he came to Thucydides, where the Athenian ambassadors observe to the Lacedæmonian magistrates, that "men are much more provoked by injustice than violence, inasmuch as injustice coming as from an equal, has the appearance of dishonesty, while mere violence, proceeding from one stronger, seems but the effect of inevitable necessity." Steering from grave to gay, and throwing in some Oxford puns, he anticipated that the new Kings, who were to supersede the directors, might in their turn be pronounced inadequate to the government of so remote a country; "and then," said he—

. . . . . "de te
Fabula narratur."

He at last concluded by pathetically comparing the Directors of the East India Company to the wife of Othello, about to be murdered in her bed: "They cry out for some respite,—they plead, like Desdemona, 'Kill me to-morrow—let me live to-night—but half-an-hour.' When that prayer was rejected, a deed was done which was repented too late."[1]

The House seems to have listened with much amazement to this pedantic jumble of profane and scriptural, humorous and pathetic, quotations from the mouth of a lawyer. But he was the cause of wit in other men, and much merriment followed in allusions to him during the remainder of the debate. Sheridan, in particular, feeling that his province was invaded, is said to have been cruelly severe upon legal oratory: but, luckily for our order, all that the "Parliamentary History" records is, that "he cited, with most happy ease and correctness, passages from almost the same pages—which controverted these quotations, and told strongly for the Bill; he quoted three more verses from the Revelation, by which he metamorphosed the beast with seven heads with crowns on them, into seven angels clothed in pure and white linen."[2]

Mr. Scott was sadly chagrined by the result of his attempt to be lively; and henceforth, reading the Bible

[1] 24 Parl. Hist. 33. [2] Ib. 51.

only for spiritual edification, he renounced the other books which he had quoted, and all such trumpery, for the rest of his days. In his parliamentary efforts he trusted thenceforward to legal learning, metaphysical subtlety, strong good sense, and frequent appeals to his conscience. He never acquired the fame of a good debater, but he sometimes spoke with considerable weight and effect, and he was a useful ally in both Houses of Parliament.

The Coalition Ministry being dissolved on the rejection of Fox's India Bill in the House of Lords, and Mr. Pitt being Prime Minister, it was thought legal promotion was now open to Mr. Scott; and it is believed that Lord Thurlow, on recovering the Great Seal, made an effort to have him made Solicitor General. But Mr. Pitt insisted on appointing Pepper Arden, saying that "the member for Weobly,—for whom he professed much respect, notwithstanding his quotations,—must be contented to take his turn in professional promotion after his seniors."

Although the party to which Mr. Scott had attached himself was, by a combination of lucky chances, and by the splendid talents of its chief, firmly possessed of power, he had been five years in Parliament before he attained office; which ought to soften the discontent of young lawyers, who are apt to think that they are ill-used, and to despond, if they are not made law officers of the Crown, or Judges as soon as they are returned to the House of Commons. During this interval he steadily supported the Government, although he once or twice followed a course which prudence as well as conscience, recommends, by showing that he could form an opinion of his own, and that, if not properly appreciated by the Minister, he might become a formidable antagonist.

He gallantly combated the motion of the Coalitionists to stop the supplies when the King refused to dismiss his Ministers on the Address of the House of Commons, saying, "I advise Ministers not to think of a resignation: at present they have the people on their side,—many of whom, in petitions to the Throne, speak very different language from that of their representatives in this House."[1]

[1] 24 Parl. Hist. 616.

As the struggle proceeded, the King and the Premier becoming daily more popular, and public indignation being strongly roused against Mr. Fox and Lord North, the time was come—which had been wisely "*bided*"—for an appeal to the people. While this was expected, Mr. Scott wrote to his friends at Newcastle: "No dissolution to-day; life promised by Pitt till Monday, and no longer promised; but whether to be enjoyed, doubtful. Both our Newcastle members voted against us last night; but the majority, you see, crumbles; and if it was not for North's myrmidons, which he bought with the Treasury money, we should have a complete triumph. I told the Chancellor to-day, that he ought to resign, or dismiss us. But what will be done, or what will become of the country, God knows. I have the offer of two other seats in Parliament *gratis;* but I shall keep my old one."[1]

Accordingly, on the general election, he was again returned for Weobly; and, close as the borough was, he was obliged to show himself there—leaving his briefs and fees at the Lancaster Assizes--which he said "he could ill afford,"—although he must now have been in the receipt of a large professional income.

The first occasion of his speaking in the new Parliament was on the Westminster scrutiny—when he justly gained great credit. The election for this city, instead of being over in one day, according to our fashion, had lasted from the 1st of April to the 16th of May, the day on which Parliament was summoned to meet; and although Mr. Fox ought clearly to have been returned, the High Bailiff, from corrupt motives, at the request of Sir Cecil Wray, granted a scrutiny. This proceeding was most improperly countenanced by Mr. Pitt and the majority now at his command. But in the month of March in the following year the scrutiny had made little progress, and there seemed a strong probability that before it was concluded Parliament would be dissolved. The case was so flagrant, that after several divisions, on which the numbers in favor of the Government gradually lessened, a resolution was carried, ordering the High Bailiff to make an immediate return,—and this Mr. Fox followed up with a motion, that all the former proceedings respecting the scrutiny should be expunged from the Journals. The motion was supported

[1] Twiss, i. 113.

by Mr. Scott, against whose prior votes on this subject some sarcasms were leveled. He seems to have taken a most masterly view of the whole subject, although the printed report of his speech is so defective that we can form but an inadequate notion of its merit. From the principles of the common law, and the statutes for regulating elections since the reign of Henry VI. down to that of George III., he deduced the doctrine, " That the election must be *finally* closed before the return of the writ, and that the writ must be returned on or before the day specified in it : "—

"At the same time," he added, "that I condemn the scrutiny, I should be sorry to be supposed to impute improper motives to those who have voted for it. I am willing to give them credit for purity of intention; they were wrong only in judgment. They had a very unnecessary tenderness for the conscience of the High Bailiff, which they say they would not torture by compelling him to make a return before he should have thoroughly scrutinized his poll; but surely his oath does not bind him to anything more than to make his return to the best of his judgment, in the time which the law allowed him to satisfy his conscience. To make him do this speedily, is no more to torture his conscience, than you torture the conscience of jurymen by compelling them to find their verdict before they are permitted to eat, or drink, or warm themselves at a fire. Indeed, the prompt obedience he has paid to the order of the House, communicated to him in consequence of the vote of last week, shows that his conscience is not of the most delicate texture; for, as it would have been tyrannical in the House to attempt to force his conscience, so it would have been unchristian in him to violate his conscience merely to obey an unjust order. But he did not require, it seems, much time to make up his mind when the House commanded him. Why, then, should he not have paid as prompt an obedience to the mandate of the King's writ ? I confess I do not like that conscience in returning-officers, under color of which they may prevent the meeting of Parliament forever, or at least present the nation with the rump of a Parliament on the day when the representatives of the whole nation ought to assemble."

He was not only listened to with the marked attention

which any member speaking against his party is sure to command, but his playfulness on "*conscience*" exceedingly tickled his hearers, and he sat down amid loud shouts of applause from the Opposition benches.[1] Mr. Fox, commenting on the speeches of the different speakers who had taken part in the debate, said, 'One learned gentlemen in particular (the honorable member for Weobly) has entered into the whole of the case, with a soundness of argument, and a depth and closeness of reasoning, that perhaps has scarcely been equaled in the discussion of any topic within these walls, that turned on the statute and common law, on the analogy of writs, and the combination of technical and constitutional learning. So well and so ably, indeed, has that learned gentleman argued it, that nothing like an answer has been offered to any one of his appeals to his brethren of the long robe. In truth, I am convinced it is out of the power of ingenuity itself to overthrow the positions laid down by that learned gentleman—to whom I will offer no apology for any allusion I may have made to him on a former day ; and I consider myself peculiarly happy in having been able to say anything that could draw forth so masterly and instructive a speech." Mr. Scott found himself in a minority of 137 against 242 ; but he enhanced his importance with the Minister by this instance of independence, and he secured respectful treatment from the leader of Opposition. Towards the close of his life he observed, 'Fox never said an uncivil word to me during the whole time I sat in the House of Commons; and I tell you to what I attribute that. When the legality of the conduct of the High Bailiff of Westminster was before the House, all the lawyers on the Ministerial side defended his right to grant the scrutiny. I thought their law bad, and I told them so. I asked Kenyon how he could answer *this*,— that every writ or commission must be returned on the day on which it is made returnable? He could not answer it. Fox afterwards came to me, and said something very civil and obliging."[1]

Mr. Scott, immediately after this *escapade*, returned to his allegiance to Mr. Pitt—from which he never again swerved. He still considered himself, however, as more particularly under the auspices of Lord Thurlow, to whom

[1] 25 Parl. Hist. 120. [1] Twiss, i. 121.

he owed his seat, and who evinced a strong desire to push him forward. For this reason he warmly espoused the cause of Warren Hastings, and made a speech in his favor on the very serious charge of the Rohilla war. In concluding, he alluded, with just severity, to an observation made the preceding day by Mr. Fox, who had said "that he would always watch gentlemen of the profession of the law in their arguments." Mr. Fox now very handsomely declared, "that none but a fool or a madman would disparage or despise the legal profession. He had a very high regard for it, and for the learned gentleman in particular, whose great abilities and high character entitled him to universal respect. He assured the House and the learned gentleman, that he meant nothing more by saying that 'he would watch the arguments of gentlemen of that profession,' than the gentlemen of the law, from being in the habits of a peculiar style of reasoning, were apt to infuse that style into their arguments in that House."[1]

In the following session of Parliament, Mr. Scott spoke ably in defense of the principles of free trade in supporting the commercial treaty with France against the very unjust and illiberal attacks of the Whigs. Having charged them with having had a similar plan in contemplation when they were in office, he said, "I am happy that the measure is now accomplished in a manner which promises a great accession of wealth to England, and holds out the most liberal encouragement to her artisans,—whose industry, skill, and perseverance, joined to their prodigious capital, must ever insure them superiority over all competitors."[2]

He now received his first judicial appointment, being named by Bishop Thurlow Chancellor of the County Palatine of Durham. He therefore ceased to attend the assizes at Durham as a counsel, and presided in his own Court with all proper solemnity. Here he was very little troubled with equity business. We only know of one case which came before him, and that was not *contentious;* but he made the most of it. Upon an application to direct an allowance to a minor, then at college, who would be entitled, when of age, to an income of about £300 a year, he thus addressed the ward of the Court:—
"Young gentleman, you will shortly become entitled

[1] 25 Parl. Hist. 58. [2] 26 Parl. Hist. 505.

to a small property, which may prove to you either a blessing or a curse, according as you use it. It was, perhaps, fortunate for me that I was not situated in my early life as you are now. I had not, like you, a small fortune to look to; I had nothing to depend on but my own exertions: and, so far from considering this a misfortune, I now esteem it a blessing; for if I had possessed the same means which you will enjoy, I should in all probability not be where I now am. I would therefore caution you not to let this little property turn your mind from more important objects, but rather let it stimulate you to cultivate your abilities, and to advance yourself in society."

Mr. Pitt, for some mysterious reason, having suddenly abandoned Hastings, and—contrary to the wish of Lord Thurlow, who had a scheme for making him a Peer, perhaps a Minister—having given him up to impeachment, Mr. Scott took no part in the subsequent proceedings against him;[1] but he resolutely defended Sir Elijah Impey, charged with having illegally hanged the great Brahmin, Nuncomar; and he struggled against the attempts to prejudice the cause of the accused Judge by the admission of improper evidence,—enlarging on the necessity for adhering to the rules of law in all proceedings in any sort tending to a judicial determination. In consequence, Mr. Fox, in a tone very unusual with him, "attacked the lawyers with a good deal of warmth and asperity, for coming down in a body to juggle and confound the members of that House."[2]

Mr. Scott, before he was Solicitor General, chiefly made himself prominent in the House of Commons by speaking in favor of a bill—which caused much excitement at the time, but has now lost all interest—for declaring "that the East India Company, according to the just construction of the India Bill, 24 Geo. 3, c. 25, was liable to repay to the Government at home the charges of sending a military force to the East Indies." Erskine, then out of Parliament, was heard at the bar of the House of Commons, as counsel for the Company, and strongly animadverted on certain arguments of Mr. Scott to prove

[1] I have not been able to ascertain even how he voted on the Benares charge, when Mr. Pitt went over so abruptly that his own Attorney General would not follow him. [2] 27 Parl. Hist. 37, 38.

the liability of his clients, contending that, at all events, the Legislature was here usurping judicial functions, and that the question ought to be decided by a Court of law. —Mr. Scott, on several occasions, defended his opinion, and insisted that this was a fit occasion for Parliament, by a declaratory Act, to pronounce what its intentions really were. Mr. Sheridan, Colonel Barré, and other Opposition members, furiously assailed the arguments of the honorably and learned member for Weobly in this controversy;—but the position he had acquired in the House may best be estimated from the labored attack upon him by Mr. Francis (pretty generally supposed to be Junius), in which the orator, with much unmerited abuse of the individual and his order, animadverts with some felicity on his inveterate habit of lauding his own honesty:—

" This is not a legislative question, and it is absurd for Parliament to ask lawyers what it meant by its own act and deed? In this House, to be sure, we have every assistance that learning and practice can afford. We have a learned person (Mr. John Scott) among us, who is universally acknowledged to be the great luminary of the law, whose opinions are oracles, to whose skill and authority all his own profession look up with reverence and amazement. Well, Sir, what information have we gained from that most eminent person? I will not attempt to follow or repeat so long, and, as I have been told, so ingenious an argument. Ingenuity, it seems, is the quality which is chiefly wanted and relied on, on the present occasion. But I well remember the course of it. The first half hour of his speech, at least, was dedicated to himself. He told us who he was: he explained to us, very distinctly, the whole of his moral character, which I think was not immediately in question; and assured the House that his integrity was the thing on which he valued himself most and which we might with perfect security rely on. Of his learning, I confess he spoke with more than moderation—with excessive humility. He almost stultified himself, for the purpose of proving his integrity. For the sake of his morality, he abandoned his learning; and seemed to dread the conclusions that might be drawn from an overrated opinion of his excessive skill and cunning in his profession. In my mind, Sir, there was no occasion for this extraordinary parade. The learned gentleman's

reputation in private life, I believe, is unimpeached.
What we wanted, what we expected of him, was his learning, not his character. At fist, however, he proceeded to the subject of debate. Here we were all in profound silence: attention held us mute. Did he answer your expectation? Did you perfectly understand him? Did he perfectly understand himself? I doubt it much. If he had understood, he could have explained himself to the meanest capacity. If you had distinctly understood him, you might distinctly remember what he said. Now, setting aside those who have been initiated in the mysteries of the profession, is there a man here who can remember and is able to state the learned gentleman's arguments?— I believe not. For my own part, though it is impossible for me to listen with more attention than I did, I confess I soon lost sight of him. At first, indeed, he trifled with the subject, in a manner that was intelligible at least, perhaps dexterous, though not conclusive. He argued some little collateral points with a good deal of artifice; he made many subtle argumentative distinctions; he tried at least to involve us in nice, logical difficulties, and to drive us *ad absurdum* by what he called unavoidable inferences, from false premises. In short, he attacked or defended some of the outposts of the questions, with what I suppose is held to be great ability in Westminster Hall. He skirmished well at a proper distance from the main body of the subject. All this I acknowledge. But when he came at last to the grand point, at which we had waited for him so long, at which we had impatiently expected the predominant light of his superior learning,— the decision of the oracle,—did he resolve your doubts? Did he untie, or did he cut, the Gordian knot? Did he prove to you, in that frank, plain, popular way in which he ought to have addressed this popular assembly, and which he would have done if he had been sure of his ground,—did he demonstrate to you, that the Act of 1784, clearly and evidently, or even by unavoidable construction, gave the power declared by the present Bill? Sir, he did no such thing. If he did, let us hear it once more. He who understands can remember. He who remembers can repeat. I defy any man living, not a lawyer, to recite even the substance of that part of his argument. The truth is, he left the main question exactly where he found

it. So it generally happens. It belongs to the learning of these genetlemen and to their prudence not to decide. It is so now. It was so 2,000 years ago."—Having given an account of the consultation in T.erence, after which the old gentleman who had desired the opinion of three lawyers on the validity of his son's marriage, exclaimed *Incertior sum multo quam dudum*, he continued, "Well may the Court of Directors,—well may this House make the same observation on the present occasion. In the name of God and common sense, what have we gained by consulting these learned persons? It is really a strange thing, but it is certainly true, that the learned gentlemen on that side of the House, let the subject be what it may, always begin their speeches with a panegyric on their own integrity. You expect learning, and they give you morals; you expect law, and they give you ethics; you ask them for bread, and they give you a stone. In point of honor and morality, they are undoubtedly on a level with the rest of mankind. But why should they pretend to more? Why should they insist on taking the lead in morality? Why should they so perpetually insist upon their integrity as if that objection were *in limine*, as if that were the distinguishing characteristic, the prominent feature, of the profession? Equality is their right. I allow it. But that they have any just right to a superior morality, to a pure and elevated probity, to a frank, plain, simple, candid, unrefined integrity, beyond other men, is what I am not yet convinced of, and without new and unexpected proofs never will admit." [1]

The Bill was sure to be carried by the overwhelming majorities which the Minister commanded, but the credit of the Government on this occasion was mainly supported by Mr. Scott—the Attorney and Solicitor General not having any weight in the House.

The expected promotion in the law had been long delayed by intrigues respecting the appointment to the offices of Chief Justice of the King's Bench and Master of the Rolls, but at last, on the resignation of Lord Mansfield, Sir Lloyd Kenyon succeeded him,—Pepper Arden, in spite of Thurlow, was made Master of the Rolls,—and Sir Archibald Macdonald being promoted to be Attorney

[1] 27 Parl. Hist. 263. For Mr. Scott's speeches on this subject, see 27 Parl. Hist. 37, 86, 186, 196.

General, John Scott, Esq., was, to the high contentment of the Bar, and the general satisfaction of the public, appointed Solicitor General.

There were great rejoicings at Newcastle, particularly when the good folks there knew that their townsman had become SIR JOHN. He modestly wished to avoid knighthood, but George III. then laid down a rule, which has been adhered to ever since, that the Attorney and Solicitor General, and the Judges, if not " honorable " by birth, shall be knighted,—to keep up the reputation of the ancient order of Knights-bachelors,—and the ceremony ought to be cheerfully undergone by them, as an accompaniment of professional promotion. On this occasion, Macdonald, who, though Solicitor General for some years, had remained " plain Archy," now knelt and rose SIR ARCHIBALD.

Sir John Scott gave an amusing account of his elevation in the following letter to his brother Henry:—

"DEAR HARRY,

"I kissed the King's hand yesterday as Solicitor General. The King, in spite of my teeth, laid his sword upon my shoulder, and bid *Sir John* arise. At this last instance of his royal favor, I have been much disconcerted; but I can not help myself, so I sing—

' Oho, the delight
To be a gallant knight !'

"I was completely taken in, having no idea that the King had any such intention. My wife is persecuted with her new title, and we laugh at her from morning till evening. —Be so good as with my best love to communicate this intelligence to my brother and sisters. Bessy joins in affection to your wife and Mary, and I am

"Yours faithfully,
"J. SCOTT." [1]

He had to go through the form of a re-election for Weobly, and he again treated the electors with a speech, in which he assured them that, "though in office under the Crown, he would continue to be a faithful guardian of the rights and liberties of the people."—The session of Parliament was closed almost immediately after he resumed his seat in the House of Commons, and there was an unexampled cessation of all political excitement. The

[1] Twiss i. 131.

Whig party seemed for ever annihilated; its leaders, still laboring under the unpopularity they had incurred by the "Coalition," had almost entirely ceased to offer any show of opposition to the measures of Government,—and the country, rapidly advancing in wealth and prosperity after the disasters of the American war, hailed the choice of the Sovereign as a "heaven-born minister." There was likewise profound peace abroad, and England was respected and courted by all foreign nations.

It was expected that the new law officer, till in due gradation he was raised to the Bench, would never have any more anxious duty to perform than to sign a patent of peerage, or to prosecute a smuggler in the Court of Exchequer.

In the absence of all official business, he took the very unusual step of going the round of the Northern Circuit —although professional etiquette has always been understood to require that a barrister, being appointed Attorney or Solicitor General, shall immediately gave up his circuit —which often produces great peril, and sometimes serious loss, when the administration which he joins is in a state of caducity. But I do not find that any complaint was made on this occasion, as when Mr. Wedderburn first joined the circuit with a silk gown. There was not even an "Information of Intrusion" filed against Sir John Scott by the Attorney General in the Grand Court, and he ever continued on the best terms with all his professional brethren. He took final leave of the circuit at Lancaster, but for the rest of his days his great delight was to talk of the "Grand Court,"—and we shall see that when he was ex-Chancellor a new generation of circuiteers took occasion to testify unabated regard for him.[1]

[1] By a special grace (passed unanimously at a Grand Court held at York on the 12th of July, 1847, for which I am most deeply grateful), I have had access to the Records of the Northern Circuit, and I extract from them some interesting entries respecting Lord Eldon:—

"York Grand Night, Sat. Mar. 16, 1782.

"Mr. Atty. Gen. Scott* mention'd, that he had no sooner arriv'd in York than a play-bill was put into his hands, in which, to his great astonishment, he found the respectable names of many of his brethren on the Circuit. The play of the Clandestine Marriage was to be performed for the benefit of Mr. Back. Mr. Smith was to lay aside the peaceful gown and array himself in a

* He had been appointed Attorney General to the Circuit, with the duty of prosecuting all offenses before the Grand Court presided over by our Lord the Junior.

CHAPTER CXCV.

CONTINUATION OF THE LIFE OF LORD ELDON TILL HE BECAME ATTORNEY GENERAL.

NEVER was there in England such a sudden change in the aspect of public affairs as in the autumn of this year: scarcely had the Solicitor General returned to London, contemplating an indefinite prolongation of ease and office, when he found himself involved in military habit; and a very distinguishable and conspicuous part was to be perform'd by Mr. Taylor, who appear'd there in his proper character, not as the two former gentlemen, in such a masquerade dress that Mr. Atty. Gen. cou'd not produce any witness who cou'd take upon him to swear to the identity of their persons, but Mr. Law being called upon, depos'd that he saw Mr. Taylor appear on the stage in his bar wig acting the part of Counselor Traverse in the Clandestine Marriage, and tho' Mr. Taylor acted the Counselor then, as he always does, in an inimitable manner, yet the Court was of opinion that, by appearing on the stage in that habit, he rather lessen'd the Dignity of the Wig, and therefore fin'd him 1 Bottle. p^d.

"Mr. Arden* in a speech this morning had made use of the following expressions,—'No man wou'd be such a damn'd fool as to go to a lawyer for advice who knew how to act without it.' In this he was consider'd as doubly culpable—in the first place as having offended against the laws of Almighty God by his profane cursing, for which however he made a very sufficient atonement by paying a bottle of claret; and, secondly, as having made use of an expression which, if it shou'd become a prevailing opinion, might have the most alarming consequences to the profession, and was therefore deservedly consider'd in a far more heinous light: for this last offense he was fin'd 3 Bottles. p^d."

"Mr. Scott laid Mr. Davenport 5 guineas that Lord Ashburton† will be Chief Justice of the King's Bench before he dies. The bet was made at York in the presence of Mr. Withers, but not being communicated to the Junior at that time, he had no opportunity of recording it sooner."

"Lancaster Grand Night, Saturday, 29th March, 1783.

"Jno. Scott, Esqr., for having come into Lancaster the day before the Commission day, and having taken up his abode that evening at the King's Arms in Lancaster, fined one gallon, p^d. £1. 1s."

"York Grand Night, Thursday, 7th August, 1783.

	£.	s.	d.
'Mr. J. Scott was congratulated on his Patent of Precedence, 2 gall^s. p^d.		2	2	0
"Mr. J. Scott was also congratulated on his Election for Weobly, 1 gal. p^d.		1	1	0

* Pepper Arden, afterwards Master of the Rolls and Lord Alvanley.
† Dunning.

the most tremendous political crisis that had occured since the Revolution of 1688—with almost a certainty of being immediately turned adrift with all his party. The rumors spread of the King's aberration of mind were unhappily confirmed by his Majesty's demeanor at a levee, which he insisted on holding in the end of October : and on the 20th of November, the day to which parliament stood prorogued, the royal authority was in complete abeyance, his Majesty's intellect being much disturbed, and his person being under restraint.

"Lancaster Grand Night, 27 March, 1785.
"Mr. Serg^t. Bolton rose and moved (having first prefaced his motion with an eloquent address to the Court), 'that John Scott, Esq., be congratulated in a bottle on his lively expectations of succeeding to a Directorship in the East India Company'—ordered accordingly—p^d. 1 bottle.
"John Scott, Esqr. having pleaded guilty to a charge exhibited against him by an honble and learned member, of having condescended (in derogation of the honor of this Court, and in contempt of its great authority) to ask leave of absence of the House of Commons, was fined 1 gll^n. paid.
"Ordered accordingly."

"Lent Assizes, Lancaster Grand Night, 1 April, 1786.
"Mr. Scott for having debased himself so much as to ask leave of the House of Commons to attend this Circuit, was fined 1 gallon, p^d."

"Mr. J. Scott having been appointed Chancellor of Durham, was congratulated thereupon by the title of 'HIS HONOR,' in 3 gallons: by consent, p^d.
"Mr. Lee, as a suitor to His Honor's Court, was congratulated on the security of his title to his estate under the administration of His Honor. 1 gall. p^d."

"Lancaster Grand Night, Augt. 6th, 1788.
"The Soll^r. Genl., J. P. Heywood, rose and mov'd that Sir John Scott, Kn^t., Soll^r. Genl. to his Majesty, might be congratulated on his appointment to the high office of Soll^r. Genl., and on his being made a Kn^t.,—that he might be condoled with for having lost his seat in Parl^t.,—and congratulated on his re-election.

	£.	s.	d.
"He was accordingly congrat^d. on his being made Soll^r. Genl.	2	2	0 p^d.
Knighted, ...	2	2	0 p^d.
Condoled with for the loss of his seat in Parl^t. .	1	1	0 p^d.
Congra^d. re-election, ...	1	1	0 p^d.

"S^r. J. Scott then rose, and stated that by ye Act 14 Hen. 8, c. 36, s. 72, he had a right to appoint a chaplain, and that he wished to show every respect to the Court : he there mov'd that the L^d. Bishop* immediately ordain Peters, and that he would sign his nomination. He was immediately ordain'd: a grand procession with flambeaus conducted him round the table to the Bishop."†

---

* The Circuit had then an officer called "Bishop."
† This is the last time Scott appears on the Circuit.

Sir John Scott ably supported the course which the unpopularity of the Heir Apparent and his Whig favorites enabled Mr. Pitt successfully to take on this occasion, contrary (I think) to all the principles of an hereditary monarchy; which was to assert a right in the two Houses of Parliament to elect any person Regent whom they should prefer, with such powers as they should think fit to bestow upon him.—When the resolution embodying this doctrine was moved in the House of Commons,—

" The Solicitor General contended that the King was in contemplation of law as perfect as ever, and the positive right of the Prince of Wales to the regency was in the present case clearly undefined. No precedent, no analogy, could be furnished from the legal records of the Constitution, that established it as a right ; no provision, then, having been made by law in the present conjuncture of affairs, Parliament was called upon to establish a precedent, which the contingency of past ages had not furnished.

On a subsequent day he thus reasoned the question, whether the form should be adopted of putting the Great Seal, during the King's incapacity, to a commission for opening Parliament, and giving the royal assent to the Regency Bills :—

" Will any man dare to express a doubt whether the King sits on the throne or not? For my part I am determined to support the law, because the law supports the King on the throne. The throne is at present full of the Monarch, and no man dares to say that his Majesty is deficient in his natural capacity. I will therefore vote for the Commission upon the simple ground of preserving the forms of the Constitution; and be it remembered that upon the preservation of the forms depends the substance of the Constitution. The parliament held in the first year of Henry VI. was a perfect legislature, consisting of King, Lords, and Commons, although the Seal was put to the Commission for opening it by a babe of nine months old. It has been said, that if the two Houses can thus procure the Royal assent to the Regency Bill, they may proceed to pass other Bills in the same way. But the right which necessity creates, is limited by the same necessity. As a justification of the use of the Great Seal in the King's name, I must observe that, notwithstanding his Majesty's temporary incapacity,—in the eye of the law his politic capacity remains entire. Therefore, there would be no illegality in passing a Regency Bill in his name, and in no other way can a regent be lawfully appointed. The succession to the throne is undoubtedly hereditary, but the wisdom of ages has left it to the two Houses of Parliament to provide for the exercise of the Government on an emergency like this. If a commission had been sealed for opening the Parliament before the two Houses met on the 20th of last month, I am of opinion that it would have been legal.[1] Gentlemen may talk as they please about *legal metaphysics;* the law is as I have explained it. An honorable member has said, 'If you can by putting the Great Seal to a commission make a legislature, why did they not drag the Thames for the Great Seal at the Revolution, and go on passing bills, without calling in William and Mary?' I answer to the honorable member, Let the throne be vacant, and I care not where the Great Seal is! When the throne is vacant, every function of the Executive Government is at an end; the Courts of justice do not sit. But let the House remember that the Courts of justice are now sitting, and the Judges are administering justice in the King's name upon the very maxim that the political capacity of the King is entire. At the Revolution, the throne being vacant, the Great Seal was inoperative, there being no Sovereign in whose name acts of state could be done; but William, the great deliverer of the nation, after the legislature was complete, passed a statute giving legal validity to the proceedings of the two Houses during the interregnum. I conclude with solemnly protesting that the opinion I have given proceeds from principle only—and is uninfluenced by any motive but a regard for the Constitution and a reverence for the wisdom of ages." [2]

When the proposal came to be debated of vesting in the Queen the power of appointing to all the offices in the Household, Sir John Scott said,—

"When gentlemen tell me that by withholding from the Regent the patronage of the Royal Household they would

---

[1] This bold doctrine, which even supersedes the two Houses of Parliament —vesting supreme power in the person who, for the time being, is in possession of the Great Seal, may, perhaps, account for Lord Eldon's conduct on some occasions as Chancellor,—when he put the Great Seal to commissions under warrants signed by the King while in the custody of his medical attendants. [2] 27 Parl. Hist. 825.

be guilty of a breach of the Constitution, let them explain how I am to discharge my allegiance to the Sovereign on the Throne, without taking care that his resumption of his royal authority may be rendered as little difficult as possible. I do not speak with indelicacy towards the Prince of Wales if I show that jealousy which belongs to my character as a member of Parliament—which it is my duty to show to the other branch of the Legislature, and to the Executive Government. If the sense of the people be taken at your bar, or in any other way, the language they would hold would undoubtedly be, ' What! could you not do your duty for three short months? Were you so hasty to dethrone your lawful Sovereign, that you treated him with the grossest disrespect, and stripped him of every mark of regal dignity and distinction, after he had been ill no longer than a month?' Do gentlemen seriously argue that the Regent, with the army, the navy, the Church, and all the offices connected with the public revenue at his command, can not carry on a vigorous and effective government? Where is the integrity of the House, if such arguments are used? Are there no men who will act from the impulse of a higher feeling—from a sense of duty, and from what they owe to their country and to their own character? I ask, is not his Majesty alive, and afflicted with a severe malady?—and is not this a reason for giving him additional attendance, rather than taking away what he before had? It has been said, that to give this patronage to the Queen would be so much influence thrown into the hands of Opposition; but it would be a gross and indecent reflection on that exalted and virtuous personage, to suppose that she would employ her power for the purpose of opposing the government of her son. No plan can be suggested which is not clogged with some evil; but upon my honor, and upon my conscience, that which we are called upon to adopt I sincerely believe the most safe, the most constitutional, and the most expedient."[1]

Finally, on a motion that the Great Seal should be put to a commission for opening Parliament, Mr. Solicitor said,—

"This is the only legal mode of proceeding; the other —that of addressing the Prince to take upon him the

[1] 27 Parl. Hist. 1033.

Regency (a term unknown to the law), is wholly illegal. You must proceed by Act of Parliament; and the Great Seal once put to it gives it all the authority of law, so that no inquiry can be instituted as to the mode in which it has been passed. If letters patent are sealed with the Great Seal, without the King's warrant having been previously granted, —however criminal may be the conduct of the person who has so acted, they are of full force, and bind the King himself as much as if signed with the King's own hand. We are not now discussing a party question, and I know that my opinion is not influenced by any party bias. If the Prince were to accept the regency on an address, he must represent the King in the House of Lords without authority, and he must give the royal assent to a Regency Bill,—thereby appointing himself Regent,—so that he might be exposed to future difficulties from grave questions arising as to his authority. The commission is a fiction, I admit; but there are many fictions of law, and from some of these fictions arise the best security of the rights of the subject. The present may be called a wholesome fiction, inasmuch as it saves the Constitution from danger, and proves this constitution to be so admirably constructed that it contains in itself a provision for every emergency."[1]

Such arguments prevailed in England; although, after the consideration I have repeatedly given to the subject, I must ever think that the Irish Parliament proceeded more constitutionally by considering that the Heir Apparent was entitled to exercise the royal authority during the King's incapacity, as upon a demise of the Crown, and by presenting an address to him, praying him to do so, instead of arrogating to themselves, in Polish fashion, the power of electing the supreme magistrate of the republic, and resorting to the palpable lie of the proceeding being sanctioned by the afflicted Sovereign. While the bill was still pending in the House of Lords, all these speculations were cut short, for this turn, by George's happy recovery.

The disappointed Whigs tried to assuage their grief by ridiculing Sir John Scott, and the others who had fought

[1] 27 Parl. Hist. 1155.

most stoutly against them, in the following *jeu d' esprit*, which they published in the "ROLLIAD :"—

"INCANTATION,

OR RAISING A PHANTOM; IMITATED FROM 'MACBETH,' AND LATELY PERFORMED BY HIS MAJESTY'S SERVANTS IN WESTMINSTER.

Thunder.—A Caldron boiling.

Enter three Witches.

First Witch. Thrice the Doctors have been heard,
Second Witch. Thrice the Houses have conferr'd.
Third Witch. Thrice hath Sydney cock'd his chin,
Jenky cries—Begin, begin.
First Witch. Round about the caldron go,
In the fell ingredients throw.
Still born fœtus, born and bred
In a lawyer's puzzled head,
Hatch'd by ' Metaphysic Scott,'
Boil thou in th' enchanted pot.
All. Double, double toil and trouble;
Fire burn, and caldron bubble.
Second Witch. Skull, that holds the small remains
Of old Camden's addle brains;
Liver of the lily's hue,
Which in Richmond's carcass grew;
Tears which, stealing down the cheek
Of the rugged Thurlow, speak;
All the poignant grief he feels
For his Sovereign—or the Seals;
For a charm of powerful trouble,
Like a hell-broth, boil and bubble.
All. Double, double toil and trouble;
Fire burn, and caldron bubble.
Third Witch. Clippings of Corinthian brass
From the visage of Dundas;
Forg'd address, devis'd by Rose,
Half of Pepper Arden's nose;
Smuggled vote of City thanks,
Promise of insidious Banks;
Add a grain of Rollo's courage,
To inflame the hellish porridge.
First Witch. Cool it with Lloyd Kenyon's blood.
Now the charm is firm and good.
All. Double, double toil and trouble;
Fire burn, and caldron bubble.

Enter HECATE, *Queen of the Witches.*

Hecate. Oh! well done! I commend your pains,
And ev'ry one shall share i' th' gains."

The losing party likewise raised a laugh against their antagonists, by pretending that Lord Belgrave, afterwards Marquis of Westminster, who, on this occasion, declared against them, and quoted, in debate, a passage from the Greek text of Demosthenes, had actually spouted the following line from Homer,—

"Τὸν δ' ἀπαμειβόμενος προσέφη πόδας ὠκὺς Ἀχλλεύς"—

publishing translations of it (for the benefit of the country gentlemen) by those who had chiefly combated the right of the Prince of Wales during the late crisis.

TRANSLATION BY SIR JOHN SCOTT.
" With metaphysic art his speech he plann'd,
And said—what nobody could understand."

However, we have "ANOTHER BY THE CHANCELLOR," in honor of his *protégé* :—

" To him Achilles, with a furious nod,
Replied 'A very pretty speech by —— !'"[1]

The ultra-loyal lawyer was abundantly compensated for all these gibes by a message, some little time afterwards, from George III., requesting a call from him at Windsor. Being ushered into the Royal presence, the King most graciously said to him, "I have no other business with you, Sir John Scott, than to thank you for the affectionate fidelity with which you adhered to me when so many had deserted me, in my malady."[2]

Sir John Scott led a very quiet life from this time for four years,—till he was promoted to be Attorney-General, and the "Reign of Terror" began. During this long interval, he hardly ever had occasion to open his mouth in the House of Commons:—there were no state prosecutions ; and, answering a few Government cases, which could have given him little trouble, he had only to attend to his business in the Court of Chancery. There, those who came next to him were at an immense distance behind him, and his gains must have been enormous.

[1] Rollaid, 20th edition, p. 531.
[2] Lord Eldon used to discredit the report of Thurlow's double-dealing on the late occasion, saying, "I was at the time honored with his intimacy; scarcely a day passed in which there was not much interesting conversation upon that subject between Lord Thurlow and the King's friends, with which I was acquainted, and I do not believe there was a word of truth in the charge." But the truth of it has been established beyond all possibility of contradiction or doubt. (See Vol. VII. Chap. CLX.) I have heard it insinuated that Sir John Scott himself was privy to these intrigues, and had a hope, under Thurlow's auspices, of being Solicitor General to the Regent; but I do not believe that there is any foundation for this. He never seems to have been privy to Thurlow's negotiations with the Whigs ; and I make no doubt that he acted on the occasion of the Regency with entire singleness of purpose. Gratitude made him eager to disbelieve anything to Thurlow's disadvantage, as well as to magnify his good qualities.

Yet he was at great pains to inculcate the doctrine that a
successful barrister is a loser by becoming a law officer of
the Crown; and in the "Anecdote Book" he gives this
account of a dialogue with George III., in which I must
say he seems considerably to have mystified his worthy old
master:—
"Soon after I became Solicitor General, his Majesty
George III., at Weymouth, with the kindness which he
uniformly manifested to me, said, 'Well, I hope your promotion has been beneficial to you?' I asked his Majesty,
if he meant in professional income? He said 'Yes, in
that and in other respects.' I told him, *what was strictly
true*, that in annual receipt I thought I must lose about
two thousand pounds a year. He seemed surprised, and
asked how that could be accounted for? I stated to him
that the attention of his law officers was called to matters
of international law, public law, and the laws of revenue,
and other matters, with which not having been previously
familiar, they were obliged to devote to them a vast deal
of time, and to withdraw it from those other common
matters of business which were very profitable; and I concluded by stating what was then the habit of the solicitors
of the public offices, to give the Solicitor General only
three guineas with his Majesty's (the Government's) cases,
which required more time and attention fully to consider,
and satisfactorily to answer, than the cases of private individuals, with which their attorneys frequently left fees of
ten, fifteen, twenty, or twenty-five guineas. 'Oh!' said
the King, 'then for the first time I comprehend what I
never could before understand, why it has been always so
difficult to get any opinions from my law officers!'"

I must be permitted to doubt whether, in the tranquil
times of his Solicitor Generalship, he ever sacrificed a
particle of private practice to his public duty: and his
professional emoluments—with the higher fees given by
ordinary clients to a counsel who enjoys the highest dignity at the Bar—must have abundantly indemnified him
for giving up his circuit.—In spite of his heavy losses, instead of being again reduced to buy six-penn'orth of sprats
for supper in Fleet Market, in the course of a few years
he bought the fine estate of Eldon, in the county of Durham, from which he afterwards took his title.[1]

[1] Since writing the last paragraph, I have met with an exact statement of

Parliament being dissolved in June, 1790, he was again returned for Weobly, and made a speech to the rustics on the blessings enjoyed under the English Constitution,—cautioning them against French principles, of which he early became apprehensive.

The first subject discussed in the new House of Commons was "whether the impeachment against Mr. Hastings had abated by the dissolution?" and this being considered an open question, although Mr. Pitt and Mr. Dundas held the negative, Mr. Solicitor, under the influence of Lord Thurlow, contended strongly for the affirmative. In answer to the argument, that this would enable the Crown at all times to defeat an impeachment by dissolving Parliament, although it be declared by the Bill of Rights that a pardon under the Great Seal can not be pleaded in bar to an impeachment,—he went so far as to aver, that "the Crown ought to have the right of dissolving for the express purpose of abating an impeachment, saying that the new House of Commons, if they think fit, may commence proceedings *de novo*."[1] But this most preposterous doctrine, which I am sorry to say several lawyers of eminence supported, was overruled by the good sense of the House, and is now universally allowed to be untenable.—It seems to have been absurdly insinuated in the newspapers, that Sir John Scott and his associates of the long robe had been bribed by Mr. Hastings; for, a few days after the decision, writing to Henry, at Newcastle, to give an account of an Sir John Scott's gains from his own fee-book—abundantly corroborating my conjectures; for it appears that the first year he was in office, instead of losing £2,000, he made more than £1,000 beyond the receipts of the preceding year, and that his income went on constantly increasing:—

		£.	s.	d.
	1786	6,833	7	0
	1787	7,600	7	0
	1788	8,419	14	0
Solicitor General	1789	9,559	10	0
	1790	9,684	15	0
	1791	10,213	13	6
	1792	9,080	9	0
	1793	10,330	1	4
	1794	11,592	0	0
Attorney General	1795	11,149	15	4
	1796	12,140	15	8
	1797	10,861	5	6
	1798	10,357	17	0

—*Twiss*, i. 218. Some of the fees then received by the law officers of the Crown have fallen off, but we have been pretty well indemnified by "patents of invention."   [1] 28 Parl. Hist. 1074, 1028, 1150.

attack of the gout, he refers to this calumny, and takes occasion to mention that his opinion was unchanged:—
"Oh! the dignity of the cloth shoe! How hard it is upon me that I, the youngest, and most temperate and abstemious of the three, should, the first of all the brothers, arrive to this dignity! I hope most heartily you may escape; because, between the pain felt and the pain of being laughed at, the complaint is quite intolerable. . . . . You would see by the papers how unmercifully we poor lawyers have been treated in the House of Commons.— But the *black squadron*, as we are called, are an obstinate little handful, and in the long run, in a right cause, we shall at least fall gloriously. As to newspaper slander, all which to my knowledge is paid for, I hold that cheap,— and, in spite of it, I shall have, at our next meeting, another tumble down with Charles Fox and William Pitt, who, for once at least, agree in a business in which they are both wrong."

The only other measure on which he spoke while Solicitor General was Mr. Fox's Libel Bill. This he was not permitted directly to oppose, for Mr. Pitt and Lord Grenville, to their immortal honor, were determined to carry it against the efforts of Lord Thurlow and the bigoted opinion of all the Judges: but he did what he could to disparage and to weaken it. According to the Parliamentary History, "the Solicitor General began by professing a most religious regard for the institution of juries, which he considered the greatest blessing which the British Constitution had secured to the subject. He had his doubts, however, whether the bill then before the House would add to the utility of that invaluable institution." He then stood up for the old doctrine that *libel or no libel?* was a question of a law for the Judges, and suggested that "a bill to unsettle a well-established rule, by which the courts had been guided for a century, ought not to pass with precipitation."[1] Finding that the bill must pass, he afterwards added a proviso which was very unnecessary, and which for a good many years proved very injurious, "that on trials for libel the Judges should, according to their discretion, give their opinion and directions to the jury on the matter in issue between the King and the defendant, in like manner as in other criminal cases."[2]

[1] 29 Parl. Hist. 592, 594, 602.   [2] 32 Geo. 3, c. 60, s. 2.

A few days after the Libel Bill received the Royal assent, Lord Thurlow was forced to surrender the Great Seal. On this occasion Sir John Scott acted a very honorable and spirited part, of which we have an extremely interesting narrative from his own lips, delivered to his brother-in-law, Mr. John Surtees:—

"Having received a message from Mr. Pitt, begging that I would call upon him, I called accordingly. Mr. Pitt said,—' Sir John Scott, I have a circumstance to mention to you, which, on account of your personal and political connection with Lord Thurlow, I wish that you should *first* hear from myself. Lord Thurlow and I have quarreled, and I have signified to him his Majesty's commands that he should resign the Great Seal.' I replied, ' I am not at all surprised at the event which has taken place; I have long looked forward with great pain to the probability of such an event, and my resolution is formed. I owe too great obligations to Lord Thurlow to reconcile it to myself to act in political hostility to him, and I have too long and too conscientiously acted in political connection with you to join in any party against you. Nothing is left for me but to resign my office as Solicitor General, and to make my bow to the House of Commons.' Mr. Pitt reasoned with me, and implored me not to persist in that resolution—in vain,—but at length prevailed upon me to consult Lord Thurlow before I proceeded any further. After I had stated to Lord Thurlow what had passed between Mr. Pitt and myself, he said, ' Scott, if there be anything which could make me regret what has taken place (and I do not repent it), it would be that you should do so foolish a thing. I did not think that the King would have parted with me so easily. As to that other man, he has done to me just what I should have done to him if I could. It is very possible that Mr. Pitt, from party and political motives, *at this moment* may overlook your pretensions; but sooner or later you *must* hold the Great Seal. I know no man but yourself qualified for its duties.' I yielded; and, preserving the friendship of Lord Thurlow, I continued to act with undiminished cordiality with Mr. Pitt."[1]

His last prominent act as Solicitor General was, very properly, to appeal to the laws of his country against a

[1] Twiss, i. 148.

gentleman who sent him a challenge for words spoken by him as counsel, strictly in the discharge of his professional duty. There was no reason to doubt his personal courage, but a display of it on such an occasion would have been a wanton exposure of his own valuable life, and would have established a precedent highly detrimental to the interests of suitors in courts of justice. His conduct was entirely approved of by the Bar and by the public. The challenger, who thus sought to repair his reputation from the damage which the evidence in the cause had cast upon it, was sentenced by the Court of King's Bench to fine and imprisonment.—But scenes were at hand in which our hero appeared with little advantage.

CHAPTER CXCVI.

CONTINUATION OF THE LIFE OF LORD CHANCELLOR ELDON TILL HE WAS MADE CHIEF JUSTICE OF THE COMMON PLEAS.

I NOW with unaffected pain approach Sir John Scott as Attorney General, for I shall be obliged to censure him severely in this capacity. I doubt not that he acted all the while in strict conformity to his own views of justice and expediency, but I consider that in several instances these were most erroneous. It must be admitted that the times were perilous. Although the vast bulk of the inhabitants of this country were steadily attached to the monarchical government under which they and their ancestors had so signally prospered—in the movement produced by the French Revolution there were some ill-designing men who wished to introduce public confusion, in the hope that they might suddenly attain the high station in society for which they were unwilling to strive by patient industry; and there were some well-meaning enthusiasts, who thought that the happiness of the community might be promoted by a considerable change in our institutions. Both classes ought to have been repressed— and might easily have been repressed by a firm and temperate administration of the existing law; but the existing law was strained and perverted, and new penal enactments were introduced by which the most important rights of the subject were suspended, and the Constitution was seriously endangered. Of this system, by which discontent was aggravated, and odium was brought upon courts of justice and upon the legislature, Sir John Scott was a most strenuous instigator and supporter.

On the 13th of February, 1793, he became public prosecutor, succeeding Sir Archibald Macdonald, promoted to the office of Lord Chief Baron, and on the 27th of May following he brought to trial John Frost for some foolish words spoken after dinner in a coffee-house. I have already given an account of this most *un-English* prosecution, and expressed my opinion pretty freely upon it.[1] In fairness I now give the Attorney General's justification of himself in his reply—premising that Erskine had tried to apologize for him by suggesting that he persisted in the prosecution, not because it had his own approbation, but because it had devolved upon him from his predecessor:—

"I protest against that doctrine, that the Attorney General of England is bound to prosecute because some other set of men choose to recommend it to him to prosecute, he disapproving of that prosecution. He has it in his power to choose whether he will or not, and he will act according to his sense of duty. Do not understand me to be using a language so impertinent as to say, that the opinions of sober-minded persons in any station in life, as to the necessity that calls for a prosecution, ought not deeply to affect his judgment. But I say it is his duty to regulate his judgment by a *conscientious* pursuance of that which is recommended to him to do; and if anything is recommended to him which is thought by other persons to be for the good of the country, but which he thinks is not for the good of the country, no man ought to be in the office who would hesitate to say, 'My conscience must direct me; your judgment shall not direct me.' And I know I can do this; I can retire into a situation in which I shall enjoy what, under the blessings of that constitution thus reviled, is perhaps the best proof of its being a valuable constitution— I mean the fair fruits of a humble industry, anxiously and conscientiously exercised in the fair and honorable pursuits of life. I state, therefore, to my

[1] *Vide* antè, Vol. VII. p. 452.

learned friend, that I can not accept that compliment which he paid me, when he supposed it was not my act to bring this prosecution before you, because it was not what I myself could approve. Certainly this prosecution was not instituted by me ; but it was instituted by a person whose conduct, in the humane exercise of his duty, is well-known ; and I speak in the presence of many who have been long and often witnesses to it ; and when it devolved upon me to examine the merits of this prosecution, it was my bounden duty to examine, and it was my bounden duty to see if this was a breach of the sweet confidence of private life. If this was a story brought from behind this gentleman's chair by his servants, I can hardly figure to myself the case in which the public necessity and expediency of a prosecution should be so strong as to break in upon the relations of private life. But is this prosecution to be so represented? When a man goes into a coffee-room, who is, from his profession, certainly not ignorant of the respect which the laws of his country require from him as much as from any other man, and when he in that public coffee-house (provided it was an advised speaking) uses a language which I admit it is clear, upon the evidence given you to-day, provoked the indignation (if you please so to call it) of all who heard it— when persons, one, two, three, or more, come to ask him what he meant by it—when he gives them the explanation, and when he makes the offensive words still more offensive by the explanation that he repeatedly gives,—will any man tell me, that if he goes into a public coffee-house, whether he comes into it from up-stairs, or whether he goes into it from the street, that he is entitled to the protection that belongs to the confidence of private life, or that it is a breach of the duties that result out of the confidence of private life to punish him?"[1]

I will only draw attention to the admission, that the prosecution could only be defended provided it was "an *advised* speaking," and remark that, instead of being "an *advised* speaking," the words were elicited by rude provocation from a man who had been indulging in wine. Yet, being in the rank of a gentleman, he was not only sentenced to six months' imprisonment in Newgate, and

[1] 22 St. Tr. 510.

to be expelled from his profession of an attorney, but to stand one hour in the pillory at Charing Cross!!!

This was a fit prelude to the famous State Trials which took place in the following year. The blame of these rests chiefly with Mr. Pitt, and I am sorry to say that it fixes a deep stain upon his memory. If he had sincerely changed his opinion on parliamentary reform, it was not right in him to try to bring his former associates to an ignominious death for zealously treading in his footsteps. Lord Loughborough, then Chancellor, was next to blame; for he, too—though for a short space—had been a reformer, and he had *agitated* at public meetings, holding language almost as intemperate as the members of the "Corresponding Society." Sir John Scott, from his earliest years, had been the steady and consistent enemy of all innovation, and had looked with alarm on every popular movement. He might, therefore, better be excused for believing that those who advocated parliamentary reform were very dangerous characters, and were resolved to subvert the established government of the country. It must likewise be recollected, that in these proceedings he never displayed anything like rancor or bitterness against any individual, and that his language and his manner were uniformly mild and forbearing. Yet, in spite of the self-complacency with which he spoke and wrote upon this subject till the close of his life, I am afraid that impartial history must condemn his conduct; for, as a great lawyer, he ought to have known that seditious harangues and publications were only to be treated as *misdemeanors*, and that to say men "compassed and imagined the death of our Lord the King," and ought to be executed as traitors, because they were liable to an *ex-officio* information on which they might be fined and imprisoned, was to confound offenses of a very different character, and to do away with the security which the Statute of Treasons, so long ago as the reign of Edward III., had conferred upon the citizens of this free land.

In the manner in which the prosecutions were conducted, I can blame nothing, except that an attempt was made to prejudge the case by parliamentary committees, and by passing an act of the legislature, which recited the existence of the traitorous conspiracy—and that when the prisoners were apprehended and examined before the

Privy Council, the judges who were to sit upon their trials were called in to listen to the evidence, and to join in the commitment. Such a course would not be endured at the present day, and no Government composed of any party in the state would venture to propose it.

To avoid repetition, I must now abstain from entering into the details of the trials of Hardy, Horne Tooke, and Thelwall—which will be found in the life of Erskine. I would willingly give the whole of the Attorney General's opening speech of nine hours, but I am afraid that my work may be already considered too *lengthy* and too *weighty*, and I must confine myself to the following sketch of it, which has been adopted by Mr. Twiss:—

"The Attorney General, in opening the various circumstances to the jury, as evidence to prove the treason of compassing the King's death, stated that the proofs, which it would be his duty to adduce, would sufficiently establish the fact of a conspiracy to depose the King, which in point of law is an overt act of compassing his death: and he argued that it could not be less an overt act of compassing the King's death for being included in the still wider design of subverting the entire monarchy and substituting a commonwealth, which was the real object aimed at under color of 'a full and fair representation of the people.' If a conspiracy to depose the King is an overt act of compassing his death where the conspirators intend to supersede him by another king, it is equally so where they intend to supersede him by a republic. The convention contemplated by these conspirators was intended to claim all civil and political authority; which authority it was to exercise, by altering the government independently of the legislature and of the statutes by which the King is sworn to govern. The conspiracy to assemble such a convention was a conspiracy to depose the King from his sovereign power; and the insufficiency of the force by which the object might be attempted could make no difference in the character of the object itself, which must be equally treasonable whether successful or unsuccessful. Nor would it make any difference whether the first assembly to be convoked was to be itself a convention assuming all civil and political authority, or was only to devise the means of forming such a convention. Neither would the conspiracy be the less a treasonable one for purposing to continue the name and office of King in the person of George the Third, if that continuance was intended to be coupled with a proviso that he should govern with a new kind of legislature, to be constituted by the convention. A king who should consent so to govern would no longer be the lawful king; he would have been deposed from his character of king as established by law. But he *could not* so consent; for so to govern would be to violate his coronation oath: therefore he must refuse, must resist, and, in consequence of resisting, his life must be in danger. In either case he would have been deposed: for the meeting of a convention, assuming all authority, must in itself have been, at least, *pro tempore*, a deposition of every other power. But in this case the evidence went beyond that kind of incidental deposition of the King: it proved that his actual deposition was the direct and express object of appointing a committee to constitute this convention. Beside the overt act of conspiring to depose the King by means of a convention, there were other overt acts of conspiracy to depose the King by other means: by endeavoring to introduce into this country, through the agency of affiliated societies, the same principles which had been set at work in France, and to follow them out to the same end. The doctrine put forward by the societies was that of 'equal active citizenship,' on which they sought to found a representative government. That was the principle upon which was formed the French constitution of 1791 —a constitution preserving the office of king, and setting up a sort of royal democracy. But in August, 1792, that constitution was destroyed: and the transactions of the English societies, in and after the October succeeding that date, proved that, if not earlier, yet at least from October, 1792, they meant to destroy the kingly office in England. They sought to advance this object by stimulating their members to arm: and various divisions did arm, and clandestinely practice the manual exercise."[1]

Lord Eldon used to relate very amusing anecdotes of this trial. "Every evening, upon my leaving the Court, a signal was given that I was coming out, for a general hissing and hooting of the Attorney General. This went through the street in which the Court sat from one end of

---

[1] See 24 St. Tr. 941. Of this last allegation no evidence could be produced.

it to the other, and was continued all the way down to Ludgate Hill and by Fleet Market."—" One evening, at the rising of the Court, I was preparing to retire, when Mr. Garrow said, 'Do not, Mr. Attorney, pass that tall man at the end of the table.' 'And, why not?' said Mr. Law, who stood next. 'He has been here,' answered Mr. Garrow, 'during the whole trial, with his eyes constantly fixed on the Attorney General.' 'I will pass him,' said Mr. Law. 'And so will I,' was my rejoinder. As we passed the man drew back. When I entered my carriage, the mob rushed forward, crying, 'That's he, drag him out!' Mr. Erskine, from whose carriage the mob had taken off the horses to draw him home in triumph, stopped the people, saying, 'I will not go without the Attorney General.' I instantly addressed them: 'So you imagine, that if you kill me, you will be without an Attorney General? Before ten o'clock to-morrow there will be a new Attorney General, by no means so favorably disposed to you as I am.' I heard a friend in the crowd exclaim, 'Let him alone! let him alone!' They separated, and I proceeded. When I reached my house in Gower Street, I saw close up to my door, the tall man who stood near me in Court. I had no alternative; I instantly went up to him: 'What do you want?' I said. 'Do not be alarmed,' he answered; 'I have attended in Court during the whole of the trial—I know my own strength, and I am resolved to stand by you. You once did an act of great kindness to my father. Thank God, you are safe at home. May He bless and protect you?' He instantly disappeared.

"Erskine was, of course, extremely popular. He was received with universal plaudits, and there was nothing to disturb his enjoyment of this contrast, or to soften my mortification, until one evening the multitude which had thought proper to take his horses from his carriage that they might draw him home, conceived among them such a fancy for a patriot's horses as not to return them, but to keep them for their own use and benefit.[1]

"The jury retired to deliberate. Upon their return, their names were called over. I never shall forget that awful moment. 'Gentlemen of the jury,' said the Clerk of Arraigns, 'are you agreed in your verdict? What say

---

[1] This imputation upon his admirers Erskine himself denied,—saying that it was "a weak invention of the enemy."

you? Is Thomas Hardy guilty of the high treason whereof he stands indicted, or not guilty?' 'Not guilty,' in an audible voice, was the answer. It was received in Court without noise—all was still—but the shout of the people was heard down the whole street. The door of the jury box was opened for the jurymen to retire: the crowd separated from them as the *saviours of their country*."[1]

Mr. W. E. Surtees, in his "Sketch of the Lives of Lords Stowell and Eldon," says: "Scott, not long afterwards, said 'the evidence was, in his opinion, so nicely balanced, that had he himself been on the jury, he did not know what verdict he should have given.'"[2] Surely the other prisoners ought to have had "the benefit of this doubt;" —and I have always been wholly at a loss to conjecture his motive for proceeding to the trial of Horne Tooke.

The expedient was tried of making Sir John Mitford, the Solicitor General, open the case,—the Attorney General reserving the reply to himself. Speaking of the design imputed to the conspirators to compel the King to govern against his coronation oath, Mr. Attorney rather incautiously said, "*He ought to lose his life*, and I trust would be willing to lose his life, rather than to govern contrary to that coronation oath." *Mr. Tooke:* "What! is the Attorney General talking treason? I should be unhappy to mistake you: did you say the King ought to loose his life?" *Attorney General:* "It is really difficult to decide for one's self, whether this interruption is or is not proper." *Mr. Tooke:* "I ask pardon of the learned gentleman; and I promise I will not interrupt him again during the whole of his reply. I only wished to know whether, in prosecuting me for high treason, the Attorney General intentionally said something far worse than anything he has proved against me." *Attorney General:* "I am very much obliged to the gentleman. I say this: that the King of Great Britain is bound by his coronation oath to govern according to the laws established in Parliament, and the customs of the realm; that he is bound by that coronation oath to resist every power that seeks to compel him to govern otherwise than according to those laws; that it must, therefore, be understood that the King of Great Britain would resist such a power

---

[1] Twiss, i. 186-87.   Page 87.

as that, because he would be acting only in the exercise
of his sworn duty ; and in resisting such a power as that
he must inevitably lose his life."

Before concluding, Mr. Attorney (as might have been
expected) pathetically appealed to his *conscience*—" I here
declare," said he, "that not one step would I take in this
prosecution repugnant to the dictates of my own judgment, exercised according to what my conscience prescribes
to that judgment, not for all which this world has to give
me. Gentlemen, why should I ? You will allow me to say,
after all that has passed, that I have no desire with respect
to myself in this cause, but that my name should go down
to posterity with credit. I can not but remember *this* is
an interest most dear to me. Upon no other account my
name will be transmitted to posterity :—with these proceedings it must be transmitted. That name, gentlemen,
can not go down to that posterity without its being understood by posterity what have been my actions in this
case. And when I am laid in my grave, after the interval of life that yet remains for me, my children, I hope
and trust, will be able to say of their father, that he endeavored to leave them an inheritence, by attempting to
give them an example of public probity, dearer to them
than any acquisition or any honor that this country
could have given the living father to transmit to them."
—The Solicitor General, who was not generally of the
melting mood, to the surprise of the beholders sobbed violently in sympathy, and some one exclaiming " Just look
at Mitford ! what on earth is *he* crying for ?" Horne
Tooke sarcastically answered,—" At the thought of the
little inheritance that poor Scott is likely to leave to his
children."

When the verdict of NOT GUILTY had been pronouuced,
it is said that the reverend and witty philologist—instead of expressing any exultation—with waggish solemnity declared that "if he should again have the misfortune
to be indicted for high treason, he would immediately
plead *guilty*, as he considered hanging and beheading pref-
erable to the long speeches of Sir John Scott." However,
he acknowledged that the prosecution had been very fairly
conducted, and, meeting the Attorney General a few weeks
afterwards in Westminster Hall, he walked up to him and
said,—" Let me avail myself of this opportunity to express

my sense of your humane and considerate conduct during the late trials."

As I have ventured to condemn Lord Eldon rather sharply for instituting these prosecutions, it is fit that he should be fully heard in his defense. Thus he wrote in his "Anecdote Book," for the information of his grandson and of posterity:—

"The trials, in 1794, of Hardy, Tooke, &c., for high treason, at the Old Bailey, were the most important proceedings in which I was professionally engaged. As I was blamed by some, perhaps by many, for indicting them for high treason, instead of indicting for misdemeanor and sedition only, I record here the reasons which led me to take the course I adopted, and to produce that great mas of evidence before the jury, which many thought perplexed them so much, that they were unable to draw the true inferences. When the societies of which these individuals were members were broken up by order of Government, and many of the members (among others, the individuals indicted and tried) were, together with all their papers, and particularly those respecting the proceedings of the different affiliated societies, seized by warrants, on suspicion of high treason, *such of the Judges as were Privy Councillors, and were present at the many and long examinations of the parties apprehended, at the reading of the papers seized, and at the examination of the witnesses, being called upon for their opinion, stated that in their judgment the parties were guilty of high treason.* The warrants of commitment for trial treated them as parties committed on account of high treason. The cases, as treasonable cases, were the subject of communications to, and debates in, Parliament. As Attorney General and public prosecutor, I did not think myself at liberty in the indictments to let down the character of the offense. The mass of evidence, in my judgment, was such as ought to go to the jury for their opinion, whether they were guilty or not guilty of TREASON. Unless the whole evidence was laid before the jury, it would have been impossible that the country could ever have been made fully acquainted with the danger to which it was exposed, if these persons, and the societies to which they belonged, had actually met in that national convention, which the papers seized prove that they were about to hold, and which was to have superseded Parliament itself, and it *appeared to me to be more essential to securing the public safety that the whole of their transactions should be published, than that any of these individuals should be convicted.* They, too, who were lawyers and judges, having stated their opinion that these were cases of high treason, I could not but be aware what blame would have been thrown upon the law officers of the crown if they had been indicted for misdemeanor, and the evidence had proved a case of high treason, which, proved, would have entitled them to an acquittal for the misdemeanor; and then the country would not have tolerated, and ought not to have tolerated, that, after such an acquittal, their lives should have been put in jeopardy by another indictment for high treason. It was true that a charge for misdemeanor might have been so conducted as not to risk the danger of acquittal on the ground of guilt of a higher nature, viz. by giving no more of the evidence than just enough to sustain the charge of misdemeanor; but then the great object of satisfying the kingdom as to the real nature of the case could not possibly have been attained. The Judge who summed up the evidence, after hearing both sides, had more doubt whether the case of high treason was made out than he had when he attended the Privy Council. Erskine and Gibbs, the prisoner's counsel, ably took advantage, particularly the latter, of the prejudices against what is called constructive treason : the jury were fatigued and puzzled ; and, in the state in which they were, it can not be surprising that they acquitted the accused. When a little time had enabled the public to judge coolly about the proceeding, the public mind seemed satisfied with the result."

But I must pronounce this apology to be wholly insufficient. The preliminary opinion obtained from the Judges before the Privy Council ought not to have been referred to without a blush, and the voice of the two Houses of Parliament was only the echo of the Attorney General's own. The necessity for communicating information to the country is a poor reason for exposing the lives of men to peril, and it might have been as well gained by a prosecution for a misdemeanor. The risk of an acquittal in that case, on the ground that the offense might have been pronounced to amount to high treason, every lawyer must know to be a mere pretext. In several

Chartist cases which, while Attorney General, I prosecuted as *misdemeanors*, the evidence came far nearer to high treason, and I obtained convictions without such an objection being made or thought of in any quarter.[1]

I must now attend to the new penal enactments which had passed in the meantime. For these the Attorney General is less responsible, and, though they were unconstitutional, they do not deserve so much censure as an attempt judicially to pervert the criminal law. First came *The Traitorous Correspondence Bill*, brought in by Mr. Attorney, which, departing from the statute of Edward III., our second MAGNA CHARTA, made an agreement to furnish naval or military stores to France,—the investing of English capital in French funds or land, and other such acts,—high treason;[2]—next, he brought in the *Habeas Corpus Suspension Act*,[3]—and then the *Seditious Practices Act*, by which the holding of public meetings, unless with the consent of certain functionaries, was forbidden, and serious impediments were opposed to the right of petitioning.[4] The Attorney General carried through these measures with great vigor, and his opinion on all legal points was listened to with much respect by the House of Commons. He particularly distinguished himself in successfully opposing the bill to disfranchise the borough of Stockbridge,[5]—in defending the conduct of Government respecting the employment of Hessian troops,—in showing the legality of voluntary subscriptions to the public revenue,[7]—and in palliating the savage proceedings in political cases of the Court of Justiciary in Scotland.[8]

When Parliament met after the State Trials, they were made the subject of strong animadversion; and the Attorney General, in moving for a continuance of the suspension of the Habeas Corpus Act, attempted to defend the manner in which they had been instituted and conducted. He thus argued—very disingenuously, for the result had not depended upon any technical rule of law, but upon the clear merits of the case:—

"A legal acquittal is not necessarily a moral one. I will put a case upon this subject. Suppose, upon a

[1] 24 St. Tr. 241. 25 Ib. 497.   [2] 30 Parl. Hist. 581.
[3] 31 Parl. Hist. 520.   [4] Ib. 929.   [5] 30 Parl. Ib. 955.
[6] Ib. 1381. 31 Ib. 21.   [7] 31 Ib. 107.   [8] Ib. 80.

charge of treason, any gentleman of unblemished honor were to give evidence of an overt act, to the satisfaction of every man who heard him, still, if there was no other evidence, the prisoner must be acquitted, because the law says there must be two witnesses. Here would be a case of a verdict of not guilty, in which every person must be satisfied of the real guilt of the person acquitted. There are cases even in which the confession of guilt by the party accused could not legally be received against him in evidence. In such cases, though a jury might be bound by law to acquit the person, could any man think that the verdict of not guilty was a proof of moral innocence?" We are told that " he then inveighed against the mischievous writings of some authors very popular with the revolutionary party, and censured the language of members of the Opposition, who applied the light and inadequate epithets of 'idle,' and 'foolish,' to the conduct of those who had adopted revolutionary doctrines, and had expressed a desire for a national convention in England. He asked whether, while such opinions were in motion, was it not absolutely necessary that Government should be armed with extraordinary powers to resist them?"[1]

The coerceive system, however, was rapidly falling into discredit,—when it was revived with double fury by taking advantage of insults offered to the King on his way to the House of Lords to open the next session of parliament. These his Majesty himself—with the courage he ever displayed at the appearance of danger—treated with indifference, but they were much exaggerated by the courtiers about him, who, converting the scandalous outrage of throwing pebbles at the King's carriage into a traitorous attempt upon his life, talked of "the *shot* striking the window of the state coach," and reported that "one of the windows was perforated by a bullet from an air-gun." An address was very properly presented to his Majesty by both Houses of Parliament, expressing their indignation at the treatment which he had experienced. But the enthusiastic loyalty which was excited on the occasion Ministers culpably made the instrument of further injuring the Constitution.

The Attorney General immediately prepared the " Treasonable Attempts' Bill," which he called "a legislative ex-

[1] 31 Parl. Hist. 1153.

position of the statute of Edward III., greatly extending the provision of that famous law, which for many centuries had sufficiently guarded the safety of the throne and the liberties of the people. Instead of the simple enactments against " compassing the King's death," or actually "levying war against him," the penalties of high treason were applied to the vague charges of *imagining* to do any bodily harm tending to the wounding, imprisonment, or restraint of the person of the King, or to depose him from the style, honor, or kingly name of the imperial Crown of this realm, or imagining to levy war against him, or imagining to put any form or constraint upon or *to intimidate or overcome both or either Houses of Parliament*—such imaginings being expressed by *publishing any writing* or by any overt act or deed.[1]

Mr. Attorney seems to have been haunted by an absolute horror of libels, which, where they do not incite to the commission of crime, we have found out to be very harmless, and we suffer to be forgotten with impunity. In defending his Bill he said, " he considered it as not extending the law of treason beyond the true intent of the statute of Edward III., but only as defining and explaining that statute, which had itself provided that in all cases of doubt upon its exposition, recourse should be had to Parliament for a more definite exposition. Persuaded as he was, by the unprecedented assemblages and libels of the time, that a design existed to subvert the Government and Constitution, he would not incur any merited charge of supineness. He had done his utmost to repress the evil by the already existing laws, *for in the last two years there had been more prosecutions for libels than in any twenty years before*. But the of-

[1] 36 Geo. 3, c. 7, made perpetual by 57 Geo. 3, c. 6. The object seems to have been to include within these words such cases as those of Lord George Gordon, and Hardy and Horne Tooke, so as, by this " legislative exposition," to establish the doctrine of *constructive treason*, which juries and the whole nation had repudiated. Upon a strict construction of the act I doubt very much whether the proceedings of Mr. Cobden, praised so highly by Sir Robert Peel, might not be brought within it, in a speech of nine hours from an ingenious counsel. It still remains on the statute book—but may be considered a dead letter. When I, as Attorney-General, prosecuted Frost and his associates for high treason, at Monmouth, in the year 1840, I proceeded entirely on the old statute of Edward III., and I obtained a conviction against them without difficulty. I will venture to say that every offender who ought to be prosecuted for high treason may easily be brought within this statute.

fense had now swelled to a magnitude with which the existing laws were no longer adequate to cope ; and unless some further aid were given by Parliament for its suppression, the House would too late regret that they had not encountered it by a timely remedy."[1] In subsequent discussions on this Bill, and another, which was fortunately only of a temporary character, forbidding the meeting of more than fifty persons for the purpose of petitioning or deliberating upon grievances, and suppressing unlicensed places for political discussions or discourses, he said, "there were people now who lived by libels; it was become a trade. It was not unusual to see the wares of useful trades exposed to sale on one side of a shop, and libels on the other. Such were their numbers, that it was his conscientious opinion they could not be effectually checked if some law were not made to stop their progress. However irksome it was for a lover of the Constitution to feel his liberty abridged, every wise man would admit, that when everything dear to him was in danger from the daring herd of rash innovators and the licentious doctrines of the dealers in sedition, valuable as British freedom was, a part should be sacrificed for a time for the safety of the whole."[2]—He again boasted, that, "*in the last two years there were more prosecutions for libels than in any twenty years before.*" He said that "if every libel were punished as a mere misdemeanor, there were many men whose lives, if protracted to the greatest extent of human longevity, would not see the end of their punishments. The object of the societies was to degrade and destroy every principle of virtue, and all natural religion, and all political order. He could with confidence declare, that there had never been a case in which he had been called upon to prosecute, that he did not state to the jury, that he would rather have the gown stripped from his back, than to ask them to give a verdict contrary to their consciences."[3]

The bills were carried through Parliament by large majorities; but while the Administration gained some temporary strength from the alarm they propogated in the country, their tendency was to inflame public discontent, and to lessen the effect of the contrast which was then exhibited to the world between the blessings of

[1] 31 Parl. Hist. 1153.   [2] 32 Ib. 370.   [3] 32 Ib. 627, 634.

regular government in England and the horrors of anarchy in France.

The Whig leaders, although with a very slender following, made a noble stand against these encroachments on public liberty. But they incur almost equal blame for a prosecution which they originated, and which exemplifies a remark I have often made to myself in perusing both ancient and modern history, that where two parties in a state have been long struggling for superiority, moderation, wisdom, and justice are never to be found exclusively with either of them, and the excesses of one side are sure to be pretty nearly matched by those of the other. Mr. Fox, instigated by Mr. Sheridan, Mr. Grey, and Mr. Erskine, and actuated, I am afraid, by the recollection that Mr. John Reeves was an active partisan of the Government, and had made himself conspicuous by placing himself at the head of an association professing to put down republicans and levelers, made the motion against him which I have already had occasion to reprobate,[1]—that on account of some antiquarian researches respecting the original constitution of Parliament, he was guilty of a breach of the privileges of the House of Commons, and ought to be prosecuted by the Attorney General. Sir John Scott very temperately observed, that "it had been found in former instances of complaints sent from the House, a jury, after a long investigation of the facts charged, differed in opinion, and acquitted the party prosecuted. Indeed, if the construction which gentlemen had put upon this passage was that which the author meant to convey, then most unquestionably it was a gross libel; but upon that point he would not give his opinion. He always considered it an unfortunate circumstance when a jury felt themselves bound to pronounce a different opinion from that of the House of Commons. However, honorable members were to divide upon the question, and if he was ordered to prosecute he would discharge his duty faithfully."[2]

The prosecution being ordered, Mr. Attorney filed a criminal information against Mr. Reeves, and, having brought him to trial, very fairly stated to the jury, "If you are of opinion that this is an ill-advised execution of a purpose which was really not criminal, it is not conson-

[1] Antè, p. 124.   [2] 32 Parl. Hist. 627. 634.

ant to the lenient, genuine spirit of the law under which
we live, that in such a case you should press a man with
the consequences of guilt. But if, on the other hand, you
are satisfied, on attending to the whole of this book, that
the purpose of the author was criminal, as it is charged in
this information—that he has attempted to shake the
foundation of that security which is afforded to a British
subject by our Constitution under a British King and a
British Parliament, you are called upon to pronounce the
verdict of guilty, which is due to God and to your country."

The defeated House of Commons did not venture to
make any complaint against their counsel, who, though in
his heart not sorry to fail, was allowed to have done sufficient justice to their case.[1]

The only other occasion of Sir John Scott taking part
in the proceedings of the House of Commons, to which I
shall feel it necessary to advert, was his introduction of a
"Bill to regulate the publication of Newspapers." Hitherto, serious difficulty had often been found in proceeding
either civilly or criminally for libels contained in newspapers, from the concealment of the names of the printer
and proprietor; but it was now required that the proprietor
and printer of every newspaper should make an affidavit,
to be filed at the Stamp Office, stating the proprietorship
and place of publication; that every copy of a newspaper
should set forth the names of the printer and proprietors,
with the place of publication; and that a copy of such
newspaper, bearing the title and purporting to be printed
at the place specified in the affidavit, should be *primâ facie*
evidence against those by whom the affidavit was made.
The bill was strongly opposed, but was not, in my opinion,
any encroachment upon free discussion, and, on the contrary, had a tendency to raise the character of the newspaper press, by discouraging the scurrilous and licentious
journals which subsisted by attacks on private character.
The bill passed, and has, I think, in practice been found
very beneficial.[2]

We must again attend our Attorney General into the
Criminal Courts, where it was his fate frequently to be defeated, even when he had law and justice on his side. I
believe that this arose from the alarming multiplicity of
his prosecutions, and the suspicion which juries enter-

[1] 26 St. Tr. 529–545.   [2] 38 George 3, c. 78. 33 Parl. Hist. 1415, 1482.

tained that he was unfriendly to freedom. He now very properly brought to trial for high treason Stone, who had corresponded with the enemy and had invited an invasion; but Erskine, by insinuating that this was like the case of Hardy and Horne Tooke, and that it was founded on the late odious acts of Parliament, obtained an acquittal.[1] The next state trial was that of Crossfield and others for high treason in conspiring to discharge a poisoned arrow at the King. There could be no doubt here about the law, and the fact was sworn to by several witnesses; but the jury did not believe them, and found a verdict of Not Guilty.[2]

Sir John Scott's last prosecution for high treason was against Arthur O'Connor, the Rev. James O'Coigley, John Binns, and others, for corresponding with the Executive Directory of France, and inviting foreign invasion. Mr. Gurney, afterwards a Baron of the Exchequer, then in the "sedition line," being counsel for one of the prisoners, made it a powerful topic with the jury that the Attorney General had always failed in his prosecutions for high treason:—

"The Attorney General in his opening told you, with a a seriousness and solemnity well becoming the occasion, that he should make out such a case against the prisoners at the bar that he thought it was not within the compass of possibility for them to give such an answer to it as to entitle them to a verdict of acquittal. Gentlemen, that language may be somewhat new to you, but it is not new to me. I have heard the same language from the same learned gentleman, delivered in the same solemn manner, more than once, or twice, or thrice, or four times; but I never knew that jury, in a case of high treason, who at the conclusion of the trial coincided with him in judgment."

On this occasion one prisoner, O'Coigley, was convicted,[3] but all the others, though undoubtedly implicated in the traitorous conspiracy, were acquitted.[4]

Mr. Attorney was more successful with his *misdemeanors*, but I can not say that he thereby increased his credit.

[1] 25 St. Tr. 1155.   [2] 26 Ibid. 1-225.
[3] It was soon after this conviction that Sir James Mackintosh, then groundlessly supposed to have gone over to the Tories, having observed to Dr. Parr, "There never was, nor can there be, a worse man than O'Coigley," the Doctor retorted—"You are wrong, Jammy, you are wrong: he was an Irishman; he might have been a Scotchman: he was a priest; he might have been a lawyer: he was a traitor; he might have been an apostate."
[4] 26 St. Tr. 1191. 27 Ib. 1.

He obtained a conviction followed up with fine and imprisonment, of the proprietor and printer of the Courier newspaper, for a paragraph which appeared in that journal, stating that " the Emperor of Russia (Paul) was rendering himself obnoxious to his subjects by various acts of tyranny, and ridiculous in the eyes of Europe by his inconsistency."[1] Then came the scandalous verdict against Mr. Cuthell, the respectable bookseller, because, without his authority or knowledge, a few copies of Gilbert Wakefield's pamphlet had been sold in his shop. I must do Mr. Attorney the justice to say, that he seemed heartily ashamed of this case, for he hardly said more to the jury than laying down for law, that " every man that publishes a book is answerable for the contents, whether he knows them or not; and when a man publishes a book, he takes his chance; if it be an innocent book, it is well—if a libel, the publisher is answerable for its contents;" but he did not venture to grapple with the question, whether, in fact or in law, the defendant was the publisher."[2]

Mr. Attorney's last exploit in this line was prosecuting the Rev. Gilbert Wakefield himself for the pamphlet, which contained, with much sound learning, much that was absurd and censurable, but which was not calculated to do any serious mischief.[3] The defendant having addressed the jury as his own counsel, with ingenuity and erudition, but little discretion,—Sir John Scott observed, " From what the reverend gentleman has said, he seems to conceive that there should be one law for him, and another for all the rest of his countrymen. I should think that I degraded myself, and insulted you, by offering to make any reply to what has fallen from him." The defendant was sent to prosecute his studies two years in Dorchester jail.[4]

I by no means impute these proceedings to any harshness in the character of Sir John Scott, which, on the contrary, was mild and benevolent,—but to the rancorous

[1] *Rex* v. *Vent*, 27 St. Tr. 617. Ante, p. 141.   [2] Ib.
[3] 27 St. Tr. 641.
[4] 27 St. Tr. 679. Upon this trial Lord Kenyon, laying aside " latet anguis in herbâ," introduced a new quotation—saying, in allusion to the defendant's great classical acquirements,—
"———ingenuas didicisse fideliter artes
   Emollit mores—
is an expression which has often been used; but the experience of this case has shown that it is not always correct."

policy then adopted by the party to which he belonged. It is agreeable to think that there is no danger of again seeing a "Reign of Terror" in this country. Of late years such prosecutions would as little have been instituted by Sir Frederick Pollock or Sir Frederick Thesiger as by Sir John Campbell or Sir Thomas Wilde.[1]

The last appearance of Sir John Scott in a criminal court was in prosecuting the Earl of Thanet and Mr. Cutlar Fergusson for a riot in attempting to rescue Arthur O'Connor after his acquittal at Maidstone. If all that the witnesses for the Crown swore was true, there had been a grave insult offered to the administration of justice in the presence of the King's Judges, and little blame was incurred by bringing the case before a jury; but the defendants showed that they had tried to quell the disturbance instead of exciting it; and they would probably have been acquitted, had it not been for the foolish declaration of Mr. Sheridan, when examined on their behalf, that he "*believed* they. secretly wished Mr. O'Connor to escape, although he observed nothing in their conduct to show that they felt such a wish."

In reading this and other trials in which Sir John Scott was concerned, I have in vain desired to select passages which might convey a favorable opinion of his style as an advocate. He confined himself to a detail of facts, mixed up with protestations of his own honesty and good intentions, quite careless as to the structure of his sentences, or the order of his. discourse. I can offer nothing better than the following very sensible statement of his duty as public prosecutor: "The Attorney General of the country, as it appears to me, has a public duty to execute in reference to which he ought to conceive that he has properly executed that duty if he has brought a fit and proper accusation before a jury, and has proceeded to the length of honestly and fairly examining the several circumstances given in evidence in support of,

---

[1] The ideas of that age are strikingly illustrated by a letter written in 1801 by Sir John Mitford, the new Attorney General, who was likewise a very mild, good-natured man :—" I flatter myself that the *very temperate exercise* of the office of Attorney General while Lord Eldon held it, and since it has been in one who has carefully followed his steps, has had an effect in producing a general persuasion that the powers of that officer have never been used but where the case manifestly demanded that they should be put in force."

and in answer to that accusation; always recollecting that the jury will finally hear, from that wisdom which can not mislead them, the true inferences that will arise upon facts which have been given in evidence on both sides." When sentence was to be pronounced on Lord Thanet and Mr. Furgusson, he said, "My Lords, I owe it to the noble Peer who stands before me, and I owe it to the learned gentleman who has been bred to my own profession, and I owe it to myself and to the public, to declare to your Lordships, that no inducement could have persuaded me to institute this prosecution, but a conviction produced by that evidence which was laid before me, that the noble Lord and the other defendant were justly implicated in the charge. Having done my duty to the public, according to what my notions of my duty require of me, I can not do better than to leave the case where it is, and to call upon your Lordships to do that which is right between these defendants and the public." [1]

I wish I could enliven these dull details of criminal proceedings by some professional *facetiæ;* but I must not introduce well-known stories on no better plea than that Lord Eldon was in the habit of telling them. One or two, in which he was an actor as well as narrator, perhaps, deserve to be recorded. "Lord Thurlow, when Chancellor, had asked me if I did not think that a wooden machine might be invented to draw bills and answers in Chancery?[2] Many years after this, when he had ceased to be Chancellor, and I was Attorney General, a bill was filed against his friend Macnamara, the conveyancer,—and Lord Thurlow advised him to have the answer sent to me to be perused and settled. The solicitor brought me the answer; I read it. It was so wretchedly ill-composed and drawn, that I told him not a word of it would do—that I had not time to draw an answer from beginning to end— that he must get some gentleman to draw the answer, from beginning to end, who understood pleading, and then bring it to me to peruse. I went down to the House of Lords the same day, to plead a cause at the bar there. Lord Thurlow was in the House, and came down to the bar to me, and said, 'So I understand you

[1] 27 St. Tr. 821-986.
[2] Mr. Babbage is said to have taken from this the idea of his "calculating machine."

think my friend Mac's answer won't do.' 'Do!' said I, 'my Lord, it won't do at all: it must have been drawn by that *wooden machine* which you formerly told me might be invented to draw bills and answers.' 'That's very unlucky,' says Thurlow, 'and impudent, too, if you had known the fact—*that I drew the answer myself.*'"[1]

"I was generally successful against those who committed frauds on the revenue—but one smuggler beat me completely. There being a great rage among the ladies for French kid gloves, which were contraband, he imported from Calais 3,000 right-hand gloves, which being immediately seized and sold by the Custom-house, he bought them for a trifle, as they were of no use without the left-hand gloves. He then imported 3,000 left-hand gloves, and these he contrived to buy in a similar manner, as they were of no use without the right-hand gloves. Having got both sets, he was entitled to sell them at his own price, under the authority of the Government, to every milliner in London.

"Jemmy Boswell called upon me at my chambers in Lincoln's Inn, desiring to know what would be my definition of *Taste*. I told him I must decline informing him how I should define it, because I knew he would publish what I said would be my definition of it, and I did not choose to subject my notion of it to public criticism. He continued, however, his importunities in frequent calls, and in one complained much that I would not give him my definition of taste, as he had that morning got Henry Dundas's (afterwards Lord Melville), Sir Archibald Macdonald's, and John Anstruther's definitions of taste.— 'Well, then,' I said, 'Boswell, we must have an end of this. Taste, according to my definition, is the judgment which Dundas, Macdonald, Anstruther, and you manifested when you determined to quit Scotland and to come into the South. You may publish this if you please.'"[2]

But perhaps there is nothing more amusing than the account of his *soldiering*, for when the dread of invasion spread over the land, he, too, wished to become a soldier, and bought a gun and a bayonet. But this was not the line in which he was destined to acquire a high reputation and to serve his country. "During the long war," said he, "I became one of the Lincoln's Inn volun-

[1] Twiss, i. 207.   [2] Ib.

teers, Lord Ellenborough at the same time being one of that corps. It happened. unfortunately for the military character of both of us, that we were *turned out of the awkward squadron for awkwardness*. I think Ellenborough was more awkward than I was, but others thought that it was difficult to determine which of us was the worst." It should be mentioned, however, for the honor of the house of Scott, that Sir William used to say "*militavi non sine gloriá*," for he actually comanded a corps of *Civilians* at Doctors' Commons, who were exceedingly *warlike*, their profitable practice in the Admiralty Court being threatened with annihilation by any rumor of peace.[1]

As Sir John Scott is forthwith to be raised to the Bench, I am desirous of taking friendly leave of him as a barrister; I can not do this more effectually than by quoting the testimony in his favor left us by William Wilberforce: "Sir John Scott used to be a great deal at my house. I saw much of him then, and it is no more than his due to say, that when he was Solicitor and Attorney General under Pitt, he never fawned and flattered as some did, but always assumed the tone and the station of a man who was conscious that he must show he respects himself, if he wishes to be respected by others."[2]

I likewise copy, with pleasure, the simple and forcible praise of Townsend: "For six years of active official and extra-official duty, during which he screwed the pressure of his power more tightly than any Attorney General before or since, with the single exception of Sir Vicary Gibbs, he still retained a large share of personal good-will, and was the favorite alike of the Bar, of suitors, and the public."

[1] Mr. Attorney, in a letter to his brother-in-law, Mr. Surtees, dated 6th June, 1799, thus speaks in modest terms of his own military prowess and Sir William's:—" We had a most glorious exhibition here on the King's birthday, in the review of the volunteer corps, which furnished much the most magnificent spectacle I have ever seen. As a non-effective in an awkward squadron, I had the modesty not to show myse'f in arms, though I have military character enough to attend the drill occasionally in a more private scene. Your friend Major Sir William Scott's corps, not havin,, yet been bold enough to attempt the strong measure of firing, were also absent."— *Twiss*, i. 216.

[2] Life of Wilberforce, vol. v. p. 214.

CHAPTER CXCVII.

CONTINUATION OF THE LIFE OF LORD ELDON TILL HE WAS MADE LORD CHANCELLOR.

ON the 8th of July, 1799, died Sir James Eyre, Chief Justice of the Common Pleas,—and the Attorney General claimed his "pillow." Mr. Pitt and Lord Loughborough, the Chancellor, wished much to retain him in his office,—representing to him how important it was for the Government to have his assistance in the House of Commons, and suggesting that for his own sake it would be better to wait for higher promotion. But his health and comfort requiring repose, he insisted on his right, and it was conceded to him, under an arrangement that he should be raised to the peerage. He used always to add: "The King, likewise, made it a condition that I should promise not to refuse the Great Seal when he might call upon me to accept it,—and this condition I thought I was bound to accede to."[1]—While deliberating about his title and his motto, he thus wrote to Sir William: "There seems to be, as suggested by Mitford, a difficulty about Allondale. The whole dale belonging to Mr. Beaumont, and I having no connection with it, it's thought it may give offense to trepass upon it. If the Chancellor thinks so and you, I must resort to something else; there's hardly any that don't open to some such objection, and I may be driven to Eldon at last.—' *Sit sine labe decus,*'—is the best motto by far that I heard of; and John told me he had it from you.

"As the ring is to be a compliment to the King, I have thought of Virgil's description of the hive when the king is secure, as applicable to the unanimity of the country in the present security of its monarchy.

'Rege incolumi, mens omnibus una.'[2]

---

[1] George III. certainly had felt a high regard for him ever since the Regency question, and entirely approved of all his conduct, both in Parliament and as public prosecutor; but, perhaps, Lord Eldon a little magnified his Majesty's fondness for him, with the view of showing that he held the Great Seal directly of the Crown, and that he was at liberty to take part, if he chose, against the Prime Minister.

[2] This alludes to the ceremony of his being called to the degree of

"Pray, my dear brother, send me a line when you receive this. I am going to spend my last day in the Court of Chancery, and then I am to dine with the Chancellor, so that I fear I can not get to the Commons; and, the moment I come out of Court, I could only come under strong emotion of spirits. I can find nobody that can think that Scott[1] will do, except Lord R.; and I won't have it unless you bid me."

At last, resolving to take his title from his estate, he became John, Lord Eldon, Baron Eldon, of Eldon, in the county palatine of Durham; and, being sworn of the Privy Council, and his patent as Chief Justice having passed the Great Seal, he thus addressed his venerable parent, who survived to rejoice in his elevation :—

"Lincoln's Inn, 19th July, 1799.

"MY DEAR MOTHER,

"I can not act under any other feeling than that you should be the first to whom I write after changing my name. My brother Harry will have informed you, I hope, that the King has been pleased to make me Chief Justice of the Common Pleas and a Peer. I feel that under the blessing of Divine Providence I owe this—I hope I may say I owe this—to a life spent in conformity to those principles of virtue which the kindness of my father and mother early inculcated, and which the affectionate attention of my brother, Sir William, improved in me. I hope God's grace will enable me to do my duty in the station to which I am called. I write in some agitation of spirits, but I am anxious to express my love and duty to my mother, and affection to my sisters, when I first subscribe myself

"Your loving and affectionate son,
"ELDON."

I prefer the letter to his brother :—

"MY DEAR HARRY,

"I would write you a longer letter, but I am really so oppressed with the attention and kindness of my friends,

---

Sergeant-at-Law, which was a necessary preliminary to his being made a Judge. Rings are distributed by a new Sergeant, with an appropriate motto. An act of Parliament was passed (39 Geo. 3, c. 113) to allow him to be called Sergeant in vacation.

[1] The title of LORD SCOTT, if he had taken it, would by this time have appeared sounding and historical, like Lord Say or Lord North. The surnames of Pitt and Fox, now so illustrious, must once have appeared very mean.

that I can't preserve a dry eye. God bless you and my sister; remember me affectionately to Mr. and Mrs. Foster. You shall hear from me again. With the same heartfelt affection with which I have so often subscribed the name of J. Scott, I write that of your affectionate brother,

"ELDON."

When these letters reached Newcastle, the members of the family threw themselves into each other's arms in a transport of joy, and the good old lady exclaimed, "To think that I, in this out-of-the-way corner of the world, should live to be the mother of a lord!"

In the midst of all these distinctions, one object for which he struggled he could not yet obtain. To please Lady Eldon, who had a just horror of the wigs with which Judges were then disfigured in society, he prayed the King that when he was not sitting in Court he might be allowed to appear with his own hair—observing, that so lately as the reigns of James I. and Charles I. judicial wigs were unknown. "True," replied the King, "I admit the correctness of your statement, and am willing, if you like it, that you should do as they did; for though they certainly had no wigs, yet they wore long beards."

Lord Eldon took his seat in Court on the first day of Michaelmas Term following.

All accounts admit that he was a most admirable Common-law Judge. At this period of his life he was not even deficient in decision or dispatch,—whether sitting with his brethren in *banc*, or by himself at *nisi prius;*—and, though the business before him sensibly increased from the reputation he acquired, he did not suffer any arrears to accumulate. His judgments are well reported by *Bosanquet and Puller;* but they are almost all on abstruse and technical subjects. I have looked through them with a desire to select a few that might be interesting to my readers; but I find generally such points as these: that, "If the tenant in a writ of right pray *aid* after a general *imparlance*, it is good cause of demurrer,"[1]—and that, "On a joinder in demurrer without a sergeant's hand, there may be a *non pros.*, as a sergeant must be met by a sergeant."[2] One case turning on a principle of general jurisprudence he determined,—respecting the arrest in this

[1] *Onslow* v. *Smith*, 2 B. & P. 384. [2] 2 B. & P. 336.

country of the Comte d'Artois (afterwards Charles X. of France) for a debt contracted by him at Coblentz, in raising a corps of French emigrants, jointly with his brother (afterwards Louis XVIII.). Lord Eldon, after stating that "the case of this illustrious person must be decided on the same grounds that would operate in favor of the meanest individual," went on to examine the facts as they appeared in the affidavits, and gave it as his opinion that the defendant was not liable to be arrested,—regard being had to the nature of the debt, and the circumstance of the defendant being an alien.[1]

On another question, which caused much excitement at the time, although fortunately it has become unimportant, I must take the liberty to think he was wrong; and I am afraid that, unconsciously to himself, his opinion was a little biased by religious prejudice. This was, "whether Roman Catholic peers had a right to frank letters sent by the post?" They received a writ of summons to Parliament like all other peers; they might have sat and voted any day, on taking the oaths of supremacy and abjuration; no one could tell that they might not have chosen to do so; they were admittedly entitled to all other privileges of the peerage; and Protestant peers were allowed to frank without taking the oaths and their seat,—nay, began to frank forty days before the time appointed for the meeting of Parliament. The fact that Catholic peers, in practice, had not enjoyed the privilege, was only proof that they had been oppressed, and could not operate as a forfeiture. Yet Lord Eldon, thinking, perhaps, that this might be the first step towards Catholic emancipation,—a measure which he ever conscientiously believed would be the ruin of the country,—persuaded himself and his brother Judges that, as the Catholic peers did not, *de facto*, sit in Parliament, and as they had no petitions sent them to be presented to the House of Lords, and as they did not take a part in any parliamentary proceedings, the right of franking given to the members of the legislature—the better to enable them to do their duty in Parliament—ought to be confined to Protestants.[2]

Lord Eldon, while Chief Justice of the Common Pleas, introduced the excellent custom of giving *reasons* for the

[1] *Sinclair* v. *Charles Philippe*, 2 B. & P. 363.
[2] *Lord Petre* v. *Lord Auckland*, 2 B. & P. 139.

certificate of the Judges upon a case from a Court of Equity upon a legal question; but, when Chancellor, he so carped at the *reasons* of Lord Kenyon and other Common-law Judges, that they refused to do more than simply to give an answer in the affirmative or negative to the questions put to them.¹

I find in "the books" the report of only one case that came before him on the circuit. At Exeter he had to try a number of tailors who were indicted before him for a riot arising out of a combination for a rise of wages. Jekill, for the defendants, cross-examining a witness as to the number present, the Lord Chief Justice reminded him that, as according to law "three may make a riot," this inquiry was irrelevant. *Jekyll:* "Yes, my Lord, Hale and Hawkins lay down the law as your Lordship states it, —and I rely on their authority; for if there must be *three men* to make a riot,—the rioters being *tailors*, there must be nine times three present, and, unless the prosecutor makes out that there were twenty-seven joining in this breach of the peace, my clients are entitled to an acquittal." *Lord C. J.* (joining in the laugh): "Do you rely on common-law or statute?" *Jekyll:* "My Lord, I rely on the well-known maxim, as old as MAGNA CHARTA, *Nine tailors make a man.*" Lord Chief Justice Eldon overruled the objection; but the jury took the law from the counsel instead of the Judge, and acquitted all the defendants."²

He took his seat in the House of Lords on the 24th of September, 1799, when Parliament was suddenly called together for an augmentation of the regular army, by permitting voluntary enlistment into it from the militia.— He had considerable weight here; but this arose from his high station, from his repute as a great Judge, and from the earnestness and seeming sincerity of his mode of speaking; for he never was much of an orator, or even of a debater, —having no natural felicity of diction,—being utterly reckless as to the construction of his sentences,—and having no scruple or remorse in using the same word several times in the same sentence with a different meaning, or in

---

¹ See *Thompson* v. *Lady Lawley*, 2 Bos. & Pul. 303, where will be found an admirable dissertation by him in a " certificate case," on the point whether, under a general devise of "all manors, messuages, tenements, and hereditaments," *leasehold messuages* shall pass?   ² Joe Miller, 23rd edition, p. 235.

using different words in the same sentence with the same meaning.¹ There was not the slightest effort of arrangement in his discourses, and his reasoning on political subjects was often shallow and illogical. But, to give effect to his arguments, he appealed to his conscience; and, if he was at a loss for language, he could always shed tears.

His maiden speech in the House of Lords was on the third reading of a bill to continue the snspension of the Habeas Corpus Act. Lord Holland having thrown out a taunt that notwithstanding the alleged frequency of high treason, and the vast crowds who had been charged with that crime in England, O'Coigley, the priest, was the single individual who had been found guilty; Lord Eldon said, "the person so convicted was proved to have been planning, with disaffected bodies of men in this country, the destruction of the British interest in Ireland; and surely the noble Lord need not be told that a person attempting to sever the crown of Ireland from that of England was guilty of an overt act of treason. The noble Lord had argued that none should be apprehended but such as could be brought to trial; but he should know that cases might occur, in which, for want of two witnesses, persons could not be legally convicted, though no doubt remained of their guilt. But would the noble Lord say that therefore no danger existed? Would the noble Lord argue, that, because sufficient legal proof could only be brought against one of the men who were put upon their trial at Maidstone, the legislature should not have endeavored to prevent the mischief? He would venture to say, that to the suspension of the Habeas Corpus Act was owing the preservation of the crown in the house of Hanover; and that, by it, late and former conspiracies had been broken to pieces."²

He warmly supported Lord Auckland's bill to forbid a marriage between a woman divorced for adultery, and her paramour. He said, "he did not think it would be *sufficient* to prevent the enormous crime, for so he regarded it, of adultery, but because he thought it would have a *tendency* to such prevention. It was true that the contract of a seducer to marry his victim was invalid in law; but a simple and silly woman might be likely enough to act on

¹ The accuracy of his phraseology is not to be judged of by the reports, which generally greatly improved it. ² 34 Parl. Hist. 1488.

the opinion that it would be fulfilled, and that might be one of the terms on which she surrendered her virtue. Let her, therefore, be told by this bill that she would be effectually prevented from marrying her paramour. He was certain that nine out of every ten cases of adultery that came into the Courts below, or to that bar, were founded in the most infamous collusion, and that, as the law stood, it was a farce and a mockery, most of the cases being previously settled in some room in the city; and that juries were called to give exemplary damages, which damages were never paid to, nor expected by, the injured husband."[1] The bill passed the House of Lords, but was thrown out in the House of Commons.

The Irish Union chiefly occupied the attention of Parliament during the present session; but he took no part in the discussions on this measure. Had he been aware of Mr. Pitt's ulterior views with respect to the Roman Catholics, he no doubt would have opposed it.

When on the point of still greater elevation, Lord Eldon was deprived, by death, of two dear relatives, whose loss rendered prosperity of less value in his eyes. In the end of the year 1799 expired his brother Henry, to whom he had been tenderly attached. Writing to one of his sisters, he said:—"I have felt very acutely upon this event; and my mind has been running back through scenes of infancy, youth, and manhood, which I spent with poor Harry, till my firmness has occasionally quite failed me, and my spirits have been depressed excessively." In the following summer the worthy coal-fitter's widow paid the debt of nature, after seeing her eldest son universally revered as Judge of the Court of Admiralty, as well as her youngest making her "the mother of a lord;" and although, as she was in her ninety-first year, her "boy Jack," as she continued to call him, must have felt grateful that she had been preserved to him so long, it must have been a sore reflection to him, that on any future good fortune that might befall him, the pleasure of making her happy by announcing it to her was gone forever.

In the life of Lord Loughborough I have entered minutely into the history of the crisis which ended in the resignation of Mr. Pitt, and the appointment of Mr. Ad-

[1] 35 Parl. Hist. 233, 237, 280.

dington as Prime Minister.¹ I do not think that Lord Eldon was concerned in it till the King at length received Mr. Pitt's proposal for Catholic Emancipation. He is supposed then to have been consulted at Buckingham House, and to have concurred in the answer, that "his Majesty, highly disapproving of the measure, would apply himself, as speedily as possible, to the reconstruction of the Cabinet." He rejoiced much to see a man of Mr. Addington's inflexibly Protestant principles placed at the head of the Treasury, but he ever eagerly asserted that the offer of the Great Seal was made to him directly by the King, and he delighted in the appellation of the "King's Lord Chancellor,"—making a distinction unknown to the Constitution—and thinking, erroneously, that his relation to the First Minister of the Crown was different from that of a Chancellor appointed in the ordinary manner on the composition of a new Government.

Early in February it was generally rumored, and, I believe, definitively settled, that the Great Seal should be intrusted to him, both the King and the new Premier having unbounded confidence in his anti-Catholic zeal. Congratulations poured in upon him from all quarters; but by the following letter it appears that he was resolved not to "take joy" till the bauble was actually in his custody;—a caution the more necessary on account of the alarming state of the King's health.

"14th February, 1801. Common Pleas.

"DEAR LORD KENYON,

"I feel a good deal of uneasiness to protect myself against the possibility of your Lordship's thinking that I am wanting in the respect and duty which I owe to you, and which I can truly say has ever been accompanied with the most grateful and affectionate regard. May I therefore be allowed to assure you that, whatever other persons may have thought it becoming to mention in conversation respecting themselves or me, nothing has passed yet with respect to me, that would warrant me, consistently with propriety, in making that communication to you which it would be my duty to make, as I wish to make it to you, whenever the matter is settled the one way or the other? I can say no more than that there is

¹ Vol. VII., Ch. CLXXIV.

a probability that I may be compelled to quit this little Court, in which I should have wished to end my days.

"Your obliged and faithful friend and servant,
"ELDON."

Thurlow, probably still more delighted with the dismissal of Loughborough, against whom he continued to cherish the deepest hatred, than with the promotion of his own *protégé*, poured forth his feelings in the following effusion to him whom he considered the new Lord Chancellor :—

"MY DEAR LORD,

"Though I don't know the circumstances which induced you to give up the Common Pleas, I have no doubt your decision upon them was guided, as upon all occasions, by wisdom and honor; and I rejoice sincerely in the event.

"But I congratulate still more with the House and the country. Their judgments will be no less illustrated by sound principles and clear deductions than supported by authority; not let down by unsatisfactory attempts to argue, or shaded by surmises of mean partialities and prejudices. . . . .

"If I can shake off this painful disorder, my first exertion will be an endeavor to see you. There is not enough remaining of me to be useful; but I shall take great satisfaction in finding arranged the fundamental principles of that conduct, which is to extricate the present difficulties incurred by the mere want of such principles. . .

"I am ever, my dear Lord,
"Your very faithful and affectionate friend,
"THURLOW.

"Wednesday, 18th Feb. 1801."

After a month of unexampled confusion, during which it was difficult to say in whom the executive government was vested, the attempt to retain Mr. Pitt at the head of affairs, on his renouncing all his measures for the relief of the Catholics, failed, and his administration came to a close. The transfer of the Great Seal took place on the 14th of April, in an interval when his Majesty was better, but still in a state of much excitement. Lord Eldon used to give the following account of the scene—which he represented as a striking proof of the King's fondness for him :—" When I went to him he had his coat buttoned thus (one or two buttons fastened at the lower part), and, putting his right hand within, he drew out the Seals from the left side, saying, '*I give them to you from my heart!*'" Mr. Twiss observes, "It is not impossible that the unusual demonstration with which the King accompanied the transfer of the Great Seal to Lord Eldon may have been partly occasioned by the then unsettled state of the royal mind."[1]

Lord Eldon, at the commencement of his career as Chancellor, was placed in a situation of extreme difficulty, and he has been severely blamed for the course he pursued. It is now incontestably proved that for above two months the King, with short intermissions, was in a state of mental alienation, and was under the care of physicians particularly skilled in the treatment of his peculiar malady. His Chancellor always stoutly asseverated that the royal signature was never obtained, nor the royal pleasure taken on any act of state, when the royal mind was not clear and collected. This statement it is very difficult to credit. The following extract from Lord Eldon's "Anecdote Book" shows the King's general situation :—

" His Majesty not being able to hold a council, and his recovery being doubtful, it was not judged fit that the Chief-Justiceship of the Common Pleas should be resigned, the offices of Chancellor and Chief Justice being by law capable of being held together, and in case his Majesty did not recover, it being thought certain that the Great Seal would be taken from my custody, and that I should not be restored to the Chief-Justiceship if I had resigned it. During all the period, therefore, in which his Majesty's indisposition continued, I remained in the very singular situation of a person both Lord Chancellor and Lord Chief Justice of the Common Pleas, exercising publicly the duties of both offices."[2]

Yet his Majesty was allowed to sign commissions as usual. He could write seemingly rational notes like the

---

[1] 1 Twiss, 251. We may judge of the opinion of the new Ministers on this subject from an entry in the Diary of Mr. Abbot (afterwards Lord Colchester), lately published in the Memoirs of Lord Sidmouth:—"April 15th. Mr. Addington told me in the House that the alternative yesterday was, whether the King should only transfer the Great Seal from Lord Loughborough to Lord Eldon, or be requested to do several other things ; and the unanimous opinion was, that *his Majesty should only do one thing that day.*"—Vol. i. p. 401.

[2] Twiss, i. 252.

following; but they did not deceive the Chancellor, who was in correspondence with his medical attendants and with members of the royal family:—

"Kew, April 29th, 1801,—past One, P. M.

"On returning from walking, the King has found *his* Lord Chancellor's letter, and desires the commission for passing the bills now ready for his assent may, if possible, be sent this evening to the Duke of Portland's office, from whence it will be forwarded early to-morrow morning. His Majesty is pleased at finding the bill against Seditious Meetings got through the House of Lords yesterday with so little trouble.

"The King would by no means have wished that his Lord Chancellor should have omitted sitting in the Court of Chancery to-morrow, for the mere matter of form of bringing himself the commission, as his Majesty is so fully convinced of the satisfaction the suitors must feel at that Court being presided over by a person of real integrity, talents, legal knowledge, and good temper. He can not but add having felt some pleasure at hearing that the Lord Chancellor sat the other day on the Woolsack between Rosslyn and Thurlow, who ever used to require an intermediate power to keep them from quarreling. How soon will the shins of Pepper permit him to take the coif? "GEORGE R."

After his Majesty's health had considerably improved, Dr. John Willis thus addressed the Chancellor:—

"May 16th, 1801.

"MY LORD,

"We have not seen the King better than this morning. Your Lordship's conversations with his Majesty have not hitherto produced all the effect we wish. He seems rather to select and turn any part to his purpose than to his good. The Council, he tells us, you propose to be in London. Of course, we wish much that your Lordship should see the King again soon—that every means possible should be used to reconcile his Majesty to the present control: for till a consciousness of the necessity of temperance arises in his own mind, it is absolutely necessary to have resort to artificial prudence. I have the honor to be

"Your Lordship's obedient humble servant,
"J. WILLIS."

The public, however, were kept in ignorance of the "control" and "artificial prudence" exercised, and at times the excitement seemed entirely to have subsided. Prior to a Council, at which his Majesty was to appear, and important acts of state were to be sanctioned, thus wrote the Prime Minister to the Chancellor:—

"Downing Street, 21st May, 1801.

"MY DEAR LORD,

"I came so late from Kew, and was so hurried afterwards till half-past twelve, when I went to bed, that it was not possible for me yesterday to write to you, as I wished and intended. During a quiet conversation of an hour and a half, there was not a sentiment, a word, a look, or a gesture, that I could have wished different from what it was;—and yet my apprehensions, I must own to you, predominate. The wheel is likely to turn with an increasing velocity (as I can not help fearing), and if so, it will very soon become unmanageable. God grant that I may be mistaken! We have, however, done our best. The Council, as your Lordship has probably been apprised by Mr. Fawkener, is to be held at the Queen's House at one.

"Ever sincerely yours,
"HENRY ADDINGTON."

In a few days after, Dr. Thomas Willis, the clergyman, supposed to be the most skillful of the family, wrote to the Chancellor as follows :—

"Kew House, May 25th, 1801.

"MY LORD,

"Dr. John [Willis] is residing with the King, but we conferred together before he set out, and he desired that I would write the letter which your Lordship had requested to have this morning.

"The general impression yesterday, from the King's composure and quietness, was, that he was very well. There was an exception to this in the Duke of Clarence, who dined here. 'He pitied the family, for he saw something in the King that convinced him that he must soon be confined again.'

"This morning I walked with his Majesty, who was in a perfectly composed and quiet state. He told me, with great seeming satisfaction, that he had had a most charming night, 'but one sleep from eleven to half after four;'

when, alas! he had but three hours' sleep in the night, which, upon the whole, was passed in restlessness, in getting out of bed, opening the shutters, in praying at times violently, and in making such remarks as betray a consciousness in him of his own situation, but which are evidently made for the purpose of concealing it from the Queen. He frequently called out, 'I am now perfectly well, and my Queen, my Queen has saved me.' Whilst I state these particulars to your Lordship, I must beg to remind you how much afraid the Queen is lest she should be committed to him; for the King has sworn he will never forgive her if she relates anything that passes in the night.

"The only thing that he repeated of your Lordship's conversation is, that you told him to keep himself quiet. He certainly intends going to Windsor to-morrow morning early for the day. Had not your Lordship, therefore, better write to his Majesty, that you had proposed, agreeably to his permission, to have paid your duty to him to-morrow, but that you understand he is going to Windsor,—where you may endeavor to fix your audience for Wednesday?

"It is too evident, my Lord, that it can not be proper, since it can not be safe, for the King to go to Weymouth as soon as he intends. Your Lordship will, therefore, no doubt, think it requisite to take steps to prevent it as soon as possible. I have the honor to be

"Your Lordship's most obedient servant,
"THOMAS WILLIS."

Lord Eldon, accordingly thus addressed the King:—

"The Lord Chancellor, offering his most humble duty to your Majesty, presumes to submit to your Majesty's most gracious consideration, that it appears to him that great difficulties may arise in matters of public concern, if your Majesty should be pleased, during the time of the sitting of Parliament, which he conceives can not now be long, to remove to any considerable distance from Parliament. It can not but happen that before Parliament can be closed, some intelligence should be received from abroad, upon which it may be absolutely necessary to learn promptly, and perhaps instantly, your Majesty's pleasure, and to learn it by communications more ample than your Majesty could possibly allow to your servants, if they were not personally attending, in the discharge of their duty, upon your Majesty. Communications, in the form of messages to Parliament, not admitting of delay, may also become necessary. Impressed at this moment with a deep sense that it is extremely important on all accounts to your Majesty's welfare, that your Majesty should be graciously pleased to secure to your servants the means of personally communicating with your Majesty, at least during the short interval which must elapse before Parliament separates, at the close of which they may, in obedience to your Majesty's commands, attend your Majesty anywhere, the Lord Chancellor ventures to hope that your Majesty will not think it inconsistent with his duty, that he should have most humbly, but most earnestly, submitted to your Majesty the expression of his conscientious conviction upon this subject.

"The Lord Chancellor also requests your Majesty's gracious permission to introduce to your Majesty the Master of the Rolls and the Solicitor General previous to your Majesty's birth-day. As Tuesday is the seal-day in your Majesty's Court of Chancery, your Majesty may probably have the goodness to give that permission on Wednesday."

From his Majesty's answer, it might be supposed that his recovery was complete:—

"Kew, May 31st, 1801.

"The King can not allow any difficulty to stand in the way of his doing what may be most useful to the public service. He will, therefore, postpone his journey to Weymouth till the close of the session of Parliament, relying that the Lord Chancellor and Mr. Addington will bring it as soon as possible to a conclusion. He will not, therefore, change any arrangement for removing the things necessary to be sent to Weymouth, but he and his family will remain at hand till that period. His Majesty will be glad to receive at the Queen's Palace the Master of the Rolls and Solicitor General on Wednesday, any time after one that may best suit the Lord Chancellor; when he hopes to hear who may be most eligible to be appointed Solicitor General to the Queen. GEORGE R."

Yet, a week after, the Princess Elizabeth thus writes to Dr. Thomas Willis:—

"June 6th, 1801.

"After receiving one note you will be surprised at this;

but second thoughts are sometimes best; besides which, I am commanded by the Queen to inform you by letter how much this subject of the Princess is still in the King's mind, to a degree that is distressing, from the unfortunate situation of the family; and Mamma is of opinion that the Lord Chancellor should be informed of it, as he has mentioned the subject to Mr. Dundas to-day. The Queen commands me to add, that if you could see her heart, you would see that she is guided by every principle of justice, and with a most fervent wish that the dear King may do nothing to form a breach between him and the Prince,—for she really lives in dread of it; for from the moment my brother comes into the room till the instant he quits it, there is nothing that is not kind that the King does not do by him. This is so different to his manner when *well*, and his ideas concerning the child so extraordinary, that, to own to you the truth, I am not astonished at Mamma's uneasiness. She took courage, and told the King, that now my brother was quiet, he had better leave him so, as he never had forbid the Princess seeing the child when she pleased; to which he answered, 'That does not signify; the Princess shall have her child, and I will speak to Mr. Wyatt about the building of the wing to her present house.' You know full well how speedily everything is *now ordered* and done. In short, what Mamma wishes is, that you would inform the Lord Chancellor that his assistance is much wanted in preventing the King doing anything that shall hurt him. The Princess spoke to me on the conversation the King had had with her, expressed her distress, and I told her how right she was in not answering, as I feared the King's intentions, though most kindly meant, might serve to hurt and injure her in the world. I hope I was not wrong, but I am always afraid when she speaks to me on such unfortunate subjects. I think the King heated and fatigued, which I am not surprised at, not having been one minute quiet the whole day. I assure you it is a very great trial, the anxiety we must go through; but we trust in God,— therefore we hope for the best. Your friend,

"Elizabeth.'

In another letter to him, dated 9th June, her Royal Highness, after mentioning the Queen's name in connection with some indifferent subject, thus proceeds:—

"She commands me to say to you that she wishes the Lord Chancellor would show Mr. Addington, that, as the King is contented with it, that he had better not hurry our going, as he is so much better that there is hope that in gaining strength it will insure us from having a relapse, which you may easily believe is her earnest and daily prayer. He has been very quiet, very heavy, and very sleepy, all the evening, and has said two or three times, yesterday was too much for him. God grant that his eyes may soon open, and that he may see his real and true friends in their true colors! How it grieves one to see so fine a character clouded by complaint! But He who inflicted it may dispel it, so I hope all will soon be well. Your friend,
"ELIZABETH."

Finally she writes to him on the 12th June:—

"I have the pleasure of saying, yesterday was a very good day, though the sleepiness continues to a great degree. I am told the night has been tolerable, but he has got up in his usual way, which is very vexatious. I am commanded by the Queen to desire you will say everything from her to the Lord Chancellor, and thank him in the strongest terms for the interest he has taken in her distress. She so entirely builds her faith on him, that she doubts not his succeeding in everything with his Majesty, who, to say true, greatly wants the advice of so good a friend and so good a head. How providential is it that he is, thank God! placed where one can know his worth! I have just seen Brown, who is very well satisfied. This morning, therefore, I trust all is going on well, though I feel that there is still fear. Your friend,
"ELIZABETH."

Near a week after, Dr. Thomas Willis wrote the following alarming letter to the Lord Chancellor:

"Kew Green, June 16th, 1801. Eight o'clock, P. M.

"MY LORD,

"Dr. John, who has not seen the King, will bring this to town. I have nothing to say that is in truth very favorable. His Majesty rode out this morning at ten o'clock, and did not return till four; he paid a visit in the course of the day to Mr. Dundas. His attendants thought him much hurried, and so think his pages. He has a great thirst upon him, and his family are in great fear.

His Majesty still talks much of his prudence, but he shows none. His body, mind, and tongue are all upon the stretch every minute; and the manner in which he is now expending money in various ways, which is so unlike him when well, all evince that he is not so right as he should be. My Lord,
"Your Lordship's most obedient servant,
"Thomas Willis."

His Majesty seems now to have become very impatient of the control of the Willises, and very desirous to get rid of them; whereupon Lord Eldon, who was supposed to have the greatest influence over him, wrote to him, earnestly requesting that at least Dr. Robert might still be allowed to be in attendance.

His Majesty returned the following very touching answer, which it is difficult to peruse with a dry eye:—

"Kew, June 21st, 1801.

"The King would not do justice to the feelings of his heart, if he an instant delayed expressing his conviction of the attachment the Lord Chancellor bears him, of which the letter now before him is a fresh proof; but, at the same time, he can not but in the strongest manner decline the idea of having Dr. Robert Willis about him. The line of practice followed with great credit by that gentleman renders it incompatible with the King's feelings that he should, now by the goodness of Divine Providence restored to reason, consult a person of that description. His Majesty is perfectly satisfied with the zeal and attention of Dr. Gisborne, in whose absence he will consult Sir Francis Millman; but can not bear the idea of consulting any of the Willis family, though he shall ever respect the character and conduct of Dr. Robert Willis. No person, that ever has had a nervous fever, can bear to continue the physician employed on the occasion: and this holds much more so in the calamitous one that has so long confined the King, but of which he is now completely recovered. George R."

The Lord Chancellor was ready enough to take the King's word for his recovery: and having sent him a commission to sign, for giving the Royal assent to Acts of Parliament, received the following answer:—

"Kew, June 23rd, 1801.

"The King is much pleased with the whole contents of

the Lord Chancellor's letter, and returns the commission, having signed it, for passing the bills now ready for the Royal assent. He can not avoid adding, as he knows it will give pleasure to the person to whom it is addressed, that appetite and good sleep is perfectly, by the goodness of Divine Providence, restored, and that no degree of attention shall be wanting to keep those necessary assistants of perfect health.   GEORGE R."

In spite of the apprehensions of his family and his physicians, his Majesty's health soon after really was restored, and he remained pretty rational for several years. Lord Eldon, I think, has been much too severely blamed for his personal dealings with the King under such circumstances. In a letter which he wrote at this time to Lord Ellenborough he says:—" I think Dr. Reynolds told us one day in your absence, that the King was better when he was speaking to us than he was for a *long while* after he began to go out again in 1789. Taking this to be as improper as may be in Thurlow, Camden, &c., still we may do great prejudice if we do not attend to it—and assume, upon an incorrect view of fact, a ground of despair."[1] When there was a moral certainty, that if entirely conscious and in possession of his faculties, the King would have approved of the steps to be taken, and that he would be sure, if again conscious and in possession of his faculties, to sanction and ratify what had been done in his name,—and when the most serious detriment would have arisen to the public service from suspending the exercise of the Royal authority,—I must say that loud complaints against Lord Eldon for acts of state done in the King's name, during the King's temporary incapacity, savor a little either of prudery or of faction. Nor could it be expected that in public the Chancellor would admit the full truth —though I could much wish that he had made his statements on the subject in Parliament with less of emphasis and solemnity.—He will more easily be forgiven for the manner in which he mystified his friends who put impertinent questions to him on the subject in private society. " Eldon," says Wilberforce in his Diary, " had just received the Great Seal, and I expressed my fears that they were bringing the King into public too soon after his late indisposition. ' You shall judge for yourself,' he answered,

[1] MS. letter in the papers of the Earl of Ellenborough.

'from what passed between us when I kissed hands on my appointment. The King had been conversing with me, and when I was about to retire, he said, 'Give my remembrance to Lady Eldon.' I acknowledged his condescension, and intimated that I was ignorant of Lady Eldon's claim to such a notice. 'Yes, yes,' he answered, ' I know how much I owe to Lady Eldon; I know that you would have made yourself a country curate, and that she has made you my Lord Chancellor.'"[1]

Till the happy and unexpected turn which took place in the King's health in the end of June, Lord Eldon had been contemplating a Regency, and a speedy change of Administration; but he now looked forward to a long tenure of office, although he would not have believed any wizard who should have foretold that he was to be Chancellor, not only under George III., by whom he was so much liked, but under George IV., by whom as yet he was mortally hated,—and that he was to hold the office longer than any of his predecessors since the time of St. Swithin.

On the first day of Easter Term he headed a grand procession from his house in Bedford Square to Westminster Hall, and he was installed in the Court of Chancery, being attended by all his colleagues in the Cabinet, and the whole profession of the law.[2]

[1] Life of Wilberforce, iii. 9.
[2] " Alexander, Lord Loughborough, Lord High Chancellor of that part of the United Kingdom of Great Britain and Ireland called Great Britain, having delivered the Great Seal to the King at the Queen's House on Tuesday, the 14th day of April, 1801, his Majesty the same day delivered it to John Lord, Eldon, Chief Justice of the Court of Common Pleas, with the title of Lord High Chancellor of that part of Great Britain and Ireland called Great Britain, who was then sworn into the said office before his Majesty in Council. His Lordship sat in Lincoln's Inn Hall during the Seals before Easter Term, and on Wednesday, the 22nd day of April, 1801, being the first day of Easter Term, he went in state from his house in Bedford Square, accompanied by the Earl of Chatham, Lord President of the Council, the Earl of Westmoreland, Lord Keeper of the Privy Seal, his Grace, the Duke of Portland, one of his Majesty's Principal Secretaries of State, the Earl of St. Vincent, the Earl of Rosslyn, Lord Hobart, one other of his Majesty's Principal Secretaries of State, Lord Kenyon, Chief Justice of the Court of King's Bench, the Right Hon. Henry Addington, Chancellor and Under Treasurer of the Exchequer, the Right Hon. Sir Wm. Scott, Knight, Judge of the High Court of Admiralty of England, the Judges, King's Sergeants, King's Counsel, and several other persons. The Lords accompanied him to the Court of Chancery, where (before he entered upon business), in their presence, he took the oaths of allegiance and supremacy, and the oath of Chancellor, the same being administered by the Deputy Clerk of the Crown, Master Holford, the Senior Master in Chancery, holding

His promotion had been very generally approved of, and, although it can not be said that he continued to enjoy the same unmixed applause which had been showered down upon him as Chief Justice of the Common Pleas, the public expectation of him in his new position was by no means disappointed. I reserve for the conclusion of this memoir a deliberate estimate of his qualities as an Equity Judge, and a review of his decisions. At present it must suffice to say, that if there was still something to desiderate, the "marble chair" certainly had not been so ably filled since the time of Lord Hardwicke.

CHAPTER CXCVIII.

CONTINUATION OF THE LIFE OF LORD ELDON TILL HIS FIRST RESIGNATION OF THE GREAT SEAL.

LORD ELDON'S first speech in the House of Lords as Chancellor I myself heard, and I have mentioned it in my account of the striking scene when Lord Thurlow, after years of absence, reappeared, to support the right of a woman to be divorced from her husband, who had committed incest with her sister.[1]

He next came forward to support a bill brought in to indemnify those who had acted in arresting and detaining persons suspected of high treason during the suspension of the "Habeas Corpus Act." This was violently opposed by Thurlow, from spite to Mr. Pitt and Lord Loughborough; but Lord Eldon gallantly defended it, saying that "one of his earliest maxims in politics was, that political liberty could not be durable unless the system of its administration permitted it to be occasionally parted with, in order to secure it forever. When it was otherwise,

---

the book (the Master of the Rolls being prevented from attending by indisposition); which being done, the Attorney General moved that it might be recorded, and it was ordered accordingly. Then the Lords departed, leaving the Lord Chancellor in Court."—*Minute Book*, No. 2, fol. 80.

I ought to have mentioned that, on the arrival in his own country of the news of his appointment as Chancellor, all the bells in Newcastle and Gateshead were set a ringing, and all the ships in the Tyne hoisted their flags. The "Hoastman's Company" must have been particularly proud of their brother freeman. [1] Ante, Vol. VII. 35 Parl. Hist. 1432.

liberty contained the seeds of its own destruction. With respect to the consideration of necessity, he was aware that it was often the plea of tyrants; yet it was that consideration on which the most moderate men, when they took prudence for their guide must sometimes act. In all periods of our history, their Lordships would find that the benefits of the Habeas Corpus Act were occasionally relinquished; but the suspension of the Habeas Corpus Act did not take away the responsibility of Ministers. There were cases in which, if a Minister did not act, he would deserve to lose his head. Such, for instance, and he stated no hypothetical case, was the occasion of ambassadors passing from Ireland through England to France, and *vice versâ*, for purposes of a treasonable nature. In such a case, where the information was such as could not be doubted, if a Minister refused to act, what would he not deserve? And yet such a person could not be indemnified for his conduct, without such a bill as that before their Lordships." The Bill was carried by a majority of 54 to 17.[1]

The only other debate in which he took a part, before the conclusion of the session, was on the Bill directed against HORNE TOOKE "to prevent priests in orders from sitting in the House of Commons"—when he had, again, to combat Lord Thurlow, who insisted that it was an encroachment on the rights of the clergy. The ground taken by Lord Eldon was, that, by the canons of the Anglican Church, orders are indelible—but this does not seem to show very conclusively that a clergyman, without cure of souls, or benefice, may not sit in the House of Commons, while bishops, with a still more sacred character impressed upon them, and with all their episcopal duties to perform, sit in the House of Lords, to the general contentment of the nation.[2]

A few days before the prorogation his Majesty set off on his long talked of excursion to Weymouth, and in his way paid a visit at Cuffnels in Hampshire. While he was there, Mr. Rose, the master of the mansion, wrote a very alarming letter to Lord Eldon,—in which, after giving an account of the King, when riding to Lymington, being caught in a heavy shower of rain,—being wet through, as no entreaties would prevail with him to put on a great

[1] 35 Parl. Hist. 1537. [2] Ib. 1543.

coat,—remaining three-quarters of an hour conversing with the mayor,—proceeding to Sir Harry Nicoll's, and dining without changing his clothes,—and again getting wet as he rode home, adds—

"There is no describing the uneasiness I felt at his Majesty keeping on his wet clothes, because I recollect Mr. Pitt telling me that his first illness, in 1788, was supposed to be brought on by the same thing; but there was no possible means of preventing it. The exercise, too, must have been, I fear, too much after the disuse of riding for some time. His Majesty intends going to Southampton (ten miles) on horseback to-day, and returning to dinner. I mention these circumstances to your Lordship, deriving some relief to my own mind from it, without a hope of your being able to take any *immediate* step in concert with Mr. Addington or others of his Majesty's servants, but trusting that it may induce your Lordship to make as early a visit to Weymouth as possible."

Lord Eldon hurried down to Weymouth on pretense of carrying important papers for his Majesty to sign, but, finding him perfectly tranquil, returned after a stay there of three days.

Nothing was now talked of but the negotiation with Bonaparte. It was generally understood that the Chancellor was of the section in the Cabinet bent on carrying on the war, and in this belief Windham wrote him a letter on the measures which ought to be taken to guard the country against invasion, thus concluding—"With all my dread of invasion, I hope you do not suppose me to consider the danger of invasion as by any means equal to those of peace. A man may escape a pistol, however near his head, but not a dose of poison. If I am not mistaken, you do not materially differ from me in this opinion." This conjecture was pretty near the truth, but within a fortnight Lord Eldon wrote the following letter to his brother, Sir William:—

"The preliminaries of peace with France were signed last night. The terms, I understand, I am not at liberty to mention. With my head and heart so full as they have been for ten days past, I have felt, most deeply, the want of such a friend as you here. I am perhaps, at this moment, one of the most anxious of mankind. I think, upon the whole, the peace, as to its terms, not objectionable, if we could forget the damnable principles upon which France has acted and may continue to act. You would excuse a great deal upon all subjects if you knew the state of mind I am in."

When the preliminaries were about to be discussed in the House of Lords, he thus addressed his predecessor, in the hope of mollifying him and of obtaining his vote or his proxy:—

. "MY DEAR LORD,

"I received the honor of your Lordship's letter from Bath, and shall give all due attention to the subject of it.

"His Majesty has put into my hands the paper which your Lordship gave him at Weymouth respecting the Princesses, and in the course of next week that business will be finished.

"I most sincerely hope that your Lordship's health is re-established. My vacation, which has been spent in great anxiety of mind and depression of spirits arising from apprehensions, is coming to its close, leaving me little relieved from either. If your Lordship had been within the reach of conversation, I might occasionally have unburdened that mind to you so far as I understand the principles upon which a person who has the misery of being in a cabinet is to act would have allowed me. Your Lordship will conjecture that I am alluding to what has passed as to the peace, with reference to which the grounds upon which I have acted can not perhaps with propriety be stated upon paper, or without mischief be insisted upon in debate. They are such, that if I can rejoice in the peace it is with trembling, and I am not surprised that many men whom I honor and revere, tremble without rejoicing. I have satisfied myself that, attending to all considerations, such as can and such as can not be publicly stated, the measure is justifiable and right; but your Lordship, I think, can sufficiently conjecture what are my principles to believe that I feel considerably on this subject. I have written thus much under a persuasion that your Lordship will receive in confidence what is written from respect, and from respect due from me to you, whatever may be your opinion upon what has been passing. Whatever that may be, I sincerely hope your health and your inclination will bring you to Parliament. If you there approve what has been done, it will give great sanction to the measure, and great consolation to me personally. If you disapprove, I shall nevertheless, I am sure, have the satisfaction of seeing you repressing by the weight of your authority those who will approve upon the principles broached at the Shakespeare Tavern, and which you and I abhor. I do not know whether your Lordship will or will not blame me for what I have written, but I had my pen in my hand, and I could not refrain from unburdening a mind laboring with anxiety. You'll be so good as commit it to the fire after you have read what remains— which is only a cordial expression of all good wishes for your health, with an assurance that I am, with much respect and regard, my dear Lord,

"Your obliged and obedient humble servant,

"ELDON."

"October 24, 1801."[1]

Stiff and formal as is this production under the pretense of great openness, it produced the desired effect, and Lord Loughborough offered him his proxy, although he said he could not make a speech in defense of the peace. A proxy was sent for signature in the following letter:—

"MY DEAR LORD,

"I return your Lordship a great many thanks for your very kind and obliging letter. I shall certainly think myself much honored in having your Lordship's proxy. I did not think myself authorized to hope for it to-morrow night, and therefore have not sent the inclosed sooner. In fact, upon a point of such magnitude as will form the subject of to-morrow's debate,—the peace,—I think your Lordship's great character would hardly admit of your voting in absence. I find Lord Grenville objects also to the Russian Convention, which is to be debated on Friday. May I crave your opinion upon that? I confess I can not bring myself to think much of some of the objections.

"With every good wish for your Lordship's health, permit me to add that I am, with very sincere regard,

"Your obliged and faithful friend and servant,

"ELDON.

"Monday."[2]

---

[1] Rossl. MSS.   [2] Ibid.

Lord Eldon spoke late in the debate, and said,—" In advising his Majesty to make peace, I would perish sooner than I would sacrifice any of the essential interests of the country; but when I say this, I must not be understood to vapor in praise of the peace as if it were a very honorable one. Again, upon the motion for approving of the Defensive Treaty, he observed:—"I am not ready to assert that the present is a glorious peace, but I have discharged my duty conscientiously in advising his Majesty to sign it, and I trust that, if candidly viewed, it will be found as good a peace as was likely to be obtained, all the circumstances under which it was made taken into consideration." On both occasions he went over all the articles in a very minute and I must admit very tiresome manner, as if he had been discussing exceptions to the Master's report in a chancery suit.[1] But in the debate on the Russian Convention he gave an able exposition of our belligerent rights with regard to neutrals,—probably having the invaluable assistance of his brother, Sir William, whose judgments in the Court of Admirality have placed them on an imperishable basis.[2]

He did not, for a long time after, take any part in debate, except in answering the Earl of Suffolk, who praised the present Administration at the expense of Mr. Pitt, whom he accused of detaining for a long time persons suspected of treasonable practices, without ever bringing them to trial. "The Lord Chancellor declared, with much warmth, that he would sooner suffer death upon the spot than hear the conduct of the late Administration aspersed. If it was criminal, he was as deeply criminal as they; and the only reason for pursuing a different conduct now was, that the country was under different circumstances." He concluded with a panegyric on Pitt, under whom alone, he began to think, he could hold the Great Seal with any security.[3]

Lord Eldon interfered little in politics from this time till the spring of the year 1804, when, through his agency, while the King was again seriously indisposed, the plan was perfected of turning out Mr. Addington aud restoring Mr. Pitt to his post as Prime Minister. During this interval the Chancellor still grew in royal favor, and his Majesty was in the constant habit on returning papers sent

[1] 36 Parl. Hist. 171, 596, 724.   [2] Ib. 236.   [3] Ib. 1134

for the royal signature, to write him letters, showing his affection for his "friend," and his minute attention to public business. Of these, many will be found in Mr. Twiss's valuable work—but I must be content with giving two or three as a specimen:—

"Windsor, April 15th, 1802.

"The King returns the Commission for passing the Bills this day to the Lord Chancellor, having signed it. He at the same time expresses a most sincere wish that the recess may be crowned with the restoration of the Lord Chancellor's health, and strongly recommends that he will not, at first coming out, be quite so assiduous as he was in business before his confinement, to which he rather attributes the duration of the fit of the gout.

"GEORGE R."

"Queen's Palace, April 30th, 1802.

"The King returns to the Lord Chancellor the Commission, which he has signed, for giving his assent to the Bills now prepared for that purpose. At the same time the King avails himself of the opportunity to express the satisfaction he receives from the assurance of the Lord Chancellor's gout having entirely subsided. That a degree of lameness and weakness still remains is the natural effect of the disorder, but will daily diminish; and the King therefore strongly recommends to the Lord Chancellor the not coming next Wednesday to St. James's, but the coming on Thursday for the Recorder's report, which will avoid the necessity of going up stairs; and Wednesday is the first day of Term, which must in itself be a day of some fatigue. GEORGE R."

"Weymouth, August 14th, 1802.

"Yesterday the King received the Lord Chancellor's letter. He trusts that the fatigue of sitting in this warm weather in Lincoln's Inn Hall has not proved so inconvenient as might have been expected. The King is much pleased at Dr. Ridley's being placed in the Isle of Wight. His being of the family of so celebrated a man as the Bishop that bore that name, in addition to his connection with the Lord Chancellor, very properly entitle him to that situation. GEORGE R."

"Windsor, Nov. 13th, 1802.

"The King returns the Commission for opening the Parliament, which he has signed. Having had the curiosity of reading the Commission, have found a mistake, the insertion of George, Earl of Leicester, instead of William, Earl of Dartmouth, as Lord Steward of the Household, which can easily be corrected by the Lord Chancellor ordering this change of names, though the King has signed the Commission. GEORGE R."

"Windsor, Feb. 27th, 1803.

"The King has, with great satisfaction, signed the Commission for passing the Bill to restrain the Bank of England from paying cash, as he is convinced of the utility of the measure, and ardently hopes it may be prolonged the next year; or, if the situation of public affairs should at that time prove more favorable, that the Bank will at least be restrained from paying cash above a certain proportion of each payment it may have to issue.

"GEORGE R."

About this time Lord Eldon, being appointed High Steward of the University of Oxford, was alarmed by news that he must return thanks in a Latin epistle, and in consternation he wrote to Sir William, "Pray, pray, give me two sentences thanking them, and assuring them that to the best of that *judgment* (the talent they are pleased to allow me) I wish to dedicate my old age with '*diligentia*,' and more of it than adorned my '*adolescentia*' to 'literis, virtuti, probitati et pietati.'"[1] But he was greatly relieved by an intimation from the Duke of Portland, then Chancellor, that in expressing his gratitude, he might make use of his mother tongue. This incident must have caused much pleasantry in his family, where, although he was regarded with a high degree of respect as well as affection, he amiably allowed himself to be treated with considerable familiarity.

Soon afterwards his eldest son played off a good-humored hoax upon him, by writing him a metrical application for a living, supposed to come from a poor parson, who had been at school with him—but without signing his name—merely dated it, "No. 2, Charlotte Street, Pimlico." Thus it began:—

"Hear, generous lawyer! hear my prayer,
Nor let my freedom make you stare,
In hailing you, Jack Scott!

---

[1] These were words in the address to him from the Convocation.

>   Tho' now upon the woolsack placed,
>   With wealth, with power, with title graced,
>   *Once* nearer was our lot.
>
> " Say, by what name the hapless bard
>   May best attract your kind regard,
>   Plain Jack ?—Sir John ?—or Eldon ?
>   Give, from your ample store of giving,
>   A starving priest some little living,—
>   The world will cry out ' Well done !'
>
> " In vain, without a patron's aid,
>   I've pray'd and preach'd, and preach'd and pray'd—
>   *Applauded*, but *ill-fed*.
>   Such vain éclat let others share ;
>   Alas ! I can not feed on *air*,—
>   I ask not *praise*, but *bread*."

The Chancellor himself went to Charlotte Street, Pimlico, to inquire after the writer, but could find neither poet nor parson in those regions.[1]

We must now attend to much graver matters. While Parliament was sitting, in February, 1804, deliberating upon the measures necessary to be taken for the military defense of the country, in consequence of the renewed hostilities with Napoleon, now become Emperor,—afflicting rumors were spread of a return of the King's malady ; and there can be no doubt that he was then attended by Dr. Willis, and kept under restraint. A question upon the subject being put in the House of Commons, Mr. Addington very guardedly answered that "there was not at that time any necessary suspension of such royal functions as it might be necessary for his Majesty then to discharge."[2] Two days after, Lord Hawkesbury having held the same vague language in the House of Lords, Lord King and Lord Fitzwilliam urged that more explicit information should be given by the noble and learned Lord on the woolsack, who, as keeper of the Great Seal, was peculiarly and personally responsible. *Lord Eldon:* " I can assure the noble Lords who have personally alluded to me in such pointed terms, that I am fully sensible of the responsibility which attaches to me in particular. I have considered—and that deeply—the duty which is incumbent upon me at this trying crisis. I am aware that, while I am, on the one hand, constantly t

---

[1] The poem is said to have originated in an assertion by the Chancellor, that his son could not disguise his handwriting so as to deceive him.

[2] 1 Parl. Deb. 1134.

keep in view what is due from me in point of delicacy to my Sovereign, I ought, on the other, never to forget that I have a duty to perform to the legislature and to the public. I have settled in my own mind what line of conduct I ought to pursue on this occasion, and that line I have pursued. I am anxious that there should be no misapprehension on this subject, and therefore I declare that my noble colleague has correctly stated the convalescence of his Majesty. Delicate as this subject is, I certainly would not have mentioned this much if I had not been compelled to it; but, as I have been compelled to it, I will state that, *at this moment there is no suspension of the royal functions.*"[1] Lord Grenville complaining that the noble and learned Lord had conveyed no information to the House, Lord Eldon added: "From that attachment and duty which I owe to his Majesty, no consideration shall make me swerve so far as to go into what I conceive an unnecessary and improper explanation."[2]

The country was now in a most perilous situation. The Mutiny Act was about to expire in a few days, and unless it were renewed, the army could not lawfully be kept on foot. A Bill to renew it had passed both Houses along with several other bills, which, for the public safety, ought to receive the royal assent without delay.

Lord Eldon boldly, and I think excusably, obtained the King's signature to a commission for passing these bills, at a time when it is quite clear that, if His Majesty had been a private person, any deed or will executed by him would have been adjudged to be a nullity. The Commission being produced in the House of Lords, Lord Fitzwilliam said "he entertained doubts as to the state of his Majesty's mind—which induced him to call upon the Lord Chancellor for further information, before the very important exercise of the prerogative which had been announced was carried into effect."

Lord Eldon: "I can assure the noble Earl and the House, that in everything connected with so grave, important, and momentous an occasion, I have proceeded with all due delicacy, deliberation, and caution; even with fear and trembling. Not satisfied with the reports

[1] Ib. 639. [2] Ib. 641.

of the medical attendants of His Majesty, I have thought it proper and necessary to have a personal interview with the Sovereign, when due discussion took place respecting the Bills offered for the royal assent, which assent was fully expressed. I would sooner suffer my right hand to be severed from my body, than act in such an instance upon light or superficial grounds; and I have no hesitation to aver, that the result of all which took place on the occasion amply justifies me in announcing his Majesty's assent to the Bills specified in the Royal Commission. I know and feel with gratitude my obligations to the best of Sovereigns, and to his person I bear the warmest affection. But I can most conscientiously say, that no considerations whatever, not even those to which I have alluded, shall ever induce me to break that sacred covenant which I have made with myself not to suffer that anything shall warp my judgment, or bear me from the rule of strict duty and rectitude. I am fully aware of the high responsibility under which I stand, and with reference to which I act on this occasion."[1]

It will be observed that his Lordship on this occasion avoids making any assertion as to the competence of the Sovereign—does not at all disclose what the rule of rectitude and duty was which he had covenanted with himself to observe—nor exclude the possibility of his having obtained a release from the covenant,—which it is so easy to obtain when covenantor and covenantee happen to be the same indiuidual. However, the clerk having read the commission, concluding with the words, "By the King himself—signed with his own hand," and "Le Roy le veut," being pronounced over each of the Bills, they all became law.

The following is an account of this transaction, written by Lord Eldon many years after; and, even assuming that he has neither colored nor suppressed any of the circumstances of the interview, it is plain that he relied mainly upon what he considered "the competency of the King, as king, notwithstanding his indisposition," and that he would by no means have become witness to the act and deed of a private individual in such a state of mind:—

"During one of his Majesty's indispositions, and when there was a doubt whether he was sufficiently recovered

[1] Parl. Deb. 808.

to make it fit to take his royal sign-manual to a commission for passing Acts of Parliament, the time approached when, if the Mutiny Bills were not renewed and passed, the establishments of the army and navy, in the midst of war, must be broken up. It became, therefore, absolutely necessary to have his royal sign-manual to acts for continuing those establishments. The Chancellor is the minister responsible for that. I waited upon his Majesty, and carried with me the commission, and a brief abstract of the several intended acts, but in much more of detail than the previous statements made upon such occasions. I began reading that abstract,—a caution not usual when the King was well; and he said, 'My Lord, you are cautious.' I entreated his Majesty to allow *that*, under the then circumstances. 'Oh!' he said, 'you are certainly right in that; but you should be correct as well as cautious.' I said I was not conscious that I was not correct. 'No,' said he, 'you are not: for if you will look into the commission which you have brought me to sign, you will see that I there state that I have fully considered the bills proposed to receive my sign-manual to be correct; therefore, I should have *the bills* to peruse and consider.' I stated to him that he never had had the bills while I had been Chancellor, and that I did not know that he had *ever* had the bills. He said during a part of his reign he had always had them, until Lord Thurlow had ceased to bring them; and the expression his Majesty used was, that Lord Thurlow had said it was nonsense his giving himself the trouble to read them. I said his Majesty had satisfied me that I had used caution enough, took the sign-manual and went to the House of Lords; and when about passing the commission, Lord Fitzwilliam arose and said, 'I wish to ask whether the Chancellor declares his Majesty is equal to the act of signing the commission with full knowledge upon the subject,' or to that effect. I answered, 'Your Lordship will see the commission executed immediately.'

"I have committed this to paper, having been much abused on account of this transaction, and for the purpose of stating that it was my determination, if I thought his Majesty sufficiently well as an individual to give his assent, to take the royal sign-manual to the commission, and execute it without making observation; if, on the other hand, I did not think him so well as an individual,—inasmuch as the competency of the King, as king, was what the law authorized me to consider as belonging to him, notwithstanding his indisposition, I determined to take the royal sign-manual to the commission, and after executing it, to state to the House in what condition of his Majesty I had taken this step, and to throw myself on Parliament's consideration of my case, and my having so acted, in order, in a most perilous period, to prevent the establishments necessary for the defense, and indeed the existence, of the country from going to pieces. Many thought I acted too boldly in this proceeding; but I could not bring myself to think that I ought to countenance the notion that the King's state of mind, considering him as an individual, was such as I in my conscience did not believe it to be; and I did think that it was my duty to expose myself to all that might happen, rather than give a false impression of the actual state of my Sovereign and Royal Master to his people.

"God grant that no future Chancellor may go through the same distressing scenes, or be exposed to the dangerous responsibility which I went through, and was exposed to, during the indispositions of my sovereign! My own attachment to him supported me through those scenes. Such and so cordial was the love and affection his people bore to him, that a servant meaning well, and placed amidst great difficulties, would have been pardoned for much, if he had occasion for indemnity.

"When I went to take the King's sign-manual, some other ministers wanted it in their department. They sent the papers to me, instead of coming themselves to support me by their acts. I refused to tender any of them to the King."[1]

Lord Eldon told the following anecdote, referable to the same period:—

"In one of his Majesty, George III.'s, illnesses, when he was at Buckingham House, it was conceived to be my duty as Chancellor to call at that house every day. This was constantly done, to the interruption of the business of my Court to a great extent, for which the public opinion made no allowance. Upon one day, when I went to make my call of duty, Dr. Simmons, the medical attend-

[1] Twiss, i. 285.

ant constantly there, represented to me the embarrassment he was exposed to, being persuaded that if his Majesty could have a walk frequently round the garden behind the house it would be of the most essential benefit to him; that if he took his walk with the doctor, or any of his attendants, he was overlooked from the windows of Grosvenor Place, and reports were circulated very contrary to the truth respecting his Majesty's mental health; that, on the other hand, his Majesty's family were afraid of accompanying him; and that he, the doctor, did not know how to act, as the walk was of vast importance to his Majesty's recovery. It was to me plain that he wished that I should offer to attend his Majesty, and walk with him in the garden. I offered to do so, if he thought it likely to be useful to the King. He then went into the next room, where the King was, and I heard him say, 'Sir, the Chancellor is come to take a walk with your Majesty, if your Majesty pleases to allow it.' 'With all my heart,' I overheard the King say, and he called for his hat and cane. We walked two or three times round Buckingham House gardens. There was at first a momentary hurry and incoherence in his Majesty's talk, but this did not endure two minutes; during the rest of the walk there was not the slightest aberration in his Majesty's conversation, and he gave me the history of every Administration in his reign. When we returned into the house, his Majesty, laying down his hat and cane, placed his head upon my shoulder, and burst into tears; and after recovering himself, bowed me out of the room in his usual manner. Dr. Simmons told me afterwards that this had been of infinite use towards his recovery."

The wary Chancellor, when in a communicative mood, also related that the King complained to him that a man in the employ of one of his physicians had knocked him down. "When I got up again," added the King, "I said my foot had slipped, and ascribed my fall to that: for i would not do for me to admit that the King had been knocked down by any one."

His Majesty continued in this unsatisfactory state of mind till the month of June following, some members of the Cabinet not having nerve to transact business with him; but, during this period, Lord Eldon not only obtained his assent to acts of state, such as giving the royal assent to bills that had passed both Houses of Parliament, but actually induced him to dismiss Mr. Addington, and to take back Mr. Pitt as his Prime Minister. The Sovereign being sometimes better and sometime worse, and occasionally appearing to talk and to write rationally, and the physicians all agreeing that he was likely to recover soon,—although, if a private person in the care of a committee under the jurisdiction of the Court of Chancery, it is quite clear that he would not have been restored to liberty,—perhaps Lord Eldon did well in continuing to treat him as competent fully to exercise all the prerogatives of the crown. Not being completely disabled, as he was in 1788 and in 1810, any proposal to suspend his functions, or to supersede his authority, might have led to a public convulsion; and the smaller evil to be chosen might be to consider his legal competence as unimpaired, —there being advisers for every act that was done, responsible to Parliament and to the country.

But I can by no means offer so good a defense to another charge against Lord Eldon—that, in the intrigue by which the change of Government was effected, he betrayed his political chief. This charge, which has been several times advanced, is reiterated in the recent Life of Lord Sidmouth, by Dr. Pellew; and, I am sorry to say, I think it is completely established.

When Mr. Pitt, not pleased to see those whom he considered his own creatures assuming an independent existence, had become impatient for a return to power, and had coalesced with the two parties, in regular opposition, under Mr. Fox and Lord Grenville, the existing Government was in jeopardy, and its majorities decreased on every division. Nevertheless, the King, highly satisfied with his Prime Minister, was resolved resolutely to stand by him; and, till the result of the debate on the 25th of April respecting the defense of the country against invasion, in which the different sections of opponents heartily concurred, neither King nor Prime Minister had any thought of a change. But, long before this, Lord Eldon, without the knowledge of the King, and without the privity of any of his colleagues, was in secret communication with Mr. Pitt, now the declared enemy of the King's Government. He might most reasonably have thought that Mr. Addington could no longer be allowed to be at the head of affairs with safety to the state—but then it would have been his duty, boldly and openly, to have said so to Mr. Addington, and it would have been his duty instantly to resign the Great Seal into his Majesty's hands. Retaining the Great Seal,—professing to serve under Mr. Addington,—and regardless of the "wishes of his Royal Master," about which, when it suited his purpose, he could be so pathetic, he, of his own accord, through the medium of a note sent by his son, then a member of the House of Commons, opened a negotiation with Mr. Pitt for Mr. Addington's overthrow.[1] This fact is incontestably established by the following letter from Mr. Pitt to Lord Eldon:—

"York Place, Tuesday night, March 20th, 1804.

"MY DEAR LORD,

"Mr. Scott was so good as to give me your note this evening in the House of Commons.[2] I am very glad to accept your invitation for Saturday, as, whatever may be the result of our conversation, I think the sooner we hold it the better. The state of public affairs makes it impossible that the present suspense should last very long, and nothing can give me more satisfaction than to put you confidently in possession of all the sentiments and opinions by which my conduct will be regulated. Believe me, my dear Lord, Yours, very sincerely,

"W. PITT."

All that we know of their proceedings in March is, that after their secret meeting, thus arranged, they had "a tete-à-tete dinner."[3] It is supposed that the negotiation was interrupted by the King being so much under the influence of his malady, that he could not be produced to hold a conncil, or have any political communication made to him.[4]

On the 23rd of April Mr. Fox was to lead a grand

[1] All possibility of a coalition between Mr. Pitt and Mr. Addington had long gone by, Mr. Pitt having declared that he would not even become head of the Treasury without first dissolving Mr. Addington's Administration.
[2] This refers to the Chancellor's eldest son, then M.P. for Boroughbridge.
[3] This is proved by an entry in the journal of Mr. Abbot (afterwards Lord Colchester), copied in Pellew's "Life of Lord Sidmouth," ii. 277.
[4] The following note from the Queen to Lord Eldon seems to show that his Majesty was worse about the middle of April:—

"MY LORD,

"Something having occurred last night which I wish to communicate to you, I take advantage of your promise to apply to you when under any assault of the combined Opposition, which it was thought might prove fatal to the Government; and, the day before, Mr. Pitt thus wrote to the Chancellor:—

"York Place, Sunday, April 22nd, 1804.

"MY DEAR LORD,

"Under the present peculiar circumstances, I trust your Lordship will forgive my taking the liberty of requesting you to take charge of the inclosed letter to the King. Its object is to convey to His Majesty, as a mark of respect, a previous intimation of the sentiments which I may find it necessary to avow in Parliament, and at the same time an assurance, with respect to my own personal intentions, which I might perhaps not be justified in offering, uncalled for, under any other circumstances, but which you will see my motive for not withholding at present. I certainly feel very anxious that this letter should be put into His Majesty's hands, if it can with propriety, before the discussion of to-morrow; but having no means of forming myself any sufficient judgment on that point, my wish is to refer it entirely to your Lordship's discretion, being fully persuaded that you will feel the importance of making the communication with as little delay as the nature of the case will admit. *I shall inclose my letter unsealed for your inspection, knowing that you will allow me in doing so to request that you will not communicate its contents to any one but the King himself. I am the more anxious that you should see what I have written, because I can not think of asking you to undertake to be the bearer of a letter expressing sentiments so adverse to the Government with which you are acting, without giving you the previous opportunity of knowing in what manner those sentiments are stated.*

"Believe me, with great truth and regard,
"My dear Lord,
"Faithfully and sincerely yours,
"W. PITT."

It would appear that Lord Eldon had sent back the letter, to have some alteration made in it,—expressing a readiness to deliver it when the King should be in a state of mind in which he could receive it.

difficulty, and beg to see you for a moment, in case you call at the Queen's House this morning, before you go to the King.

"CHARLOTTE.

"Q. H. April 14th, 1804."

'York Place, Sunday night, April 22nd, 1804.

"MY DEAR LORD,

"I have no hesitation in availing myself of your permission to return into your hands my letter to the King. My wish is to leave it entirely to your discretion, whether it can with propriety be delivered before the debate tomorrow. If not, I anxiously wish that it should be known to His Majesty in due time, that it was deposited with you in order that it should be so delivered, if you should judge that it could with propriety.

"I am, my dear Lord,
"Faithfully and sincerely yours,
"W. PITT."

Mr. Twiss,—not having seen Dr. Pellew's statements,—after mentioning the Council held on the 23rd of April, at which the King was well enough to appear, good-naturedly observes, "The attempt to remodel the Government seems to have been immediately resumed through the agency of the Lord Chancellor, on whom alone, in a matter where the personal intervention of Mr. Addington was necessarily out of the question, the King inclined to rely." The public now most certainly know that till the 29th of April the King did not employ the agency of Lord Eldon in communicating with Mr. Pitt, whom he then regarded as little better than a Whig, and that he eagerly hoped Mr. Addington might continue Prime Minister.

Mr. Fox's motion was actually made on the night of the 23rd of April, and was warmly supported by Mr. Pitt, but was defeated by a majority of 52; and Mr. Addington still resolved to retain his post, the King backing him, and expressing high resentment at the contents of Mr. Pitt's letter which had been shown to him. But rumors—spread by whom was never known—became rife that the King was desirous of changing his Minister; and when a similar motion was repeated on the 25th, although there was no increase in the numbers of the Opposition, Mr. Addington's supporters fell off, and his majority was reduced to 32. He thought he could stand his ground no longer, but he did not communicate to any of his colleagues his intention to resign till Sunday, the 29th of April. On that day a Cabinet was held, when he reproached the Chancellor for having been the bearer of a letter from Mr. Pitt to the King, containing expressions so injurious to the Government with which he was acting, and for the head of which he had always expressed so much regard. All present agreed in the necessity of immediate resignation. Lord St. Vincent afterwards "expressed, as one main ground of the Government being defeated, when, with the hearty support of the King, he considered the struggle as anything but desperate, the secret understanding between Lord Eldon and Mr. Pitt, or as he phrased it, 'the enemy having a friend in the citadel, who opened the gates to him.'"[1]

The resolution of the Cabinet being communicated to the King, his Majesty, who had been kept in ignorance of the previous intercourse between Mr. Pitt and Lord Eldon, and of the fact that Lord Eldon was privy to the contents of Mr. Pitt's letter, of which he had been the bearer, was made to see the absolute necessity for parting with his favorite Minister, and authorized Lord Eldon to desire Mr. Pitt to attend him at Buckingham House with the view of forming a new Administration. The following is Mr. Pitt's answer to the confidential note which he received, begging a prior personal interview with the Chancellor:—

"York Place, Sunday, April 29th, 1804.

"MY DEAR LORD,

"I am very much obliged to you for your letter, and must feel great satisfaction in learning the manner in which the assurances contained in my letter were received. I shall be at home till half past two to-day, and afterwards from five to six, and any time before two to-morrow, if you should find occasion to call here; or if you prefer seeing me at any other hour, or at your house, you will have the goodness to let me know, and I shall be at your commands. I am, my dear Lord,

"Sincerely and faithfully yours,
"W. PITT."

Great difficulties arose in the negotiations which were now begun, for I believe that Mr. Pitt was sincere in his wish to introduce Mr. Fox, as well as Lord Grenville, into the Cabinet, and Mr. Fox was most odious both to the King and the Chancellor.

[1] Lord Brougham on his personal knowledge, in a very able article in the Second Number of the Law Review.

The Marquis of Stafford, leagued with the Opposition, had a motion standing in the House of Lords for the Monday, respecting the defense of the country. At the meeting of the House, Lord Hawkesbury, as the organ of the Government, stated, that "he had reasons of the highest and most weighty importance, which induced him to request the noble Marquis to postpone his motion. These reasons, it was true, were of that delicate and peculiar nature that he could not at the present moment, consistently with his duty, enter into them further." Lord Grenville and other lords expressing a wish for further explanation, the Lord Chancellor quitted the woolsack and said: "Being of opinion, my Lords, that sufficient grounds exist for your Lordships to exercise your good sense and discretion upon the point under consideration, I shall say no more, being determined, for my own part, to fulfill, as long as I have a drop of blood in my veins, my duty to his Majesty and the country,—for these terms, my Lords, mean the same thing; to do my duty to his Majesty, is to do my duty to the country; and to perform my duty to the country, is to perform my duty to my Sovereign. And upon my most awful sense of what I think my duty to both, my conduct has been, is, and shall ever be regulated, and this paramount consideration now induces me to go the length of joining my noble friend in recommending the noble Marquis—as far as the opinion of an humble individual may be deserving of attention—to postpone his motion." Who could have conjectured the manner in which the noble and learned Lord had been performing his duty to his Sovereign and his country during the preceding month?

On the 2nd of May Mr. Pitt wrote a long letter to the King, which has never been published, but in which he must have fully explained his views about the formation of the new Government. This he sent, with the accompanying note, to Lord Eldon:—

"York Place, Wednesday, May 2nd, 1804,
Three-quarters past one, P. M.

"MY DEAR LORD,

"I inclose a letter addressed to you, which I shall be much obliged to you if you will lay before his Majesty. I am sorry not to have been able to make it shorter, or to send it you sooner. As I think it may probably find you at the Court of Chancery, I will, at the same time that I send it, ride down to Mr. Rose's, at Palace Yard, in order that I may be easily within your reach, if anything should arise on which you may wish to see me before you go to the Queen's House. If you should not be at the Court of Chancery, I shall order my letter to be carried to your house, unless my servant should learn, where it can be delivered to you sooner. Ever, my dear Lord,

"Yours very sincerely.
"W. PITT."

It seems that Lord Eldon added to Mr. Pitt's communication a soothing missive from himself, and that the King, much excited, and unable to conceal his dislike of the change forced upon him, had returned an answer to Mr. Pitt, testifying even contempt for the sentiments and style of that Minister. This answer will probably never see the light; but the following letter from the King to Lord Eldon shows very strikingly how his Majesty stood affected:—

"Queen's Palace, May 5th, 1804,
"19 minutes past six, P. M.

"The King is much pleased with *his* excellent Chancellor's note: he doubts much whether Mr. Pitt will, after weighing the contents of the paper delivered this day to him by Lord Eldon, choose to have a personal interview with his Majesty; but whether he will not rather prepare another Essay, containing as many empty words and little information as the one he had before transmitted.

"His Majesty will, with great pleasure, receive the Lord Chancellor to-morrow, between ten and eleven, the time he himself has proposed. GEORGE R."

Lord Eldon most earnestly denied that he exercised any influence over the King in disinclining him to the admission of M. Fox into the Cabinet. If he believed that such a step would be detrimental to the public service, I can not see the harm of the Chancellor, when consulted, expressing his opinion upon it; and unless some such influence had been used, I am persuaded that his Majesty would now have assented to it, as he very readily did in 1806.

The King, of his own accord, or by persuasion, remaining inflexible, the Grenvilles would not separate themselves from Mr. Fox, and the memorable Administration was to be formed in which all the power of the State was to be centered in one individual. The new Prime Minister Elect thus addressed the King:—

"May 7th, 1804.

"Mr. Pitt humbly begs leave to acquaint your Majesty, that he finds Lord Grenville and his friends decline forming a part of any arrangement in which Mr. Fox is not included. Mr. Pitt hopes to be enabled by to-morrow to submit, for your Majesty's consideration, the most material parts of such a plan of Administration as, under these circumstances, he wishes humbly to propose."

Although Mr. Pitt was now in direct communication with the King, he never moved unless in concert with the Chancellor, on whom he chiefly relied for intelligence respecting the state of the King's health. Thus he addressed him when the arrangements were complete, and only required his Majesty's sanction:—

"York Place, Tuesday, May 8th, 1804.

"MY DEAR LORD,

"I shall be much obliged to you if you can send me a single line to let me know what accounts you have from the Queen's House this morning. I shall be very desirous of seeing you in the course of the day, and will endeavor either to find you near the House of Lords between four and five, or will call on you in the evening. It will probably be desirable that I should see the King again to-morrow. "Ever, my dear Lord,

"Sincerely yours,

"W. P."

At this meeting the Ministry was settled, the King evidently being in a state of mind in which, as a private man, he would not have been allowed to sign an ordinary contract. When it was over, he thus addressed Mr. Addington:—

"Queen's Palace, May 9th, 1804, 48 m. past six, P. M.

"The King has this instant finished a long, but most satisfactory, conversation with Mr. Pitt, who will stand forth, though Lord Grenville, Lord Spencer, and Mr. Windham have declined even treating, as Mr. Fox is excluded by the express command of the King to Mr. Pitt. This being the case, the King desires Mr. Addington will attend here at ten to-morrow morning with the Seals of Chancellor of the Exchequer. The King's friendship for

Mr. Addington is too deeply graven on his heart to be in the least diminished by any change of situation; his Majesty will order the warrant to be prepared for creating Mr. Addington Earl of Banbury, Viscount Wallingford, and Baron Reading; and will order the message to be carried by Mr. York to the House of Commons for the usual annuity, having most honorably and ably filled the station of Speaker of the House of Commons. The King will settle such a pension on Mrs. Addington, whose virtue and modesty he admires, as Mr. Addington may choose to propose. . . . "GEORGE R."

The same evening Mr. Pitt thus addressed his confidant:—

"York Place, Wednesday night, May 9th, 1804.

"MY DEAR LORD,

"I have had another interview to-day, not quite, I am sorry to say, so satisfactory as that of Monday. I do not think there was anything positively wrong, but there was a hurry of spirits, and an excessive love of talking, which showed that either the airing of this morning, or the seeing so many persons, and conversing so much during these three days, has rather tended to disturb. The only inference I draw from this observation is, that too much caution can not be used in still keeping exertion of all sorts, and particularly conversation, within reasonable limits. If that caution can be sufficiently adhered to, I have no doubt that everything will go well; and there is certainly nothing in what I have observed that would, in the smallest degree, justify postponing any of the steps that are in progress towards arrangement. I am, therefore, to attend again to-morrow, for the purpose of receiving the Seals, which Mr. A. will have received notice from his Majesty to bring. If I should not meet you there, I will endeavor to see you afterwards at the House of Lords.

"I am, my dear Lord,
"Ever sincerely yours,
"W. PITT."

The following day the change of Government formally took place, and Lord Eldon was confirmed in his office under the new chief. "The upshot of the whole intrigue is that Mr. Pitt shoves Mr. Addington out of his place, which he takes himself, and retains his coadjutor in the business as Chancellor, '*his ally within the besieged garrison, who opened the gate to him under the cloud of night while the rest slept."*[1]

I add Lord Eldon's own account of his part in the transaction, as recorded in his autobiography entitled the "Anecdote Book," showing with what caution this work is to be perused; for he would represent that the King was quite recovered when the change took place,—he entirely suppresses his own previous intercourse with Mr. Pitt, as if the idea of this Minister's return had originated in a spontaneous order of the King requiring an immediate interview,—and he would induce a belief, that, after Mr. Pitt was installed it became matter of deliberation whether he himself should continue Chancellor,—whereas all mankind must now believe that this was as well understood between them, as that George III. should continue on the throne :—

"When Mr. Addington went out of office, and Mr. Pitt succeeded him, the King was just recovered from mental indisposition. He ordered me to go to Mr. Pitt with his commands for Mr. Pitt to attend him. I went to him, to Baker Street or York Place, to deliver those commands. I found him at breakfast. After some little conversation, he said, as the King was pleased to command his attendance with a view to forming a new Administration, he hoped I had not given any turn to the King's mind which could affect any proposition he might have to make to his Majesty upon that subject. I was extremely hurt by this. I assured him I had not; that I considered myself as a gentleman bringing to a gentleman a message from a king; and that I should have acted more unworthily than I believe myself capable of acting, if I had given any opinion upon what might be right to his Majesty. Mr. Pitt went with me in my carriage to Buckingham House, and, when we arrived there, he asked me if I was sure his Majesty was well enough to see him. I asked him whether he thought that I should have brought him such a message if I had any doubt upon that, and observed that it was fortunately much about the hour when the physicians called; and, it turning out that they were in the house, I said he might see them in an adjoining room. He asked me to go with him into that room. After what had passed, I said I should not do so, and that it

[1] Law Review, No. xi. p. 264.

was fit that he should judge for himself, and that I should be absent. He then left me, and, after being with the physicians a considerable time, he returned, and said he was quite satisfied with their report, and expressed his astonishment at what he had heard from them: that he had learnt, he thought from unquestionable authority, only the day before, that I never had seen the King but in the presence of the doctors or doctor who attended him on account of his mental health. He intimated that this was intelligence which had come from C——n House, and which he had now learned was utterly devoid of truth. He was soon after introduced to the King, and he remained with his Majesty a considerable time. Upon his return he said he found the King perfectly well,—that he had expressed his full consent to Lord Grenville's being a part of the new Administration, but that all his endeavors to prevail upon his Majesty to consent to Mr. Fox also being a member of it had been urged in vain in the course of a long interview and conversation. It is well known that Mr. Pitt was obliged to form an Administration without either.

"After Mr. Pitt had formed the rest of his Administration, he conversed me as to remaining Chancellor. I told him that I must first know whether he had any reason to believe that it had been necessary to ask me whether I had given any turn to the King's mind that could affect any proposition he had to make to the King. He said, that when he left his Majesty he was convinced that nothing had passed between his Majesty and me relative to the formation of an administration, as to any person who should or should not form a part of it; and that, if I desired it, he would give me a written declaration, in any terms which would be satisfactory, that he had no reason to think that I had in any way influenced his Majesty's mind. I told him that what he had said was enough."

But, conscious that his plotting against Mr. Addington could not be concealed from the world, and that, *primâ facie* he was liable to the accusation of treachery, he was ever after indefatigable in repeating the assertion that he was the "King's Chancellor," and not Mr. Addington's. He harped upon his promise to accept the Great Seal, when he was made Chief Justice of the Common Pleas: he said, "Upon the duty of a subject to obey the commands of the sovereign as to accepting office, I have some notions that, I believe, are much out of fashion;" and he declared, "With respect to the Chancellorship, I was indebted for that office to the King himself, and not, as some supposed, to Mr. Addington, and as some of Mr. Addington's friends supposed." But if we give entire credit to these representations, they in no degree mitigate the censure due to his indirect proceedings; for the duties of his situation were the same, however he obtained it; and no degree of royal favor could entitle him to deceive a colleague who placed implicit confidence in his honor.[1]

Lord Eldon must, at all events, be allowed to have been a most consummate master of political intrigue; and, always persuading himself that his objects were laudable, he gained them without any unnecessary artifices. On this occasion, although thwarting the royal wishes, he contrived to persuade the King that he lived but to obey him; and when Mr. Addington had by his means been violently torn from the King's embrace, his Majesty was more than ever charmed with the Chancellor. At the end of the first week of the new *régime*, thus wrote the delighted and deluded Sovereign:—

"Queen's Palace, May 18th, 1084, 5 m. pt. 10, A. M.

"The King having signed the commission for giving his Royal Assent, returns it to his excellent Lord Chancellor, whose conduct he most thoroughly approves. His Majesty feels the difficulties he has had, both political, and personally to the King;[2] but the uprightness of Lord Eldon's mind, and his attachment to the King, have borne him with credit and honor, and (what the King knows will not be without its due weight) with the approbation of his Sovereign, through an unpleasant labyrinth."

Commissions continued to be signed by the King for passing bills, and all other acts of state were done in his name, in the ordinary course of business: but the following two letters show that the Chancellor still acted on his

---

[1] "However the debilitated energies of the country might demand that some change should be wrought suddenly, however the tottering mind of the King might require that the change should be wrought quietly, still it would have been more analogous to the ordinary principles and common conduct of gentlemen if he had himself retired from the Ministry when he considered it too weak to serve the country efficiently, before he entered into a secret negotiation, which might end, as it did end, in its subversion."—*W. E. Surtees* p. 103.

[2] *Sic.*

distinction between his Majesty's *natural* and *political* capacity;—

The Duke of York to Lord Eldon.

"Horse Guards, May 25th, 1804.

"MY DEAR LORD,

"Having missed the pleasure of seeing your Lordship to-day as I had intended, I trust that you will excuse my troubling you with this letter, to put you in mind of the necessity of speaking as early as possible to his Majesty upon the propriety of the Queen's keeping his birthday at St. James's; as, if it is not announced in the Gazette to-morrow night, persons who mean to appear at the drawing-room will not have time to prepare their dresses. I am afraid, from what I have heard, that things were not comfortable at the Queen's house this morning, and wish that you would inquire of Sir Francis Millman and Dr. Simmonds before you go in to the King, as he seems to dwell much upon the illegality of his confinement, and is not aware of the dreadful consequences which may attend him if any unfortunate circumstance can be brought forward in Parliament.   "Believe me ever,
"My dear Lord,
"Yours most sincerely,
"FREDERICK."

Mr. Pitt to Lord Eldon.

"Bromley Hall, Saturday Evening, May 26th, 1804.

"MY DEAR LOBD,

"As I was leaving town this evening I learned (in a way on which I can entirely depend) some circumstances of a conversation in one of the audiences on Thursday, which seem very alarming. The topics treated of were such as did not at all arise out of any view (right or wrong) of the *actual state* of things, but referred to plans of foreign politics, that could only be creatures of an imagination heated and disordered. This part of the discourse, however, though commenced with great eagerness, was not long dwelt on, and in the remainder there was nothing in substance wrong. This information has been given me, as you may imagine, in strict confidence; but I desired and received permission to communicate it to you, and to mention it to Dr. S. I will tell you the name of my informant when I see you, and you will probably not find it difficult to guess him in the meantime.

There is nothing very material to be known as to the particulars (as far as it strikes me), except that they related to plans, political and military, about the Netherlands. I mention thus much now, because it may enable you to learn from Dr. S. whether anything has before passed on this point. I would have endeavored to see you in town to-morrow morning, but I understand you will be setting out early to Windsor. On your return, either that evening or Monday morning, I shall be very anxious to see you at any hour that suits you best, and will beg you to send to Downing Street to let me know.

"Ever, my dear Lord,
"Sincerely yours,
"W. PITT."

Even so late as the 30th of June, the King wrote a letter to the Chancellor—in which, after lamenting that business in Parliament had been protracted to so late a period of the session, he says, " But, in truth, part of this must inevitably be laid this year to the door of the King's long, tedious, and *never-ending* confinement, which has thrown much perplexity in every quarter, but which he is resolved, with the protection of Divine Providence, carefully to avoid in future." The determination to avoid "confinement" in future, rather seems to indicate a present necessity for it. However, his Majesty's health soon after rallied greatly, and till his attack in the year 1810, when he was permanently disabled from performing any of the functions of royalty, he displayed the same acuteness and vigor of intellect, as well as mental activity, which had formerly distinguished him—ever devoted to what he considered his duty—but ever retaining the prejudices of education which led to the misfortune of his reign.

During the remainder of Mr. Pitt's life, Lord Eldon was not very conspicuous in politics. I do not think he was at all consulted about foreign affairs, and he is not answerable for the new continental coalition against France, which ended in the capitulation of Ulm and the battle of Austerlitz. He took some part in the proceedings of the House of Lords, but these were not very important, as the Whig leaders had in a great measure seceded from Parliament. He ineffectually opposed the bill for disfranchising Aylesbury, and giving the right of election to the adjoining hundreds,[1]—he succeeded in throwing out the bill for the abolition of the slave trade,[2]—and he strenuously opposed all relaxation of the law of imprisonment for debt, which in its then state he contended was essentially necessary for our prosperity as a commercial nation.[3]

The question of Catholic Emancipation being started, on a petition from the Roman Catholics of Ireland, he made a long speech against it—bringing forward very boldly the religious principles to which he ever after most steadily adhered. He maintained that whatever was required by toleration had already been conceded to the Roman Catholics, and that their numbers should be disregarded, the legislature looking only to the reasonableness of their demands. He argued that the Roman Catholics of Ireland were highly favored, as they had a greater latitude in the form of their oath of allegiance than was allowed to the Protestant Dissenters of England; for the Irish Roman Catholics were required only to swear allegiance to the King and his family, whereas the form of the English oath was, to the King and his family, *being Protestants*. The British Constitution, he contended, was not based upon the principles of equal rights to all men indiscriminately, but of equal rights of all men conforming to, and complying with, the tests which that Constitution required for its security.[4] By such arguments he carried with him a majority of 178 against 49.[5]

Lord Eldon was employed during the summer and autumn of 1804, and the spring of 1805, in a very difficult negotiation between the King and the Prince of Wales, who had long been at open enmity with each other. The spirit in which it was begun by his Majesty may be discovered from a note to the Chancellor, in which he says,— "Undoubtedly the Prince of Wales's making the offer of having the dear little Charlotte's education and principles attended to, is the best earnest he can give of returning to a sense of what he owes to his father and, indeed, to his country, and may to a degree mollify the feelings òf an injured father; but it will require some reflection before the King can answer how soon he can bring himself to receive the publisher of his letters."[6] The Chancel-

[1] 2 Parl. Deb. 517, 532, 681–82.   [2] Ib. 931.   [3] Ib. 1130.
[4] 4 Ibid. 783.   [5] Ib. 843.   [6] 18th July, 1804.

lor prevailed upon the King to agree to an interview, but afterwards received a note from him annexing this proviso—that "no explanations or excuses should be attempted by the Prince of Wales, but that it should merely be a visit of civility, as any retrospect would oblige the King to utter truths which, instead of healing must widen the breach."[1] The Prince agreed to these terms, but, before the appointed time arrived, became deeply wounded by discovering what he considered undue partiality in favor of the Princess of Wales. His Majesty had written another note to the Chancellor, containing the following expressions respecting her Royal Highness:—"In the interview he had yesterday at Kew with the Princess, her whole conduct and language gave the greatest satisfaction. She will entirely be guided by the King, who has directed her to state whatever she pleases to the Lord Chancellor as the person alone to be trusted by her in any difficult occasions that may arise. She is deserving of every attention, and therefore strongly recommended by the King to his Lord Chancellor." The Chancellor in consequence having spoken favorably of the Princess to the Prince, his Royal Highness positively refused to meet the King, and desired that the Chancellor would carry a message from him to his Majesty to that effect. The Chancellor venturing on expostulation, the Prince replied, —"Sir, who gave you authority to advise me?" *Lord Chancellor:* "I express very sincere regret that I have offended your Royal Highness by doing so; but then, Sir, I am his Majesty's Chancellor, and it is for me to judge what messages I ought to take to his Majesty: your Royal Highness must send some other messenger with that communication; I will not take it." It was agreed that the Chancellor should write to the King to put off the interview on the ground of the Prince being much indisposed, as we find by the following note from his Majesty to his Chancellor:—

"Kew, Aug. 22nd, 1804, 10 m. past one, P. M.

"The King, soon after his arrival here with the Queen and his daughters, found the Dukes of Kent and Cambridge, since which the Lord Chancellor's letter has been brought by a servant of the Prince of Wales. The King authorizes the Lord Chancellor to express to the Prince

[1] 20th Aug. 1804.

of Wales his sorrow at his being unwell; that, in consequence of this, his Majesty will postpone his interview with the Prince of Wales until his return from Weymouth; and then, as was now intended, it will be in presence of his family at Kew, of which the Lord Chancellor will be empowered to give due notice to the Prince of Wales. GEORGE R."

After the King's return from Weymouth, an interview did take place between him and the Prince, which his Majesty declared "was every way decent, as both parties avoided any subjects but those of the most trifling kind." And, after a long and tedious negotiation, the Chancellor succeeded in bringing about an arrangement, whereby the care of the Princess Charlotte was transferred to the King, although his Majesty and the Prince of Wales still continued in a state of irreconcilable hostility.[1]

Lord Eldon had a difficult part to play during these altercations; but, although naturally unwilling to make an enemy of the Heir Apparent, he seems to have conducted himself with becoming spirit, if not always with the best tact. In Lord Malmesbury's diary we have the following account of a fracas between him and the Prince, which must have happened soon after. Lord Eldon said to the Prince, "The Princess hoped her dignity and comfort would be attended to." *Prince:* "I am not the sort of person to let my hair grow under my wig to please my wife." *Lord Eldon* (respectfully but firmly): "Your Royal Highness condescends to become personal. I beg leave to withdraw." He accordingly bowed very low, and retired. The Prince, alarmed at this, could find no other way of extricating himself than by causing a note to be written the next day to Lord Eldon, to say that "the phrase he made use of was nothing personal, but simply a proverb—a proverbial way of saying *a man was governed by his wife.*" Lord Malmesbury adds, "Very absurd of Lord Eldon, but explained by his having literally done what the Prince said."[2] It was then little expected that

[1] "The Prince declared a statement that he would not see the Chancellor to be 'a strange fabrication of the King;' while the King declared that 'fair dealing was the honorable line to combat misapprehension, chicane, and untruth;' and thus concluded his last missive on the subject: 'The Lord Chancellor is desired to take a copy for the King of this returned paper of instructions, and prepare the paper to be transmitted to the Prince of Wales, *who certainly means further chicane.*'"—*Lord Malmesb.*, 10th March, 1805.
[2] Vol. iv. p. 223.

George IV. would call Lord Eldon *his* Chancellor, and address him by the familiar and endearing sobriquet of "Old Bags."

In the midst of these distressing disputes in the Royal Family, to which it will be my painful duty ere long to return, it is refreshing to find the following letter to the Chancellor from another son of the King, who seems uniformly to have conducted himself with propriety in all the relations of public and domestic life:—

The Duke of Kent to Lord Eldon.

"Saturday morning, Feb. 9th, 1805,
Kensington Palace.

" MY DEAR LORD,

" Fearful lest your Lordship should, in the multiplicity of business in which your time is so much engaged, forget what I did myself the pleasure of saying to you (relative to my attendance in Parliament) on the day when the session was opened, and from that cause, that I may at any time be absent, when my presence would have been wished for by his Majesty's Government, I now do myself the pleasure to address you these lines, in order to repeat my readiness to attend in the House of Peers, whenever your Lordship is so good as to send me the slightest direct intimation that my appearance is wished for. In doing this I am anxious your Lordship should understand, that I am actuated by that principle I have ever professed, of supporting the King's Government, and never taking any part in political disputes, for which I have the utmost abhorrence, and indeed am less fit than any other member of the House, having never given my attention to any other pursuit but that of my own profession. *The King* is *my* object: to stand by *him* at *all* times, my *first* duty and my *inclination;* and I think I can not prove this more strongly, than by pledging myself, as I did when first I received my peerage *spontaneously*, always to support *his* servants, where my feeble voice could be of use. I *have* ever acted up to this profession, and I ever *will;* but it is not my system to attend Parliament otherwise; therefore, I solicit to be informed by your Lordship, *when* I *am* wanted, that I may not *then* be absent. Having said this, I now beg leave to add, that, as the King remains at Windsor till Tuesday, the 19th instant, it is my wish to be a couple of days with him in that time, and I therefore am anxious to learn from your Lordship if I shall be wanted in the course of the next week, and *on what days*, so as not to be from here on such as you shall name.

"With a thousand apologies for this intrusion, and sentiments of the highest regard and esteem, I remain,
"My dear Lord, ever yours,
"Most faithfully and sincerely,
"EDWARD."

Towards the close of this session of Parliament, the Ministry was in a very unprosperous condition. The strength which it had gained by Mr. Addington being prevailed upon to forget his wrongs, and to accept a peerage and a seat in the Cabinet, was more than counterbalanced by the vote of the House of Commons against Lord Melville, in consequence of which that minister was dismissed from office, and his name was struck out of the Privy Council. Lord Eldon had now the prospect of presiding in the House of Lords on the trial of his former colleague; but prior to his resignation of the Great Seal the preliminary arrangements had not been completed, and he was only called upon to give his opinion respecting the Bill for indemnifying the witnesses, when he very properly laid down, that "liability to a civil action was no sufficient reason for a refusal to answer a question," and the indemnity was confined to criminal proceedings.[1] At last, to the great relief of the Government, Lord Eldon, under a commission from the King, pronounced the prorogation.

Before Parliament met again, death had committed ravages which deeply affected the Chancellor, both in domestic life and as a public character. He had the heavy misfortune to lose his eldest son, to whom he was tenderly attached as his first-born, and, for ten years, his only child,—who, about a year before, had been married to an amiable young lady, now in an advanced state of pregnancy,—and who, though not of brilliant talents, had ever been most exemplary in his conduct, so that Pope's lines on the son of Lord Chancellor Harcourt might well have been applied to him:—

"Who ne'er knew joy but friendship might divide,
Or gave his father grief but when he died."

I am afraid that the subject of this memoir not unfre-

[1] 45 Geo. 3, c. 126.

quently pretended to deep sensibility when his heart was unmoved; but the following letter, written by him to Sir William, speaks the genuine language of nature, and touchingly shows the anguish of a bereaved parent:—

"December 24th.

"MY EVER DEAR BROTHER,

"With a broken heart I inform you that, before I had written the last paragraph of the letter I sent by this day's post, my poor, dear, dear John was no more. I am so distressed, and all around me is such a scene of distraction and misery, that I know not what to do. May God Almighty preserve you and yours from what we suffer! His mother is living in my arms out of one hysteric into another, and his poor widow is in a state which can neither be conceived nor described. For myself, I am your ever, ever affectionate, but ever, ever unhappy brother, ELDON."

Sir William hurried to the house of mourning, and wrote to his daughter an affecting account of what he beheld: " Her (Lady Eldon's) grief is still as wild and passionate as ever, without the least abatement. She takes hardly any sustenance, and is falling away in such a degree, that I should not be surprised at any consequences that were to follow from the decay of her strength. It is impossible to describe the degree in which my brother is worn down by the constant attentions he is obliged to pay to her. She will hardly suffer him to be out of the room, and, during the whole time he is there, he is a witness to the indulgence of such sorrow as it is quite impossible for any man to stand. He is much affected in his health."

Lord Eldon met with much sympathy on this melancholy occasion, and he received letters of condolence from Mr. Wilberforce, Lord Ellenborough, and many other friends. Even Mr. Pitt, although struck by the illness which proved fatal to him, and still more depressed by the fatal result of his measures for humbling the power of Napoleon, thus wrote to Sir William Scott:—

"Bath, Dec. 27th, 1805.

"MY DEAR SIR,

"It is with great regret I break in upon you in the moment of a calamity in which you so nearly participate; but I feel too deeply for the loss which the Chancellor and all his family have sustained, not to be anxious to inquire how

he and they support themselves under this heavy affliction.
I know how vain every topic of consolation must be in
the first impression of so much just sorrow, but I trust he
will gradually find the relief, which even the sympathy
and affection of his friends can not administer, in the resignation and fortitude of his own mind. You will, I am
sure, pardon my giving you this trouble, and will oblige
me much by any account you can give me. I much wish
he may be induced to try for a time the benefit of change
of scene, and of a place of quiet.
"Believe me, my dear Sir,
"With great truth and regard,
"Most faithfully and sincerely yours,
"W. PITT."

Lord Eldon was necessarily recalled to the discharge of
his public duties by the very embarrassed state of public
affairs. Parliament was to meet on the 21st of January,
and when that day approached, Mr. Pitt, broken-hearted,
having returned from Bath to his house at Putney, was
known to be dying. In the midst of the deepest gloom,
the session was opened by a speech which Lord Eldon delivered to the two Houses as Lord Commissioner, and a
generous forbearance was exhibited by the Opposition.
On the 23d of January the proud spirit of the Premier
took its flight to another sphere of existence; and there
really seems to have been more solicitude to do honor to
his memory by voting a public funeral for his remains, and
money to pay his debts, than to struggle for the power
which was in abeyance. All parties were now disposed to
look upon him as a noble-hearted Englishman, who had
ever been the champion of his country ; and while the par-
tialties of many dwelt upon his efforts against French
conquest and French principles, others remembered his
early struggle in the cause of reform, and, justly asserting
that he had always been true to the principles of free
trade, and that if not thwarted by bigotry he would have
united Ireland to England by the indissoluble bond of affection, they palliated his encroachments on the Constitution, and the persecution of his old associates, by the
pressure to which he was subjected, and the unknown dangers arising out of the great revolutionary movement then
in operation over the world.

But a ministry must be speedily formed. I do not find

that during this crisis Lord Eldon engaged in any intrigue to patch up a Tory Government, or to exclude Mr. Fox. Either unnerved by domestic sorrow, or submitting quietly to what appeared to be an inevitable misfortune, he seems passively to have looked on while Mr. Fox and Lord Grenville were forming their arrangements, and to have made no attempt to retain the Great Seal.

On the 3d of February he announced his resignation, and said that he should not sit in the Court of Chancery after the following day. In rising to quit the chair on the 4th, he thus, in a tremulous voice and with real emotion, addressed the Bar:—

"Before I take leave of this Court, I wish to address a few words to you, gentlemen, expressive of the feelings I entertain for the respectful attention I have on all occasions experienced from you. I had doubted whether the more dignified manner of parting would not be simply to make my bow to you, and retire; but observing that I have been represented, yesterday and the day before, to have addressed you on the subject, I shall not resist the impulse I feel to say a few words. I quit the office I hold without one painful reflection. Called to it by authority of those whom it was my duty to obey, I have executed it, not well, but to the extent of my humble abilities, and the time which I have been able to devote to it; and I enjoy the grateful feeling that there is no suitor of this Court who can say I have not executed it conscientiously. There is yet, however, one painful emotion by which I am assailed—it is the taking leave of you. In retiring into private life, I am upheld by the hope that I shall carry with me the continued esteem of a profession for which I feel an attachment that will descend with me to the grave. For the great attention, respect, and kindness I have always received from you, accept, gentlemen, my sincerest thanks, accompanied by my best wishes for your long-continued health and happiness, and uninterrupted prosperity."

In the evening of the same day he thus wrote to his wife, showing the high self-complacency which stuck by him to his last hour:

"DEAR BESSY,

"I took leave of the Court of Chancery this morning: I don't mean to go to the Woolsack in the House of Lords to-morrow, or any more. I am to resign the Seal at two o'clock on Friday." . . . . . "I can not describe my own situation in point of health and feeling otherwise than as excellent,—as that which a man has a right to possess, who, having done his duty to God, his King, and to every individual upon earth, according to the best of his judgment, has a right to support himself under heavy afflictions by the consciousness of proud and dignified integrity."

The transfer of the Great Seal took place at the Queen's house, on the 7th of February. In a narrative which he wrote at the time, he merely said, " When his Majesty took the Seal from my hands, his Majesty's demeanor and assurances were in all respects satisfactory to me." But he afterwards stated, in his old age,—" The King appeared for a few moments to occupy himself with other things: looking up suddenly, he exclaimed, 'Lay them down on the sofa, for I *can not* and I *will not* take them from you. Yet, I admit, you can't stay when all the rest have run away.'"

The ex-Chancellor certainly carried with him the respect of the Bar and of the public. For five years he had presided in the Court of Chancery with consummate ability. In spite of the doubts and delays by which his usefulness was so much marred, the business of the Court had been transacted very satisfactorily, and there was yet no such accumulation of arrears as called forth the complaints which disturbed his second Chancellorship. The appeals in the House of Lords he had with hardly any assistance decided in a manner which pleased the English— and the Scotch still more.

He gained popularity by puffing himself (which he was never slow to do upon any subject) respecting the reform he introduced in considering the Recorder's Report of prisoners capitally convicted at the Old Bailey. " The first time I attended," he said, " I was exceedingly shocked at the careless manner in which the business was conducted. We were called upon to divide on sentences affecting no less than the *lives* of men, and yet there was nothing before us to enable us to judge whether there had or had not been any extraordinary circumstances ; it was merely a recapitulation of the judge's opinion and the sentence. I resolved that I never would attend another report without having read and duly considered the whole of the evidence of each case; and I never did. It was a considerable labor in addition to my other duties, but it is a comfort to reflect that I did so, and, that in consequence, I saved the lives of several individuals." We know, on undoubted authority, that he did take great pains with this department of his duty, but he surely very unjustly disparages his predecessors and his colleagues, and there is no reason to suppose that such men as Lord Kenyon and Lord Ellenborough could be so grossly negligent and reckless as he describes them.

Erskine was now Chancellor. "All the Talents" were in their palmy state, and the old Tory party, which was soon to recover power and to retain it many years, seemed extinguished. Lord Eldon did not by any means relish his position. He had a pension of £4,000 a year, under the recent Act of Parliament;[1] but this was a poor consolation to him for the loss of the profits of the Great Seal, and he thought to himself, that if he had continued at the Bar he should have been in possession of a much larger income.

CHAPTER CXCIX.

CONTINUATION OF THE LIFE OF LORD ELDON TILL HE WAS RESTORED TO THE WOOLSACK.

I COULD have wished to relate that our ex-Chancellor now eagerly resumed his classical studies, and tried to discover what had been going on during the last thirty years in the literary world,—but he spent his time in poring over the newspapers, and gossiping with attorneys, in whose society he ever took great delight. "The form of the ex-Chancellor was then often seen to haunt the Inns of Court, the scenes of his departed glory; and often would he drop in to the chambers of his old friends, and, in the enjoyment of his pleasing conversation, make others as idle as himself."[1] He says that he now again read over "Coke upon Littleton;" but he certainly did nothing more, while he remained out of office, to enlarge

[1] 39 Geo. 3, c. 110.   [1] W. E. Surtees, p. 105.

his mind or to improve his taste. He found no delight in leisure, even for a little month, and he was more and more eager for his return to office. At first he was sanguine, —from the King's known dislike to Mr. Fox; but he was dreadfully alarmed by reports, which from time to time reached him, that the new Foreign Secretary was rapidly doing away with the prejudices against him in the royal bosom, and was likely to become a favorite at Court.

He did not speak often in Parliament from the Opposition bench; but he censured the appointment of Lord Ellenborough to a seat in the Cabinet while at the head of the criminal law. With mildness of manner and apparent candor, "that such an arrangement was not illegal he admitted: and he would not say that it was unconstitutional; but he thought it inexpedient, because it tended to excite a suspicion of political partiality in the administration of justice. It was observable that Lord Mansfield, whose case formed the solitary precedent, had become extremely unpopular after his entrance into the councils of the Government; and the jealousy which then arose in the minds of the people, however ill-founded, had been sufficient to weaken the confidence which ought ever to be reposed in a judge. Lord Eldon declared himself persuaded that a tenure of a seat in the Cabinet would not in the slightest degree affect the purity of Lord Ellenborough's judicial administration; but he thought, that, for the satisfaction of the country at large, it was undesirable to have the Lord Chief Justice in such a position; and he trusted that, on reflection, the learned Lord himself would not wish to retain it. It would not be proper that the same individual should act, first as a minister to institute prosecutions for treason and sedition, and afterwards as the Judge to preside at the trials. A Lord Chief Justice, it was true, might, in such cases, absent himself from the Council, or delegate the trial at law to some other judge; but in either of these cases he abandoned some duty appertaining to one of his two appointments. There might occur prosecutions, not for offenses affecting the general foundations of government, but for mere libels on the party in office; and the person accused, in any such case, would never be satisfied of the fairness of his trial, if the presiding judge were a member of the Cabinet directing the prosecution. Lord Eldon added, that he had himself been connected with Lord Ellenborough, for nearly thirty years, by the sincerest friendship: and even if he could suppose that this personal regard could be at all weakened by anything which he had then said, still he felt himself so strongly impelled by a sense of duty, that he could not refrain from expressing his opinion. He concluded by a suggestion that the best way of disposing of the matter would be to leave it to the consideration of Lord Ellenborough himself; and he was convinced that his noble friend would arrive at that result which would be satisfactory to the feelings of the public as well as to his own."[1]

During the trial of Lord Melville's impeachment, Lord Eldon did not take an active part in examining the witnesses, or arguing questions of evidence, Lord Chancellor Erskine here having a decided advantage over him. When it came to the verdict, he said NOT GUILTY on all the charges, although on one or two of them he was in a narrow majority.

The session having passed off prosperously for the new Government, the hopes of the Opposition were revived by the death of Mr. Fox; but the Whigs all rallied under Lord Grenville, and it seemed as if the King himself had gone over to them, for he consented to a dissolution of Parliament for the purpose of giving them strength. Although the existing House of Commons had been very quiescent, it was known to be of good Tory materials, and ready on the first opportunity to stand up for the restoration of Tory rule. The Tory leaders had not dreamed that the King, who had so reluctantly parted with them, would consent to Parliament being prematurely disbanded. It was only four years old; and since the passing of the Septennial Act, nearly a century ago, there had not been an instance of a dissolution till the Parliament had completed its sixth session,—with the exception of the precedent set by Mr. Pitt in 1784, considered necessary from the difference between the two Houses, and the rebellion of the House of Commons against the King and the people.

In the whole history of Lord Eldon's life there is nothing more extraordinary than the effect which the news

---

[1] 6 Parl. Deb. 263.

of this measure produced upon him. Not only did he
suspect that Canning and many Pittites were going over,
but he thought and wrote most unkindly, and I must say
most disrespectfully and irreverently, of his "dear old
master, George III.," who, while favoring him, had been,
and again became, the God of his idolatry. Thus he
pours out his indignation to his brother, Sir William
Scott :—

"I am not in the least surprised at what you say about
C. I have for some time thought that much less than a
dissolution would serve him as a cause of separation, and
I suspect that Lord G. has known him so well as by flattering his vanity on the one hand, by making him the person
of consequence to be talked with, and alarming that
vanity on the other, by disclaiming intercourse through
anybody with the Pittites as a body, to make him the
instrument of shaking, among the Pittites, that mutual
confidence which was essential to give them weight, and
thus to keep them in the state of a rope of sand till a dissolution, when he won't care one fig for them all put together. The King's conduct does not astonish me, though
I think it has destroyed him. His language to me led me
to hope better things; and, in charity, I would suppose
from it, that his heart does not go with his act. But his
years, his want of sight, the domestic falsehood and
treachery which surround him, and some feeling (just
enough, I think) of resentment at our having deserted
him on Mr. Pitt's death, *and, as to myself particularly,
the uneasiness which, in his mind, the presence of a person
who attended him in two fits of insanity excites,* have conspired to make him do an act unjust to himself. I consider it as a fatal and final blow to the hopes of many, who
have every good wish of mine. As to myself, personally,
looking at matters on all sides, I think the Chancellorship
would never revert to me, even if things had taken another
turn, and it is not on my own account I lament the turn
they have taken. As to any other office, I could have no
motive, on my own account, to wish for any, and, with a
disposition to co-operate for the good of others who have
public objects, I have only to pray God to continue to me,
if it be His pleasure, the other sources of happiness of a
private kind. I have had a letter from Lord Redesdale,
also very dismal, and, in its contents about the Prince,

like yours. The Duke of Cumberland sent me a military express to inform me of the dissolution.

"Ever yours affectionately,
"ELDON."

Can any one who reads this letter doubt that, if the Whig Government had stood, George III. steadily supporting it, Lord Eldon would, ere long, have personally assailed him, and, if his "dear old master" had been reduced to the same situation in which he was in 1801 and 1804, would have denied his capacity to govern?

The ex-Chancellor had about the same time, probably in more guarded language, unburdened his mind in a letter to the Duke of Portland. Fortunately, his Grace's answer is preserved:—

"Bulstrode, Nov. 24th, 1806.

"I will add little to the length of this letter, except to contradict the rumors you have heard of any intimation having been made to me, either directly or indirectly, of H. M.'s sentiments upon any political subject whatever. H. M. was pleased to come to this place on the Saturday before the dissolution of Parliament, accompanied only by the Queen and Princesses, and the Dukes of York and Cambridge; but not a syllable, or even allusion, to the present state of things, or to the event then impending (with which, however, I have some reason to think he was at that time unacquainted), except, if it can bear such an interpretation, his repeatedly, for three or four times, expressing his regret at having a good memory, and lamenting it as a serious misfortune. Believe me, my dearest Lord, nothing can relieve my mind so much as unburdening it to you at the present crisis. The friendship I have for so many years experienced for you, teaches me to believe that I can not use any argument so likely to induce you to gratify my wishes. I therefore conclude with the most cordial assurances of regard and attachment.

"Your Lordship's most faithfully ever,
"PORTLAND."

The elections went strongly in favor of the Whigs, and Lord Eldon really was in despair. Yet he judged it good policy that he should not appear dejected, and that active preparations should be made for opposing the Government. In a long letter to Lord Melville, he says:—

"I had also, for twelve months past, observed, not without grief, that all my exhortations to plan, to union, to system, had been thrown away upon everybody here. If they had not, I think I should at this moment have seen a very different state of things. I certainly did express strongly, at the Priory, my fears that the opinion expressed by your Lordship (to which so much respect would be paid because it was due to it) upon this measure, would greatly augment the panic that existed, while it did not appear to me that it could do any good. Upon the matter of fact (what this dissolution does prove as to the mind or intention *of anybody concerned in it*) we may live to converse together;[1] but whatever my belief of the actual mind and intention of any person concerned in it may be, though you know I am no politician, I should deservedly be thought an idiot, if I did not feel with what universality it will be deemed to import that mind and intention which you think it imports, and how impossible it is to give weight, generally, to any grounds of belief to the contrary, unless they are furnished by acts or declarations for which it can not be reasonable to look. That mischief, great mischief has been done, let the truth of the case be what it may be, can not be doubted. My poor opinion is, that it will be augmented, and unnecessarily, if we act upon the supposition that it will not bear dispute what the truth of the case is."[2]

But Lord Eldon places all his hopes upon a scheme which had been actively going on for some months, but which, being confined to a small junto, he did not venture to state or hint at to Lord Melville, who probably would have strongly condemned it.

The Prince of Wales having laid certain charges, of a very serious nature, touching the honor of his wife, before the King,[3] four members of the Cabinet, Lord Chancellor

[1] A very cautious but significant allusion to the King.
[2] He afterwards goes on to blame, very severely, Mr. Pitt's attempts to bring in Mr. Fox. Lord Melville wrote him back a very manly answer, in which he justifies what Mr. Pitt did; and having shown that no evil could have arisen if the King had taken his advice, thus concludes:—"Compare that state of the King and country with the state of both now, and then judge of the wisdom and rectitude of Mr. Pitt's views!"—*January*, 1807.
[3] This investigation originated in the advice of Lord Thurlow. See Sir Samuel Romilly's Memoirs, ii. 140, 142, 144.—Lord Grenville thought that the alleged birth of a child "would render it impossible to avoid making the matter public, and the subject of a parliamentary proceeding."

Erskine, Earl Spencer, and the Lords Grenville and Ellenborough, were appointed commissioners to inquire into the charges, with Sir Samuel Romilly, the Solicitor General, as their secretary. They conducted the proceeding with a sincere anxiety to arrive at the truth, but not very regularly or discreetly,—for they gave the Princess no notice of what was alleged against her, and she had no opportunity to contradict or to explain the evidence, which placed her conduct in an equivocal point of view. It likewise turned out that, in taking down the examination of the witnesses, they only stated the substance of what each was supposed to have sworn—not giving the questions as well as the answers—so that the exact effect of their testimony could not be accurately judged of.[1]

The unhappy lady, when she heard from rumor of what was going on against her, applied for advice and assistance to the ex-Chancellor, who was delighted to become her *patron;* for he thought that he might thereby please the King, who he believed secretly favored her, although his Majesty had sanctioned this investigation;—he was pleased to thwart the Prince, whom he regarded as a political enemy;—he expected that an opportunity might arise for censuring the conduct of the Ministers, and bringing unpopularity upon them for their attack upon the persecuted Princess; and let us charitably suppose, that, convinced of her innocence, he had something of a disinterested desire to see her righted.[2] Accordingly, a very intimate intercourse, both by visits and letters, was established between him and her Royal Highness. "Lord Eldon at that period would often dine with her at Blackheath; and to him she used to assign the seat of honor on her right hand. In Germany it had not been the custom for gentlemen to help the ladies near them to wine; but each sex fill their own glasses at their option. The Princess, however, as Lord Eldon related, used to reverse in some sort our old English fashion in his favor; for she would quietly

---

[1] See Sir S. Romilly's Memoirs, iii. 92.
[2] It requires a considerable effort to make us ascribe to him much of good motive in his treatment of Caroline of Brunswick. Although at this time he maintained that she was the chastest and most injured of her sex, he afterwards said, in confidence to Lord Grey, in reference to the charge now brought against her,—" My opinion is, and *always was*, that though she was not with child, SHE SUPPOSED HERSELF TO BE WITH CHILD."—*Romilly's Memoirs*, iii. 104.

fill his glass herself,—and so frequently, that he seldom left her house without feeling that he had exceeded the limits of discretion. Those, indeed, who recollect the proverb, 'that though one man may take a horse to the well, ten men can not make him drink,' will moderate their commiseration for the hard lot of the ex-Chancellor."[1]

The following are two of the letters which she addressed to him, before she heard of the result of the "Delicate Investigation."

"Blackheath, June 24th, 1806.

"MY DEAR SIR,

'I must mention to your Lordship that the two letters from Lady Douglas to Mrs. Fitz Gerald, which your Lordship saw on the occasion, never to enter again to my house, (which would have been very great proofs against Lady Douglas, and show her true character,) have been taken out of my drawers, in which all the papers were, and upon each was written what were the contents of each different parcel. Yesterday, to my greatest astonishment, I missed that parcel. Every search in the world has been made, in case my bad memory had led me to put it in some other place; but I have not succeeded to find them, and am led to believe, that the same person, who was able to take a hundred pound note from Carlton House, could easily take this parcel, which was so great a proof *against* Lady Douglas's character. No step has been taken by me to find out if he is the guilty one. In case you wish to see me, I shall be very happy to receive you to-morrow, or on Thursday morning, at any hour, and I beg to entreat of your Lordship, to take it well into consideration, that it is quite impossible for me to remain any longer silent upon this subject, in which my honor is so much implicated, and which is so much the talk of the public at this moment, that I hope your Lordship will take it in the most serious light, and to take some steps which will lead to any conclusion, whatever it may be. My health, as well as my spirits, suffer too much to be left any longer in suspense; and you, who have always shown yourself as a sincere friend to me, will feel as I do upon this subject. I remain forever, with the truest sentiments of high regard, esteem, and friendship,

"Your Lordship's sincere friend."

[1] Surtees, p. 116.

"Blackheath, July 25th, 1806.

"The Princess of Wales entreats and desires Lord Eldon to go as to-morrow to Windsor, and ask an audience of his Majesty, and deliver to his Majesty the inclosed letter. The Princess is under very great apprehension, that the report made from the examination, to his Majesty, has not been fairly and literally delivered to his Majesty. She wishes for that reason that Lord Eldon should verbally explain, and open his eyes on the unjust and unloyal proceedings of his Ministers. The Princess can not help thinking that his Majesty has been led into error, otherwise he would have by this time shown his usual generosity and justice, by declaring the Princess's innocence. The Princess is quite resigned to her cruel fate, from the period that her honor was in the hands of a pack of ruffians, and who are only devoted, and slaves, to her most inveterate enemy. The Princess hopes that on Sunday Lord Eldon will be able to give her a satisfactory account of the reception he received of his Majesty, and the Princess has been now for seven weeks in the most dreadful and tormenting suspense. The Princess will be very much obliged if Lord Eldon will do her the favor of losing no time for setting off for Windsor and of seeing the King. The Princess sends to his Lordship the letter to the King for his perusal. If he should wish to alter any part in the letter, the Princess desires that Lord Eldon will mark it down and send it back; the Princess would in less than an hour send it to him again.

"The Princess remains, with the highest esteem and regard, his Lordship's most sincere friend,

"C. P."

The Report of the Commissioners to the King, dated the 14th of July, 1806, acquitted the Princess of the charge that she had given birth a child long after her separation from her husband, but stated "that evidence had been laid before them of other particulars respecting the conduct of her Royal Highness, such as must, especially considering her exalted rank and station, necessarily give occasion to very unfavorable interpretations."[1]

[1] Sir S. Romilly says,—" The result of this examination was such as left a perfect conviction on my mind, and I believe on the minds of the four Lords, that the boy in question is the son of Sophia Austin; that he was born in Brownlow Street Hospital, on the 11th of July, 1802, and was taken by the Princess into her house on the 15th of November in the same year."—*Mem.*,

On the 11th of August a copy of this Report was sent to her by Lord Chancellor Erskine, with an intimation that "she was to be admonished by his Majesty to be more circumspect in her conduct." Under Lord Eldon's advice, she several times wrote to the King, complaining of the manner in which the proceeding against her had been conducted by his Ministers; solemnly denying the levities which the Report imputed to her, and praying "that she might again be admitted into the presence of her uncle—her father-in-law and her Sovereign—who had ever hitherto proved her friend and protector."

The King, melted by these expressions, and still exasperated against his son, was supposed to be favorably inclined towards her, although, as her conduct had been made an affair of state, he could not now, against the advice of his Ministers, receive her at Court as if free from blame.

Lord Eldon was prudent enough not to commit his sentiments on this subject to writing. The two following are the only other letters to him from the Princess which have been allowed to see the light:—

"Blackheath, Oct. 13th, 1806.

"The Princess of Wales, with the most grateful sense, is most sincerely obliged to Lord Eldon for his kind inquiry through Lady Sheffield.

"Her body as well as her mind have naturally much suffered from the last melancholy catastrophe, having lost in so short a time, and so unexpectedly, a most kind and affectionate brother and a sincere friend. The afflictions which Providence has sent so recently to her are very severe trials of patience and resignation, and nothing but strong feelings of religion and piety could with any sort of fortitude carry the Princess's dejected mind through this. She puts her only trust in Providence, which has so kindly protected her in various ways since she is in this kingdom.

"The Princess also has the pleasure to inform his Lordship that the Queen has twice made inquiry, by Lady Ilchester, through Lady Sheffield, about the Princess's

---

ii. 144. Yet, although there is no pretense for the notion that "Billy Austin" was the son of the Princess of Wales, or that she was ever in a state of pregnancy after the birth of the Princess Charlotte, it is now ascertained that he was of totally different parentage, and born in Germany.

bodily and mental state. The Duchess of York, through her lady to Lady Sheffield, and the Duke of Cambridge in the same way made their inquiries. The Duke of Kent wrote himself to the Princess, which of course she answered herself. The Duke of Cumberland, who has twice been with the Princess after the melancholy event took place, desired her to announce, herself, to his Majesty the unexpected event of the death of the Prince Hereditary of Brunswick. She followed his advice, and the letter was sent through Lady Sheffield to Colonel Taylor. The answer was kind from his Majesty, and full of feeling of interest for the severe loss she sustained in her brother. Lady Sheffield's health did not allow her to stay longer with the Princess. Mrs. Vernon, one of her ladies, is now at Montague House, in case his Lordship wished to write by her to the Princess.

"The Princess trusts that soon she will have comfortable and pleasing tidings to relate to Lord Eldon. She has, till that moment, nothing further to inform him of, than to repeat her sentiments of high regard, esteem, and gratitude, with which she remains forever his Lordship's most sincere friend,   "C. P."

"Blackheath, Nov. 16th, 1806.

"The Princess of Wales makes her apology to Lord Eldon for her unfortunate mistake. The letter which was intended for his Lordship is gone to Altona to the Duke of Brunswick. The contents of the letter consisted in desiring his Lordship to agree to the request of the Princess to discharge the three traducers and slanderers of her honor from her household, of which some are even yet under the Princess's own roof at this present moment. The Princess, by not having yet discharged them, is liable to receive great affronts from them, which Mr. Bidgood has tried in all means by hurting the Princess's feelings. The pew at Church, which is only appropriated for the Princess's servants, is close to her own at Greenwich, where she constantly goes, if not illness prevents her. Mr. Bidgood shows himself there every time, and even had not the proper attention of appearing lately in mourning, which all the servants of the Princess are accustomed to be as long as their Royal Mistress is in deep mourning.

"The Princess begs Lord Eldon to take all these matters into consideration. Mr. Perceval, who is also informed on the same subject, is perhaps more able to explain the whole circumstance to his Lordship than the Princess can. The Princess flatters herself that his Lordship will do her the honor and pleasure to come on Tuesday at six o'clock to dinner to meet Sir William Scott."[1]

Lord Eldon and Mr. Perceval then set their wits to work, and (as it was supposed, with the assistance of Mr. Plumer, afterwards Solicitor General, Vice Chancellor, and Master of the Rolls) composed and printed "THE BOOK," long so mysterious in its origin, its nature, and its history. This was to be used not only as an instrument for the restoration of the Princess, but for the ruin of the Ministry.[1]

Her Royal Highness now intimated to his Majesty, that "unless she were relieved from further suspense, her case must be immediately laid before the public." This threat so far operated, that in the end of January, 1807, Lord Chancellor Erskine transmitted a message to her, by order of the King, acquainting her that "his Majesty was advised it was no longer necessary for him to decline receiving her into the royal presence." The Prince of Wales then interposed; and Lord Chancellor Erskine, from ancient attachment, taking his part, and believing

[1] Sir William became such a favorite with her Royal Highness as to be the subject of a good deal of raillery among his friends; and after the Queen's trial, being questioned respecting the footing on which they had lived together, he would give no other answer than " Non mi ricordo."—Though the most moral of men, he would indulge in a little free badinage,—insomuch that, being asked by a Duchess "what would happen if he, the supreme Ecclesiastical Judge, should himself be guilty of a peccadillo?" he replied, "I have been considering that ever since I became acquainted with your Grace."

[1] Sir S. Romilly, under date 27th Nov., 1806, says of this production,— "Instead of the dignified defense of an injured and calumniated Princess, it is a long, elaborate, and artificial pleading of an advocate; and no person, as much accustomed as I am to Plumer's manner, can doubt that he is the author of it. As a pleading, however, it is conducted with great art and ability. It is manifestly intended to be at some time or other published, and is likely, when published, to make a strong impression in favor of the Princess." He adds in a note, that he had afterwards ascertained that, although Plumer had altered and corrected it, it was drawn up by Perceval, and printed under his superintendence. He does not specify the hand which Lord Eldon had in it,—being always rather chary of the reputation of the Chief of his Court. But there can be no reasonable doubt that Lord Eldon was privy to the whole transaction. Mr. Surtees says that "Mr. Perceval had the sanction of Lord Eldon, of the Duke of Cumberland, then in confidential communication with his Majesty and Lord Eldon, and of (it may hence be fairly inferred) a still more exalted personage." (P. 117, 118.) See 24 Parl. Deb. 1132, 1144; Edinburgh Review, No. cxxxv. 29, 32.

that, although there was no proof of the Princess having broken her marriage vow, her levity of manner should be seriously discouraged, the King consented to her restoration being deferred. This was good news for Lord Eldon and Mr. Perceval, and by their advice she wrote again to the King, "that unless justice were speedily done to her, she should appeal to the public, and make a disclosure to all the world of the infamous charges against her, and the irrefragible evidence by which they were repelled." There was thus every prospect of "The Book" being published; and although it might have brought much discredit on the Royal Family, and must have been injurious to the morals of the people, it probably would have answered the purpose of the authors, and would have caused a rupture between the King and his Ministers.

The return of the Tory Opposition to power was effected, however—not, as had been projected, by a cry of "The injustice of the Delicate Investigation," but by the cry of "The Church is in danger."—We must now attend to the proceedings of the new Parliament.

The session opened very auspiciously for the Whig Government. After a little grumbling at the dissolution, the Address being carried in both Houses without a division, and thanks being voted for the battle of Maida, Lord Grenville introduced his Bill to abolish the Slave Trade. This was strongly opposed by Lord Eldon, who cavilled at its title,[1] and contended that, admitting the trade to be contrary to justice and humanity, the circumstances, the mode, and the time of its abolition were proper matters of consideration. He said he did not believe the measure now proposed would diminish the transport of negroes, or that a single individual would be preserved by it; at the same time that it would be utterly destructive of the British interests involved in that commerce. He tauntingly asked, "was it right, because there was a change of men, and of public measures in consequence, that the interests of those who petitioned against the bill should be disregarded, and what was before considered fit matter of inquiry should now be rejected as material and inapplicable?"[2] The bill nevertheless passed,

[1] 8 Parl. Deb. 257.   [2] Ib. 614.

as it would have passed years before if Mr. Pitt had been sincere in his support of it;—and the next time that a Liberal Government was established in England, slavery was abolished in all the dominions under the British crown.

Lord Eldon did not take a prominent part in Parliament in resisting any other measure of the present administration, but he was very actively and effectively employed in bringing about the restoration of his own party to power. His principal associate at this time, and for many years after, was his Royal Highness the Duke of Cumberland, a prince of very considerable talents, as well as energy, and a very zealous and steady friend of the Tories. His Royal Highness had unbounded influence over his father, and was ready to take advantage of any incident which could be used to remove from office those whose principles he so much disliked.

While the Tory Opposition were very low, placing their sole reliance on their advocacy of the cause of the Princess of Wales, their spirits were suddenly revived by a notice in the House of Commons, by Lord Howick, of a motion "for leave to bring in a bill to allow Roman Catholics to hold commissions as field-officers in the army." Notwithstanding the success of the Government at the late general election, considerable distrust had been shown of them from the suspicion that they favored Catholic Emancipation, and a strong anti-popery spirit was known to exist in the country. Under such circumstances it was, I fear, an instance of gross imprudence to bring forward a measure which, though laudable in itself, was not very important, nor very pressing, and was sure to give the King and all the enemies of the Government a formidable advantage. A resolution was taken by the Tory leaders that it should be strenuously opposed, and that an alarm should be given of danger to the Established Church. Accordingly, on the day on which it was introduced and explained in an admirable speech by Lord Howick, Mr. Perceval declared that "he felt himself bound to oppose its principle, and to call the attention of the House and of the public to one of the most important and most dangerous measures that had ever been submitted to the judgment of the legislature." He then proceeded, in a very inflammatory harangue, to address himself with much dexterity to the religious prejudices of the nation, and foretold, that "if the measure were agreed to, all our most valued institutions must be swept away."[1]

A panic was spread over the country; and the King, roused by the Duke of Cumberland, sincerely believed that he was now called upon to give his assent to a dangerous measure, contrary to his coronation oath. With the sagacity and decision which ever distinguished him on such occasions, he perceived that he unexpectedly had an opportunity of getting rid of Ministers who had been forced upon him, and whom he still regarded with aversion. He therefore not only insisted upon the Bill being dropped, but, when this concession was made to him, he demanded a written engagement from all the members of the Cabinet, that they never in future would advise him to make any further concession to his Roman Catholic subjects. They unanimously refusing to give such a pledge, he dismissed them all from their offices. There is no proof that Lord Eldon suggested this most unconstitutional proceeding, although he had the opportunity of doing so in an interview which he then contrived to have with the King at Windsor; but he certainly made himself responsible for it by approving it, and by taking advantage of it. There is much plausibility in the doctrine, that new Ministers, by accepting office, make themselves answerable for the grounds on which their predecessors were turned out, as otherwise the King does an important act without any one being answerable for it, and he might be supposed to *have done wrong:* but in this instance Lord Eldon did not hesitate positively to applaud all the King's proceedings in effecting the change.

When the new arrangements were completed, Lord Eldon, finding that the Great Seal was to be restored to him, was happy,—although not very proud of the Duke of Portland as his new chief,—and, although, he felt a little regret at the exclusion of Lord Sidmouth, the manner in which he had behaved to his former chief having occasionally caused him some remorse, in spite of the oft repeated assertion that he was the "King's Chancellor." He was soon quite satisfied, however; and thus he wrote to his brother, Sir William :—

[1] 9 Parl. Deb. 9.

"I am most sincerely hurt that Lord Sidmouth is not among us. My earnest wish and entreaty has been, that he should—and many others have wished it; but it has been urged by some, that, at this moment, it can not be; that not an individual connected with Lord Melville would join or support, if it was so; that a large part of Mr. Pitt's friends would secede; that among Lord Grenville's majority there are persons not adverse, and likely enough to be friendly, who are so desperately angry at Lord S., that, with him in Administration, they would be against it to a man; that Canning declines office if Lord S. was to have office now, but would not object a few months hence; and all the Pittites, who talk to me, hold themselves bound, by their view of past transactions, not to desert Canning in a question between him and Lord S. Note, the language which those two have held respecting each other has done infinite mischief. And, finally, to make bad worse, (with a determination formed, as I understood, to offer a continuance of their situations to Bragge, Bond, &c., &c., of Addington's friends, as laying the foundation of their future junction with himself,) about the very moment that it was formed, they sent resignations—a step which has had a very bad effect. In short it's a sickening scene that's passing; but I can present it to you more conveniently in conversation than correspondence. When do you return to town? I have written to Sir W. Wynne. I take the Great Seal again to-morrow, if it pleases God. The 1st of April is an ominous day. It will not be in my possession a month, if there is not a dissolution. On my own personal account, I have no wish about it—much less than I thought I should have had."

The same day he sent the following most characteristic effusion to his brother-in-law, Dr. Ridley:—

"The occurrence of again taking the Great Seal, Harry, gives me but one sentiment of comfort,—that it is possible I may be of use to others. The death of my friend, Mr. Pitt, the loss of my poor, dear John, the anguish of mind in which I have been, and ever must be, when that loss occurs to me,—these have extinguished all ambition, and almost every wish of every kind in my breast. *I had become inured to, and fond of retirement.* My mind had been busied in the contemplation of my best interests,—those which are connected with nothing here. To me, therefore, the change is no joy :—I write that from my heart. But I can not disobey my old and gracious Master, struggling for the established religion of my country ; and I hope all good men will join in our efforts, and pray for the peace of Jerusalem. But all good men must join in his support, or he and our establishments will fall together.

"I am to receive the Great Seal to-morrow. Whether party will allow me to keep it a fortnight, I know not. On my own account I care not."

Before making any comment, I add an extract of a letter to his old friend, the Rev. Dr. Swire, written the day after he was actually Chancellor the second time :—

"While dreaming of a visit to you, I have awaked with the Great Seal in my hand, to my utter astonishment. But this attack upon the Establishment has brought forward on the part of the King, governed by his own determinations and without any assurance of support, a firmness which, I confess, astonishes me. The world should not have induced me to take the Seal again, if his commands had been of such a nature as to leave me any choice ; or the circumstances, which must inevitably lead to difficulties in Parliament, probably insuperable, and appeals to the people, perhaps, without sufficient effect, had not shamed me into decision, that this great and excellent man, for great as well as excellent he has now shown himself, shall not want the aid of every effort I can exert.

"He considers the struggle as for his throne ; and he told me but yesterday, when I took the Seal, that he did so consider it ; that he must be the Protestant king of a Protestant country, or no king. He is remarkably well—firm as a lion—placid and quiet, beyond example in any moment of his life. I am happy to add that, on this occasion, his son, the Prince has appeared to behave very dutifully to him. Two or three great goods have been accomplished if his new Ministers can stand their ground. First, the old ones are satisfied that the King, whose state of mind they were always doubting, has more sense and understanding than all his Ministers put together : they leave him with a full conviction of that fact. Secondly, the nation has seen the inefficiency of 'All the Talents,' and may perhaps therefore not injure us much by comparison. When he delivered the Seal to me yesterday, he told me he wished and hoped I should keep it till he died. If we get over a few months we may support him."

Very different language this of the restored Chancellor to that of the discontented ex-Chancellor on the dissolution of the late Parliament!!! The King is now one of the most rational, right-headed, best-disposed, and best conducted of men. His Majesty no longer feels uneasiness at the presence of "the person who had attended him in *two fits of insanity*," and, instead of being " surrounded by domestic falsehood and treachery," even his eldest son "*appears* to behave very dutifully to him." But, in perusing these letters, disgust is chiefly excited by the hypocritical lamentations which they express upon the writer being again compelled to take the Great Seal. While excluded from office, he had been the most discontented, and restless, and turbulent, and impatient of his whole party. I do not presume to criticise his feelings, or blame his activity, while in opposition, although I may wish that he had discovered more creditable subjects for his intrigues than the "Delicate Investigation," and the "Danger to the Church;" but when, by good luck and skillful conduct, he had gained the object so near his heart, it is too bad that in writing to his bosom friends— having nothing to gain by dissimulation—he should pretend that he considered his resumption of the Woolsack a grievous calamity, to which he never would have submitted had it not been for the promise extorted from him by George III. at the time he was raised to the office of Chief Justice of the Common Pleas, and the peremptory manner in which that promise was enforced. A distinguished writer in the Law Review[1] says, perhaps rather harshly, "there is a positive certainty that this can not be an honest representation of the fact;" and, believing that by the frequent repetition of such sentiments the noble and learned Lord at last really became his own dupe, I would rather adopt the candid defense of him by his kinsman, Mr. E. W. Surtees, who says, "The reiterated attempts to represent the highest honors of his life as to him only grievous incumbrances, forced upon his reluctant

[1] Vol. i. No. xii. 256.

acceptance, were in all probability the mere result of that inveterate habit of canting, which, whether originally caught from the example of his old schoolmaster, Dr. Moises, or adopted to acquire admiration or disarm envy, disfigured and degraded a character in which there was much to admire and love."[1]

The Great Seal was again put into Lord Eldon's hand, with the title of Lord Chancellor, on the 1st of April—many jests being passed upon him and his colleagues for their selection of "All Fool's Day" for the solemnity of their installation.[2]

He was warmly welcomed on his return to the Court of Chancery—where even the Whig lawyers had, for thirteen months, felt very uncomfortable. It happened that, on the first day of his sitting in Lincoln's Inn Hall, he was delayed from taking his place on the bench by the want of his wig. Sir Samuel Romilly, hearing of this *embarras* went into the private room where the Chancellor was sitting, and with some apology offered him the use of *his*. *Lord E.:* "I willingly accept your offer, Sir Samuel; but I can not help feeling how very much better the wig would be worn on this occasion by its proper owner." *Sir S.:* "I thank your Lordship for your kind speech—and let me avail myself of the opportunity which it gives me of assuring you, in all sincerity, that, greatly as we differ in our political views, there is no man who

[1] Lives of Lords Stowell and Eldon, p. 97.
[2] The chronicler of the Court of Chancery, however, proceeds with his accustomed gravity:—"1st April, 1807. Thomas, Lord Erskine, Lord High Chancellor of that part of the United Kingdom of Great Britain and Ireland called Great Britain, having delivered the Great Seal to the King at the Queen's Palace, on Wednesday, the 1st day of April, 1807, his Majesty the same day delivered it to the Right Hon. John, Lord Eldon, with the title of Lord High Chancellor of Great Britain, who was then sworn into the said office before his Majesty in Council; and on Wednesday, the 15th day of April, being the first day of Easter Term, he went in state from his house in Bedford Square to Westminster Hall, accompanied by the Judges, King's Sergeants, King's Counsel, and several other persons. The Lord Chancellor proceeded into the Court of Chancery, where, before he entered upon business, in the presence of the Earl of Camden, Lord President of his Majesty Council, and Lord Hawkesbury, one of his Majesty's Principal Secretaries of State, and a full Court, he took the oaths of allegiance and supremacy, and the oath of Chancellor, the same being administered by the Deputy Clerk of the Crown, his Honor the Master of the Rolls holding the book, and three other Masters being present, which being done, the Attorney General moved that it might be recorded. Then the Lords Camden and Hawkesbury departed, leaving the Lord Chancellor in court."—*Min. Book*, No. 2, fol. 85.

rejoices more heartily than I do at your resuming your place in this Court."¹

In a debate which took place in the House of Lords soon after the new Ministers were installed, upon the unconstitutional manner in which their predecessors had been dismissed, Lord Eldon was charged with having taken advantage of the private interview which he had with the King respecting the disputes between the Prince and Princess of Wales, to advise his Majesty to insist on the "pledge" which was the immediate cause of their dismissal. We have only the following short sketch of the answer which he then made: "The Lord Chancellor represented the present discussion as wholly new, irregular, and unparliamentary. Indeed, he thought the sense of their Lordships should be strongly marked to that effect on their Journals. As to the insinuations which had been personally thrown out against himself, as having been one of those who secretly advised his Majesty to dismiss his late Ministers, he should treat them only with the contempt they deserved. The circumstance of his having had the audience of his Majesty he had stated to the noble Baron (Lord Grenville), and he trusted that the noble Lord was perfectly well satisfied with the sincerity of his statement. The only pledge he had given was, the uniform tenor of his public life. His Majesty asked no other, and he should continue to serve his Sovereign, to the best of his abilities, without fearing any responsibility that might attach to his official conduct."² Afterwards, in the year 1813, when Earl Grey was sitting by him on the woolsack, and they were talking on the subject of the Princess of Wales, he said, "I do assure you—*you may believe it or not, as you think proper*—but I do assure you, that when I had the conference with the King, in 1807, which I requested, it was solely for the purpose of representig to him what mischief might follow if Perceval was not prevented from publishing the book which he was then bent on publishing."³ As he confessed that he did not expect to be believed, we may be allowed to entertain some doubts as to the accuracy of his recollection of all that passed in the interview with the King. In the

---
¹ On the authority of a Right Reverend Prelate, to whom Lord Eldon related the anecdote. ² Parl. Deb. ix. 422.
³ Mem. of Sir S. Romilly, iii. 104. Twiss, ch. xxiv.

"Anecdote Book" he says (I believe with strict truth), "In order to disarm political jealousy, I communicated to Lord Grenville, then Minister, that I was going to Windsor, and the nature of the business which led to my visiting his Majesty." He goes on flatly and circumstantially to deny the charge,—but he materially weakens the force of his denial by introducing it with this insincere sentence:—"It happened, *unfortunately*, about this time, that the Administration meditated a bill in Parliament which was favorable to the Roman Catholics, and that there was that misunderstanding in consequence of it which led to the King's dismissing his Administration." He must have thought that those were very credulous who could be persuaded that he considered the blunder of the Whigs in bringing forward the "Roman Catholic Officers' Bill," and their consequent dismissal, as *misfortunes*,—and he could not have sifted very nicely the facts which he was to lay before them.

It would appear that for a short time after the formation of the new Government,—for the purpose of wreaking vengeance on the discomfited Whigs,—there was an intention to publish "the Book." Lady Hester Stanhope, in a conversation with her physician, in the year 1837, referring to this subject, said,—"I prevented the explosion the first time, and I will tell you how. One day the Duke of Cumberland called on me, and in his accustomed manner began:—'Well, Lady Hester, it will be all out to-morrow. We have printed it;' and to-morrow it will be all out.' I knew what he meant, and said to him, 'Have you got the Chancellor's leave? I, for my part, don't like the business at all.' 'Why don't you like it?' asked the Duke. 'Because,' answered I, 'I have too much respect for Royalty to desire to see it made a subject for Grub-street songs.' I did not say this so much on the Prince of Wales's account as for the sake of the Princess. I dreaded the *other* disclosures to which a business like this might lead. The Duke turned away, and I saw that the same idea struck him; for, after a pause, he resumed his position, and answered,—'You are quite right, Lady Hester; by God, you are quite right; but what am I to do? We have gone too far; what am I to do?' 'Why, I think,'

[1] It was printed at a private press in the house of Mr. Perceval, on the west side of Lincoln's Inn Fields.

rejoined I, 'the best thing you can do, is to go and ask the Chancellor.' So off he packed ; and I fancy Mr. Perceval, and the Chancellor, and he talked it over, and decided on quashing the business."[1]

It has been said that the chief opposition to the suppression came from the King, who, "hating his eldest son with a hatred scarcely consistent with the supposition of a sound mind," wished that he should be exposed to public obloquy.[2] The true end for which "the Book" had been composed having been accomplished, the authors themselves soon became very much ashamed of it, and were eager to destroy every trace of its existence. Some copies, however, surreptitiously got into circulation, and in the "Phœnix" Sunday newspaper, published on the 21st of February, 1808, there appeared the following announcement and mottoes:—

"INFORMATION MOST EXTRAORDINARY.

'I have news to tell you !!!' *Hen. VIII.* Act 4.
'I'll astonish the natives!' *Reynolds.*
'Better late than never!' *Old Proverb.*
'I'll show your Grace the strangest sight
 think your highness saw this many a day!' *Hen. VIII.* Act. 5.
'The tidings that I bring will make my boldness manners.' *Ib*
'At what ease
 Might corrupt minds procure knaves as corrupt
 To swear against you! Such things have been done . *Ib.*
'———When I am dead, good wench,
 Let me be used with honor; strew over me
 With maiden flowers, that all the world may know
 I was a chaste wife to my grave ; embalm me,
 Then lay me forth ; although unqueen'd, yet like
 A queen and daughter to a king, inter me !' *Ib.*

---

[1] Vol. i. p. 395. Lady Hester afterwards states, in a manner which rather impairs her credit, that Mr. Perceval paid £10,000, out of the secret service to recover one copy of " the Book," which had been stolen from his table.
[2] Lord Brougham.

> 'After my death, I wish no other herald,
> No other speaker of my living actions,
> To keep mine honor from corruption,
> But such an honest chronicler as Griffith.'   *Ib.*'

The Chancellor and Mr. Perceval were grievously alarmed; and Sir Vicary Gibbs, the Attorney General, with a view to stop the publication by injunction, filed an information in the Court of Chancery, stating that a commission had issued by the King's orders to certain privy councillors, to inquire into certain charges against her Royal Highness, the Princess of Wales; that they had made a Report upon the subject to his Majesty; that Francis Blagdon, the proprietor of the Phœnix Sunday newspaper, pretended to have got a copy of this Report, and that he was about to publish it with certain scurrilous commentaries, and praying that he might be prevented by injunction from doing so, and that by a decree he might be ordered to deliver up the same to the Attorney General for the use of his Majesty.

Strange to say, the case came on before the Lord Chancellor Eldon, one of the authors of " the Book." He adjourned the hearing of it from Lincoln's Inn Hall to his private room. There the motion was made by the Attorney General in person,—assisted by Sir Arthur Pigot, Sir Samuel Romilly, Mr. Bell, and Mr. Mitford, "that an injunction might be awarded to restrain the defendant from parting with and from printing or publishing the Report in the Information mentioned, or any document or proceeding made or had in the prosecution of the said commission, or any abstract or extract of or from the same." I have not been able to learn what passed during the discussion, but, from an office copy of the Order made, which lies before me, along with the information and affidavits, it appears that the injunction was granted in the terms prayed for.

One would have expected that the matter would have been handed over to the Master of the Rolls, but I do not suppose that there was any impropriety in Lord Eldon himself sitting and giving judgment on this occasion, for the application did not proceed on the piracy of any original observations on the Report from his pen, as a violation of literary property, contrary to the law of copyright, —but merely upon the title of the Crown to prevent the publication of a Report made by privy councillors in such an inquiry; and there could be no doubt respecting the law upon this subject, although it seems to have been utterly forgotten by those great lawyers, Lord Eldon, Mr. Perceval, and Mr. Plumer, when they themselves composed and printed "the Book" for general circulation.

Although "the Book" was suppressed, the unhappy Princess was received at Court, and was treated with much kindness and respect by her present protectors, till her husband became Regent and King, and they became his Ministers.

www.ingramcontent.com/pod-product-compliance
Lightning Source LLC
Chambersburg PA
CBHW032027150426
43194CB00006B/181